A. M. Fairbairn

The place of Christ in modern theology by A. M. Fairbarn

A. M. Fairbairn

The place of Christ in modern theology by A. M. Fairbarn

ISBN/EAN: 9783743330955

Manufactured in Europe, USA, Canada, Australia, Japa

Cover: Foto ©Lupo / pixelio.de

Manufactured and distributed by brebook publishing software (www.brebook.com)

A. M. Fairbairn

The place of Christ in modern theology by A. M. Fairbarn

THE PLACE OF CHRIST

IN

MODERN THEOLOGY

BY

A. M. FAIRBAIRN, M.A., D.D.

MANSFIELD COLLEGE, OXFORD; GIFFORD LECTURER IN THE
UNIVERSITY OF ABERDEEN; LATE MORSE LECTURER IN UNION SEMINARY, NEW YORK;
AND LYMAN BEECHER LECTURER IN YALE UNIVERSITY

NEW YORK
CHARLES SCRIBNER'S SONS
1896

IS DEDICATED TO

MY WIFE,

WHOSE

QUIET HELPFULNESS AND FAIR COMPANIONSHIP

HAVE MADE

THE TWENTY-FIVE YEARS OF OUR WEDDED LIFE

YEARS OF HAPPY LABOUR

AND

GRACIOUS PEACE.

BATHGATE, *February 27th*, 1868.   OXFORD, *February 7th*, 1893.

PREFACE.

TREATISES in Systematic Theology are not so common as they once were, nor are they so easy either to write or to read. Criticism has become so much a mental habit and has changed so many things that we find it hard to be patient with any process that is not critical, or to agree with any principle or method that professes to be constructive. Construction, indeed, without criticism is sure to be invalid; but the criticism which does not either end in construction or make it more possible, is quite as surely without any scientific character or function. Hence, though modern criticism, philosophical, literary, and historical, has made systematic treatises of the old order impossible, it has only made a new endeavour at construction the more necessary. This book does not profess or claim to be a system of theology, but it is an attempt at formulating the fundamental or material conception of such a system; or, in other words, it is an endeavour through a Christian doctrine of God at a sketch of the first lines of a Christian Theology.

This endeavour is due to the feeling that criticism

has placed constructive thought in a more advantageous position than it has ever before occupied in the history of the Christian Church. It has done this by making our knowledge more historical and real, and so bringing our thought face to face with fact. But, for the Christian theologian, the most significant and assured result of the critical process is, that he can now stand face to face with the historical Christ, and conceive God as He conceived Him. What God signified to Jesus Christ He ought to signify to all Christian Churches; and here all can find a point from which to study themselves and their systems. Theology as well as astronomy may be Ptolemaic; it is so when the interpreter's Church, with its creeds and traditions, is made the fixed point from which he observes and conceives the truth and kingdom of God. But theology may also be Copernican; and it is so when the standpoint of the interpreter is, as it were, the consciousness of Jesus Christ, and this consciousness where it is clearest and most defined, in the belief as to God's Fatherhood and His own Sonship. Theology in the former case is geocentric, in the latter heliocentric; and only where the sun is the centre can our planetary beliefs and Churches fall into a system which is but made the more complete by varying degrees of distance and differences of orbit.

Of the two Books into which this work falls, the

first is concerned with historical criticism, the second with theological construction; but the critical process is an integral part of the constructive endeavour. We must understand the factors and forces that have moved and shaped the theologies of the past before we can, even in rudest outline, draw the ground-plan of a theology for the present. Hence came the necessity for the discussion, even within our narrow limits, of so large and complex a question as the evolution of theology and the Church. The origin and action of elements alien to the consciousness of Christ had to be discovered, and the development of those native to it traced. Then, it was no less necessary that we should follow the course of the speculation and criticism that have compelled the Churches, often against their wills and in spite of their own inherent tendencies, to return to Christ. The two histories—the evolution of theology on the one hand, and the return through criticism to Christ on the other—raise the question of the Second Book: the significance for theological thought of the Christ who has been, as it were, historically recovered. And here the Author regrets that he has been forced to move within limits which have prevented more detailed discussions and elucidations. The omission of these, especially in the third division of the Second Book, has been to him a real, though possibly a necessary, act of self-denial.

It remains for him only to thank certain friends

who have helped him by kindly reading the proofs, and with criticisms and suggestions as well as corrections; and among these he would name, in particular, the Rev. Dr. Mackennal, of Bowdon; Mr. P. E. Matheson, M.A., Fellow of New College; and Mr. Vernon Bartlet, M.A., Tutor of Mansfield College. In a very special degree he has to thank Mr. J. Gordon Watt, B.A., of Mansfield College, for two careful and excellent pieces of work—the Table of Contents and the Index.

This book appears as the Morse Lecture, but it contains matter that was also delivered in the Lyman Beecher Lectures at Yale, besides much matter that has never been delivered at all. The author does not, for both literary and scientific reasons, like to see either the limits or the form of the lecture preserved in the book; and so he has not attempted here to reproduce the lectures, but simply to discuss his subject in the form and within the limits its importance seemed to demand. He is grateful for the opportunity here afforded of expressing his sense of the honour done him both by Union Seminary and Yale University in the appointment to these Lectureships.

TABLE OF CONTENTS.

INTRODUCTION.
THE RETURN TO CHRIST.

                                                                  PAGE

i. THE NEW ELEMENT IN THEOLOGY.
- The growth of the historical spirit 3
- Its interpretation of Christ and revivifying of theology . . 6

ii. THEOLOGY AS THE HISTORICAL SPIRIT FOUND IT.
- Schools in theology: the Evangelical and the Anglican . . 9
- The theological library as it was.
    - Its wealth of apologetics 11
    - Biblical exegesis and dogmatics 13
    - But lack of any history of Christ 17

iii. THE RECOVERY OF THE HISTORICAL CHRIST.
- The theological library as it is 18
- The revivification of the New Testament 19
- The significance of the change for theology 20

BOOK I.
HISTORICAL AND CRITICAL.

DIV. I.—*THE LAW OF DEVELOPMENT IN THEOLOGY AND THE CHURCH.*

CHAPTER I.
THE DOCTRINE OF DEVELOPMENT.

i. ON THE HISTORY OF THE DOCTRINE.
- Introduction of term and idea into English theology by Newman   25
- History of the doctrine in Protestant and Catholic controversy   27
- Newman's theory of development 32

ii. THE IDEA OF DEVELOPMENT.
- Its character dependent on its field of activity . . . 34
- Historical development must be biological 35
- Newman's theory merely logical 36

iii Development in the Church.
   Its environments: how these affected the interpretation of
      Christ 38
iv. The Realm of the Law.
   Christ equally for all Churches the test of development . . 42
   The law universal and impartial in its scope 44

CHAPTER II.
DEVELOPMENT OF THE ANCIENT CHURCH.

i. The Creative Organism.
   Jesus Christ the creative and normative Person . . . 47
   His religion, priestly in character, yet priestless . . . 48
ii. The Primitive Environments.
   Originally Judaic, but soon Gentile 50
   Judaism the enemy of Christianity, yet medium for its inter-
      pretation 52
iii. The Immediate Result.
   The sub-Apostolic age guided by vulgar tradition rather than
      by Apostolic thought 55

CHAPTER III.
NEW FACTORS AND NEW LINES OF DEVELOPMENT.

Summary of Positions Determined. 58
i. The New Factors: the External.
   1. Greek philosophy 59
   2. Roman polity 60
   3. Popular religion 61
   Interpreted through these, Christianity became Catholicism . 62
ii. Ancient Philosophy and Theology.
   Two internal factors: Hebrew religion and Christian history . 63
   Hebrew religion, through Philo, changes philosophy into
      theology 64
iii. Christian History and Theology.
   Christian history creates the problems of Christian theology . 66
   Theology Eastern and soteriology Western 70

CHAPTER IV.
THE GREEK MIND AND THEOLOGY.

i. Two Minds and Two Churches.
   Greek philosophy and Roman law in the Greek and Roman
      Churches 71
   Contrast of thought and systems 73

ii. THE GREEK AND LATIN FATHERS.	PAGE
The Greek metaphysical and speculative	75
The Latin political and forensic	76
iii. THE GREEK THEOLOGY.	
It continues, completes, and reflects Greek philosophy	78
Sketch of ante-Nicene development of theology	81
iv. THE TERMINOLOGY.	
Derived from Greek philosophy	85
Elaborated and defined through controversy	86
v. THE MERITS AND THE DEFECTS OF THE THEOLOGY.	
God a unity, more metaphysical than ethical	89

CHAPTER V.

THE LATIN THEOLOGY AND CHURCH.

i. THEIR DISTINCTIVE FACTORS.	
Organization and thought	93
Imperial Church and legal theology	94
ii. TERTULLIAN.	
His Stoic philosophy	95
His Roman jurisprudence	98
His sacerdotalism and forensic soteriology	100
iii. THE OLD RELIGIONS AND THE NEW.	
The Church at its origin without an official priesthood	101
The sacerdotal tendency in Tertullian and Cyprian	104
Its Hebrew and Gentile causes	105
iv. THOUGHT AND ORGANIZATION IN THE WESTERN CHURCH.	
The Church supersedes and inherits Roman Imperialism	107
SUMMARY AND CONCLUSION	110

CHAPTER VI.

SCHOLASTICISM.

i. THE NEW RACES AND THE OLD.	
The seat of the Church in Rome	111
Scholastic philosophy provincial, the work of the new Northern peoples	112
ii. THE NEW RACES AND THE OLD PROBLEMS.	
The problems Augustine's: his innate dualism	115
The transitional period significant for polity	117

iii. Scholasticism.

A theological period: Anselm and Aristotle 118
   1. The religious question: the relation of Reason and Faith 119
   2. The theological question: the Atonement . . . 122
   3. The philosophical question: Nominalism and Realism . 124

CHAPTER VII.
THE RENAISSANCE AND THE REFORMATION.

i. The Time and the Men.
The decay of Mediævalism 127
The Italian and Teutonic Humanisms 130

ii. The Renaissance in Christian Literature: Erasmus.
Contemporary comparison of primitive Christianity and Catholicism 131
Erasmus: his labours on the New Testament 132
His criticism of Catholic doctrines and practices . . . 134

iii. The Reformation: Luther.
Protestantism and Humanism 137
Luther, a reformer by necessity: his doctrine of grace . . 138
The new movement: its leaders and its failures . . . 141

iv. Calvin and Geneva.
Calvin and Luther contrasted 144
His doctrine of God; his unconditionalism in theology and polity 145
Calvinism the conscious and constructive antithesis to Rome . 148
The influence of Geneva 150

CHAPTER VIII.
THE MODERN CHURCHES AND THEIR THEOLOGIES.

The Return to the Religion of the Sources . . . 152

i. Relation of Church to Theology.
Institutional Theologies and theological Churches . . . 154
The material conceptions of the modern Churches . . . 155

ii. Catholicism and Theology.
Catholic theology political and polemical 156
Tradition and Scripture 158

iii. The Lutheran Theology.
Its determinative idea: justification by faith 159
The Scriptures and the Sacraments 161
The *communicatio idiomatum* and scientific Christology . . 161

iv The Reformed Theology.

Its determinative idea: the sovereignty of God	162
1. The supralapsarian school	163
Its affinity to Stoicism and Pantheism	164
2. The sublapsarian school	168
The double criticism of Calvinism.	
A. The Arminian: its conditionalism	169
B. The Socinian	172
Consequent modifications in soteriology and theology	173
The modern evangelical theology	175

v. Theology and the English Church.

The institutional schools, the High Church and the Broad	176
The theological schools, the old Puritan and the modern Evangelical	179
Puritan and Anglican ideals compared	180
Anglican theology	182
Its apologetic and antiquarian character	183

vi. Retrospect and Conclusions.

The modern return to the historical Christ	186
Note to p. 182	188

Div. II.—*HISTORICAL CRITICISM AND THE HISTORY OF CHRIST.*

CHAPTER I.

THROUGH LITERATURE AND PHILOSOPHY TO CRITICISM.

The Anglican Revival and German Criticism	191
i. The Beginnings of Historical Criticism: Literature.	
1. Lessing, its founder: on revelation and religion	192
2. Schiller	195
3. Goethe	196
ii. Historical Criticism: Romanticism and Theology.	
Herder's influence on theology and Biblical study	199
iii. Philosophy and Historical Criticism.	
1. Philosophy English and German	203
2. Kant's ethical Theism	205
3. Jacobi's Intuitionalism	206
4. Fichte's Idealism: his Johannean theology	207

iv. PHILOSOPHY AND THE INCARNATION: SCHELLING.	PAGE
His speculative Christianity	209
The Incarnation, the Church, Redemption	211
v. PHILOSOPHY AND HISTORICAL CHRISTIANITY: HEGEL.	
His philosophy historical, but not critical	214
The absolute religion, one with the absolute philosophy	217
Philosophy transfigures dogmatic	221
vi. HISTORICAL CRITICISM AND THEOLOGY: SCHLEIERMACHER.	
His versatility and enthusiasm	223
The feeling of dependence in religion	224
The consciousness of Christ and the Christian consciousness	226

CHAPTER II.

PHILOSOPHICAL CRITICISM AND THE HISTORY OF JESUS.

THE BEGINNINGS OF CRITICISM OF THE GOSPELS	230
i. STRAUSS AND HIS MASTERS.	
Strauss in Berlin	232
The influence of Hegel and Schleiermacher	233
ii. THE "LEBEN JESU."	
Strauss a speculative philosopher	235
The mythical theory	240
iii. THE COUNTER CRITICISM.	
The criticism of panic	242
Relevant criticism	245
iv. CONCESSIONS AND CONCLUSION.	
His irenical attitude	247
Jesus the religious genius	248
Withdrawal of concessions	252

CHAPTER III.

LITERARY CRITICISM.—THE TÜBINGEN SCHOOL.

i. THE CRITICAL PROBLEM AND CHRISTOLOGY.	
Historical criticism corrects speculation	254
The new Christologies	257
ii. FERDINAND CHRISTIAN BAUR.	
His mental history	259
His conversion to Hegelianism	261

TABLE OF CONTENTS. xvii

iii. How BAUR CAME TO HIS PROBLEM.
His speculative Christology 263
To him the historical problem positive 265
The Pauline and Petrine antitheses 267

iv. How BAUR SOLVED HIS PROBLEM.
The Catholic Church the synthesis of these antitheses . . 269
The theory of tendencies and the Gospels 270
The Tübingen School 272

v. WHERE THE TÜBINGEN CRITICISM FAILED, AND WHY.
The criticism subjective and one-sided 273
Its want of historical veracity 275

CHAPTER IV.

THE NEWER HISTORICAL CRITICISM AND THE HISTORICAL CHRIST.

i. THROUGH CRITICISM TO HISTORY.
Histories of Christ, French, English, and German . . . 278
"Vie de Jésus" 278
"Ecce Homo" 279
The New Strauss and other German works 280

ii. THROUGH HISTORY TO THEOLOGY.
1. Contemporary history more fully studied 286
2. Constructive historical criticism 288
3. The newer literary criticism 291
4. Biblical theology 292

iii. RESULTS AND INFERENCES.
1. The recovery of the historical Christ 294
2. The new feeling for Him in literature 294
3, 4. He is the norm for all Churches 295
5, 6. And the starting-point for criticism and theology . . 296

BOOK II.

THEOLOGICAL AND CONSTRUCTIVE.

Div. I.—*THE NEW TESTAMENT INTERPRETATION OF CHRIST.*

CHAPTER I.

THE EXPOSITORY BOOKS.

	PAGE
THE INTERPRETATION OF CHRIST IN THE NEW TESTAMENT	302

i. THE PAULINE CHRISTOLOGY.
A. Historical relations and characteristics 303
B. I. The theology.
  Jesus, the Messiah 306
  His Divine Sonship 307
 II. The soteriology.
  1. The system of the earlier Epistles 310
   Christ, the Second Adam 310
   The Pauline philosophy of history; the old order
    and the new 314
  2. The later system 317
   The Son, alike Creator and Saviour; His cosmical
    relations 318

ii. THE CHRISTOLOGY OF HEBREWS.
A. Its specific character 320
B. Its theology: Jesus the Son of God 322
 The essential relation of the Son to the Father . . 323
 The finality of the New Covenant: a series of contrasts . 324

iii. THE MINOR CHRISTOLOGIES.
A. The Jacobean 328
B. The Petrine 330
C. The Apocalyptic 332

CHAPTER II.

THE HISTORICAL BOOKS.

i. THE SYNOPTIC GOSPELS.
A. Mark 334
B. Matthew 335
C. Luke 337

TABLE OF CONTENTS.

	PAGE
ii. THE FOURTH GOSPEL.	
A. Relations and characteristics of the Gospel	338
B. Christology: the Word and the Son	341
The history symbolical of the ideal	342
iii. THE IDEAL PERSON AND THE REAL HISTORY.	
Jesus supernatural, yet human	346
The Temptation: the normal humanity of Christ	348
His supernatural office and work	353

CHAPTER III.
THE CHRISTOLOGY OF CHRIST.

i. SIGNIFICANCE OF HIS NAMES.	
A. The Christ	358
B. The Son of God	359
C. The Son of man: its personal and its official sense	361
ii. THE NAMES AND THE MISSION.	
The double Sonship	364
Correlation of the terms in the Fourth Gospel	365
Sonship and Fatherhood	368
iii. HIS PERSON AND PLACE.	
His message to man—the interpretation of Himself	369
The necessary, sufficient, and accessible Mediator	371

CHAPTER IV.
THE RELATIONS AND THE REASON OF THE CHRISTOLOGIES.

i. COMPARISON OF THE APOSTOLIC CHRISTOLOGIES WITH CHRIST'S.	
Affinities, historical, religious, philosophical, and theological	373
ii. CONCLUSORY AND TRANSITIONAL.	
The Apostolical and naturalistic interpretations of Christ	377
The verdict of history on the Person and His work	378
The vindication of the Apostolical theology	381
Its influence on the thought and life of men	382

DIV. II.—*CHRIST THE INTERPRETATION OF GOD.*

CHAPTER I.
THE GODHEAD.

i. THE DOCTRINE OF THE GODHEAD AND REVELATION.	
God and the Godhead	385
Revelation changes idea of God into knowledge of the Godhead	386

TABLE OF CONTENTS.

	PAGE
ii. THE DOCTRINES OF GOD AND THE GODHEAD.	
Their history and function in Christian theology	388
Consequent conceptions of the sonship of man	390
iii. CHRIST AND THE GODHEAD.	
Father and Son in the Godhead	391
The Christian Trinity and ethnic parallels	395
iv. THE GODHEAD AS A DOCTRINE.	
The Sonship of Christ and the sonship of humanity	397
The essential distinctions in the unity of God	398

CHAPTER II.
THE GODHEAD AND THE DEITY OF NATURAL THEOLOGY.

i. GOD IN THEISM AND THEOLOGY.	
The philosophical and the religious conceptions of God	401
ii. THE GODHEAD AND THE CHARACTER OF GOD.	
Unethicized conceptions of God	403
The Christian conception completely ethicized	405
iii. THE GODHEAD AS IT AFFECTS THE NOTIONS OF CREATOR AND THE CREATION.	
Theistic difficulties: the relation of God to the world	406
How mitigated by the conception of the Godhead	408
The eternal love of God the motive of the creative act	410
iv. THE GODHEAD AND PROVIDENCE.	
Deism and Pantheism	414
Deity transcendent, yet immanent	415
v. THE GODHEAD AND THE EXTERNAL RELATIONS OF GOD.	
The instrumental and the personal worlds	417
Nature a middle term between God and man	419
The personal world alone real to God	421
The creative Will, eternal and universal	421
Resultant ethicized conception of the universe	423

CHAPTER III.
THE GODHEAD AND THE DEITY OF CONSTRUCTIVE THEOLOGY.

i. THE THEISTIC CONCEPTION AND THEOLOGY.	
A *communicatio idiomatum* between God and the Godhead	426
ii. THE JURIDICAL DEITY.	
In Catholicism, as political and legal	429
In Calvinism, as the sovereign Will	430

iii. WHETHER AND IN WHAT SENSE GOD IS A SOVEREIGN.
Dr. Candlish's position examined 432
Paternity and sovereignty indissoluble 434

iv. THE SOVEREIGNTY OF LAW AND OF GOD.
Legal v. paternal sovereignty 436
God in the filial consciousness of Christ 439

v. GOD AS FATHER AND AS SOVEREIGN.
The unity of love and righteousness 441
Both necessary to God 443

vi. PATERNITY AND SONSHIP.
Fatherhood primary and determinative of sovereignty . . 444
The sonship of nature and the sonship of grace . . . 446

Div. III.—A. *GOD AS INTERPRETED BY CHRIST THE DETERMINATIVE PRINCIPLE IN THEOLOGY.*

CHAPTER I.
THE FATHERHOOD AND SIN.

i. THE FORMAL AND THE MATERIAL PRINCIPLE OF THEOLOGY.
The formal, the consciousness of Christ 449
The material, the Fatherhood of God 451

ii. THE DOCTRINE OF SIN.
Sin how defined and conceived 452
The peculiar creation of Christianity 454

iii. THE PERMISSION AND DIFFUSION OF SIN.
Sin and obedience as related to sonship 456
Original sin and heredity 458

iv. SIN COMMON AND TRANSMITTED.
The sin of nature 459
The unity and solidarity of the race 460

v. SIN AND THE REGAL PATERNITY.
The Father wills the salvation of man 463
The Sovereign wills the expulsion of sin 465
Neither annihilation nor compulsory salvation . . . 466

CHAPTER II.
THE FATHERHOOD AND SOTERIOLOGY.

i. THE INCARNATION.
Jesus Christ, the incarnate Son of God 470
The two natures: Sonship involves their affinity . . 472
The attributes of God and the *kenosis* 475
The relation of the natures within the incarnate Person . 478

TABLE OF CONTENTS.

ii. THE ATONEMENT.
	PAGE
The condemnation of sin the ground of salvation	479
The sacrifice of the Son and the revelation of the Father.	483
A new consciousness of God and of sin	485
Principles deduced	486

iii. THE HOLY SPIRIT.
The immanent presence of God in man	487
The Spirit in the teaching of Christ and the Church	488
The Holy Spirit, the renewer and revealer	491

CHAPTER III.
REVELATION AND INSPIRATION.

i. RELIGION AND REVELATION.
Revelation a necessity to religion	493
The place of an historical revelation.	495

ii. REVELATION AND INSPIRATION.
Their correlation and functions	496
The Scriptures and the Church	498

iii. THE SCRIPTURES AND CRITICISM.
Catholic and rationalist polemic	500
The legitimacy of the higher criticism	502
The authority of the Scriptures as a revelation.	504

iv. THE BIBLE AS THE AUTHORITY IN RELIGION.
Function of canonization	506
Authority attribute not of book but of revelation	508

v. WHETHER A CONSTRUCTIVE DOCTRINE BE POSSIBLE.
The essentials and the accidents of revelation and religion	509
The Spirit and the Word	510

B.—*GOD AS INTERPRETED BY CHRIST THE DETERMINATIVE PRINCIPLE IN THE CHURCH.*

CHAPTER I.
THE DOCTRINE OF THE CHURCH IN THE NEW TESTAMENT.

i. THE CONCEPTIONS OF GOD AND THE CHURCH.
The Monotheism of Jesus Christ	513

ii. CHRIST AND THE IDEA OF THE CHURCH.
The kingdom of God	515
Its ministry not sacerdotal	517

iii. THE APOSTOLIC IDEA OF THE CHURCH.
    The Church or *ecclesia* 519
    Local *ecclesiae*: their autonomy 520
    The universal *ecclesia*, the body of Christ. 522
    The mystical Church, the spouse of Christ 525

iv. THE CHURCH AS THE KINGDOM AND PEOPLE OF GOD.
    Ideas of Church and kingdom 528
    The Church the filial society 529

v. THE CHURCH AND ITS ORGANIZATION.
    Apostolic succession 531
    The priesthood 533

CHAPTER II.
THE CHURCH IN THEOLOGY.

i. THE CHURCH AND ITS POLITY.
    Material and formal character 535
    Polity and community 537
    Apostolic descent of the Church 540

ii. THE CHURCH VISIBLE AND INVISIBLE.
    Doctrine and difficulties of Augustine 541
    Doctrine of Reformers 543

iii. THE CHURCH OF GOD—HOLY, CATHOLIC, AND APOSTOLIC.
    His people 545
    The Church is as God is 547
Index 549

INTRODUCTION:
THE RETURN TO CHRIST.

Καὶ ὁ Θεὸς αὐτὸν ὑπερύψωσε, καὶ ἐχαρίσατο αὐτῷ τὸ ὄνομα τὸ ὑπὲρ πᾶν ὄνομα· ἵνα ἐν τῷ ὀνόματι Ἰησοῦ πᾶν γόνυ κάμψῃ ἐπουρανίων καὶ ἐπιγείων καὶ καταχθονίων, καὶ πᾶσα γλῶσσα ἐξομολογήσηται ὅτι Κύριος Ἰησοῦς Χριστός, εἰς δόξαν Θεοῦ πατρός.—PAUL, Phil. ii. 9-11.

Δύο γὰρ, ὡς ἔοικεν, ἱερὰ Θεοῦ, ἓν μὲν ὅδε ὁ κόσμος, ἐν ᾧ καὶ ἀρχιερεὺς, ὁ πρωτόγονος αὐτοῦ θεῖος λόγος. ἕτερον δὲ λογικὴ ψυχὴ, ἧς ἱερεὺς ὁ πρὸς ἀλήθειαν ἄνθρωπος ἐστιν.—PHILO, "De Som.," i., § 37; tom. i., 653.

Παραπωλώλει γὰρ ἂν τὸ τῶν ἀνθρώπων γένος, εἰ μὴ ὁ πάντων δεσπότης καὶ Σωτὴρ τοῦ Θεοῦ Υἱὸς παρεγεγόνει πρὸς τὸ τοῦ θανάτου τέλος.— ATHANASIUS, "De Incar. Verbi," ix. 4.

Hunc ille Platonicus non cognovit esse principium; nam agnosceret purgatorium. Neque enim caro principium est, aut anima humana, sed Verbum per quod facta sunt omnia. Non ergo caro per se ipsam mundat, sed per Verbum a quo suscepta est, cum *Verbum caro factum est, et habitavit in nobis.*—AUGUSTINE, "De Civ. Dei," x. 24.

Quatenus autem Christus mundum vivificat: hinc est quod deus deique filius est, non quod caro est.—ZWINGLI, "Ep. ad Alberum," Opera, vol. iii., p. 595 (1832 ed.).

Der eigentliche Inhalt des Christenthums ist aber ganz allein die Person Christi: ... Man kann also sagen: In einer Philosophie der Offenbarung handle es sich allein oder doch nur vorzüglich darum, die Person Christi zu begreifen. Christus ist nicht der Lehrer, wie man zu sagen pflegt, Christus nicht der Stifter; er ist der Inhalt des Christenthums.—SCHELLING, "Philos. der Offenbarung," Vorlesg. xxv.

§ I.—THE NEW ELEMENT IN THEOLOGY.

THE most distinctive and determinative element in modern theology is what we may term a new feeling for Christ. By this feeling its specific character is at once defined and expressed. But we feel Him more in our theology because we know Him better in history. His historical reality and significance have broken upon us with something of the surprise of a discovery, and He has, as it were, become to us a new and more actual Being. It is certainly not too much to say, He is to-day more studied and better known as He was and as He lived than at any period between now and the first age of the Church. There is indeed this difference between then and now—He is studied now through the intervening history and in its light; He was studied then only in the light of His personal history and the past that lay behind it. But, apart from this necessary difference, we feel His personal presence in all our thinking more in the manner of the apostolic than of any other age; and so we are being forced to come to the theology of the schools and the conventions of the Churches through Him rather than to Him through these. This may be said to be the distinction between the old theology and the new: the former was primarily doctrinal and secondarily historical; but the latter is primarily historical and secondarily doctrinal. The old theology came to history through doctrine, but the new comes to doctrine through history; to the one all historical questions were really dogmatic, but to the other all dogmatic questions are formally historical. This does not mean the surrender of doctrine, but rather the enlargement of its meaning and scope. For when history is read through doctrine, the realm of realities is reduced to the size and beaten into the shape of a very restricted and rigorously ordered world of ideas; but where doctrine is read through history, the realm of ideas must be so widened and articulated as to represent the realm of realities. Harmony of history with belief was the note of the one school; harmony of belief with history is the note of the other; and of these harmonies the second, as the more natural, is at once the more necessary and the more difficult to attain.

This recovery of the historical Christ, and consequent new feeling for Him, is due to many causes, mainly to the growth of the historical spirit. This spirit is not new, though its methods are; but it is more scientific, sympathetic, veracious, than of old. In its more modern form it may be said to have begun with Romanticism, or the attempt by a poetic interpretation of the past to escape from the prosaic realities of the present. Romanticism differed from the classical Renaissance in the field it selected for its imaginative activity and appreciation, but agreed with it in the tendency to idealize and in the endeavour to imitate what it found and admired in its selected field. The ideals of the Renaissance were all classical; the literatures of Greece and Rome were to it the standards of taste, imitation of their flexible yet stately elegance at once its inspiration and its despair; it studied classical art, derived from it all its ideas of the beautiful, and laboured to embody them in a sculpture and architecture that were judged to be most excellent when most like their models. The dream of the Renaissance was to escape from the Italy of the fifteenth century into the Athens of Pericles or Plato, or into the Rome of Cicero or Augustus. But the ideals of Romanticism lay in the past of the Western

European peoples and of their religion. Its field was the Middle Ages; it glorified their chivalry, legends, poetry, art, faith, and what it glorified it could not help attempting to imitate. Literature became disdainful of the cold and artful elegance of the classic style, and grew warmer, more vehement, quicker to feel and to reflect the more rudimentary emotions of human nature, those primitive and spontaneous passions which culture tends to tame or expel. In Painting there was formed the pre-Raphaelite school, which studiously aimed at breaking away from a classicism that had become conventional and attaining a more realistic idealism, an art that should in the interests of the ideal be frankly natural, though in its members, according to their native tempers, now the natural and now the ideal predominated. In Architecture the movement found expression in the Gothic revival; ruined abbeys were curiously studied, old churches incautiously restored, new churches built in every variety of Gothic, hideous, hybrid, and historical, and, in general, the idea zealously preached and industriously realized that Gothic was the only fit style for the religious edifice. In Worship the imitative mediævalism which is known as ritualism came to be, and vestments, acts, articles, and modes proper to the worship of the period represented by the buildings were so used as to make the revival complete.

The course and the phenomena of the classical and the mediæval revivals are thus exactly parallel; each is alike imitative, in each imitation runs into extravagance, and extravagance ends in the exhaustion whose only issue is death. But neither passed away resultless. Out of the Renaissance came, after the season of imitative subserviency to Greece and Rome had ceased, the mastery of classical literature and the knowledge of classical art that have made them the great instruments of culture, though their power lies in their being instruments commanded by the mind, not commanding it. Out of Romanticism there has come, for all save those who are still in the stage of servile reproduction, love of the past, the knowledge of it that can come only through love, and the sense of the connection and the continuity of man in all the periods and in all the places of his being. Both had, therefore, a kindred though not an identical function; each, by creating knowledge of a specific past, helped to supply history with the ideas and the spirit that made it a science. They taught us to see events in their relations, to search into their causes, to study persons through their times and the times in the persons, to discover the conditions that regulated the growth and decay of institutions, to find in what seemed a chaos of conflicting wills a principle of order and a law of progress. And just as we have learned to read the past truly we have come to understand man really; what makes the race re-live its life to the imagination makes the reason know not only the race but the units who compose it. To penetrate the secret of man is to discover the truth of God; in a sense higher than Feuerbach dreamed of anthropology is theology.

Now, the historical spirit could not do its now destructive and now constructive work and ignore the Supreme Person of history. He has left the mark of His hand on every generation of civilized men that has lived since He lived, and it would not be science to find Him everywhere and never to ask what He was and what He did. Persons are the most potent factors of progress and change in history, and the greatest Person known to it is the One who has been the most powerful factor of ordered progress. Who this is does not lie open to dispute. Jesus Christ is a name that represents the most wonderful story and the profoundest problem on the field of history—the one because the other. There is no romance so marvellous as the most prosaic version of His history. The Son of a despised and hated people, meanly born, humbly bred, without letters, without opportunity, unbefriended, never save for one brief and fatal moment the idol of the crowd, opposed by the rich, resisted by the religious and the learned, persecuted unto death by the priests, destined to a life as short as it was obscure, issuing from His obscurity only to meet a death of unpitied infamy, He yet, by means of His very sufferings and His cross, enters upon a throne such as no monarch ever filled and a dominion such as no Cæsar ever exercised. He leads captive the civilized peoples; they accept His words as law, though they confess it a law higher than human nature likes to obey; they build Him churches, they worship Him, they praise Him in songs, interpret Him in philosophies and theologies; they deeply love, they madly hate, for His sake. It was a new thing in the history of the world; for though this humble life was written and stood vivid before the eye and imagination of men, nay, because it veritably did so stand, they honoured, loved, served Him as no ancient deity had been honoured, loved, or served. We may say, indeed, He was the first being who had realized for man the idea of the Divine; He proved His Godhead by making God become a credible, conceived, believed, real Being to man. And all this was due to no temporary passion, to no transient madness, such as now and then overtakes peoples as well as persons. It has been the most permanent thing in the history of mind; no other belief has had so continuous and invariable a history. The gods of Greece lived an even more changeful life than the Greek men; the Zeus of Homer and of Plato, though one in name, is in character not only two, but two radical opposites. The history of religion in India is but a record of the variations and the multiplication of deities. The mythologies of Mesopotamia and Egypt were never fixed; they bewilder by the number and extent of the changes in the crowd of figures they present for analysis. But the belief in Christ has for now almost two thousand years lived under a criticism the most searching and scientific that ever assailed any idea of mind or fact of history, and yet this criticism has only made the belief more active, more vigorous, more sure of its intrinsic truth and reasonableness. What makes the result more wonderful is, that the criticism was at its thoroughest when the faith seemed at its weakest. In the first centuries of its existence, when it had to suffer from the reproach of its recent and mean origin, the infamy of its Founder's death, the poverty and ignorance of its adherents, and its varied offences against Greek culture and Roman policy,—it had to bear the malignant yet searching criticism of Celsus, the witty satire of Lucian, the vindictive and insolent invective of the rhetors and their schools. Yet the men of the new religion were, even within the arena of letters, victorious over the men of the old learning. And both in the last century and in this, when it seemed weak through continued supremacy, the exercise of a too secular lordship, and the reproach of lives which it nominally guided but did not really command, it received but renewal at the hands of the subtle scepticism of Hume and the destructive criticism of Strauss. The wonderful thing in the story is, that what in the abstract would have seemed impossible romance is in reality the most sober fact; while out of the story, when viewed in relation to the course of human development, rises for philosophy the problem, Can He, so mean in life, so illustrious in history, stand where He does by chance? Can He, who of all persons is the most necessary to the orderly and progressive course of history, be but the fortuitous result of a chapter of accidents?

Now, how has this new feeling for Christ affected constructive Christian theology? We have just seen that historical inquiry raises questions that belong to the philosophy of history, which is but the most concrete form of the philosophy alike of nature and man. We cannot conceive and describe the supreme historical Person without coming face to face with the profoundest of all the problems in theology; but then we may come to them from an entirely changed point of view, through the Person that has to be interpreted rather than through the interpretations of His person. When this change is effected, theology ceases to be scholastic, and becomes historical; and this precisely represents the change which it has undergone or is undergoing. The speculative counterpart of the new feeling for Christ is the rejuvenescence of theology.

But that we may understand what this new factor in theology means, we must briefly review the state of theological knowledge and inquiry in the period which saw the birth of our modern historical criticism.

§ II.—THEOLOGY AS THE HISTORICAL SPIRIT FOUND IT.

When the new historical spirit began to concern itself with theology, the field of dogmatic thought was with us occupied by two opposed schools—the Evangelical and the Anglican— then just entering upon the specific phase known as the Tractarian. The Evangelical represented the beliefs that had during the previous century been the most active and vigorous, the most charged with creative enthusiasm and recreative energies; the Anglican represented beliefs that had been long decadent, and were now blindly and stormily struggling towards a second birth. The Evangelical, though touched with a Puritan tendency, had almost lost the Puritan spirit, having become individualistic in a sense and to a degree the Puritans would have abhorred; the Anglican, though with some Catholic impulses and many claims to an historical temper, was still strongly provincial and arbitrary, not to say violent. The Evangelicals had accomplished the religious revival of the eighteenth century, had contended against its sordid earthliness, its low morals, its sodden and conventional unbelief, and had created the great philanthropies that improved the prisons, reformed manners, befriended the lower races, and emancipated the slaves; but the Anglicans had the spirit and the passion that were to achieve the distinctive revival of the nineteenth century. The speech of the Evangelical was of doctrine, *i.e.*, revealed truth correctly taught, conceived, and received; the speech of the Anglican was of dogma, *i.e.*, truth as defined, formulated, and enforced by the decree of a body politic, or the heads of such a body. The Evangelical position, as in essence doctrinal, conceived the relations of God and man as determined by certain beliefs which, articulated in fixed formulæ, were alternatively represented as "the truth" or "the Gospel" or "the plan of salvation"; but the Anglican position, as in its essence political, conceived and represented the relations of God and man as regulated by certain fixed and persistent institutions, as dependent for their happy realization on a specific polity and certain offices, rites, and instruments variously designated as "Apostolical Succession," "the Priesthood," "the Sacraments," and "the Church." The Evangelical position, as mainly doctrinal, was intellectual and individualistic; the Anglican, as mainly political, was historical and collective: but the collectivism of the one was less universal than the individualism of the other. The Evangelical tended, by his distrust of mere institutions, to a reluctant Catholicity; the Anglican, by so emphasizing special offices, persons, and acts, tended to as reluctant a particularism. They both agreed in their evidential method or process of proof—it was an appeal to actual authorities; but they differed in the authorities appealed to—the Evangelicals were Biblical, the Anglicans less Biblical than Patristic. In handling their authorities they were alike uncritical and unhistorical; the authority of the Evangelicals was a Bible which the higher criticism had not been allowed to touch, while the Anglicans, with more need for science, and a larger yet easier field for its exercise, were in their use of the Fathers still more strenuously unscientific. But while they differed as to their authorities, they agreed not only in method but in the principle which underlay it—viz., what the authority appealed to could be made to prove must be accepted as the very truth of God.

But the character of the theology will become more apparent if we survey the then current theological literature. What were the great books, and what their special questions and method? Suppose we had entered while the century was yet in the thirties a well-stocked clerical library—what should we have found? Apologetics would be represented by Butler and Paley, and the most popular of the Bridgewater Treatises, especially Chalmers and Whewell. For Theism the argument from design was in the ascendant; adaptation was as charmed a word then as evolution is now; everything was judged by its fitness for its end—the more perfect the contrivance the more irrefragable the evidence. Design was discovered in the organs of sense, in the hand of man, in the relation between the functions of digestion and the chemistry of food, in all the adaptations of man to nature and nature to man. Christianity was proved to be divine, partly, by its being an instrument or institution so excellently adapted to the improvement of man, especially in the conditions in which he here finds himself; and, partly, by the testimony of its first preachers, who must be believed as honest men, because rogues would not and fools could not have endured the sufferings and made the sacrifices they did for the sake of the Gospel. It was characteristic that Butler's "Analogy" was more esteemed than his "Sermons on Human Nature"; an argument that proved natural religion which yet never was a religion of nature, to be more heavily burdened by intellectual and moral difficulties when taken by itself than when completed and crowned by revealed, was much better adapted to the age than one built on the supremacy of conscience. The latter was so little considered that its fundamental inconsistency with the doctrine of probability on which the "Analogy" is based, was never perceived. But while these were the typical apologetical works others would not be absent. Hume, of course, as a highly respectable and deeply subtle opponent, would be there, but flanked by Reid's reply to his philosophy, possibly supported and supplemented by James Beattie's "Essay on Truth," and by Campbell's answer to his argument against miracles. If the deistical controversy was exceptionally well represented, then Leland would give the general survey of the field and the men who had worked in it; Samuel Clarke would by "the high priori road" demonstrate the being and attributes of God; Berkeley by his new theory of knowledge would show how the vanity of the new materialism could be exposed and spirit made the only real thing in the universe; Sherlock would examine his witnesses to prove the Resurrection no fraud; Conyers Middleton would prove how miracles restricted to the apostolic age simplified the controversy, and strengthened the apologist by relieving him from the cruel necessity of either defending ecclesiastical miracles or sacrificing to their manifold incredibilities the credibility of the Biblical; Warburton would maintain his audacious paradox, and argue that the legation of Moses was revealed and divine, because, while every other legislation created, ordered, and enforced obedience by the penalties of a life to come, he alone never invoked the sanctions of a future state; Jeremiah Jones would tell how the canon was formed and ought to be defended; while Nathanael Lardner's large and massive scholarship would bring the cumulative evidence of antiquity to prove the credibility of the Gospel history. By the help of these the theologian could do his apologetical work, and marshal his evidences and his arguments against Voltaire or Bolingbroke, Collins or Tindal, Hume or Gibbon, Rousseau or Tom Paine, who, though dead, yet lived in the only infidelity then known.

But apologetics could not stand alone; the Scriptures must be explained as well as defended. So Horne's "Introduction" would be on hand, possibly also Michaelis' as Englished, augmented, and amended by Marsh; and if his " Introduction " was known, so also would be his " Commentaries on the Laws of Moses," which had been translated by a Scotch minister, Alexander Smith, of Chapel of Garioch. Commentaries would be numerous; the rich collections and erudite dissertations of the *Critici Sacri* and the industrious compilations of the *Poli Synopsis Criticorum* would be at command; while Grotius and Vitringa, Coccejus, Geierus, Calovius, and Clericus, represented the older scholasticism, Ernesti and Gesenius, Rosenmüller and Eichhorn, would shed the newer and drier light of the rationalism that was just ceasing to be. If the minister was very venturesome, he might have acquainted himself with the daring critical speculations of Bretschneider's "Probabilia," or the ingenious theories of Schleiermacher, whose essay on Luke a bold young man of the name of Thirlwall had translated and published in 1825, though even he had not dared to avow the work. If the library was a scholar's, he would, of course, have Brian Walton and Mill, and would turn hopefully to a new critical text of the New Testament which a young German, Lachmann by name, had just published; and he would seek help from the great patristic commentators, Origen, Theodore of Mopsuestia, Theodoret, Theophylact, Chrysostom, Augustine, and Jerome. Or if it was a working cleric's, he would, according to his taste, have Whitby and Hammond, or Patrick and Lowth, Matthew Henry, or Thomas Scott, or Adam Clarke. There would, of course, be the classical books on certain special subjects, periods, or persons. Prideaux "On the Connection of the Old and New Testaments," Lowth on Hebrew Poetry and on Isaiah, Horne on the Psalms, Luther on Galatians, Brown of Whamphray on Romans, Owen on Hebrews, Leighton on Peter. For his archæology and philology he would have Lightfoot and the Buxtorfs, as well as such fresh and unexpected light as had just been supplied by the lexicons and grammars of Gesenius and Winer, and by the researches of Robinson, while

Josephus would be a standing authority, and the sacred text itself the most certain and fruitful of all his sources.

But what would give its distinctive character to the library would be its dogmatic theology. If it were an Anglican's, his books would have much to say about the Calvinistic and Arminian controversies, the divine origin or the excellent expediency of Episcopacy, the mind of the Fathers and the meaning of the Creeds. There would be a curious absence of what the Lutheran and Reformed Churches understood by "systematic theology"—great systems, in their sense, being quite unknown in the English Church. The book that approaches most nearly to this idea could not but be there; it bears the characteristic name, "The Laws of Ecclesiastical Polity"—*i.e.*, religion is considered as institutional, a theory of social order, a state whose laws may be explicated as they must be enforced. Beside it, almost as much honoured, though standing on a far lower plane, would be Pearson "On the Creed," and with him would be Bull, maintaining against Jesuit and Socinian alike the Nicene orthodoxy of the ante-Nicene Fathers, and Waterland, with all the apparatus of a most elaborate and well-equipped scholasticism, vindicating the same faith against the Arians of his own Church. Burnet "On the Articles" would find a less favoured place; while Whitby "On the Five Points" and Tomline's "Refutation of Calvinism" would be memorials of what was even then a burnt-out controversy. Of course, as one who held the faith of Ken, he would hold in peculiar reverence the Fathers who lived before the division of East and West, and would study the ancient Church, its constitution and customs, by the help of Bingham. If, however, the library belonged to an Evangelical or Presbyterian or Independent, the books would differ in character and range; those already named would almost certainly be present, but amid companions that modified their speech. The burning controversy was now the Calvinistic and Socinian, which was very unlike the Arian controversy of the days of Waterland and Clarke. Then the emphasis fell on the person of the Redeemer, but now it fell on His work, or on the person just so far as it was concerned in the work. The Evangelical revival was largely responsible for the change; its watchword had been "Salvation," and it had, on the one side, magnified conversion as its subjective condition, and on the other the Atonement as its objective ground. Hence came the inevitable question— In what relation did Jesus Christ, and especially His supreme act, His sacrifice or death, stand to the forgiveness of sins? What was the precise thing it was meant to accomplish? And what must it be to accomplish this thing? The Socinian said, He is an example, He saves by the moral influence of His life and death; the Evangelical said, He is a sacrifice, He saves by making expiation on our behalf and propitiating Divine justice—*i.e.*, by becoming our substitute He bears our punishment, and so enables God justly to forgive our sins. The books written during the controversy form a library in themselves. They were, in form at least, largely Biblical. While the theories of inspiration differed, yet on both sides the authority of the Scriptures was assumed, the Socinians, indeed, venturing in their own interests on an "Improved Version of the New Testament," which was often remarkable for its deft defiance of grammar. In the doctrinal question their champions were Priestley and Belsham, Toulmin and Kentish, Lant Carpenter and Yates, who skilfully made the worst of their opponents' case and the best of their own, especially by contrasting the grace and love of the Gospel with the severities of Calvinism, and by transferring the rather vindictive jurisprudence of its representatives from the abstract forms they loved to the concrete which they wished to avoid—*i.e.*, from impersonal law to personal God. On the Calvinistic side the critics and apologists were a multitude. Horsley's charges and letters against Priestley would be sure of a place, not simply because of their racy and merciless polemic, but as forming the link that connected the new Socinian with the old Arian controversy. In one of the most striking pieces of autobiography in the language, Thomas Scott, of Aston Sandford, makes his own experience testify to the verity of his beliefs, and certainly his "Force of Truth" would be among the books of every Evangelical. There, too, would be his friend, sturdy and stalwart Andrew Fuller, with his comparison of the Calvinistic and Socinian systems, and his vigorous assault on the new Unitarians. Archbishop Magee would be in evidence with his two discourses, which were brief, and his notes, which were voluminous, in proof of the scriptural doctrines of the Atonement and Sacrifice. Edward Williams, too, would unfold his doctrine of Sovereignty, which showed that God, as rector or ruler of the moral universe, was bound to uphold law, and could uphold it only by enforcing its sanctions, though He would, when His mercy required it and the common good allowed it, so modify the form of infliction as to accept the sufferings of an innocent Person in lieu of the penalty due to the guilty. His distinguished pupil, John Pye Smith, was certain of a place for his works on the "Priesthood of Christ," which showed how well he had learned the principles and method of Williams, and on the "Scripture Testimony to the Messiah," which showed that he had studied to higher purpose under masters then much feared because foreign. Beside him would stand the lectures and treatises of George Payne, Ralph Wardlaw, Joseph Gilbert, and Thomas Jenkyn, who all on similar principles, though with various modifications of method and terms, described, explained, and defended the theistic grounds, but legal nature, necessity, functions, and ends, of the Atonement. The relations of God and man were expressed and explicated through the categories of a special jurisprudence; theology was, as it were, done into the language of the bar and the bench. Yet the system was not irrational; indeed, its rationalism was its most remarkable feature. It was built up with elaborate care, and exhibited such rare architectonic skill that one could not but confess, were the universe a constitutional state which had broken out in rebellion, and God its monarch, thus and not otherwise, if He were to be at once merciful and just, would He be obliged to act. Of course, the principle or essence of the thought might be correct; it was the forms or categories of interpretation that were inadequate.

But what was not found in the library would be to us more remarkable than what was, especially its poverty in books dealing with Jesus as an historical person. Books of a kind would indeed be here abundant. Harmonies of the Gospels bearing great names, like those of Gerson and Jansen, or Chemnitz and Lightfoot, or Bengel and Greswell, and exhibiting extraordinary feats of conciliatory exegesis; . defences of miracles, and especially the Resurrection, against deists and deniers of every sort; poetic presentations of sacred history, and especially its most dramatic events; edifying and devotional works, calling us with à Kempis or Jeremy Taylor to the imitation of our "Great Exemplar," or with Bishop Hall to the "contemplation" of Him. But hardly a book attempting to conceive and represent Him just as He appeared in history would have been found. Of course, Fleetwood was everywhere, especially in the homes of the people, but seldom read, scarcely worth reading, certainly not worth a place amid the books of a serious theologian. If Milner's "Church History" was taken down, it began with the Apostles; if Mosheim, he gave only an insignificant chapter to Jesus; if the newer Waddington, he started with A.D. 60. It was indeed a strange and significant thing: so much speculation about Christ, so little earnest inquiry into His actual mind; so much knowledge of what the creeds or confessions, the liturgies or psalmodies, of the Church said; so little knowledge of the historical person or construction of the original documents as sources of real and actual history. It is still more significant that the men who were then most seriously intent on the revival of religion through the revival of the Church, were the very men who seemed least to feel or conceive the need of the return to Christ. They were possessed of the passion to find and restore the Church of the Fathers, and to the Fathers they appealed for direction and help ; but in no one of their multitudinous tracts or treatises is there any suggestion or sign that Christ, as the Founder, supplied the determinative idea of His own Church. The men were true sons of their generation, and for it the historical sense, especially in this province, was not yet born.

§ III.—The Recovery of the Historical Christ.

But what a contrast does the workshop of a living theologian present to the library of the older divine! Dogmatics and apologetics have almost disappeared from it, and in their place stand books on almost every possible question in the textual, literary, and historical criticism of the Old and New Testaments. Harmonies have almost ceased to be, and instead we have discussions as to the sources, sequence, dependence, independence, purpose, dates, of the four Gospels. Lives of Christ by men of all schools, tendencies, churches, abound, each using some more or less rigorous critical method. Beside these, and supplementary to them, are histories of New Testament times, which show us 'the smaller eddies as well as the greater movements, and supply both the background and the light and shade needed to throw the central Figure into true perspective. Then we have monographs on Jewish and heathen teachers, on Hellenistic and Talmudic beliefs, on Judaic sects and Gentile schools and usages, on early heresies and primitive societies, with the result that the age of Christ and His apostles is experiencing such a resurrection as Ezekiel saw in his valley of vision. Paul is studied not simply as the pre-eminent dialectician of the apostolic period, but through his psychology, his personal experience, his antecedents, discipline, relations —in a word, as a man who lived among living men; and in consequence his work and his epistles have grown full of meanings once altogether overlooked. The Gospels are no longer studied simply in relation to each other, but also in relation to the other literature of the New Testament and the thought of sub-apostolic times, and so have helped to make us conscious of the forces that organized and built up the Christian society. The Apocalypse has ceased to be read and interpreted as a mysterious prophecy which conceals even more than reveals all the destinies of all the empires that rule the Christian centuries, and has become one of our most significant documents for the interpretation of the mind of the parties within the primitive Church. The analytical process is not yet complete, and the synthetic has hardly well begun; yet enough has been achieved to warrant us in saying that the second half of our century may be described as the period when the history of the New Testament has, through its literature, been recovered, and in this history by far the greatest result is the recovery of the historical Christ.

We are speaking meanwhile only of a result which we owe to historical criticism; we are not as yet concerned with its religious or theological import. The claim does not for the moment transcend the sphere of historical inquiry and knowledge. It is neither said nor meant that our age is distinguished by a deeper reverence or purer love for the Redeemer, or even a stronger faith in Him. In these respects we might claim pre-eminence for other ages than our own. In the hymns of the early and mediæval Church, of the Lutheran and Moravian Churches, of the Evangelical and Anglican revivals, there is a fine unity of spirit, due to all possessing the same simple yet transcendent devotion to the person of the Christ. This devotion it is impossible to excel; we confess our sense of its truth, its intensity, elevation, humble yet audacious sincerity, by the use of the hymns that were its vehicle. So true is the faith of those hymns that they compel all Churches, even the most proudly exclusive, to forget their differences and divisions, and in the high act and article of worship to realize their unity. The high Anglican praises his Saviour in the strains of Luther and Isaac Watts, Gerhardt and Doddridge; the severe Puritan and Independent rejoices in the sweet and gracious songs of Keble and Faber, Newman and Lyte; the keen and rigid Presbyterian feels his soul uplifted as well by the hymns of Bernard and Xavier, Wordsworth and Mason Neale, as by the Psalms of David. And this unity in praise and worship which so transcends and cancels the distinctions of community and sect, but expresses the unity of the faith and fellowship of the heart in the Son of God. In the regions of the higher devotion and the purer love all differences cease. And as in worship so in theology; the greatest of the older divines were those who most laboured to do honour to Christ. The very goal of all their thinking, the very purpose of all their systems, was to exalt His name, to assist and vindicate His supremacy in thought and over His Church. Here East and West are agreed; Augustine vies with Athanasius, John of Damascus with Anselm, Luther with Loyola, Calvin with Bellarmine, Howe with Hooker, Rutherford with Milton. In the homage of the intellect to Christ no Church or age can claim to be pre-eminent; here there has been unity, an almost passionate agreement, intensest and most real when the Church or age was most in earnest. The statement, then, that our age excels all others in the fulness, objectivity, and accuracy of its knowledge of the historical Christ must not be construed to mean the superiority of our age in its sense of dependence on the Redeemer and reverence for Him. It knows Him as no other age has done as He lived and as He lives in history, a Being who looked before and after, within the limits and under the conditions of time and space, influenced by what preceded Him, determining what followed. What the theological consequences of this larger and more accurate knowledge may be is more than any one can tell as yet. To deduce or indicate some of these is the purpose of this book.

Our discussion will fall into two main parts: one historical and critical, and one positive and constructive. The historical and critical will deal with two questions: first, the causes that have so often made theology, in the very process of interpreting Christ, move away from Him; and, secondly, the causes that have contributed to the modern return to Him. The positive and constructive will also be concerned with two questions: first, the interpretation of Christ given in the Christian sources; and, secondly, the theological significance of Christ as thus interpreted.

BOOK I.

HISTORICAL AND CRITICAL.

DIV. I.—THE LAW OF DEVELOPMENT IN THEOLOGY AND THE CHURCH.

DIV. II.—HISTORICAL CRITICISM AND THE HISTORY OF CHRIST.

Ἐν ἀρχῇ ἦν ὁ Λόγος, καὶ ὁ Λόγος ἦν πρὸς τὸν Θεόν, καὶ Θεὸς ἦν ὁ Λόγος. οὗτος ἦν ἐν ἀρχῇ πρὸς τὸν Θεόν. πάντα δι' αὐτοῦ ἐγένετο, καὶ χωρὶς αὐτοῦ ἐγένετο οὐδὲ ἓν ὃ γέγονεν. ἐν αὐτῷ ζωὴ ἦν, καὶ ἡ ζωὴ ἦν τὸ φῶς τῶν ἀνθρώπων, καὶ τὸ φῶς ἐν τῇ σκοτίᾳ φαίνει, καὶ ἡ σκοτία αὐτὸ οὐ κατέλαβεν. —JOHN i. 1-5.

Quod initium sancti Evangelii, cui nomen est secundum Ioannem, quidam Platonicus, sicut a sancto sene Simpliciano, qui postea Mediolanensi Ecclesiæ præsedit episcopus, solebamus audire, aureis literis conscribendum, et per omnes Ecclesias in locis eminentissimis proponendum esse dicebat.—AUGUSTINE, "De Civ. Dei," x. 29.

Unicus enim natura Dei Filius, propter nos misericordia factus est filius hominis, ut nos natura filii hominis, filii Dei per illum gratia fieremus. Manens quippe ille immutabilis, naturam nostram in qua nos susciperet, suscepit a nobis; et tenax divinitatis suæ, nostræ infirmitatis particeps factus est; ut nos in melius commutati, quod peccatores mortalesque sumus, eius immortalis et justi participatione amittamus, et quod in natura nostra bonum fecit, inpletum summo bono in ejus naturæ bonitate servemus. Sicut enim per unum hominem peccantem in hoc tam grave malum devenimus; ita per unum hominem eundemque Deum justificantem ad illud bonum tam sublime veniemus. —AUGUSTINE, "De Civ. Dei," xxi. 15.

Der Sohn kommt von dem Vater herunter zu uns und hänget sich an uns, und, wir hängen wiederum uns an ihn und kommen durch ihn zum Vater. Denn darum ist er Mensch worden und geboren von der Jungfrauen Maria, dass er sich sollt in uns mengen, sehen und hören lassen, ja auch uns also zu sich ziehe und an ihm halte, als dazu gesandt, dass er die, so an ihn glauben würden, hinauf zöge zum Vater, wie er in dem Vater ist.—LUTHER on John xiv. 20.

Die Welt ist eine Blume, die aus Einem Saamenkorn ewig hervorgeht.—HEGEL, "Geschichte der Philos.," iii. 615.

DIVISION I.

THE LAW OF DEVELOPMENT IN THEOLOGY AND THE CHURCH.

CHAPTER I.

THE DOCTRINE OF DEVELOPMENT.

§ I.—ON THE HISTORY OF THE DOCTRINE.

THE term and idea of development were introduced formally and explicitly into English theology by Newman. With him, indeed, it was not so much a scientific doctrine as a form of personal apology, exhibiting, as it were, the logic of his conversion. With his premises the logic was invincible, but its significance is personal and biographical rather than general and historical. His thought moved uneasily between two poles, both of which he owed to Butler, though the one was Butler's own, the other Locke's. Butler's was the doctrine of conscience, Locke's the doctrine of probability. Conscience was Butler's real contribution to the philosophy of human nature; probability was the first principle of his analogy, or special apologetic for the Christian religion. The two positions were full of implicit incompatibilities; the supremacy of conscience made a constitutional authority the guide of life, but, according to the doctrine of probability, the guide was a sort of logical calculus. The one doctrine was transcendental—*i.e.*, conscience meant that human nature brought with it and had imbedded in it a law for the governance of man or the regulation of his conduct; but the other doctrine was empirical—*i.e.*, man had by balancing probabilities to discover the faith he was to hold, and so the spiritual laws he was to obey. The imperious but narrow logic of Newman's mind, quickened by his passionate yet intellectual mysticism, forced these incompatibilities into sharp antitheses. The reason could only deal with probabilities, but the conscience possessed supremacy and authority; while it was the nature of the one to question and analyze and weigh, it was the nature of the other to reign and to command. Now, religion was associated with the authoritative, not with the ratiocinative, faculty. Conscience was the source of natural religion, and its supremacy the one valid authority; and so the supersession of natural by revealed religion meant the "substitution of the voice of a lawgiver for the voice of conscience."[1] The intellect, as governed by the law of probability, was naturally critical of authority, and had to be beaten down and forced under, that it might be disciplined and filled with religious contents. And so Newman began a quest after "the invisible Divine Power" or "external Authority" whose supremacy was "the essence of revealed religion." This could not be the Scriptures, for they were a book that needed interpretation, and the real authority was the interpreter rather than the interpreted. It could not be the Anglican Church, for it had no organ through which to speak: its bishops were worse than dumb; their voices were often contradictory, oftener without authority, and too frequently attuned to the measures of a selfish and worldly wisdom. So he was forced to turn to the time when there was neither Anglican nor Roman nor Greek Church, but only the undivided Church of East and West. In this Church, its Fathers

[1] "Development of Christian Doctrine," p. 124 (2nd ed., 1846).

and its Councils, he found the authority he craved; what was then always and everywhere believed by all was the truth. Skilful and dexterous interpretation made the theory work awhile; but though the conversion of a disputant by his opponents is the rarest of events, yet where they fail the logic of the situation may succeed. And so it happened with Newman. The primitive Church was soon seen to be anything but a united Church; within it were many minds and many differences of doctrine and custom, and of it no living Church was an exact reproduction or reflection. Compared with it, the Roman was different, but continuous; while the Anglican was both discontinuous and different. In no respect, therefore, could the Anglican be saved or vindicated through the Church of the Fathers; but in two respects the Roman could be vindicated—by its manifest historical continuity, and by a theory of development which not only explained the differences, but turned them into proofs of the Roman claim. This theory became, then, at once the justification of Newman's consistency, the condemnation of the Church he forsook, and the vindication of the Church he joined.

To sketch the history of the theory would carry us far beyond our present limits. On one side it represented the victory of Protestant criticism, and confessed that the Catholicism of Trent was not the Catholicism of the ancient Church; but, on the other side, it evaded the Protestant conclusion by construing the Church, Roman and Catholic, as a living and therefore growing body, which not only had the right to defend its life by augmenting or developing its creed, but was bound on due occasion to exercise the right. The earlier form of the theory resulted from the controversies of the sixteenth and seventeenth centuries. Calvin,[1] Flacius and the other Magdeburg

[1] "Epistola Nuncupatoria," "Inst.," pp. 18-25 (ed. 1536). Calvin here argues that the Reformed is nearer the Fathers than the Roman faith,

centuriators,[1] Chemnitz,[2] Amesius,[3] and Daillé,[4] had strenuously affirmed what Bellarmine and Baronius as strenuously denied —that the new Catholicism was not the old Christianity; and their evidences and arguments were too cogent to be

which exhibits radical and revolutionary additions to their creed and customs. It is the negation rather than the development of the patristic theology. Cf. his "Supplex Exhortatio ad Cæsarem Carolum Quintum," Opera, vol. vi., pp. 453-534 (in "Corpus Reformatorum"), and "Acta Synodi Tridentinæ. Cum Antidoto," *ibid.*, vol. vii., pp. 365-506; but especially "Inst.," bk. iv., cc. iv.-viii. (ed. 1559).

[1] "Ecclesias. Historia, integram ecclesiæ Christi ideam complectens, congesta per aliquot studiosos et pios viros in urbe Magdeb." (1559-1574). This was the claim of Protestantism, made in thirteen folio volumes, to be "historical Christianity." It traced, century by century, the fall of Catholicism, partly by ignorance and neglect, partly by the potency of idolatry or sin and evil custom, from the purity and simplicity of the Apostolic age to the tyrannies and impurities of the Mediæval Papacy. Yet it did justice to the saintliness and truth that had never ceased to illumine the Church. The man who planned and carried through the enterprise was Matthias Flacius, often, from his birthplace, named Illyricus. With him were various collaborateurs: Wigand, a man most indefatigable in the theological polemics of his most polemical age, yet whose spirit is well expressed in his epitaph—

"In Christo vixi, morior vivoque Wigandus:
Do Sordes morti, cætera Christe tibi";

Matthæus Judex, who died before the work had far advanced; Basilius Faber; Andreas Corvinus, Wigand's son-in-law; and Thomas Holzhuter. To it belongs the significance of being the first serious appeal to history as a whole, and as a process of change and enlargement. It was in reply to these "centuriæ Satanæ," that had advanced "e portis inferis in Ecclesiæ detrimentum," that Baronius wrote his "Annales Eccles." ("Gratiarum Actio Ph. Nereo," tom. viii., p. vii.).

[2] "Examen Decret. Concil. Trid." (1565-1573). The fundamental principle of this book is "Nostram antiquitatem esse Christum et Sacram Scripturam" (p. 670, ed. 1641). But he throughout argues: the Fathers, so far as representatives of the true and pure antiquity, are against Rome —its customs and dogmas are not theirs. His arguments are derived, not simply from Scripture, but also "ex orthodoxorum Patrum consensu." Yet the Fathers are to be judged by Scripture, not Scripture by the Fathers (cf. pp. 477, 495, 503, 526, 726, 768). For they all, as subject to the customs and pre-judgments of their time, erred in opinion and in interpretation; and while their errors were to be forgiven, they were not to be imitated (cf. pp. 285, 469, 480-482, 542, 543, etc.).

[3] "Bellarminus Enervatus," tom. i., lib. i., c. vi. (1628).

[4] "Traité de l'Emploi des Saintes Pères pour le jugement des différends

ineffectual. Petavius[1] struck out a happier answer than Bellarmine. He carried the question out of the region where there was difference into the region where there was agreement between the Roman, the Reformed, and the Lutheran Churches. He said, in effect:—on such vital matters as the Trinity and the Incarnation, the ante- and

qui sont aujourd'hui en la Religion" (1632). This book has an interesting history, but what concerns us is its modern spirit. It was written in answer to the Roman Catholic plea, "We have antiquity and the Fathers," and argues:— the questions of the Fathers were not ours, and do not decide our controversies; their doctrine was not uniform, and they have often contradicted one another; they have not written as representatives of the whole Church, nor have they ever claimed to be for us authorities in religion, nor are they ever used as such save for offensive or defensive purposes. Every Church differs from them, and vindicates, as well as exercises, its right to differ. Growth everywhere involves change, most of all in religion, and it is mere pretence, discarded wherever inconvenient, for any Church to say, "We follow the Fathers,"—since by the very nature of the case they can neither be pure nor ultimate authorities, and as a matter of fact in many fundamental matters are not treated, nor are even capable of being treated, as authorities at all.

[1] "De Theologicis Dogmatibus," published at Paris, 1644-50. It was republished with additions, mainly from the polemical tracts of Petavius himself against Grotius, Salmasius, and the Jansenists, by Clericus under the pseudonym of Theophilus Alethinus at Antwerp, 1700; and again under the editorship of Father Zacharia at Venice in 1757. A new and very sumptuous edition began to appear at Rome in 1857. The book is classical, the first attempt at a scientific history of dogmata, and is notable as suggesting to modern theology the term "Dogmatics." He uses dogmata that he may denote Christian ideas, as known through the Scriptures and tradition, but as formulated by the Church. It was a well enough understood patristic sense, but prior to its modern use there were instructive differences in the nomenclature of the science of interpretative theology. The first systematic treatise bore the significant name Περὶ ἀρχῶν; scholasticism began by the use of *Libri Sententiarum—i.e.*, sentences from the Fathers were selected, systematized, and subjected to dia'ectical elaboration; then, as the schoolmen became more independent of the Fathers and more dependent on Aristotle, their systems took the name *Summæ Theologicæ*, which were in scheme and construction philosophical and deductive rather than inductive and interpretative. The Lutheran theologians used the name *Loci Communes—i.e.*, their systems were built on principles or commonplaces derived, not from the Fathers, but from the Scriptures. The Reformed took the characteristic title *Institutiones Christianæ Religionis—i.e.*, they conceived their systems as methods

the post-Nicene Fathers did not agree.[1] Measured by the later and authoritative standards the ante-Nicene Fathers were almost all on one point or another heretical; but they were not heretics because the Church had not spoken, and it was their very differences and inchoatenesses that made it necessary for her to speak. She watched and preserved the truth, whose pillar and ground she was, by timely definitions and developments.[2] Jurieu, from the Protestant side, by changing the emphasis, so applied Petavius that the differences between the Papal and the Apostolic and ancient Christianity were from developments translated into innovations, and a Church that came into its creed by fragments and in stages proved by the very terms of its being to be no infallible and immutable Church.[3]

of education and instruction in the Christian verities. With the name *Theologica Dogmata* came in the notion of fixed principles variously interpreted and formulated, therefore with a development and a history. Protestant theologians did not take kindly to it, though it was used by Reinhart in 1659, and by Buddæus in 1724; yet as late as 1780 Doederlein, "Inst. Theol.," p. 192, complained "theologiam theoreticam male nostris temporibus dici coeptam esse dogmaticam." And his reason was: "Nam theologia dogmatica propria est, quæ agit de placitis et opinionibus theologorum." But this did not suit the usage of Petavius. Cf. for the classical and patristic use of the term C. L. Nitzsch, "Sys. der Christ. Lehre," pp. 50-53; Baur, "Vorles üb. d. Christ. Dogmengesch.," i. 8 ff.

[1] "De Theol. Dog.," "De Trin.," lib. i., cc. iii.-viii. He holds that the ante-Nicene Fathers spoke in certain cases "Ariano pæne more"; and, in c. v., § 7, names Athenagoras, Tatian, Theophilus, Tertullian, and Lactantius as holding that the Son was made (*productum*) that He might be used as a kind of assistant or servant (*administrum*); while others, like Origen, held the Father superior in age, dignity, and power to the Word, and, although made from the substance of the Father, yet He no less than creatures had had a beginning. In c. viii., § 2, he describes Arius as a "germanum Platonicum," who followed the dogma of those ancient writers, "qui nondum patefacta constitutaque re ad eumdem errorem offenderunt." Cf. Bishop Bull, "Defensio Fidei Nic.," Proem., §§ 7, 8.

[2] "De Theol. Dog.," Prolegomena, c. i., ii. The *cautiones* he appends are very instructive. Cf. "De Trin.," Præfatio, and the Appendicula, in which the editor gives an attempt at an *Apologia* for the doctrine of his author. The boldness of Petavius involved him in serious charges of dealings with heresy; his doctrine and illustrations exercised great influence on Newman.

[3] "Lettres Pastorales addressées aux Fidèles de France, qui gémissent

Catholic doctrine was often but successful heresy: "The authors of heresies and superstitions which are rejected are indeed loaded with infamy, but the makers of those that are received are canonized and revered." Bossuet did his best to rid Catholicism of a theory[1] which so completely removed the basis from his famous argument against the Protestants. That argument, so far as it was constructive, rested on two positive principles—viz., "que la foi ne varie pas dans la vraie Eglise et que la vérité venue de Dieu a d'abord sa perfection"[2]; but the doctrine of evolution changed the first into an historical untruth, the second into a philosophical error. But the "Histoire" as a whole is only a splendid example of a polemic successful by its very want of truth and reasonableness. It moves upon the same level as the performances of those modern writers who imagine that

sous la Captivité de Babylon" (2nd ed., 1686). See in particular letters ii., iii., v., vi. Bossuet had affirmed "l'impossibilité des changemens insensibles." Jurieu argues—the history of the immutable Church of Rome has been a succession of variations, insensibly introduced, but slowly working out a radical revolution. These letters are pathetic reading; fugitive leaflets addressed to the dispersed and persecuted Churches of France, containing now learned discussions in history and doctrine, now impassioned exhortations to steadfastness, and again sad and touching narratives of the sufferings and heroisms of the proscribed. It is a signal example of the waywardness of literary fame; it is a more learned, more modern, more scientific book than Bossuet's, yet the militant bishop has received honours which were denied to his antagonist. Jurieu went to the root of the matter, formulated a doctrine of development, held that the Church grew in mind, did not understand its own faith and meaning at first, learned to understand only by degrees; illustrated his contention from the Fathers and from history, and troubled the equanimity of Monsieur de Meaux by roundly affirming that the man who denied it must have a brow of brass, or be of a crass and surprising ignorance. The letters were translated into English and published, with a dedication to the Prince of Orange, in 1689.

[1] See the Avertissements to the "Histoire des Variations." They are instructive reading, full of the arts of the disputant who to evade the issue starts a false charge against his opponent. They are in extent equal to a third of the "Histoire," and showed how thoroughly the Aigle de Meaux had been winged.

[2] "Hist. des Variations," vol. iii., Avert., p. 5 (ed. 1845).

to exhibit the differences of critics is to refute criticism. The most perfect work of this type must always remain the least significant. Such is Bossuet's, and its insignificance is seen in this—that as the ideas of order and progress in history became explicit in philosophy, the development he so disliked reappeared in a new and more scientific shape in theology. It took a twofold form: the French, which was more social and political; and the German, which was more philosophical and theological,—the former, whose main exponent was Joseph de Maistre, being due to the speculative tendencies which culminated in Comte; the latter, which had in Moehler its most brilliant representative,[1] exhibits the combined influence of Hegel and Schleiermacher. But Newman's theory, though its real affinities were with Petavius rather than de Maistre or Moehler, was yet distinctively his own, explicable through his own history, the peculiar product of his experience, the logical issue of the position he had years before assumed. In him, therefore, it is too much a matter of personal development to stand in need of explanation from without.

What, then, was Newman's theory of development? He described it as "an hypothesis to account for a difficulty"[2]— viz., the procession or evolution of Catholicism from what was in many respects so radically unlike it, as to be its very opposite, if not contradiction—primitive Christianity. It "came into the world as an idea rather than an institution, and has had to wrap itself in clothing and fit itself with armour of its own providing, and to form the instruments and methods of its prosperity and warfare."[3] The process by which it has done this is called "development," "being the germination, growth, and perfection of some living, that

---

[1] "Symbolik," § 40. Cf. Perrone, "Prælect. Theol.," tom. ii., pp. 165, 166.
[2] "Development of Doctrine," p. 27.
[3] *Ibid.*, p. 116. This notion Newman owed to Guizot, but he failed to see how completely it bore the features of Guizot's Protestantism. The primary and essential thing in Christianity was to Newman the institution, not the idea; but to Guizot, the idea, not the institution.

is, influential, truth, or apparent truth, in the minds of men during a sufficient period. And it has this necessary characteristic—that, since its province is the busy scene of human life, it cannot develop at all, except either by destroying, or modifying and incorporating with itself, existing modes of thinking and acting."[1] In antithesis to development stands " corruption," which is defined as " that state of development which undoes its previous advances," " a process ending in dissolution of the body of thought and usage which was bound up, as it were, in one system," " the destruction of the norm or type."[2] The " tests " which distinguish " true development " from corruption are seven—" the preservation of the Idea," "continuity of principles," " power of assimilation," "early anticipation," " logical sequence," "preservative additions," and " chronic continuance."[3] This is an impressive apparatus for the determination of true developments from false, but the moment we attempt to apply the theory to history we are pulled up with a sudden shock. For it turns out to be a theory not for historical use, but for polemical or apologetical purposes. The developments are to proceed under the eye of "an external authority,"[4] which is to be the only and infallible judge as to whether they are true or false. But this remarkable provision calls for two remarks: first, "infallibility" is not an "idea," but a very definite "institution," and so hardly conforms to the terms under which Christianity was said to have "come into the world"; and, secondly, to exempt "the infallibility of the Church" from the law of development is to withdraw from us the most flagrant example of its operation. If anything has a history which exhibits growth, it is this doctrine; to make one development the judge of the right or wrong of all the rest, is to mock us by refusing to enforce at the most critical point

[1] "Development of Doctrine," p. 37.
[2] *Ibid.*, pp. 62, 63.
[3] *Ibid.*, 64 ff.
[4] *Ibid.*, p. 117: cf. chap. ii., § 2.

the law which has been so solemnly enacted. This may be expediency, but it is not justice ; and injustice in history is no service to the cause of truth.

§ II.—The Idea of Development.

The theory of development as formulated and applied by Newman had three great defects : it was logical and abstract, not biological and historical or real; its starting-point was too late, a picture of the created society rather than of the creative personality ; and its end was a mere fraction or section of the collective organism isolated from all the rest, and invested with functions whose origin evolution could well have explained, but was not allowed to touch. These defects indicate the lines our exposition of the positive doctrine will follow.

What does development mean? The term meets us in all sciences and all branches of inquiry ; it denotes an idea that is in the air, working, consciously or unconsciously, in all minds. Darwin did not discover it, nor was it first formulated by Spencer ; but it is as old as philosophy, and has been more or less implicit in the methods of all great inquirers. What is distinctive of to-day is our more conscious or common use of it, our clearer sense of the problems it sets us, our greater mastery of the factors necessary to their solution, and distincter conception of the limits within which we and our problems move. Development may be defined as at once a subjective method and an objective process,—as a method it seeks to conceive and explain a being or thing through its history ; as a process it denotes the mode in which the being or thing becomes as a mode of progressive yet natural change worked by two sets of factors, the inner and outer, or organism and environment. In each branch of study it assumes a form appropriate to the matter which is handled : in philosophy it becomes either, subjectively, an inquiry into the process by which man comes by his knowledge or grows into the intelligence he is, or, objectively, a dialectical explication of the Idea, the Cause, or Force which unfolds or is unfolded into the system which we name "the universe" or "the known" or "the manifold of experience"; in science it is in its subjective sense the method which seeks in the immanent and correlated forces of nature a reason for all the changes and variations which natural things undergo—in its objective sense it is the process by which out of old forms or species new ones arise, organs being modified, lost, recovered, or developed in the struggle for existence; in history it describes the method which studies beliefs, customs, institutions, and events through the factors of their origin and in their reciprocal and correlated being, and the process by which out of the simpler the more complex societies, states, and religions emerge. But the distinctive element in all the senses may be stated thus: in development the thing is studied as it grows and where it grows, and through the causes and conditions of its growth, in order to the truer knowledge alike of its special forms and of the forces through whose operation they are.

If this is an approximately correct description of development, then it must, from its very nature, so far as concerned with real persons or organisms, be biological—*i.e.*, it must study life as living, as lived, and as perpetuating life. It cannot be merely logical—*i.e.*, proceed as if nature could be reduced, as it were, to the forms of the syllogism, or stated in its terms. The distinction between logical and biological development may be represented thus: the one is evolution conceived as an immanent process, and proceeding either without any environment or independently of any formative energies active within it; but the other is evolution exhibited in an organism which lives within a living world, affected by all its forces, and sensitive to its every change. In the field of history the logical is simply an abstract deductive process stated and conducted in concrete or historical terms—*i.e.*, it assumes principles and reasons to conclusions that history may be used to illustrate, but cannot be allowed to decide or to determine. But the biological or scientific is essentially concrete and inductive : *i.e.*, it keeps its feet on reality and studies things in their relations ; begins to observe the organism or new form at the earliest possible point ; carefully analyzes and describes the various environments into which it enters, notes how it is modified by each and modifies each ; seeks to discover whether the great factors of change are inner or outer ; and accurately measures and registers at every definite stage the degree and path of change. Logical development is a simple process, but biological is most complex : the former is selective, defines what it wants to prove, and fixes the conditions and lines of proof; but the latter is comprehensive, finds in the facts and phenomena before it what has to be explained, and attempts, by following their history, to find the explanation.

Now, Newman's theory revealed its essentially logical and dialectical character in this—it was an argument which used historical formulæ for the maintenance of a given thesis, not for the interpretation of history. He took what he was pleased to call the Church out of the world in which it lived and through which it was organized—so declining to study these in their correlation and reciprocal action ; and he did not study either the Christ who created the society, or the society as it was created by Christ. He indeed elucidated his theory by historical illustrations ; but though the illustrations were historical, they did not constitute history ; they had all the insignificance of texts isolated for special polemical purposes from their context. In human as in natural history the action of the environment is as real as the action of the organism. They may differ as regards function and quality, but they agree in being alike efficient as factors of change. The organism is creative, the seat and source of life ; but the environment is formative, determines the shape which the life assumes. Without the organism there would be no life, no victorious energies, no being that struggles to be more and more; without the environment there would be no arena that at once exercises and disciplines the energies, no field full of forces that must be now resisted and now assimilated. This mutual being and correlated activity of organism and environment is but the form under which, as regards the question specifically before us, we express this fundamental principle:—the Church, so far as it exists in all or in any of its organized forms, lives within the world, subject to the laws which govern all related being. Its history is a section of universal history, in the proper sense as secular as the history of any empire or state. It belongs to time, conditions and is conditioned by the agencies active within it, is inseparable from the other fields of human activity, moral and social, individual and collective. The history of belief, of custom, of institutions, of political action and change, of industry and policy, of personal morals and international relations, cannot be written apart from the history of the Church, nor its history apart from theirs; at every fundamental and significant point the one shades into the other. And this interpenetration is independent of any theory as to the constitution of the Church, or its relations to the State; it is as complete on the Presbyterian as on the Papal, on the Congregational as on the Anglican theory, and is as little escaped by a voluntary as by an Erastian Church. But if every Church must so live in the world as to be a part of its collective being, then it must always be construed in and through the place and time in which it lives. Apart from these it can as little be explained or understood as can an organism apart from nature and its order. In both cases there must be the co-ordination of the living being and its home in order to any scientific theory of development.

§ III.—Development in the Church.

Now, in the field of inquiry which concerns us, what has been termed the organism is not the Church, but the historical Christ—not the created society, but the creative Personality. What He involved will be seen by-and-by. What we have meanwhile to note is this : He entered into a double environment—the society He created, and the world within which it lived. He founded the society, and the society was bound to interpret Him ; indeed, it was only as He could be made to live explicated and reasonable to its intellect that He could command its conscience or abide in its heart. But the interpretation could not be simply in the terms He Himself supplied ; to have secured this the world as well as the society would have had to be made wholly new. The inherited experiences and instincts of centuries could not be dissolved and discharged by an act of faith or by a simple change of associations. The men who entered the Church did not cease to be Jews or Greeks or Romans ; though their spirit and temper were changed, yet their faculties, activities, modes and instruments of thought, remained the same. Nothing is so certain or so evident as the activity of racial idiosyncrasies and the prevalence of local and provincial varieties within the ancient Church. These differences affected doctrine, polity, worship, morals—in a word, the whole field of religion. Judaism was most varied, a thing of many schools and types; there was a Judaism of the Temple and of the synagogue, of the desert and of the mart, of the rabbinical school and of the ascetic's cell ; there was a Sadducaic, Pharisaic, and an Essenic Judaism —a Judaism of Judæa and Galilee, of Jerusalem and Alexandria, of Italy and Asia Minor. And traces of all the rich varieties can be found in ancient Christian literature, in the history of the Church and the sects. And Hellenism was as varied; the local cults were an innumerable multitude; the intellectual tendencies, and as a consequence the types of philosophical thought, differed almost as much; the schools of Athens and Alexandria, of Antioch and Tarsus, were all as distinct and dissimilar as were their respective races and histories. And in the West paganism was no less varied; North Africa and Gaul, Spain and Italy, alike lived under Rome, yet in religion each went its own way, retained its ancient worship, but did not scruple to add new to its ancient deities. And these local differences affected the local Churches. They were first organized on the lines of municipal and provincial or territorial differences, and then on the lines of imperial and Roman policy. The episcopal constitution did not rise all at once, nor, when it had risen, did it move altogether with equal step in all places. In some localities it sprang into sudden being; in others the old congregational and presbyterial simplicity lingered on. Ancient customs persisted even though the religion changed; and the longest struggle Rome had—a struggle in which it has not been even yet completely successful—was against the old local cults continued in the local Churches. But even more persistent were the old intellectual tendencies. There is as much ancient philosophy in Justin Martyr as in Marcus Aurelius, in Origen as in Celsus. The literary spirit of Alexandria, eclectic yet idealist in philosophy and allegorical in interpretation, is as evident and active in Clement as in Philo, in the Catechetical School as in the New Academy. The history of Neo-Platonism is Christian as well as pagan; it had almost as much to do with the formation of Athanasius and Augustine as of Plotinus and Porphyry. If Tertullian had not been a jurist, his theology would not have been what it is, especially as regards those very elements and terms by which it has most powerfully affected the development of dogma. His Greek mind and training make it impossible that Chrysostom should ever have written the Anti-Pelagian Treatises, while they are as full as they well could be of the intellectual principles and tendencies that had once made Augustine a Manichean. The causes and conditions that so helped to shape the Fathers helped no less to form the Church whose mind they made and expressed. Change their philosophy, and their theology would not have been what it was. Without Aristotle in the Middle Ages we should not have had scholasticism, at least not in the distinctive form it now possesses; and without ancient philosophy all the many types and varieties of patristic and scholastic theology would be different from what they are. If, therefore, the men who made the thought and formulated the faith of the Church have been so powerfully affected by external forces, it is evident that its development cannot be dealt with as if it had been governed entirely from within. The internal were indeed the creative forces, but the external were factors of form and of formal change.

This argument, so far as it has proceeded, must not be construed to mean that the action of the environment was either illicit or unnecessary. It had, quite as much as the organism, a place and function in the order of Providence. If there had been no creative Person there could have been no society; if no society, conscious of being a creation and with faith in its Creator, there could have been no reason for the interpretation of Him; if no world with its antecedent history, there could have been no interpretative faculty, method, or means. This does not in any way question the necessity of metaphysics or philosophies, which exist simply because man is man, and he must always ask a reason for the being of himself and his universe. And the dogmata of a Church are but what may be described as its philosophy of its Founder or of its own being, and as such necessary to it if it would have a justified or rational existence. Nor is there any question raised as to the legitimacy of using the terms philosophy had elaborated and the methods it had followed in its quest after truth, nay, such use had the right which belongs to simple necessity. The past did not accumulate its riches in vain : they were made to be used, not to be lost. The philosophy of Greece had a divine function in the world as well as the law of the Hebrews, and its art and polity had a mission as high and as real as its philosophy. The mere fact, therefore, that religious customs, or social institutions, or doctrinal forms, or even doctrines themselves have been borrowed by the Church, or assimilated and incorporated from without, does not condemn them,— if it did, what would survive? But it does this—it helps us to see what they are by showing how they came to be. The natural history of an organism or an institution is its explanation, not its condemnation ; if it cannot bear to be explained, it wants the most rudimentary of all rights to being and to belief. And here, while the formal factor is found in the environment, the material factor must be sought in the organism, and the truth of the one must be tested by its adequacy as a vehicle or mode of expression for the other. Christ remains the regulative as He was the originating mind ; He is, as it were, the eternal norm, the law by which the spirit, offices, institutions, of the Church must be measured and judged. It cannot escape from Him, or make Him after any one of its own changeful moods ; for the literature which describes His history has made His Presence universal and immortal. It is as if the ideals of the creative mind stood disclosed for comparison with the realities of the creation. Supremacy and permanence then belong to Him alone ; the determinations of every man or council or age have a merely local and temporal character, and the earlier even more than the later. For Christ must be formed within that He may be read and articulated without, but the growth into His spirit has been a matter of centuries and proceeds but slowly even yet. The literature of to-day is worthier of Him than the literature of the second or third century ; the religious consciousness has fewer pagan and more Christian elements now than it had then, and its interpretation of Him, as it has more accurate knowledge at its command, ought to have more truth and more validity than belongs to the symbols of Nicæa and Chalcedon. If there has been development, it must mean greater competence to interpret the Christ, and greater truth in the interpretation.

§ IV.—The Realm of the Law.

But the discussion as to the idea of development and the action of the material and formal factors in it involves another—viz., as to its scope or range. The facts and phenomena to which it ought to be applied may be described as of two classes—the quantitative or extensive, and the qualitative or intensive. The quantitative or extensive concern the evolution not simply of a given Church, but as it were of Christendom, of the varied forms of thought and society under which men have attempted to realize the religion of Christ. This indeed represents an immense area of inquiry, for the religion is so rich and so multiform as to be almost incapable of definition or even description. It is not a single system or organization; it is a multitude of systems, a crowd of the most diverse organizations; yet it is none of these, but rather the common spirit they all labour to realize, the common purpose they all endeavour more or less blindly to fulfil. Newman said [1]: "Whatever be historical Christianity, it is not Protestantism," and we may add, still less is it Catholicism. "If ever there were a safe truth, it is this." The religion of Christ is too rich, too subtle, too incorporeal and infinite to be exhausted in any single system, or embodied even in so finely articulated and rigorous an organism as the Church of Rome. That Church, immense

[1] "Development of Christian Doctrine," p. 5.

as it is, is but a fraction of Christendom; on the one side of it lies the Greek, on the other side the Anglican, and beyond these the Churches, in all their branches and varieties, that have been in a peculiar degree the creators of the modern world—the Lutheran and the Reformed. No Church can claim to be "historical Christianity"; for it is equal to all the Churches, yet it is much more than they all. Each may have played its own part in history, but its part has been small compared with its Founder's. His religion is co-extensive with His influence; under its vast canopy the stateliest Church and the meanest conventicle alike stand, and in His presence all degrees cease, grandeur is abased, and lowliness is exalted. But if Churches are to be understood, it must be not through the claims they make for themselves, but through their relations to Him; each is an example at once of His power and action on the world, and of the world's power and action on Him through His people. Development cannot concern itself with less than this. If it did so, then it could be no theory or law exhibiting the growth of the faith and life of Christ in man. Both of these have existed outside as well as inside the Churches, often in nobler forms without than within; and everywhere they have been His and from Him. Certainly, if all good and holy living be due to Him, it comes dangerously near impiety to limit His "covenanted mercies" to systems which the hands of man have built and the vanity of man has called the Church of Christ.

The phenomena we have called qualitative or intensive are those attributes or elements which Churches have claimed as their distinctive characteristics. These may be matters of polity, or doctrine, or offices and worship, or discipline and conduct, or all these combined. A scientific theory of development must seek to explain all the Churches and theologies of Christendom, with all they claim to be, making all equally and in all things subjects of investigation and of equal investigation. We must carefully guard against assumptions which either exempt from its action the phenomena which it is most needed to explain, or which affirm it in the region where it is a convenient apologetic while excluding it from the region where it becomes a reasonable but unwelcome explanation. Thus Newman's development postulates the being and claims of the Roman Church, its infallibility and truth; but while he skilfully used it in justification of his Church, he as skilfully avoided its use in the explanation of its genesis. Concede the Roman claim, and his theory was an ingenious "hypothesis to account for a difficulty"; regard it as a claim which must be read through its natural history as a problem in evolution, and the "hypothesis" cannot be got upon its feet; it is absolutely without reason or function. Again, it is equally impossible to limit development to a process of formal without substantial change, which the Church is said to conduct with a view to adjusting herself to the changed conditions of the time.[1] For it is evident that the Church and its Creed are assumed to be exempted from its operation—*i.e.*, the developmental process is not one which can be applied to this Church and Creed, but one which they direct. Their being and truth must be granted before it can be called into action, and even then it can act only under their superintendence. But development must try whether it can explain the Church and the Creed before they can be allowed to use development; and this is the more necessary, as "Christian Church" here means not the Church of Christ, but a specific ecclesiastical body, and "Creed" the faith of certain among its members.

The theory, then, must be either rigorously applied, or not at all; exceptions in favour of particular Churches are impossible. History must be impartial; it knows no schism and recognizes no dissent; for it the claims of Churches are subjects for investigation, not sanctities beyond it. Infallibility may

[1] Moehler, "Symbolik," § 40. Cf. "Lux Mundi," pp. viii., ix.

command or satisfy faith, but it only whets the curiosity of science by presenting it with a large and complex problem. The historian sees that the Christian religion is a vaster thing than any Christian Church, or than all the Churches; he sees too that these Churches differ from age to age both in character and action. He perceives that Catholicism in the early Middle Ages helped to organize modern civilization, but has been in later times possibly the most disintegrating of all our social forces. The countries which most suffer from revolution are the countries where its rule is or has been most absolute; the countries where it has least authority most represent order and progress. The historian then cannot accept a Church at its own estimate; he must study it in relation to its place and time, ask how and why it came to be, how it behaves, and with what results. For him its offices, orders, creeds, councils, its whole systems of polity and belief, are matters for inquiry and explanation; and only when nature has been completely exhausted is there even a possible apology for an appeal to the supernatural. Start with the supernatural as a first principle, invest the forms of the society or its political framework with Divine right or infallible authority, and it is so lifted out of historical conditions that it ceases to be an object to which development can be applied.[1]

[1] Mr. Gore begins his work on "The Church and the Ministry" by making two assumptions, one being "the truth of the Incarnation" (p. 6). But one may, because of his very reverence for "the truth of the Incarnation," object to it being assumed as an apology for a polity well known outside Christianity, and within it easily capable of explanation without any such assumption. The author who proceeds in this way only assumes the appearance of the historical inquirer in order the more effectually to do the work of the dogmatic divine. He acts as would the man of science who, in order the more conclusively to prove some theory of his own, should begin by solemnly assuming the omnipotence of the Creator, so using his faith on the one hand to become independent of nature, and on the other to suggest that the opposite theory means a nature without God. But here as elsewhere the law of parsimony rules superfluous causes out of court. Apart from this there is no disproof of Mr. Gore's theory of the Church so strong as the Incarnation and the terms in which it is stated.

To speak of it in the terms of evolution is to use language that has no meaning ; to employ scientific methods in the investigation of its origin, behaviour, and growth is to force science into a region where it has no place and no problem. To ascribe development to it is only to say that it uses its Divine attributes to act on fit occasions as becomes the Divine. But in all this, as there is no nature or law, so there is no room for the inquirer whose function is to explain nature by the discovery of her laws.

CHAPTER II.

DEVELOPMENT OF THE ANCIENT CHURCH.

THE exposition of the idea or doctrine of development has implied throughout that for it there is only one method of verification—viz., the comparison and correlation of the various factors and forms of change. The primitive organism must be studied till it is known, and so must the primitive environment; the result must then be examined and compared with the forces active in organism and environment respectively. Only by a method like this can we discover what each has contributed to the total effect. Of course the old forces will not remain as old when new-combined; and so, while the forces are correlated, the changed or modified structure must always be compared with the original, in order that we may know whether there has been variation, and to what degree; whether its efficiency has been increased or decreased; and whether the organism has been more powerful to subdue the environment, or the environment the organism. All we can do here is to illustrate the process in outline; to exhibit it in detail would be to write a constructive history of the Church.

§ I.—THE CREATIVE ORGANISM.

This is the causal Person and Mind, Jesus Christ. The religion is His creation; all Churches derive, directly or indirectly, their being from Him. How we conceive Him and His Church will appear later. Enough to say here, while He institutes a new society and fills it with His own life, He gives it no fixed or formal political constitution. He is its Founder, its Head, its inspiration, its personalized ideal of religion. His people are intended to be like Him—as it were His person augmented, immortalized, multiplied into innumerable hosts, and enduring through all ages. Now, what sort of religious ideal did He personalize? What was most distinctive of Him was His consciousness of God, the kind of God He was conscious of, and the relation He sustained to Him. God was His Father; He was God's Son. What God was to Him He desired Him to be to all men; what He was to God all men ought to be. In Christ's ideal of religion, then, the most material or determinative truth is the conception of God. He appears primarily, not as a God of judgment or justice, but of mercy and grace, the Father of man, who needs not to be appeased, but is gracious, propitious, finds the Propitiator, provides the propitiation. His own Son is the one Sacrifice, Priest, and Mediator, appointed of God to achieve the reconciliation of man. Men are God's sons; filial love is their primary duty, fraternal love their common and equal obligation. Worship does not depend on sacred persons, places, or rites; but is a thing of spirit and truth. The best prayer is secret and personal: the man who best pleases God is not the scrupulous Pharisee, but the penitent publican. Measured by the standard of a sacerdotal religion, Jesus was not a pious person. He spoke no word, did no act, that implied the necessity of an official priesthood for His people: He enforced no sacerdotal observance, instituted no sacerdotal order, promulgated no sacerdotal law, but simply required that His people should be perfect as their Father in heaven is perfect. And so what He founded was a society to realize His own ideal, a kingdom of heaven, spiritual, internal, which came without observation; a realm where the will of God is law, and the law is love, and the citizens are the loving and the obedient, whose type is the reverent and tender and trustful child, not the hard and boasting man. In its collective being it has a priestly character, but is without an official priesthood. It has ἀπόστολοι,[1] προφῆται,[2] ἐπίσκοποι,[3] πρεσβύτεροι,[4] ποιμένες,[5] διδάσκαλοι,[6] διάκονοι,[7] εὐαγγελισταί,[8] but no ἱερεῖς —no man, or body of men, who bear the name, hold the place, exercise the functions, or fulfil the duties of the priest or the priesthood, as they were known in ancient religions. It has no temple, save the living man; no sacrifices, save those of the spirit and the life; no sensuous sanctities. Its Founder never called Himself a priest; stood to the priesthood of His land and time in radical antagonism; the writer who applies to Him the name High Priest carefully avoids applying this or any similar name to any class of His people, and those who describe His work as a sacrifice never attach any similar idea to any acts of any officials or their instruments of worship. And this may be said to represent on the negative side the absolutely new and distinctive character of the religion of Christ. It stood among the ancient faiths as a strange and extraordinary thing—a priestless religion, without the symbols, sacrifices, ceremonies, officials hitherto, save by prophetic Hebraism, held to be the religious all in all. And it so stood, because its God did not need to be propitiated, but was propitious, supplying the only priest and sacrifice equal to His honour and the sins and wants of man. In that hour God became a new being to man, and man knew himself to be more than a mere creature and subject—a son of the living God.

Here, then, stated in the most general yet distinctive terms,

---

[1] Luke vi. 13; Matt. x. 2; Acts i. 2, 26, iv. 33; 1 Cor. xii. 28, etc.
[2] 1 Cor. xii. 28; Eph. ii. 20, iii. 5, iv. 11.
[3] Acts xx. 28; Phil. i. 1; Tit. i. 7.
[4] Acts xiv. 23, xv. 2, 4, 6, 22, 23; 1 Tim. v. 17.
[5] Eph. iv. 11.
[6] Acts xiii. 1; 1 Cor. xii. 28, 29; Eph. iv. 11; 1 Tim. ii. 7; 2 Tim. 1-11.
[7] 1 Cor. iii. 5; 2 Cor. iii. 6, vi. 4, xi. 23; Eph. iii. 7; Phil. i. 1.
[8] Acts xxi. 8; Eph. iv. 11; 2 Tim. iv. 5.

was, as regards its essential character, the religion which Jesus Christ instituted. But how was it to be realized? under what forms and by what agencies organized? It was full of infinite possibilities of all kinds—intellectual, moral, social, political, religious. It involved new beliefs as to God, as to its Founder, as to man; as to their natures, characters, relations; as to all the religions of the world, their worth, function, history; as to all the ideas that most command men and organize society. It was a source of new moral forces, introduced higher and nobler ideals, created a finer sense of obligations towards God, and a more sensitive conscience as regards man. It formed a brotherhood that was ambitious to embrace the world. It was bound to feel after the polity or social framework that should best help it to fulfil all its functions, and to seek methods of worship and religious association that would enable it to do justice to all its own possibilities and all the needs of man. And these elements stood so related to one another that whatever touched any affected all. Here, then, is the problem: How did this parent germ or creative organism—*i.e.*, the religion instituted by Christ—behave in its various environments? What was their action on it and its action on them? How far were the forms it assumed and the elements it incorporated due to the immanent laws of its own being or to the action of the medium in which it lived? To these questions we must return as clear an answer as our limits will allow.

§ II.—THE PRIMITIVE ENVIRONMENTS.

The environment in which the religion began to be was Judaic. Its Founder was of Jewish descent. His theistic, religious, ethical, social ideals, so far as they have any prior history, find it in Judaism; institutions of its creation, as the school and the synagogue, were used by Him and His disciples for the spread of the religion; their *termini technici*,

Βασιλεία τοῦ θεοῦ or τῶν[1] οὐρανῶν,[2] διαθήκη,[3] ἐκκλησία,[4] νόμος,[5] προφητεία,[6] πίστις,[7] δικαιοσύνη,[8] ἁμαρτία,[9] ἀποκάλυψις,[10] Χριστός,[11] υἱὸς τοῦ ἀνθρώπου,[12] υἱὸς τοῦ Θεοῦ,[13] Λόγος,[14] can be construed only through the Judaism either of the motherland or of the dispersion. It creates as it were the atmosphere in which the New Testament as a whole lives; its terminology, theses, antitheses, its modes of argument and of proof, its conflicts, controversies, policies, its local colourings and questions, its very attempts to break from the bonds of the law and become spiritual and universal, are all conditioned by Judaism. The types are many, but the system is one: now it is the Judaism of Palestine, as in Matthew; of Asia Minor, as in the Apocalypse; of the tolerant metropolis, as in Romans; of a narrow and hot-blooded province, as in Galatians; of a philosophical community, which has idealized the worship and history of the Fathers, as in Hebrews; but whatever the peculiarity of local type the thing remains. John and Luke are as full of it as Matthew and Mark; it as subtly penetrates Epistles to Gentile Churches, full of the passion of spiritual universalism, like Corinthians and Colossians, as those expressly addressed to Jews, like James and 1 Peter. But these conditions hardly outlived the first generation. Two things happened almost simultaneously: Jerusalem was destroyed, depriving

---

[1] Matt. vi. 33, xii. 28; Mark i. 15, iv. 11, 26, 30, etc.
[2] Matt. iv. 17, v. 3, 10, 19, 20, xiii. 11, 24, 31, 33.
[3] Matt. xxvi. 28; 1 Cor. xi. 25; 2 Cor. iii. 6; Heb. vii. 22, viii. 6, 8, 9, 10, etc.
[4] Matt. xvi. 18, xviii. 17; Acts v. 11, viii. 1, xiv. 23, etc.
[5] Matt. v. 17, vii. 12, xi. 13; Rom. ii. 12, 14, 15, iii. 19, 20, 21, etc.
[6] 1 Cor. xii. 10, xiv. 6, 12, etc.
[7] Rom. i. 5, 17, iii. 22, v. 1; 1 Cor. xv. 14, 17; Gal. i. 23, iii. 9, etc.
[8] Rom. i. 17, iii. 21, 22, 25, 26, x. 3; 2 Cor. v. 21.
[9] Mark i. 4, ii. 5; John i. 29; Rom. v. 12, 13, 20, 21, vii. 7, 8, 14, 17.
[10] Rom. xvi. 25; 1 Cor. i. 7, xiv. 6, 26; Eph. i. 17, iii. 3.
[11] Matt. xxii. 42, xxiv. 5, 23, xxvi. 63.
[12] Matt. xii. 8, 32, 40, xiii. 37; Mark ii. 10, 28, etc.
[13] Matt. xvi. 16, xxvi. 63; Mark iii. 11; John i. 34, 50, iii. 18, xi. 27.
[14] John i. 1, 14; 1 John i. 1.

the Jewish religion of its Temple and priesthood, and reducing it to a mere system of customs and instruction accommodated to the needs of a homeless people ; and the Church, opened by the preaching of Paul, became more Gentile than Jewish. This meant a change at once of race and of home ; the cradle of the religion ceased to be its nursery. So it forgot the tongue of its birthplace and learned the speech of its new motherland ; in other words, while it was still in its infancy all the historical conditions with all their determinative factors, everything that could be denoted by the terms blood, language, institutions, associations, traditions, habits, customs, mind, culture, religious consciousness, literature, history, were completely changed, with the inevitable result that new evolutionary forces were called into being by the new conditions. And these forces became factors of both formal and material changes, and their power was enhanced rather than weakened by the action of old agencies within the new medium.

But while Christianity escaped from Judaism, yet it was not delivered from the Jews ; they represented its bitterest enemies, its acutest opponents, the source of its most serious dangers. The heresies it had most to fear, the differences and divisions that had been most threatening and most nearly disastrous, the tales that had most deeply affronted its ethical and reverent spirit, had been of Jewish origin.[1] Hence came an attitude to Judaism and the Jews[2] which had its strongest possible contrast in the ideal attitude to their history and religion and Scriptures. Jesus had been born a Jew. He had come to fulfil the law and the prophets ; to their authority

[1] Justin, "Apol.," i., cc. 31, 36 ; "Dial.," cc. 16, 95 ; "Martyr. Polyc.," cc. 17-19 ; Origen, "Contra Cels.," i. 28-39.

[2] Barnabas, iv. 6-8, says that they lost the covenant as soon as they had received it; ix. 4, were instructed by an "evil angel" ; and xiv. 1, did not receive the covenant because of their sins. So *Præd. Petri*, in Clem. Al. "Strom.," vi. 5, 41, affirms that they do not know God, and worship, instead of Him, angels and archangels, moons and sabbaths. Cf. Justin, "Apol.," i. 36, 37, 47, 53 ; "Didache," viii. 1 ; "Ign. Ep. ad Mag.," x. 2. Judaism is described as τὴν κακὴν ζύμην τὴν παλαιωθεῖσαν καὶ ἐνοξίσασαν.

He and His disciples alike appealed. So while the Gentile Christian rejected Judaism, he had to do it under sanction of the Jewish Scriptures,[1] which were to him canonical, authentic, and inspired.[2] Then, though the Apostolic writings existed, the New Testament did not; its parts had an isolated or dispersed being, but they had not been joined into a whole, collected, canonized, and made authoritative.[3] The antecedents of the sub-Apostolic literature and thought are oral and actual rather than written and ideal Christianity[4]—a Christianity simple, inchoate, as it were intellectually inarticulated, often ill-informed as to its own sources and history,

---

[1] Barn., cc. vi.-x. The Old Testament ceremonies are all abolished and spiritually fulfilled in the new people of God. Clem., 2 Ep. xiv. 2, where τὰ βιβλία denotes the Old Testament. Justin, " Dial.," cc. 11, 16, 18, 20, 30, 40-46, argues—Christians are the true Israel, their new law was predicted and prefigured in the old, and has superseded it. Cf. Harnack, " Dogmengesch.," vol. i., pp. 146, 147, text and notes; but especially " Texte u. Untersch.," vol. i., pt. iii., " Altercatio Simonis," pp. 56-91; Engelhardt, " Das Christenthum Justin's," pp. 245-261 and 310-320.

[2] The modes of citation are significant. In Clem. R. the Old Testament is quoted as ἡ γραφή, cc. 23, 34, 35; as τὸ γραφεῖον, 28; as αἱ ἱεραὶ γραφαί, 53. Its words are quoted as Christ's own, spoken διὰ τοῦ πνεύματος τοῦ ἁγίου, 22; or as God's own, λέγει (sc. Θεός, or Κύριος). Cf. Barn. i. 7, iv. 7, 11, v. 7.

[3] Of course, the reference in the text is a strictly limited one; it does not deny the use of Apostolic writings in the sub-Apostolic. The extent of this can be seen from the indexes to Gebhardt and Harnack, or Lightfoot's "Apostolic Fathers," or any good book on the canon—Credner or Reuss, Holtzmann or Weiss, Westcott or Zahn. What is affirmed is not only that the New Testament had not been co-ordinated with the Old, but that it did not exist as a canon or body of authoritative religious books. It is, of course, the case that certain texts can be quoted as evidence that certain New Testament books or sayings were referred to as Scriptures (*e.g.*, 2 Peter iii. 16—" all the epistles " of " our beloved brother Paul "; Ep. Polyc. xii. 1 quotes Eph. iv. 26 with Psalm iv. 5 as Scriptures, Barn. iv. 14 cites Matt. xxii. 14 with the formula ὡς γέγραπται, 2 Clem. ii. 4 introduces Matt. ix. 13 with the phrase καὶ ἑτέρα δὲ γραφὴ λέγει, while in xiii. 4 the formula λέγει ὁ Θεὸς is used relative to Luke vi. 32, 35); but these in no way affect the statement of the text. As a simple matter of fact, broadly stated, the sacred authoritative book of the sub-Apostolic Church was the Old Testament, not the New.

[4] Cf. Papias ap. Euseb., bk. iii., c. 39.

its own reason and significance, full of local varieties and many gradations of mind and culture. The later is then not the continuation of the earlier thought, but of something at once simpler and less primitive, what we may term vulgar and mixed tradition. This tradition, which represented the Word as it lived in the memories and mouths of men, was more intelligible to the new mind than the New Testament, and so was more capable of interpretation by it.[1] The Church, too, was not an organized whole, or even a homogeneous body; it did not form the men it incorporated after a single or uniform type. Hence, though the Gentile became a Christian, he did not cease to be a Gentile, or to think in the terms and under the categories he had inherited, and so he could not construe the religion exactly in the sense of its first preachers. The difference is not due to purpose, but as it were to nature and history, and exists where there is the utmost desire to express and maintain harmony with the Apostolic mind. It springs from many and complex causes, which were all natural in their origin and inevitable in their action. The Gentile Christian did not and could not come like the Apostles to the New Testament through the Old, or like the Hellenists to the Church through the synagogue; he rather read the Old Testament through the

[1] There is no doctrine more in need of scientific discussion than that of tradition. It is most vaguely used in much of the theological literature of the day. Before there was a New Testament there could not but be a Παράδοσις, but it was the note of a young community and a transitional age. The longer it continued the more unsafe it grew; the remoter from the source the less it could be used as an authority. The written word is valuable because it remains for ever primitive—the oldest testimony crystallized, as it were, in the very act of expression; but tradition, so far as it remains oral, ceases to be primitive, is augmented or modified by time, and ever assumes the hue or tone of the age through which it is passing. It must always remain more significant of the present that receives it than of the past whence it professes to come. The only true parallel to the modern Catholic doctrine—whether Roman or Anglican—is to be found in the Παράδοσις of the Pharisaic and rabbinical schools (Matt. xv. 2, 3, 6; Mark vii. 3, 5, 8, 9, 13; Gal. i. 14; Col. ii. 8).

New, the synagogue through the Church, and all through his inherited consciousness, his Greek philosophy and Roman polity.

§ III.—The Immediate Result.

And as were the conditions, such was the theology. If the Apostolic and sub-Apostolic ages be studied through their highest and most characteristic beliefs, then we may say—they are successive rather than continuous, the later is the sequent in time but not in thought of the earlier, the legitimate resultant of all the factors and conditions, but not a normal or logical or lineal evolution from the ideal of the New Testament. Its literature is concerned with the same subjects as the Apostolic, but almost everything in it is different—the atmosphere, the altitude, the proportion of parts, the emphasis on terms or ideas, the regulative principles of thought. It would be easy so to exhibit differences as to conceal harmonies, or to draw up a harmony which would mask differences; what is difficult is to show the precise significance and exact proportion of both.[1] Of the Apostolic literature we may say—it is even more important as a body of religious authorities than of historical documents; but of the sub-Apostolic—there are no more important historical documents, but no poorer religious authorities. What is absent is even more remarkable than what is present. We have reminiscences of sacred history, now correct, now incorrect. We have often large explicit use of the Old Testament and echoes of the New, becoming now

---

[1] Bull's "Defensio Fidei Nicænæ" is full of examples of forced harmonies in the region of dogma. So are some of Newman's tracts, his "History of the Arians," and his notes to his edition of Athanasius' "Orations." His "Development," on the other hand, contains examples of an opposite kind. The differences and agreements between the two ages have equal, yet contrary, historical significance. The agreements show the continuity of the society, but the differences exhibit the changes within the society, due to the changes of men and time and place. Recognition of both is needed if there is to be any real philosophy of the genesis and history of the Church.

and then, as it were, articulate as distinct quotations. We have examples of old customs like the weekly assembly or baptism or the Lord's Supper, either modified or in process of modification. We have insight into the state of the young communities; their offices and their ideas of office; their order, troubles, hopes, fears, sufferings; their mutual relations; their manifold differences alike as regards opinion, discipline, and conduct; and, above all, we are made to feel the reality of the new life which has come through Jesus Christ—the beautiful reverence and pure love for Him that lives in all hearts, and represents His continuous being in His society. But the moment we enter the region of thought we feel the change of atmosphere; whole classes of beliefs are absent or inadequately expressed.[1] We miss the great Pauline or Johannine conceptions, the unity and continuity of man, sin and grace, law and gospel, works and faith; the meaning of the Son for the Father, of the Father for the world; the significance of the Word for God and His work for men. Religious thought has become more legal and less ethical; a new emphasis falls on knowledge; the antithesis to the Old Testament is lost, and its ceremonial ideas are seen, disguised as to form but unchanged as to essence, returning to power. The heresies are different, and so are the orthodoxies. The relation of God to the world, of spirit to matter, of the Fall and Redemption, of the beginning, course, and end of the world, are, within as

[1] In measuring in the region of theology the difference between the Apostolic and sub-Apostolic age, two standards must be employed—the quality of the thought that is absent, and the inadequate character of what is present. Each has a different yet complementary significance. What is absent shows how the new mind had failed to grasp not only the whole truth, but even some of its most fundamental principles; what is present shows that what it did grasp it did not fully understand. This concerns, *e.g.*, such matters as the Pauline doctrines of sin and death (1 Clem. iii. 4, cf. iv.), faith and justification (1 Clem. xxxii. 4, cf. x.-xii.; Hermas Sim. v. 3. 1-2-3). The person of Christ and the Holy Spirit are identified (Hermas Sim., ix. 1. 1: cf. 12. 1, 2; v. 2 ff.). The kingdom of God is made more future and less ethical, and God is conceived in a manner more Judaic than Christian.

without the Church, conceived from a new standpoint, and determined in the light of other principles. Speaking broadly, we may say, from the intellectual point of view the men have hardly begun to understand the alphabet of the religion; their world is smaller, meaner, emptier, than the Apostolic, is in relation to it neither a development nor a decline, but rather a thing of another order—the first endeavour of the child-mind to understand the truth. The men are not yet prepared to know the religion. They excellently illustrate the influence of tradition without Scripture, and the inability of an undisciplined and inchoate Christian consciousness to interpret Christ.

CHAPTER III.

NEW FACTORS AND NEW LINES OF DEVELOPMENT.

OUR discussions, so far as they have proceeded, have helped to determine some positions of primary importance. First, ecclesiastical development, especially as concerns thought or doctrine, does not begin at the point where the New Testament leaves us, but, as it were, behind and outside it—from tradition, the oral Gospel, the narration and exposition, often inadequate and ill-understood, of the wandering prophet.[1] Secondly, since the men who received the tradition mostly differed in tongue, mind, ancestry, moral and religious inheritance, from the men who delivered it, the change of hands could not but involve some change of meaning. Thirdly, this change was made the more serious by the fact that the Scriptures through which the new men interpreted the tradition, were mainly those of the Old Testament. It is curious but significant that the orthodox and heretical tendencies were here the exact converse of each other; while the latter discredited and dismissed the Old Testament and made their appeal to the New, the former did not so much co-ordinate the two as subordinate the later to the earlier Scriptures, reconveying the legal spirit and idea of the one into the other. We may say, then, that the thought of the ancient Church starts rather from the vulgar than from the Apostolic mind, and so far as it can be placed in relation

[1] "Didache," xi.

to the latter is rather a mirror of difference than a point in a line of continuous development. But the full significance of these positions will appear more in the next stage of the discussion—viz., the study of the modified organism and the new environment in their reciprocal and evolutionary action By the modified organism is meant the Christian society as affected by those changes in its conditions, which have been already indicated; by the new environment, the Greco-Roman world into which it had come. The factors of evolution are, so far as they belong to the former, internal, to the latter, external, but their force is due to their relation and interdependence, not to their isolation.

§ I.—The New Factors.

The most potent external factors may be reduced to three: Greek Philosophy, Roman Polity, and Popular Religion.

1. The philosophy, though Greek in origin and largely also in form, was yet varied both in distribution and in character. Eclecticism was then as distinctive of philosophy as syncretism of religion, and its materials were selected not simply from philosophical but also from religious or hieratic systems. In Asia Minor dualisms or theosophies which had filtered from the farther East, or spontaneously developed upon the congenial soil, assumed forms at once intellectual and religious, and became (a) philosophies like the neo-Pythagorean, ecstatic, theosophic, miraculous, penetrated with the true Oriental spirit of sensuous asceticism and speculative licence; or (β) mixed systems of thought and ritual like Gnosticism, dualisms through and through, societies of the initiated dividing themselves by their Gnosis from the vulgar crowd, and God from the world by a multitude of personalized abstractions, by charms protecting themselves from matter, and by Æons protecting God; or (γ) religious doctrines like Manicheism, which attempted in the manner of the Zoroastrian

faith to solve our intellectual and moral difficulties by the theory of rival deities.[1] In Alexandria three great tendencies met : (a) the Egyptian, with its rich and complex symbolism, its hieroglyphic and hieratic language, its esoteric thought and ancient priesthood ; (β) the Jewish, with its theistic passion and large outlook upon nature and history; and (γ) the Greek, with its constructive temper, scientific method, literary education and genius. Here philosophy became neo-Platonic, possessed of the imaginative idealism which loves to find nature symbolical and history an allegory, yet cosmopolitan, eclectic, construing Greek speculation through Egyptian mysticism, and finding in Hebrew monotheism the unifying and determinative principle. In Rome and the West Stoicism reigned, and by its help the ideal man was studied, virtue cultivated, law magnified, the State made to experience a sort of apotheosis. The elevated Pantheism that was its speculative basis was so conceived as to deify the Empire and make worship of the Emperor a reasonable service. Thought in all its forms was as active as in the palmiest days of the Academy, but it was without the old lucid serenity ; it had become, save in the case of the nobler Stoics, feverish, sophistic, mystic, curious to know the beliefs and try the ways of other times and other peoples.

2. While such was the philosophy, the polity was Roman in the widest sense, imperial, provincial, municipal, social, and industrial—*i.e.*, the polity of the Empire as a whole, of its several parts, though as modified by the whole, of the cities that even when they had become Roman did not cease to be Greek or Greco-Syrian or African, of the peoples and classes who endeavoured to preserve their nationalities,

---

[1] Of course this refers to the earlier Gnostic schools and the sources of the elements they compounded. Later the chief seat of their activity was Alexandria. Cf. Lipsius, "Der Gnosticismus," pp. 105 ff.; Baur, "Manichäische Religionssys.," pp. 404-493. As to the neo-Pythagoreans, there is an interesting discussion in Réville, "La Religion à Rome sous les Sévères," pt. ii.

protect their rights, husband and distribute their resources within the limits of the Roman law, provincial and imperial. With the actual and organised polity must also be taken the theoretical, the philosophical interpretation and expansion of the law which was so characteristic of the Roman jurists.

3. The popular religion was the system of worship which anywhere prevailed, whether as public or private, an affair of the city and temple and priesthood, or of the home and the mysteries. The period was a period of syncretism; the universalism of the Empire had resulted in a mixture of all its religions; the old deities lived no more within their ancient limits; the gods of Egypt and Syria, of Phrygia and Persia, of East and West, invaded Rome, and in their train came their respective worships.[1] In the sphere of religion a sort of assimilative or encyclopædic frenzy was abroad, and men and cities did not feel happy or safe unless they had offered hospitality to some of the many migrating deities.

Now, Christianity could not live amid these varied forces or tendencies, and remain unaffected by them. Each became a factor of distinct yet parallel lines of thought,—philosophy affected doctrine; polity, organization and thought; religion, cultus. Ancient philosophy passed into theology; Roman polity survived in an ecclesiastical, which was too wise to disguise its true descent; and the old religions were perpetuated in the new worship. Yet they did not all operate with equal or uniform force within the same areas. The theological development was most active within what had been the home of philosophy, the countries of Greek speech and blood; the political was at first richest in Syria,[2] but

---

[1] Réville, "La Religion à Rome sous les Sévères," pt. I.

[2] For the irregular distribution in the growth of episcopacy, see Lightfoot's essay on "The Christian Ministry," 206 ff. His examination of the causes of its early development in Syria and Asia Minor seems inadequate and partial. The tendency had rather a common and native than a personal origin, and the persons involved are, save in one case, little better than mythical.

was later perfected in the West, mainly in and through Rome; the religious was more uniform in its operations, though as varied in its elements as were the cults within the Empire. These factors did not indeed in any sense generate the life of the society, but they determined the forms that its life assumed. In their collective and correlated action they by a twofold process secured its naturalization as a citizen of the world—a process, on the one hand, of interpenetration, and, on the other, of mediation and reconcilement. It is the one because the other; the old and the new faiths interpenetrate that the new religion may the better win and master the ancient mind. Catholicism is the interpretation of the Christian idea in the terms and through the associations of the ancient world, and as such represents on the largest scale the continuity of religion in history. Its work was a needed work, for man is incapable of transitions at once sudden and absolute; the construction of Christianity through the media of the older philosophies and religions was a necessary prelude to its construction by a spirit and through a consciousness of its own creation. The absolute ideal had, in order to be intelligible, to use constituted and familiar vehicles, but only that it might win the opportunity of fashioning vehicles worthier of its nature and fitter for its end.

§ II.—Ancient Philosophy and Theology.

But "factor" is a very ambiguous and elastic term, and so it may be as well here to define the idea it is meant to denote. This can best be done by the discussion of the concrete question, In what sense can Greek philosophy be described as a factor of Christian theology? Theology is the universe construed through the idea of God; philosophy is the universe construed through the idea of man, but man as mind. Theology is as necessary to faith as philosophy to reason. If a man asks, Why and what am I and my universe? the result is a philosophy; if a man or society asks, What does the truth we believe mean? the result is a theology. Each is a science of being, but the highest constructive principle of the science is in the one case the thought or consciousness of the thinker; in the other, it is his highest and most necessary idea. The standpoint is in philosophy subjective, a particular reason is made determinative of the universal, the means by which truth is to be discovered and explicated; the standpoint in theology is objective, a universal intelligence is made the explanation of the intelligible world with all its intellects and all their mysteries. This distinction shows at once their difference and their relation. They differ because theology starts with an idea which philosophy has to discover and define; but they are related because, while all the problems of theology do not emerge in philosophy, all those of philosophy emerge in theology, though in a different order and from a changed point of view.

Now, the relations of Greek philosophy and Christian theology illustrate this distinction. These relations were both historical and material. In history the philosophy preceded the theology; the century that saw the one begin to be saw the other cease from being. In a sense ancient philosophy died into theology, and for centuries all the life it had was in this form and under this name. The last of the Greek philosophers were theologians, Plotinus, Porphyry, and Proclus quite as much as Clement, Origen, and Dionysius. But the change in name implied a change in the thing named. The new theology was not the old philosophy, nor can the one be stated in the terms of the other and yet remain the same. The cause of the difference was this: beside Greek philosophy as an external factor of theology two internal factors must be placed—Hebrew religion and Christian history. The philosophy determined all that was formal in the problems to be solved, and supplied the speculative faculty, the dialectical temper, the logical and evidential method, and the scholastic terminology needed for their solution. The religion gave the material theistic ideas, the historical perspective required for their concrete being, and the literature by which they could be illustrated and verified. The history furnished the Person and events which alone could, by being interpreted, interpret the ideas and turn the highest of all theological into the most fundamental of all philosophical questions. It was by virtue of the religious and historical factors that the new theology differed from the ancient philosophy.

The action of Hebrew religion was the earlier and preparatory, qualifying philosophy for the new work it had to do. The philosophies that had owed their being to the Greek genius were made in the image of Greek man, but even he had too narrow a humanity behind and around as well as within him to be just to man universal, and so his systems had feeling enough for the Hellenic individual and State, but not for mankind, collective and historical. They were too appreciative of the philosophers who ought to govern to be just to the manhood which needed government. They started outside religion, and became religious only by force of reason and in its terms. Their theistic conception was metaphysical rather than ethical; never even in its ethics transcending metaphysics, ever remaining an object of contemplation or thought, never becoming an object of worship and conscience. In other words, the Deity was reached through subjective criticism, and had all the qualities of an objectified idea. He was more impersonal than personal, a regulative notion rather than a conscious reason and an active will. This was equally true whether the Divine was with Plato conceived under the form of the Good or the True, or with Aristotle, of the End or the Reason, or with the Stoic, of Law or the immanent Order. The universe interpreted was in a sense as limited as the interpreting manhood. Now, to this most specifically Greek philosophy Hebrew religion came, and by filling it with the idea of a living God gave it a larger life, a nobler and vaster outlook. This God was what no Greek deity, so far forth as a religious being, had been conceived to be—the creator of all things, the ruler of all men. He was no pale abstraction or personalized idea, but a conscious will which moved in all things and lived in all, one and personal, ethical and infinite. The man who brought the two together was Philo. As a philosopher he cannot be compared with Plato, but for the history of religion and religious thought he is even more important. Two streams meet in him, and flow henceforth in a common bed. From the moment that he attempted to unite Israel and Greece, Moses and Plato, the prophets and the philosophers, a new goal was set before the reason, and philosophy struggled towards theology. The men who came after him were not as the men who went before; he made neo-Platonic and Christian speculation alike possible, and these two agree in the very point that distinguishes both from the older Platonism; it was a philosophy, they are theologies. And just where they agree, and because of their agreement, modern is different from ancient thought. God holds a place in all systems subsequent to Philo such as He had never held in those prior to him. And this point of distinction is a sign of pre-eminence. For the thinker who seeks to construe man and history through the idea of the one moral and personal Deity, attempts a grander and more rational problem than is possible to him who would read the universe through even Hellenic man. For the universe must be so conceived as to be worthy of its God, the God so conceived as to be equal to all the needs of His universe. Where He runs through all history, its periods must exhibit reason and law. Where He is equally related to all men they must all be equal in lowliness and in dignity before Him. In their very differences they must be akin, all their truths and all their religions be of Him and through Him. All is sublimer and vaster interpreted through a universal God than through the Greek ideal of man, sublime though it be.

§ III.—CHRISTIAN HISTORY AND THEOLOGY.

But while Hebrew religion enlarged and enriched all the problems of philosophy, the Christian history made them much more concrete, imperious, and acute. This history must be understood to mean both the creative Person and the sacred literature which described at once His actual being and ideal significance. It is necessary to emphasize the place of this literature; the rise of a coherent and comprehensive theology was coincident with its recognition and a symbol of its function and power. The remarkable phenomena that meet us at the beginning of the second century, before the literature, as distinct from tradition, had made its collective appeal to mind, continue into the middle and even towards the end. Apostolic Christianity is not apprehended as a whole, and so far as its parts are apprehended they are apprehended only in part. It has all the defects of an apprehension attained through tradition and in fragments by the unprepared and undisciplined mind, unexercised and uncorrected by the study of a normative sacred literature. The apologists are not strictly Christian theologians; their thought is Christian, they exhibit Christianity in process of assimilation by philosophical minds, but the last thing that can be claimed for them is that their theology is Apostolic. In Justin there is much more of Plato than of Paul; indeed, we may say he is often as antipathetic to the one as he is sympathetic with the other.[1] But when we come to the end

[1] There is a careful and judicial discussion of Justin's relation to Paul in Engelhardt, "Das Christenthum Justin's," pp. 352-369. Cf. exposition of the opposed views in Ritschl, "Altkath. Kirche," pp. 303 ff.; and Baur, "Kirchengesch. der drei erst. Jahrhs.," 140, Eng. trans., vol. i., p. 147.

of the century we find men who have stood face to face with the Christian history, and endeavoured to construe the literature. Irenæus is not a philosopher, but a Biblical theologian, the first of the kind, with the Christ and not the Logos as the centre of his system. Many things had gone to his making; he had learned from his early masters how to love and follow the truth, how to treasure the words of the holy and the good, from the Gnostics how to value the intellect in religion, from Marcion how to make a direct appeal to the Scriptures, yet what to avoid in making this appeal; but most of all he had been formed by his study of the Apostolic mind. He is the earliest example of what has been illustrated often since—that for the Christian spirit there is no secret of rejuvenescence like a bath in the original sources. But tradition enfeebled and obscured his vision. Though steeped in Paul, and owing to him his noblest and most characteristic ideas—the ἀνακεφαλαίωσις, the unities which he opposes to the Gnostic dualisms, the unity of God, of the person of Christ, of the human race, of history, of the purpose of God and the plan of salvation, of the Church —yet he often misses or fails to read aright the Apostle's mind, or even quite perverts it.[1] Tertullian and Clement, each in his own way, illustrate the same truth, but Origen more than either. He is a Christian thinker because a Biblical scholar. With him constructive theology begins to be, and it was but fit that the most learned of all the Fathers should

---

[1] Proof of this position would require a more detailed exposition than is here possible, but the points we should emphasize are these:—What we may term the residuary dualism which, in spite of his loved unities, still works within his theistic conception, his whole doctrine of the devil, with his established and, as it were, recognized place over against God, and the consequent external and adventitious doctrines of sin and redemption; the related legalism in his conception of the Gospel, which makes it not so much a fulfilment as an enlargement and republication of law, involving a most unapostolic prominence to the institutional as distinguished from the fiduciary element in Christianity; his views as to forgiveness and grace, his tendency through inadequate appreciation of what they mean to de-ethicize

also be the first systematic theologian and the source of the most fruitful ideas in Greek patristic thought.

Now, this Christian history was transacted, as it were, within the Hebrew religion, and incorporated its most fundamental ideas; nay, appeared as its historical end and final cause. As such it came to the philosophy which had already become theological, demanding to be interpreted and explained. But to attempt this was to read the universe and all its mysteries from an entirely new point of view. Here was Christ born as all men are, said to be the Son of man, yet no man's son, Son of God, second Adam, source of a new race, Saviour of men,—how, then, was He to be conceived alike as regards His nature, His person, and His relation to God and man? Two things were necessary: His person must be held a historical reality, and must be so construed as to make God more real, living, credible, than He had been either in Greek philosophy or Hebrew religion. The history could not be allegorized or the Person evaporated into a semblance, resolved into a phantasm of the imagination or a freak of nature. Allegory was well known to the current philosophies, especially the Stoic and neo-Platonic. By its help the most offensive incidents in the ancient mythologies had become symbolical of hidden sciences or rarest moral wisdom. Philo had known it, and so used it as to bring out of the Mosaic histories the philosophies of Greece. The Christian Fathers followed the fashion of their day, and found both history and nature rich in allegory and ideal symbolisms. But they could not use this prevailing fashion to turn their sacred history into vehicles

the great Pauline ideas, and by emphasizing the accidents to lose the very essence of the ἀνακεφαλαίωσις. If we regard his historical position and function, we must speak of his importance in very bold and clear terms; but he is in the history of doctrine simply a scholar who has with mingled success and failure tried to take up a dropped line of development. Cf. the monograph of Werner (which is, however, rather one-sided and so unjust), "Der Paulinismus des Irenæus," in *Texte und Untersch.*, vol. vi., and Lipsius, "Irenæus," in *Dictionary of Christian Biography*.

for their own too luxuriant ideas. If the Person was not real, reality could not belong to anything He did or said; but if He was real, then His history must be the same. The reality of the Person and the integrity of the history thus stood together as complementary and co-essential elements of the truth. But neither the Person nor His history could be, as it were, cut out of the bosom of humanity. As the Son of man His roots were in the whole past of man collective; as Creator and Head of the new mankind His branches must reach into all the future; as Son of God His organic relations to all the universe were completed by relations to the God whose Son He was.

Now, out of this history with its necessary implications came a multitude of problems, subtler, more penetrating, more masterful, charged with more vital moral energy and metaphysical meaning than any ancient philosophy had known. If God had a Son, in what sense was the Son Son, and God Father? Did the Son begin to be? If He did not, then is He not the equal of the Father and as old as He? How, then, can He be Son any more? And does His necessary and eternal being mean that we have two Gods and not simply one? But if He did begin to be, then He must have been created; and how do Son and creature, or Sonship and creation, differ? Then, if He had necessary being with God, yet became man, did not this place God in organic relations with man collective as he lived his life in all times and all places. If God's Son was part of this race—rooted in its past, living in a recent present, creating its future—then to this race God must be bound, He in some sense also its Father, it in some sense His Son. If one who had lived as Son of man was yet Son of God, then how were God and man related? in what sense were they akin? in what sense different? Are all the sons of men, as was this Son of man, sons of God? And if they differ, can they belong to the same orders of being—He man as they are men, or they as He is? Then does not an organic relation of God to the race imply that the race is an organism with its every unit connected with every other, and all with its Father or Head? If God and the Son of God are thus connected with the race, what is their relation to evil? how has it come to be? how is its being to be ended? And what is the relation to it of the organism as a whole and of all its several units? What was man's primary, what is to be his ultimate relation to the Father? And as regards these relations, what function has the Son and His being in time?

Such were some of the questions raised by the Christian history, and it would be hard to find in the whole realm of thought problems at once more essentially philosophical or more vitally theological. They fall into two classes: those specially concerned with God, the Son of God, His relation to God and man, the constituents and function of His person; and those specially concerned with man, as a unit and as a race, his relation, individual and collective, to God, to sin, and to salvation. The former were questions in theology, and became the distinctive problems of the Greek Church; the latter were questions in anthropology, and became the problems characteristic of the Latin. The choice was not accidental, nor without a reason in history. The theology found its organon in Greek metaphysics, especially as then cultivated in the eclectic schools, and continued under new relations problems they had for centuries discussed; the anthropology had in Roman law, qualified and interpreted by Stoicism, its fit formative medium.

CHAPTER IV.

THE GREEK MIND AND THEOLOGY.

§ I.—Two Minds and Two Churches.

THE distinction just indicated is of significance enough to justify more detailed discussion. It will help us the better to understand the persistence of the classical in the Christian mind, and show how through the former the latter achieved some of its most characteristic results. Thought was as active in the West as in the East, but had other interests and other objects, and, as a consequence, other forms. Law was distinctive of the Latin and philosophy of the Greek people; the great jurists were as typical of Rome as the great philosophers were typical of Greece. All the philosophy of the West was derivative. The most original Latin philosopher was the poet who

> "denied
> Divinely the Divine,"

but Lucretius was only the expositor of the *Graius homo* he so splendidly praised. The philosophy that may with best reason be described as native to the Romans was Stoicism; but though it had a quite specific character of its own, yet it was not a native or even a naturalized Roman philosophy. With Seneca it was more a literary habit, a mental tendency, a means for the cultivation of character than a reasoned system; it is in its ethical tone and form, not in its intellectual contents, that it has affinity with Paul's.

With Marcus Aurelius it was Greek in form and source, though Roman in spirit; and of Epictetus we may say the same. But in law Rome is easily pre-eminent, and the jurist has his golden age in the second and third centuries of our era. His jurisprudence, indeed, is not simply positive and consuetudinary, but is penetrated and organized by great ideas, illumined, as it were, by the light of nature. Law is not simply the arbitrary and the conventional, but is what is always and everywhere equal and good. To know it is to know things Divine and human, just and unjust, the order constituted of nature among men. The jurists have thus under their law a philosophy, and through this philosophy they seek to read and interpret the law. They stand, indeed, upon the actual, the positive, the instituted, but labour to bring it into harmony with the ideal. Yet their nature is the nature of the jurist; they do not escape his categories. The function of all abstract right is to create right institutions; the state organized according to a Divine idea is the ultimate achievement of Divine wisdom. The quest, then, of the jurist is order, as of the philosopher truth; what thought is to the one, institutions are to the other. If the philosopher touches law, it is that he may incorporate an idea; if the jurist appeals to philosophy, it is that he may vindicate or interpret law. What the one seeks is the interpretation of man and his universe; what the other seeks is the creation of a well-ordered state, with all the relations of man to man regulated by just laws justly interpreted.

Now, the contrast between Greek philosophy and Roman law is repeated and reflected in the contrast, which is a commonplace of history, between the Greek and Latin, or Eastern and Western, Churches. Each by its very name bears witness to the supremacy of the special factor that formed it. The one is Orthodox, the other Catholic; the note of the first is its theological truth, of the second its imperial and continuous and comprehensive polity, ever enlarged and actualized by an ever-living law, because a law ever anew interpreted. The genius that made philosophy the creation of classical Greece made theology the determinative basis of the Greek Church. The political strength and capacity that gave to Rome the sovereignty of the world, the juridical and forensic genius that made its law almost ideal, developed the Roman Church into the Catholic. Each became what it did through the past it inherited. Without the philosophers the Eastern Church would never have had her theologians; without the Cæsars and their jurists the Western Church would never have had her popes and canonists. It was but natural that men who had the Greek mind or who had come under its influence should construe Christianity through the categories of the reason, and feel its fitness, as it were, for intellectual manipulation, its capability of being formulated in the terms of the intellect. And it was no less natural that men who had the Roman mind, or had been made in its image and inured into its ambitions and ideals, should see in Christianity a new state, a new form of empire, a new method of authority and rule. Though these are different, yet they are not opposites; nor do they exclude each other. Theological ideas could not live or be formulated and enforced without a polity; the polity could not be a coherent and living whole unless filled and organized by an idea. But in each case the determinative principle was different—in the one case a theology, in the other a polity. In the East the Church is to be obeyed and believed because she teaches the truth; in the West the truth or doctrine is to be believed because defined, delivered, and authenticated by the Church. The contrast affects the very form and quality of the doctrines. The system native to the Greek Church is a doctrine of God and the Godhead; but the system native to the Latin is a doctrine of man, his state and constitution, his relations and duties, government and responsibilities, individual and collective, all forensically construed. The Eastern theology was accepted by the West, but with a modification or change (the *filioque*) which showed its feebler metaphysical ability and lower speculative standpoint; the Western anthropology was never accepted by the East, and was to it, because of its abiding though weakened Hellenic ideal of man and the city or state, not only alien, but incredible. In soteriology the Greek notion was metaphysical and personal, and so found its centre and symbol in the Incarnation; but the Latin was legal and forensic, and so emphasized justification and atonement, or the Incarnation so far as it made more possible the apotheosis of the Church and its Sacraments. The former was the direct result of the relations between God and man being conceived in the terms of a philosophy, with its metaphysical categories; the latter was due to these same relations being construed in the terms of a polity, with its principles of civil and criminal jurisprudence. These differences, then, are neither superficial nor accidental, but are fundamental and real, due to causes that are as old as Greece and as Rome. They do not belong to the religion that came to the men, but to the men who came to the religion, and who made it a continuation in the one case of the thought they inherited, in the other of their realized polity and idealized law.

§ II.—The Greek and Latin Fathers.

But there was between East and West a contrast of personality and character no less than of thought and system. The great Fathers of the East were theologians, men who dealt with the facts and ideas of their faith in the method of the philosopher and in the terms of the schools. The great Fathers of the West were jurists or statesmen, men who looked at their faith through the associations and ideals of a society governed by constituted authorities, settled customs and formal laws,

This does not mean that the Greek mind was philosophical but not practical, the Latin practical but not philosophical—a position that may be so construed as to be either a superficial truth or a fundamental falsehood—for in Augustine or even in Tertullian there is as much philosophy as in any Greek Father, while in pre-eminence and intellectual influence they have no rival in the East, unless indeed it be the heretical Origen. But it means this—that the constructive ideas of the Greek Fathers were metaphysical, of the Latin political and juristic. Thus with the Greek apologists as a whole Christianity was fitted into a framework of Hellenic and Hellenistic speculation, and dealt with as if it were a philosophy which differed from all other philosophies only in being revealed, and so truer to reason. Aristides, Justin, Athenagoras, did not leave off either the garb or the name or the function of the philosopher.[1] The natural parallel of Christ was Socrates, who was indeed a Christian before Him.[2] Pantænus, the first known head of the Catechetical School of Alexandria, was educated in Stoicism.[3] His disciple and successor, Clement, sees in philosophy the preparation for Christ, holds the truth he has received to be the true philosophy, and finds perfection in knowledge rather than faith.[4] Origen was a scholar of Clement, and a hearer of Ammonius, and educated in Greek studies,[5] and the vivid picture of him as a master which we owe to the love of a pupil shows him forbidding no subject, keeping none hidden and inaccessible, that he might the better lead through heathen to Christian philosophy.[6]

Heraclas and Dionysius, who succeeded Origen in the school, were one with him in mind and spirit. Athanasius

[1] Aristides, "Apol.," inscr.; Justin, "Dial.," 1 ff.; "Apol.," II. 13; Tatian "Orat.," 31, 32, 35, 40.
[2] Justin, "Apol.," II. 10, 1. 46.
[3] Euseb., v. 10, cf. vi. 19.
[4] Strom., i. 5, §§ 28, 32; iv. 21-23; vi. 14, § 114; 15, §§ 115-123.
[5] Euseb., vi. 18, 19, cf. 14.
[6] Greg. Thaum., "Orat. de Orig.," vi.-xv.

had carefully studied "Plato and the Greek philosophers in general," and his earliest book recalls "not in form but in essence the Platonic dialogue."[1] The eloquence of Basil and Chrysostom shows the influence of their common master Libanius, while the School of Athens left its mark on the minds of Basil and his friend Gregory.[2] The Apollinares, elder and younger, studied under Epiphanius of Petra, and were excommunicated in consequence, some holding pagan philosophy injurious to true religion.[3] Theodore of Mopsuestia was also a pupil of Libanius, and educated in rhetoric and philosophy.[4] The neo-Platonism of Synesius is, to say the least, as real as his Christianity, while it was not without influence on the asceticism of Isidore of Pelusium. Indeed, of the Greek Fathers as a whole we may say that the influence of their schools, with their opposed metaphysics, psychologies, ethics, can be quite distinctly traced in all their controversies. Dogma in their hands assumes its true philosophical sense, definition is made to play the same part in regard to it and to knowledge as in the philosophical sects, and theology is as much concerned with right thinking as ever philosophy had been.

The Latin Fathers stand in these respects in marked contrast to the Greek. Tertullian, though he becomes a Christian, yet remains in thought and feeling a Roman lawyer; he loves his religion because it is so unlike philosophy, and can speak with so much authority. The more this authority insulted the pride of reason the more he loved it; "credibile est, quia ineptum est; certum est, quia impossibile est."[5] Minucius Felix was an "insignis causidicus Romani fori,"[6]

[1] Moehler, "Athanasius der Grosse," p. 108.
[2] Greg. Naz., "Orat.," xx.
[3] Socrates, ii. 46, cf. iii. 16; Sozomen, vi. 25.
[4] Sozomen, viii. 2.
[5] "De Carne Christi," 5. The "credo quia absurdum" does not occur in Tertullian, though he had moods when it would have expressed his mind.
[6] Jerome, "De Vir. Illust.," lviii.; Lact., "Inst.," v. 1.

and his *Octavius* shows us how empty the Roman conception of Christianity is unless clothed in institutional forms.[1] Callistus, whatever view we may take of Hippolytus' narrative,[2] has no claim to remembrance save as a man of political and practical gifts. Cyprian, orator and teacher of rhetoric, has the mind of a Roman patrician, and is a statesman and administrator, one we can only describe as the first prince of the Church, which to him, as to all princes, was not an ἐκκλησία, but a *civitas*. Hosius is the typical diplomatic bishop, active in councils and courts, but represented in literature by a solitary letter to an emperor.[3] Ambrose was the son of a Roman præfect, and was himself a lawyer and magistrate before he became a bishop. The class of orators, whose training and models were as distinctly legal and forensic as those of the corresponding class in Greece were literary and philosophical, furnished the names of Arnobius, Lactantius, Victorinus Afer, and, though he transcends all such categories, Augustine; yet he may be cited as the palmary example of the philosophic mind governed by the political idea. The Hilaries, of Poictiers and of Arles, were intended for secular life, and only later assumed ecclesiastical office. Leo the Great does not seem to have been trained in the heathen philosophies or literatures, while Gregory the Great was by his legal studies educated for his senatorial rank and duties.

Thus, then, in the Fathers of the Church the characteristics of East and West appear—the Greek with his literary and philosophical ambitions, the Latin with his forensic and political. The sacred literature of the East finds its antecedents and models in the schools of the rhetors, of the

[1] The *Octavius* has this interest for us: it is the nearest Western parallel to the Greek apologies, but its point of distinction from them is its deficiency in all specifically Christian elements. See Kühn, Inaugural Dissertation, "Der Octavius des Minucius Felix" (Leipzig, 1882).
[2] "Refut. Omn. Hæres.," ix. 11 ff.
[3] Cf. Athanasius, "Hist. Arianor.," 44.

West in the eloquence of the forum and the bar. The sophist loved to distinguish himself by his skill in handling the subtleties of logic and thought, but the orator by his ability so to argue a cause, real or imaginary, as to gain a verdict. And in each case there survived in the new subject the old method with all its categories, making the new spirit work within the forms created by the old.

§ III.—The Greek Theology.

The theology of the Greek Church may, then, be described as the last characteristic creation of the Greek genius. It had as natural a genesis as the philosophy in which it was rooted and out of which it grew. The Hebrew religion and the Christian history would not of themselves have sufficed to beget or evoke this theology. Without the Greek mind with its speculative achievements and capabilities it could not have been; with this mind, and because of it, the theology could not but be. Philosophy had come to be of the very essence of the Greek spirit; to it the question was a thing of nature, the cultivation of centuries had trained it to inquire, to speculate, to seek causes, to discover ends, or examine and determine means—in a word, to philosophize. It had tried many lines of thought, had vigorously developed single principles into elaborate systems, and now in despair of truth from any one school was seeking it by combining elements from all. In its earliest speculative period it had attempted to explain nature in natural terms, but did not find that nature grew more intelligible by water or air, fire or atoms, being made the mother of all things. Anaxagoras had come, "the sober man among drunkards,".and bidden reason mix the elements; and then Socrates had collected the evidence of its action, Plato had speculated as to the creative relation of the permanent and ideal to the transitory and real, Aristotle had tried to discover an intelligible order within the actual, a reason and an end that, unmoved, moved all things. The philosophy that had begun as an attempt to explain nature had culminated in the attempt to formulate the notion of its cause. And precisely at this point was found its supreme difficulty, yet imperious necessity; for it was by the attempt to formulate this conception that the successive Greek philosophies had lived, and, failing, had died. And the difficulty was not lessened but rather increased by Hebrew religion and the Christian history, while the necessity was made more imperious. God indeed was not now to be reached through nature; rather thought was to start with Him, and nature was to be read through God and God through the history; but what did this mean save that a new theology, a science of God through the history and a science of the universe through God, must be attempted? But did not such a theology already exist in the sacred literature? True, a theology was there, but it wanted adaptation or relation to the new mind. It lived in an element of emotion, of spiritual apprehension, of religious reminiscence and association that had not yet become native to the Gentile Christian. God was presented as a religious idea, but the demand was for a scientific conception. The minds that made the New Testament were penetrated with Him; they lived and thought as in His presence; they had no difficulty in conceiving His relation to them or theirs to Him, or in believing that He was the personal Creator, Sovereign, Father of men; in a word, their God was religious, not metaphysical, revealed in the sweet light of faith, not hidden in the dark definitions of the schools. But to the Greek mind God, as distinguished from the gods, was primarily metaphysical; He was Being, abstract and infinite, found and defined by thought, at once its supreme necessity and difficulty. Without Him an intelligible world could not be conceived; but then it was even harder to conceive how He as infinite could be related to the finite, as perfect could be in contact with evil, as above all time and space, and yet existing in their forms and under their categories. To the two minds God was a very different being; the difficulty of the Apostolic mind was how to do without Him, the difficulty of the Greek mind was how to bring Him into the terms of a rational and coherent conception. And the difficulty was enormously increased by the new elements which the Christian history had introduced; yet how could this history be believed unless it could be so construed as to leave God intelligible to an intelligence made by centuries of speculation a sort of organized yet automatic metaphysic? and how could God be invested with religious significance unless by being, as it were, vitalized and transfigured by this history?

The scientific character, then, and antecedents of the Greek mind were such that a scientific theology was necessary to it and necessary in proportion to its very difficulty. If God was to live in faith, He must be made to live, intelligible and reasonable, for thought, in harmony with the history on the one hand, and nature and man on the other. Certain things were *in limine* evident. He must remain sole, sovereign, one, neither multiplied nor lowered nor divided. No return to the mythological deities was possible; they were only personalized forces or passions, mixed in nature, promiscuous in intercourse, with an innumerable progeny, here of gods, there of men. Nor must there be any return to the old Judaic Deism; there God and the world were so divided that it in a sense perished in His presence and lived only by His will. As a monotheism it was cancelled by the political restrictions of the religion—for a God limited to a single people cannot be the only God—and as a theism it was denied by the absence of all recognition as to any organic relation between God and man. If, now, Christian thought could neither fall back into a kind of classical mythology allegorically construed, nor into a Judaic Deism, which would have dissolved or negatived all the real or characteristic elements in its own history, then there remained for it only a third course—it must advance to such a new conception of Deity as would enable it to maintain His unity, yet His organic connection with man as Sovereign, Saviour, and Judge. And the only way in which this advance could be made was by the old dialectic, the use of the old logical instrument and means. The result was the formation of those doctrines of the Godhead and the Incarnation which we owe to the speculative genius of the Greek theologians.

This theology, then, viewed under its formal aspect and in relation to its formative factors, must be conceived as a continuation and expansion of Greek philosophy. It is the attempt of the Greek mind to formulate the new theistic idea, to construct in its peculiar method and by its distinctive terminology a reasonable and reasoned theory of the new material that had come to it as a religion and in a history. All the phenomena that attend the genesis and formulation of philosophical theories attend the genesis of this. It comes into being by a process of development, explicative of the idea, determinative of the form. The very process that is exhibited in the history of Greek philosophy as a whole, and in each of the great Greek schools, is repeated here. At first the idea is imperfectly apprehended; it is mixed with old yet alien elements; its meaning and bearings are not distinctly discerned; then under discussion it grows clearer, under analysis purer, through experience more vivid and real. Attempts at formulation break down, now because too general, now because not general enough, till a special terminology is created, and a consensus secured. But out of the very formulation new questions rise, which divide the school into sections, each repeating the process till the possibilities of the philosophy are exhausted, and inquiry or speculation must proceed on other lines to other and more scientific results. Thus had philosophy developed, and so did theology now. The theology of the Apostolic Fathers is mainly one of reminiscence; they repeat what they have heard or read, yet often so as to show that they have either not heard aright or not fully understood. The Gnostics are the first theologians; their speculations are absurd enough as they lie, unfolded by the hand of the enemy, in the pages of Irenæus and Hippolytus; but they had a reason in them which the Fathers have carefully not allowed us to see. They attempted to translate the Christian history into an ethical cosmology. They did not love evil, but they loved God, especially as an object of speculation, and they laboured so to separate God from the world as to save Him from all participation in its evil. All that was of sense was sin, all that was of spirit was good; the movement downward to sense was the fall, the movement upward to spirit was redemption. This was instituted by the Æon Christ, and in order to do it He entered into the man Jesus. These two were distinct and different. Jesus belonged to the world of sense and suffering, which was evil; Christ to the realm of spirit and knowledge, which was good. The theory made the historical person of Christ unreal, with all its events, especially the Passion and Death, God an inaccessible monad, existence a perplexed dualism, Creator, creation and its history all evil, escape from sense the one real good; but it showed the necessity of a constructive doctrine of Christ and Christianity based on the New Testament, and not simply on the Old. The Apologists approached the matter from another side; they began with the history; it was real, veracious, but it was the history of a teacher, the record of a philosophy, Jesus was the second and perfect Socrates, giving the truth to man. But their limitations came out when they attempted to determine His relations to God. In Him the Logos became flesh, but this Logos was a sort of cosmological principle, a means of mediating in a philosophical sense between God as the object and man as the subject of knowledge, akin to man who participates in Him, akin to God whom He makes articulate. He was thus needed rather to enable God to do His work and reveal Himself, and man to find God and know His truth, than to save from sin. They did not make their monotheism and history so interpenetrate as to produce a theology of salvation. Irenæus, as became a Biblical theologian, was more soteriological. Christ is the Son of God, in Him the Divine and human natures are united; but he expressly declines to philosophize as to the relations these terms imply, and leaves us at the critical point with unrelated and unarticulated ideas. Tertullian, who, though Latin, has here great significance for Greek thought, is bolder; he sees, as Irenæus had done, that salvation must be as real as creation, and therefore the Redeemer must be as Divine as the Creator; but he attempts, as Irenæus did not, to formulate a conception of God which shall reconcile plurality with unity. "Unitas," he says, "inrationaliter collecta hæresim facit, et trinitas rationaliter expensa veritatem constituit"[1] But when he comes to expound his Trinity it turns out to be not essential, but œconomical, a matter of disposition in order to administration.[2] The Son once was not, is derivative, a portion of the Divine essence, "secundus a Deo constitutus."[3] But this οἰκονομία or administrative unity seemed a clumsy expedient; was it not simpler to say, "God is one; it is the same person who now reigns as Father, now suffers as Son"? So said the Patripassian; but does not the One so construed make the Incarnation impossible, and the history a semblance, while there can be nothing in God correspondent to what is realized on earth? Origen showed how both the Œconomical and the Patripassian theory could be transcended. He emphasized the idea of the Son: it is the distinction of a son to be born of the essence of the Father; their relation is a process of gene-

---

[1] "Adv. Prax.," 3.
[2] *Ibid.*, 2, 3. See *infra*, p. 99.
[3] "Adv. Hermog.," 3; "Adv. Prax.," 7, 9.

ration ; and, since here all the categories are infinite, the process must be eternal.[1] In this conception there are these elements: (a) Father and Son both are and are real; (β) unity, both are of one essence ; (γ) relation, the one generating, the other generated ; and (δ) eternity, the process ever has been and ever must be. One notion proper to absolute Deity was absent—the generation was by the will of the Father, not by necessity of nature, and hence the Son was θεός, or ὁ δεύτερος θεός, not ὁ θεός or αὐτόθεος.[2] "Exactly so," said Arius ; "then once He was not, *i.e.*, before the Father willed Him to be; since made by will He is made out of nothing; since made out of nothing He is a creature, dependent, variable, in need of grace to keep Him from falling." "Nay," replied Athanasius, "if He is a creature made by will out of nothing, then He is but as we are: in coming to Him we do not get to God, nor does God in Him get to us. He is an anomaly, unequal to creation, unequal to redemption, a mere divisive person, whose place in the universe is to keep apart God and man. We must develop and define our idea of the Godhead. Generation is not a matter of will, but of nature, therefore of necessity. The Father did not choose to have a Son; Fatherhood and Sonship are of the very essence of God; without these there were no God. As they are of the Divine essence and that essence is one, God is one, and the 'persons' are consubstantial. This unity gives us a single but not a simple God ; He is complex, manifold, ever has been, ever must be, a society, a Godhead; within His unity Paternity and Sonship are immanent, and as such necessities of His being."[3]

[1] "De Prin.," iv. 28; Proem, 4.
[2] "In Evang. Joh.," tom. ii., §§ 2, 3, vol. i., pp. 92, 93 (Lomm.); "Cont. Cels.," v. 39.
[3] See the two forms of Arius' Confession of Faith in Hahn, "Bibliothek der Symb. u. Glaubensreg. der alten Kirche," pp. 188-190.

§ IV.—The Terminology.

As with the thought so with its form; its terminology was slowly elaborated, each distinctive term being tried disputed, rejected, recalled, and finally adopted and adapted, in a special sense to a special purpose. The conflict of terms is but a conflict of ideas, the struggle towards adjustment of old and new, and by their use or disuse causes can be discovered, change marked, and growth measured Thus λόγος has a history in Greek philosophy before it has a being in Christian theology. Heraclitus and the Stoics know it as well as the Apocrypha and Philo, and we must understand its history outside the theology before we can understand its usage within it. Justin Martyr differs as much from John as from Athanasius; his idea is inchoate, partly philosophical, partly theological; his Λόγος is a Θεὸς ἕτερος,[1] created yet divine,[2] appointed Creator by the will of God,[3] existing wholly in Christ, partially or seminally in man;[4] He is innate in all, and in Him all participate.[5] Theophilus contrasts the λόγος ἐνδιάθετος and the λόγος προφορικός almost exactly in the Stoical manner; creation, providence, and prophecy are but the externalization of the internal Word.[6] In certain writers the idea of the Λόγος pushes into the background the idea of the Υἱός; in others the Υἱός eclipses the Λόγος, and according as the emphasis falls on the one or on the other, we have a different set of terms or ideas

---

[1] "Dial.," c. 56, vol. ii., p. 184 (Otto): cf. "Apol.," i. 63. Engelhardt, "Justin," p. 277, contrasts the attitude of the Dialogue and the Apologies to this question. Justin, addressing the heathen, shows that a man may be the Son of God and an object of worship; but, addressing the Jew, that there is "another God" beside the one God.

[2] "Dial.," 61, 62, pp. 204-206, 210.

[3] "Apol.," ii. 6; i. 32, 22.

[4] *Ibid.*, ii. 8, 10; i. 44.

[5] *Ibid.*, i. 46; ii. 8, 13.

[6] "Ad Autol.," ii. 10. Cf. Möller, "Kosmologie," pp. 133 ff.; Drummond, "Philo Judæus," vol. i, pp. 110 ff.

defining the relation to the Godhead. Οὐσία is a term common to various philosophical schools.[1] To the Stoics the universe was but the οὐσία of God[2]; a thing was only so far as it participated in the οὐσία,[3] and hence in relation to phenomena it might be described as the ingenerate, while they were the generated,[4] though God, who, speaking strictly, was the alone ἀγέννητος, could retract it into Himself and produce it from Himself again.[5] With Plutarch it is the synonym of being, simple, abstract, impassible, imperishable, from which all that happens or appears proceeds and becomes.[6] He distinguishes indeed a σωματικὴ from a νοητὴ οὐσία, the one being ὕλη or ὑποκείμενον, the other μορφὴ or εἶδος, and out of the union of these the world arises.[7] But the relation of God the creator is not one and the same to matter and to soul; He is in the one case maker, artificer (ποιητής), in the other case generator, parent (πατήρ). As regards matter, his mode of action is a ποίησις, but as regards souls a γέννησις, and so they are not so much His work as a part of Him, have arisen not so much through Him as from Him and out of Him.[8]

From philosophy the term passed into Gnostic theology,[9] and thence into the terminology of all the Greek schools, heretical and orthodox.[10] With its application to the

[1] Cf. Hatch's "Hibbert Lectures," pp. 269-279; Bigg's, "Christian Platonists of Alexandria," pp. 163-165, text and notes. Dr. Bigg says: "Οὐσία is properly Platonic, while ὑπόστασις is properly Stoic." But this is hardly correct. Οὐσία, especially in its specific Alexandrian sense, is more Stoic than Platonic.

[2] Diog. Laer., vii. 148.
[3] Stob., "Ecl.," ii. 90.
[4] Diog. Laer., vii. 134.
[5] *Ibid.*, 137: Ὅς (sc. Θεός) δὴ ἄφθαρτός ἐστι καὶ ἀγέννητος, δημιουργὸς ὢν τῆς διακοσμήσεως, κατὰ χρόνων ποιὰς περιόδους ἀναλίσκων εἰς ἑαυτὸν τὴν ἅπασαν οὐσίαν καὶ πάλιν ἐξ ἑαυτοῦ γεννῶν.
[6] "De Is.," 45, 53.
[7] "De An. Procr.," iii. 3, 4. Cf. *ibid.*, ix. 1, xxvii. 1; "De Is.," 53, 54.
[8] "Quæst. Plat.," II. i. 4 ff.; ii. 1, 2. Cf. "De An. Procr.," ix. 6.
[9] Irenæus, I. v. 1; Ptolemæus, ap. Epiphan., xxxiii. 7.
[10] "Clem. Hom.," xx. 3; xix. 12, 13. Melito, in Routh, l. 121, where

Christian Deity it took on a specific sense; He could not be changed into the world, nor could it or anything within it be regarded as a modification or individualization of Him. His οὐσία was distinct from all created being and incommunicable to the creature. To affirm that any one possessed the Divine οὐσία was to affirm of Him necessary existence—*i.e.*, Deity. And as the Deity was one, the essence was indivisible[1]; but as philosophy had construed the term, a single essence did not exclude the idea of personal differences and distinctions. To denote these the terms πρόσωπα and later ὑποστάσεις were used. Ὑπόστασις had also a history in philosophy, was introduced into theology by the Gnostics,[2] was employed at first and throughout the Arian controversy as the synonym of οὐσία,[3] but while the latter remained the name for the more abstract being, as it were the unqualified or undifferentiated Deity, the former came to denote the more concrete, or Deity realized in personal modes, distinguished and distributed into personal forms. It was in order to emphasize their real and abiding, as opposed to a phenomenal and modal, character that ὑπόστασις was substituted for πρόσωπον.[4]

But the ὑποστάσεις had not only to be distinguished; they had to be related as well; and this relation was expressed by the famous term ὁμοούσιος. It, too, came from philosophy

τὰς δύο αὐτοῦ οὐσίας refers to the two natures of Christ. From this point onward the term grows ever more common and specific.

[1] Athanasius, "De Synod.," 51 ff.

[2] Irenæus, I. i. 1; v. 4; xv. 5. But Tatian speaks of God, ὁ δεσπότης τῶν ὅλων, as ἡ ὑπόστασις τοῦ παντός, "Or. ad Gr.," v.

[3] So the Nicene Symb., ἐξ ἑτέρας ὑποστάσεως ἢ οὐσίας. Cf. "Athan. ad Afros," 4.

[4] See important notes in Harnack, vol. ii., pp. 252, 257. Ullmann, "Gregorius von Nazianz.," pp. 246-248. It was in the hands of the three great Cappadocians that the distinction between οὐσία and ὑπόστασις became finally fixed. See Greg. Naz., "Or.," XLII. 16, p. 759. But ὑπόστασις and πρόσωπον continued to be used interchangeably, though with a distinct preference for ὑπόστασις.

through Gnosticism into theology,[1] and had there a troubled history. For using it Paul of Samosata was condemned, and Arius for not using it.[2] The condemnation may or may not have been right, but what it is cited here to illustrate is this—the gradual elaboration and articulation of thought within the Church by the progressive use of terms formed without it, such terms working their way to enforcement by criticism, adoption, and definition exactly as in the schools. The terms, too, that denote the distinctive properties of the persons have a similar history. Ἀγέννητος is by Philo applied to God so as to distinguish Him on the one hand from man as γεννητός and on the other hand from the Λόγος who stands between partaking of the nature of both.[3] So the Gnostic Valentinus describes the Father as μόνος ἀγέννητος, but as He did not choose to be alone He generated νοῦν καὶ ἀλήθειαν.[4] The first real indication of the later usage occurs in the Clementine Homilies, where the Father and Son are distinguished as respectively unbegotten and begotten, and affirmed to be outside comparison[5]; but even more explicit is a passage where Ptolemæus contrasts the begotten God with the one unbegotten Father.[6] Over against the μόνος

[1] Irenæus, I. v. 1, 5, 6. In those three instances the later usage is exactly anticipated. So, too, Hippol., "Philos.," vii. 22, 78; "Clem. Hom.," xx. 7; Ptolemæus "ad Floram," ap. Epiphan., xxxiii. 7. Harnack, vol. ii., pp. 192, 193, note 7, has called attention to the striking way in which Ptolemæus forecasts the ecclesiastical terminology of the future.
[2] Athanasius, "De Synod.," 42-53; Basil, "Ep.," 52; Sozo., iv. 15. See discussions in Routh, iii. 360-365; Newman's note, pp. 165-176 of his translation of the Anti-Arian Treatises, and Harnack, i. 641 ff.
[3] "Quis Rer. Div. Her.," § 42, p. 502.
[4] Hippol., "Philos.," vi. 29.
[5] xvi. 16.
[6] "Ad Floram," ap. Epiphan., xxxiii. 7. The contrast to the precise Gnostic use is the undeveloped and incorrect Ignatian, Eph. vii. Cf. Lightfoot's "Excursus," vol. ii., pp. 90-94. In Justin, "Apol.," ii. 6, where the Father is qualified as ἀγέννητος and the Son or Logos as γεννώμενος, we see the action of the same philosophical influences as had shaped the Gnostic terminology. This is only the more emphasized by the doctrine as to the relativity of the names and knowledge of God which the passage affirms.

ἀγέννητος stands the μονογενής, the Father can be Father only as He has a Son; and here, too, as regards theological use, the Gnostics, in direct dependence on John, anticipated the Fathers.[1]

§ V.—THE MERITS AND THE DEFECTS OF THE THEOLOGY.

But it is needless to multiply examples: the facts are patent enough; all that we need to do is to see their significance. The Fathers could not help themselves; the terms were there, and they must speak in the language of their people and day and school. But to use the language was to admit the thought; to translate their beliefs into the formulæ of the schools was to make them scholastic formulæ, translated in matter as well as in form. The matter construed was not the old scholastic matter, and so the new definitions and theorems were not identical with the old; but they were definitions and theorems all the same, exactly as scholastic in character, value, and function as those they superseded. What entered the speculative Greek intellect a religion and a history came out a theology, as much a creation of the metaphysical mind as if the place had been an academy or a school instead of a council. But the theology was as little the ultimate science of the religion or of the history as Plato or Aristotle is the ultimate science of nature and man and society. It was simply a philosophy of the new material in the language of the old schools.

It is no part of our purpose to discuss here the truth or value of this theology, only to indicate how it came to be. Yet

[1] See a careful analysis of the evidence as to this dependence on John in Hort, "Two Dissertations," pp. 30 ff. The history of the terms used in Greek theology has still to be written, and only when it has been will the continuance within the theology of old philosophical questions be made apparent. All the contemporary schools, philosophical as well as theological, were grappling with the same questions, hitting upon kindred solutions, and looking for light along similar lines. The text attempts neither a history nor an explication of the terms; it only seeks to indicate that they belong to theology, because to the speculative tendencies and endeavours of the time.

there are two points of view from which it may be regarded: the philosophy it continued or the material it construed. From the first point of view the theology of Nicæa and Chalcedon is a bold and splendid piece of constructive metaphysics, the completion of the ancient Greek quest after a scientific conception of God and His relation to man. It combines elements that had before been held to be incompatible in thought. It endeavours to translate God from an abstract into a concrete, related, living Absolute; to conceive Him as a Godhead which has within itself all the constituents and conditions of a real intellectual, moral, and social existence, as if He were a universe while God. This is the meaning of its heroic struggle to affirm at once the unity of the Divine Essence and the distinction of the Divine Persons. The unity is not a simplicity, but, as it were, a rich and complex manifold, an absolute which is the home of all relations, a unity which is the bosom of all difference, the source and ground of all variety. Such a conception saves us from the Deism which shuts up God within the limitations or impotences of His own infinitude, and from the Pantheism which loses Him within the multitudinous and fleeting phenomena of an ever-changing universe. But the re-articulation of the theistic idea was only one side of the endeavour; the other side was the adjustment or adaptation to it of the idea of man. This was accomplished in a twofold way: by a general doctrine of human nature, and by a special doctrine as to the person of Christ. By the first the Divine and human natures were made to approximate, to become sympathetic, capable of related and even allied being; by the other, the Divine had actually so realized this relation with the human that it had come to have a sort of corporate being in the race. God's transcendence had stooped to immanence, and by the incarnation of One the Divine life of the whole had been assured. These gracious and sublime ideas were the aim rather than the achievement of the theology; they were more what it aspired to than what it reached. But even so they compel us to regard it as the completion, under the impulse of the Christian history, of the quest of ancient thought after a scientific conception of Deity.

But from the point of view of the material construed the theory was much more defective. It did most inadequate justice to the theistic contents of the Christian history. Metaphysics had triumphed over ethics, scholastic terms over moral realities. It is hard to say whether the Nicene theology did more eminent service or disservice to the Christian conception of God. In contending for the Deity of the Son, it too much forgot to conceive the Deity through the Son and as the Son conceived Him. In its hands, and in consequence of its definitions and authority, the metaphysical Trinity tended to supersede the ethical Godhead. The Church, when it thought of the Father, thought more of the First Person in relation to the Second than of God in relation to man; when it thought of the Son, it thought more of the Second Person in relation to the First than of humanity in relation to God. The immanent relations may be the essential and real, but they are not interpreted unless made the basis of the outward and actual. The Fatherhood in the Godhead loses its moral and religious meaning unless it be translated into the Fatherhood of God; the Sonship within the Trinity is without its most majestic and gracious sense till it finds its consequent and correlate in the sonship of man. The Nicene theology failed here because it interpreted God and articulated its doctrine in the terms of the schools rather than in the terms of the consciousness of Christ. It would have better served the Church and the truth if it had done the first not less, but the second much more. For its too metaphysical Godhead injuriously affected in all its branches all later theology. The persons of the Godhead, from being metaphysically, came, especially in the hands of Western theology, to be ethically distinguished; and on this distinction theories of salvation were based which represented it as transacted within God, though applied and carried out in time according to the terms of the eternal covenant. The division of the Persons within the Godhead had as its necessary result the division of God from man, and the exaltation of miraculous and unethical agencies as the means of bridging over the gulf. The inadequacy in these cardinal respects of the Nicene theology would be inexplicable were we to regard it as a creation of supernatural wisdom or the result of special Divine enlightenment; but it is altogether normal when conceived as a stage in the development of Christian thought. In it Greek philosophy was translated into Christian theology, and, of course, its translation did not mean its death.

CHAPTER V.

THE LATIN THEOLOGY AND CHURCH.

§ I.—Their Distinctive Factors.

THE action of the Latin mind on Christianity was quite as characteristic as the action of the Greek. They differed indeed as tendencies rather than as antitheses—*i.e.*, they were not conscious contradictions or even opposites, but distinct habits and tempers unconsciously working out dissimilar results. This did not exclude mutual influence. Tertullian created as to the Godhead modes of thought and representation that affected the Eastern mind; Dionysius of Rome admonished and corrected Dionysius of Alexandria. If Athanasius was the theologian of the Nicene Council, Hosius was its diplomatist, and Leo was even more potent at Chalcedon. On the other side, the Greek apologists powerfully influenced Tertullian, much as his principles and methods differed from theirs, while neo-Platonic thought modified the minds of Victorinus the Rhetor, Hilary, Ambrose, and, above all, Augustine. But this mutual influence does not exclude independent development; nay, it helps us all the more to measure and to value the action of the different minds and conditions in the creation of ecclesiastical thought and institutions.

Two quite distinct questions are here before us: the one touching the relation of Roman polity, taken in its widest possible sense, to the organization of the Church; the other touching the action of the thought which at once accompanied, conditioned, and sanctioned the movement. It was here as in the Roman Empire; as was the jurist to the one, such was the theologian to the other. While soldiers and statesmen gave to the Empire visible form, the jurists found for it a philosophy, which not only idealized the reality, but helped to secure its stability and the greater happiness of its citizens and subjects. While the Church was in the process of formation the Empire was undergoing a sort of apotheosis, becoming in a sense a church rather than a state. The worship of the Emperor was only a symbol of the common reverence for the Empire, a confession that the system under which they lived was Divine, a religion even more than a government. Two parallel movements went on, a political and an intellectual; the one a development of the State as an organism, the other of the ideas by which it was penetrated, illumined, justified; and the result was a double transformation, a civil and a religious. The more highly organized the State became the more distinctly it grew into a religion; the change in civil organization from what it was under the later Republic to what it had become under the Empire at the end of the second century but feebly reflected the far greater change in religious thought.

As in the Empire, so in the Church; organization and thought went hand in hand, each conditioning the other and both affected by the world in which they lived. As to the organization, little can here be said; happily, it has of late been amply, though far from finally, discussed from various points of view.[1] What stands out clear from these discussions is this: the organization of the Church has a history, and is therefore capable of scientific explanation. It can be

[1] The literature concerned with this question is far too extensive to be here noticed. Happily, it is beginning to be discussed with something of the scientific spirit. Among the works meant in the text are Ritschl's "Altkathol. Kirche"; Lightfoot's dissertation on "the Christian Ministry"; Hatch's "Bampton Lectures"; Harnack's translation of Hatch, with his

seen growing, its growth measured, and the causes discovered and determined. It does not issue from the mind of the Master as it now exists in the Greek, the Roman, the Anglican, or any one of the Reformed Churches; and what can be explained by local causes and conditions is only made inexplicable when traced to miraculous power. Of these causes the most potent was the polity, public and private, of the societies, the cities, and the empire into which it entered. By a process gradual but inevitable it came to be construed in the language of the State, and so organized by the empire that it superseded as to be its only qualified and possible successor. But what concerns us here is the thought which, developing with the organization, became, as it were, its immanent reason, the philosophy that gave it meaning, the spirit that was its power.

§ II.—TERTULLIAN.

The point at which our discussion can best begin is with the man who, because he was the first, distinctly and luminously, to embody the Western spirit, did so much to shape its later course: Tertullian. He is a man of marked individuality; indeed, with him, as with Paul and Augustine, personal character is the most determinative element in his history and thought. But the formal factors of his mind may be described as two: Stoic philosophy and Roman jurisprudence. We cannot agree with Ritter when he says[1] that in Tertullian a more philosophical spirit lived than had as yet appeared in Latin literature; but it is certain that, in spite of his hot and scornful invective against philosophy, he was one of the very first to philosophize in a Christian

---

own "Analecten"; his discussions in the "Dogmengeschichte," in the "Didache," and in various parts of the "Texte u. Untersuchn."; Gore's "The Church and the Ministry"; Loening's "Gemeindeverfassung des Urchristentums," with Loofs' review in the *Studien u. Kr.* for 1890.

"Gesch. der Christlich. Philos.," vol. i., p. 417.

sense.[1] This he did on the basis of Stoicism, though, to use Neander's phrase, in harmony with the "massive one-sidedness of his nature."[2] He may not always mean so to use it, but he so uses it all the same. Thus he employs the term "natura" in the Stoical sense,[3] which was also the sense most familiar to the Roman jurists. It denotes the transcendental ideal or law or reason embodied in the constitution alike of man and the universe. But, of course, with Tertullian "natura" never becomes the synonym of God or supersedes Him; on the contrary, it simply expresses His mind and will. And so to act against nature is to disobey God; the contra-natural is the ungodly, is sin. God is the teacher of the reason[4]; it testifies before Scripture and independently of Scripture to His being,[5] to the immortality of the soul,[6] nay, even to the truth of Christianity.[7] As with "natura," so with "substantia." This term most frequently translates the Stoical ὑποκείμενον; it is the substratum of things, the essence or basis of all reality[8]; as such it is the corporeal, is body, for what is without body is without being.[9] Spirit is a kind of body, and save as body soul is not.[10] And

[1] "Gesch. der Christlich. Philos.," vol. i., p. 379.
[2] "Antignosticus," p. 4.
[3] "De Corona," 5, 6: "Natura quæ prima omnium disciplina est." "Quærens igitur Dei legem habes communem istam in publico mundi, in naturalibus tabulis." "Ipsum Deum secundum Naturam prius novimus." "De Pænit.," 1: "Quippe res Dei ratio; quia Deus omnium conditor, nihil non ratione providit, disposuit, ordinavit, nihil non ratione tractari intellegique voluit." Cf. "De Spect.," 2, 18, 23, 27.
[4] "De Test. An.," 5: "Magistra Natura, anima discipula. Quicquid aut illa edocuit aut ista perdidicit, a Deo traditum est, magistro scilicet ipsius magistræ."
[5] "Adv. Marc.," i. 10: "Nec hoc ullis Moysi libris debent. Ante anima quam prophetia. Animæ enim a primordio conscientia Dei dos est." Cf. cc. 13-18.
[6] "De Test. An.," 2-4.
[7] "Apol.," 17: "O testimonium animæ naturaliter Christianæ."
[8] "Adv. Herm.," 34-36; "Adv. Prax.," 7, 9; "Adv. Marc.," iii. 10.
[9] "De Carne Chr.," 11: "Omne quod est, corpus est Sui generis. Nihil est incorporale nisi quod non est." Cf. "Adv. Herm.," 35.
[10] "De An.," 7: "Nihil enim, si non corpus." He finds in the parable

these categories apply to God as to the soul; He is body because He is substance[1]; though "substantia," He is "spiritus," while the soul is "afflatus," which is an inferior kind of substance.[2] Since the soul is corporeal, it is passible; because it feels, perceiving; because it perceives, suffering.[3] As our knowledge is sensuous, we can know God only in part; the body which fills all space can never be fully perceived by a body localized, however well equipped with senses.[4] As He is body, He has hands, feet, and eyes[5]; and as He is substance, He is capable, as it were, of distribution without division into various forms or portions[6]; and it is because of such distribution or, let us say, specialization of the Divine substance, that the *Logos* or Son arises, who must possess this substance in order to be Divine, and He must be corporeal or He could not be. Since, then, substance is necessarily corporeal, body becomes of the very essence of humanity; only in its terms can the Incarnation be stated on the one hand and the race be conceived and described on the other. This explains the emphasis he lays on the flesh, alike as regards Christ[7] and man. It supplies, too, the basis for the legalism and the correlative materialism (for the one is but the political, the other the metaphysical side of the same thing) which underlie all forms of sacerdotalism, of Dives and Lazarus the clearest evidence of the "corporalitas animæ." Cf. 9-11. Augustine animadverts on this dictum, "De Genesi ad Lit.," lib. x., *ad fin.*

[1] "Adv. Prax.," 7: "Quis enim negabit deum corpus esse, etsi Deus spiritus est? Spiritus enim corpus sui generis in sua effigie." Cf. the Stoical σῶμα ἐστιν ὁ Θεός; Clem. Al., "Strom.," i. 11, § 51.
[2] "Adv. Marc.," ii. 9. Cf. "De Pænit.," 3.
[3] "De An.," 7.
[4] "Adv. Marc.," ii. 16; "Adv. Prax.," 14.
[5] "Adv. Marc.," ii. 16. But, he argues, these members are not to be compared with man's.
[6] "Adv. Prax.," 8, 9, 14.
[7] In resisting Docetism Tertullian fell over into the opposite and equally serious error of what can only be described as Materialism. His conception alike of the Person and the Passion is much too sensuous to be true either to the divinity or the humanity. Cf. "Apol.," 21; "Adv. Marc.," iii. 8; but especially the treatise "De Carne Chr."

especially in its cardinal doctrines of ordination and sacraments, and determines all the doctrines touching man and his native depravity co-ordinated under the generic name of original sin. With Tertullian these doctrines take their rise, inchoate in form, but consistent and complete in principle. The "propagatio animarum per traducem" is with him the logical consequence of his doctrine of being. If souls are bodies, they must be capable of propagation. Adam becomes the common root or womb of mankind; from him all have proceeded, in him all were contained.[1] But if this is so, then Adam is the unevolved race, the race is the evolved Adam—he with all its sins and all its souls latent within him, it with his sin evolved in the evolution of all the souls that make up its collective and continued being.[2]

But quite as determinative as his Stoicism is his Roman jurisprudence. As a theologian he remains a jurist, his theology, in spite of his Montanism, being stamped with the image of the forensic mind. Thus it is as a jurist rather than as a Stoic that he construes the Godhead.[3] It is to him "una substantia, tres personæ." By the former term God is distinguished from man. Tertullian was too good a theist to take "substantia" like the Stoic in a pantheistic or monistic sense, and so he writes "Deus substantiæ ipsius nomen."[4] He was not the sole substance; for "substantia" was rather the name of an individual existence, "substantia propria est rei cuiusque," and so denoted difference, while "natura" denoted what was common.[5] It was by virtue of their respective substances that God and the world differed, and this difference was developed in what we can only describe as the terms of

[1] "De An.," 9, 20, 21, 25-27; "De Res. Car.," 45; "De Carne Chr.," 11.
[2] "De Test. An.," 3: "Per quem (Satan) homo a primordio circumventus, ut præceptum Dei excederet, et propterea in mortem datus exinde totum genus de suo semine infectum suæ etiam damnationis traducem fecit." Cf. "De An.," 41.
[3] "Adv. Prax.," 2, 3.
[4] "Adv. Herm.," 3.
[5] "De An.," 32.

jurisprudence. Deus was always "substantia," but not always "dominus." He became Dominus because of creation, and Judex because of sin.[1] But while He exercises rule over the creature, He has communicated of His substance to the Son and the Spirit, who constitute together with the Father the "tres personæ." "Persona" is a legal term, denoting the party or name to a suit, and "substantia" floats between its legal and philosophical sense. The "personæ" differ "gradu," "forma," "specie," which were all juridical terms, often used as synonyms; and they agree "statu," "substantia," "potestate,"[2] terms also juridical and synonymous. The "personæ" were thus distinguished, but the "substantia" was not divided, a state of things most intelligible to one who thought as a Roman lawyer; and this distinction he conceives as a matter of disposition, dispensation, or οἰκονομία. Under suggestion from this term he passes from legal to political nomenclature, and speaks of the "personæ" as "officiales," the agents of an administration. The Godhead is a monarchy, and monarchy signifies nothing else than "singulare et unicum imperium," but the authority does not cease to be one by having more than one minister. And so, speaking like a Roman jurist, he describes the Son and the Spirit as "consortes substantiæ Patris,"[3] with whom He speaks "quasi cum ministris et arbitris ex unitate Trinitatis." To be this were they created, for Son and Spirit alike owe their being to the Father.[4] In harmony with this idea of the Godhead is his notion of man's relation to God. He is under law, and law positive—to be obeyed, not because it is right, but simply because it is law instituted by the Supreme Legislator.[5] Hence man becomes by sin a criminal; his sins

[1] "Adv. Herm.," 3.
[2] "Adv. Prax.," 2. See Dirksen, "Manuale Lat. Fon. Jur. Civ. Rom.," *sub* vv.
[3] "Adv. Prax.," 3, 4, 12.
[4] *Supra*, p. 83.
[5] "De Pænit.," 4: "Neque enim quia bonum est, idcirco auscultare debemus, sed quia Deus præcepit." Cf. Scorp., 2, 3.

are "crimina," "delicta interdicta," punished as such things must be.[1] The legal idea Paul struggled so hard to expel thus returns in a more aggravated form, not as a Divine institution to purify, but as an instrument of judgment and justice, which those it condemned could yet propitiate. With it enters the notion, so offensive to Paul, of merit, and with merit the idea of the means of creating it, and of its worth or function with God. Hence comes the belief in a God who needs to be satisfied, and in penance as a method of satisfaction.[2] In a moment, as twins born of the same idea, forensic theology and legal morality came to be. Both have a common basis, a God so much a personalized law that He needs by suffering to be satisfied for the dishonour done by sin. If the sin be conceived to be so great that only a God can satisfy God, we have the scholastic theory of the Atonement. If the offence be such that satisfaction can be given by the act or suffering of men, we have the Catholic doctrine of merit and intercession. On such a basis and with such ideas, we only need to have a positive institution to have a system of jurisprudence translated into a Church.

§ III.—The Old Religions and the New.

But now, in order to include other elements necessary to this discussion, we must turn to the action of the third factor—the religion.[3] As the field here is so immense, we must confine ourselves to a single point—the ministry; but, happily, it involves almost all that is essential. Here our question is not political, concerned with sources,

[1] "De Pænit.," 3.
[2] *Ibid.*, 5, 9. The doctrine of merit, or the satisfaction of God by penances or works, as it appears in Tertullian, deserves a fuller discussion than we can give to it here. It was simply an adaptation of the principle of Roman law: "Qui enim accepit satisfactionem, injuriam suam remisit" ("Digest," lib. xlvii. 10, 17, § 6: cf. iv. 2, 14, §§ 9, 11). But this adaptation represents the substitution of the legal for the evangelical idea. See Harnack, "Dogmengesch.," iii. 16-18, note 1.
[3] *Supra*, p. 61.

succession, or degrees in office, but material, concerned with what the ministry was and what it became.[1]

We begin with the position already stated—the Church at its origin had no official priesthood.[2] Regarded through the relation of its constituent members, it was a family, a brotherhood, a household of faith[3]; from the standpoint of its privileges and liberties it was an ἐκκλησία, or society of the enfranchised, where every man was free and a citizen[4]; from its relation to God it could be variously described as a "kingdom," an "elect people," a "royal priesthood," or a "temple built of living stones."[5] As the priesthood was the collective spiritual society, so all its sacrifices were spiritual or ethical, never sensuous. Men were to present their bodies a "living sacrifice," which was a "reasonable service," "holy, acceptable unto God."[6] Beneficence and charity are "sacrifices" with which "God is well pleased."[7] "Praise" is a "sacrifice"[8]; the gifts of love are "an odour of sweet smell, a sacrifice acceptable, well pleasing to God."[9] The special function of the "holy priesthood," formed as it is of the "living stones" which God has built into

---

[1] The political and the sacerdotal questions are quite distinct. Both are historical, but the question as to episcopacy and episcopal succession is altogether political—*i.e.*, a question of polity or constitution; while the question as to the priesthood touches the very nature and character of the religion. Men may hold the episcopal theory and deny the sacerdota'; and they may hold the sacerdotal without accepting the episcopal. Of works that deal with the specific question there may be named: Ritschl's "Altkathol. Kirche," pp. 362, 368, 394, 461, 555, 560, 576; Rothe, "Vorles üb. Kirchengesch.," pp. 208-231, 299-313; Harnack, "Dogmengesch.," i. 283 ff.; Höfling, "Die Lehre der ältes. Kirche vom Opfer," and a1 essay of my own in Jubilee Lectures (1882), on "Ecclesiastical Polity an l the Religion of Christ."

[2] *Supra*, pp. 48, 49.
[3] Eph. iii. 15; 1 Peter ii. 17; 1 Thess. iv. 9; Gal. vi. 10; Eph. ii. 19.
[4] 1 Cor. i. 2; 2 Cor. viii. 19, *et passim*.
[5] John xviii. 36, 37; 1 Peter ii. 9; Titus ii. 14; Heb. viii. 10; 1 Peter ii. 5; 1 Cor. iii. 16-19; 2 Cor. vi. 16; Eph. iii. 21.
[6] Rom. xii. 1.
[7] Heb. xiii. 11.
[8] Heb. xiii. 15.
[9] Phil. iv. 18.

a "spiritual house," is to "offer up spiritual sacrifices acceptable to God through Jesus Christ."[1] This view is common to all the writers of all tendencies in the New Testament. James defines "pure religion before God and the Father" to be this: "to visit the widow and the fatherless in their affliction, and to keep himself unspotted from the world."[2] And the definition is made the more impressive by his using a term ($\theta \rho \eta \sigma \kappa \epsilon i a$) which denotes the body or outer form of religion, not its inner essence or spirit.

And these ideas did not at once die, though the process of deterioration or materialization began very soon. They live throughout the second century, but in the face of tendencies at once creative and prophetic of change. We see them first successful in heresy, which here, as in so many things—tradition, Apostolic succession, sacramental theory and practice—anticipates what later becomes orthodoxy[3]; while the Apostolic usage survives in the Apostolic Fathers, though they have no very clear consciousness of what it involved. The episcopate in Ignatius has high political or congregational significance, but no sacerdotal. His bishop is no priest, and to him $\theta \nu \sigma \iota a \sigma \tau \eta \rho \iota o \nu$ and $\nu a \delta s$ are alike spiritual. This was the more remarkable as the priesthood of the Old Testament was early used as a standard of comparison or ideal of the order that ought to be realized by the ministry of the New, which yet is not invested with priestly character or functions.[4] In the $\Delta \iota \delta a \chi \eta$ the prophet has displaced the priest.[5] The apologists

[1] 1 Peter ii. 5.
[2] James i. 27.
[3] To attempt detailed proof of this position is more than our limits will allow, but one may say the ecclesiastical significance of Gnosticism is only beginning to be understood. Since the text was written, Harnack's examination of the "Pistis-Sophia" has appeared; and it bears directly on the points mentioned. See pp. 59 ff. Cf. Koffmane's "Gnosis nach ihrer Tendenz u. Organisation."
[4] Clemens, i. 40, 43, 44.
[5] xiii. 3.

labour strenuously to explain how Christianity, though without the sacerdotalism characteristic of the then recognized worships, is yet a religion; how its temples, altars, and sacrifices are all inner and spiritual, its incense the secret prayer and the pure conscience, its statuary the new man with his graces and virtues, its adornments or priestly vestments his temperance, courage, wisdom, piety.[1] To Justin Martyr, Christians were the true high-priestly race; they offer the sacrifices well-pleasing to God, the prayer and thanksgiving which He loves to accept when offered by the worthy.[2] With Irenæus the sacerdotal dignity is the portion of the just, and the sanctified heart, the holy life, faith, obedience, righteousness, are the sacrifices God loves.[3] The choicest altar was the service of the needy; to minister to man was to sacrifice to God. Clement of Alexandria refused to regard any as priest save the Gnostic, him who can offer the sacrifice of praise and burn the incense of holy prayer.[4] There was a distinction of offices, but no sacred order exercising their functions by virtue of some inalienable grace. The Eucharist was congregational—it was a common meal and a collective thanksgiving, not a sacrifice dependent on officials for its efficacy[5]; there was "liberty of prophesying"; the individual

[1] "Cont. Cels.," viii. 17. Cf. vii. 62; Minuc. Felix, "Oct.," 8, 10, 32.
[2] "Dial.," 116, 117, vol. ii., pp. 392 ff. Cf. "Apol.," i. 13, 67.
[3] iv. 8, 3; 17, 4: v. 34, 3.
[4] Strom., vii. 7, § 36: Οὗτος ἄρα ὄντως ὁ βασιλικὸς ἄνθρωπος, οὗτος ἱερεὺς ὅσιος τοῦ θεοῦ. Cf. iv. 25, ii. 18; Pæd., iii. 12. For the sacrifice which is acceptable to God, Str., v. 11.
[5] Clem.; 1 Cor. xli. 1; Did., ix., x., xiv.; Ig. Smyr., 8; Eph., 20; Philad., 4; Justin, "Apol.," i. 65-67. The evidence seems to warrant the inference that the congregation was necessary to the act, but not a clerical order or person. The injunctions of Ignatius imply that customs other than those he recommended prevailed, and his words are hortatory rather than authoritative. Justin's president is no priest, but one of the brethren: προεστὼς τῶν ἀδελφῶν, not ἱερεύς or ἀρχιερεύς. Tertullian's words are clear: "Nonne et laici sacerdotes sumus? . . . Differentiam inter ordinem et plebem constituit ecclesiæ auctoritas, et honor per ordinis consessum sanctificatus. Adeo ubi ecclesiastici ordinis non est consessus, et offers et tinguis et sacerdos es tibi solus Sed ubi tres, ecclesia est, licet laici. . . . Omnes nos Deus

society or church could exercise discipline, could even institute or depose its officers.

But change is in the air; the fatal word is spoken by Tertullian, who in this shows the legal mind below the Montanist temper. He speaks of the "sacerdotale officium" which virgins cannot enter,[1] of a "sacerdotalis disciplina" and the "jus sacerdotis,"[2] of an "ordo sacerdotalis" and the "sacerdotalia munera."[3] He names the bishop "summus sacerdos" and "pontifex maximus."[4] Hippolytus in Italy claims for himself, as successor of the Apostles, the high-priesthood [5]; while Origen in Alexandria, though he holds to the universal priesthood and spiritual sacrifices,[6] yet taxes his ingenuity to unfold the likeness of the new ministry to the ancient priesthood.[7] In the Apostolic constitutions the bishop is frequently designated ἱερεύς,[8] and even ἀρχιερεύς.[9] But it was the hands of Cyprian that studiously clothed the new clergy in all the dignities of the old priesthood, and provided it with appropriate sacrificial functions and intercessory duties. With him the bishop is uniformly "sacerdos," his colleagues "consacerdotes," and the presbyters are those "cum episcopo sacerdotali honore conjuncti."[10] But, of course, the creation of a priesthood involves the institution of a priestly service; the "sacerdotium" cannot live unless there be a "sacrificium." There was only one rite that could be made to serve this purpose; and so the simple and beautiful institution of the Supper

ita vult dispositos esse, ut ubique sacramentis ejus obeundis apti simus" ("De Exh. Cast.," 7). Cf. "De Monog.," 7, 11, 12.

[1] "De Virg. Vel.," 9.
[2] "De Monog.," 12; "De Exh. Cast.," 7.
[3] "De Exh. Cast.," 7; "De Præscr. Hær.," 41.
[4] "De Baptis.," 17; "De Pudic.," 1.
[5] "Refut. Omn. Hær.," Proem, ἡμεῖς μετέχοντες ἀρχιερατείας τε καὶ διδασκαλίας.
[6] "Homil. in Lev.," ix. 9, 10 (ed. Lom., vol. ix., pp. 360-364).
[7] "In Evang. Ioh.," tom. i. 3 (ed. Lom., vol. i., p. 9).
[8] ii. 34, 35, 36; vi. 15, 18.
[9] ii. 27, 57.
[10] "Ep.," 61, 2. Cf. 1, 3; 4, 4; 65, 2; 66, 3; 67, 1; 72, 3; 73, 7.

shares the transformation of the ministry. It becomes the "sacrificium dominicum," and the priests who stand in the place of Christ offer a true and full sacrifice in the Church to God the Father, and can say, "Passio est domini sacrificium quod offerimus."[1] While the old and noble conception, which was so integral an element of the Apostolic Gospel, of the collective spiritual priesthood, altogether disappears, the officials become sacrosanct and "dispensatores Dei."[2] The development is not complete, but it is begun. The ancient ideal died hard; reminiscences of it may be found in Cyprian himself, in Augustine, in Leo the Great, even in Aquinas, nay, in the very Catholicism of to-day, but they only help to illustrate the continuity of the evolutional process and measure the vastness of the change.

But, now, what were the causes of this change? Neander thinks that the idea of an official priesthood came into Christianity from Judaism[3]; Ritschl that it was due to the inability of the Gentile Christians to understand the Gospel.[4] Both factors are needed—the one acted upon the religion from within, the other from without. The men who interpreted the New Testament through the Old interpreted first the law and then the priesthood of the Old into the New. They were made parallel—the later and spiritual was assimilated to the older and sacerdotal, the antitype was resolved into the type, the substance into the shadow. What Cyprian shows us is a rejuvenescent Judaism, the kingdom of the truth translated into a kingdom of priests. But this internal

---

[1] "Ep.," 63, Ad Cæcilium, 14, 17: cf. 4, 5, 6, 7, 9.

[2] "Ep.," 59, 6. It is hardly possible to measure the distance between the ideal minister of Christ or the apostle of Paul and the priest of Cyprian. Indeed, the two things are quite incommensurable; they belong to altogether different orders. If we study epistles like the fifty-ninth or sixty-third after the Gospels or Paul, we feel how the return of the priest has effected a revolution in the religion.

[3] "Church History," i. 270, 271 (Bohn's ed.).

[4] "Altkathol. Kirche," 394.

factor could not have sufficed without the external. Men who had never known any but priestly religions could not easily understand one altogether priestless. At first two things helped them: its very strangeness, its absolute antithesis to the familiar and the received; and, next, its appearing as a new opinion or belief, which spread by preaching or discourse, and could be taken as a philosophy. But the more it established itself as a religion, the more men, both without and within, tended to expect or seek in it the forms and offices that everywhere else prevailed. They found it easier to adjust the religion to themselves than themselves to the religion. Their minds were not sheets of clean white paper on which its truths could be clearly written, but pages crowded with the records, habits, customs, beliefs, of immemorial yesterdays; and the lines of the new could not but often mingle and blend with those of the ancient writing. A religion without a priesthood was what no man had known; a sacred order on earth seemed as necessary to worship as the very being of the gods in heaven. The temple was the centre of the State, but it was idle without a priesthood, and without it the oracle was dumb. And so these two forces, inveterate and invariable association and the Hebrew Scriptures, combined to work the change. Without the universal sacerdotalism there would have been no adequate impulse or occasion, without the Scriptures no sufficient authority or warrant; it was the correlation of the two that made the change at once natural and inevitable.[1]

[1] Tertullian may be said to represent the heathen tendency, Cyprian the Hebrew. The former allows himself a large rhetorical latitude, and glides easily into the use of the same terms for the Christian as for the heathen office (cf. "Ad. Uxor.," i. 6, 7; "Scorp.," 7; "Ad Nati.," i. 7, "De Monog.," 12; "De Ieiun.," 16; "De Pall.," i. 4); but the latter is careful and discriminative alike in the terms he uses and his sources and modes of proof. His thought is governed by the ideal of the Old Testament priesthood.

§ IV.—Thought and Organization in the Western Church.

These indeed so move together as to be different aspects of one process; the thought a man expresses in speech or in a system, a society expresses in its institutions or laws. That the thought of the most eminent man in the then Christian society was penetrated by the principles and ideas of Roman jurisprudence, is evidence that the spirit or genius of Rome had begun to organize the Church. It was not by chance that it came to be conceived as a "civitas"; the name expressed the simple truth. It was no mere substitution of a Latin for a Greek term; "civitas Dei" did not translate ἡ πόλις θεοῦ ζῶντος. Πόλις and "civitas" might alike denote a society of men organized under a common authority and governed by common laws, but the πόλις was a city of free men living within defined geographical limits, while the "civitas" had become a universal empire with its chief citizen as emperor. The πόλις could not be without its ἐκκλησία, its assembly of free citizens, or the "civitas" without its Cæsar, even though he might condescend to mask his power under the forms of the Senate. Now, in the West the Greek sense and connotation of πόλις and ἐκκλησία were lost, but the Roman sense and connotation of "civitas" remained; and so the Church was conceived not as a society of freeborn men, governed by its choicest because wisest sons, but as an *imperium* under an *Imperator*, ruled by ministers he alone could appoint and he alone depose. In other words, the clergy became the Church, the Church the religion, and the religion a transformed Roman Empire, with the Pope for emperor, bishops for procurators, and the priesthood for the magistrates and legionaries that levied the taxes, enforced the laws, upheld the unity, and maintained the peace of the civilized world. Papal infallibity is but imperial supremacy transfigured and spiritualized. The Catholic Church could not have been without Christianity, but still less could it have been without Roman imperialism. It owes its life to the one, but its distinctive organization to the other. The very forces that disorganized the civil body helped to organize the ecclesiastical. Apart from Rome, and Rome decadent, with the imperial ideal and organism, but without the imperial spirit, Catholicism could never have come into being. If the Church had passed the first five centuries of its existence under an Oriental despotism or amid free Greek cities, its structure would have been altogether different. It seemed to vanquish the Empire, but the Empire by assimilating survived in it; the name was the name of Christ but the form was the form of Cæsar.

The more elaborate the organization became, the more it reacted on thought, demanded idealization and justification at its hands. The philosophy of Tertullian was worked into an anthropology, and stated in terms derived from Paul. Man lived in Adam, bore his nature and inherited his sin. But now a jurisprudence unknown to Paul and quite alien to him was so introduced as to create a new and fateful system of ideas. As the whole race was of one sin because of one descent, it was also of one guilt—stood before God culpable, condemned. The individual was lost in the race; the collective sin involved personal blame and penalty. At one stroke, then, humanity in its natural state became a mass of perdition, and certain of the most distinctively Pauline positions forgotten or their antitheses frankly affirmed. But over against this lost mass was placed the saved society, construed, too, through the law and polity of Rome. The attributes of Christ were transferred to the Church; yet to a Church radically transformed by being made into a Roman "civitas." To be in it—*i.e.*, to be a naturalized citizen—was to be saved; to be outside it was to have no part or lot in its privileges, to be without all its good. The conditions of entrance were in the hands of its officers; baptism naturalized, admitted to citizenship; the Eucharist maintained and developed what baptism had given. And then, as thought and organization corresponded, they could be made to justify each other. Augustine argued at one point: "Men must be by nature guilty and lost, otherwise the baptism of infants would not be necessary"; and at another he with equal conviction and reason argued: "Since infant baptism is necessary, man must be by nature depraved and condemned." The race was not so much sinful in the religious as guilty in the forensic sense, and the Church which saved it was, while instituted by grace, yet political in form, legal in method, and juristic in its regulative principle. Of course the thought and organization did not stand alone. The East did not cease to influence the West. Augustine studied theology and the Church through Plato as well as through Roman polity, and to this source he owed the lofty idealism which gave to his system all its dignity and all its power. Indeed, the Roman institution received its final apotheosis through neo-Platonism at the hands of the pseudo-Dionysius; as he conceives it, symbolism reigns in heaven and on earth, a celestial hierarchy holds the approaches to God above, an ecclesiastical hierarchy guards and regulates them below, and men are graduated according to the degree of their initiation in the holy mysteries which at once reveal and conceal the ineffable Godhead. No book exercised a mightier influence on Catholicism, did more on the one hand to foster its mysticism, on the other to develop its sacerdotalism. It moulded in an equal degree men so dissimilar as Scotus Erigena and Thomas Aquinas, Hugo of St. Victor and Thomas à Becket, Grosseteste and Dante; and yet it was but neo-Platonism made to speak with the Catholic tongue.

We may then summarize the results of our discussion thus: While Greek philosophy, as the main formal factor of

Greek theology, had worked out a scientific conception of God, metaphysically rich, though ethically poor, especially in those elements most distinctive of the Christian religion and history, Roman polity and law, as the main formal factors of the Latin mind, had combined to effect the evolution of a system that made the Church a new empire and man by nature criminal, condemned because of alienation from his sovereign. The popular had incorporated with the Christian religion ideas which changed it from a system priestless and spiritual into one sacerdotal and sensuous. The result of these changes was a radical change of the religion. The life it had it owed to its Founder, the form it owed to its conditions; and there is nothing that so proves His divinity as His being able still to live and still **to act** within forms so little congenial to His Spirit.

CHAPTER VI.

SCHOLASTICISM.

WITH the formation of the Greek and Roman Churches change did not cease. It went on under conditions and factors old and new. We cannot trace it in the East, and must be content with the briefest possible sketch of its course in the West.

§ I.—THE NEW RACES AND THE OLD.

As the Church had superseded the Empire, it was but natural that she should occupy its ancient seat. The place was a necessary part of the idea. Rome was accustomed to rule the world, and the world was accustomed to the rule of Rome. In the capital the habits of direction and administration had become instinctive, and in the provinces those of reverence and obedience. And, indeed, with a conservatism greater than the later empire had known, the reigning head of the Church lived in Italy, and was selected almost always from men of Italian birth. And so it happened that a religion Palestinian in origin and Greek in theology became as Roman in polity, Roman also in power. Its Holy Land of reminiscence and imagination was in the East; but the Holy Land of its experience, as seat of the authority it recognized and source of the laws it obeyed, was Italy. And Italy was satisfied with possessing the power its inherited ambitions and capacities so well qualified it to organize and administer.

But alongside the centralization of power stands what we may call the distribution of thought. While the Empire survived as the Papacy, philosophy survived as Scholasticism; and in obedience to the law which has always governed their relations, authority resided in the capital, but philosophy consulted her dignity and independence by living in the provinces. So it was when the Cæsars ruled, so it remained when the Popes governed. Athens and Alexandria, Tarsus and Antioch, offered a more congenial home to learning and philosophy than imperial Rome, and ecclesiastical Rome left the kindly nursing of Scholasticism to Paris, Oxford, and Cologne. Authority is apt to be jealous and philosophy to be critical, and so the two agree best when their respective seats are distant enough to prevent the shocks of too sharp and too frequent collision. Philosophy, when remote from authority, can idealize it, and even render it a generous, because a not too exacting, obedience; authority, when it feels free from a criticism too intimate and curious, can tolerate philosophy and even accept its courteous homage. And so it has invariably happened that seats of empire have not been homes of living philosophies; the men to whom the machinery of Church or State is everything have, as a rule, but little taste and less patience for those ideas and ideals which are at once the puzzle and the joy of the speculative reason.

Hence we have within the bosom of the Latin Church a distinction between North and South which curiously reflects and repeats the distinction between East and West. The newer peoples stood to the intellectual or philosophical material in the religion more as did the Greek, the older to the political and administrative more as did the Roman. Indeed, one of the most remarkable facts in history is the way in which, as the speculative energies of the old races decayed, those of the new peoples developed and grew. What excited their enthusiasm and roused them to strenuous exertions was the endeavour to translate the belief they had received into a reasoned philosophy. And so from the eighth century onward, right through the period of Scholasticism, the constructive intellect was as specifically Northern as the political and administrative was Italian. The questions and controversies that mark the end of the old world and the beginning of the new are grouped round the names of Bæda and Alcuin, Paschasius Radbertus and Ratramnus, Rabanus Maurus and John the Scot, Gottschalk and Hincmar of Rheims—men all sprung from the new stock. And their pre-eminence becomes even more evident in the high days of Scholasticism. Anselm, though of Italian birth, was of Northern blood and culture; the same may be said of Peter the Lombard; and of Thomas Aquinas it is enough to say that he had in his veins the blood of the Norman and the Hohenstaufen, and his activity as learner and teacher is mainly associated with Paris and Cologne. Even Bonaventura could not have been the schoolman he was without Paris and its great masters. But when we turn from these, the action of the pure Northern mind on all the tendencies of mediæval religious thought is seen to be enormous. Roscellinus and Abelard were alike sons of Brittany. Of the names connected with the famous school of St. Victor, its founder, William of Champeaux, was a Frenchman, Hugo was a German, Richard a Scot. The greatest scholar of all the schoolmen, Albertus Magnus, was a German, and Germans, too, were the noblest representatives of the highly transcendental form of piety we call mysticism, Eckhardt and Tauler, Henry Suso, and the anonymous author of the "Theologia Germanica;" while of immediate kin were Ruysbroeck, Thomas à Kempis, and the Brothers of the Common Lot. England, too, had its famous Schoolmen,—men like Robert Pulleyn, who, though not the oldest "Magister Sententiarum," was yet older than Peter Lombard; John of Salisbury, critical, sceptical of speculation and speculative methods, but full of admiration for the saintly life; Alexander of Hales, who had the strength and the foresight to naturalize in the Christian schools the Aristotle that had issued, rehabilitated and living, from the Moorish; Duns Scotus, acutest of schoolmen, high ideal realist, metaphysical as became a Scot, yet practical as one to whom the ultimate reality was the all-efficient Will; Roger Bacon, student of nature as of theology, seeking to reform the study of both by the use of new methods, and to rescue man from the dominion of a pseudo-Aristotle; William of Occam, nominalist, yet Franciscan, making his scepticism the more potent a solvent that it was veiled under the most rigorous respect for authority. But it would become a mere tedious catalogue of now-forgotten names were we to attempt to enumerate the men of Northern blood who served the mediæval Church by turning her traditions and her creed into a living philosophy. Great as were the services of the Roman Church to the young peoples, their services to her were greater still. If she gave them a polity and a ritual, they gave her a reasoned if not a reasonable faith. She, because of her imperial ancestry, was able to give the ideas and mechanism of law, the love of order, the spirit at once of authority and obedience; but they, because of their fresh enthusiasms, unexhausted and unvexed with centuries of fruitless attempting to read the riddles of the race, were able to labour at building her inchoate intellectual material into a living and articulated body of reasoned beliefs. And theirs was the nobler work: the Church was but the vehicle of ancient custom and law; but the new mind was the first to naturalize reason in religion, to claim that its whole realm should lie open to the searching eye of constructive and interpretative thought. Its action in the first instance was in the service of the Roman Church, but only that it might in the last instance be more effective in the service of the truth.

§ II.—THE NEW RACES AND THE OLD PROBLEMS.

This new mind, then, came, with all its unexercised energies and untempered curiosities, to the old problems, and endeavoured to solve them by the help of the only factors it knew. For it the earlier theology of the East could hardly be said to exist; it was written in a little-known tongue, used by men who denied the *filioque*, and were heretics. The belief in the dignity and sanity of human nature, in the freedom of the will, in the affinity of God and man which was native to Greek theology in its golden age, was foreign to the later Latin, nor had it the literary and historical sense, so necessary to the interpretation of a religion that lives by its sacred books, which had marked the great scholars of the East, especially Origen, Theodore of Mopsuestia, and Chrysostom. Scotus Erigena had indeed something of the Oriental mysticism and speculative audacity, but his system was a theosophy, not a theology, and his master no veritable Greek Father, but the late fantastic and hierarchical pseudo-Dionysius. The man that set the problems of the new mind was Augustine, and his theology was full of unreconciled antitheses. It reflects at once his intellect and his history; the dualism that was native to his soul is inherent in his system. He never transcended it in experience, and it always dominated his thought. The basis of his intellect was, as it were, neo-Platonic, but the forms under and within which it worked were Manichean. These, indeed, had many and subtle interrelations. Neo-Platonism hated matter, feared the senses, cultivated asceticism and ecstasy as means by which they could be transcended. The Manichee believed the spirit to be alone good and real, the flesh to be altogether evil and devilish. And this dualism remained within the system of Augustine, but under forms which were determined by his experience. He read it into Paul, and expressed it in the forms of the Pauline antitheses. He read it into the civil and ecclesiastical forms which confronted him, and articulated it into his theory of the two *civitates,*—of God, which was the Church; of man, which was Rome republican and imperial. He was forced to develop the political form in his controversy with the Donatists, and the theological in his controversy with the Pelagians; but he never reduced either his principles or their forms to consistency. His "Confessiones" and his "Retractationes" but exhibit from his own point of view the history of a mind whose external conflicts were faint echoes of his internal. He never made his theology penetrate his anthropology, his mysticism qualify and clarify his ceremonialism, his spiritual create and control his political ideal. His works are almost all occasional, torn from him by the necessities of the moment, exhibiting all the one-sidedness and exaggerations of a singularly rich and restless mind, that throws itself successively on single aspects of the truth, and deals with each aspect as if it were the whole. He had all the excellencies proper to one who is in the field of controversy perhaps the supremest master; but his system has all the defects proper to his pre-eminence in this field—*i.e.*, it is in no respect a system, but only a succession of positions polemically maintained.

In a system whose character so corresponds to its genesis, two things are significant for us here: the polity, or ideal of the Christian society; and the theology, or ideal of the Christian truth. As regards fundamental or determinative principle, the one was conditional, but the other was absolute. The conditionalism belonged to the very essence of the polity, because baptism and the Eucharist, while respectively the means of entrance into the Christian body and the terms of continuance within it, were also sacraments which men, on the one hand, could give or withhold, and men, on the other, accept or refuse. And the absolutism was of the essence of the theology, because God was conceived as the omnipotent and ubiquitous Will that fixed all destinies and determined all events, and man was conceived as unable to will any good thing till he was changed of God. If the conditionalism of the polity had been consistently worked out, it would have qualified the absolutism of the theology; for if fulfilled conditions could incorporate and maintain a man in the body of the saved, the will of God no longer acted without regard to the acts of man. And, on the other hand, the absolutism of the theology, rigorously applied, would have repealed the conditionalism of the polity; for where the will of God is conceived as refusing to act in view of motives or conditions supplied from without, no system of qualifying acts or rites can be in place. On this point the history of religious thought is conclusive; no real and rigorous sacerdotalism has been able to build on an absolute theology, and no absolute theology has been able to make its home within a real and rigorous sacerdotalism.

Out of Augustine, then, came questions enough for the new mind, and we can see it from the seventh to the eleventh century attempting to master the world into which it had come, and, especially, to work out what we may call the rudimentary principles of orientation. These were centuries of great intellectual and political activity. The genius of the Empire was around and upon and within the Church, working out its organization. By a series of felicitous fictions laws were found for its regulation, and history made to authenticate its claims and authorize its right to the imperial city and seat. By the wisdom first of statesmen, then of churchmen, the clergy were schooled, disciplined, and qualified for their place in the stupendous organism which under the name of the Catholic Church had now come to be. And the whole went on without fear of external criticism. The schools of philosophy were dead; the ancient world with its literature and literary mind had perished; the realities that lived were those that belonged to the Church, and these were construed in its spirit and under its eye. And so, though the questions in theology were set by Augustine, they were selected, understood, and handled in a manner which became the minds thus situated. Directly out of his Christology, which made Jesus as Son of man the recipient of grace, rose the controversy touching the natures and the person of Christ,—whether the humanity was Son of God by adoption or through the unity of the person shared in the essential sonship of the Deity. Out of the anti-Pelagian polemic came the question as to the "duplex Predestinatio,"—whether the will of God was absolute as to both election and reprobation, or only as to one; and, further, whether in matters affecting salvation the will was in any respect free or altogether bond. Out of his more spiritual view of the Sacrament, as confronted by the growing practice of the Church to make the Mass the central act of worship, came the Eucharistic controversy, whether the elements do or do not undergo substantial change. The greatest book [1] of the period is concerned with this question, and marks a moment when the development of the political idea evoked a correlative change in the theological. If these elements do not become the veritable body and blood of Christ, how can the Sacrament be His perpetuated sacrifice, means by which men are reconciled to God and participate in His life?

§ III.—SCHOLASTICISM.

But if this period was more significant for polity than for theology, the next, which extends from the twelfth to the sixteenth century, was more significant for theology than polity. The former ends with Gregory VII.; the latter begins with Anselm and is governed by Aristotle. The Church could not escape from ancient philosophy; when its authority was most absolute, its dependence on it was most complete. If

---

[1] Radbertus, "Liber de Corpore et Sanguine Christi." Migne, "Patrol.," vol. cxx.

tradition was the organ of the material factor in theology, the Greek mind still supplied the formal. By a curious nemesis the Aristotle whom the Eastern Fathers had neglected for Plato, became the Father of Scholasticism. If Churches always canonized their benefactors, he would long ago have been at the head of the Roman calendar. There were many Schoolmen, but they all had one master, and they built by his help and to his honour systems that even he would have acknowledged to be encyclopædic and marvels of architectonic craft. Their aim was to exhibit the unity in thought which the Church manifested in society and politics; the Pope was king of men, theology was queen of knowledge. The hour of his ascendency and of its coincided. The Papacy and Scholasticism grew together, lived and decayed together. The forces that dissolved mediæval thought disintegrated the Mediæval Church.

Scholasticism had three great questions—a religious, a theological, and a philosophical; but though formally different, they were all essentially one. The religious concerned the relations of faith to authority on the one hand and to knowledge on the other; the theological concerned the nature, function, and forms of the redemptive work; the philosophical concerned the conditions, the methods, and the objects of knowledge. Anselm, distinctly the most original and creative of all the mediæval theologians, may be said to have determined either the rise or the special form of all three.

1. The religious question was directly raised by the relation of the Church to the awakening intellect. That relation had become something quite other than it was in the patristic period. Organization had increased, and, as it were, individualized authority; the claim to command kings involved the right to control mind, to legislate for thought. But just as this claim became acutest philosophy awoke from its long sleep, and men were forced suddenly and consciously to face

the whole furniture and contents of their own minds, and to ask, Whence? how? in what manner and according to what order did we come by this wonderful body of beliefs which we hold, this marvellous structure of doctrine we confess? Was reason first? or was faith—*i.e.*, the Church? Do we believe because we know? or do we know because we believe? Anselm said: "Neque enim quæro intelligere, ut credam; sed credo, ut intelligam."[1] Abelard replied, in the words of Jesus, the son of Sirach: "Qui credit cito, levis corde est,"[2] and argued that reason was of God, and had, as philosophy showed, found God. Men believed not because a thing was spoken, but because they were convinced of its truth. Faith alone was the supposition of things not seen, but knowledge the experience of the very things themselves; and so only through knowledge will faith be made perfect.[3]

They thus differed as regards the sequence or relative priority of faith and reason, but not as regards their ultimate harmony. Without this harmony neither faith nor reason could be satisfied; were they to remain in conflict, either the one or the other must be sacrificed, and the sacrifice of either would be the sacrifice of something directly created and sanctioned of God. Hence Anselm was as anxious to satisfy reason as Abelard—his intellectual life was one long struggle to make the objects or material of faith become the content of the reason—but he wanted to make sure of the objects before he began the process of reconciliation. Yet his whole endeavour, alike in the "Cur Deus Homo," the "Monologium," and the "Proslogium," was a confession that a satisfied reason was necessary to the completion, the continuance, or even the reality of faith. Beneath, therefore, the difference as to the order or sequence of the acts, there was agreement as to their equal necessity and validity; a faith that could not be

---

[1] "Proslogium," i., Opera, p. 30 (ed. 1721).
[2] "Introd. ad Theol.," Opera, p. 1051 (Migne). Cf. Ecclesiasticus xix. 4.
[3] *Ibid.*, pp. 1050 ff. Cf. "Deutsch," Peter Abālard, pp. 96 ff., 433 ff.

explicated by reason and justified to it, neither thinker could have conceived as of God or possessed of authority over man. And this remained a characteristic of the great constructive scholastic systems; they were essentially rationalisms, attempts to make the matter of faith reasonable to the reason.[1] And the difference as to the sequence or relative priority of reason and faith was more apparent than real. It is evident that here the chronological order is one and the logical order another. If the first be regarded, Anselm is right; if the second, Abelard. In the actual history or experience of the soul faith precedes reason; in the logical or ideal process, where the intellect, by the method of analysis and synthesis, deals with the material submitted to it, reason precedes faith. In the realm of experience man begins with facts; he believes those who know. He does not start life with a matured and furnished intellect, but as one who must believe that he may understand. Parents, school, church—and parents and school are but a form of church—supply him with a body of beliefs; and when he begins to think, he finds himself in possession of such a body. But these beliefs become his own by a process of ratiocination, more or less conscious. They are not the property of his intellect till they have been by his intellect understood and assimilated. Should they turn out to be beliefs contrary to his reason, either they must cease to be his or he must cease to be reasonable; should they be agreeable to his reason, then they become the beliefs of his reason, or, more simply, of the man. What was first was inherited rather than personal; what was last was personal rather than inherited. In the one case faith

[1] This is admirably expressed by Anselm in the "Cur Deus Homo" as the aim of his dialectic: "Ut rationabili necessitate intelligam esse oportere omnia illa, quæ nobis fides Catholica de Christo credere præcipit, si volumus salvari" (Lib. i., § 25, p. 86). Again: "Per unius quæstionis, quam proposuimus, solutionem, quicquid in Novo Veterique Testamento continetur, probatum intelligo"; and this solution is so reached by reason alone as to be fitted to satisfy both Jews and pagans (ii., § 22, p. 96).

precedes reason, in the other reason precedes faith. The first is a preparatory and transitional state; the second alone is permanent, personal, and final.

2. The theological question was expressed in the title of Anselm's best-known treatise, "Cur Deus Homo?" Its aim, true to the spirit and tendency of the West, was soteriological rather than Christological—*i.e.*, concerned more with what the Person did than what He was, conceiving the Person through the work and as a condition necessary to it. With this treatise constructive theories of the Atonement begin to be. For a thousand years the Church had lived without making any approach to a reasonable doctrine of the death of Christ. Its connection with redemption and the remission of sins had always been affirmed, but there had been no discovery of any real or valid reason for the connection. Eminent and orthodox Fathers, like Irenæus and Augustine, had made its final cause the devil rather than God, the rescue of man by purchase from his power[1]; but Anselm found its final cause in God rather than the devil. He worked out his theory on the forensic lines familiar to Latin theology. His cardinal principles were these: Sin withholds from God the honour that is His due; it is therefore a debt. Where such sin is the creditor must either be satisfied or the debtor punished; and satisfaction must mean not only that the original debt is paid, but that compensation is offered

---

[1] This was not indeed, as is so often represented, the uniform doctrine before Anselm. It was expressly denied by John of Damascus; and Athanasius had long before him conceived it as a sacrifice for the Father against whom man had sinned. Yet the notion was a favourite one with the Greek as well as the Latin Fathers. It took scientific shape with Origen (in Matt. xvi. 8, tom. iv. 27: Lom. ed.), though he made the transaction an illusion operated by God; it was developed by Gregory of Nyssa, translated into a "pia fraus" by Ambrose, is stated in more judicious and respectful language by Augustine: "In hac redemptione tanquam pretium pro nobis datus est sanguis Christi"—and in Gregory the Great the humanity of Christ is the bait with which God hooked that fish, His old enemy, the devil. Anselm dismisses this ancient theory very sharply (i. 7), and with him it may be said to disappear from theology.

for the loss sustained or the dishonour inflicted by the withheld payment. To give such satisfaction is impossible to man or any creature, for the utmost the creature can do is to fulfil the duties of the hour. He can do no more than obey, cannot collect such a surplusage of merit as would satisfy man's infinite Creditor. The being who does it must be one who has man's nature, that he may act in man's name; but he must also have God's dignity, that he may satisfy the infinite claims of God for the damage inflicted by man's infinite sin. To do this God became man, and He did it by His sufferings and death. The theory was throughout a piece of forensic speculation; it was the relations of God and man interpreted in the terms of Roman law, though as modified by Teutonic, and as applied in the penitential discipline of the Church.[1] As such it was fatal to the kingdom of God as a reign of grace. The satisfaction which compensated the offended secured the legal quittance of the offender; the debt paid could not be a debt forgiven; to deny salvation or reward to any man so redeemed was to

---

[1] These three sources of the Anselmic idea must be recognized; in his discussion elements can be recognized peculiar to each of the three. Cremer's essay in the *Studien u. Krit.*, 1880, pp. 1-24, lays too much stress on the affinity with Teutonic law. It may be true that this law allowed the alternative "aut satisfactio aut pœna," but the alternative was not as unknown to Roman law as Cremer would make out. Satisfaction for a debt could be made by a stranger without the knowledge of the debtor and even against his will, provided it were, with the free consent of the creditor, made in his name, and on his account. If the creditor were satisfied, though he did not receive an exact equivalent for the debt, the debtor was liberated (cf. Dig., xlvi. 3, 17, 23, 52; 1. 16, 47, and 176). The processes by which this could be accomplished were significant, as *e.g.*, "cessio nominum," by which a new creditor took the place of the old, and "delegatio" or "intercessio," by which a new replaced the old debtor. Both as regards principle and process the Anselmic theory owed more to Roman than to Teutonic law. Of the latter Anselm can have known little; his legal ideas must have come mainly from the Church courts and the Norman courts, where the rules were derived through the Frankish from the Roman legislation. As to "satisfacere" and "satisfactio," see Dirksen, *sub* vv., and *supra*, p. 100.

deny him his most manifest rights. If grace was saved by God being made to provide the person who satisfied, then the whole became a preconcerted transaction, a sort of commercial drama, a legal fiction sanctioned by the offended for the good of the offender. Or if the notion of forgiveness was retained by the act being transferred from the satisfied Father to the satisfying Son, then the ethical unity of the Godhead was endangered and the most serious of all heresies endorsed. Yet defective as was the theory, it was the most rational word which had been spoken on the question, and introduced a method of speculation which has endured even to our own day.

3. The philosophical question was the famous one as to universals, or Nominalism and Realism. The question was raised by a passage in Boethius' translation of Porphyry's introduction to the logical writings of Aristotle, and concerned at once the nature of general terms and their relation to individual objects. Anselm, in a polemic against Roscellinus, denounced those heretical dialecticians "qui non nisi flatum vocis putant esse universales substantias,"[1] and his influence made Realism for long the dominant philosophy. There were three positions; *universalia* were either *ante rem*, *in re*, or *post rem*. The first was Platonic Realism, and had as its representative Duns Scotus; the second was Aristotelian, and was held by Aquinas; the third was Nominalism, and had as its great exponent William of Occam. The first and second as both realisms affirmed that universals were realities—the one that they were before things and creative of them, the other that they were in things, as it were the ordering and unifying spirit of the whole. Nominalism, on the other hand, made universals mere names, abstractions formed by thought for its own convenience. These terms, then, implied the questions fundamental to all thought, which according as they are conceived, stated, and answered, differ-

[1] "De Fid. Trin.," c. ii., Opera, p. 42.

entiate all schools of philosophy. Scholastic Realism is akin to our transcendental Idealism. It assumed the priority of thought, reasoned downwards from the universal to the particular, and explained all phenomena of sense by the action of the spirit or idea which alone was real and rational. Of its two forms the one was more speculative, the other more practical or experimental,—the speculative deducing what is from the *realia*, *i.e.*, the ideas; the experimental using the ideas to explain the realities. Duns Scotus, because the more purely speculative or *a priori*, was more of a rationalist than Aquinas; Aquinas, because more experimental, *i.e.*, standing more on his own experience and the Church's, was more of a supernaturalist, one who used his speculation to justify his experience. To Duns the rational was the real, but to Aquinas the real was the rational. Nominalism, on the other hand, is like our empiricism. It started from the priority of sense, reasoned from below upwards; held that mind in acquiring knowledge proceeded from particulars to universals, which, as simple generalizations from a multitude of individuals, were mere names.

The two schools acted in the region of theology in accordance with their respective principles Realism was more constructive and conservative, Nominalism more critical and disintegrative; and was always most so when its criticism was skilfully masked under deference to authority. The system that does not start with a constructive reason cannot rationally or logically translate religious beliefs into the terms of the reason. What it does not find within and has to construe as simply given from without, it can only regard as a thing more or less arbitrary because more or less external. On the ground of reason it cannot find the most transcendental of all ideas reasonable; and hence, if it accepts them, must accept them on the word of an authority which it has somehow been persuaded to regard as sufficient. This was the position of the later and more scientific Nominalism, especially of Occam. He was more conscious of the difficulties than the faculties of belief, and his ultimate reason for it was an appeal to an authority whose words could be more easily quoted than its right or reason justified. Hence Nominalism was a sign that Scholasticism, and with it mediæval Catholicism, had begun to decay; the hour had come when the materials it had so audaciously built into system could be assailed by a criticism which was most disintegrative when it seemed most conservative.

Scholasticism, then, in its essential character was a philosophy, determined by the philosophies which had been before it. The world it attempted to interpret was composed of the Church and such remains of the ancient order as it had been able to incorporate; the method it pursued was one it learned from Aristotle. The limitations that mark it belong to its world on the one hand, and its method on the other, but it is only when construed as a sort of belated ancient philosophy that it can be construed at all. This philosophy came to it as a logic or dialectic rather than a metaphysic, affecting the substance through the forms of thought, by teaching it the art of definition and distinction, of statement and argument. It was exactly the sort of philosophy the age needed to construe the material offered to it, the Church and its tradition receiving at its hands a sort of intellectual apotheosis. But just as the *ne plus ultra* of the constructive endeavour was reached by the schools of absolute and of modified Realism, or the Scotists and the Thomists, a subtle and sceptical Nominalism, fatal to the assumptions of both, came out of the North, showing thought critical where once it had been only constructive. And coincident with this appeared other causes which were to work even more efficiently for the birth of new than for the death of the old theologies.

CHAPTER VII.

THE RENAISSANCE AND THE REFORMATION.

§ I.—THE TIME AND THE MEN.

OF the causes external to Scholasticism which contributed to the decay of the mediæval system, the most potent, and for us by far the most significant, was the Renaissance. It was made possible by the then state of the Catholic Church, and actual by the recovery of the ancient literatures; the one may be described as the condition, the other as the cause of its being. It found the Mediæval Papacy in a state of decay, and it hastened the decay into a dissolution. If Christianity assimilated while it dissolved the Greco-Roman world, the resurgence of that world dissolved the Papacy, whose energies had been exhausted in the creation of modern Europe. By the middle of the fifteenth century it was manifest that the old system had in every point—thought, polity, religion—broken down. Just as the intellect had ceased to be constructive in theology, the Church had ceased to be creative in religion, or adequate to the realization of even its mediæval ideal. In politics the Papal system had lost its ancient imperialism, had forgotten the high ideals that governed it, and had degenerated into a cunning statecraft, meddling, selfish, vicious. The Popes had allowed themselves to be swept into the whirlpool of Italian intrigue, and, greedy of power, of patronage, and, still more, of money, fought, schemed, bribed, betrayed, broke or kept faith, on the purest Machiavellian principles, and for strictly consonant ends. The acutest political and most typical Italian mind of the century calls Italy *la corruttela ed il vituperio del mondo*, and so connects its moral debasement with the Church as to show that patriotism could hardly bear other fruit than the ecclesiastical revolt. But even more utter was the religious decadence. There is no need to invent scandal: the literature of the period is the most scandalous in history, that which concerns the Papacy the most scandalous of all. The vow of celibacy was not construed as a vow of chastity, and the obscurest offender could plead in apology the example of illustrious princes and heads of the Church. Impure Popes signified impure courts, cardinals and conclaves that made light of sin. The dreadful thing about Innocent VIII. or Alexander VI. was not his personal character, but his election by men who knew his personal character only too well. The whole system was moribund, and a decaying body politic is never a wholesome body, least of all in the head.

This century, then, of decaying mediævalism was the century of the Renaissance. Men who lived under a once proud and noble Church system, now fallen into impotence and unreality, found themselves face to face with an ancient literature, and, through it, with an older world. Comparison became not only possible, but necessary; through the medium of the older the newer world came to know and to criticize itself. The ancient literature was finer, the ancient world fresher, than anything the moderns knew. Man had changed since the literature had been lost to him; and the change made it at its rebirth the more vivid and him the more ready to learn its lesson. The old world knew no Church and had no sense of sin; the new world had been fashioned by the Church and was possessed with the sense of sin, though the Church had fallen into feebleness, and sin lived more in symbol than in sense or conscience. Each world had thus its naturalism, but with a difference: the nature of the old world was innocent, and so its naturalism was open and unashamed; the nature of the new world was sinful, and so its naturalism was furtive, guilty, debased. And this radical difference made minds conscious of many sharp, unreconciled, even irreconcilable antitheses. The recovered literature created a sense of style, and the elegant Latinity of Poliziano made scholastic Latin, and all that had been written therein, seem barbarous. With the sense for style the faculty of criticism awoke, and Lorenzo Valla was able to prove the donation of Constantine a forgery, the tradition as to the origin of the Apostolic symbol a fable, the language of the Vulgate faulty and inaccurate. The study of ancient philosophy proved more educative and ennobling than the study of mediæval theology. Aristotle, in the hands of Pomponazzi, took a subtler and broader meaning than he had had in the schools; the heroes and sages of antiquity were drawn into the circle of the saints—baptized, as it were, into current ecclesiastical ideas and usages; Socrates became a type of Christ, Plato the Attic Moses; before his bust, laurel-crowned, Marsilio Ficino kept a lamp burning, cultivating piety at the shrine of the man he taught to speak Latin. Pico della Mirandula, loving the old, yet loyal to the new, strove to reconcile the two, sought the aid of the Kabbala, and, by the help of cunning allegory, made doctrine and history and philosophy speak the language he wished. But an eclectic mysticism, though devout and sufficient for the individual, is never final or scientific, or sufficient for the time. The old recovered world could not thus be reconciled with the new world on which it had broken. There were falsities in both, and also veracities in both, and the veracity in each was to be fatal to the falsity in the other. The moribund body ecclesiastic was sensitive all over to the touch of the new historical spirit; nascent criticism showed that some of the Church's proudest claims were based in fraud;

the lofty spirit of Plato, now unsphered, rebuked its empty, dogmatic formulæ ; and a passionate patriot and preacher of righteousness at Florence stood forward sternly to denounce its sins against the liberties of man and the laws of God. The times were ripe, but the Italy that the Papacy had so helped to debase could not embody the new thought in victorious action. The spirit of Machiavelli guided the policies of Italy ; and out of the mean, ambitious, and selfish intrigues of princes, uprising and restoration, in any large sense, political or religious, can never come.

But along with the classical the ancient Christian literature and world were recovered, and became objects of historical study and knowledge. And in relation to these two worlds and literatures the characteristic differences between North and South were again repeated. The transalpine was exceedingly unlike the cisalpine Humanism. The Teutonic, as we may call it, was notable for its intense ethical seriousness, the religiousness, the Christian temper and aims of its representative men ; but the Italian for its unethical character, its spirit of revolt against religion, its recoil towards classical forms of philosophical belief, Epicurean, Peripatetic, Platonic, culminating in systems like the Pantheism of Bruno and the Atheism of Vanini. Primitive Christianity was, indeed, not so intelligible to Italian as to German men. For one thing, it came in a literature that offended classical taste, that had none of the grand style which the men of the Renaissance loved, and they feared that too much study of it might injure the elegance of their Latinity. And so it was a literature that the great Italian scholars did not care to edit, or great houses to publish. The famous presses of Italy sent forth editions of the Greek and Latin classics, but not one of the Greek New Testament ; intellectual centres like Florence affected the Platonic academy rather than the Christian school. For another thing, Italy could construe Christianity better as a political than as an intellectual system; the men who knew it only as New Rome did not care to know it as it had been before it was Roman; its roots in the Eternal City were more intelligible to them than its roots in the paternity of God and the sin of man. But in the transalpine countries it was altogether different; there classical antiquity had immeasurably less significance and ancient Christianity immeasurably more. The two Humanisms, then, may be distinguished thus: the Teutonic Humanism studied classical that it might the better know Christian antiquity, but the Italian studied the literature that it might the better imitate the life of the ancient classical peoples. Hence Italy had scholars and painters, but the Teutonic countries scholars and reformers. Reuchlin, though no official theologian, was a Humanist, that he might be a better divine. He studied language that he might be qualified to interpret religion. Colet, the most typical English Humanist, studied Greek that he might the better know and teach St. Paul. Erasmus, the purest embodiment of Teutonic Humanism, was editor of the first Greek New Testament published, paraphrased it, annotated it, and worked throughout his long and laborious life mainly on early Christian literature. The Teutonic mind made the literature more of a means, but the Italian made it more of an end,—where it was more of an end, the characteristic result was the new birth of art; where more of a means, the result, no less characteristic, was the new birth of religion.

§ II.—The Renaissance in Christian Literature: Erasmus.

The recovered knowledge of Christian antiquity could thus, as little as the recovered knowledge of classical, remain without result. Where men profoundly believed their religion, they could not discover anew its sources without being profoundly moved by the discovery. To come suddenly face to face with the personalities and ideas creative of the Christian faith as they lived in the marvellous literature of the period of creation, was like being translated into a new and strange world. For while the Christianity the Church had made was known, the Christianity that had made the Church was not. And so long as the Church, simply as Church, was known, man did not feel the need of getting behind and beneath it to its Maker, did not conceive the necessity or even the possibility of comparing it with His mind and purpose. But when they found themselves in possession of the original literature, and were able to deal with it as literature, yet as the sacred and authoritative source of the Church and her faith, comparison of the parent form and the living organism became inevitable ; and, of course, could not but involve judgment as to the degree in which the organism had departed from the primitive type.

The inevitable though altogether undesigned result of this return to the sources of the religion was therefore the rise of such questions as—How did the Church and Churchmen of to-day compare with Christ and His Apostles and Apostolic Christianity? Whether was the difference to the advantage or disadvantage of religion? Whether ought the established order to be accommodated to the primitive law, or the primitive law to be superseded and supplemented by the established order? We may see the answer of Humanism, more or less again undesigned, in Erasmus, who was, like Reuchlin, no Protestant, and, like him, lived and died a Catholic. It is no reflection on him to say that his primary interest was literature, his secondary religion. That is but to say that he was a Humanist, not a reformer. To the work of a reformer no man was ever by nature less destined, and no man was ever more obedient to the nature he had. He loved peace, culture, good society ; he was delicate, fastidious, sensitive, " so thin-skinned that a fly would draw blood," as was most truly said of him ; he hated the obtuse, the ignorant, the vulgar, the men who could not see or feel the sarcasm within its veil of compliment, or the irony hidden in a graceful allusion or ambiguous phrase. He feared revolution, with its sudden release of incalculable forces, the chaos, the collisions, the brutalities it was certain to evoke. The possible evils incident to radical change more alarmed his imagination than the evils actual in the existing order touched his conscience. He loved his esoteric world, desired nothing better than to be left in possession of it, free to criticize from its point of view the world exoteric, yet, with due regard to the benefits of studious peace, always preferring to insinuate rather than express an opinion, to pronounce a conditional rather than an absolute judgment,[1] But in spite of the nature that bound him to the old order, and so held him a Catholic, no man did more for reform, or formulated principles that more demanded it. His New Testament was here his greatest achievement. Some of the great presses had indeed first and chiefly busied themselves with editions of the Vulgate, which, as the Church's version of the Bible, stood under its sanction, raised no question of translation, of criticism, of relation to prior and creative sources, but was rather, as it were, its authorized and printed tradition. But with Erasmus' New Testament it was altogether different. Here stood the Book in its original speech, with attempts to fix certain dubious readings, with one most significant text omitted, with a new version alongside it said to be more elegant and accurate than the old: how did the sanctioned and authoritative version translate this original? and could the

---

[1] No man ever more frankly enthroned authority, or professed the spirit of submission. At the bidding of the Church he was ready to condemn his own critical conclusions (Opera ix., p. 864, B.), and he could, he said, have agreed with the Arians and Pelagians, if the Church had sanctioned their doctrine. See letter to Wilibald Pirkheimer, "Epistolæ," p. 1029 (Leyden ed.). We know what confessions of this kind would mean in the mouth of a cynic—no two things may be nearer allied than submission to authority and indifference to truth. He would be a brave man who would say what they mean in the mouth of Erasmus.

translations beside the original be authoritative any more? Here, too, was the Head and Founder of the Church, the Church He founded, the men through whom He did it, all presented in the lucid pages of authentic and contemporary history: did the Catholic truly represent the Apostolic Church, embody its spirit, interpret its doctrines, maintain its laws and institutions? What of Rome, and the Papacy, and the priesthood, and the whole sacerdotal organization was there in the Christianity of Christ and His Apostles?

These questions were inevitable, and the answers as clear and emphatic as they could be made by a man of Erasmus' temper and habits and tastes. Christ was the one Teacher appointed of God Himself; supreme authority belongs to Him alone.[1] He marvels that men should have made Christ's words to Peter bear exclusive reference to the Pope; they refer indeed to him, but to all Christians as well.[2] By Church he does not understand priests, bishops, or popes, who are merely its ministers, but the whole Christian people or collective community[3]—that is, "A certain congregation of all men throughout the whole world, who agree in the faith of the Gospel, who worship one God the Father, who place their whole confidence in his Son, who are led by the same Spirit of Him, from whose fellowship every one who commits deadly sin is cut off."[4] As to the Sacraments, were

[1] "Annotationes in Nov. Test.," *sub loc.*, Matt. xvii. 5.

[2] *Ibid.*, Matt. xvi. 18. It may be noted that Stunica laid special emphasis on Erasmus' attitude to the primacy of Peter and the Papal Chair. The charges were: (1) Erasmus has affirmed that it cannot be argued from Peter standing first in the Apostolic catalogue in Matthew that he was the first of the Apostles. (2) He denies that the words, "Thou art Peter," etc., etc., refer to Peter alone. (3) He maintains that the Pope's title in earliest times was "Pontifex Romanus," not "Summus Pontifex." (4) He holds the monarchy of the Pope to be later than Jerome; the authority now ascribed to the Roman See was unknown even to Augustine. —"Apologia ad L. Stunicam," opera ix., p. 381.

[3] "Epist.," 1029, A.; "Adagiorum Chiliades," p. 589 (Basel ed.).

[4] "Colloquia": "Inquisitio de Fide," 298 (Amsterdam ed.).

it not that the judgment of the Church was adverse, he would incline to the reformed doctrine; even as it is, he does not see any good in a body imperceptible to the senses, or any use in it, provided only spiritual grace be present in the symbols.[1] Besides, no one but the priest can know that the Host has been properly consecrated, and Erasmus can find no place in the sacred Scriptures which certainly proves that the Apostles consecrated bread and wine into the body and blood of the Lord.[2] The elements are but symbols that signify the indissoluble unity of Christ, the Head, and His mystical body, the Church. Indeed, the sacerdotal tendencies and practices of the time, with their inexorable and demoralizing fetishism, had no more unsparing critic than Erasmus, and his criticism proceeded from principles that were fatal to all the penances, claims, and ordinances of Catholicism. Relic-worship invariably provoked his severest and most pungent satire, and even moved him to gravest censure as a new and meaner Pharisaism, which became, even more than the old, the hideous caricature of godliness.[3] To escape from it men must return to the Gospel. The rule is, men go to Rome to come back worse; what best ensures amendment of life is the Word of Truth.[4] Neglect of the Gospel has caused a double evil to come upon the Church, more than heathenism of life and a ceremonial Judaism in worship. In the ceremonies the whole Papal system was for the mind and conscience of the day summarized; it was here that it most directly touched life, subverted morals, debased worship, estranged man from God.

[1] "Epist.," 941, A.
[2] *Ibid.*, 1193, D. E. Of course this represents the view of the familiar epistles—Erasmus' private, confidential opinion, what would have been most agreeable to his reason. His public view, accepted because of the judgment of the Church, may be found in the letters to Conrad Pelican *ibid.*, 963-966, and his "Detectio Præstigiarum Cujusdam Libelli," occasioned by an anonymous German work on this subject.
[3] "Annotationes in Nov. Test.," *sub loc.*, Matt. xxiii. 5.
[4] "Colloquia": "Adolescens et Scortum," p. 251.

So Erasmus assailed the ceremonies from every point of view. They were unscriptural: in the whole New Testament there is no command which refers to ceremonies; against them are warnings enough by Christ, arguments enough by Paul, but nowhere from any one any word of commendation.[1] They were irreligious too; where they flourished, piety, morality, common decency even, decayed. And the reason was not far to seek. Positive laws, made by bishops or councils, popes or orders, could not supersede or set aside the laws of nature or of God. These had the prior and higher authority, but they were ever being invalidated or repealed by the ceremonies. If a priest lets his hair grow or wears a lay habit he is punished, but if he debauches himself and others "he is still a pillar of the Church." Men who would die rather than eat flesh when forbidden, yet did not scruple to live lasciviously. In language of appalling plainness he described the obfuscation of conscience by the ceremonies; they abrogated the law of God, caused disrespect and disobedience to the most rudimentary, yet imperative, moral laws, blinded and blunted the moral sense, created an artificial and utterly unveracious conscience in persons, orders, and even whole communities.[2] No man had ever less of the Puritan temper than Erasmus; but no man so helps us to understand the need for the Puritan spirit and character. Sacerdotal ceremonialism had done in Christianity what it has done in every religion it has ever got control of—what, Erasmus again and again argued, it had done with most tragic results in Judaism: ended the reign of the moral ideal, subordinated the Divine categorical imperative to some trivial positive ordinance, to the ritual or routine of the caste or the cloister or the school. Humanism, in the light of the literature it loved, saw the evil, and in its elegant,

[1] "Ratio Veræ Theolog.," p. 94; "Enchiridion," pp. 60 ff.
[2] "Colloquia: Ἰχθυοφαγία." This colloquy presents a full and most vivid view of Erasmus' position.

incisive, satirical, yet humorous way criticized what it saw; but criticism, while it may entertain and even amend life, neither can nor will do what was then most in need of being done—reform religion.

§ III.—THE REFORMATION: LUTHER.

But the new reading of history involved a new effort not only at the interpretation, but also at the realization of the religion. Hence out of Humanism Protestantism soon came. Both were creations of the historical spirit—the one in the sphere of literature, the other in the realm of religion. The recovered literature of classical and Christian antiquity alike acted on the imagination, but with a characteristic difference: in the one case, the imagination was reached through the reason, in the other the reason was reached through the imagination and conscience. The result in the former case was culture, the exercise and enjoyment of balanced and regulated faculty; the result in the latter case was religion, the genesis of new beliefs as to God and man, and the impulse to embody them in action—*i.e.*, in the creation of a new world correspondent to the new faith. The historical spirit in the sphere of literature is objective, handles its material as facts or phenomena that have to be understood and criticized, construed and explained; but the historical spirit in the realm of religion is subjective, handles its material as transcendental and eternal realities related to an immortal subject, as symbols or revelations of the cause and end of being, and of the law by which life ought to be ordered. Now, the access to the original sources meant to the quickened conscience and imagination a sudden coming face to face with the Christ, who was at once the maker of the Christian religion and the Saviour of the soul. The more earnest the man who stood there, the more inevitable would be the question—Is the Church's way Christ's? Does it truly represent Him and realize His religion? This was Luther's question, but not his only—it was the question of the time; yet to understand the form in which it was raised we must understand him. He was no Humanist, in the strict sense, though Humanism had contributed to his making. Some of its brightest sons were amongst his oldest and truest friends; but he himself had none of the fastidiousness, the dubious temper, the love of elegance, the refining, though not necessarily refined, spirit, which makes the study of literature a culture and an end in itself. He was a stalwart man, sensuous, passionate, imaginative, tender, easily moved to laughter or to tears, capable of the strongest love or hate possessed of the simpler emotions, a stranger to the more complex, indifferent to the abstract, open to the concrete. Good had for him no being without God, and evil none without the devil. He was never meant by nature for an intellectual innovator; his changes were never due to any speculative process or logical concatenation of thought, though in decisive moments he was often guided by a supreme, yet courageous, common sense. Like all men of strong and simple emotions, his instincts were all conservative; he hated change, changed only under the compulsion of an over-mastering feeling or need, and with a sort of convulsion of nature, conservative changes taking always more or less the form of a catastrophe. Hence the large dramatic element· in Luther's life; he resisted change till resistance became impossible, and then he changed with a noise that startled Europe. So was it with the publication of his Theses, his burning of the Pope's Bull, his appearance at Worms, and his marriage. Hence, too, the inconsistencies of Lutheranism; it has no logical coherence, is explicable when studied through Luther's history and experience, but inexplicable if regarded as a reasoned and articulated system. In dealing with justification by faith his mode of handling Scripture was the freest; in dealing with the Supper his method was a slavish literalism. And the case is typical: in him lay two opposite worlds; he was a revolutionary without being a radical, or, as it were, a Protestant under protest, which means that the work he did grew out of the conflict between character and position, but was not the spontaneous outcome of an innovating and reconstructive mind.

Now, this was precisely the sort of man needed to change the literary or Humanistic into a religious and reforming movement. It could not have been done by a designing man, or a cloistered student, or a malcontent, or a doctrinaire radical; it could only have been done by a man compact of passion and imagination,—of a passion that, when roused, could move with irresistible force, blind to the obstructions in its path; of an imagination that, when quickened, could see further than the colder reason, and also compel others to see. We are to imagine a man so constituted possessed of what is perhaps the most awful and imperious creation of Christianity, the sense of sin; and with this sense in kind and quality and degree as it had been in Paul and in Augustine, and as it was to be later in Bunyan. Such a sense is at root a passion for the possession of Deity by a man who feels Deity too awful in His goodness to be possessed by him. It does not argue a bad man, but it argues a man who knows the impossibility of being worthy of God, yet feels the necessity to him of the God who seems so unapproachable, so inaccessible. To such a man, reconciliation, to be real, must be of God and to God, a work of infinite grace; and religion to be true must be the way or method of such reconciliation. The Christian doctrine of sin would be intolerable were it not transfigured by the Christian doctrine of grace; indeed, it is the splendour of the one that makes the shadow lie so dark upon the other. Sin without grace is the creed of cynicism or despair; it is only through grace that it becomes an integral part of Christianity.

Such a man was Luther, and to him the New Testament

comes, not as the voice of the Church, but as God's voice. The first Christian age rises before him, wakes into life, stands out in vivid contrast to his own. Here are no indulgences, penances, pilgrimages; all is simple, of grace, through faith, without works. He feels affinity with Paul; new Catholicism is but old Judaism, with its fathers, traditions, law, ceremonial, righteousness after the flesh; and the new must be combated by the weapons that had vanquished the old. He stands in the immediate presence of Christ, and learns that His conflict with the Pharisees has the same reason and meaning as Paul's with Judaism. In the light of the New Testament duty becomes clear: there must be a return to Apostolical Christianity. For Luther this return was summed up in the idea of Redemption by the free grace of God in Christ, justification by faith, without any work or contributory merit on the part of man; and by this idea he measured the Church. What he saw before him was an immense system of salvation by works, the works mere ceremonial, not ethical, with a merit that came of obedience to positive or ecclesiastical, not to absolute or Divine law. But such merit as purely external is a transferable, even purchasable thing; while he conceived that what ought to be was a salvation altogether of God, which allowed no place and no value to the ceremonial performances of man or the profitable but unethical enactments of a body ecclesiastical. The question was not to him as to the modern scholar, How did the ecclesiastical system come to be? That question implies a standpoint much more scientific than his; one that can do justice to the Catholic Church even while indifferent to its claims. But if his method was less scientific, it was more efficacious than the modern; for while the modern seeks to explain, it does not care to overturn or supersede; but Luther could only seek to overturn, while he did not care to explain. For to him it was impossible that both the New Testament and Rome could be right; whatever was wrong, it could not be the New Testament; there stood the mind of Christ and the interpretation of His Apostles; and to accept the one and attempt to realize the other was the absolute duty of the Christian man.

To men, then, who believed that for Christianity the mind of Christ was the creative and normative mind, the appeal to the sources was irresistible; and the ranks of the Humanists soon confessed that it was so. The older men, Reuchlin and Erasmus, stood aloof, but the younger men were carried away. Crotus Rubianus, Luther's "Crotus noster suavissimus," the most brilliant of the putative authors of the "*Epistolæ Obscurorum Virorum*," though he was later to repent and return; Eobanus Hess, "regius poeta et poeticus rex"; Philip Melanchthon, scholar and divine, hope and pride of his famous grand-uncle, designated heir of his splendid library; Justus Jonas, most eloquent of the Humanists and Reformers, Melanchthon's typical "orator," "der Mann der kann die Worte des Textes herrlich und deutlich aussprechen, erklären, und zum Markt richten"; Ulrich von Hutten, knight, patriot, man of letters, devoted to a liberty near akin to licence; Œkolampadius, erudite enough to be consulted and esteemed by the great Erasmus; Camerarius, perhaps best Grecian of his age, one of the true fathers of modern scholarship, the *fidus Achates* of Melanchthon; and above all, though he acted from his own initiative, not Luther's, the most heroic of the early Reformers, Ulrich Zwingli,—these, and many others, driven by the inexorable logic of the situation, became leaders in the small but resolute army of men who were trying to return to the Christianity of Christ. If Protestantism was not created by learning, yet without learning it could not have been; and there was nothing more natural or noble or necessary than that the men who had discovered the use and meaning of the primitive Christian literature should endeavour to recover and to return to the religion it revealed.

The recovery of the ancient literature had thus resulted in an attempt to realize the ancient and original idea. But though the attempt was inevitable, the achievement was not possible. Facts cannot be annihilated or centuries eliminated from the life of man ; the past will control the present, the present reverence the past, whatever logic may say. There is nothing so impossible as the restoration of a lost state ; the attempt is made by men under conditions and by means of material all so different from the original that, while it may imitate the old, it can never be the old it imitates. And here every sort of obstacle stood in the way: Lutheranism was full of inconsistencies, spared much which ought to have perished, over-emphasized its great idea, bound itself hastily to definitions and formulæ which produced new divisions and a scholasticism more bitter, controversial, and unfruitful than the old. It affirmed man's immediate relation and sole responsibility to God ; yet it organized, by the help of German princes, a most Erastian Church. Then the new movement became a sort of Cave of Adullam ; men resorted to it whose only reason was discontent with the existing order of things. It is granted to no revolution to be accomplished by perfect men, but the religious revolution most needs good men, and it is hardly judged, often fatally hindered, when men figure in it who are not good : its own misfortunes injure it more than do the mistakes or crimes of the enemy. Then the most reasonable revolution awakens unreason, the dissolution of an old order begets the wish for a dissolution of all order and the reign of chaos. So after Luther came Carlstadt, after Carlstadt came Münzer, after Münzer the Peasants' War ; and of course for these the new return to the old faith was held responsible. Kings, with faith in their own Divine rights, grew grave ; where the old ecclesiastic only troubled the new reformer threatened to overturn—he therefore deserved no mercy. Timid men, too, who always see double when singleness of eye is most needed, argued: "The old order was bad, still it was order; we must stand by it against these new ideas, which will subvert all things." The moment of dismay was the opportunity of reaction. Rome drew herself together and confronted her disorganized foe. In a system like hers there were and are recuperative energies of incalculable potency, and these, when summoned to act, acted. The enthusiasm of her noblest sons rose in the presence of danger; the meaning of her idea and mission dawned once more upon her. She contrasted her unbroken uniformity with the formless movement that had risen against her, her venerable doctrines with the mad imaginations of the German Anabaptists, and asked: "Have not I ruled the world these fifteen hundred years both beneficently and wisely? But if this Protestantism, which has produced these lawless and levelling sects, be allowed to exist and conquer, what will become of our rights, properties, civilization?" The question seemed so unanswerable that kings and nobles, thinking there was no choice between anarchy and Rome, marshalled armies and fought battles to end what to them was less a pestilent heresy than a disorganizing and destructive political movement.

§ IV.—CALVIN AND GENEVA.

But in Luther and Lutheranism we have only one form of the attempt to return to the religion of the sources; in Calvin and Calvinism we have another. These two are very different. The moving impulse was in Luther the sense of sin, but in Calvin the love of truth alike as ideal and as reality. Luther finds in the sources a way of escape from sin, Calvin an ideal which men are bound to realize. Luther's passion was to believe and teach a true soteriology, Calvin's was to build a system and a state in the image of the truth of God. In him the movement has its supreme constructive genius. He is one of the best-hated men in history; round his name fierce controversies have raged, and still rage; and controversies begotten of disputatious hate and unreasoning love are things the judicious, who love to pass for judicial men, do not care to touch. There is something imposing in the multitude and variety of aversions that converge on Calvin. He was hated by the Catholics as the author of the system that opposed the proudest and most invincible front to Rome; by princes and statesmen, as the man who instituted a Church that acted as a revolutionary force in politics; by Anglican bishops and divines, as the father of the Puritanism that so long disturbed their power; by Arminian theologians as the inventor and apologist of a *decretum horribile*, which they detested, without always making sure that they understood; by Free Thinkers, as the man that burned Servetus, who, because he was burned, must have been a saint, and Calvin, because he burned him, a shameless sinner; by Secular Republicans, because he founded a religious State, and dealt hardly with sins they were inclined to; by the sons of Light and Culture, for the imperious ethical temper that did not leave room for the free play of elements needed to constitute their whole of life. But the man who has touched so many men, discordant in everything but this concordance of hate, must have been a man of transcendent power, whose character and work deserve close and impartial study from all men who would understand the sixteenth and the later centuries.

Calvin was in almost every respect a contrast to Luther,— less sensuous and more intellectual; intenser, but not so impassioned; less obstinate and self-willed, but more imperious and inflexible; not so amiable, but of a far loftier and more ethical spirit; possessed of a severer conscience and more scrupulous will, but of a nature less roomy and human-hearted. Luther was ever boisterous, a man of open sense, of buoyant and irrepressible speech, whose words were half battles, whose eye was quick to see, whose heart was quick to feel, whose judgment was always in danger of being mastered by passion or blinded by pity. Calvin, on the other hand, was a man of invincible calm, of balanced speech, gentle towards weakness, severe towards vice, severest of all towards himself, for he had, as Beza tells us in his quaint French: "Une telle intégrité de conscience, qu'en fuyant toutes vaines subtilitez sophistiques avec toute ambitieuse ostentation, il n'a jamais cerché que la simple et pure vérité."[1] Calvin could never have been guilty of the mistakes of Luther, especially such a disastrous blending of the blunder and the crime as was made in the matter of the Landgrave Philip; but Luther could as little have been guilty of the severities of Calvin. Luther was incapable of conceiving, to say nothing of approving or enforcing, Calvin's legislation: his pity for human weakness would have proved stronger than his love of an ideal that showed it no mercy; but Calvin was still more incapable of allowing, with Luther, the Church to be a creature of the State. To him it was impossible that the society which existed for the realization of the Divine law should stand under a society whose laws were made and enforced by men for strictly temporal or civil ends. The singular simplicity of his nature made him love symmetry and system in all things, consistency in character, the veracity that made conviction, speech, and conduct all agree. It is characteristic that his fundamental thought is not, as with Luther, justification by faith or the mode in which the guilty man may be made right with God, but it is grace, or the absoluteness and sufficiency of the will of God, as the gracious will which purposes and achieves salvation. Calvinism is Stoicism baptized into Christianity, but renewed and exalted by the baptism. It has the fortitude of Stoicism, the quality that enables men to bend without being broken, to submit without being

[1] Dedication to the Duchess of Ferrara of the "Petits Traictez de M. Jean Calvin," Opera, vol. v., p. xv (Corpus Ref.).

conquered; it has its indifference to suffering, its scorn of the sentiment that simply pities evil and loses love of existence in horror at pain; it has its optimism, believes with it in the efficiency yet benevolence of the universal Will, in moral law as absolute, in obedience as a thing which lies "non extra omnem modo controversiam, sed deliberationem quoque." But it far transcends Stoicism, for its Will is personal while infinite, gracious while absolute, so real and efficient in its working as to have made sure of all its means and all its ends. Man is placed in time to know and to obey this Will, it is revealed in nature, conscience, grace; and these are so related that knowledge of God and of ourselves are not two knowledges, but one and the same. To be obedient is but to follow nature in its ideal sense and fulfil the law of God. In its speculative elements Calvin's theology is one with Augustine's, but not in its political or ecclesiastical. In Augustine, as we have seen,[1] the speculative and the political are contradictory; the speculative was an unconditional, but the political a conditional system; the high necessities belonging to his theistic thought were qualified, and indeed negatived, by his regulative sacerdotalism, his *Civitas Roma* metamorphosed into a hieratic *Ecclesia Christi*. But in Calvin the speculative and the political are so related that the one is a deduction from the other; his theology is the basis of his polity, his polity is the application of his theology to society and the State. His Church was an attempt to organize society through his theistic idea, to build it into a sort of articulated will of God. The defects of his theistic idea were expressed in his political ideal, exhibited in their harshest form in his legislation and the endeavour to enforce it. But the defects were not those of weakness or earthliness; they were those of a too lofty severity, a too unyielding moral rigor, due to the belief that God's will was gracious in order that man might be righteous,

[1] *Supra*, pp. 115, 116.

and man's duty was so to live as to cause this will to be realized in himself and by all men. These defects may have showed ignorance of human weakness, and its strength; it has yet to be proved that they showed anything ignoble, either in the mind that made the system, or in the system the mind made.

In order to understand the mind and purpose of Calvin he ought to be studied in the first edition of his "Institutio," printed 1535, published 1536. It was written when he was but twenty-six, an exile from France, who had tried many places, but found a home in none, yet who had, in the face of all his danger and unrest, worked out the main lines of his system. But only the main lines: the first edition is a mere sketch, yet a sketch which lives, with this characteristic—that the emphasis lies less on dogma than on morals, worship, polity. What mainly concerns him is the new order, what it ought to be, how it best may be. It is the work of a man penetrated with the conviction that the new Gospel is a new law, that the law must be embodied in a new life, individual and collective. The justified man is elect unto obedience; the good man cannot be contented with bad moral conditions; the perfect person needs a perfect society; and so he must labour to bring about the conformity of all things, but most of all the lives of men and states to the will of God. The motive of the book stands expressed in the famous prefatory letter addressed to Francis I.; it was meant to be a sort of rudiments by which men touched by a zeal for religion might be formed *ad veram pietatem*. But behind this stands another motive: it is an apology for the Reformed Faith, which is dying of odium, charged with being the enemy of order, law, peace, and all things that civilized men hold dear. He demands that the King hear him; an unheard cause cannot be condemned, and the cause is not his; it is that of all the godly—nay, of Christ Himself. The graver the cause the greater the duty of the sovereign, who is bound "agnoscere se in regni administratione Dei ministrum." But he must judge by a fit standard, by the *Verbum Dei*, interpreted according to the analogy of faith. So tried the cause is sure of victory. "Quid enim," he asks, "melius atque aptius fidei convenit, quam agnoscere nos omni virtute nudos ut a Deo vestiamur, omni bono vacuos ut ab ipso impleamur, nos peccati servos ut ab ipso liberemur, nos cæcos ut ab ipso illuminemur, nos claudes ut ab ipso dirigamur, nos debiles ut ab ipso sustentemur, nobis omnem gloriandi materiam detrahere, ut solus ipse glorificetur et nos in ipso gloriemur?"[1]

He follows up his claim for a hearing by a frank discussion of the charges against the Reformed Faith. These are: The doctrine is new, doubtful, and uncertain; ought to be confirmed by miracles; is against the consent of the Fathers and the most ancient custom; is schismatical; and, finally, may be known by its fruits—the sects, seditions, licence, it has produced. These charges he answers thus: The doctrine is as old as Christ and His Apostles, as sure as their word, is confirmed by their miracles, is supported by the Fathers, maintains the unity of the true Church, which may exist without apparent form, and needs no external splendour; but is only "pura Verbi Dei prædicatione et legitima Sacramentorum administratione."[2] Nor will he allow that sedition or licence marks the new faith: the men are godly; loss and suffering, imprisonment and persecution, have been their only reward. And here in his book it may be seen what they believe and mean: they stand by those great realities, the moral law, which tolerates worship of none but God, and forbids all sin against Him and against man; the Apostolic faith, which stands lucid, simple, sufficient in the Apostolic symbol; prayer, which has its perfect type in the *Pater Noster*; the Sacraments which Christ instituted, and the Church which He founded to secure Christian liberty, both

---

[1] "Inst.," "Epis. Nuncup.," pp. 12, 13.
[2] *Ibid.*, p. 21.

to man and society. Here, at least, is no Lutheran individualism, no emotional conservatism, broken into, but not broken up, by the forces of a moral revolution; but here is a constructive work, coextensive with the whole man and the State. Calvin was as radical as Luther was conservative, but, while radical, he was also constructive, just as Luther had the true conservative instinct to retain, but its no less real impotence either to design or to build.

Calvinism was thus, in a sense quite unknown to Lutheranism, the conscious and consistent antithesis to Rome. For one thing, a rigorous and authoritative system was met by a system no less rigorous and authoritative. The Roman infallibility was confronted by the infallibility of the *Verbum Dei*; the authority of tradition by the authority of reasoned yet Scriptural doctrine; salvation through the Church by salvation through Christ; the efficacy of the Sacraments by the efficacy of the Spirit; the power of the priesthood by the power of the ever-present Christ. The strength of Calvinism lay in the place and pre-eminence it gave to God: it magnified Him; humbled man before His awful majesty, yet lifted man in the very degree that it humbled him. Catholicism is essentially a doctrine of the Church; Calvinism is essentially a doctrine of God. In days when men have little faith in the supernatural and transcendental, Catholicism is an enormous power; its appeal to history is an appeal to experience, and men will cling to its traditions in the very degree that they have lost faith in God; but in days when men are possessed by faith in an all-sufficient Reason that knows all and never can be deceived, in an all-sufficient Will that guides all and never can be defeated or surprised, then the theology that holds them will be the theology that makes God most real to the intellect and most authoritative to the conscience. And it was at this point and by this means that Calvinism so seized and so commanded men, faith in God being ever a less earthly and a sublimer thing than faith in a Church. Then, for a second thing, Geneva served in an equal degree the cause of freedom and of order. Calvinism was the very genius of system in theology and of order in polity. These two stood together; the one was a logical corollary from the other, yet appeared also as a copy of the ancient Scriptural model. But while order was as necessary to Geneva as to Rome, it was for reasons so different that the order did not remain the same. The order Rome maintained was autocratic, personalized in the Pope, incorporated in the Church, realized by its authority; the order Geneva created was democratic, personalized in God, incorporated in the Apostolic Society, realized by the authority of conscience. Roman order was external, imposed from without; Genevan order internal, evoked from within. Hence while Rome could, in alliance with an absolute monarch, realize its order, the Genevan could be realized only by and through the people. It might be tyrannical in exercise; it must be popular in basis, and the basis was determinative; in it lay all the possibilities of freedom and progress. With it a regal supremacy in things spiritual and ecclesiastical was as incompatible as a papal; and where it prevailed, rule based on a single will became impossible. It thus allied itself with the rights of the people and the spirit of political progress, the countries which were most penetrated by it being precisely the countries which have become the most conspicuous examples of ordered freedom. For a third thing, Geneva became the Protestant city of refuge; hither came Spanish, Italian, French, German, Netherlandish, English, and Scotch refugees and exiles. Each saw the order that reigned in the city, felt Calvin's powerful influence, acknowledged his superlative genius, beheld his splendid success. And so each came to admire and love the Genevan Church model as the most perfect realizable on earth, and went home determined to labour even unto death for its introduction and establishment. Then Calvin acquired and exercised a patriarchal authority. He corresponded with all the Churches; advised, instructed on all questions of internal organization, doctrine, and discipline ; on the relation to the State, whether friendly or adverse ; on the relation to other Churches, whether Protestant or Popish ; indeed, on all subjects which then arose of general or local importance. And, besides, Geneva was a sort of college, where young men were trained for the ministry, and whence they were despatched to their own countries to teach the new faith. And of the men trained there Michelet truly says: "If in any part of Europe blood and tortures were required, a man to be burnt or broken on the wheel, that man was at Geneva, ready to depart, giving thanks to God, and singing psalms to Him." Can we wonder that the faith propagated by men who feared no human face should have spread so far, and become so prolific a nurse of heroes?

CHAPTER VIII.

THE MODERN CHURCHES AND THEIR THEOLOGIES.

WE have said that the attempt to return to the religion of the sources was an impossible attempt; but this statement requires a double qualification. First, the Church, so long as it believes in the divinity of its Founder, is bound to have a history which shall consist of successive and progressively successful attempts to return to Him. He can never be transcended; all it can ever be is contained in Him; but its ability to interpret Him and realize His religion ought to be a developing ability. It was as a little bit of leaven that the Christian faith entered the consciousness of pagan man, and only by the slow process of expansion and penetration can it expel the pagan and create the Christian. And each attempt to return is at once a condition and a measure of this growth, springing from a new sense of the necessity and supremacy of Christ, and exhibiting the degree in which it has become possible truly to apprehend Him. Secondly, the causes that in this case made the return impossible did not prevent the attempt becoming a revolution that was almost equal to a return. For one thing, it made other and later attempts both possible and necessary, with more promise of success for the later. For another thing, it showed that as the cause of the attempt was the new knowledge of the sources, so the cause of the failure was the persistence of the old consciousness. In other words, the theology remained for all specifically Western, under forms more or less Augustinian, though no longer co-ordinated as in Augustine. It was this change in the co-ordination that was the significant thing. It is the essence of all revolutions that nothing continues as it was before; certain institutions may survive, but they are not the old institutions; for they are made different by the different world they live in, and where a common change has come there all the old things have passed away and all things have become new.

§ I.—RELATION OF CHURCH TO THEOLOGY.

What we have now to study, then, is how the changed conditions and the new and different factors affected the development of theology. With the modern Churches, their formation, constituents, constitution, history, we have no concern, save in so far as they are related to our question. This relation varies according as the determinative idea belongs to the Church or to the Theology. We may describe this idea as, in the former case, political or institutional, in the latter, intellectual and ethical. If the primary and material conception is the Church, then the Theology is read through it, and as authenticated and determined by it; but if this conception be the Theology, then the Church is construed through it, and judged, either justified or condemned, by the truth it professes to hold and to be bound to incorporate. In the one case the society is conceived as possessed of a given constitution, say monarchical or oligarchical, which is necessary, not only to its *bene esse*, but to its very *esse*; in the other case certain beliefs are conceived as means used of God to change and command men and organize a new spiritual society. Where the political idea comes first, the Theology has more or less a legal character, appears as consuetudinary or as constitutional law,—as the one it is thought or opinion received or allowed; as the other it is opinion fixed, formulated, legalized, become dogma. In dealing with it men have all the latitude and all the limitations so familiar to the interpreters of written and unwritten laws,—some reading the great ecumenical creeds literally, others liberally, as mere delimitations, marking off the forbidden, some taking them in the sense of the great constitutional lawyers—*i.e.*, the Fathers and Schoolmen; others carrying into them, with more or less regard to the ancient forms, the sense of their own day. But in every case the idea of the relation is the same; the Church is the prior; Theology has no being apart from it; is defined, articulated, authenticated by it; and the function of the theologian is simply to interpret in terms intelligible to living men what has been so constituted. He, too, has thus no being apart from the Church; he must be of it to have Theology, or to know and be under the laws which govern its interpretation. And so it becomes a thing institutional, legal, dogmatic, moving within the region of positive law. On the other hand, where the theological idea comes first, the Theology appears as a body of beliefs or regulative ideas, creative and life-giving truths which the Church must receive that it may live, study and explain that it may live more abundantly. In other words, these truths are at once creative and normative, not so much the possession as the possessors of the Church, the medium in and through which it has its being. It receives them, not once for all, but ever anew, from the hand of its Creator, and as He is personal they become the means of cultivating personal relations. And so there emerges a further distinction; the institutional can never be historical, save in so far as history is identical with the being of the institution, but the theological must be historical, for apart from its source, and its true apprehension and assimilation of the same, it has no right to be. Where the political idea reigns, the action of God outside the political area is conceived as irregular, illicit, or uncovenanted; where the theological idea reigns, the Church must be as it were His visible image,—He too large to be confined within the institutions of men, they too hard and narrow to be equal to His penetrative and expansive grace.

Now, the Churches that emerged at the Reformation may be divided into three classes,—the strictly institutional, or Roman Catholic; the strictly theological, or Lutheran and Reformed; and the mixed, where both characters exist as distinct and conflicting schools, or the Anglican.

These Churches are all at once ancient and modern; each represents in a different aspect at once the continuity of history and the changes effected by the religious revolution. These changes were equally radical in all the Churches, though in each differently formulated, the elements, old and new, being by each specifically combined and organized. In Catholicism we have the continuity of Western institutions, Roman, political, and ecclesiastical; in the Reformed communities we have the continuity of Western religious thought; while in all we have the only real form of Apostolic succession, the continuity of holy persons, convinced and reverent Christian men. Rome accepted and developed the polity of Augustine, but qualified his theology into what he would have considered its negation. Luther and Calvin both rejected his polity; but the one made his theories of human nature and grace the bases of a doctrine of justification by faith, the other his theory of the Divine sovereignty and will the regulative idea of a more consistent and absolute system. In the Anglican Church the Catholic or institutional school has least represented the continuity of thought, and the theological and evangelical has least emphasized the historical institution. They but exhibit on a diminished scale and in a more modified form the characteristics and conflicts of the larger Churches with their larger controversies. Each of these Churches, then, has its special material and determinative conception of the Christian religion; in Catholicism it is the Papal Church, in Lutheranism justification by faith, in

Calvinism the sovereignty of God, in Anglicanism now, to the Catholic, the episcopate in the Church, now, to the Evangelical, the doctrine of grace or salvation or the second birth. The development of Theology in these Churches has been governed by this material conception conditioned by the external factors or the events of history.

§ II.—CATHOLICISM AND THEOLOGY.

Within Catholicism the place and history of theology have been determined by its essentially political or institutional character. Catholic Theology is only a branch of Catholic politics; it does not transcend the sphere of jurisprudence, or the scientific interpretation of law, positive or consuetudinary. The theologian can never get behind the institution; it surrounds him, fills him, teaches, guides, superintends him, allows him as a theologian no independent being of his own or apart from it. For him to attempt to return to the sources would be to contradict his material conception. If he would go, he must be taken by his Church, to find what it has found, to think what it has determined. But since the Church is primarily the source and basis of the Theology, the Theology must be explicative of the Church, a science of its being, adapted to its character, suited to its condition and needs. Here, then, is involved a twofold formal factor, one springing from the character of the institution, the other from its circumstances. What these were and how they affected Catholic Theology we must now seek to understand.

Modern Catholicism dates from the Council of Trent, as Lutheranism from the Confession of Augsburg, and Calvinism from the appearance of the "Institutes" and the Genevan Catechism. The earlier creeds affected the later; the Roman is the polemical antithesis of the Protestant; but though it professed only to formulate, yet, by the very nature of the case, it changed by formulating. A custom ceases to be old and kindly and fluid when fixed in a hard-and-fast decree. Besides, it is with a Church as with a country which has lived for many centuries without a written constitution, but is suddenly, by a revolution and in face of it, forced for defensive and offensive purposes alike, to frame a constitution. What is so extorted will not be a pure, unmixed transcript of the ancient customs and beliefs, for the State will be unable to forget the revolution, or do other than adapt its old laws to its new needs. And so the decrees and canons of Trent mark the transition of Rome from the freedom of an unwritten to the bondage of a written constitution. Conflicting views and interests, indeed, helped by trained diplomacy, made carefully framed and skilfully qualified formulæ mitigate the evil, but it was too real an evil to be capable of complete mitigation. In definitions all things are not possible even to the choicest ambiguity. The institution, with all its anomalies, is maintained; the emphasis everywhere falls on it, determining the place, relation, and form of every doctrine; but still the maintenance is qualified by being in the face of the enemy. The claim of the Church to be authoritative and continuous is never forgotten, but neither is the necessity of opposition to the Reformed communities. But the polemics were not always compatible with the continuity, and so the Theology leans to the semi-Pelagian, as the Reformed to the Augustinian. The action and grace of God are limited and conditioned by the institution, or the need of finding a place and a function for the Sacraments. Men, too, must have some ability as well as reason for obedience to the Church, and so room has to be found for works and a freedom of will which the theological soul of Augustine would have loathed. The value of direct and decided antagonism was well understood at Trent, though qualified by the division of mind and school in the council; but later it was made efficient by the policy of the Jesuits. In their hands theology became at times even Pelagian, that it might the better contradict the high Augustinianism of Calvin; and their hostility to Jansenism was due not only to its affinities with the Reformed faith, but to their keen insight into its fundamental incompatibility with the autocratic and sacerdotal institution which they called the Church.

Then necessities at once political and polemical compelled the council to formulate a doctrine of the Scriptures and define their relation to the Church; and though these necessities seemed coincident, they were in reality diverse. If only Catholicism could have lived under an unwritten constitution, it might have been capable of indefinite adaptation to its many and most dissimilar environments; but to this the written law set a limit, especially in the doctrine as to the Scriptures. Tradition and Scripture were made the joint sources of revelation; but the canon and the version that had been in use in the Roman Church were sanctioned, and the office of interpreter was reserved for the Church. These were all antitheses to the Protestant theses. By the first the Church and the Scriptures were so bound together that neither could be had alone, or live or be believed alone; by the second the Apocrypha was made as canonical as the Hebrew books of the Old Testament or the Apostolic books of the New; by the third a most manifestly incorrect version and corrupt text was made authoritative; and by the fourth the Church was made master of the whole situation by being alone possessed of the power to read what was written. Trent here attempted what no Church or council had dared to attempt, and the Fathers, by following their keen political and polemical instincts, lost their great opportunity. They made the attitude of Rome to the Bible as abjectly traditional as that of Protestantism was strenuously historical; criticism of the Scriptures as canonized and sanctioned at Trent is as fatal to Catholicism as the critical use of them is necessary to the continued being of the Reformed Churches. The Church that is bound to a given canon, version, and text by its own decisions is more the slave of the letter than the Church that must find the spirit within the letter in order to be able to live. The time came when Rome could have accomplished great things in polemics and even in science if only Trent had never spoken, and she had sons enough both able and willing to attempt it, but its speech compelled their silence. The Nemesis that overtook it was the inability to handle critically the books its enemy lived by, for if it had done so the result would have been the disproof of its own decisions and the invalidation of its own claims.

This relation to the Church deprives Catholic Theology of all independent character. In its service men of large scholarship and polemical genius have worked, but they have been unable to make it a free and full science of God, because the first necessity was to make it a servant of their Church. We ought never to forget our obligations to the learning of the Benedictines and the Jesuits, but the necessity of making every way lead to Rome has prevented the rise of systems that seek to transcend the institutions of man and to be worthy of the majesty and grace of God. The development which is but a form of political activity may have theological interests, but is not the development of a Theology.

§ III.—THE LUTHERAN THEOLOGY.

The Lutheran Theology, on the other hand, created the Lutheran Church. It was organized by a body of beliefs and in order to their realization. These beliefs were of a kind that could not live under Catholicism, nor could it allow them to live. They were throughout the negation of the right of a sacerdotal institution to be, to hold any place or exercise any function as between God and man. Luther, when he said that justification by faith was the article of a standing or falling Church, stated the exact truth. He meant to say, in the terms of the New Testament, especially of Paul, that God in Christ is the sole and sufficient Saviour. He affirmed what was to him no abstract doctrine, but the most concrete of all realities, incarnated in the person and passion of Jesus Christ, drawing from Him its eternal and universal significance. But because its source and being were so august, no institution or society of sinful men could limit it, or be the sole channel of its distribution, none could command the approaches to it, or frame other terms for its acceptance than God Himself had framed. Hence the Church must be adjusted to this fundamental belief; it could not be accommodated to the rites or laws of any Church.

The Theology, then, was primary and normative, the Church secondary and normated, which may seem to mean that the religion had again become an ideal seeking a fit medium or society in which to live. But in order to see what it means and how it affected the development of the Theology we must recall the historical conditions. Luther came to the principle he found in Paul through his own experience and the theology of Augustine. The antithesis was the same in both—sin and grace. He conceived his sin and his relation to God under forms more or less forensic; he conceived God's relation to him in terms more or less evangelical —*i.e.*, as relations above law, gracious, spontaneous, immediate. As guilty he was condemned, deserved nothing but punishment; law could not help him, and he could do nothing to merit its help. If any help came it must be from God; and He could not help because of anything in a creature who was without merit, but only because of His own free love. Christ was God's means of sending this help, and faith the condition of our participation in Him. This faith was no meritorious act; it was simply the immediate opening of the soul to God, enabling God, by changing all the soul's affections and relations, to make it a changed soul. The Lutheran theology came into being as a philosophy of these acts and relations; it is essentially a soteriology, a science of the Redeemer's person and work, profoundly conscious of man's sin and the grace by which he is saved. But this theology had to be worked into relation with history and experience. It could not recognize the truth of an institution which had usurped the august predicates of Christ, and so been guilty of blasphemy against the most holy God, and it would not divorce the religion from all forms of realized being. To it two things were necessary,—the Scriptures, the source of all our knowledge of the justifying Person; and the Sacraments, means by which His people communicated with Him, especially in the act of His passion and death. As regards the Scriptures, the early Lutheran doctrine was clear and brave. It did not, like the Roman, make the Church the slave of the letter. The Scriptures were our sources, but they must be read in the light of the central idea. The truth was not true because they contained it; they were true because of the truth they contained. Hence the freedom of the Lutheran criticism; it was bound by no ecclesiastical canon, did not commit the blunder of confounding canonization with inspiration, but made the sacred literature a living literature, authenticated by its power to give life. As regards the Sacrament of the Supper, transubstantiation was denied; but, owing to Luther's strong conservative instincts, consubstantiation, or the presence of the body and blood within the elements, was affirmed. Hence came certain problems for Lutheran Christology: How was this presence and distribution of the body to be conceived? The Redeemer was in heaven, and where He was His body must be: how, then, could it be at once there and here? The attempted solutions were many, all centring in the relations of the natures not to the person, but to each other, elaborate theories of the *communicatio idiomatum* taking shape and forming schools in what seems the bitterest and most unfruitful controversy of even the sixteenth and seventeenth centuries. But things are not always what they seem; the question represents the great contribution of the Lutheran Church to constructive theology. The Incarnation has been its problem as it has been the problem of no other Church, not even of the ancient Greek. In the nineteenth century, as in the sixteenth, it has travailed at a scientific Christology, though from the opposite end of the scale. It laboured at it then by attempting to make the manhood capable of receiving the Deity, but now, by reversing the process, at making the Deity capable of losing itself, though only anew and more gloriously to find itself, in the manhood. In all the kenotic theories there are exaggerations and suppressions and mysteries, that grow more mysterious by being looked at; but one thing they have done—they have made men see that the Incarnation is the symbol at once of the highest mystery and the highest truth. It holds the key to the problem of the relation of God and man; it is that problem summarized, recapitulated, impersonated. The philosophers who have most strenuously handled and most nearly solved the problem have been sons of the land and Church of Luther; and the theologians of other lands and Churches that have to-day attempted through the Incarnation to vivify theology and relate it to modern knowledge, are only paying unconscious but deserved homage to the faith and insight of the reformer and his sons.[1]

§ IV.—THE REFORMED THEOLOGY.

In the Reformed as in the Lutheran Church, the theology was primary and normative; but the determinative conception was different. Calvin, like Luther, read theology through Augustine and without his ecclesiology, but from an altogether opposite point of view. Luther started with the anthropology, and advanced from below upwards; Calvin started with the theology, and moved from above downwards. Hence

[1] Cf. *infra*, pp. 257, 258.

his determinative idea was not justification by faith, but God and His sovereignty, or the sole and all-efficiency of His gracious will. Reformed theology is, therefore, throughout in character and in essence a doctrine of God, and its history is but a record of changes or modifications in this ultimate and normative conception. As God was construed from the standpoint of the anti-Pelagian Augustine, He was conceived, under the category of will, as the absolute *Imperator* or Sovereign of a revolted state or *civitas*. While He had the attributes both of justice and grace, and because of the one punished and because of the other saved, yet both were more qualities of will than of character. As a consequence there emerged very early two types or schools of thought, distinguished by the different emphasis they laid on the scope and efficiency of the Divine will—the supralapsarian and the sublapsarian. The former placed the Divine decrees above or before the Fall, the latter below it. The schools hold too important a place in the development both of philosophy and theology to allow us to pass them over in silence.

1. The supralapsarian is the highest speculative Calvinism, and may be described as a philosophy based on a rigorous theory of the Divine will as conditioned and qualified by the Divine nature, and by nothing else.[1] The nature of God determined both His ends and the means necessary to their realization.[2] As it was they must be; nothing in the creature could move the Creator, for only an infinite motive could move the infinite mind, and it did not

[1] Zanchius, "De Natura Dei," lib. iii., cap. iv., quæs. xi., thesis iii.: "Quod Deus suam gloriam, suam bonitatem, denique seipsum velit; hoc facit neque ab ulla re permotus neque secundum beneplacitum voluntatis suæ neque in aliquem finem: sed ex necessitate naturæ."

[2] *Ibid.*, quæs. vi., thesis:' "Quæ Deus vult de seipso, necessario vult: quæ autem de creaturis, ea vult libere." This is an important distinction, but is made in the interests of a doctrine of freedom and necessity which practically anticipates Spinoza's, *ut infra*, p. 166. There must be no constraint or even sufficient motive from without if God is to be a perfectly free Being.

become the majesty of the Supreme to find reasons for His action in any realm or form of being below His own.[1] Hence the ends of God were all contained in the nature of God; and as the last or absolute end was His own glory, His must also be the means to realize it, for only an infinite will could work out the ends of the · Infinite, and it was impossible that the Sovereign of all could allow any subject or any number of subjects to frustrate His purpose. The system was worked out from these premisses with relentless logic, and a moral severity worthy of Stoicism. It was Stoical in its ethical temper, in its ideal at once of obedience and submission, in its love of virtue and scorn of vice; while on the intellectual side it was, as Stoicism was, Pantheistic in all its fundamental conceptions. God's was the only efficient will in the universe, and so He was the one ultimate causal reality.[2] Calvin was as pure, though not as conscious and consistent a Pantheist as Spinoza,[3] and some of the inconsistencies that he spared the later supralapsarians did their best to remove.[4] While they conceived God as conscious and voluntary, and therefore personal, yet they cancelled this conception by the now implicit,

[1] Zanchius, lib. iii., cap. iv., quæs. xi., thesis iii., § 3: "Finis autem ultima, cujus causa Deus reliqua omnia quæ sunt, fecit et facit; fuit sempiterna ipsius gloria." ... "Atque ita deinceps, pulcherrimo ordine, ad hos primarios fines, omnia voluit et sapientissime ordinavit. Atque omnia hæc sanctissima decreta, ab omni æternitate facta sunt in voluntate Dei sapientissima atque justissima. Deinde vero suo tempore ventum est et quotidie venitur ad æternorum istorum decretorum executionem. Ac juxta ordinem naturæ quod primum fuit in intentione (ut solent loqui omnes scholæ), illud postea ultimum fuit et est in executione. Et contra, quod posterius fuit in intentione; illud primum in executione fuisse videmus."

[2] Amesius, "Theologia," lib. i., cap. vii., § 18: "Si enim decretum aliquod Dei penderet proprie ex ejusmodi prævisione, tum Dei Idea adveniret ei aliunde, quod ejus naturæ haudquaquam convenit." ... § 38: "Hinc voluntas Dei est prima causa rerum. Per voluntatem tuam sunt et creata sunt (Apoc. iv. 11). Voluntas autem Dei ut velit operari ad extra, non præsupponit bonitatem objecti, sed volendo ponit et facit."

[3] Calvin, "Inst.," iii., cap. xxiii., § 8: "Voluntas Dei est rerum necessitas."

[4] Turretinus, "Instit. Theol. Elenc.," loc. vi., quæs. iii., § 1: "Nos vero

now explicit principle, that His will always was as His nature was, that if His choices were with a view to His ends, His ends and therefore His choices alike depended on His nature, and could not but be in harmony with it. He was free in the Edwardian sense—*i.e.*, He had not so much freedom of volition as freedom of action and execution; all His choices were necessary, but all His acts were free.

This affinity with Pantheism in fundamental idea is often represented by agreement in what seem matters of detail. In Spinoza's system will and understanding—*voluntas* and *intellectus*—were one and the same, and the higher Calvinism always tended to identify the intellect with the will, foreknowledge with foreordination. To both the highest good was the knowledge of God, and clear knowledge became intellectual love of Him, which was eternal beatitude. Both had at root the same idea of sin and of virtue, both had the same sense of the awful majesty of order or law, both came to the individual through the universal, and read all things phenomenal in the light of the one substance or the alone efficient will. Calvin may be said to have anticipated Spinoza in his notion of God as *causa immanens*.[1] Spinoza,

omnia sine exceptione, sive cælestia, sive sublunaria, sive magna, sive parva, sive bona, sive mala, sive necessaria et naturalia, sive libera et contingentia Providentiæ divinæ subesse credimus, ut nihil in rerum natura possit dari vel evènire, quod ab ea non pendeat."

[1] Calvin, "Instit. Christ. Relig.," lib. i., cap. v., § 5: "Fateor quidem pie hoc posse dici, modo a pio animo proficiscatur, naturam esse Deum." . . . Cap. xiii., § 14: "Spiritus divinus, qui, ubique diffusus, omnia sustinet, vegetat et vivificat in cælo et in terra." One of the most distinctive features of the Reformed theology was the emphasis it laid on the doctrine of the *præsentia essentialis*, which it applied alike to man and nature. Thus Turretinus, loc. iii. quæs. i., § 13: "Homo non eget longe corrogatis testibus, vel ut exeat ex seipso, cum habeat in sinu suo domesticum hujusce veritatis Doctorem. . . . Hæc sane imago prototypum suum refert, et nemo est, qui, si attendere velit, Deum in se præsentem non tantum audiat et videat, sed etiam quodammodo tangat et palpet." And so also Zanchius, lib. ii., cap. vii., quæs. iii., § iii. 4: "Sunt autem omnia creata a Deo non alia quam suæ essentiæ virtute. Quicquid igitur in rebus creatis a Deo positum est, similitudo aliqua essentiæ Dei est; sicut et

in his definition of freedom, "Ea res libera dicetur, quæ ex sola suæ naturæ necessitate existit, et a se sola ad agendum determinatur," and in his application of it to God, "Deus ex solis suæ naturæ legibus et a nemine coactus agit,"[1] may be said to have perfected and reduced to philosophical consistency the Calvinistic conception of Deity.[2]

But the higher Calvinism was not an abstract system; it was developed into an applied theology—*i.e.*, it was made to explain the history of man with all its anomalies, alike as regards evil and good. Its high speculative idea was boldly explicated and articulated into a system that seemed at once to represent and explain all human experience. Life was complex, man was varied, the home of evil and good; virtue and vice, holiness and sin, lived and contended in the individual, while on the broader field of

Esse creaturarum, similitudo quædam est Esse Dei; et vita creaturarum, imago quædam est vitæ Dei." . . . Lib. ii., cap. vi., quæs. ii., thesis i.: "Deus autem inest rebus a se conditis, ut causa duntaxat efficiens, conservans, movens. . . . Quare sic propositionem intelligamus, Deum vere et reapse in singulis esse rebus sua essentia, et ex consequenti, sua potentia ac virtute, præsentem."

[1] "Ethices," pars i., def. vii., propos. xvii.

[2] Zanchius, lib. iii., cap. iv., quæs. vi., thesis, § 1: "Quando igitur dicimus, Deum, quæ de seipso vult, ea necessario velle: de necessario absolute et simpliciter dicto, intelligimus; quod nullo scilicet modo se aliter habere potest suapte natura. Fieri enim simpliciter et absolute non potest, neque potuit unquam; quin Deus seipsum, suam bonitatem et gloriam velit. Neque hoc quidpiam detrahit de liberrima ipsius voluntate aut omnipotentia. Non enim est hæc necessitas coactionis, sed naturæ; sicut etiam cum dicimus natura bonum esse, et natura genuisse filium." Burmann, a Dutch theologian, who was born the same year as Spinoza, and died two years after him in his "Synopsis Theologiæ," published six years before the "Ethics," thus states his idea of the organic unity of the universe, vol. i., p. 146: "Nam cum tota rerum natura non sit nisi unicum ens adeoque homo sit pars naturæ, sequitur," etc. And he holds that if only we knew things as they are we should discover their necessity (*ibid.*, p. 145): "Si homines clare totum naturæ ordinem intelligerent, omnia æque necessaria reperirent, ac illa quæ in mathesi tractantur." The antecedents of Spinoza in the Reformed theology—*i.e.*, the theology which was in his day actively and daringly speculative in Holland—have not been examined as they deserve. The field would repay the diligent inquirer.

history they struggled for the possession of the race. Yet where a Divine will reigned these anomalies could not be conceived as the result of accident. "Chance," indeed, is but a term denotive of ignorance; the man who uses it confesses that he can find no reason in the universe, and all that he knows is that things fall out—he knows not how. But this is a confession that can never be made by the man who believes in a Divine will efficient in all and over and through all. He is bound to read all anomalies through the all-ordering will, and ordered anomalies are anomalies no more. Hence when the high Calvinist saw that this world though made by God, was possessed by sin, he said: "The sin was ordained not as an end, but as a means; it is here because there was something God could not accomplish without it; what is first in the Divine intention is last in the Divine execution; find out this first which is to be the last, and sin will be explained." This thing first intended and last executed was a necessity to the Divine nature, and could be nothing less than the manifestation of the godliest qualities of God, the attributes which were His glory and marked Him off from all created and dependent being; and so it was said: "The most essential attributes of God are holiness—or justice, which is but holiness in exercise—and grace; and His most necessary function is sovereignty; but He can be seen to be a holy and gracious Sovereign only provided there are subjects to whom He can show the awful severity of His holiness and the sweet and saving condescension of His grace. In order to the exercise of these attributes there must be men to be judged and men to be saved; and in order to the being of such men there must be sin. So God ordains it as a means, not as an end; not for its own sake, but as a condition necessary to the acts that shall most manifest His glory." Then he saw that some men were good in spite of most evil conditions, some were bad though their conditions were good, and so he said: "This evil and this good are of God, and not of the will of man; reprobation and election are both of Him, happen as He has predestined." Then, as the reasons for this choice could not be placed in man without conditioning and so cancelling the absoluteness of the Divine will, without, too, finding motives outside God which would deprive Him of the freedom and spontaneity of His action, it was said: "Election is unconditional; there is and can be nothing in the creature which moves God to the exercise of His grace; He saves because it becomes His mercy, and He judges because it becomes His justice, though, of course, neither were possible without sin." The system was thus one where the sole efficient factor of all things—therefore the one abiding and causal reality—was the Divine will. It was audaciously, yet with fear and awe, worked out in the terms of Divine sovereignty and human subjection, of sin and salvation, election and reprobation, into a theology which conceived and represented the universe, all beings and all the phenomena and accidents of being as but forms under which the eternal will realized itself. Man became, if not a mode of the infinite substance, yet a mode or vehicle of the infinite will, and the universalized Divine will is an even more decisive and comprehensive Pantheism than the universalized Divine substance.

2. But there was a lower Calvinism—the sublapsarian.[1] This, by placing the decrees of God below the Fall instead of above it, escaped some of the difficulties of the supralapsarian, but only to encounter those proper to a less thorough and consistent system. The Divine will was called into action because of the conditions created by the Fall; but while sin had thus a less intelligible and, as it were, justified being, the lot of the sinner seemed at once harder and more inexplicable. The

[1] The greatest of the Reformed divines were supralapsarian; but it never received confessional expression, not even in the "Formula Consensus Helvetica." In the Westminster Confession the general outline is supralapsarian—*i.e.*, the decrees come in before both the Creation and the Fall; but the particular statement is sublapsarian.

Fall became more of an accident, and so sin lost much of its awfulness, the character it had as an evil made necessary by the infinite ends. The fate of the reprobate appeared all the darker because God took occasion to act as He did from the wilfulness of a single, even though he were a representative, man. The very degree in which evil in its origin ceased to be necessary was the measure of the Divine injustice in dealing with it as if it were an infinite offence. And so the modification increased rather than lessened the openness of the system to criticism. This criticism was due to a double reaction against Calvinism within the Reformed Church, the one assailing it through the idea of man, the other through the conception of God. The former was the Arminian, the latter the Socinian movement.

A. The Arminian criticism of Calvinism rested on two main ideas—that of equity and that of man.[1] The former made

[1] The special points on which Calvinist and Arminian differed were five: (*a*) Predestination: The Calvinist held it to be absolute and unconditional—*i.e.*, the decree to elect was without foresight of faith or good works, an act of the Divine will unmotived from without, moved only from within, *ex gratia* or *ex necessitate naturæ divinæ*; while the decree to reprobate had as condition no special demerit of the sinner, but was just because of sin, though it was a sin that as common involved all in equal guilt and liability to penalty. But the Arminian held the decree, whether elective or reprobatory, to be throughout conditional—*i.e.*, election depended on foreseen faith, reprobation on foreknown unbelief. (β) Atonement: The Calvinist held that it was strictly limited, made for the elect alone, and that it so satisfied Divine justice on their behalf that they could not but be saved; for were any lost, then the penalty of sin would be twice inflicted—once on Christ, and again on the sinner for whom He died,—a thing impossible to Divine justice. But the Arminian held the Atonement to be universal, designed and accomplished for all, making the salvation of no man actual, but the salvation of all men possible, the result being conditional on faith. (γ) Depravity: The Calvinist held it to be total, involving bondage of the will and inability to all spiritual good; but the Arminian considered it as a bias or tendency, which yet left the will free, and so the man responsible for his own destiny, belief, or unbelief. (δ) Conversion, or the work of the Holy Spirit: The Calvinist believed grace to be irresistible, the calling of God to be both effectual and efficacious, due to the immediate operation of the Spirit on the soul; but the Arminian maintained the Divine action to be mediate, through the truth, and so to be moral and

moral principles or laws condition the Divine will; the latter set physical limits to the Divine action. The Calvinistic idea of justice was based altogether on the supremacy or rights of God, but the Arminian so construed justice as to place the rights of man over against God's. Sin had not turned man into a mere vessel of wrath or of mercy, a creature who was damned because of guilt he had inherited, or saved by a grace that acted without reason or any regard to foreseen faith or good works. The worst criminal had his rights, especially the right to a fair trial before a fair tribunal; and these rights did not cease simply because the judge was God, and the accused, or even the condemned, was man. The Creator owed something to the creature He had formed, and these obligations did not cease because the first man had sinned. In a perfectly real sense sin had only increased the duty of God to be just. If original sin was what Augustine had stated it to be, and what the Calvinist maintained it was, then it

persuasive as distinguished from physical and necessitating. (*e*) Perseverance of the saints: The Calvinist held their indefectibility, the men unconditionally elected, absolutely purchased by the death of Christ, and irresistibly called out of their depraved and lost estate by the direct operation of the Holy Spirit, could not possibly fall from grace; but the Arminian maintained their defectibility, as indeed on the basis of his other doctrines he could not but do. The Arminian positions contradicted the sublapsarian quite as much as the supralapsarian position, as each was alike rigid so far as concerned the destiny of man. The exposition in the text is not concerned with the special doctrines of the two systems, but with their underlying and determinative ideas.

In the history of the two systems there are many instructive features. On the Calvinistic side we have more of the speculative and scholastic spirit, the intellect is deductive and architectonic; on the Arminian the spirit is more humanistic and literary. The great names in Calvinism—Calvin, Zanchius, Gomarus, Twisse, Rutherford—are all men of speculative genius; but the great names in Arminianism—Grotius, Episcopius, Brandt, Limborch, Le Clerc—are all men of literary faculty and humanistic temper. In the realm of opinion Calvinism did not spontaneously incline to toleration, but Arminianism did. Some of its earliest representatives were among the earliest advocates of religious freedom. There seems a curious reversal of this, the natural order, in their relations in England, where the Arminians were Laudian, with the notable exception of irrepressible John Goodwin. Why this was so is discussed below.

would be truer to name it the radical wrong of man. The race had not been consulted by the first man; he was not their representative, for they had no will in his appointment and no veto on his acts. And so by every law of justice they ought to be pitied rather than blamed for what they had suffered in consequence of him; and it was impossible to conceive anything nearer infinite injustice than allowing it to involve millions of men in every age and of every age in eternal death. The criticism was irresistible; the moment the idea of equity was admitted to a place in the relations of God to man, the old absolute unconditionalism became untenable. If justice reigned, it meant that God must be just to man, even though man was disobedient to God; and there was no justice in condemnation for a sin which came without personal responsibility, or in a salvation which had no regard to personal will or choice.

The correlate to the idea of equity was the idea of man. He was free and rational; sin had not destroyed either his reason or his freedom. By the one he had the ability to believe, by the other the ability to choose; and in justice God must deal with him as one possessed of such abilities. Thus the free will of man came to condition the absolute will of God. In the realm of nature His omnipotence and all His physical attributes ruled, but in the realm of mind His love and moral attributes governed. The destiny of man could not then be deduced by a logical process from the premiss that God is the sovereign will which can do as it chooses; for He has chosen to make man free and responsible, and His conduct to man will be conditioned by the nature He has made. If He has willed to create man moral, it is certain that He will not deal with him as if he were merely physical. But if Creator and creature are alike moral in character, it follows that necessitating action on the one side and necessitated on the other are both excluded. By His own voluntary act God has limited the range and exercise of His physical attributes, and so the terms which express His relations to man must be those of reason and freedom, not those of will and compulsion.

B. But the Socinian criticism struck the Reformed theology in a still more vital point—viz., the doctrines of the Godhead and Atonement. These represented the agencies and means by which the gracious became the redemptive will, at once efficacious in its action and limited in its extent. This was accomplished by incorporating the forensic ideas of Western with the metaphysical ideas of Eastern theology; but it was so done that while the metaphysical unity of the Godhead was preserved the ethical was not. If God was conceived as Creator, His will was simple and absolute; but if as Redeemer, it became complex and conditioned. But because of the very principles from which the theology started, the conditioned action must still remain God's—*i.e.*, be a transaction within the Godhead, carried out by and between the Divine Persons. His justice demanded the punishment of the guilty; His mercy desired their salvation; but this could be only on terms which satisfied the justice. The Godhead was made to represent how this happened; the Father became, as it were, hypostatized justice, the Son hypostatized mercy, and the Spirit their joint or resultant will. These united in a sort of pretemporal covenant. The justice of the Father was to be upheld by the Son becoming man and bearing all the penalty of all the sins of those men whom the eternal council had decreed to save. Of these no one could be lost, since the penalty could not be twice exacted, and the Father once satisfied would become unjust were He to allow the man to be lost. The theology was an absolute Monotheism, but this soteriology seemed to involve an ethical Tritheism. So the Socinian criticism concentrated itself on two points—the unreality of the hypostatized distinctions and of the transactions they were made to represent. The will of God was one, and His relation to man was one. Three dispositions or wills representing different moral tempers and attitudes within the Godhead were fatal even more to the ethical than to the metaphysical unity of God; and the Son, as more benevolent than the severe and vindicative Father, was the more Godlike. But apart from the wills, what was the use of this transaction conducted within the eternal council? If God was willing to forgive the guilty, why should He not? Who could dispute His will? If man could forgive a penitent son, why could not God? And what was Christ but an example of the good man submissive to God and a pledge of His readiness to forgive?

This Socinian criticism was of value as a severe and mordant analysis of a formal and scholastic theology, especially as it appeared in certain vernacular versions; but it had little independent and no constructive worth. It often succeeded in criticism because it failed in insight, and it was too intent on contemporary polemics to be either a speculative or historical interpretation of Christianity. Negative criticism has its place in history, and it is a place not to be despised; its function is to remove the partial or the perverted, that room may be made for the more adequate and the truer. The Socinian criticism simply applied to the profoundest mysteries of theology our every-day logical and ethical categories. It represented the play of the prosaic understanding in the region of the speculative imagination. But for this very reason it was effective, and compelled in the system it criticized a twofold modification, one in the theology, the other in the soteriology. The first was effected by the Subterlapsarian School, which had hypothetical universalism as its note.[1] The will of God was a will of universal

[1] This was the school of Saumur, and no school of the seventeenth century can exhibit a roll of more distinguished names. It took its name from the Protestant academy or university which the wisdom and munificence of Du Plessis-Mornay had founded at Saumur, and so long as it was allowed to live it served well the one and common cause of religion and letters and liberty. Its most distinguished representatives were John

benevolence; the Godhead desired the salvation of all men, and the death of Christ was adequate to this desire, atoned for the sins of the whole world. But in order that it might not be without effect, the salvation of the elect was decreed; theirs, therefore, was necessary, other men's was only made possible. But to this theory the old doctrine of atonement did not correspond. According to it, if Christ made absolute satisfaction for the sins of any man, the man could not be lost; if the satisfaction was less than absolute, the man could not be saved. Hence, if the Atonement was to be either really or hypothetically universal, some other idea of its nature must be formed. This other idea represents the modification in soteriology, and came from the ranks of the Arminians; its author was the famous jurist Grotius, and its character juridical, but based on the notion of political as distinguished from absolute justice. In effect, it replied to the Socinian by saying,—We do not live under a system of rigorous and absolute justice, which would make all atonement impossible; or a system of private benevolence, which would make one unnecessary; but of public justice, where it may be expedient. God is not an individual, a being with purely personal relations; He is a Governor, He governs

Cameron, one of several Scotchmen who entered the service of the French Protestant Church (in the Faculty of Saumur alone there were two besides Cameron—Mark Duncan and William Geddes), and though he was recalled and made Principal of Glasgow University, yet he preferred the freedom of the French to the bondage of the Scotch Church; Moses Amyraut, from whom the system got its name of Amyraldism; and Louis Cappel (Ludovicus Cappellus, second of the name). The last named was member of an illustrious Huguenot family which may be said to have served their religion by the sacrifice of all their worldly goods and the devotion of their intellect and learning. This Louis was one of the most famous Biblical scholars in the heroic age of sacred scholarship. It is worthy of mention that on the recommendation of Cameron he came to Oxford and studied Arabic. While Amyraut represented Saumur in its freer attitude to doctrine, Cappel represented its freer attitude to the Scriptures, and their combined positions occasioned a famous counterblast, the "Formula Consensus Helvetica," which forms the high-water mark of the Reformed Church in its doctrine both of the Decrees and the Scriptures.

a very mixed universe, and He must so govern it as to uphold order, which means the greatest good to the greatest number. In order to this He must cause law to be respected both among those who have and those who have not broken it, and a law unenforced by sanction and penalty is not respected; it is really, if not formally, repealed. But it is not necessary that He enforce the penalty in the express form and to the last word threatened, for a threatening differs from a promise thus: the one must be fulfilled to the letter, the other need not. The infliction of penalty is therefore a necessity, but its form and degree may vary The law may be relaxed; the Governor may forgive for a consideration. The Atonement is such a consideration; because of it God can remit the penalty, and save the sinner from the law. But as there is no absolute satisfaction, only a ground for relaxation, the result is conditional, the salvation of all men is made possible, of no man necessary. Only because of faith does the relaxed law acquit, God forgive, and the man find acceptance.

The modern evangelical theology may be described as a fusion of the Saumur hypothetical universalism with the Grotian jurisprudence. It built on the sovereignty of God; but its sovereign was no longer the absolute of the higher Calvinism, where the power was too sole to be responsible and too supreme to be qualified, but rather the limited Monarch of a constitutional universe, where the justice is public and the benevolence is universal. The defects of theory are obvious; it is the interpretation of God and His highest act in the terms of a forensic school jealous for the vindication of law and the maintenance of order.[1] It is a freer and less rigid law than Tertullian's or Augustine's; it is not so calculating and mercantile as Anselm's; it is the law of a free and constituted state, benevolently administered; it is the law of the Dutch Republic or the English Common-

[1] See *supra*, pp. 14-17.

wealth, where the law is king, not the law of an empire or an autocracy where the king is the law. But it is still law, God, if one may say so, translated into the terms of a lawyer's law, not law penetrated, transfigured, glorified, by the indwelling of God. Yet by this very defect the theory illustrated the truth that every change in Reformed theology has but expressed some modification in the theistic conception. And here it also expressed in a form now more, now less forensic, the intense conviction that to man the greatest possible evil was to be alienated from God, and the greatest possible good to be reconciled to Him. In spite of its defects the theology helped to make so many lives holy that we may be sure that it had a message from God to man.

§ V.—Theology and the English Church.

English theology must be construed through the schools of the English Church. In that Church there have always been parties as strictly institutional as the Roman, and parties as strictly theological as the Lutheran and the Reformed; and though their coexistence has often modified their action, yet it has as often sharpened their doctrinal antitheses. The institutional school exists to-day in two sections—the High Church and the Broad; the theological is also represented by two distinct types—one old and historical, the Puritan, the other modern and living, the Evangelical.[1] The two former have this as their generic characteristic:—they emphasize the institution, the episcopal body as now constituted and now existing within the English State and under its sanction. But they are distinguished thus:—the High Church emphasizes the ecclesiastical and traditional elements in the institution, but the Broad Church emphasizes the civil and national. What justification by faith was to Luther the episcopate is to the High Anglican, the article of a

[1] *Supra*, pp. 9, 10.

standing and falling Church; while in contrast to Calvin, who held the State to be but the Church in its civil aspect, the Broad Anglican holds the Church to be the State in its religious character. The High Anglican so emphasizes all in the polity that distinguishes the Church from the State, especially the episcopate and the episcopal succession, with the sacraments or the articles of adminstration, as to affirm, or tend to affirm, if not their common and mutual independence, at least the independence of the Church on the State. But the Broad Anglican so loves not so much to minimize their differences as to discover their affinities and coincidence that he now and then almost loses in the State the separate being of the Church. Yet widely as they seem to differ their generic characteristic indicates agreement in fundamental idea—in each case the Church is political, and *is* by virtue of its political qualities. And this agreement has its historical interest and evidence. The same "Ecclesiastical Polity" to which the Broad Churchman appeals, is one of the High Churchman's most loved authorities; and the old High Church was as civil in its basis as is the modern Broad. The ultimate Divine right with Laud, the ground of all his policy, the warrant of all his action, was the King's; and it was by the same party that the headship of the second Charles over the Church, with all the baneful tyrannies that flowed from it, was most broadly stated, fulsomely praised, and strenuously defended. The Act of Uniformity is a monument of the identity of the historical High Church with the Broad as regards civil or political doctrine. Their distinctive features are, because of this agreement in fundamental idea, largely due to developments in civil politics. The modern Broad Church is a theory as to how the old connection of the civil and ecclesiastical states may be maintained under a democracy; the modern High Church is a theory as to how the Church may, while living within and under a democracy, yet be independent of it. What occasioned the rise of the two were the same events differently regarded; love of the liberalism which had gained the ascendency in the State made the Broad Church, fear of it created the High. Both parties may have since then learned to temper their feelings, and, as a consequence, their judgments, with wisdom or discretion; but of the historical fact there can be no doubt. And the fact is significant of the essentially political character of both ideals.

The institutional character of these two schools is expressed in their respective attitudes to theology, and their theologies repeat and reflect the differences of their institutional ideals. The theology of the Broad Church represented the revolt against the past, the attempt not to dishonour it, but to loosen the bonds with which it bound the present; but the theology of the High Church represented the revolt against the present, and the apotheosis of the past with a view to its control of the new mind. What was to Thomas Arnold the evidence of God's action in the present—viz., its enlarging liberty, widening knowledge, saner morals, purer love of truth as truth and man as man—was to Newman, who read it through the ecclesiastical changes he both hated and feared, Liberalism, or the apostasy of modern man from God, and constituted the need for bringing out of a period when God most manifestly reigned, forces and motives to restrain and order and govern the present. The theology of Maurice had its basis in philosophy, and he read Scripture and history and institutions in the light of illuminating philosophical ideas; but the theology of Pusey had its basis in men and documents which he regarded as authoritative and normative, and his special method of proof was by catenas of texts—Biblical, patristic, and scholastic—and an exegesis that was seldom historical, because so often traditional or dogmatic, though when occasion demanded he could induce his authorities to speak with an opportune or more modern voice. What appealed to Kingsley was not the ecclesiastical past of England, but its national and heroic elements and persons, which were to him therefore religious; but what appealed to the Anglican Newman or to Hurrell Froude was men who could be described as saints because they had served the Church rather than the nation or the people. The scholarship of Stanley was as picturesque and imaginative as the poetry of Keble, but he always made the past speak as to a learner who was yet a critic, while Keble made his attitude to the past a sort of religion, the wisest and the most pious men being those who most revered the names sacred to ecclesiastical mythology. And these persons express tendencies. Theology is to the one class dogma, something given and defined, something regulated by tradition, creed, or canon--*i.e.*, it is here, as in Catholicism, part of the written or unwritten law of the institution, with no real or valid existence apart from it; but theology is to the other a form of modern thought, personal rather than collective, the activity of a mind whose field and obligations are more civil than ecclesiastical. There are signs that these distinctions may be transcended. Minds that are High Church by conviction and association have assimilated a philosophy that may yet through their theology transform their ecclesiology.

The Puritans and the Evangelicals are not related like the High Church and the Broad. They have hardly any historical connection, and differ greatly in temper, tendency, and quality of theological mind. The Puritans were primarily theologians, possessed with the passion of realizing in personal and collective life the ideals of their theology; but the Evangelicals are primarily pastors and preachers, who accept the order under which they live as the one which best enables them to save souls. The Puritan was essentially a son of the Reformed theology, profoundly convinced of its truth, conceiving it as a sort of ideal world existing in the mind of God, and by Him communicated to His people that it might be embodied in the whole of life ; but the Evangelical is essentially a son of the Evangelical revival, with its intensely individual spirit, its love of souls, its belief in the truth as the instrument for saving them, with a certain feeling that things which do or even might endanger this are evil, and a certain timid tendency to regard a too inquisitive mind or a too extensive and varied intellectual activity as undesirable or even possibly profane. Their respective theologies correspond ; there was a large idealism in the Puritan, as became the work of men who were no less distinguished as thinkers than as scholars, and there is an immediate practical and edificatory purpose in the Evangelical, which prevents it ever becoming as large or as courageous as either its Puritan predecessor or its High Church contemporary.

This analysis of the English schools may help us to understand the various forces that have made English theology so mixed yet so uniform in character. It has never, save with some of the Puritans or their immediate scholars, been theoretical or *a priori*—*i.e.*, given to constructive speculation ; but its main interest or determinative idea has been either political or historical, which indeed is here only another form of the political. The earliest controversies in the English Church may be said to have been between two conceptions— whether the actual Church ought to be brought into harmony with the ideal, or whether the actual was not the ideal Church. This of course involved a difference of ideals rather than of actuals: the ideal in the one case was theological and abstract, a society constructed according to the mind and word of God ; but in the other case it was political and concrete, the society which the wisdom of the past had created and the piety of the present was bound to preserve and administer. The former was the Puritan ideal, the latter the Anglican ; the one was the home of the dynamic forces, the other of the static, that shaped the English Church, though in the end the static proved stronger than the dynamic. But this difference was not at first due to a difference in theology—for the prevailing and even official tendency was Calvinistic—but to the relative primacy of the theological or political idea. With the Puritan the theology was primary, and so his doctrine was essentially High Church; but with the Anglican the polity was primary, and so his doctrine was, under the conditions then existing, as essentially Erastian. The Puritan said: "God is the supreme Sovereign; His will ought everywhere to be obeyed, in State as in Church. He has revealed in His Word and by the act and process of institution an order or law for the Church which He has not done for the State; therefore the Church must be constituted according to the revealed ideal, and on it the State cannot be allowed to impose another law or discipline than those so manifestly Divine. In the kingdom of God the king is a vassal or minister, who may as a man be allowed to serve, but who cannot as sovereign or head be allowed to rule. The headship belongs to Christ, the King; and He rules over His saints, and His saints are known by their obedience to His rule. The Church is the people of Christ living according to His laws." But the Anglican replied: "Harmony is of heaven, law is of God, and the Church ought to be so ordered by law as to be the home of harmony. Your discipline would throw all things into chaos; but the Church we know is distinguished by seemly and heavenly liturgies, which the past for good reason created and the present for good reason has retained. This Church is composed of the English people; that people is under one aspect the State, under another aspect the Church; the sovereign is the symbol and organ of their corporate unity, and therefore it is but reasonable that he should be the common source of authority, and as the head of the one be the head of both." These ideals were thus not so much different as opposite; they made their appeal, as it were, to different senses, started from opposed premisses, reasoned to conclusions which had to the one party all the cogency of logical deductions from accepted principles, to the other party all the invalidity of a process whose false beginning vitiated its logical end. But what is evident is this: the premiss in the one case was a theology, a God who had revealed a discipline His people were bound to realize and obey; the premiss in the other case was a polity, a system rooted in the past, actual in the present, part of the order which had grown with the people, and at once interpreting to it and realizing for it the faith by which it ought to live. The God the Puritan conceived was a being of so absolute a moral purity that He could not allow His Church to be merged in the State or controlled by the civil magistrate or served by ministers of his creation, or composed of any but the pure in heart and in life; nor could He love any ceremony, however beautiful, that might hinder His immediate control of the conscience, or change the essence or even the emphasis of service from conscience and reason to sense. But what the Anglican conceived was a worship so in harmony with the forms and customs and traditions of the past, and so expressive of common moods and sentiments, that the Church and its services should, as much as the State, represent in its own sphere the collective and the continued being of the people. The differences were thus radical, and the fundamental point is touched when we say, The determinative idea was to the Puritan theological, but to the Anglican political; in other words, the regulative notion of the one was the theology, of the other the institution.[1]

Now, the Anglican or institutional idea, so soon as it became defined and, as it were, conscious, acted on theology in a characteristic manner, modifying all its absolute elements, shrinking, if we may so speak, from the direct and naked sovereignty of God. There is a remarkable change

[1] See note at end of chapter, pp. 188-190.

in what we may call the official theology of the Church between Elizabeth and the first Charles. Under Elizabeth Calvinism was dominant; the Thirty-nine Articles are in their doctrine higher than the old *Confessio Scoticana*; the Bishops' Bible, as sanctioned by Elizabeth's bishops, contains the true Genevan doctrine; Parker and Grindal, Whitgift and Bancroft, were quite as Calvinistic as Goodman or Jewel, Cartwright or Perkins; the Lambeth Articles are as high as the Genevan Catechism; Hooker thinks Calvin "incomparably the wisest man that ever the French Church did enjoy," and though he opposed the Genevan discipline, he had nothing to say against the theology. But under Charles the Anglican tendency was Arminian, the milder theology and the high polity going hand in hand. The significance of the change does not so much lie in the new theology as in the more elastic political doctrine it allowed. Laud was not an Arminian simply because he was able the better to resist the Puritans by contradicting their theology, but because his theory of Divine right of kings and bishops had freer scope and could have a more justified existence under a conditional theology than under one which so magnified the Divine sovereignty as to leave no room or place for any absolute sovereignty of man over the people of God. And Laud did not stand alone; the Anglicans, like Jeremy Taylor, Bull, Sancroft, Barrow, became the severest critics of Calvinism; and never again do we see, as under Elizabeth and James, the highest offices of the Church held by Calvinists, and representative theologians sent as delegates to help a Calvinistic synod to formulate a high, aggressive, and uncompromising Calvinism.

But this was not the only result of the action of the now determinative institutional idea. Anglican theology became, we cannot say historical, for it was too special and apologetic in its scope to be entitled to this name, but retrospective, traditional, patristic. It had a twofold polemic—against the Puritan and against the Catholic; and its appeal from both was to the ancient and undivided Church—an appeal whose legitimacy the one opponent might admit, but the other could only deny. Hence the most characteristic works in Anglican theology became, as it were, antiquarian rather than constructive. The idea that a theology was the most comprehensive of all philosophies ceased to live for the Anglican—at least, there was a cessation of all attempts to realize it. The only real exception to this law was the Cambridge Platonists, but they were men trained in Puritan colleges during the Puritan ascendency, and are significant as indicating what sort of schools this ascendency, if it had continued, would have developed in the Church. The institutional idea has so governed the theological development that even questions of pure and Biblical theology have been read through it. The Trinity and the Incarnation have been discussed as branches of patristic, and as determined by the œcumenical creeds and definitions of the specific period to which the Anglican made his appeal. The result has been a remarkable difference between the theological activity of the Anglican and the other Reformed Churches. These latter have been great in scientific systems, rich in interpretative ideas, fertile in constructive endeavours. The Lutherans elaborated the scholastic *communicatio idiomatum* into a consistent and logical doctrine; their attempts at a more reasonable Christology have instructed all the schools of Christendom, even those of the later Roman and Anglo-Catholicism. The Reformed Church had many theologies that were whole philosophies, seeking to interpret the universe, man with all his good and evil, history with all its failure and achievement, in the terms of the theistic idea. From these Churches came the doctrine of the covenants which did so much to create the notion of order and progress in history, and a scientific because a historical interpretation of the Bible. And they more than any others have created science in sacred learning, the criticism that has restored the Scriptures to reason and conscience and life. But the Anglican has lived within a narrower range, and has worked for a more specific purpose. He has made the Fathers and the history of a particular period emphatically his own, and he has done it that he might vindicate the polity, the creed which the polity carried with it, and the political rights and privileges of his own Church. He may have done well in so doing; all that concerns us is to note that he has done it, and has thus given to his theology its peculiar and distinctive characteristic.

§ VI.—Retrospect and Conclusions.

But, now, what is the significance of this discussion?

1. We have been able to distinguish the various factors that at once govern the formation and growth of theology and determine its specific character in a given period or Church. The consciousness of the time, whether personal or collective, supplies the factor determinative of form; and the dominant element in the consciousness determines the particular point from which the matter will be construed.

In the ancient Eastern Church the formal factor was Greek philosophy. Its theology was the endeavour of the old philosophical mind to construe the new Christian history in the old philosophical terms. The construction had all the excellencies and all the defects of the minds in and through which it took its rise. On the one hand, it fitly closed and completed the history of Greek philosophy by means of a scientific doctrine of God and the Godhead, which held within it the germs of the conciliation of the old antinomies of transcendence and immanence. On the other hand, it fitly began a series of endeavours to interpret the highest truths of the reason through the surest realities of the faith.

But it was only a beginning, for the construction was more philosophical than religious, so purely metaphysical that it failed to preserve and express those august yet gracious ethical elements that were the very essence of the conception of God that came in Jesus Christ.

In the ancient Latin Church the formal factor was represented first by Stoical and then by neo-Platonic philosophy and Roman polity. These acting together, and strengthened by the popular religion, resulted in the gradual assimilation of the polity by the Christian society, its apotheosis when assimilated, and the interpretation of man's relations to God in the terms of law.

In the mediæval period the formal factors were the Church, which had incorporated the Empire while transmitting the religion, Law, Roman and Teutonic, and Greek Philosophy, especially as a dialectic or doctrine of logical forms; and the result was that we had three great questions due, respectively, to the translation of political sovereignty into spiritual supremacy, the terms of man's reconciliation with God into those of a legal process, the order and process of our knowledge into the determinative principle in theology.

In the modern Churches the ancient and mediæval formulæ have survived, but have been variously articulated and modified according as the regulative idea was political or theological.

2. But alongside the formal factor stands the material—*i.e.*, the matter whose meaning is to be determined. This is represented by the creative Personality of the Faith and His authentic history. This history being written, is invariable, but not so the history of the Christian mind or consciousness in relation to it. Variation has, from the very nature of the case, been here the law. The longer the history lives in the consciousness and penetrates it, the more does the consciousness become able to interpret the history in its own terms and according to its own contents. The old pagan mind into

which Christianity first came could not possibly be the best interpreter of Christianity, and the more the mind is cleansed of the pagan the more qualified it becomes to interpret the religion. It is therefore reasonable to expect that the later forms of faith should be the truer and the purer.

3. Every great period of progress or development in theology has been marked by the ascendency of the material and inner over the formal and outer factors; in other words, the direct effect of every fresh return to the sources has been the enlargement and re-formation of religious thought. This is true in the case of the anti-Gnostic Fathers, whose use of the sources is seen in the way they transcend rather than repeat tradition, and leave a theology richer than anything that had preceded it, especially in those elements most distinctive of the original and Apostolic Word. Augustine marks another moment of return; and his pre-eminence over Tertullian is due to his deeper reading of Paul. The Reformation is a similar moment, the only possible result of the recovered knowledge of the Scriptures by men who believed that they revealed the mind of Christ and His Apostles. In each of these periods the return to the sources has enriched the faith and purified the life of all Churches, even the most resistant.

4. Our day has also been marked by a return to the sources of a quite specific character,—it has been more distinctly than any other a return to the historical Christ. The most potent influence in the Scriptures for the anti-Gnostic Fathers, Augustine, and the Reformers was the Pauline. Paul has been in all times what he was in his own—the greatest of all the Apostolic forces that work for evolution and change. But the modern return is to Christ, and to Him as the Person who created alike the Evangelists and the Apostles, by whom He is described and interpreted. He has become the centre from and through which all are studied, and is not simply looked at through the eyes of Paul or John.

5. This is not an individual or incidental thing, but represents the tide and passion of the time; is, as it were, the sum and essence of the living historical, philosophical, and religious spirit. This is what we must now attempt to understand and describe, that we may see how the consciousness of the time has become full of Christ, and its reason been called anew to His interpretation. He is the end of critical and historical inquiry, but the starting-point of constructive thought. The determinative idea of theology is not the Church, but the Christ. In harmony with His mind must it be built, and by agreement with Him its truth determined.

NOTE. See p. 182.

THE differences between the Puritan and the Anglican positions may seem to be stated too sharply and antithetically in the text, and with too little regard to changes of men and times; but they represent the essential points that emerged in the controversy between Cartwright and Whitgift, and determined the later developments of the two tendencies. Cartwright's positions may be stated thus: the Church is prior in being and superior in authority to the State, has the right as a distinct and separate and higher society to make its own laws, appoint its own officers, enforce its own discipline, frame its own creed, and regulate its own ceremonies; it is bound to do so in accordance with the mind and will of its Founder as revealed in the New Testament, and not to allow any prince or civil magistrate as such to impose laws upon it or occupy a place in it that was not assigned to him by Christ. Whitgift's positions were the exact antitheses of these: "the Church could not as a visible society" with "an external government" be established without the civil magistrate, who may also in respect to it as such be called its head by virtue of "the supreme authority given of God to the prince over his people in all causes"; he had therefore those powers as regards laws, ministers, creed, and ceremonies which Cartwright had claimed for the Church alone, though of course he was not qualified to exercise specifically priestly functions. Cartwright, indeed, held that in "ruinous decays and overthrows of religion," when there was "no lawful ministry to set good orders," "that then the prince ought to do it"; and that even if any "lawful ministry" agreed to "any unlawful or unmeet order, that the prince ought to stay that order." But his very exceptions define his rule: Reformation was the duty of every man, especially the man most able to effect it. It was characteristic that Cartwright maintained that "the Commonwealth must be made to agree with the Church," but Whitgift that "the Church must be framed according to the Commonwealth"; Cartwright that "although the godly magistrate be the head of the Commonwealth, and a great ornament unto the Church, yet he is but a member of the same," but Whitgift that this was to "overthrow monarchies," since it made the prince "a servant, no master, a subject, no prince, under government, no governor, in matters pertaining to the Church"; Cartwright that "infidels under a Christian magistrate are members of the Commonwealth, but not of the Church," nor are known "drunkards or whoremongers," and the excommunicated, "though sundered from the Church," may yet retain his "burgeship or freedom in the city," but Whitgift that while "in the Apostles' time all or the most that were Christians were virtuous and godly," yet "now the Church is full of hypocrites, dissemblers, drunkards, whoremongers." It is this latter that gives its religious significance to the controversy, and makes apparent the moral passion that was at its heart. On the Puritan side what they wanted, and were by their theological idea bound to want, was a Church in which the moral will of God should be supreme.

The operation of the two principles was not on either side uniform. The Puritan principle took a double line,—one section held to the collective idea, and wished the Church, without ceasing to be national, to be organized on the Genevan or Presbyterian model; another section adopted the Separatist idea, and held that the way to proceed was by persons rather than parishes, or the method of the Apostolic age. The one received its logical and historical expression at the hands of the Westminster Assembly; the other in the societies of the Separatists under Elizabeth and James, and though they have little real historical connection and are distinguished by specific differences, in the later Independents whose representatives are the "five dissenting brethren" at Westminster, and in John Milton. The note of the former was the place it assigned to the "civil magistrate"; it was his duty "to take order that unity and peace be preserved in the Church, that the truth of God be kept pure and entire, and that all blasphemies and heresies be suppressed." Hence toleration was no part of this creed; indeed, round it the fiercest of the controversies within and around the Assembly raged, the Scotch delegates storming against it with a perfervid zeal the English people have never forgotten, and Milton has immortalized in the famous sonnet which described "New Presbyter as old priest writ large." On the other hand, the note of the early Separatist and the later Independent was that the function of the "civil magistrate" was, as Robert Browne phrased it, "only to rule the commonwealth in all outward justice," and not to "compel religion," or "force submission to ecclesiastical government by laws and penalties." For as John Robinson, the Pilgrim Father, argued, "civil causes could never bring forth spiritual effects"; "compulsive laws" might create hypocrisy, but not the spirit that "received the Word gladly." And so John Milton said, "Though the civil magistrate were able, yet hath he no right to interfere with conscience or anything that pertaineth to the Church of Christ." "To compel the profane to things holy in his profaneness is all one under the Gospel, as to have compelled the unclean to sacrifice in his uncleanness under the law."

The Anglican principle also took a double line, according as the power that established the Church or the established polity—*i.e.*, the episcopate—was emphasized. In the earlier period Bancroft and Bilson represent the latter, as Whitgift the former. Bilson denied that princes could "authorize pastors to preach the Word or to administer the Sacraments"; but though to them the discipline and ministry of the Church are committed, they are not in a Christian state to do these things without the consent and help of the "civil magistrate." But the emergence of the question as to the ultimate authority in the State, king or people, raised the same question as to the Church, with the result that there arose the theories on the one hand of the double Divine right, king's and bishop's, characteristically the bishop's being secondary, the king's primary, and on the other its popular correlate, that the polity was a matter of indifference, its specific form a thing to be determined by the people through their representatives. Laud is the typical name on the one side, John Selden on the other. Laud is an autocratic or monarchical Erastian, but Selden a democratic or parliamentary. The Laudian theory made the bishop depend for his jurisdiction and authority on the king, and out of this came what can only be described as the apotheosis of the king by the Anglican theology of the seventeenth century. On the basis it supplied the Act of Uniformity was passed; and though the Act still survives, the theory died before the hard and disillusioning facts of the Revolution Settlement and the Hanoverian dynasty. As a consequence, the relations between the royal and ecclesiastical powers were conceived more in the manner of the Separatists, and indeed their very phraseology was unconsciously repeated. Thus Leslie's famous treatise on the "Regale" was described in words strangely suggestive of the document that may be said to have occasioned the rise of the name "Independents," as "concerning the Independency of the Church upon any power on earth, in the exercise of her purely spiritual authority and power." The modern High Church is on this point, so far at least as concerns theory, more of the mind of Cartwright than of Hooker. While they hold with the latter as to the framework or outward structure of the Church, they hold with the former as to its separate authority and distinction from the State. In theory, too, they here agree more with the Separatists than with Laud, and hold in principle, though not in practice, with the men who refused obedience to the Act of Uniformity, and agree in practice, though not in principle, with the men who enforced it.

DIVISION II.

HISTORICAL CRITICISM AND THE HISTORY OF CHRIST.

CHAPTER I.

THROUGH LITERATURE AND PHILOSOPHY TO CRITICISM.

THE history of the process which has made the historical Christ the starting-point of constructive theology lies outside our present purpose; but a brief sketch, exhibiting its relation to modern tendencies, is necessary. While the ecclesiastical revival in England was making its first blind and impassioned attempts at a beginning, the philosophical and critical tendencies that were to do so much for our knowledge of the primitive Church were in Germany endeavouring to concentrate themselves on Christ and the literature of the New Testament. The two movements were in spirit, temper, design, and agencies very different, and it would have been well if each could have qualified the other. If the Anglican men had combined with their own profound love of the Church and devotion to its Head, the scientific conscience, the intellectual courage and veracity, the literary and historical sense, of the German theologians, they might have accomplished the most catholic revival in history, without any of the violences to reason, to truth, and to charity that attended both the manner and the results of their work.

If the German critics had, in addition to their own great qualities, possessed the reverence, the love of the beautiful, and the sense for the holy that distinguished the Anglicans, then their work, while no less thorough and fruitful, would have been more religious. There is nothing that so strikes a student of the Anglican revival as the complete unconsciousness in its representative men of the deepest of all the problems which their own theory and contentions involved, and which, for altogether different reasons and purposes, the greatest of their contemporaries were trying to face and to formulate; and there is nothing that so surprises the student of German criticism as its want of awe in touching beliefs quick with those loves and hopes that are dearest to the human heart. Of these two movements, started and conducted in such total unconsciousness of each other, it is hard to tell which will have the most enduring influence. But one thing is evident: knowledge and thought are in the long-run mightier than institutions and offices, and we may well leave the issue to the truth of God and the reason of man.

§ I.—THE BEGINNINGS OF HISTORICAL CRITICISM: LITERATURE.

But our concern is simply with the critical movement in its relation to the history and, at least so far as it bears upon the person of Christ, the literature of the New Testament. In order to understand this movement we must survey the tendencies out of which it grew. It belongs to our own century, and is part of its reaction against the hard and narrow rationalism of the preceding. It has nothing to do with the pragmatical and negative criticism of the Deists, but represents the larger and more constructive spirit that distinguishes the nineteenth from the eighteenth century, especially in all that concerns philosophy, literature, science, history, and religion.

1. The literary revival preceded the critical, helped to determine both its spirit and its problems, the attitude of the mind

as well to religion as to religious ideas, their forms and their history. Lessing, though he belongs to the eighteenth, was the prophet and forerunner of the nineteenth, century; he, by his theological no less than his literary activity, stands between and unites the two worlds. By him the Wolfenbüttel Fragments, the last words of the dying Deism, were edited, and by him the new critical thought was first consciously expressed.[1] His earlier intellectual sympathies were with Deism; his later, if Jacobi is to be believed, with Pantheism.[2] The shallower minds of his day thought that religion stood or fell with certain words and events: the Deist imagined that he had only to prove certain words derived or erroneous or insignificant, certain events impossible or fictitious, in order to prove revealed religion false; the rationalist, that he had only to prove what were supposed to be miracles to be unexpected coincidences or the hasty interpretations of an unillumined mind, in order to harmonize religion with nature and maintain the truth of its history; the apologist, that he had only to prove the literal veracity of the word and the probability of the event in order to vindicate religion and save it altogether. But Lessing endeavoured to free it from the pragmatic literalism of all three, and sought

[1] Lessing's attitude to Christianity is too vexed a problem to be discussed here. Many things make it hard to determine; so much of his theological activity was polemical, and so much of his polemic was either γυμναστικῶς or simply *argumenta ad homines*. But as the controversy turned so much on the function and meaning of the Bible for religion, his contributions to it bear directly on the questions of criticism and religion. His most polemical treatises are full of constructive ideas; but of course it is when he sets himself to positive work, as in his "Nathan der Weise" and the "Erziehung," that we find him at his best. We should take a more positive view of his personal religion than Hebler does—"A Christian non-Christian" ("Lessingstudien," p. 103).

[2] Jacobi's "Werke," vol. iv., pp. 37 ff. (ed. 1819). But though there are distinct enough traces of Spinoza in Lessing, yet he is no Pantheist; Spinoza influenced him more on the historico-critical than the philosophical side. His God was supernatural, though not extra-natural, a free, conscious Spirit, the eternal Providence who determined His own ends.

its essence in the contents of conscience and the truths of reason.[1] The sensuous, whether as written word or miraculous act, could neither constitute nor prove the spiritual. Books could be only transitory vehicles of eternal realities. Religion had existed before the Bible—could exist without it.[2] Revelation, which was the communication by God of new or higher truths to the mind, was necessary because of human weakness, which without such Divine action would hinder and hamper human progress. Humanity was a colossal man whose education was in process, and education was revelation.[3] In his childhood he was instructed by symbols and ruled by laws whose sanctions were physical rewards and penalties; in his youth, by personal authority and motives drawn from a future life appealing to his imagination and heart. God was the Educator of man; the Divine Spirit was active in the race. But the theory allowed to no positive or revealed religion an absolute value. Each had only a "pædagogic" worth, was a sensuous form needed to make the full truths of reason intelligible to sense-bound man. To speak with the philosophy of the time, revelation was the method by which the ideas of religion were conveyed into the intellect and impressed as laws upon the conscience. And here the fundamental thought of his "Nathan" comes in to complete his doctrine of revelation and religion. It pleaded for toleration by vindicating the right of other religions than our own to exist, based on their power to produce intellectual veracity and moral excellence. The three rings, which are the symbols of the three religions, are in an equal measure gifts of the one Father. A Moham-

[1] "Ueber den Beweis des Geistes u. der Kraft," "Theol. Streitschriften," pp. 3 ff. (ed. 1867). Here he argues: "Accidental truths of history can never be evidence for necessary truths of the reason: that Christ raised a dead man does not prove that God has a Son co-essential with Himself" (pp. 6, 7). In his doctrine of the relation of the Bible and religion Lessing was as much opposed to his own Fragmentist as to the orthodox. Cf. " Axiomata," vii.-ix.
[2] "Axiomata," the second of the Anti-Goeze pamphlets. Cf. Axioms, i.-viii.
[3] "Die Erziehung des Menschengeschlechts," §§ 1-5, 17, 26, etc.

medan or Jew, realizing the ideal truths his religion expresses is as truly a religious man as a Christian.[1] And so Lessing was not a disciple of the Christian religion or the systems which Churches have built on the Gospel, but only of what he called the religion of Christ—*i.e.*, the religion which Jesus as a man knew and practised,[2] and which every man can have in common with him. His whole tendency was to release the spirit from the letter, and to reconcile the free handling of sacred histories and records with reverence of mind. For, according to Lessing, there was no intrinsic or absolute necessity for revelation; once it has perfectly educated man, he can dispense with it. The letter with its symbolism, which is a necessity to the man still in the sensuous stage, is a mere superfluity to the man who has so grown as to be able to walk according to the spirit. The theory which made religion so independent of the letter could not but contribute to the growth of the criticism which was concerned with the written word. It needed time to show whether it was possible to handle the letter without touching the spirit.

2. Schiller, too, acted powerfully, if indirectly, on religious thought. His spirit was too moral to allow him to be other than a Theist, characteristically of the Kantian type. Life was full of ethical significance; the stage, he thought, ought to be an ethical teacher, showing the world the moral law in action. And just because the ethical in him was so intense he loved the ideal, though not the actual, Christianity. In its

[1] Though "Nathan der Weise" seemed to establish a sort of equation between the three great religions, yet its whole conception was due to the Christian spirit; within neither of the other two religions could it have risen. Character is an old test of truth. It is remarkable if we compare "Nathan" with "Die Erziehung," that in the latter Islam has no place or function.

[2] This was a distinction which Lessing owed to Reimarus, and made the title of a suggestive little tractate. Lessing has some claim to notice as a speculative theologian. His construction of the Trinity, "Die Erziehung," § 73, contains, indeed, no new element, but it is remarkable as a forecast of many later attempts at the speculative restoration of what had been critically dissolved.

pure form, the representation of moral beauty, or the incarnation of the holy,[1] the Christian religion was in practical life a depraved, an offensive, and a mean, because broken, representation of the highest. Its distinctive quality or character as ideal lay in its moral energy, its power to change the categorical imperative into free inclination, to create the beautiful soul possessed of the virtue which is nothing else than "an inclination to duty." With it and as its essence he sings the gospel of the love which impelled God to create man, which uplifts man to God, and makes all men brothers. But yet its ethical majesty was not all gain; the apotheosis of the spirit, by undeifying nature, impoverished man. He needed the fair humanities of old religion; and so, though admiring Monotheism, the poet mourned the loss of the old gods.

> "Einen zu bereichern unter allen
> Musste diese Götterwelt vergehn."[2]

3. Goethe's influence on the religious province was much more extensive and intense than Schiller's. He touched life and thought more deeply, and on more sides, was less ethical, yet more universal. He conceived the perfect culture to be too wide, too varied and rich, to be based on a single religion, or to be realized by the imitation of a single person. His own ideals were Hellenic, not Hebrew; but his Hellenism was not uniform or monotonous—it was variously qualified and enriched. He owed much to Mysticism, much to Herder, and much to Spinoza; they taught him to read order and unity into nature, and he loved to feel himself in harmony with the life that filled the universe and became conscious in man. He could not conceive spirit without matter or matter without spirit; God and the world stood together inseparably, He existing in it—it the woven and flowing garment which at once hid and manifested His essence.

---

[1] "Briefwechsel zwischen Schiller und Goethe," vol. i., Br. 86, p. 67 (ed. 1881).
[2] "Die Götter Griechenlands."

"Ihm ziemt's, die Welt im Innern zu bewegen,
Natur in sich, sich in Natur zu hegen."

Spinoza might be to others *Atheus*, but to him he was *Theissimus et Christianissimus*. From him he learned what he conceived to be the fundamental principle of all religion: "He who truly loves God must not desire that God love him in return." There was nothing he more resented than Lavater's dilemma: "Either Christian or Atheist." He held, on the contrary, that it was indifferent what a man believed—that he *believed* was everything. He would be a Christian in his own way, but in the way of no other person.[1] The ordinary categories were too small for him; he was at once Polytheist, Pantheist, and Theist—the first as poet, the second as interpreter of nature, the third as moral being. God he knew by *scientia intuitiva*, and to him blessedness upon earth was to acknowledge God, wherever and however He may reveal Himself. So he conceived Christ as one, but not the sole, revelation of God, the highest in the moral world, but not so sufficient or exhaustive as to be adequate alone; and he described himself as not an unchristian nor an antichristian, but as yet a decided non-christian[2]—*i.e.*, he did not, like the first, stand outside Christianity, nor, like the second, oppose it, nor did he claim to be all or only what it required, nay, rather he comprehended so much of it as was good, and much besides. So he said to Lavater, "You find nothing more beautiful than the Gospel; I find a thousand pages written by both ancient and modern men, graciously endowed of God, quite as beautiful and useful and necessary to mankind." He believed in the aristocracy of the cultured rather than in the monarchy of Christ. So he will not allow His sole or solitary supremacy; he names it unrighteous and robbery to pluck all the beautiful feathers from the thousands of birds under heaven in order to adorn a single bird of Paradise. And as he limits the authority of Christ,

[1] "Wahrheit und Dichtung," bk. xiv.
[2] "Briefe an Lavater," 39, p. 144 (Hirzel).

he denies His miraculous character; an audible voice from heaven would not persuade him that water burned and fire extinguished, or that a virgin became a mother, or that a dead man rose again; nay rather, he held such things to be blasphemies against the great God and His revelation in nature So he conceived Christ to be one in a multitude of forms under which God was manifested. Yet the God He manifested was the essence of His own beautiful soul, full of goodness and love.[1] He was therefore the highest in His own order, the moral and spiritual. And this determined his attitude to the Gospels: the genuine he defined as the really excellent, that which stood in harmony with purest nature and reason, and contributed even to-day to our highest development; the spurious was the absurd, the hollow, and the stupid, what brought forth no fruit, at least none that was good. In this defined sense all four Gospels—though Mark and Luke were written without immediate experience, and John only in extreme age—he held to be thoroughly genuine; for in them there is the radiance of a majesty which proceeded from the person of Christ, and which was of as Divine a kind as ever the Godhead has assumed upon the earth. Before this Christ he bowed in devoutest reverence as before the Divine revelation of the highest principle of morality.[2] Hence Goethe tended to transfer the idea of the true from the supernatural in Christ and the historical in the Gospels to the moral and spiritual in both, and to these as beautiful and impressive yet natural creations of the spirit within the universe. The cross did not and could not signify to him any act of Divine sacrifice for human redemption, but it grew into a beautiful symbol of self-renunciation, and life through it.

> "Und so lang Du das nicht hast,
> Dieses 'Stirb und Werde!'
> Bist Du nur ein trüber Gast
> Auf der dunklen Erde."

---

[1] Eckermann, "Gespräche mit Goethe," ii. Th., p. 199 (ed. 1868).
[2] *Ibid.*, iii. Th., p. 255.

§ II.—Historical Criticism: Romanticism and Theology.

But the most potent influence in historical theology from this period and circle was Herder. He was, as has been well said, the theologian among the classics and a classic among the theologians.[1] A many-sided man, open, capable, susceptible on all his sides, he touched and was touched by literature and art, philosophy and history, as well as theology, and with him to touch was to quicken and to mould. His idea of God owed much to Spinoza and to Leibnitz; for the former's category of substance he substituted the latter's category of force—not as material simply, but as rational and spiritual. God was the absolutely active Being, physical yet intellectual: "Die selbstständigste Ur- und Allkraft," "Der Ursprung, Gegenstand und Inbegriff aller Erkenntniss."[2] As such God was to nature no *extra* or *supra*; if He did not exist in the world, then He existed nowhere; yet immanence did not mean identity; God was not the world, nor was the world God. He was the highest, most living, most active Existence, who had given to His creatures what is highest—viz., existence, reality. He stood manifested alike in nature and man, especially man; yet these two were so related that man could not be understood save through nature, or nature perfected save in man. He, indeed, is the middle term that unites two worlds; on the one side he is rooted in the earth, on the other he is a free citizen of the spiritual and eternal; and in the unity of his natural and spiritual being we have a twofold revelation of God. The God we seek in nature is the same as we find in history,

---

[1] A. Werner, in Herzog-Plitt, "Real-Ency.," vol. v., p. 791.
[2] "Gott, einige Gespräche über Spinoza's System," Theol. Werke, viii.: cf. pp. 148, 176, 246 ff. (Müller's ed.). Herder set the example of the extravagant praise of Spinoza which became a sort of *mode* in the Romanticist School. Schleiermacher's famous tribute, "Dem Heiligen Spinoza," and Novalis' much-quoted "Gottertrunkener Mensch," are but echoes of him.

and the greatest person in history is the unique Son of God because the pre-eminent Son of man. The Divine element in our race is the culture of humanity; to it every great and good man, every lawgiver, discoverer, philosopher, poet, artist, every noble man in his rank and place, in the education of his family, in the fulfilment of his duties, by example, deed, and word—has contributed. Humanity is so great that he knows no nobler word to define and describe man than simply man himself. This was explicated in religion, which was like a holy triangle whose several angles were poetry, philosophy, and religion; or she was like a goddess, and these represented the priest of her temple, the prophets who revealed her truth, the providence that exhibited her actions. Religion, then, is the realized idea of humanity, Christ its highest embodiment, His religion the purest humanity reached in the purest way. Humanity is what He proved in His life and confirmed by His death. What His few words witness to is the truest humanity. To this religion of humanity He consecrated His life; in His heart it was written, "God is My Father, Father of all men, and all men are brothers."[1]

Herder emphasized, like Lessing, the distinction between the religion of Christ and the religion built on and round Christ; and in order to reach both it and Him his cry was, "Study the sources, back to the original documents."[2] He was pre-eminently a Biblical theologian; the Bible was to him Divine because it was the most human of books, written by men for man; and the man who would read it must be inspired by it, possessed of a new sense, a new feeling for the greatness of its contents. Lessing's dictum—revelation is education—he translates into this more concrete form: revela-

---

[1] " Ideen zur Philos. der Gesch. der Menschheit." Cf. bks. iv., v., xv., xvii., and "Von Religion, Lehrmeinungen und Gebräuchen," especially sect ii.

[2] " Briefe, das Studium der Theologie betreffende," pts. i. and ii. These letters are in the best sense modern: the first part concerns the study of the Old, the second of the New, Testament.

tion is the mother, reason is the daughter.[1] Neither can take the other's place, supersede or be superseded. Revelation, so construed, is of course neither co-extensive nor identical with a book, but represents the action of God in, on, and through man in history. It had, as it were, been immanent in man from the beginning; not indeed as compacted or articulated or finished knowledge, but as a form or faculty underlying all ideas of the reason, the feeling for the invisible in the visible, the one in the many, the cause in the effects. But to educe this feeling and translate natural into Divine revelation, God sends select spirits, men who as His organs become the guardian angels of our race, with their spirit outshining and illuminating centuries, with their hearts embracing nations, with their giant power exalting them even against their wills. The process which effected the revelation was inspiration, which was no frenzy or demoniac passion, but illumination, the reason so awakened and clarified that it can see God face to face, speak with the God it sees and tell man what it has seen and heard. The revelation that comes to man comes through him by exaltation of all his faculties. "He who formed the eye, must He blind it in order that we may see? The Spirit who breathed the breath of life into creation, and who quickens all our powers, shall He destroy them in order that He may in their place kindle in us light?" But what has so come to educate man by revealing the immanent God man must ever anew enter into, that he may be educated and exalted more and more. The Schoolman, the Churchman, the system-builder, have obscured, have even lost, the Bible; we must go back to it as men, read it as the book at once of the poetry and the religion of humanity. It is Oriental, and needs imagination and heart for its interpretation. For Anselm's "Believe, that you may know," Herder substituted "Love, that you may understand," for love quickens intelligence and appreciation. What men have taken as a prosaic

[1] "Briefe, das Studium der Theologie betreffende," pt. iii., Bre. 26, 27.

or matter-of-fact record of the manner of making the world, is a Divine poem, which introduces, as it were, the drama of God's action in history, educating man by means of special peoples. The actors in this drama are persons, but the force that moves them is God. To Herder sacred history is not true because it is miraculous, but because it is and works for good; yet the miracle has its place, "the three luminous points of a heavenly attestation of the Anointed of God" are the Baptism, the Transfiguration, and the Resurrection. Since he so conceived the history he was bound to consider the literature. His attitude to the Gospels was significant and characteristic. The oldest was Mark, an anticipation of our latest criticism, more instructive for its reasons than in itself; the second was the lost Gospel of the Hebrews, and these together were the two sources used by Luke; while our Matthew was a free translation of the Hebrew source with some omissions and additions. In John we had an echo of the older Gospels in a higher tone;[1] it was the Gospel of the spirit and the truth. Its speculative and constructive purpose makes John's the most permanent, the most modern, the most instructive of all the Gospels.

Our purpose is simply historical, and our expositions are too brief to warrant criticism. But Herder's defects and excellences are alike obvious. He enlarged the outlook of the theologian, filled theology with human interest by inviting it to occupy the whole field of human history, bound all its great ideas to great persons and tendencies. He lifted

[1] "Regel der Zusammenstimmung uns. Evang.," Werke: zur Rel. u. Theol., vol xii., pp. 54, 55. The discussions on the Gospels in vols. xi. and xii. are not without their interest even now. It is wonderful how Herder's literary insight kept him right when more skilled critics went astray. In all that pertains to external criticism he is long out of date, but in internal he is still suggestive. His position is: the Gospel existed before the Gospels; they are but a written echo of the oldest common tradition, and he sets himself through their internal characteristics and differences to explain their origin, order, and purpose. He has most affinity with John, whose use of miracles as "symbolical facts" was altogether to his mind.

religion out of the hands of the ecclesiastics, placed it above and beyond as well as within all the Churches, and made the ideas of God and man approximate and even touch. He vivified the Bible, changed it from a dead and closed to a living and open book; he compelled dogma to return to its source, and there dissolve its hardened terminology in order that it might crystallize into truer and more perfect forms. He showed that to approach Jesus through history was to make Him a more real, more living, more universal figure, and that to construe Him was to be forced to deal with the Gospels as histories and as literature. But his work was scattered, diffuse, thrown out in fragments and on occasions, was rhetorical, imaginative, and, where it touched theology, it was full of the intuitions of genius, but without the architectonic of the reason. Yet where he was weak the philosophy he did his best to criticize was strong; not, indeed, so much in itself as in what it caused to be.

§ III.—PHILOSOPHY AND HISTORICAL CRITICISM.

Philosophy exercised on theology a far more powerful influence than either literature or history. There has been since the Platonic period no more splendid or fruitful cycle in speculation than that which begins with Kant and ends with Hegel, or one more governed by religious ideas and problems. Each of the transcendental philosophies involved a speculative Christology, and it was the attempt to apply the last and greatest of these to the history of Christ that resulted in the birth of modern criticism. We must therefore come to it through them; not, indeed, with the minute exposition and illustrative detail that would be necessary were we writing a history of religious thought, but with the utmost possible brevity.

1. In England philosophy and theology have stood to each other in very different relations from those which they have sustained in Germany. Here they have affected one another

more as antagonists than as allies. Hobbes had no place for religion in his system save as a legalized superstition, whose source was the belief in witchcraft and in ghosts. Locke was the parent of English Rationalism and Deism; his empiricism could not but tempt men to strip religion of all its mysteries, in order that it might be reconciled to a reason emptied of all transcendental contents. Hume had but to use Locke as modified by Berkeley in order to evolve a scepticism so universal that it did not spare even the ego. The Mills, father and son, inherited their full share of the impotences and aversions of our insular empiricism; and though it has in Spencer changed its terminology, and even boldly essayed to become constructive, yet it remains at heart what it has ever been; for Agnosticism is just scepticism become too proud or too perverse to confess to its own real nature. And so our traditional philosophy has either attempted to explain religion out of existence as a congeries of illicit or fictitious ideas, or it has presented theology with the problem which produced the distinctive apologetics of the eighteenth century —how to get religion into a mind which has no religious constitution or contents. If men would be religious under such a philosophy it must be by the help of some external authority which supplies them with a faith and becomes the guarantee of its truth. The theological evolution of such philosophy was seen in Newman, the speculative in Hume and the Mills.

But the tendency in Germany has been exactly the opposite. It has started with the transcendental in mind, and has laboured to discover the transcendental in nature and history. The endeavour has been either to sublime philosophy into theology, or to make the two so interpenetrate as to become one; at least the goal of all its strivings has been the speculative and positive interpretation of our religious ideas and their historical forms. And, as a consequence, the ambition of the greater German philosophers has been to be speculative theologians, and of the theologians to be constructive philosophers ; in the one case the philosophical thought has become religious, in the other the religious has aspired to be philosophical. And so every speculative has had its corresponding theological tendency and crisis. Leibnitz and Wolff made the theologians of the eighteenth century ; were, indeed, themselves so eminent theologians that the philosophy of the one culminated in a *Théodicée*, of the other in a *Theologia Naturalis*. Kant created Röhr and Wegscheider ; Jacobi and Schelling contributed to form Schleiermacher ; Daub and Marheineke made theology Hegelian in matter and method ; Strauss was more a philosophical than a theological nursling ; while all the phases of the neo-Kantian and the neo-Hegelian philosophies have reproduced themselves in theology. Hence this relation of the speculative to the religious criticism must never be left out of sight.

2. The earlier phases of German Transcendentalism which begin with Kant and end with Fichte, hardly concern us. In the region of religion Kant could not be said to have been really waked out of his dogmatic slumbers. He remained where the eighteenth century placed him, content to conceive religion very much in the manner and form of the current Rationalism. Hence he did not directly accomplish in the religious sphere anything like the revolution he accomplished in the philosophical. The Critique of Pure Reason tended indeed to paralyze theology; according to it no real science of God was possible. The super-sensuous, as lying outside experience, lay outside knowledge. But the God the pure reason abolished the practical restored. Kant was an ethical Theist, God was the centre of his moral system, and his categorical imperative made Deity a new power for the conscience of his time. Religion became a mere vehicle of morality, the knowledge of our duties as Divine commands. The value of Christianity depended on the purity of its moral spirit, that again on the person of its Founder. His

historical character was important only so far as it exhibited a humanity, which, as realizing the Divine ideal of man, was well pleasing to God. This ideal was eternal, the only-begotten Son of God, no created thing, but proceeding out of His essence, His express image, and so in His mind as to be for ever before Him, His delight, on account of which He made and now loves the world. Since this ideal so lives in God, men did not create it, but it descended from heaven in order to incorporation in man, and in its union with us it may be represented as the Son of God in a state of humiliation. Such a descent and humiliation do not imply the occasional being of the ideal or the miraculous being of the man who embodies it, since the ideal is implicit in the moral nature of the normal man. But the man who does realize it becomes a type generative of a higher humanity by virtue both of the character He presents for our contemplation and the society of like-minded persons He institutes. Incarnation in the Kantian sense was simply the personalization of the moral ideal, and the Church a society to help towards its realization. Christ, by embodying this ideal, showed us what God had created man to be; and by founding the Church He created an ethical society, or kingdom of God, which was meant to train man for a reign of pure reason, and for a morality under a God who is all in all. Christ is, as it were, the symbol of religion thus embodied, duty apprehended as the Divine will;[1] and His Church is an institute for the cultivation of personal virtues, or for helping to create men of a similar type to its Founder. That exhausts His and its significance for man.

3. Jacobi marks a reaction against the Kantian criticism;

[1] For Kant's construction of Christianity see, in particular, his "Religion innerh. der Grenzen der blossen Vernunft." This may be described as a translation of Christian dogmatics into the terms of a moral Rationalism. It is curious to see how doctrines like Original Sin, Satisfaction, the Trinity, the Church, can, by deft manipulation, be made into the empirical modes and agencies by which a transcendental morality may be realized.

Fichte a development of its subjective idealism. For Jacobi belief, not knowledge, was ultimate.[1] God was reached by intuition, by the heart. The issues of the critical philosophy were escaped by denying the right of the reason to be either the critic or the architect of faith. Faith was saved by excluding reason from religion; yet not so much saved as lost. For Jacobi confessed that, while with the heart a Christian, he was with the understanding a heathen, and so swam between two streams, borne up by the one, but sinking continually in the other. Just because he shrank from every attempt to express or represent God, he could not allow any absolute worth to historical Christianity. The anthropomorphic was the idolatrous; Christ as the God-man was not so much the creator as the creation of faith. Whatever indeed could be regarded as Divine, and as such calculated to awaken man to virtue and a Divine life, might be represented under the image and by the name of Christ. But it was only the inner and ideal Christ that could be so used; any attempt to transfer such an idea to the historical was religious materialism, the humiliation of reason and morality by idolatry.[2]

4. Fichte's earlier system, egoistic Pantheism as it was, had this great worth for German religious thought—a pure and exalted morality was its centre and end. Man lived to be moral; the world existed as an arena on which his being could realize its moral ends. These implied a living and active moral order, which was the only God we needed or could conceive— an *ordo ordinans*, not an *ordo ordinatus*. Religion is faith in the reality of such an order or law. To do every moment what duty commands, without doubt or speculation as to consequences, was

---

[1] "Idealismus und Realismus," Werke, vol. ii., pp. 124 ff., especially pp. 156-163. Cf. "Einleitung," which is for Jacobi a rather sober exposition of his philosophical principles. But even more characteristic is his discussion, "Ueber eine Weissagung Lichtenberg's," the said prophecy being: "Our world will yet become so superfine that it will be quite as ridiculous to believe in God as it is now to believe in ghosts."

[2] "Von den Göttlich. Dingen," Werke, vol. iii., pp. 285, 286.

the true faith; its opposite was Atheism. From this doctrine it followed that, since the order was realized in and through men, then in the man who completely surrendered himself to the order, and embodied it, God Himself was individualized or incarnated, the Eternal Word became flesh. But Fichte later developed a more objective theistic idealism, which involved a corresponding change in his historical doctrine.[1] It was characteristic that for him John's was the only real Christ. Paul, who supplanted John, remained always half a Jew.[2] Now, the essential note of the Johannean Christ was this— God was conceived not as abstract or absolute being (*Sein*), but as conditioned (*Dasein*); consciousness, revelation, knowledge, was of the essence of God. The idea of a creative act is a fundamental error, the idea of the eternal consciousness the standard of all religious truth. John does not say, "In the beginning God created the heavens and the earth," but, "In the beginning was the Word, and the Word was God," *i.e.*, consciousness or revelation is eternal, and the eternal being of the Word is the eternal being of man, or of the incarnation of God, *i.e.*, the eternal unity of the Divine and human, which is the innermost essence of religion. In the person of Jesus, and in a manner belonging to no other man, the eternal appeared in time, God became incarnate; but the radical matter is the eternal significance, not the temporal appearance. Fichte's cardinal principle is, only the metaphysical, not the historical sense saves[3]; the latter may instruct the intellect, the former alone redeems the soul. And the metaphysical sense into which he construed the historical Person was this: in His real and whole being He is the greatest miracle in the whole course of creation. It is true that He has both appeared in time and been generated out of God from eternity; but mathematics and philosophy have also both alike issued out of God

[1] "Die Anweisung zum Seligen Leben," Werke, vol. v., pp. 476-491.
[2] "Die Grundzüge des gegenwart. Zeitalters," Werke, vol. vii., p. 99. Cf. vol. v., p. 477.
[3] Werke, vol. v., p. 485.

and been in God from eternity. And Christ's appearance was a necessity to the order of the world and of history; grant law to be in history, and within its being His was necessarily involved. Without Him the system could not be realized, or man attain his end as a religious being. Religion was conceived as the union of God and the soul, and Jesus as the great miracle in the field of humanity, because the first to realize this unity. By a Divine genius He was what He was—personalized religion. He was historically necessary, for all who attain unity with God do it through Him. In every one who does so the Logos becomes incarnate.

§ IV.—PHILOSOPHY AND THE INCARNATION: SCHELLING.

Philosophical interpretations and reconstructions of Christianity were thus familiar to German Transcendentalism even in its earlier and subjective phases. But they become much more characteristic of its later and objective. Religion, as the highest manifestation of spirit, became its final problem. Schelling inaugurated the change, led philosophy from subject to object, from mind to nature, from knowing to being. He passed through so many phases that it is difficult to seize and exhibit his precise significance for our history. But his changes only increase his importance, show philosophy becoming ever more conscious of mind as the root of the universe, of religion as an essential characteristic and product of spirit. For us two things are important: first, his doctrine of the Absolute, and his consequent notion of history; and, secondly, the way in which he combined these into a speculative construction of historical Christianity. The first involved a new conception of God and the world and their relation to each other. His idea of the absolute was, on the negative side, a doctrine of indifference, denial of the antithesis between subject and object; on the positive side it was a doctrine of identity, the affirmation that whatever is, is within, not without, the Absolute. It was thus not abstract, dead, but concrete, living. Nature and spirit, like Spinoza's modes of expansion and thought, were the co-ordinate forms in which the Absolute Identity appeared; they were by a ceaseless self-generation or birth of the Divine Essence. History, as the field in which spirit is revealed and realized, becomes the revelation and realization of God. By this idea two things seemed to be accomplished; the dualism which had been the basis of the eighteenth-century thought, and which survived in the antithesis of the pure and practical reason with Kant, was overcome; and religion ceased to be confined to the moral relations of man and God, and, as posited in their respective natures, was necessarily identical and co-extensive with their reasoned co-existence.

From this point of view Schelling attempted a speculative construction of Christianity, which was destined to exercise extraordinary influence on the most dissimilar phases and schools of thought—critical, catholic, and evangelical.[1] Theology he conceived as "the highest synthesis of philosophical and historical knowledge," and its positive function was "the historical construction of Christianity." The fundamental characteristic of Christianity was that it represented the universe as history, as a moral kingdom, and so stood in antithesis to the ancient religions: in other words, they knew

[1] "Die Methode des academischen Studiums," Vorlesn., viii. and ix.; Werke, vol. v., pp. 286-305. Schelling's construction affected Strauss through Hegel; through Hegel and Schleiermacher, Moehler and the Catholic Hegelians, the former elaborating it into his doctrine of the Church as a continued incarnation; through Moehler it influenced the later Anglicans; and in the latest phase of the Anglican theology, which has been, of all modern theologies, the most changeful, it has, developed by the partially assimilated philosophy of Green, assumed for a while a more pronounced, though not a very coherent, form. Its basis is Pantheistic; its history properly begins with Spinoza. It is significant that just where neo-Platonism agrees with German Transcendentalism it inclines to a similar theory, which shows its presence in a few sporadic texts in certain Alexandrian Fathers.

a Fate; it knows a Providence. In Hellenism nature revealed God, but in Christianity man revealed Him; and the two systems were related as nature and spirit. As the sphere of nature is space, so the field of history is time, and every particular element or force (moment) of time is the revelation of a particular side of God, in every one of which He is absolute. In nature God is, as it were, exoteric—the ideal appears through another than itself; but in the ideal world, therefore pre-eminently in history, He lays aside the veil, appears in His own proper quality as spirit, and His kingdom comes. Now the difference of the natural and historical is seen in their supreme acts. Greek religion was essentially the apotheosis of nature, but the Christian is the incarnation of God; and each result is reached by a reverse process: Hellenism deified nature and placed man on its summit; but Christianity, as it were, humanized God. By apotheosis man is magnified; but by incarnation the finite, in the very act and moment as it were of its highest dignity, is sacrificed, overcome by being freely and personally surrendered and reconciled to the Infinite. These two ideas distinguish the old world and the new. "The first idea of Christianity is necessarily the incarnated God, Christ as apex and end of the ancient world of the gods." But while the idea has an historical beginning, embodiment in a single Person, yet it represents an eternal and universal truth, and must be construed as such. What He expresses has its symbolic and ideal being continued in the Church, but its real or essential in collective man. Round its idea the Church has allowed a mythology to gather, which may have been needed as a body for the preservation of the soul—viz., the idea; but philosophy translates the empirical form into this universal truth: "The Eternal Son of God, born from the essence of the Father of all things, is the finite itself as it exists in the eternal intuition of God, appearing as a suffering God, subjected to the fatalities of time; and this God, in the moment of His appearance in Christ, ends the world of finitude and opens that of infinitude, or of the dominion of the Spirit."[1] The universalism of this truth is confirmed by the presence of the idea in religions before and without the Christian, yet in forms that may be termed immanent—as really present, though imperfectly realized—and prophetic, as looking towards a more perfect realization. And as universal it is eternal, and so independent of all questions as to whether certain books be genuine or spurious, or certain histories are real or imagined. Christianity, as speculative and transcendental, must never be confounded with a series of empirical facts.

Schelling six years later introduced some modifying elements into his speculative construction, laying a new emphasis on the need of redeeming personal freedom from personal evil.[2] The spirit has its Iliad, its tale of struggle with brutal and natural forces, and then its Odyssey, when out of its painful wanderings it returns to the Infinite. This is accomplished by a double act: on the one side, of revelation—God shows His heart, which is love; on the other side, of discovery—man sees it, and surrenders freely his particular to the universal will. But in order to this a Mediator in human form is necessary. "For only the personal can heal the personal, and God must become man in order that man may come again to God."[3] He becomes man in the archetypal Divine Man, who as in the beginning with God is by His nature the highest peak or apex of the Divine revelation. By this Man nature is transfigured to spirit and God becomes a personal and intelligent Being. But who is this archetypal Man? It can only be Christ, but Christ conceived not as an individual, but as universal, ideal man; what is true only of collective humanity cannot be limited to

---

[1] Werke, vol. v., p. 294.
[2] "Philos. Untersuchungen üb. das Wesen der menschl. Freiheit," Werke, vol. vii., pp. 331 ff.
[3] *Ibid.*, p. 380.

the historical individual, though without this individual the truth could not have come to be or to be known. To conceive and embrace the ideal principle is to be incorporated with Christ, to be of His community, realizing His unity of nature and spirit, participant, as it were, in His incarnation. His history thus ceases to be single and empirical, and becomes universal, the history of a Divine Spirit so incorporating itself with humanity as to organize it into a great body whose head is Christ. History conceived from this point becomes in consequence of Christ, as it were, the progressive incarnation of God.

The theory of the *Freiheitslehre* was by no means Schelling's last endeavour in this direction, and while growing more mystical he also grew more Biblical. As his thought ripened the personal element became more essential to religion, and so he conceived in a more natural way the historical side of Christianity. He persisted indeed in construing religious doctrines as philosophical principles, and in treating Christianity as the exoteric form of his esoteric transcendental theosophy. But his tendency remained throughout the same. God and man were not so conceived as to exclude each other. Divine life was seen active everywhere. Providence ruled human history. Nature and man were penetrated with God. Religion was not opposed to morality, or made a lower and more childish form of it, but treated as the most splendid and perfect flower of the human spirit. It was not given to Schelling either in his brilliant youth or in his sober age to read the riddle of the universe, but certainly he was one of the men who have helped man nearer to it.

§ V.—PHILOSOPHY AND HISTORICAL CHRISTIANITY: HEGEL.

But now we come to the man and the philosophy which were by far the greatest formative and reformative forces in theology. It were folly to attempt to interpret Hegel in a paragraph or two; but it were still greater folly to attempt to understand modern movements in theology without him, especially those that circle round the history and person of Christ. It is certain at least that without him we should never have had the "Leben Jesu" of Strauss, and without it all our modern developments in theology would have been different. There may be room for doubt as to whether Strauss understood Hegel, or made a logical application of his principles, but there can be none as to his having learned in the school of Hegel the principles he attempted to apply. The Hegelians of the right and centre tried to disown the distinguished member of the left whose revolutionary radicalism threatened the school with disgrace and dissolution, but he defied their efforts and made good his claim to rank as a representative, though the side he represented was almost the antipodes of theirs. Strauss was, as it were, the Frankenstein of the Hegelian philosophy. The master was sacrificed to the disciple in fear rather than in fairness, and has not even yet emerged from the eclipse caused by the man that seemed his most characteristic child.

With Hegel's philosophy as a whole we have here no concern, only with its construction of the person and history of Christ. This, indeed, was fundamental to it, of its very essence, and may be said to hold within it every element distinctive of the system as a philosophy both of being and of history. By a most fateful evolution, the rock on which the school was shipwrecked was exactly the point which the master most avoided; at least, where his speech became most obscure and oracular. The point which he laboriously emphasized, the fact and function of incarnation, elicited little but agreement and approbation; the point he touched most delicately, the relation of the idea and fact of incarnation to the historical Jesus, occasioned the storms amid which the school may be said to have perished. The course of this fateful but inevitable evolution is what we have to trace.

While the Hegelian philosophy was pre-eminently a philosophy of history, taken, in the widest sense, as comprehensive of nature and man, with all his institutions and achievements, yet it was not in the strict and proper sense a critical philosophy. Hegel's was not a critical mind; it was too constructive, loved large and synthetic views too much to appreciate easily the analytical and dissolving processes of criticism. He had little sympathy with the Homeric dissertations of Wolf, or with Niebuhr's destructive and constructive feats in Roman history. His dialectical process could be better illustrated by the main factors and general tendencies of history than by minute yet often revolutionary inquiries into its details. His system, as an absolute as distinguished from a subjective idealism, easily tended to become a mere theory of the real, a philosophy that justified what was by finding a sufficient reason for it. This meant that at root it was an optimism, not emotional like Leibnitz', but intellectual, using the language of thought rather than of the imagination or the heart. Hence Hegel did not say, "This is the best of all possible worlds"; but he said, "What is real is rational, and what is rational is real." Yet, unless carefully guarded, the latter implies a more unqualified optimism than the former, for it does not apologize for evil by pleading the necessity that belongs to all created and therefore limited and imperfect being, but it boldly justifies evil by turning the actual into the rational. Of course, this did not happen in Hegel's own hands, but it represented a tendency in his school. What did happen in his hands, however, was that his system became more constructive or interpretative of history than critical of historical facts. He was critical enough of criticism and critics, but not of the literature and phenomena they handled. His function was to explain these by relating them to his system, making them parts of a whole, not by dealing with them specifically and looking at his system from the standpoint they supplied. Applied to our question this meant two things : (1) the Christianity he construed was the traditional, as it lived in the Scriptures, the creeds, and the institutions of the Church he knew ; and (2) he looked at it through his philosophy and as it affected his philosophy ; he did not look at his philosophy through it and at it as affected by his philosophy. It was when men of more purely theological interests and training came to do this that the revolt and revolution happened.

But this represents only a general attitude and tendency, not the determinative doctrines of the philosophy. These touched our question at two points, a formal and a material : the one was connected with the Hegelian dialectic, or theory of knowing ; the other with the metaphysic, or theory of being. Hegel's doctrine as to the process and conditions, or method and nature, of knowledge determined his notion of religion. He did not, like Schelling, storm and reach the Absolute by intuition or immediate knowledge—this, Hegel said, was to begin with an Absolute that was shot, as it were, out of a pistol ; but he reached it by a reasoned process which exhibited the progress of the consciousness from sensuous perception to pure knowledge—a progress governed by thought in the successive phases or stages of its evolution. Nor did he, like Schleiermacher, seek the roots of religion in feeling, but in thought. The object of religion, as of philosophy, was eternal truth, God, and nothing but God, and the explication of God. They were identical as to matter, differed only as to form. God existed to philosophy as a notion, as an object of pure thought in the form of thought, but to religion as an idea or figurate conception—*i.e.*, thought still clothed in a sensuous form. This Hegelian distinction must here be recognized. Unless it be understood subsequent discussions and expositions will be unintelligible. Strauss selected this distinction as the most important point for theology in the Hegelian system. The notion (*Begriff*) is the highest form of thought, the mind's grasp or comprehension of an object in its totality, as it exists in and for itself. The idea (*Vorstellung*) is thought in a picture, a general conceived in an individual, the imperishable in a transient vehicle, the boundless and eternal in the conditions of space and time. The notion seizes the truth as it is in itself, above the limits and forms of the senses; but in the idea thought is still bound in the fetters of the sensuous, floats in continual unrest between perception and pure thought. What the notion contains in the unity and totality of its elements the idea exhibits only relatively and subjectively, on this or that side, and under given relations. The one is but a reflexion in which the pure light, which is the element of the other, appears in the most varied colours. Now, the Hegelian distinction between these forms of thought constitutes the Hegelian distinction between philosophy and religion. The matter was in each case the same; the forms under which it was conceived alone differed. Whether the difference in form did not involve an essential difference in matter, is a question that need not here be discussed. Enough to know there was for Hegel, as for Homer, one speech for the gods, another for men. Religion was the form in which truth existed for mankind, a lantern here of horn, there of glass, in which beams of the eternal light were carried, making humanity, even in its dark course, conscious of the right way.

Now, this formal involved the material question. Philosophy and religion were formally different, but materially identical: philosophy was religion in the form of thought, with all its truths reasoned, articulated, explicated; religion was philosophy in the form of the idea, with all its truths expressed in language, customs, and institutions, more or less sensuous, symbolical, figurative. Religions differ as to the measure or degree in which they hold or embody the truth, but the Christian stands distinguished from all others as the absolute religion—*i.e.*, one whose substance or contents agree with those of the absolute philosophy, needing, in order to become it, only to be translated into the terms of the notion. Now, the point where their coincidence and material identity becomes most apparent is as regards their common basis or ultimate object—the Absolute of philosophy is the God of religion. The Christian religion was nothing but the realization or embodied activity of the Christian doctrine of the Godhead, while the philosophy was nothing but the dialectical explication of the Absolute ; nature and man were but forms and results of its self-manifestation. As the Absolute and the Godhead differed in name but agreed in essence, so did the religion and the philosophy. Hegel's Absolute was not, like Schelling's, indifference or identity— that, he said, was but the night in which all cows look black ; but it was a process, a development, by and out of which all difference was evolved. In the place of Spinoza's Infinite Substance he set the Infinite Subject, and instead of its two mechanically opposed attributes, extension and thought, and its transient modes, he emphasized the eternal movement of the Subject, the process by which it died that it might live, as it were sacrificing its infinitude to finitude, dissolving its abstract and universal in order to concrete and particular being, yet ever only that it might return out of the finite and the particular into the infinite and universal again, though as articulated and reconciled consciousness. Or, to express it otherwise, the Absolute as thought must in thinking distinguish Himself from Himself, make Himself to Himself an object, must as it were limit and objectify Himself, but only that He may in this form return to Himself—*i.e.*, know Himself as thus distinguished and objectified as identical with Himself.

But this highest truth in philosophy is only the reasoned counterpart of the highest truth in religion—the Godhead or Trinity.[1] That doctrine was at once the whole substance or

[1] "Philosophie der Religion," Werke, vol. xii., p. 184. For Hegel's own exposition of his doctrine see pp. 177-288, and "Phaenomenologie des

essence of religion, and a complete philosophy of God and the world. The Absolute as pure being and pure thought is the Father; it belongs to His being, to His very essence, to be Creator; thought to be thought must posit an object, must beget another; spirit as spirit must reveal itself, revelation is of its essence, and the process of positing another, of revealing self, is eternal. Without this process thought would not be thought; apart from the eternal generation, God would not be God. What is posited, generated, sublated, is the Son: God in eternally distinguishing Himself from Himself eternally begets Himself as His Son. This Son is the world of finitude existing in distinction and difference from the Infinite, yet remaining identical with it. But what is thus differentiated ever struggles towards return and reconciliation, and this achieved the difference is overcome, which means that Spirit knows itself one with the Eternal, and this Spirit is the Holy Ghost. In the Godhead the whole history of the universe is thus subsumed; the Father is God as He exists in and for Himself, in eternity; the Son is God as He exists in the form of another, in time, separated in order that He may be reconciled; the Spirit is the other returned into oneness, the particular reconciled with the universal. The process by which the Absolute is evolved into the relative and the relative returns, reconciled, into the bosom of the Absolute, represents at once the life of God and the history of the universe. The former is the latter known and read from within; the latter is the former unfolded, explicated, understood from without. By the doctrine of the Godhead God and the world are so combined that without the world

---

Geistes," Werke, vol. ii., pp. 561 ff. Professor Seth ("Hegelianism and Personality," p. 165) seems to go too far when he says: "Hegel's speculative Trinity is, in fact, simply the rehabilitation of that ancient philosopheme which, at the end of the period of enlightenment, Lessing had laid his vivifying hand upon, and made a present of to the new German philosophy." This is to overlook the genetic development of the philosophy and certain radical distinctions in the two doctrines.

there could be no God, and in all the world God is and acts; its history is but the process by which He distinguishes Himself from Himself and reconciles Himself to Himself.

But now this highly speculative construction, which has in it elements of the profoundest truth and insight, had to be applied. The most specific point of application was also the most dangerous: the Godhead was so construed as to involve incarnation, but the incarnation it involved was universal, while the Christian was particular, concerned a specific historical Person. Nothing indeed could be more explicit than Hegel's teaching as to the necessity and actuality of incarnation; it was of the very essence or content alike of his philosophy and of the absolute religion. By it the unity of the Divine and human natures was revealed; each faced the other, not as opposites, but as cognates, related as universal and particular, not as isolated and mechanically separated atoms. Man was the son, the other or object existing in separateness and distinction from the Subject. But now in order to bring this idea of a racial or universal incarnation into relation with the Christian, and specifically with the person of Christ, Hegel called another idea into court—atonement or reconciliation. Man is divided from God, and needs to be lifted from his state of division to one of union. His empirical being is one of contradiction with his ideal, and what he needs is to lose the empirical and realize the ideal, or become consciously one with God. This essential unity must be presented to the consciousness or interpreted to the experience of man by a manifest fact or sensuous reality in order that he may through knowledge attain to union. In other words, in order to save man from his state of division and estrangement, God must "in an objective manner" enter this empirical or sensuous present as man's equal or fellow, and so cause it to appear—and appearance is always for another, and the other is here the Church or the society of faith—that the Divine and the human natures are not in themselves different, but really alike, akin, able to be in the unity of a person.[1] So far good; but Hegel does not proceed to prove that a given Individual knew Himself, while man, essentially one with God; on the contrary, what he explains is: how the faith in the God-manhood has arisen—*i.e.*, what he emphasizes is the origin and reality of the faith in the Incarnation, what he does not emphasize is that a given historical Person was the conscious, incarnate God. He argues that the Incarnation has been and is because (1) it is the faith of the world; (2) the Spirit as a self-consciousness, *i.e.* as a real man, is there, a manifest existence; (3) He exists to immediate certitude; and (4) the believing consciousness sees and feels and hears His Deity. The remarkable thing is the relation of the faith to the Person rather than the Person to the faith. Christ through death became the God-man in the faith of the Church, and His history was written by those who held this faith and upon whom the Spirit had been poured out. The main thing was the consciousness not of the historical Christ, but of those who held Him to be the God-man.

The speculative construction was easy; its conciliation with historical fact was difficult. Hegel evaded the difficulty by dealing with the faith as authenticating the fact rather than with the fact as creating and justifying the faith. The evasion, with all that it involved, was not immediately seen; theologians were more disposed to be appreciative than to be critical. The new system widened, enriched, magnified, fertilized, the old theology; every dogma seemed as if possessed of a new spirit, as if it were illumined and transfigured by having become the abode of Deity. The doctrine of incarnation as now construed brought God out of His abstract and inaccessible solitude and made Him the most concrete and living of beings; emphasized His nature as spirit, love, activity; dissolved His being as a mere external Deity, whose home was the other side of nature and man and

[1] Werke, vol. xii., pp. 238-251; vol. ii., pp. 586-593.

history, and made Him present always and everywhere, in every moment of time and in every soul of man; lifted man at once out of the proud yet empty self-sufficiency in which the older philosophers had placed him, and out of the dust into which the older theologies had cast him, and made him a veritable son of God, like in nature to the God whose son he was, created for Him as created by Him, with all nature and all history so organized and directed as to impel him towards the God who was his end and home. It was small marvel that the theologians were grateful for ideas that so vivified theology. They were delighted to discover that doctrines translated into the language of the notion became high philosophical truths. Men like Marheineke discovered that orthodox formulæ as to the *homoousion* and the *agennesia* were as golden vessels of eternal truths ministered by consecrated hands; they described Sabellianism as a relapse into Judaism, Arianism as a return to heathenism, and the doctrine of Athanasius as the first speculative development of Christian truth. His theology was but absolute idealism in an empirical form; it had only to be translated into the notional form to be a system of reasoned truth. Systems of Dogmatic adopted the new terminology, and distributed their matter in three divisions: the kingdom of the Father, or God, existing in Himself; the kingdom of the Son, or God objectified, creating, revealing Himself, incarnating Himself, and so redeeming man; and the kingdom of the Spirit, or God in renewed man or the Church as returned into Himself. God became the essence of man, man the actuality of God. Theology was happy at the supreme good fortune that had come to her, her ability to speak in her own tongue the very identical thoughts of her old enemy. A beautiful and hopeful day of peace had dawned on the field of ancient strife. "The old prophecy of the patriarchs of modern philosophy appeared on the point of fulfilment, not only as regards religion in general, but Christianity in particular. A limit seemed set to the long feud between philosophy and religion by the alliance of the two houses, and the Hegelian system was saluted as the child of peace and of the promise, with whom a new order of things was to begin, when the wolf should dwell with the lamb, and the leopard lie down with the kid. Wisdom, the proud heatheness, humbly submitted to baptism, and made a Christian confession of faith; while faith, on her side, did not hesitate to certify that Wisdom had become wholly Christian."[1]

§ VI.—Historical Criticism and Theology: Schleiermacher.

But the critical defects of the Hegelian theology could not escape notice and accentuation. Its aversion to criticism on the one hand, and on the other its reluctance to bring its conception of the Incarnation into direct relation with the history and historical person of Jesus, were, though not purposely or explicitly, forced into prominence by one as eminent in theology as Hegel was in philosophy. Schleiermacher had suffered from Hegel's not very merciful or just criticism, but no other man had so quickened and modified religious thought in Germany in all its phases—speculative, critical, ethical, ecclesiastical. He made and ruled for many years from his professor's chair the theological mind of the country, attracted and instructed by his pulpit the educated classes of Berlin, and exercised through the press a commanding influence on many sections of thought. He happily escaped the two influences dominant in his early years—French Illuminism in the State, shallow Rationalism in the Church. He was born of Calvinistic parents, educated among the Moravians, and so knew religion on both its evangelical and emotional or pietistic sides. It developed, softened, inspired his always susceptible nature, but it did not save him

[1] Strauss, "Glaubenslehre," vol. i., pp. 1, 2.

from doubt, rather stimulated the critical side of his intellect. But it helped him by enlisting his heart on the side of religion to fight his scepticism, and made him peculiarly susceptible to the just budding enthusiasm of the Romanticists. He seemed for a while to become the theological spokesman of the school, the apologist of intense and emotional religion against arid Deism, especially as the Schlegels, Novalis, and Tieck helped to feed the fire and fancy that were in him; but he was too many-sided to be a scholar in any one school. He was a philosopher, a learner from Jacobi, Fichte, and Schelling, and an enthusiastic student of Plato. He was a critic, open in mind to the new methods that were breathing the breath of life into classical studies and rediscovering the ancient world. And his hand was in each department the hand of a master. Speculative, theological, critical, philological, ethical treatises came from his fluent pen, each original, suggestive, penetrative in matter, and fascinating in form. And besides his own proper work he taught, as Strauss has happily said, "Plato to speak in German, or his German readers to think in Greek."[1]

Schleiermacher helped to create the new epoch in theology. In the conflict between Rationalism and Supernaturalism he lifted the old ground from beneath their feet, and raised issues at once deeper and higher. He took his stand on religion, and saved it from friends and enemies alike. He resolved it into a thing essentially human, necessary to man. Religion was not a thought or volition, the creation of the reason or the conscience, metaphysics or ethics, conduct or cultus, but a feeling—the feeling, direct, intuitive, of absolute dependence. It was the immediate consciousness of the being of everything finite in the Infinite and through the Infinite, of everything temporal in the Eternal and through the Eternal; it was to feel amid all becoming and change, amid all action and

---

[1] Strauss, "Characteristiken und Kritiken," p. 6.

suffering, our very life as life only as it was in and through God.[1] With the nature of God it had no concern; speculation concerning Him might be philosophy or theology, but was not religion. But the feeling, as it was of dependence, could not live in isolation; the universe was in ceaseless activity, revealing itself to us and in us every moment; and to be moved by what we thus experienced and felt, not as separate units, but as parts of a whole, conditioned and supplemented by all the rest, was religion.[2] Feeling then, while the most individual and arbitrary of things, was yet, because man was at once a natural and social being, so interpreted, as to involve both a personal and collective consciousness, a feeling of dependence on an Infinite manifested at once through nature, man, and society.[3] But while this was the generic notion of religion, specific religions owed their being to some creative idea embodied in some creative person, a fundamental faith realized in a fundamental fact; their founders were persons who so realized a new and characteristic consciousness of God as to create societies in order to its propagation. Such religions were either sensuous or teleological: the sensuous, which had types in Hellenism and Islam, were religions which subordinated the moral and active emotions to the natural; but the teleological, which included Judaism and Christianity, subordinated the natural emotions to the moral and active. Of the specifically Christian consciousness Christ was the Creator; it owed its being to Him; and as He was necessary to its origin, He was no less necessary to its continuance.[4] His was an absolutely perfect consciousness, expressive of an absolutely perfect relation to God, which meant an absolutely full abode of God in Him; and so the more this consciousness, which lived in the society

---

[1] "Ueber die Religion," Werke: zur Theol., vol. i, pp. 184, 185.
[2] *Ibid.*, p. 193.
[3] *Ibid.*, p. 207. But in particular Rede V.
[4] "Glaubenslehre," §§ 7-11.

and was propagated by it, became man's, the more perfect would both the man and his religion be.

Now, it is from this point of view that we must understand Schleiermacher's construction both of the person and the history of Christ. He did not, like Hegel, come to the question from a speculative system in order to incorporate the religion with his philosophy and translate it into its terms; but he came to it from the existence and the experience of the religious person and society, in order the better to interpret the source or cause of their religious being. They seem to have this point in common: Hegel approached Christ through the faith of the Church and Schleiermacher through what he termed the Christian consciousness. But this apparent agreement veiled a deep difference: faith was to Hegel something intellectual, objective, and formulated; while consciousness was to Schleiermacher at once moral and emotional, subjective, experienced, as it were the concrete soul of the man and the society, and its history. Then once Hegel had the faith he had no need for the Person—indeed, He was to him only a growing burden which could be best got rid of by being forgotten; but Schleiermacher's need for the Person grew with his interpretation of the consciousness— without Him it could not be, nor any of its phenomena be explained or maintained. His method may be described as one of correlation and comparison; the consciousness was an effect, the Person the cause, and so he analyzed the elements and motives of the consciousness that he might discover the forces by which they were caused. The primary elements were two—sin and redemption, or guilt and grace: sin belonged to the consciousness of our collective natural being, redemption or grace to the consciousness of our renewed life. The creator of this latter was Christ; through the community with God which He established the faith in His Godhead lived.[1] In Him activity and dignity are

[1] "Glaubenslehre," §§ 91-105.

inseparable; it were vain to attribute to the Redeemer a higher dignity than the activity ascribed to Him warrants or demands, but all it does warrant must be ascribed. Well, then, in the collective life of the society redemption is worked by the sinless perfection of Jesus; this perfection He had and has communicated, His consciousness having become, as it were, communicable, transmissible, heritable. His character, therefore, is archetypal, the original of a type He not only created, but perpetuates. If neither the Church as a whole nor any single member realizes His sinlessness, still the very abiding of the consciousness of the historical Archetype, with the ever-renewed impulses to good and renewal it creates, is witness to its being and its power. The archetypal Person has thus become an ever-operating moral cause; His transcendental yet historical being, which created His society, has become an immanent yet ever-active, impulsive, and propulsive being maintaining His society. Whence came His sinlessness? It could not possibly come out of sinful mankind, could not therefore have a natural source,—must, then, have had a supernatural, been due to a creative act of God. And as His sinlessness was not simply a thing of His special nature, but a permanent possession, expressed in His whole character and all His conduct, then the creative power must have continued; His consciousness was ever full of God, God possessed Him without measure, in Him God had literal being. But did this not take from Him all identity with man? Nay, it made Him the normal man; for sin is against the essence of man, and he was made to be a home of God. The personality of Jesus, then, means that the innermost force, whence all His activity proceeded, was the being of God in Him, a Divine indwelling so real that His humanity formed only an organism for its operation and realization. His consciousness of God was therefore absolute and perfect, making Him the completion of the old and the beginning of the new creation—a real man, yet so penetrated and possessed of Deity that He became, as it were, in His own right a creator of a race or society which He was to fill as full of Himself as He was of God, in order to the realization of God's kingdom on the earth.

Schleiermacher's theology was thus essentially a Christology, a theory as to the necessity of the historical person of Jesus to the being of the Christian religion. It was God, man, and history interpreted through Him. But its distinctive feature was its starting-point and standard of interpretation, the Christian consciousness. This was, indeed, not an individual or arbitrary consciousness, but one collective and normal, the note of the new humanity as distinguished from the old, with its naturalism and sinfulness. But this starting- and standing-point involved important consequences. Christ was approached through the Church, yet not the Church of tradition or formulated dogmas or of fixed institutions, but of living experience, of loving and exercised reason, of free inquiry and reverent thought. Then the qualities most essential to Him were those most necessary to the being of the consciousness of a society redeemed by His sinlessness from its sin. As a consequence the emphasis did not fall on the attributes and acts which the old apologetic and the older dogmatic had made so essential to His person and so demonstrative of His divinity—the miracles, the supernatural conception, the Resurrection, the Ascension; but it fell upon what was ethical, spiritual, religious in Him—His sinlessness, His archetypal character, His absolute consciousness of God. These gave to Him His pre-eminence, His peculiar significance. His historical being bound Him to time, His archetypal nature and character to eternity. Through the former only could His society—*i.e.*, His religion—be explained; through the latter only could His nature, reason, end, be determined. It was characteristic that, while the speech of the Hegelian School was all of the God-man, Schleiermacher's was all of the Redeemer. In his religious system Jesus held the same place as God held in the practical system of Kant: in the one case God was a necessity to the conscience, in the other Jesus was a necessity to the consciousness; but while the former had all the severity of an inflexible moral law, the latter had all the beauty and all the grace of the Redeemer and Saviour of mankind.

CHAPTER II.

PHILOSOPHICAL CRITICISM AND THE HISTORY OF JESUS.

SO far, then, all the Christologies passed in review have had one quality in common: they were speculative and, in a sense, *à priori*. They reasoned upwards, either from an abstract philosophy or a concrete society, to a doctrine of the creative personality or fundamental fact; they did not begin with the history, construe the Person through it, and then work their way downwards to the philosophy or the society. Schleiermacher's method, though it seemed historical, was really the most subjective of all; he carried from the idealized consciousness an ideal Christ back into the Gospels, and then by its help performed a critical process which preserved all that was necessary to his ideal and surrendered all that seemed superfluous. While the speculative Christology had been so active, historical and literary criticism had been almost, though not altogether, idle. In the literary field various notable theories had indeed been propounded. Eichhorn had shown a more excellent way than was known to the old harmonistic by his hypothesis of an *Urevangelium*, or primal Gospel, which, already existing in various recensions, had been worked up by our Synoptists. Griesbach had attempted to explain Mark as a series of excerpts from Matthew and Luke, while Hug accepted the canonical as the chronological order, and conceived the later as making use of the earlier Evangelists. Gieseler had found the common source in oral tradition, and Schleiermacher himself had turned the oral into written sources, which the three Synoptists had in different orders connected and arranged. The criticism of the Fourth Gospel had been begun by Vogel, and Bretschneider's "Probabilia" had definitely raised the question of its authenticity. But the speculative Christology made its appeal to John, and would not argue the question of his authorship. His Christ was its Christ: Herder, Fichte, Schelling, Hegel, Schleiermacher, all agreed with Luther that the fourth was the golden Gospel, the very temple and pillar of the truth. And speculation was as independent of history as of criticism. While Schleiermacher had in 1821 in Berlin begun to lecture on the Life of Jesus, and Hase in 1823 in Tübingen and in 1828 in Leipzig had done the same, yet the only published works were Hase's "Handbuch" and Paulus' "Leben Jesu." As to the latter, its hard Rationalism—often more grotesque in its prosaic matter-of-factness than Romanticism in its most whimsical fantasies—has insight and enlightenment for no human soul. One of the driest of books, it has yet come to be one of the most amusing, illustrating the miraculous vagaries of an exegesis that must discover authentic facts, but can allow nothing supernatural in the evangelical narratives. It is written with the double purpose of proving that in the Gospels all the history is real, but all the miracles false, which means that for every miracle there is a natural explanation, though the explanation is often more remarkable than the miracle. The marvel is that any one should have thought the history under such conditions worth saving or Jesus a person deserving either of belief or reverence. Well said Schleiermacher, years indeed before Paulus published his "Leben": "How a Jewish Rabbi of philanthropic mind and somewhat Socratic morals, with a few miracles, or at least what others took for such, and the ability to utter some clever gnomes and parables—how One who was this and nothing more, and who, were He only this, were not fit to stand before Moses or Mohammed, could have caused such an effect as a new religion and Church,—to be able to conceive how this were possible one must first take leave of his senses!"

§ I.—STRAUSS AND HIS MASTERS.

Let us see, then, how matters stood : there were several large and bold Christologies, but no corresponding criticism of the Gospels or study of their history. There were highly abstruse yet comprehensive doctrines of the Incarnation, but no fundamental inquiry into the mind or life of the historical Person who was said to have revealed or realized it. The Redeemer was elaborately constructed out of the Christian consciousness, and the picture of Him in the sources adapted to this ideal rather than the ideal made and fashioned according to the sources. In one respect this state of matters was not exceptional ; on the contrary, it might be described as normal. In England the old dogmatic was quite as remote from historical study of the historical Person, and the new Anglo-Catholics were still more remote ; indeed, as regards the latter, there is nothing so startling in their early literature as the absence of all, not to say scientific, but even intelligent, study of the Scriptures, and especially of the creative Personality of the faith. Measured by such standards the German mind was at this period fruitfully active in this field. But what made the state of things extraordinary and unstable was the audacity of so much speculative construction without any correlative research or inquiry into the history of the Person construed. The inquiry was bound to come, and was no less bound when it did come to be of a revolutionary character. The man who opened it was David Friedrich Strauss. He had come to Berlin to study philosophy and theology under the two great masters, who from difference of nature, as well as of doctrine and method, cordially inter-despised each other. They, with scholars almost their equals, lectured in the University : Hegel

[1] "Reden üb. Rel.," v., note 14.

now massive, majestic, like a swollen river running between bank and bank and bearing down whatever stood in its course, and now strung, tense, like a charged catapult shooting out a criticism in a metaphor or an argument in a sentence that went straight and strong through any defensive armour; Schleiermacher nimble, subtle, graceful, like the streamlet that leaps as it runs, making beauty for the eye and music for the ear. The schools divided the city, emulation quickened thought. Collision sharpened their antitheses, contact deepened their contrasts. Marheineke applied absolute Idealism to theology, interpreted religious doctrines into their notional form, made the person of Jesus the point where the unity of God and man, the Divine essence in its human realization, became visible, and so manipulated idea and notion that the Augsburg Confession and the new philosophy, Luther's catechism and Hegel's logic were different only as to form, but were as to matter the same. Neander, the last of the Fathers, as his disciples loved to call him, childlike, erudite, wise by his very unworldliness, a Protestant monk or saint,[1] but no ascetic, embodied in himself and applied to Church history what, in a sense, might be termed the fundamental principle of Schleiermacher—*Pectus est, quod theologum facit.*

Men from all parts of the country—parsons from their quiet vicarages, students, tutors, doctors from the Universities —came to Berlin, ardent, admiring, to drink at the fountainhead from the undefiled wells of pure thought and the religious consciousness. Of these no man was thirstier, from toilsome wandering along the rugged way that led from Kant to Hegel, than Strauss. But to his dismay the cholera soon after his arrival carried off Hegel, and he had to fight his perplexities without the master's aid. What began his trouble was the distinction between the idea and the notion, as equal to the distinction between religion and philosophy, which had been said to involve formal, but not material, difference. But this,

[1] Schwartz, "Geschichte der Neuesten Theol.," p. 42.

in the mind of one who had been trained to study and to teach the Scriptures as well as philosophy, inevitably raised the question :—In what relation do the historical contents of the Bible, especially of the Gospels, stand to the notion? Do they belong to the matter which is the same for both idea and notion, or only to what as form is dissolved by the disembodying action of thought? Is the pre-eminent evangelical fact or Person only a concentration for the religious consciousness of the idea in its process of realization, or has it unique and absolute value for speculative thought? The Hegelians argued from the unity of the Divine and human natures to the reality of the incarnation in Christ. In Him the idea of the God-man had been actualized. But what warrant was there for this individualization? The philosophy that resolved the Absolute into a process could not concede to a single person universal and permanent and exclusive being. The maxim, too, "Whatever is actual is rational," applied to theology, justified all its doctrines, made the formulated and the persistent the valid, and so left thought no freer than before. But had not criticism questioned the credibility of the evangelical facts, the veracity of the sources, the accuracy of the narratives? Berlin was ringing with the fame of certain lectures on the life of Jesus which Schleiermacher had been delivering. He had shown how the person of Christ could be constructed from the Christian consciousness, had subtly analysed documents, transposed narratives, involved the once certain in uncertainty. Strauss had heard the master lecture, had notes of the lectures taken in two different years, though these could be as little transcribed as a dancer in full swing could be photographed.[1] But this critical method applied to the Gospels with a freedom that only a very mature and independent Christian consciousness could justify, suggested the question :—Can I not by its help work the "Life of Jesus" into harmony with the new philosophy? He thought

[1] "Der Christus des Glaubens," p. 8.

he could, and here is the original design : "(1) Positive or traditional—an objective exhibition of the life of Jesus according to the Gospels, an exposition as to how He lives in believers, and the reconciliation of both sides in the second article of the Apostles' Creed. (2) Negative or critical—the history of Jesus dissolved for the most part as history. (3) Dogmatic restoration of what had been destroyed."[1] The critical part was only the preliminary condition of the constructive ; the facts were to be abolished to leave thought free scope. The man was only twenty-four, but he had mapped out his work. His soundings were hardly well begun when he resolved to draw up a chart contradicting and invalidating those that had been made before. Three years later the scheme was realized on a much larger scale than the original design and with momentous issues in the " Leben Jesu."

§ II.—The " Leben Jesu."

This book has now to be understood. Exposition is here criticism. The work was fundamentally vitiated, falsified in character and method, by its starting-point and end. It professed to be critical, but was throughout a pure creation of the philosophical imagination. Its critical theories had been created, its exegetical method was applied, to work out a foregone conclusion. Certain narratives, which were regarded as historical, were incompatible with a given speculative doctrine, and blocked the way to a speculative end. So a critico-historical theory was invented to disintegrate the narratives and dissolve the facts. And as was the genesis such was the elaboration of the work, arbitrary, daring, skilful, most dogmatic where it ought to have been most critical. The man was a speculative, constructive thinker, blind to probabilities, forcing history to become the vehicle of an *à priori* system. The criticism never becomes scientific ;

[1] "Streitschriften," pt. iii., p. 59.

realities are nothing, idealities everything. The critic has no historical sense; seeks only to abolish, not to construct or restore. The Person whose life he means to write becomes shadowy, illusive; escapes us almost altogether. We follow from negation to negation, but never get to positive or substantial fact. There is no living background, no actual world of loving, hating, thinking men: Jews factional, fanatical, full of hopes created by the written Word, of thoughts coined in the schools and circulated by tradition; Romans superciliously pitiful to the conquered, contemptuously indulging the common hatred to sectaries. There is no delicate eye for light and shade, no realizing imagination, no attempt to live in the land and time of Jesus, or in the generation when the so-called mythical process was going on and working into final form in the evangelical narratives. The great realities for Strauss are neither the narratives nor the facts, but his antagonists, the older critics and historians on the one hand, and the theories on the other. He never forgets his speculative basis and conclusion, his critical doubts, his mythical theory as means to the end, the hard, far-fetched naturalistic explanations of Paulus, the strained and improbable conjectures and conjunctures of the harmonists. So he is no critical historian, but a dogmatic controversialist, in the might of a speculative principle so bearing down upon living men and living beliefs as never to get face to face with the facts that must be known before they can become objects of thought. The work was thus least scientific where most negative, and positive only where speculative. The speculation was too violent and arbitrary to find what it sought—the universal and permanent truth represented by the history. The criticism cleared the ground of old critical structures, and so made new ones at once possible and necessary, but it did no more.

The speculative basis on which Strauss built was simply the Hegelian doctrine of the Absolute, specifically developed and applied. The disciple narrowed ideas that the master had made large and indefinite. Hegel meant his philosophy to explain what had been and is; Strauss used it to determine what must be or have been. The eternal process became the immanent God realizing Himself in the invariable and necessary order of nature. Deity was impersonal, miracle impossible, and so the supernatural incredible. The chain of finite causes was inviolable. Strauss declared that philosophic studies had freed him in feeling and thought from the religious and dogmatic presuppositions which biassed even the most acute and learned theologians. But whether speculative are more scientific than theological assumptions is a question which need not meanwhile be discussed.

His speculative end was also given him by the Hegelian philosophy. The evangelical facts expressed in the sensuous form truths which he wished to translate into the notional. He did not see why men should be satisfied with the lower when they could by a critico-speculative process reach the higher form. So he considered his work a real service to Christianity—at least the ideal and absolute Christianity of the learned. He says: "The author knows that the essence of the Christian faith is entirely independent of his critical inquiries. The supernatural birth of Christ, His miracles, His resurrection and ascension, remain eternal truths, however much their reality as historical facts may be doubted. Only the certainty of this can give to our criticism calmness and dignity. . . . Inquiries of this kind may inflict a wound on the faith of individuals. Should this be the case with theologians, they have in their science the medicine for such wounds, as, if they would not remain behind the development of their age, cannot be spared them. The subject is not yet, of course, properly prepared for the laity, and therefore this book has been so written that unlearned laymen will soon and quickly perceive that it is not designed for them."[1] To the uninitiated the old facts were still necessary; but to those

[1] "Leben Jesu," Vorrede (1st ed.), pp. vi, vii.

who had penetrated into the Hegelian *penetralia*, the mythical theory, "with the sacrifice of the historical reality of the narrative, held fast its absolute truth."[1]

What, then, was the eternal truth which was the kernel of the historical shell thus mercilessly broken and cast away? The Hegelian conception so construed as to be reduced to consistency; in other words, the dismissal of the historical Person in order to the complete articulation of the idea. The notion of the God-man was universalized; the attributes which the Church had ascribed to Christ were made the property of the race. The unity of the Divine and human natures was realized in man, not in a man. The Incarnation was the self-manifestation of God, the realization of the Idea, not in a single person, but in humanity; not at a particular point of time, but from eternity. "This is the key to the whole of Christology, that as subject of the predicates which the Church assigns to Christ an idea is set for an individual, but a real idea; not one Kantian, unreal, subjective. Conceived in an individual, a God-man, the attributes and functions which the Church doctrine ascribes to Christ contradict each other; in the idea of the race they agree. Humanity is the union of the two natures, God become man, the infinite Spirit emptied into the finite, and the finite recollecting its infinitude. Humanity is the child of the visible Mother and the invisible Father—of Nature and Spirit; it is the Miracle-Worker, in so far as in the course of human history the Spirit becomes ever more perfectly Master of Nature, which is forced under it as inert material for its activity. It is the sinless, inasmuch as the process of its development is blameless; defilement cleaves to the individual, but is, in the species and its history, abolished. Humanity is the one that dies, rises again, and ascends to heaven, since from the negation of its natural there proceeds always a higher spiritual life; from the abolition of its finitude as personal, national, and earthly spirit there issues

[1] "Leben Jesu," vol. i., p. 52.

its union with the infinite Spirit of heaven. By faith in this Christ, especially in His death and resurrection, man is justified before God ; that means, the individual becomes participant in the Divine-human life of the species, by having the idea of humanity created and vivified within him. And this happens mainly because the negation of the natural, which is itself the negation of the Spirit, therefore the negation of the negation, is the only way to true spiritual life for man."[1] " If we know the Incarnation, Death, and Resurrection, the *duplex negatio affirmat*, as the eternal circulation, the endless pulsation, always repeating itself, of the Divine life, what single fact, which is but a sensuous symbol of this process, can claim pre-eminent importance? To the idea in the fact, to the race in the individual, our age wishes to be led. A theological system, which in its doctrine of Christ stands by Him as an individual, is no system, but a sermon."[2]

But if this transcendental construction was to stand, then the historical reality of the evangelical narratives must be sacrificed, for the universal could not assume the attributes of the particular Person if He were to remain, in the full and strict sense, an historical reality. But how was the sacrifice to be performed? By the old Deistic method, which charges Jesus with unveracity and imposition, the Evangelists with falsehood and fabrication? To adopt it was for many reasons impossible. It was a discredited and discreditable method, had broken down in the hands of the men who had used it. Then the speculative construction required the ideal truth of the facts, the ideal veracity of the narratives. To translate conscious fictions into transcendental truths had been to build an elaborate palace on shifting sands. A system which claimed to be true could never be based on intentional falsehoods. A theory thus became necessary which sacrificed the letter, but retained

---

[1] "Leben Jesu," vol ii., pp. 734, 735.
[2] *Ibid.*, p. 738.

the spirit; denied the real, but affirmed the ideal truth of the Gospels. The mythical theory seemed to do so—exactly fitted the mechanism of the work. It made the evangelical facts unconscious creations—the symbols or investitures of primitive Christian ideas. The creations were unconscious, and so written down as historical in all good faith. They were the products of the collective spirit of a people or Church, and so clothed or expressed their actual thoughts and beliefs. The myths were created by the normal action of the spirit, and so while historically false were ideally true. The theory needed but a small substratum of reality. It was only necessary to believe that Jesus had grown up at Nazareth, had been baptized by John, had called disciples, gone about Judea teaching, set Himself against the Pharisees, introduced the Messianic kingdom, and been crucified—the victim of Pharisaic hate.[1] His death disappointed but did not disperse the disciples. They had Oriental imaginations and Jewish hopes. Their literature and traditions were full of promises and prophecies to be fulfilled in the Messiah, and these so mingled with their reminiscences and thoughts of Jesus that the attributes and actions of the ideal became those of the actual person. The Messiah of their dreams and desires was gradually rounded into the historical Christ, His character adorned with the qualities, His life with the achievements, His mission with the ends attributed to the long-predicted and long-expected national Deliverer. The Messiah was to be a lawgiver, prophet, priest, and king, and Jesus was represented as having been or being each of these, in each pre-eminent over all His predecessors. The shining of the face of Moses was eclipsed by the Transfiguration. The miracles of Elijah and Elisha suggested, but paled before, the feeding of the five thousand, the raising of the dead, and the Ascension. Whatever extraordinary thing Jesus

---

[1] "Leben Jesu," vol. i., p. 72.

said or did had its suggestive source in the Old Testament or tradition. He was little more than a lay figure dressed out in Messianic prerogatives. The mythical theory, indeed, did with prophecy very much what evolution has done with design. The Messianic hope, struggling under certain conditions for life, made Jesus into the Christ.

Strauss elaborated his hypothesis with extraordinary ingenuity. The air was full of mythological theories. Wolf's "Prolegomena" had started many questions—critical, mythical, religious—as to the Homeric poems and primitive Greece. Niebuhr had carried a new light into the history of ancient Rome. Heyne had enunciated the principle, *A mythis omnis priscorum hominum cum historia tum philosophia procedit*; and he and Hermann had, though under specific differences, resolved mythology into a consciously invented and elaborately concealed science of nature and man. Creuzer had made it a religious symbolism, under which was hidden an earlier and purer faith. Ottfried Müller, in a finer and more scientific spirit, had explained myths as created by the reciprocal action of two factors, the real and ideal, and had traced in certain cases their rise even in the historical period. The same tendency had existed in Scriptural as in classical studies. Mythical interpretations had been applied long before to certain sections of the Old Testament. Eichhorn and Bauer, Vater and De Wette, had employed it with greater or less freedom and thoroughness. It had even been carried into the New Testament, and made to explain the earlier and later events in the life of Jesus, those prior to the Temptation, and those subsequent to the Crucifixion. Strauss thus only universalized a method which had been in partial operation before; made the myth, instead of a portal to enter and leave the Gospels, a comprehensive name for the whole. In doing so it was not enough to build on old foundations. The enormous extension of the structure needed a corresponding extension of the base. The man could not but fail at the end whose work at the beginning was not simply ill done but not done at all.

§ III.—THE COUNTER CRITICISM.

In order to complete our history and analysis of the book, it will be necessary to throw a hurried glance over the five stormful years that followed its appearance. It was the signal for the outbreak of an angry and bewildered controversy of the sort distinctive of religious panics. Men known and unknown, schools old and new, clergy and laity, every one who could carry a stick or even spring a rattle,[1] joined in the *mêlée*. The Prussian Government proposed to place the book under ban, but Neander protested: " Let it be answered by argument, not by authority." The Pietists and High Lutherans hailed it as the *caput mortuum* of the speculative and critical schools, and began the reaction they called revival. The Hegelians, anxious to disown their too radical *confrère*, made a valiant effort to affiliate him to Schleiermacher, but the sons of the divine victoriously vindicated his true descent. And the storm of words did not come alone; more material penalties followed. Strauss was cast out of the university where he had given and tasted the promise of a brilliant career, and had to face a world which had for him little praise and less promise. He was not a man to bear criticism in silence, and his speech now was most characteristic. He replied to his critics by counter-criticism, repelled their assault by assailing themselves. He selected from the hosts opposed to him certain men, representatives of various tendencies, and fell on them in the most vigorous way. The selected were Steudel, Tübingen professor, supernaturalist, and traditional theologian; Eschenmayer, philosopher and physician, a believer in animal magnetism, demoniacal possession, and other things

---

[1] " Das Leben Jesu für das Deutsche Volk," p. 157.

ghostly; Wolfgang Menzel, literary critic and mythologist, a layman who acted the severe moralist; Hengstenberg, High Lutheran, standing by the letter of the Scriptures and the creeds; Bruno Bauer, just beginning his changeful career, for the moment an orthodox Hegelian, conciliator of knowledge and faith; Ullmann, a theologian, modern, irenical, anxious to give to reason the things that are reason's, to faith the things that are faith's.

Strauss's criticism,[1] save in Ullmann's case, to whom he was studiously courteous, spared neither the men nor their writings. Steudel, dolorous, incompetent, was a Pietist permeated with Rationalism, heir to a past he had not mind enough to inherit or courage to renounce; Eschenmayer was but a succession of ever-repeated incoherences and contradictions; Menzel was a literary Ishmaelite, a critic without insight, who but blundered when he judged; Hengstenberg was full of latent Pantheism; and Bruno Bauer under-

[1] The replies and counter-criticisms, first published in 1837, were in 1841 issued in a collective form under the title: "Streitschriften zur Vertheidigung meiner Schrift über das Leben Jesu und zur Charakteristik der gegenwärtigen Theologie." The replies were in three parts. The first was the answer to Steudel and his school, that of a rational and reasoned supernaturalism, and was certainly a very merciless exposure of the self-illusions it had indulged. The second part contained the reply to Eschenmayer and Menzel. Eschenmayer is best known by his contributing through Schelling to the alliance of Natural and Transcendental Philosophy. He and Strauss met as antagonists on another field—spiritualism, or what would be now so called. Eschenmayer, in a book on "The Conflict between Heaven and Hell," sketched in a distantly Dantesque style the nether regions, where he places those who corrupt and falsify the Word, assail, deny, and blaspheme the Son of man Himself. There, of course, Iscariot is sent, and the Mythicists in general, who cry, "Great is the Goddess Idea of Berlin." Strauss thought such superfine wit imbecile and laughable where not disgusting (v. "Charakter. u. Krit.," pp. 355, 376). The third part contained answers to Hengstenberg, the Hegelians, and the theologians of the conciliatory school, the men of the "Studien u. Kritiken." The criticism of the Hegelians is of considerable autobiographical worth, and the letter to Ullmann is most pacific in tone and purport. A positive and constructive part was intended to follow, but it was embodied in the third edition of the "Leben Jesu."

stood neither Hegel nor theology. Literary amenities seldom distinguish theological controversies, but in this case the truculence was transcendent. Strauss compared his critics to women set a-screaming by the going off of a gun.[1] Eschenmayer, who had denounced him as the modern Iscariot, guilty of the sin against the Holy Ghost,[2] was described as no inspired man of God, the Spirit not being given to plagiarism, even from himself,[3] while his book was characterized as the child, born in lawful wedlock, of theological ignorance and religious intolerance, consecrated by a somnambulating philosophy.[4] Wolfgang Menzel thought his author like the devil, without conscience,[5] and Strauss could not read Bruno Bauer's speculations without feeling as if he were in the witches' kitchen in *Faust*, listening to the clatter of a whole choir of a hundred thousand fools.[6] Hengstenberg said the prophecy of Lichtenberg was fulfilled—the world had got so fine as to think the belief in God as ridiculous as the belief in ghosts.[7] Strauss was a man without a heart, or had one like Leviathan [8]—" as firm as a stone, and hard as a piece of the nether millstone." But, in this case, behind the verbal ferocities was a mind that knew the enemy it faced, and delighted in his absolute antagonism. Hengstenberg thoroughly understood the " Leben Jesu." To vanquish its speculative Pantheism the old Lutheran theology must be revived, subscription to the confessions, in their literal sense, enforced. To conquer the mythical theory, historical reality must be claimed for the narratives alike of the Old and New Testaments. If it was allowed a foothold in the

[1] "Leben Jesu," 2 Aufl., Vor.
[2] "Streitschriften," pt. ii., p. 3. Eschenmayer's critique bore the title " The Iscariotism of our Day."
[3] " Streitschriften," pt. ii., p. 10.
[4] " Leben Jesu " (1st ed.), vol. ii., Vor.
[5] " Streitschriften," pt. ii., p. 3.
[6] *Ibid.*, pt. ii., p. 109.
[7] *Ibid.*, pt. iii., p. 9.
[8] *Ibid.*, pt. iii., p. 18.

one, it could not be held out of the other. The spirit of the age was to be met not by conciliation, but by contradiction. To mediate was to be faithless. The Church, suckled on its old creeds, was to do its old work. The strength given by a narrow aim and definite belief favoured for a while the reaction; but the times proved too strong even for Hengstenberg. Churches, after an intellectual revolution, can as little return to their old confessions as countries, after a political, can go back to their old constitutions.

Relevant criticism was at first hardly possible. But two or three attempts at it showed insight. Tholuck[1] achieved more than a brilliant occasional success, and struck Strauss on his weakest point. He argued that a critical theory of the history must rest on a scientific criticism of the Gospels, and therefore that the inadequate criticism of the sources made the critical life of Jesus uncritical, left its mythical theory a castle in the air. Strauss flung a scornful complimentary sneer at the high horse of his many-sidedness,[2] the jewelled spoils from the ancient and modern classics sprinkled over his pages,[3] but the sting in the sneer did not neutralize the sting in the criticism. Alexander Schweitzer,[4] leader of Schleiermacher's left wing, took another line: Persons were the main factors of change and progress in history. It was not true that the first was often the least and the last the most perfect form in an historical process; the reverse was more often the case. Personal attributes transferred to the race were mere figures of speech—abstract, impotent, capable of nothing but exercising the mind; they must be concentrated in a person if they are to mean or to accomplish anything.

[1] "Die Glaubwürdigkeit der Evangel. Geschichte," 1837. F. C. Baur, whose own criticism Tholuck in a dim way anticipated, later characterized this book as "a masterpiece of scientific charlatanry and pettifogging" (Rabulisterei) "Kirchengesch. des Neunzehn. Jahrh.," p. 367.
[2] "Leben Jesu" (3rd ed.), Vor., p. iv.
[3] "Streitschriften," pt. iii., p. 13.
[4] "Studien u. Kritiken," 1837, pp. 459-510.

He thus argued for the historicity of Christ by vindicating the reality and rights of creative personalities in every province of thought and action, but especially the religious. The Founder made the religion, not the religion the Founder. Its eminence was but a reflection and consequence of His. Individual genius was here as everywhere the creative force. De Wette,[1] the then most authoritative critic in the department of sacred literature, pronounced against the uncritical method and position of the "Leben Jesu," especially as to the Fourth Gospel. Ullmann[2] criticised the mythical theory, analysed the idea of myth, distinguished its varieties, argued that the Gospels may be histories with mythical elements without being mythical histories. Nor were they our only sources. Outside the Gospels were most important witnesses. There was Paul, a writer of epistles full of history, a history in himself, man and system alike being in need of explanation; not capable of being explained if the Christ he so trusted, served, interpreted, had been only an obscure rabbi of Nazareth in process of formation into a transcendental object of faith by the mythicizing imagination. Then, too, there was the primitive Church, an historical reality if such a thing ever was—how could it be what we know it to have been if its faith and all its creative facts were but dreams of an idealizing spirit? Paul and the primitive Church had been ignored, but they show a faith rooted in fact. Christ created the Church, not the Church Christ; the seed grew into the plant, not the plant into the seed. Neander[3] opposed the historical to the mythical Christ. He was arbitrary and subjective, too anxious to find an ideal and modern in the real and ancient Christ, expected too much from a change of the contra- into the supra-natural. But his work had

---

[1] "Erklärung des Ev. Johannis," Schlussbetrachtung." Cf. "Leben Jesu,' (3rd. ed.), Vor.; "Charak. u. Krit.," Vor.
[2] "Studien und Krit," 1836, pp. 776 ff.
[3] Neander, "Das Leben Jesu Christi," 1837.

one pre-eminent quality—it was an honest effort, marked by sympathetic insight into the character portrayed, to get face to face with the facts, to construe evangelical as actual history; and so it tended to create in the reader a consciousness of reality that could confront the mythical theory undismayed.

§ IV.—CONCESSIONS AND CONCLUSION.

As the controversy proceeded some points personal to Strauss emerged, which are not without historical interest. He defended his work as a scientific search after truth, and for science there did not exist the holy, but only the true.[1] He was not the enemy, but the apologist, of the Christian faith, and had proved its essence independent of critical inquiries. He had not wished to destroy the faith of the people, only to translate its transcendental matter into a scientific form. Hence he had written for the learned alone. Why not in Latin then?[2] That had been to put new wine into old bottles, with the usual certain result. He did not mean to be unchurched, was thoroughly happy and at home in the Christian religion; could be refreshed in spirit from its old yet perennially young sources.[3] The critic did not write for edification, but for science; and science, while it denied the reality of the facts, affirmed the reality of the faith. Miracles were unreal, but the faith in them was not. The great point was not the occurrence of the Resurrection, but the belief in it.[4] He wished the clergy to preach Christ, not Schleiermacher and Hegel. But the irenical spirit apparent in these personal apologetics soon became much more pronounced. The *consensus eruditorum*, joined with his present loneliness

---

[1] "Streitschriften," pt. i., p. 92.
[2] *Ibid.*, pt. i., p. 88; pt. iii., p. 132.
[3] *Ibid.*, pt. i., p. 9.
[4] *Ibid.*, pt. i., pp. 33-48; pt. iii., p. 41. This position was later elaborated by Baur.

and cheerless outlook for the future, constrained him into concessions and efforts at conciliation. In his third "Streitschrift" (1837), in the third edition of his "Leben Jesu" (1838), and in the "Zwei Friedliche Blätter" (1839), he successively and increasingly modified the cardinal points of his position, the criticism of the sources, the mythical theory, and the speculative Christology.

In the third edition of the "Leben" the critical attitude to the Fourth Gospel was changed. Strauss confessed that his zeal against the theologians had made him unjust to John; he now doubted his own denials, could as little say John's Gospel is genuine as that it is spurious.[1] And with these doubts as to the sources, the mythical theory could hardly retain its old rigour. Jesus became more historical; his speeches, even the Johannine discourses, more genuine, the latter giving, not the master's *ipsissima verba*, but the ideas they had given to the scholar.[2] But the less nebulous Jesus grew, the more extraordinary He became; as the range of the unconsciously creative phantasy was limited, the reality of the consciously creative person was increased. While the speculative Christology was allowed to stand, the individual had his rights conceded by Jesus being raised into the world's pre-eminent religious genius, creator of the Church, maker of Christianity, the empirical or real as distinguished from the absolute or ideal Christ. At the head of all world-historical events individuals stood, were the subjectivities through whom the absolute substance was realized.[3] In the field of religion, especially where Monotheistic, the grand creative forces had been individuals. And Christianity was the product of a creative individuality. "Certainly this does not again bring Christ into the peculiar Christian sanctuary, but only places

[1] "Leben Jesu" (3rd ed.), Vor., p. v.
[2] *Ibid.*, vol. ii., p. 740.
[3] *Ibid.*, vol. ii., pp. 770-779. This conciliatory and conclusory chapter embodied the views and modifications of the third "Streitschrift," and replaced a chapter in the first edition which had given special offence.

him in the chapel of Alexander Severus, where, with Orpheus and Homer, he has to stand beside not only Moses, but also Mohammed, and must not be ashamed of the society of Alexander and Cæsar, Raphael and Mozart." But this disquieting co-ordination was qualified by two considerations: first, religion is not only the highest province in which the Divine creative power of genius can be manifested, but is related to the others as centre to circumference. Of the religious genius in a sense quite inapplicable to poet or philosopher can it be said, "God reveals Himself in him." Secondly, as Christianity is the highest religion its Author is supreme in the circle of religious creators.

But this new standpoint received its most perfect expression in the second of the "Zwei Friedliche Blätter."[1] This is one of Strauss's most perfect compositions, an irenical soliloquy, a far-off echo of Schleiermacher's "Monologen" and "Reden," which muffled, as it were, the sigh for peace of a man who was trying to conquer his own worst doubts, and wished to live in friendship with the new culture and the old faith. Culture seemed to him to be not so much hostile as indifferent to faith; and for Christianity to become superfluous was worse than to be vanquished. As a child of the culture, who had also been a son of the old faith, he could not but seek to reconcile the two, especially as a basis existed in a philosophy which was more Christian than primitive Christianity, conceived God and man as united, not at one or a few points, but everywhere and always. The new spirit could not believe in everlasting rewards and penalties; could be moral without them; needed only an immortality of conscious growth. The resurrection of Christ was an eternal and ideal truth clothed in a form suitable to

[1] "Vergängliches und Bleibendes im Christenthum" ("The Transitory and Permanent in Christianity"). It was published in 1839 along with a genial and beautiful paper on Justinus Kerner, Strauss' mystic friend, but had first appeared the year before in the "Freihaven"; in 1845 an English translation was published.

childhood, but without worth for manhood. His death was no atonement, only the absolute submission of a righteous spirit to God. His works were not miracles, the *miraculum* was only the *mirabile*. The Incarnation was incompatible with the nature of God, who could be revealed in a single person as little as the essence of harmony in a single tune. "The only worship—one may lament or praise but cannot deny it—the only worship which from the religious ruins of the past remains to the cultured mind of to-day is the worship of genius."[1] Must, therefore, the doom of Christianity be written? No; Christ descends from the throne of Divine Sonship only to assume the sovereignty of religious genius. Genius redeems and rules the world, saves humanity from ignorance and impotence, and helps it to realize its ideal. Religion is the highest creation of spirit, Christianity the highest religion, and Jesus the supreme genius of the world, who never has been, never can be, either in kind or degree, surpassed. Beyond Him no future can go:—

"As little as man will ever be without religion will he be without Christ. For to think to have religion without Christ were no less absurd than to think to enjoy poetry irrespective of Homer, Shakespeare, and their kind. And this Christ, so far as He is inseparable from the highest form of religion, is an historical, not a mythical, person, a real individual, no mere symbol."[2]

"There is no fear that He will be lost to us, even though we are forced to surrender much that has been hitherto named Christianity. He remains to us and to all the more secure and stable the less we anxiously hold fast doctrines and opinions which may be to thought an occasion of apostasy. But if Christ remains to us—remains, too, as the highest we know and can conceive in things religious, as He without whose presence in the heart no perfect piety

---

[1] P. 106.
[2] P. 131.

is possible—then there also remains to us in Him the essential truth of Christianity."[1]

But Strauss's career as the prophet of Christ, the religious genius, was doomed to find sudden pause. His irenical attitude was too full of incompatibilities to be long maintained. The notion that the first could be the most perfect form in religion, or any other creation of spirit, was alien to the Hegelian philosophy as Strauss had construed it. His new conception of Christ involved admissions as to the Gospels fatal alike to the mythical theory and the critical conclusions that made it possible. It was an approach to Schleiermacher, Alexander Schweitzer more than hinting that it was a crib from himself. It was neither an appropriate termination to the old structure, nor a buttress built to support its weakest side, but simply a fragment from a foreign school of architecture planted against the outer wall, a pillar from the florid Gothic cathedral of the Romanticists placed at the end of the severe and classic temple of the new philosophy. And the pillar was in a new revolution of thought, coincident with a revulsion of feeling, cast down and thrown out. In the spring of 1839 Strauss was invited to a professorship at Zürich. The election was the work of the Radicals, who were then in power. It alarmed the Church; the clergy roused the people to revolt and political reaction. Strauss strove to assuage the storm, explained he did not mean "to use the position given him in the university to undermine the established religion," or "to disturb the Church in her faith and worship." He meant to hold himself "within the limits of his scientific vocation," and "endeavour to make the fundamental Christian verities esteemed." But the oil did not smooth the waters, and Strauss soon ceased to pour it.[2]

[1] P. 132.
[2] The letters connected with the Zürich affair throw considerable light on the irenical attitude and mental history of Strauss. They

Whether he would or could have fulfilled his scientific vocation without disturbing the Church or its faith is a matter on which it is useless to speculate. He had hardly the stuff in him to be an exoteric Conservative while an esoteric Radical. Our modern instincts are against the opinion Augustine attributes to Varro: "Multa esse vera, quæ non modo vulgo scire non sit utile, sed etiam tametsi falsa sunt, aliter existimare populum expediat."[1] Last century, indeed, knew more than one professor a Voltaire *privatim*, but a Warburton *publice*. The relations between conviction and expression in our century are—though not what they ought to be—healthier and more honest. Later on Strauss admired in Reimarus "the martyrdom of silence"[2] which the Deist suffered that he might enjoy the fame and emoluments of a Christian. But he himself was saved by the Zürich affair from a similar or worse martyrdom. The preface to the irenical "Blätter" is dated March 15th, 1839; his call to Zürich was cancelled March 18th, and in the August following, in the preface to his "Charakteristiken und Kritiken,"[3] he withdrew his critical concessions and all they implied. Next year the "Leben Jesu" came out in a fourth edition,[4] purged from everything concessive and irenical; the section

may be found in a very wooden and wearisome little book: Boden's "Geschichte der Berufung des Dr. Strauss an die Hochschule von Zürich," 1840. Cf. Hausrath's "David Friedrich Strauss und die Theologie seiner Zeit.," vol. i., apps. iv.-xi.

[1] "De Civitate Dei," lib. iv., c. xxxi.

[2] "H. S. Reimarus und seine Schutzschrift für die vernunftigen Verehrer Gottes," p. 6.

[3] The volume contains his early essays in three divisions: Theology, Belles Lettres, and the Night-side of Nature, or Spiritualism. The essay of greatest value is one on Schleiermacher and Daub, marked by genial insight, nice discrimination, grace, and force of style.

[4] On this edition Strauss used to look back with pleasure as giving the fullest and most adequate expression of his early views. The English translation by Miss Evans, published in three volumes by Chapman (1841), is from this edition. The third edition was also translated into English, but in a second-hand way from the French. It could find no London publisher, but made its appearance at Birmingham.

on Christ the religious genius omitted, the Fourth Gospel pronounced spurious, its discourses "free compositions of the Evangelist." He was in those days caustically compared to a physician who rushed from his house, sword in hand, and assailed the people passing along the street; but who, taking fright at seeing so many done almost to death, retreated within doors, though only to sally forth the next moment, bandages in hand, to bind up his victims.

CHAPTER III.

LITERARY CRITICISM.—THE TÜBINGEN SCHOOL.

WE have seen how speculation made historical criticism necessary; we have now to see how the criticism corrected the speculation, especially during the years 1840-60 when the Tübingen criticism reigned.

§ I.—THE CRITICAL PROBLEM AND CHRISTOLOGY.

The "Leben Jesu" had indeed accomplished a revolution; up till its appearance the speculative construction of Christ's person had been the main thing, but now the supreme problem was His historical reality, His place and function in history, the character and claims of the literature which described Him and the society He founded. It was a new thing to see the most rational of all transcendental philosophies culminating in a doctrine of the Incarnation, and through it reading all religions and the whole of history. But it was due to two things: (1) the larger and more constructive spirit of the new philosophy, which saw it must explain not simply physical nature and the individual man in their correlated being and reciprocal action, but the whole of nature and the whole of man alike in the past which represented his becoming and in the present which represents what he has become; (2) the new knowledge and quickened imagination which had so enlarged the past and made it to re-live its life under the eye of the poet and thinker. As a necessary result to interpret man was to interpret his religion, and no philosophy of religion was possible without recognition of the place and meaning of the supreme religious Person of history. Hence the Transcendentalisms that rose out of two such apparently opposed, yet really convergent, streams as the criticism of Kant and the humanism of Herder, especially as modified by the Romanticists, could not but attempt the speculative construction both of Christianity and Christ. But the Christ it laboured to construe was the Christ of doctrine and tradition; His name to it was but a symbol, a formula, which had simply to be accepted and translated into the language of the school in order to be made the very crown and apex of the philosophy. Strauss took the matter in full earnest, and, that the school might be free to deal with the formula as it listed, he undertook to do away with the historical Person, dissolving Him into a mythical creation, which only the more therefore embodied the Idea. He was thus but a speculative thinker disguised as an historian; he had used his philosophy to get rid of the historical reality and to translate it as a religious idea into the terms of the transcendental notion. His criticism ought never to be taken as a serious performance; its real significance was not in what it did, but in what it caused to be done. It followed a twofold method: as literary it was a hostile analysis of current views as to the Gospels; as historical it was a dissolution of the history into myths. But in neither respect was it independent; in both it was too much governed by *à priori* considerations to have any scientific worth whatever. Yet its very failure was its greatest service to science; the noise it had made was a direct invitation to architectonic minds of every type to arise and build.

This call was equally heard on two sides—the side of faith and of science. They both for different reasons lay under the same necessity—the moral and intellectual compulsion to seek and, if possible, discover the historical truth. They started from very different principles, pursued somewhat different methods with altogether different hopes; but the quest of each was the same—the real history of Christ with all that pertained to His person, words, and work. On the one side, the men of faith suddenly found themselves confronted with the most awful of all possible losses—the going out, in the interests of the Absolute Idea, of the one Divine Person in history. If all the institutions that had grown round Him, all the doctrines that had been formulated concerning Him, all the modes of doing Him honour and rendering Him service, were to live while He Himself were to die or be as one who had never lived the Divine life save in the imaginations of men, then the life in all these institutions, doctrines, and forms of homage would be but a deeper death, with His going all that invested them with power and meaning would also go. Hence men who so felt were bound to rise and attempt to build the altar which had been destroyed; but with true instinct they saw that, while destruction had come by the path of speculation, reconstruction must come by the way of historical inquiry and literary criticism. On the other side, the men of science were equally clear as to their duty. Strauss had solved no problem, had instead raised a multitude, had made the most remarkable moment and the greatest event in history less intelligible than ever they had been before. It was, therefore, necessary by new methods, and from fresh points of view, to begin the work of research and discovery. In a constructive and positive regard the latter tendency was more important than the former; the Tübingen School contributed, directly or indirectly, more to the accurate knowledge of the primitive history, and to the new sense in its reality, than did the men they were accustomed to describe and to despise as apologists. The claim to be free from assumptions and partialities is made by almost all schools, but is true of few, if of any, and certainly of no modern school is it so little true as of Tübingen. Yet in spite of its assumptions it accomplished work that has made all Christendom its debtor.

But before we touch it something must be said as to other tendencies in theology and historical criticism. The period was one of remarkable activity in Christology. The men who had received their intellectual impulse from Hegel and Schleiermacher did not cease to think because Strauss had written, rather their speculative energy was absorbed by the doctrine of the Incarnation, and their critical by the history of Christianity and its sources. The tendency was common, the subject absorbed men of all schools and parties, so much so that this century has earned the right to be regarded as one of the great periods of constructive Christology. Of course, this has always been a great Lutheran doctrine,[1] so discussed as to involve the question not only of the relation of the Divine and human natures in Christ, but of God to nature and to man. It was the Lutheran *communicatio idiomatum* that made Schelling and Hegel, as well as Schleiermacher, possible. If the Divine attributes could be so communicated to the humanity that it could, without ceasing to be human, become, as it were, Divine, then certainly a basis was laid for a philosophy which affirmed the identity of the natures, and translated the individual or singular into a collective sonship. If, too, the consciousness of God could be so communicated to Christ and be so possessed by Him that it could be described as absolute, then the communicated was the communicable, what He had received He had only to transmit, and it became the consciousness of His society, which, by possessing, as it were, His immanent presence, became articulated into Him. And so, as Christological doctrine had been done into the philosophies, it was but natural that the philosophies should be done back into Christological doctrine again, with types corresponding to the philosophies that had given the impulse. The

[1] Cf. *supra*, pp. 160, 161.

result was the emergence of three schools, though each had within it many subordinate varieties : one started from the Hegelian idea, and, emphasizing the identity of the human with the Divine, endeavoured to relieve the humanity from the restraints and attributes of finitude ; the second, starting from the same idea, but emphasizing the identity of the Divine with the human, endeavoured by a theory of kenosis to impose certain of the categories of finitude upon the Deity ; the third, by emphasizing the ethical elements in God and man, found in a new society or humanity, possessed of Divine life, evidence that an absolute miracle, a creative and therefore Divine personality, had appeared in a human form and performed what corresponded to His personality, an absolute miracle—viz., created the society that, as it were, perpetuated both His being and His activities. The first of these tendencies used more or less the categories of Hegel ; the second forced them into a Biblical and confessional formula ; the third blended the principles of Schelling and Schleiermacher with the method of Hegel. We may term these respectively the philosophical, the kenotic, and the historical Christologies, but to attempt to deal with any in detail would carry us far beyond our present limits. It is enough for our purpose to indicate their significance. They showed (1) that in positive theology the Incarnation had for all parties become the centre of gravity ; (2) that it could not be construed without reference both to the historical Person and the faith in Him and the life from Him which had together persisted in His society ; (3) that critical activity as to the sources had only stimulated speculative activity as to the Person ; and (4) that, apart from the historical reality of the Person and the veracity of the sources, every attempt at dogmatic construction was but a byplay in a philosophical movement, without the religious value and function that could alone justify its being in a living theology.

§ II.—Ferdinand Christian Baur.

We turn now to the Tübingen School, that we may understand how it contributed towards the solution of the questions raised, but left undiscussed and unanswered, by Strauss. It was the creation of a man, whose death was also its dissolution, yet it had distinguished disciples, and certain of these so important as to be in name and achievement hardly inferior to the master. It was a progressive school, learned from experience and experiment, had a mind that was educated by research and modified by discovery. Its founder, Ferdinand Christian Baur, was in various ways most unlike Strauss. He did not reach his position, as it were, at a bound, by the sudden spring of a daring and aggressive intellect, but slowly, progressively, by the path now of speculation, now of historical investigation, now of critical inquiry, and each new position he reached supplemented or qualified his earlier inferences. And so the changes that came to him were logical, the result of broadening knowledge or deepening insight. His mental history was not, like that of Strauss, a series of impulsive revolutions, changes of mind due more often to revulsions of feeling than to the slow process of conviction or conversion, but was a consistent growth, governed throughout by rare integrity of intellect. He and his criticism are therefore much more significant, though the two were often placed in the inverse relation ; he was Strauss' schoolmaster at Blaubeuren, his professor at Tübingen, and it used to be said that the master became the scholar's pupil. This had in it enough of the appearance of truth to pass with the thoughtless for true. Meanwhile we must know something of the man that we may understand his school.

Baur was born in 1792, was the son of a German pastor, reared in severe simplicity and obedience, nursed in the peculiar mystic yet evangelical piety of Swabia. He was educated at Blaubeuren and Tübingen, while the idealisms of

Fichte and Schelling were in the ascendant. He qualified himself for the mastery of the moderns by a deep and sympathetic study of Plato, and found the Academy the best propædeutic for theology. He was an ideal student, had no enjoyment outside his study. One of his most brilliant pupils, Friedrich Vischer, has described him as to the very heart modern in spirit and work, but ancient in worth, near kinsman to the reformers, a patriarch while a modern, heroic in his industry and patient love of truth, great, simple, good, with a voice whose very tones spoke of inmost sincerity and simplicity. His influence was immense, at once stimulating and unsettling. On these points there is emphatic testimony. An extraordinary proportion of his pupils became either distinguished or well-known men. Of the nine who in Strauss's time were the *élite* of the forty seminarists, all, with one exception, after a longer or shorter trial of the Church, sought and found their way out of it into teaching or literature[1]—a curious prophecy of the fate which in the later days of its founder was to befall the new Tübingen School.

The history of his mind explains the genesis of his school. He began his theological studies penetrated with the lofty visions and *à priori* constructions of idealistic thought. Schleiermacher was then dominant in theology, and his "Glaubenslehre" helped Baur out of the old Tübingen scholasticism into a system which allowed his critical faculty freer play. He was one of the men in whom many tendencies meet, and whose strongly assimilative yet independent minds unify the conflicting currents into a single and homogeneous stream. While Strauss was his pupil, Baur published in 1824 a work on symbolism and mythology.[2] It is an attempt to discuss and exhibit, as to matter and form, the so-called

---

[1] Strauss, "Christian Märklin," p. 24.
[2] "Symbolik und Mythologie, oder die Natur-religion des Alterthums" (Stuttgart, 1824-25). The work was in three volumes, but in two parts, a general and a special. The first was taken up with questions as to

heathen religions. Its principles are those of the idealistic philosophy as qualified by Schleiermacher, its tools those of Creuzer. A symbol is the representation of an idea through a simple picture or image given in space; a myth the figurative representation of an idea through an act, an event in time. The form of the symbol is nature; of the myth, history and the persons who act in it. The essential element in both is the idea represented, which in the race as in the individual is perceived in a concrete before it can be conceived in an abstract form. Symbol and myth are necessary as forms to religion. It is given immediately through the spiritual nature of man, but finds its positive realization in history. History is a revelation of the Godhead, mythology one of its elements or members. Monotheism is the highest stage in the evolution of religion; Christianity the highest point Monotheism has reached—an ethical Idealism, which, while revealed in historical acts and events, is yet to be construed as a matter of innermost self-consciousness.

But he did not long remain in the school of Schleiermacher; he was soon caught in the fine yet strong network of the Hegelian dialectic,[1] and it became to him at once a philosophy of history and of religion and an historical method. In harmony with it he construed history as the development and

mythology and history, the second with an analysis of the main elements and ideas of the religion. The work was written before Baur had been called to Tübingen.

[1] The date of his transition to Hegel can be fixed with tolerable precision. His reply to Moehler's "Symbolik" ("Der Gegensatz des Katholicismus und Protestantismus") appeared first in 1833 (second edition 1836), and exhibits in curious but instructive combination Schleiermacher's consciousness of dependence and Hegel's doctrine of the Absolute. This is a work of remarkable breadth and power. Moehler's "Symbolik" has been translated, yet Baur's reply, which has never been so honoured, is its superior in everything but style. The two books have this in common—both are eclectic. Moehler owed almost everything distinctive in his book to the German Protestants under whom he had studied. His theory of tradition and the Church is but a modification of Schleiermacher, his theory of the Church and the Incarnation a modification of Schelling. In Baur's

the explication of the Idea. Thought stood where God or Providence used to stand; instead of an order created by a personal will we had the successions and relations of a dialectical movement. Facts, events, persons, were but bearers of the idea, factors in its unfolding and articulation. Philosophy had to do with the unity or subject which was the cause of all change; history had to do with the forms, individuals, acts, occurrences, which were its varied vehicles and ministers. The function of the thinker was so to study history as to discover and to be able to exhibit the unity in the multiplicity of its manifestations. The manifold of nature existed to sense, the manifold of history to imagination; but thought, reason, was bound to seek under all its complex manifoldness the organising idea, the causal subject, the rational unity. As a result Christianity could not be conceived as an accident; it represented a necessary stage in the evolution of thought; it was so built into the order of things that it could not but be. To study its phenomena and development was not to study a chaos or a succession of more or less fortunate chances, but an ordered and an orderly movement of mind. But a further and more important result was this—its phenomena could not be interpreted in isolation, but only as an organized and organic whole; as their cause was one, they, too, constituted a unity; the idea was explicated only when it was realized and known. Thus the polity of the Church could not be construed without the doctrine, or the doctrine and polity without the worship, or the doctrine, polity, and worship without the literature, or the literature without the manners and customs,

work one of the most instructive things is its success in showing how easily the absolute sovereignty of Calvinism can be translated into the Hegelian Absolute, and how simply the evangelical principle, that good works can never avail before God, can be turned into the philosophical formula—the human creature in himself is nothing before God. Whatever attributes to man independence of God or reality of being before Him, contradicts the principle of Protestantism.—" Der Gegensatz,' p. 49 (2nd ed.).

or all these together without the men in and through whom they had lived; and though these all differed, yet all were necessary to the realization of the idea, and the idea in all was the same. And so, as a still further result, the most vital element in religion was its thought; indeed, thought was its very essence, the one thing that was expressed in all its forms and gave unity to their infinite variety. Indeed, no man ever had a deeper or truer conception than Baur of the relation of dogma to the Church and to religion, and it was in this field that he did his really valuable and permanent work. His great monographs on the history of dogmas, on the Manichean religious system, on the Christian Gnosis, on the Atonement, on the Trinity and Incarnation, his Handbook, his Lectures, and his chapters on dogma in his Church history, are all remarkable for their solid research, patient and lucid exposition, penetrative thought and criticism. He is not always to be trusted (no man is); his philosophy often makes him wise above what is written, or tempts him to interpret ancient doctrines as provisional and anticipatory forms of modern principles, and to lay an exaggerated emphasis on the action of antitheses, their power, by contradicting, to develop each other till comprehended in a higher synthesis. But in extenuation of these defects much could be said. There is so much of Hegel in neo-Platonism, and consequently in the contemporary Christianity, that it would have been astonishing if a Hegelian had not found much of his own mind in certain ancient dogmas. Yet the very reading of an old doctrine by a new mind is a condition of its better interpretation.

§ III.—How Baur came to his Problem.

Baur was engaged in this field of study when the "Leben Jesu" appeared, and he remained an almost silent spectator of the controversy it caused. That work had had for him nothing new,[1] as he had watched its growth and discussed every point in the process with its author. This sheds light on a significant literary coincidence. The "Leben Jesu" and the most suggestive of all Baur's books on the history of religious thought appeared in the same year (1835), and they express on the fundamental matter of the speculative Christology views that, while almost identical, yet exhibit most characteristic differences.[2] "All that Christ is as God-man He is only in faith and through faith"; "what lies behind faith as historical reality is veiled in mystery." "The God-man is indeed the object of faith, but not its necessary presupposition; what faith presupposes is not Christ as God-man, but as mere man, an empirical human being." The judgment of faith is therefore a subjective process, though it finds its occasion in an historical appearance. In order to be justified, faith must become knowledge; and this happens not through any outer history, but by philosophy, which is knowledge of the Absolute Spirit, God as the Triune, and the identity of man with God. The knowledge of Christ as God-man is the truth as to the unity of the Divine and human natures. "Everything which relates to the appearance and life of Christ has its truth only therein, that in Him was manifested the essence and life of the Spirit; but what the Spirit is and does is no affair of history. For faith, therefore, the appearance of the God-man, the incarnation of God, His birth in the flesh, may be an historical fact; but to speculative thought the incarnation of God is no single event which once happened, but an eternal

[1] Baur, "Kirchengeschichte des Neunzehn. Jahrhundts.," p. 397.
[2] Cf. "Die Christliche Gnosis," pp. 707-721, with the conclusory dissertation of the "Leben." On the question of priority this ought to be stated: the second volume of the "Leben," which contains the speculative Christology, did not appear till 1836, while "Die Christliche Gnosis" had appeared the year before. On the connection between the speculative question and the method of historical proof, see Ritschl in the "Jahrb. f. deuts. Theol.," vol. vi., pp. 433 ff. He there replies to an article by Zeller on the Tübingen School which had appeared in Von Sybel's "Hist. Zeitschrift," but has since been published in the first volume of the "Vorträge."

determination of the essence of God, by virtue of which God only in so far becomes man in time (in every individual man) as He is man from eternity. The finitude and humiliation and passion which Christ as God-man endured God at every moment suffers as man. The atonement ma... by Christ is no temporal performed act, but God reconciling Himself with Himself eternally; and the resurrection and exaltation of Christ is nothing else than the eternal return of the Spirit to Himself and to His truth. Christ as man, as God-man, is man in His universality; not a single individual, but a universal individual."

As regards their speculative Christology, Baur and Strauss were near enough to be described as agreed, but in the application to the personal Christ the significant differences emerged. Strauss too utterly dissolved His historical reality to leave Him any function, but Baur allowed Him too important a function to be able to lose historical reality. He held that it was in Christ that the truth as to the unity of the Divine and human natures first attained concrete and self-conscious being, and was by Him expressed and taught as truth. Here was a double reality: in Him man achieved the consciousness of the truth and from Him received it. In respect of the form of knowledge, and in no other, did the philosopher who knew the absolute stand above Christ. So to speak of Him was to postulate a fulness and certainty of historical knowledge much beyond what Strauss could allow. In other words, the problem to Strauss had been negative, but to Baur it was positive. The former had been only anxious to dissolve the sacred history and turn it into a sensuous form of the absolute philosophy; but the latter was minded to discover what the history had really been, and how out of it so stupendous a fact as Christianity had grown. Thence came Baur's distinctive problem: how, while agreeing with the philosophical construction of Strauss, to escape the negative results of the mythical theory and discover the actual and positive process by which Christianity rose and developed on the field of history. He saw that Strauss had committed a double blunder—one in literary, another in historical, criticism: in literary, because he had attempted a criticism of the Gospel history without any criticism of the Gospels themselves; in historical, because he had neglected the one fixed and certain point·from which the history could be so approached as to be surely and scientifically construed. To do these two things was the function and end of the Tübingen criticism.

In the development of Baur's mind, the order in which he came to the problem was the reverse of that above stated—*i.e.*, the historical preceded the literary. These, indeed, he so fused as to make the distinction somewhat unreal. He so construed history through literature, and literature in history, that one may say all his literary criticism was historical, and all his historical criticism literary. His general canon may be stated thus: Find out the oldest authentic literature, through it discover the strict contemporary history, then use the knowledge thus gained to determine the earlier history and the value of its less strictly authentic literary monuments. In obedience to this canon, he approached the study of the Gospels from positions obtained through the study of the Apostolic Epistles and history. This point of approach is noteworthy, and explains much in Baur's criticism otherwise unintelligible. It grew out of his studies as an historian of dogmas which had carried him back into the post-Apostolic and Apostolic times. The very subjects he had chosen forced him to face the differences within Christianity, and to inquire whence had they come, what were their causes, affinities, distribution. As a result he came to conceive the early Church as a by no means homogeneous body, but one in which there were many minds, shaped by many influences, using ideas and terms, following customs and forming institutions that had often a long prior history. From the controversies of the post-Apostolic he approached the Apostolic age, seeking in the one the germs of the differences he had found in the other. He had, indeed, as early as 1831, in an essay on "The Party of Christ in the Church at Corinth," argued to the existence of antagonisms in the Apostolic Church; but the full extent and meaning of the differences dawned on him but slowly. In his work on "The Pastoral Epistles," published in 1835, he, full of his studies on Gnosticism, argued to their late date, indeed to their origin in the second century, because they exhibit so many and so distinct traces of the ideas, the parties, and the policies of the Gnostic period.

But it was only after he had finished the cycle of his great monographs in the history of dogma that he applied himself to the main problem. His work on "Paul," published in 1845, two years after his "History of the Trinity," exhibits with consummate critical skill the conclusions he had reached. It made an era in New Testament criticism. The significant points in it were two—one critical and one historical. The critical was:—in Romans, 1 and 2 Corinthians, and Galatians, we have authentic Apostolic documents, genuine Epistles of Paul. They are our best authorities on every question touching the origin, nature, and principles of primitive Christianity. The historical position was:—these authentic documents reveal antitheses of thought, a Petrine and a Pauline party in the Apostolic Church. The Petrine was the primitive Christian, made up of men who, while believing in Jesus as the Messiah, did not cease to be Jews, whose Christianity was but a narrow neo-Judaism. The Pauline was a reformed and Gentile Christianity, which aimed at universalizing the faith in Jesus by freeing it from the Jewish law and traditions. The universalism of Christianity, and therefore its historical importance and achievements, are thus really the work of the Apostle Paul. His work he accomplished not with the approval and consent, but against the will and in spite of the efforts and oppositions, of the older Apostles, and especially of their more inveterate adherents who claimed to be the party of Christ. The antithesis was absolute, emerged at every point. It was personal, a conflict as to apostleship—whether Paul's was or was not as authoritative and Divine in its origin as that of Peter or James or John; religious, whether the Gentiles were or were not as free to Christ as the Jews; historical, whether the old dispensation had or had not been repealed. In it the very essence and whole future of Christianity was involved; by it the whole series of Pauline antitheses was explained—grace and law, faith and works, flesh and spirit, letter and spirit, old and new covenant, law and promise, the old man and the new, righteousness by faith or of law, were but forms under which this conflict as to the meaning and mission of the Gospel proceeded. The thing might seem strange, but there it stood written on the broad face of the documents, yet illustrated in their obscurest references and minutest details. The men who had been with Jesus—chosen, called, trained, authorized, and sent out by Him—did not understand Him,—they knew Christ only after the flesh; but the man who had been born out of due time, the last of the Apostles, had, not by the ordinary historical way, but by a sort of miraculous divination, by clear and logical deduction from the cross and death of Christ, rediscovered the universalism and the freedom that were in Him, and rescued Christianity from relapsing into Judaism. Not the unity, therefore, but the differences and antagonisms, of the Apostolic age is the key to all its problems, the point on which the constructive historian must stand if he would do his work.

§ IV.—How Baur solved his Problem.

From the position thus won Baur proceeded, by the help of the Hegelian philosophy and method, to interpret primitive

Christianity, or, in other words, explain the rise of the Catholic Church. This history exhibited, as it were, in operation the fundamental law of the philosophy, was the palmary example of the dialectical movement by which out of difference and contradiction unity was evolved. There was the thesis :—Particularism, Jesus of Nazareth is the Messiah, His religion does not abolish the law, is only a reformed and ennobled Judaism, preached by Jews to Jews; then came the antithesis :—Universalism, Jesus is the Christ the Saviour of the world, known by faith, preached to all men; and, finally, these were harmonized in the synthesis :—the Catholic Church, which reconciled the discordant elements by finding place for a new law, a new priesthood, and a new ceremonial, but at the same time affirmed the Church to be for all, one and universal. In the light of this law of contradiction and conciliation primitive Christianity was read and its history reconstructed. In this work Baur was aided by a distinguished band of scholars, and so the work became from this point not simply his, but his school's. Together they used their principle and method to explain the literature, the doctrine, and the polity of the Apostolic period, yet these three so formed a unity that to explain one was to explain all.

As regards the Pauline literature the application was obvious: the Epistles that showed the antitheses in their sharpest form were the oldest and most authentic; the others had their date fixed according as they exhibited the antitheses as clear, or as modified, or as in process of being overcome. But for us the most interesting thing is the application of this law to the criticism of the Gospels. Baur did not at once see its bearing upon these; saw it only after he had made a special study of John. He perceived in it an ideal purpose; the history was dominated by an idea, written in its interest, made its medium or expression. This was a very different thing from saying that it was mythical. Everything mythical is unhistorical, but not everything unhistorical is mythical.[1] Many things that seem to be mythical owe their form to the free and creative mind of the writer. For this mind history is an easy and elastic medium; and so in the criticism of the Gospels the first question is not, What objective reality has this or that narrative in itself? but rather this, How does the narrative stand related to the consciousness of the narrator, by whose means and presumably for whose ends it has become for us an object of historical knowledge? This relation of the narration to the design or mind of the narrator Baur found most obvious in the Fourth Gospel, and so he described it as a history with a tendency—*i.e.*, not so much a history as a free spiritual creation which made facts the vehicles of the writer's ideas. The Fourth was in every respect a contrast to the Synoptic or historical Gospels; and to do as Strauss had done, use the Synoptics to discredit John, and John to discredit the Synoptics, was altogether uncritical. But John, thus appraised and relegated to a date late in the second century, because representing the very last stage in the process of conciliation and comprehension, made the theory of tendencies applicable to the Synoptics. The application was made in harmony with Baur's ideas as to the state and relation of parties deduced from the recognized Pauline Epistles. As each party had its own notion of the religion, each must have had its own conception of the Master and a history which embodied it. And so the three Gospels represented the three parties—the particularist, the universalist, and the mediatory—and each had its tendency thus determined; it so selected and arranged and handled its material as to express the views or serve the ends of its party. Matthew was the oldest Gospel, the depository of the Judaic or Petrine tradition; Luke was Pauline in its aims, made its selection of narratives and facts in the interests of universalism; while Mark was later and of a ueutral character, won by dropping the points distinctive of

[1] "Krit. Untersch. über die kanon. Evang.," pp. 72, 73.

the other two. And so the Tübingen was the very antithesis of the Straussian criticism, and consisted not in emphasizing the unconsciously creative mythicizing imagination, but in discovering the conscious design, and so using it as to explain the phenomena of the Gospel. The literary criticism thus became but a form of the historical; the conflicts and conciliation that proceeded in the Church created its literature; its idealized histories were but the mirror of its actual life. Baur blamed Strauss for attempting a criticism of the Gospel history without a criticism of the Gospels, so building a structure which floated, foundationless, between heaven and earth. Baur himself fell into the opposite extreme, gave a criticism of the Gospels without any correspondingly adequate criticism of the Gospel histories—*i.e.*, their histories were but the conflicts, or a theory as to the conflicts, of the Apostolic age carried back and made into a life of Christ.

Baur's method was admirably adapted to literary criticism of a given sort. He studied the sources in the light of his theory; searched every document for its peculiarities of style, thought, narration; and then strove to determine the time when and purpose for which it was written. The conflict and reconciliation of the Petrine and Pauline tendencies accomplished the most extraordinary feats in the realms both of Apostolic and post-Apostolic literature. Certain works were written to promote the first, certain others to promote the second, while a third class arose to reconcile the two. Every book, every fraction of a book, had thus its place and purpose in the historical evolution determined. The results seemed at first most satisfactory and permanent. The standpoint of authentic and authoritative history won in the Pauline Epistles appeared to bring certainty where there had been conjecture, order where confusion had reigned. The spirit and policy that united so many conflicting and controversial works into a single and sacred canon combined the opposed parties into one Catholic Church, and formulated their contrary and contradictory opinions into a body of Catholic doctrine. And all was done in obedience to the most scientific law the philosophy of history had been able to formulate. In applying this law to the primitive Church and its literature certain formulæ came into current use, and pity the man who refused to use or subscribe them. The damnatory clauses of the Athanasian Creed were mild in comparison with the judgment he had to bear. Petrinismus and Paulinismus, Particularismus and Universalismus, Idea and Appearance, Tendency, Parteismus, Thesis, Antithesis, Synthesis, were the keys that unlocked all knowledge; to be unwilling to use these or to believe in the discoveries made by their light was to be adjudged an ignoramus or a charlatan, or, worst of all, an apologist, which meant little else than a knave, or one whose only science was the misuse of knowledge. But the simplicity and ease of the method, the splendid results it achieved, the happy yet audacious combinations it enabled men to make, gave to the men who used it a sense of power and of new discoveries, and rallied a brilliant band of scholars round the master. The new Tübingen School was formed, and in it—

"Et pueri nasum rhinocerotis habent."

Schwegler anticipated the master in the application of his theory to collective history or the complete evolution of primitive Christianity, and in a manner which almost surpassed him in critical and constructive ingenuity, tracing the Church from its germ in a Jewish sect which believed Jesus of Nazareth to be the Messiah. Zeller brought his fine historical sense to bear on the Acts of the Apostles; Ritschl wrote the story of the genesis of the primitive Catholic Church; Köstlin busied himself with the theology as well as with the history and criticism of the Gospels. But the limit was soon reached, the formulæ grew emptier the longer they were used, the system was too symmetrical, and though the explanation was so perfect that it ought to have been true, yet somehow it did not satisfy even those who had so laboriously made it out and built it up. The scholars did not serve the school with their matured powers. Schwegler found in the history of Rome a field for the exercise of his critical faculty; Zeller, to the great profit of modern, became the historian of ancient, philosophy; Ritschl passed from the left in theology to the right; and Köstlin went over to æsthetics. The master was not, indeed, left alone: distinguished scholars still stood by him, though more and more asserting by divergences their independence. But even before his death, in December 1860, his school had in reality ceased to be.

§ V.—WHERE THE TÜBINGEN CRITICISM FAILED, AND WHY.

The break-up of the school meant that its work was accomplished, its lines of inquiry and possibilities of combination exhausted. In its earlier stages it had achieved great things; in its later it had failed in literary criticism through one-sided exaggerations, in historical through its inability to explain the facts. It had indeed forced New Testament criticism to become a science; extended our knowledge of the early Church, its men, parties, beliefs, purposes; had given life and motion to the once dead and rigid features of Apostolic and post-Apostolic literature; but it had the faults inseparable from a school that, while formally historical, was essentially philosophical. It failed because the point that was most vital for the history was least important for the philosophy. It neither discovered nor cared to discover the Person that created the processes it described. Paul was more important than Jesus. Impersonal tendencies were greater than conscious persons. Internal divisions and jealousies were forces mightier and more victorious than the enthusiasm of humanity. The genesis of a literature was made in a manner conceivable, but not the genesis of a religion, with its ideas and truths and enthusiasms.

The tendency had demolished the mythical theory. What was written out of the set purpose to serve a party could not be a product of the unconsciously creative phantasy. The conscious invention could not at the same time be an unconscious creation. But the more conscious the creative process became the more difficult grew the theory, for it the more distinctly involved the reality and the veracity of the persons who conducted the process, and demanded an exhaustive analysis of the materials with which they worked. The Tübingen criticism had this paradoxical character—it was at once most abstract in its principles and method, and most concrete and particular in its procedure; and as a consequence what its principles and method determined beforehand its critical process was made to prove. That process was one of internal criticism, uncorrected by a sufficient analysis of what may be termed the objective or external conditions. In place of this stood certain philosophical formulæ, and these were fallacious in the very degree that they were imposing. Thus Particularism was identified with Christian Judaism, and dealt with as if it were something uniform and homogeneous. But it comprehended many varieties: Palestinian; Hellenistic; men who clung to the ceremonialism of the Synagogue, but disliked the Temple; men who held to the Temple and feared the Synagogue; men who were of Essenic, of Pharisaic, or of Sadducaic sympathies; men whose tendencies were more universal than national. Paulinism, too, was not so distinctly Gentile, as Baur imagined; it was full of Judaic elements, which he overlooked, and, as a consequence, whose meaning he did not see, either for the universalism he attributed to Paul, or for the particularism he ascribed to the pillar Apostles. Then, because of his *à priori* and internal criticism, he failed to note the rise and operation of new elements in the Church of the second century. His evolutional process was too exclusive; thought was to him what the Church is to the Catholic, and in watching or describing its evolution he forgot to study the conditions that made it possible or necessary.

We must confess, then, that the Tübingen criticism failed, almost as completely as the Rationalism and Mythicism it displaced, to bring us face to face with the historical realities, especially the living Person that had created Christianity. This failure was manifold. Paul was conceived as the man in whom the Christian principle exists in its purest form, yet, as also holding that the absolute significance of Christianity depends on the person of Christ, is indeed essentially identical with it. But does this sense of the pre-eminence and absolute value of His person belong to the consciousness of Christ Himself or only to the mind of Paul? If to the former, then the Person must be a vaster factor of change than Baur ever allowed Him to be; if only to the latter, all that we have is the peculiar doctrine of a distinguished man. Then, too, if, as Baur argues in another connection,[1] it is the ethical in the person and doctrine of Jesus which constitutes His significance, how comes it that the highly metaphysical Paul is His truest exponent, while the intensely ethical James is dismissed as a typical Ebionite? Then his theory made the rival parties look real and consistent enough while conceived simply in relation to each other, but they became less real and consistent when conceived in historical relation to Jesus. How did it happen that the Petrine party, who had known Him and were the depositaries of the pure original tradition, retained so little of His spirit and teaching, while the Pauline, who had never seen Him, retained and evolved so much? How was it that two so dissimilar streams flowed from the same source? —that Peter so missed and Paul so discovered the import of Christ?—that His person and death meant so much to the one, so little to the other, their ideal thus contradicting, as it were, their actual relations? By what title could principles so antagonistic as legal particularism and evangelical universalism

[1] "Die Tübinger Schule," pp. 30 ff.

both claim to be Christian? and how could qualities that excluded each other be akin in origin and united in end? But these, though radical, were not the only failures on the historical side. The Church, as Baur conceived it, had in its first age well-known men, but almost no literature; in its second a great literature, but almost no known man. How comes it that the jealous-minded men of the first age, who wrote so little, are to us distinct and familiar persons, while the catholic-minded men of the second age, who did and wrote so much, are shadowy and nameless? How has an illiterate age been so full of historical personalities, while a most literate age has hardly one? By what chance have not only the Socrates, but the Sophists, in this case become well-defined characters, living in the full light of history, while Plato and the Platonic circle have faded into nebulous nameless forms? A theory that involves violent anomalies can hardly claim historical veracity. Baur's had enough of the first to cancel its claim to the second. But the failure of the Tübingen School was far from absolute, was indeed in some essential respects equal to the most splendid success. Their method and many of their results remain a precious and inalienable inheritance, which every explorer on the same field must possess before he can hope to succeed.

CHAPTER IV.

THE NEWER HISTORICAL CRITICISM AND THE HISTORICAL CHRIST.

WHAT, then, was the precise result of the Tübingen criticism? Simply this—it had made a more radical, and therefore a more historical, criticism an imperious necessity, and had defined as its final yet primary problem the discovery of the historical Christ. Till He was known, no single step in the scientific and constructive interpretation of primitive Christianity could be taken. The very emphasis that had been laid on the differences in the Apostolic circle compelled an appeal to the source in which they were implied. Hence the inquiry into Paulinism, which had been, as it were, the peculiar quest of Tübingen, was superseded by one more fundamental and much more complex. This was an inquiry that from its very character could not be conducted by the sole light of philosophical principles and the use of internal evidences as their special formulæ, a sort of new dialectic clothed in a peculiar technical terminology of its own, but must proceed in the spirit and method proper to sober yet constructive historical science. All that can be done here is to sketch its main lines and results, but not till we have indicated the energy with which all schools of thought now turned to the problem Tübingen had so carefully masked, yet had made so inevitable.

§ I.—Through Criticism to History.

The years that have passed since the death of Baur in 1860 may be described as the period of the criticism of the Gospels and their history. The work in this field has been at once fruitful and immense. It will be enough, through a few typical books and names, to indicate its scope and variety. In 1859 Ewald described the Tübingen "wisdom" as a "disordered dream,"[1] and he exhibited Christ as the end of the ancient and the beginning of the modern world, the alone true Messiah, the eternal King of the kingdom of God, which He alone founded; the Son of God, as no other had been in our mortal flesh and fleeting time; the purest reflection and most glorious image of the Eternal Himself.[2] It is characteristic that, in the face of all the denials of the Tübingen men, he holds that the Johannean authorship of the Fourth Gospel is "entirely certain," a certainty he had always maintained, and of late again proved; and he loses himself in wonder when he thinks how soon the most marvellous of histories had found so marvellous an historian.[3] In 1863 what has been termed "one of the events of the century" occurred. Rénan's "Vie de Jésus" appeared. Its faults were flagrant, as were all its qualities; it was inadequate, was perfunctory in its literary criticism, violent and subjective in its historical, selecting and grouping its material in obedience to an æsthetic faculty that had more appreciation of the picturesque than of the real. For the rest it was unctuous, without ethical sense or moral discernment, steeped in false sentiment, extravagant in its inverted pietism, offensive in its rapturous eulogies of One it could still represent as in the supreme moments of His life stooping to imposture. Indeed, it has been but too accurately described as the most sacred of all histories done into

---
[1] "Gesch. des Volkes Israel," vol. vii., p. xix.
[2] *Ibid.*, vol. v., pp. 496 ff.
[3] *Ibid.*, vol. v., p. 121; vol. vii., pp. 213 ff.

"a French erotic romance," and the erotics are never so intense as when the character is most impugned. "The Sweet Galilean Vision" was not distinguished by dignity or truthfulness.

But the book was symptomatic; it was the first volume of a series that increased in wisdom as it grew in number, recognizing throughout this truth—that Christianity was to be explained not through abstract principles, tendencies, differences, conciliations, but through its most creative Personality. And it was prophetic—in its train came a succession of remarkable works; two of these were contributions as characteristic of Germany and England as the "Vie de Jésus" was of France. The English[1] was the work of a scholar, but not of a theologian; it had no *apparatus criticus*, hardly any sense of the speculative, literary, or historical questions that had been exercising the theological mind; but, in part for these very reasons, it was a fresh and powerful book. It went, as it were unweakened by metaphysical or critical hesitancies, straight to the moral heart of the matter, asked the meaning of the person and message and society of Jesus. He is so real because so moral; and His morality, which seems too ideal to be practical or even possible, is made by His method and its relation to His personality eminently real and realizable. This book, indeed, was not the first attempt to read and appraise the religion through the character of the Founder; it had been made long before by the genial and sympathetic spirit of Ullmann. In the treatise that fitly introduced the review that has so long and so excellently served the reasonable and irenical school he represented, he with a singularly delicate hand exhibited at once the historical, religious, and theological significance of the "Sinlessness of Jesus."[2] This was precisely the sort of field which English thought could love and cultivate. And so Channing[3] had

[1] "Ecce Homo" (1865). [2] "Studien und Kritiken." (1828), vol. i., pp. 1-83.
[3] Sermon on the "Character of Christ."

argued from the pre-eminence of Christ's character to His
supernatural origin and the truth of His words and mission ;
Young[1] had expanded it into an argument for His Divinity ;
Bushnell[2] had made it a sort of *apologia pro religione suâ*.
But "Ecce Homo" was strong because so little theological,
so untechnical, the sort of fragment that is created not so
much by labour as by a moment of vivid intuition. It
detached Christ's society from the conventional notions suggested by the word "Church," interpreted His words as its
laws, and exhibited its ethico-social idea as the articulated
mind of its Founder. Without the knowledge or the literary
genius of the "Vie de Jésus," it yet had, in a far higher
degree, the veracity and the realism that come only with
moral insight.

The German work was the new "Leben Jesu."[3] It differed
from the old almost as much as Hume from Hegel, Reimarus
from Schleiermacher. It was addressed to the German nation,
the people of the Reformation, whose historical right it was
to lead the advance from the religion of Christ to the religion
of humanity. The tendency in the new is more earthward
than in the old. The child of a transcendental stoops to be
the apostle of an empirical and sensuous age. The love of
truth may be no less, but the hatred of adversaries is more
intense ; and while hatred sharpens the eye for the detection
of pretence, it blinds it to the soul of goodness in things which
seem evil. There is nothing of the Hegelian philosophy
save a faint aroma perceptible here in a term, there in a
turn of thought. The Church is evil, and must be abolished
that the new religion of culture may be realized. The clergy

[1] "The Christ of History" (1855).
[2] "The Character of Jesus." This is chapter x. in "Nature and the Supernatural" (1858); but was also published in separate form in 1861.
[3] "Das Leben Jesu für das Deutsche Volk bearbeitet" (Leipzig, 1864). Translated, and published by Williams & Norgate under the title, "The Life of Jesus for the People."

are compared to field mice, set down as the slaves of self-interest, averse to truth, fighting behind paper battlements which do not deserve a siege.[1] Mediating and modern theologians are written down knaves or fools.[2] Even Baur is not thorough enough to escape censure, is described as using the historical interest as a defence against fanaticism, like the legal fiction which saves the Crown by sacrificing the Ministry.[3]

The new Life is in some respects an improvement on the old. The criticism of the sources is not so utterly inadequate. It is not indeed original, only derivative, a summary of the Tübingen results; but it is a confession that history without literary criticism is worthless. The idea of historical perspective is more developed, the sense for fact keener, the worth of a background to the person and character he would portray better understood. The man, in short, is, while less of a constructive thinker, more of an artist. But while there are more of the prerequisites of a genuine life, there is almost as little of the reality. It is like the work of a decipherer, who, while ambitious to prove the date, alphabet, and language of an inscription, laboriously leaves its contents half read; or like the trick of a renovator, who, while professing to restore the painting of an ancient master, painfully washes out its main lines, and leaves only isolated patches of its principal figure. There is indeed in his Jesus, with His bright and tranquil Hellenic spirit, while less of flesh and blood, more of intellectual and spiritual reality, than in the Jesus of Rénan. But the reality is modern and contemporary rather than historical. Jesus is less a Galilean peasant than a student, consciously eclectic, receiving into Himself from various sources material to be built into unity through the action of His own consciousness. He is, too, at best ill known, has been so covered with parasites, had His features so eaten away, His sap so sucked out, as to be little else than a

[1] P. 162.   [2] P. xix.   [3] xiv. 978.

hardly recognizable ruin. Of few great men do we know so little. But enough is known to deprive Him of unique pre-eminence. He has had predecessors in Israel and Hellas, on the Ganges and the Oxus, and has not been without successors. He looks great to the Church because clothed in clouds. These are not indeed myths in the old sense. The name remains, but the thing is gone. The mythical theory is modified out of existence. Myths cease to be unconscious creations, become more or less intentional inventions. The miracles, whether worked by Jesus or on Him, like the Transfiguration and the Ascension, are myths, but made as often with as without a distinct intention. The Resurrection is the creation of subjective visions. The method is eclectic, Reimarus and Baur having contributed to it almost as much as the earlier and later Strauss. But by what it loses in ideality it gains in reality. The new theory, as less speculative and more historical than the old, is more amenable to criticism. And so the question, by being simplified, has come nearer solution.

The philosophical bases and goal of the New Life in some respects develop, but in general contradict, those of the old. There is less recognition of transcendental truth, more distinct acceptance of a natural and humanistic faith. The fundamental conception approximates to ancient Stoicism, but in its development and application is modified by modern Empiricism. The only things in Christianity said to be imperishable are not peculiar to it—"the belief that there is a spiritual and moral power which governs the world,"[1] and the conviction that "the service of this power can be only spiritual and moral, a service of the heart and mind." This faith can stand, without any supernatural aid, on the natural order of the world. It needs no future state; teaches men, when every hope of life is extinguished, not to comfort the present by drawing on the future; to live, if not as saints,

[1] Vor., xvii.

yet as honourable men; to die, if not blissfully, yet calmly. Whatever man needs lies within the terms of nature. Duty has authority only as evolved from what is involved in man. Religion is only culture, humanity in its finest bloom. Thought thus moves on a lower plane in the new than in the old life. Strauss has fallen back on a narrower and less exalted conception of the universe. There is less of Deity in it. Man has ceased to be a revelation of God. There is not in any proper sense a God to reveal. The "spiritual and moral power which governs the world" has almost nothing in common with the Absolute. The idea of God does not exclude miracles; the most cogent arguments against them are Hume's. Spirit does not now reveal itself in history in changing forms, but in abiding matter. Faith cannot now be translated into science, *Vorstellungen* into *Begriffe*. Where distinctions before existed contradictions now emerge; the Hegelian distinction is superseded by one rougher but much handier, between sense and nonsense, science and ignorance. The ideal truth is not saved, while the historical reality is sacrificed. A speculative Christology is never essayed. The attributes of Christ perish with Him, are not transferred to humanity. There is indeed an ideal Christ, but He is to be construed only as the idea of human perfection. The idea needs to be dissociated from the historical person, the religion of Christ exalted into the religion of humanity. Nothing can be admitted which transcends nature. Humanism is the final and highest goal of man.

Almost simultaneously with the new "Leben Jesu" two other Lives appeared: Schleiermacher's[1] and Schenkel's.[2] As to the former something has been already said. Schleier-

[1] "Das Leben Jesu. Vorlesungen an der Universität zu Berlin im Jahre 1832 gehalten. Aus Schleiermacher's handschriftlichem. Nachlasse u. Nachschriften seiner Zuhörer herausgegeben von Rütenik" (1864). His literary executors had withheld these lectures from publicity for more than thirty years—from fear, Strauss affirmed, caused by his own early work.

[2] "Das Characterbild Jesu" (Wiesbaden, 1864).

macher created his Christ out of the Christian consciousness, while allowing the intellect, as critic and interpreter of the sources, the freest play. Throughout his favourite source is John; while the most transcendental of all the Gospels, it is the least miraculous, most exalted in its doctrine of the Person, most sober and natural in the details of His history. What distinguishes the Christ of John is the vividness and fulness of his consciousness of God, though it does not involve His identity with the Divine, only the unity of His thought and will and life with the Father. Strauss regarded the work as a challenge to criticism, and he criticised thus: Its Christ is not the Jesus of history,[1] but an ideal creation, the last refuge of the ancient faith, built out of, not confessional, but emotional and imaginative, material—"a reminiscence from long-forgotten days, as it were the light of a distant star, which, while the body whence it came was extinguished years ago, still meets the eye."[2]

Schenkel's was mainly remarkable for the way in which he offended men of all schools, and his preference for Mark as the oldest and most trustworthy source. Keim[3] achieved higher and better things, his work being throughout distinguished by a keen, at once historical and spiritual, sense. He set Jesus within a living Judæa, analyzed the forces that played upon and helped to form Him, and endeavoured to construe His life from within, to read His history as if it were an externalization of His mind and spirit, though as such throughout conditioned by His place and time. In Keim's attitude there were many conflicting elements; he wished to remain within the terms of nature, yet ever seemed to feel as if his subject transcended them; the love of the rational and

[1] "Der Christus des Glaubens und der Jesus der Geschichte," 1865.
[2] *Ibid.*, p. 220.
[3] "Die Menschliche Entwickelung Jesu" (1861), "Die Geschichtliche Würde Jesu" (1864), "Der Geschich. Christus" (1865); but mainly the great work which incorporated all these, "Geschichte Jesu von Nazara in ihrer Verkettung mit dem Gesamtleben seines Volkes" (1867-1872).

the sense of the supernatural so contended within him that, with all its detail, and all its dogmatisms, and all its arbitrariness, his book is a book of suggestions rather than of final determinations. It is filled throughout with the conviction that in the life which had so mightily affected man there must be elements which explain its action, and these can never be understood by the man who shuts himself within a narrow and prosaic naturalism, excluding from the present he studies the future it has created.

But detailed or even incidental mention of the really significant recent works on this field is simply impossible, though all are marked by the same characteristic conviction—viz., that literary, historical, and theological criticism must here go hand in hand. They have been critical and conciliatory, like Weizsäcker's, Weiss's, and Beyschlag's, which, dealing often freely with the literature, yet regard Jesus as by indefeasible right of inner being or character belonging to an order higher than the natural. Or they have been conservative and apologetic, like the "Jesus Christ" of Pressensé, Gess's interpretation of the Person through the consciousness, Steinmeyer's "Contributions to Christology," and Luthardt's lectures; or they have been critical and negative, like Volkmar's "Jesus Nazarenus," or the books of Wittichen and Lang. And what is no less encouraging is that Catholics have been as active as Protestants, whether German, like Grimm and Neumann; or French, like Dupanloup and Bougaud, Lasserre and Didon. In England Farrar and Geikie and Edersheim are familiar names, the last having in his own line of rabbinical learning made a considerable contribution to our knowledge of the world which surrounded Jesus. "Supernatural Religion" ought not to be forgotten; it was as if Tübingen had come to life again and assumed in its resurgent state our English speech, yet with a difference. It had all the old *à priori* and doctrinaire method, but its sources were directly modern, indirectly ancient—*i.e.*, it tried to reach primitive Christianity through Tübingen ; but what it reached was Tübingen rather than Christianity. Taken as a whole—though it is a whole that admits, as certain of the above names will show, remarkable rather than weighty exceptions—we may say that more recent Lives are distinguished by a growing sense of being on firm historical ground, and of using sources that the more they are critically handled can be the more intelligently trusted. It is surely a matter on which all parties will agree, that what has so restricted the reign of speculation as to enlarge the area of reality has brought with it little but pure gain. In the region of the highest and most potent life nothing but good can come from the knowledge of the honest truth.

§ II.—THROUGH HISTORY TO THEOLOGY.

But the significant thing is that no examination of Lives can exhibit the gain ; so many distinct yet convergent lines of inquiry have helped to make our views more historical. These may be represented thus :—

1. CONTEMPORARY HISTORY.—It is but in keeping with modern scientific method that the environment should be carefully studied and minutely known in order to the knowledge of the organism. This means that the New Testament cannot be studied in isolation, but must be set against its living background ; or, to vary the figure, planted in its native soil. But it is not a single picture or plant ; it is a series of pictures with many and varied backgrounds, a collection of plants that grew on many and different soils. The Gospels move within a limited area, but it is an area crowded with conflicting forces, very varied in their distribution and in their values. The main scene of the Synoptic history is Galilee—of the Johannean, Judæa ; and these differ almost as much as if they were alien in race and religion —as, indeed, in great part they were. In Galilee the great institution was

the synagogue; in Judæa, the Temple: where the synagogue was in power the rabbi was the minister, religion was instruction, the law was ceremonial, the authority was the written Word and its oral interpretation, and worship the acts and exercises of a popular assembly; where the Temple was supreme the priest was the minister, religion was ritual, the law was sacerdotal, the authority was the sacred institution and its customs, and worship the rites and sacrifices of the altar. In Galilee the Pharisee, in Judæa the Sadducee, was the authoritative and active person in religion; the former had as the peculiar field of his activity the school and the synagogue, but the latter had as his the Temple; the scribes were mainly of the Pharisees, but the priests of the Sadducees. Now, differences like these could not but variously condition life in the two provinces; the influences, the questions, the ideas and notes of religion were all different; the same person could hardly seem the same when transplanted from the one to the other, and the difference would be in precise proportion to the strength and intensity of his action on religion. But insight into these differences and what they signified is a very recent thing; accurate discrimination of the two great parties may be said to have begun only in the latter half of our century, and the result has been to give us a more vivid and a more veracious view of the conditions under which Jesus lived. We know better the influences that surrounded Him, the forces He had to contend against, the causes of His changeful fortunes in Galilee, of the final catastrophe at Jerusalem. Of the many gains two especially concern us here. We are better able to test the veracity of the sources and to judge as to the truth and verisimilitude of the history, and we are better qualified to measure the forces then active in Judæa, what they could and what they could not do, whether they were equal to the creation of either the historical or the ideal Christ, whether He but impersonated or really transcended His conditions.

Of course, the value of this study is not confined to the Gospels; it is even more necessary to our knowledge of the Apostolic age. By giving knowledge of the various environments into which the new religion passed, it helps to explain its tendency not to indefinite variation, but to variations of given types along given lines. Without it Paul could not be understood; with it the one-sided and *à priori* Tübingen construction of him is impossible. It is teaching us to know something of the varied forces that modified Judaism at home and abroad, to distinguish the many types of Hellenism—Syrian, Alexandrian, Italian, Grecian—to analyze its action alike on the formation of heretical and catholic thought, of the separate communities and the organized Church. It is teaching us no less to study the action of Greek and Roman cities, their politics, commerce, guilds, schools, customs, on the Christian societies and their leaders, and is helping us to understand how kindred germs in different environments may become very different organisms. On the whole, it has become manifest that without accurate knowledge of contemporary history no scientific criticism or construction of ancient Christianity is in any respect possible.

2. Increased knowledge of contemporary history has made constructive historical criticism much more possible. To the new historical temper the Tübingen method is peculiarly alien, especially its notion of history as an immanent or a dialectical evolution of thought by means of antithesis and synthesis, a sort of naturalism stated in the language of the pure intellect. Its questions are matters of fact, of evidence and interpretation, not of the determination and development of the idea. Ritschl[1] challenged the right of the criticism that settled the question of miracles by philosophy, to the name historical. And it was a question Baur had at the most critical point evaded. The reality of the faith in the Resurrection had been for him the main thing; but for history the main thing—indeed, the only

[1] "Jahrb. für deuts. Theol.," vol. vi., pp. 429 ff.

real thing—was the fact rather than the faith. And this was typical; it was only the most flagrant example of his theory that history was but the evolution of the Spirit, the genesis of the Church only the conciliation of differences. Historical criticism followed the reverse process—abandoned theory for a study and analysis of all the conditions, examined the organism and environment in their mutual relations with a view to the exhibition of the final result. If the ancient Church were so approached, the Pauline differences could not be made the constructive starting-point; they were consequences rather than causes; what was necessary was to get behind them. In the matter of radical belief as to the place and person of Christ there were indeed differences, but not contradictions, in the Apostolic circle. And these differences assumed a sort of unity, or at least received explanation, when viewed in relation to Him. He had declared that He had come to found a new covenant over against the old; and here all parties were at one.[1] On this point the Synoptics were more emphatic than John; and Mark, the oldest of the Gospels, as explicit as either Matthew or Luke. But when the Apostolic men made the attempt to conceive and represent what this meant, the differences emerged; and in order to understand why they did, all the conditions and forces of the time must be considered. There was a double transformation or development—viz., of doctrine and of polity—and to each, as parallel and correlative, all parties contributed,—the men who knew the Old Testament and construed Christ through it quite as much as the men who came to the Old Testament only through Christ; but to both He was equally and essentially the Christ, founder of their society, source of their faith. This meant that the personal Christ played not only a much greater part in the creation of His society than Tübingen had assigned to Him, but a part so great that He was everything to it, source alike of the differences by which it only the more lived

[1] Ritschl, "Die Entstehung der altkathol. Kirche," pp. 27 ff. (1857).

and did Him reverence, and of the methods and reason by which they were overcome.

So much did the new lines of inquiry affect the critics of the newest Tübingen School that they abandoned metaphysics and took to psychology, yet so as only the more to emphasize the significance now given to the person and work of Christ. Thus, as they could not surrender their fixed point, Paul was interpreted through his mental constitution; he became an epileptic who could not but see visions and mistake them for realities, or a dialectician so compacted of nerves and reason, of sensitive flesh and susceptible soul, that he was forced to translate his experience into a system of the universe. As a compound of enthusiast and schoolman his formulæ came to him from various sources—the constructive impulse from his conversion, but the real material he used from his own experience. Still, psychology carries us but a very little way in historical criticism. The more Paul's idiosyncrasies were magnified the more remarkable became the force that caused him to do what he did. But this certainly, in the very degree it magnified his peculiar character, tended to exalt the personal significance of Christ: He becomes more and more evidently the cause of all that is pre-eminent in Paul and in the Apostolic age as a whole; the forces that belittle and deprave rise from the conditions into which His society enters, not from Him. And this has further resulted in emphasizing the most cardinal of all the facts which the Tübingen men overlooked—the new life that came in with Christ and through Him. Of this life the thought which Baur so dwelt on was but the expression. But the life was more than the thought—its source, reason, the soil out of which it grew, the energy by which it lived. And the life is a most manifest effect, existent in all the Apostles, creating a new literary capability, a new ethical, social, religious spirit, a society of brother missionaries, possessed of the enthusiasm to heal and to save. And once thought enters into the meaning of this new life and its value for humanity, it is forced back on its cause, and compelled to see that without Christ the greatest movement in history has neither a beginning nor an end.

3. But coincident with the historical has been a new literary criticism. With the disappearance of the old theory of sharp antitheses, the arguments which restricted the Pauline Epistles to four have lost their force, and even critics of the negative order have allowed both the Thessalonians and Philippians to find their way into the circle of the authentic. While as to the others more accurate knowledge as to the forms and distribution of Gnosticism is shedding new light on their origin, succession, and meaning. The Apocalypse, too, is seen to have another value than Baur assigned to it, and the criticism of the Gospels has simply been revolutionized. By a process of the most minute and rigidly scientific investigation the Synoptics have been proved to stand in relations fatal alike to the order and the tendencies of Tübingen. Mark is now held to be the oldest, and the discussion as to the sources and the dependencies of all the three is carrying us, alike as regards the history and the words of Jesus, to a standpoint where the ancient harmonist and the recent mythicist alike cease to trouble. The Fourth Gospel, too, is read with an opener sense, a cycle of tradition that helps to explain it is slowly recovered, and a clearer and more literary conception of the relation of the speeches both to the speaker and the reporter is being formed, while a broader notion of its method and function is filling it with a new historical content. In a word, just as the mind which comes to the New Testament has grown more historical, it has become more historical to the mind—*i.e.*, the mind has been able to discover a more historical character in the literature, has trusted abstract principles less, has studied the textual, philological, and literary matter and minutiæ more, with the natural result that the more scientific treatment has obtained more assured results. In this field the services of English scholarship have been conspicuous and

meritorious, and happily complementary to the more audacious and brilliant inquiries of Continental scholars.

4. The new historical and literary spirit has produced a more detailed and skilful handling of the thought or intellectual content of the literature. The sacred writers are not now dealt with as if their personalities had been merged into one colossal individuality, and as if the very composite material they had created were a single work which could be interpreted and quoted as a homogeneous whole. The new insight into the characters, histories, circumstances, succession of the writers, has necessitated a distinct and special treatment of their minds and words, which has, as notably in the case of Paul, enabled us to measure and register the change and expansion of their thought. "Biblical theology" means now the theology of the Bible, not of the creeds or schools. Within the New Testament the most careful and exhaustive work of this kind has been done. We can now with reverence, yet with accuracy, speak of "the theology" or "the doctrine of Jesus." And works like Wendt's[1] shed through the theology needed light upon the Person. His great terms and phrases, like "the Messiah," "the Son of Man," "the Son," "the Kingdom of God," "the New Covenant"—His great sayings, parables, discourses, like the Sermon on the Mount—His addresses to His disciples—His warnings to the Pharisees—His prayers in Gethsemane and words on the cross,—have all been analyzed, compared, explained; His speeches in John have been read at once in comparison and in contrast with those in the Synoptics; and so we have been invited, as it were, to know Him as He knew Himself, to understand His mission as it was in His mind and before it had been touched by the spirit of Paul or seized by the coarse hands of controversy.

And Paul has been even more elaborately discussed, dissolved, and, as it were, rearticulated. His own authentic

[1] "Die Lehre Jesu" (1886 and 1890).

words still throb with the passion or glow with the love that filled him as he wrote; we can follow his swift though not always obvious logic, and reconstruct his world while we interpret his mind. Hebrews and John, Peter and James, have been similarly treated and explained, and we can now look at the thought of the New Testament in its constituent parts, in its historical succession, and as a complete, if not organic, whole. Its differences, the affinities they imply but cannot conceal, its evolution and its causes, we can now trace, and one thing is beginning to stand out with a perfectly new distinctness—viz., the degree in which the mind of the Master transcends the minds of the disciples; not the way they develop His teaching, but how they fail to do it; the elements they miss or ignore, forget or do not see. Where Paul is greatest is where he is most directly under the influence or in the hands of Jesus, evolving the content of what he had received concerning Him; where he is weakest is where his old scholasticism or his new antagonism dominates alike the form and substance of his thought. So with John: what in him is permanent and persuasive is of Christ; what is local and even trivial is of himself. To exhibit in full the falling off in the Apostles cannot be attempted here; enough to say, their conception of God is, if not lower, more outward, less intimate, or, as it were, from within; nor does it, with all its significance as to the absolute Paternity, penetrate like a subtle yet genial spirit their whole mind, all their thought and all their being. They have lost also, in some measure at least, what is its earthly counterpart—the social form under which it can be realized in time, the idea of the kingdom, with all it implies as to the human brotherhood which expresses the Divine Sonship. Their ethics have lost the wonderful searching inwardness yet fine sanity of the Sermon on the Mount; their conduct is more mixed, their tempers are more troubled and troublesome; they so live as to show more of the infirmities of man and less of the calm which comes of the complete possession of God. These are differences which Tübingen overlooked, but they do more to distinguish and differentiate the schools in the early Church than any it discovered. But does not this mean that the very process which has reclaimed Christ for knowledge has tended to restore Him to faith? He stands out in a new degree and way the creator of His society, with thoughts greater than it has been able to assimilate, source of its continuous progress by making the re-interpretation of His person its constant and inevitable problem.

§ III.—Results and Inferences.

1. This history may be described as an inquiry into the causes and the process by which the historical Christ has been recovered. It has been due to no single man or book, but represents a tendency or movement which individuals have served, but no individual created. Literature, philosophy, criticism, theology, religion, have all contributed to it, and the result has been due to their common action, which has been all the more concordant that it was so undesigned. The Person that literature felt to be its loftiest ideal, philosophy conceived as its highest personality, criticism as its supreme problem, theology as its fundamental datum, religion as its cardinal necessity. The most destructive efforts became the conditions of the most constructive achievements, and the century whose middle decades were marked by a process of historical and literary disintegration, finds its last decade distinguished by a process of re-integration, or a new and profounder sense of the historical reality and pre-eminence of the Person who had been mythically dissolved or dialectically construed into a product of conflicting tendencies.

2. The new sense of His historical being and transcendence is reflected in the changed tone and attitude of literature. The ethical idealization of Schiller and the rather benevolent

or condescending allusions of Goethe, as of one speaking from a lofty height concerning another who had struggled upwards to a lower standpoint, are now unknown. The two most illustrious poets of our era were distinguished by their feeling not for the abstract and ideal, but for the concrete and historical Christ. But even more significant is the case of the most typical English man of letters in our generation. Matthew Arnold was an earnest, though we can hardly call him a serious, religious teacher. He was, indeed, anything but this at the outset—classical, almost pagan in his restraint and suppression of himself towards religion. Goethe was his saint and ideal, " Europe's sagest head," " the physician of the iron age."

> " He took the suffering human race,
> He read each wound, each weakness clear,
> And struck his finger on the place,
> And said, *Thou ailest here, and here !* "

But the more Arnold came to feel the historical reality of Jesus, the more he fell under His invincible charm and bowed before His religious supremacy. And the poet and man of letters changed his *rôle*. He tried to become the interpreter of Christ, as it were a new apostle, charged to preach His Gospel, the secret he had found in His Word, to the age of the Philistines. It might not be a great secret, many had found it before him, but the remarkable thing was not the quality or range of his truth, but the fact of his message and the reality of his vocation as he conceived it. It was a sort of spontaneous confession by one whose love was culture, that the sure way to be cultivated was to learn and follow the secret of Him who in spite of His lowly estate was yet the finest ideal of humanity.

3. But this historical Christ means much more for the Church than for literature. We cannot stand as we now do face to face with Him in a sense and to a degree unknown in the Church since the Apostolic age, and be as we were before. For this immediacy of knowledge compels the

comparison of our societies, conventions, and systems with His mind and ideal. As He is the source and the authority of all the Churches, no Church can refuse to be measured and judged by Him. No development can be legitimate that is alien to His spirit and purpose.

4. He thus becomes the determinative idea in ecclesiastical questions. The Fathers cannot explain Christ, though He can explain the Fathers. He is ultimate, but they are derivative. Their knowledge is as less historical, more defective, than ours; and where knowledge is inadequate the judgment can never be final. The old Protestant appeal to Paul was more reasonable than the Tractarian appeal to the undivided Church of East and West, or the Ultramontane appeal to a central and infallible authority; for Paul had the Apostolic knowledge that was the basis of Apostolic authority, but the undivided Church could not have the authority, for it did not possess the knowledge, while the Ultramontane authority is one the sources can better judge than it can judge the sources. The authority which the ancient Church was without the modern Church cannot possess; and so neither it nor any branch of it can be the norm of Christ, while He is the norm of the whole Church, and of all its branches.

5. This return has made evident to us the true historical method in criticism. It must proceed from the source downwards, and not simply be contented to judge the source by what we find far down the stream. Above in the fountain there is purity, but below in the river impurities that gather as the course lengthens and the fields tilled and reaped of men are drained into its waters.

6. But even less than literature and the Church and criticism can theology remain unaffected by this return, as it were, into His very presence. We all feel the distance placed by fifty years of the most radical and penetrating critical discussions between us and the older theology, and as the distance widens the theology that then reigned grows less

credible because less relevant to living mind. Does this mean that the days of definite theological beliefs are over, or not rather that the attempt ought to be made to restate them in more living and relevant terms? One thing seems clear: if a Christian theology means a theology of Christ, at once concerning Him and derived from Him, then to construct one ought, because of our greater knowledge of Him and His history, to be more possible to-day than at any previous moment. And if this is clear, then the most provisional attempt at performing the possible is more dutiful than the selfish and idle acquiescence that would simply leave the old theology and the new criticism standing side by side, unrelated and unreconciled.

BOOK II.

THEOLOGICAL AND CONSTRUCTIVE.

Div I.—*THE NEW TESTAMENT INTERPRETATION OF CHRIST.*

Div. II.—*CHRIST THE INTERPRETATION OF GOD.*

Div. III.—*THE INTERPRETED GOD AS THE DETERMINATIVE PRINCIPLE.*

       A.—Of Theology.
       B.—Of the Church.

A. Ecce oravi Deum. *R.* Quid ergo scire vis? *A.* Hæc ipsa omnia quæ oravi. *R.* Breviter ea collige. *A.* Deum et animam scire cupio. *R.* Nihilne plus? *A.* Nihil omnino.—AUGUSTINE, "Solil.," lib. i., c. 2.

Tu verò es quod es: quia quicquid aliquando, aut aliquo modo es: hoc totus, et semper es. Et tu es qui propriè et simpliciter es: quia nec habes fuisse, aut futurum esse; sed tantum præsens esse nec potes cogitari aliquando non esse. Sed et vita es, et lux, et sapientia et beatitudo, et æternitas, et multa hujusmodi bona; et tamen non es nisi unum et summum bonum, tu tibi omnino sufficiens, et nullo indigens; quo omnia indigent ut sint, et ut bene sint.—ANSELM, "Proslogium," c. 22.

Divina bonitas est finis rerum omnium.—THOMAS AQUINAS, "Summa," P. i, Q. 44, art. 4.

In illo summo bono universaliterque perfecto est totius bonitatis plenitudo atque perfectio. Ubi autem totius bonitatis plenitudo est, vera et summa charitas deesse non potest. Nihil enim charitate melius, nihil charitate perfectius. Nullus autem pro privato et proprio sui ipsius amore dicitur proprie charitatem habere. Oportet itaque ut amor in alterum tendat, ut charitas esse queat. Ubi ergo pluralitas personarum deest, charitas omnino esse non potest.—RICHARD OF ST. VICTOR, "De Trin.," lib. ii., c. 2.

Die christliche Religion hat ihren historischen Grund und Quellpunkt in der Person Jesu. Diese giebt beidem, dem Christenthum und seinem Dogma, seinen geschichtlich bestimmten, d. h. positiven Charakter.

Das religiöse Verhältniss, das als objectiv neue Gottesoffenbarung in der menschlich neuen Thatsache des religiösen Selbstbewusstseins Jesu in die Menschheitsgeschichte eingetreten ist und das Realprincip der christlichen Gemeinschaft und ihres Glaubens ausmacht, ist in der Gotteskindschaft als der unmittelbaren Selbstaussage des religiösen Selbstbewusstseins Jesu ausgedrückt. Der Inhalt dieses Begriffes ist der Inhalt des christlichen Principes: das Christenthum ist die Religion der in Jesu für die Menschheit real aufgeschlossenen Gotteskindschaft und damit des in dieser sich realisirenden Gottesreiches als des göttlichen Endzweckes der Menschheit.—BIEDERMANN, "Dogmatik," §§ 158 and 160.

DIVISION I.

THE NEW TESTAMENT INTERPRETATION OF CHRIST.

THE questions that fall to be discussed in this Second Book are mainly of two kinds,—exegetical, concerned with the source of our Christian conception of God; and constructive, concerned with its explication. We use exegesis that we may think of God as Christ did; but we construct a theology when His conception of God is made the idea through which we interpret the universe. His consciousness is the source and norm of the conception, but the conception is the source and norm of the theology. This theology must then, to use a current term, be, as regards source, Christocentric, but, as regards object or matter, theo-centric; in other words, while Christ determines the conception, the conception determines the theology. Hence, what we have to do is, first, to attempt to interpret God through the history and consciousness of Christ; and, secondly, to elaborate this interpretation into the main lines of a Christian theology.

CHAPTER I.

THE EXPOSITORY BOOKS.

THE New Testament as a whole may be described as a series of co-ordinate rather than successive attempts at an interpretation of Christ. These attempts are either historical or constructive, and by no means represent one uniform, simple idea, but rather many ideas, all complex and manifold.

We shall best discover what these are by beginning with the Epistles. In them there are five main types of thought, which we may term, after the authors or titles of the several books, the Pauline, the Hebraic, the Jacobean, the Petrine, and the Apocalyptic. These all have this in common: they are attempts to construe the person and work of Jesus Christ through the history, literature, religion, and people of Israel; but they differ in the use they make of these interpretative media, and the relative values they assign to them and to Him. Paul interprets Jesus through the Messianic promise and the prophetic ideal, and mainly in opposition to the literalism of the rabbinical schools and the Pharisaic law; Hebrews, through the idealized religious institutions of Israel, especially the priesthood and the Temple; James, through the law as understood in the synagogue; Peter, through prophecy as the organ of the Messianic hope; the Apocalypse, through the people of God, His elect, though hated and persecuted of man. These all witness to the historical reality of Jesus Christ, to the being of communities whose life is derived from Him, to a common belief in the transcendence of His person, and to a common necessity of understanding what this transcendence means and involves. They all imply that His history is known, and that their readers do not need any information concerning it, the emphasis laid on His sinless character, death, and resurrection being for doctrinal rather than mere historical reasons. Readers and writers are all monotheists; all believe in the God of Israel, the reality of Israel's vocation, the authority of his sacred literature, in the Divine origin of his religion. Grant all these things, and What are we to think of Jesus Christ? may be said to be the problem common to them all. The very fact that such a problem had at such a stage arisen, among such a people, and with such beliefs, is remarkable. What it signifies we may best discuss after we have reviewed the various interpretations.

§ I.—THE PAULINE CHRISTOLOGY.

A. Before attempting to interpret Paul's conception of Christ, several things necessary to a proper historical estimate of him and his theology must be noted.

1. The Epistles which specially concern us may be divided into three classes: (*a*) the historical and polemical, including Galatians, Romans, 1 and 2 Corinthians; (β) the transitional, Philippians; (γ) the Christological, Ephesians and Colossians. I do not think that any good reason for the denial of his authorship of any of these has been made out.

2. The polemical Epistles are, with the probable exception of the Thessalonians, our oldest authentic Christian literature. There may be older literary material in the Synoptics, and even in the Acts, but it is material which cannot with certainty be discovered and detached from its context, while the books in which it is embedded are all, as books, later than these Epistles.

3. The relation as regards theology of all these Epistles

may be stated thus: In material principle the system is throughout the same, but the later is the more developed, and is stated with formal differences due to a different antithesis and purpose. In (*a*) the antithesis is Judæo-Christian, and so the argument assumes a more limited historical form, uses terms and establishes positions determined not simply by the thinker, but by the system he opposes. In (β) the old antithesis is present in the soteriology,[1] but the Christology, which rises out of an ethical and is pervaded by a hortatory purpose,[2] escapes from the old Judæo-historical terminology into one wider and more general, though behind lies the memory of the old antagonisms.[3] In (γ) the antithesis is a *gnosis* which has both Hellenic and Hellenistic elements, requiring a discussion which is now as formally cosmical and ethical as in (*a*) it had been historical and Judæo-scholastic. We may say, then, that what these Epistles show is a developing system, reflecting the growth of a mind alive to new problems and affected by changing conditions.

4. Their common characteristic is an interpretation of Christ of so comprehensive a character as to be both a philosophy of man and history and a theology. It is, as it were, the universe, its cause, course, and end interpreted in the terms of Christ.

5. This system was not simply formulated, but received literary expression less than a generation after His death at the hands of a man who indeed did not know Him "according to the flesh," but who had lived in the city where He died, first among the men who had compassed His death, and then among the men who had known and followed Him. Paul came through Jesus as He seemed to the Jews to Jesus as He was to the disciples, and it was while face to face with the knowledge he had from both sources that his theology took its rise.

6. The system has not simply an interpretative but an

[1] Phil. iii. 5-9.   [2] Phil. ii. 5.   [3] Phil. i. 28-30.

historical significance. One or two of His sayings,[1] and of actual events, His descent and birth,[2] His institution of the Supper,[3] His death, burial, resurrection,[4] may be said to be all of the history these Epistles know. But to represent this as all the knowledge they give is to make a superficial truth suggest a complete falsehood. They are wholly filled by His personality. Its reality, the conditions under which He lived, what He did, suffered, seemed, and was, are so woven into their very texture that without the Gospels we could not make even a show of interpreting the Pauline Epistles. And what does this mean but that the history is the very groundwork of the Apostle's thought, everywhere assumed in it, inseparable from it, the element in which it lives, moves, and has its being.

7. With the biographical relations and psychological roots of the Pauline theology we have here no concern, but simply with its doctrine of Christ. Yet it may not be irrelevant to be reminded that its historical worth and action are something quite distinct from even the most accurate scientific theory as to the subjective conditions of its origin.

B. In the Christology we have two questions,—one theological, concerned with the conception of God as modified by the doctrine of Christ; another soteriological, concerned with the modes and forms under which He is conceived to live and act in time. As regards the former, the doctrine of all the Epistles is identical; as regards the latter, formal differences emerge that will necessitate distinct discussion.

I. THE THEOLOGY.—Schultz says: "Paul is the creator of the theological doctrine of the Godhead of Christ, especially of the doctrine of the Christ in distinction from the doctrine of Jesus as the Christ."[5] This means that he was the first, not to conceive Jesus as Messiah, but to conceive

---
[1] 1 Cor. vii. 10, 11, ix. 14.　　[3] 1 Cor. xi. 23 ff.
[2] Rom. i. 3, ix. 5; Gal iii. 16, iv. 4.　　[4] 1 Cor. xv. 1-8.
[5] "Die Lehre von der Gottheit Christi," p. 395.

His Messiahship as involving His divinity. This may be true so far as the dialectic expression of the idea is concerned, but it is not true as to the real contents of the idea. Jesus Himself effected the revolution in the idea, but Paul elaborated the idea so revolutionized into a theology.

The constructive thought of Paul starts with the historical person of Jesus, and his primary postulate may be said to be its truth and reality. This historical Person is to him the one and only Messiah. In the Gospels Jesus is a personal but Christ an official name, and the two are never interchanged or confounded [1]; but in the Pauline Epistles Christ has become as personal a name as Jesus [2]—*i.e.*, the Person so constitutes the office and the office is so incorporated in the Person that distinction has ceased to be possible. Jehovah started as a denominative and became an appellative, denoted first the God of Israel in distinction from other gods; but when the monotheism grew absolute, it became, as it were, generic, the synonym of God; Jehovah could be used only of God, God only of Jehovah, and other usage in either case was impious or idolatrous. So the Christ was at first like a predicate waiting for a subject; it denoted an office which no one had as yet filled; but by the time Paul began to write the office had been so occupied that it could never again be vacant: the personal name, Jesus, had become official, signified the Saviour; the official name, Christ, had become personal, denoted Jesus. But this inter-incorporation of the Person with the office and of the office with the Person had a twofold effect—the attributes of the office became those of the Person, the qualities of the Person were conveyed to the office. The rank, the place of the Messiah in prophecy and promise, His function in

---

[1] This distinction gives all their point to the words of Peter, Matt. xvi. 16; the question of Jesus to the scribes, Matt. xxii. 42; the question of the high priest, xxvi. 63, and the words of mockery, 68.

[2] Cf. 1 Thess. ii. 6, iii. 2, iv. 16; 2 Thess. iii. 5; Rom. v. 6, 8, vi. 4, 9, vii. 4, viii. 9, 10, 11, ix. 3, 5, xiv. 9, 15, 18, xv. 3, 17, 18, etc.

THE DIVINE SONSHIP. 307

Israel and for the world, were seen to belong to Jesus; the filial and fraternal spirit, the moral qualities and acts, the passion and death of Jesus became descriptive of the Messiah. The incorporation of the office in the Person meant that its history became His; the identification of the Person with the office meant that His character became its.

Now, it is the distinction of Paul that he made this unity, with all it involved, articulate, and it is also characteristic that the determinative idea in the system which he elaborated with so much dialectical passion came from the personality of Jesus and not from the Messianic office. That idea was His filial relation, His Divine Sonship. What was to him the primary fact in the consciousness of Jesus became the constitutive factor of his own thought. By the revelation of the Son in him he was made a Christian and an Apostle.[1] His Gospel concerned the Son of God,[2] who is God's own Son,[3] His beloved,[4] the Son of His love.[5] This Sonship did not begin with His historical existence, but preceded and even determined it. God sends forth His Son, who exists before He can be sent forth,[6] and comes that He may create in man the spirit of the sonship He Himself has by nature.[7] He, though rich, yet for our sakes becomes poor.[8] He comes out of heaven, descends from above that He may ascend with man redeemed.[9] Hence there follows a twofold consequence, the one affecting the Son, the other the Father. As to the Son a place and an eminence are ascribed to Him that involve Divine rank and honour. In contrast to the multitudinous deities and lords of heathendom Paul places the one God and the one Lord, and then co-ordinates while distinguishing the two thus: "All things

[1] Gal. i. 15, 16.
[2] Rom. i. 3.
[3] Rom. viii. 3, 32; Gal. iv. 4.
[4] Eph. i. 6.
[5] Col. i. 13.
[6] Gal. iv. 4; Rom. viii. 3.
[7] Gal. iv. 5; Rom. viii. 9, 14-17.
[8] 2 Cor. viii. 9.
[9] 1 Cor. xv. 47; Rom. x. 6, 8; Eph. iv. 10.

are from the Father and we unto Him; all things are through the Son and we through Him."[1] The Father is the one and universal source and end; the Son is the one and universal medium and actualizing cause. As such He is Lord of all, "both of the dead and the living,"[2] and the confession of this absolute sovereignty marks the Christian.[3] And what this means is made explicit in a most emphatic way: Old Testament texts that refer to Jehovah are applied to Christ,[4] and He is made the ultimate standard and end of action. Whether we live or die it is unto Him.[5] And so it need not in any way surprise us that Paul speaks of the Son as "He who is over all, God blessed for ever."[6] The doxology was the natural language of such a faith.

And this faith he more fully develops in a passage marked

---

[1] 1 Cor. viii. 5, 6.
[2] Rom. x. 12, xiv. 9.
[3] Phil. ii. 11; 1 Cor. xii. 3: cf. 1 Cor. i. 9; Rom. i. 4, v. 21.
[4] Rom. x. 13, cf. Joel iii. 10; 1 Cor. ii. 16, x. 22, cf. Deut. xxxii. 21.
[5] Rom. xiv. 6-9, cf. 4; Phil. i. 21.
[6] Rom. ix. 5. This is a passage where the grammar admits by a change of punctuation and emphasis several different interpretations. The late Ezra Abbot ("Critical Essays," xvi.) enumerates seven possible constructions, all grammatical, and each representing a distinct phase of theological doctrine. But his classification resolved itself into two main divisions: (a) where ὁ ὤν, with all that follows, including θεός, is referred to Christ; and (β) where ὁ ὤν introduces a new sentence and θεός denotes God, the Father. (a) may be termed the Christological, (β) the doxological interpretation. Where grammar is so little decisive we must be guided by exegesis; and it seems to me as if the Apostle's argument has its natural culmination in the Christology, while the doxology would be a most un-Pauline ending to a catalogue of Jewish privileges. Κατὰ σάρκα is one side of the very antithesis with which the Epistle opens (i. 3), and has no meaning without its other member. Were there no theological considerations in the case, ὁ χριστός would be naturally taken as the antecedent of ὁ ὤν; and this appears also as the connection which the argument requires. And if Christ can be said to be ὁ ὤν ἐπὶ πάντων, then it is a violent bit of exegesis to erect the last clause into a sentence with a new subject. For the rest, θεός is here taken as predicative, not as denominative, and is in this sense entirely suitable both to the special argument and to the general theology. Θεός is the natural predicate of one ὁ ὤν ἐπὶ πάντων. And this is but a paraphrase of passages already considered.

by epic fulness and dignity.¹ In order to see its meaning we must seize its argument. It starts from the historical "Christ Jesus." His reality is assumed, and a common conception of His person. If the readers did not agree with the writer in both these respects, his argument would lose all validity. He is not labouring the proof of a dogmatic position, but is using a common belief to enforce a neglected duty. He speaks then of the "Christ Jesus" they knew, who had been "found in fashion as a man," and was "obedient unto death." He is the supreme example of sacrifice in order to service, of the surrender of all that a self might hold dear in order to the saving of man. Why? Because, although in the form of God, He did not think the being equal with God a thing to be clutched at, but emptied Himself for our good. Prior being is here affirmed, a being so in the form of God that to be equal with Him is a thing of nature, a being, too possessed of thought and will; and a will not·bound like man's to obedience to a higher, but with the power and right to be a law unto itself, the quality of the will which is law being evident in the beneficence of the deed. It is when His prior dignity is considered that His voluntary humiliation, obedience, and death appear so wonderful, and His later exaltation so entirely natural and fit. But so to construe Christ is to modify the whole conception of God. Abstract monotheism ceases, and is replaced by a theism which finds within the one Godhead room for both Father and Son. It is the characteristic of the Pauline theology that it is a theology of the Fatherhood which is through the Sonship. Neither can be without the other; both must be together, or neither can be at all. The ideas exist in what we may term a spontaneous rather than an explicated and formulated unity, but they exist and are co-ordinated.² The divinity of both Father and Son was affirmed; later thought must

¹ Phil. ii. 6-11 ; Meyer, *in loc.*
² Gal. i. 1; 1 Cor. i. 3; Rom. i. 7; 2 Cor. i. 2.

determine how their unity could be conceived and expressed. The great thing gained was, Fatherhood and Sonship were as immanent essential to Deity.

II. THE SOTERIOLOGY.—But, now, how did Paul bring his theological idea into relation with reality? As the filial idea which he owed to the Person penetrated, pervaded, and modified his doctrine of God, so the historical and soteriological idea which he owed to the Messianic office affected his notion of man, past and present, individual and collective. By investing the Divine Son with all the attributes and functions of the Christ he brought God and man into relation; made God fill and govern all history, and history become the slow unfolding of His purpose; made man as a race appear as an organism or unity over against the one God, while man as an individual appeared in His sight as a being of peculiar value and an object of peculiar regard. It was under this aspect that the theology became a philosophy of history as well as a doctrine of redemption, and the differences between the earlier and later Paulinism emerged.

1. *The system of the earlier Epistles.*—This system is governed as to form by its double antithesis—Judaism and Judaic Christianity. He has the history, persons, institutions, terms, of the Old Testament ever before him, but only that he may reverse the process of the Judaizers; read Christ into the Old Testament instead of the Old Testament into Christ. On this the whole future of Christianity depended. Had they succeeded, the new religion would have died into the old, but by his success the new escaped from the old, and lived.

i. In Paul the Christology is, as it were, the synthesis of the theology and the anthropology; or, in other words, his conception of Christ stands organically connected with his conception of God on the one hand and of man on the other. One side of this relation we have seen: Christ is God's Son, existing in the form of God, Divine in name and dignity. But on the other side He is connected with man, born of a woman,[1] of the seed of David,[2] and the stock of Abraham.[3] He is thus twofold in origin and nature. According to the flesh, He is of man, and especially Israel[4]; according to the spirit, He is of God.[5] On this ground and for this reason He occupies a unique position; like the first man, He is a new creation, and like him the common source or parent of a race; but in every other respect they stand as direct and absolute contrasts. The first man was natural, but the second is spiritual: the one was of the earth, made from the dust of the ground; but the other is "out of heaven," as it were a pure creation of God. And so Adam was only a "living soul," a being who lived and moved within the terms of sensuous nature; but Christ was a "quickening Spirit," a Being above nature, who had life and was capable of giving it.[6] And as were the parents such were their posterities,—Adam's of the earth, and sensuous; Christ's of heaven, and spiritual. These two, and they only, are therefore universal persons, and their acts correspond alike as regards quality and universality to their persons. By Adam, the natural or sensuous man, sin enters into the world, and death by sin; by Christ, the heavenly and spiritual man, righteousness comes, and life by righteousness.[7] Hence they stand for races, species, kinds: to be in Adam is to be sinful, under the reign of death; but to be in Christ is to be righteous, under the reign of grace and life.[8] Each contains a race, and is, in a sense, the race he contains.

Hence what comes to be in each comes to be for all.[9] In Adam the race lives its natural life, sins, and dies; in Christ the race by obedience unto death, by suffering unto sacrifice, is made capable of escaping from the natural, of being purged from sin, of attaining the spiritual, of being reconciled to God.[10] In the distribution of their acts there is thus a difference which

[1] Gal. iv. 4.
[2] Rom. i. 2.
[3] Gal. iii. 16.
[4] Rom. ix. 5.
[5] Rom. i. 3-5, viii. 3.
[6] 1 Cor. xv. 45-47
[7] Rom. v. 12-14.
[8] Rom. v. 19-21.
[9] 1 Cor. xv. 2.
[10] 2 Cor. v. 15-19.

springs from the quality and character alike of the acts and the actors. The act of Adam is a transgression, but what it creates is a state rather than an act. This state, which is named ἁμαρτία, is distinguished on the one hand from παράβασις, which is the transgression of a positive law, and on the other from παράπτωμα, which is an act that involves guilt.[1] Adam creates no man save himself a transgressor or offender, though he creates all men sinners; and while Christ may be made sin for us,[2] He cannot be made transgression or offence. The act of Adam, then, creates for man a state of privation, loss, evil, which are all summed up in the term

[1] These terms Paul used in very distinctive senses, and always with careful discrimination. 'Αμαρτία occurs one hundred and seventy-four times in the New Testament, seventy-one instances being in Paul. Παράπτωμα twenty-one times in the New Testament, sixteen of them being in Paul. Παράβασις five times in Paul and twice in Hebrews. Of the two latter παράπτωμα is the more general, denotes offence against any law, natural or revealed; παράβασις the more special, denotes violation of a positive law, an express precept with its express sanction. Παράπτωμα is nearer ἁμαρτία than παράβασις. Rom. iv. 25 and 1 Cor. xv. 3 are examples of coincidence; but even here the distinction emerges. 'Αμαρτία could have been used in the singular, but not παράπτωμα. There is such a thing as collective ἁμαρτία, but παραπτώματα are individual, and save as single acts cannot be. Sin reigns, plays the lord, holds in bondage, has a sort of distinct being of its own, and is even independent of action, though action is not independent of it. But παραπτώματα have no being save through choices or as acts of will. So, too, with παράβασις. Man may be a sinner without being a transgressor, but he cannot transgress without sinning. Adam's act could be alternatively described as ἁμαρτία, παράβασις, or παράπτωμα, but the consequence to his posterity could be expressed by ἁμαρτία, but not by either of the other terms. We may express the distinction by saying that to Paul those terms did, but ἁμαρτία did not, denote the idea of culpability or guilt. Hence the fine distinction of phrase, Christ παρεδόθη διὰ τὰ παραπτώματα ἡμῶν (Rom. iv. 25), but τὸν μὴ γνόντα ἁμαρτίαν ὑπὲρ ἡμῶν ἁμαρτίαν ἐποίησεν (2 Cor. v. 21). He could be delivered for offences, but not made an offender; He could be made sin without becoming a sinner. Paul did not mean to suggest any idea as to the transfer of culpability or guilt. He would have been greatly shocked if he had imagined it possible that any one could take his phrase as equivalent to παράπτωμα or παράβασιν ἐποίησεν. Nothing could have been more abhorrent to his mind than the idea of the guiltless made guilty.

[2] 2 Cor. v. 21.

"death"; but he does not create one of guilt. And out of this state man can be redeemed, but only by an act similar in kind, but opposite in quality, to the one which involved him in it.[1] The one was an act of transgression, the other must be an act of obedience. And this act Christ, by virtue of His place and nature, office and function as the Second Adam, performs, and alone could perform. And His act becomes as to man a righteousness, which, like the sin that comes through Adam, is a state rather than an act, and can, relative to its opposite, be described as a state of salvation, or deliverance, or title to privilege and to life.[2] By natural birth or descent from Adam we inherit the ἁμαρτία, are born into the state it denotes; by faith, which is the condition of the spiritual birth that introduces into the family or race of Christ, we become possessed of the δικαιοσύνη, pass into the state it describes.[3] The conduct which becomes the state of sin is transgression, but the conduct which becomes the state of righteousness is obedience. The community which realizes the one is man κατὰ σάρκα, bearing the image of the earthly; the community which realizes the other is man κατὰ πνεῦμα, made in the image of the heavenly. The head of the one is Adam; the head of the other is Christ. We name Adam's society the world, but Christ's the Church.[4]

[1] Rom. v. 15.　　　　　　　　　　[2] Rom. v. 16-21.
[3] Rom. i. 17, iii. 21, 22, v. 1; Phil. iii. 9.
[4] In order to a clear apprehension of the Pauline theology we must never lose sight of his great antitheses. It is impossible to represent these here in all their range of significance and relation, but certain main features ought to be recalled. There is an antithesis—
　(1) Of Persons, Adam and Christ.
　(2) Of their acts—ἁμαρτία and δικαιοσύνη : sin and righteousness.
　(3) Of their consequences—θάνατος and ζωή : death and life.
　(4) Of the process of realization—κατάκριμα and δικαίωμα : condemnation and justification.
　(5) Of the conditions of the process—παράβασις or παράπτωμα, changing sin into guilt, and πίστις, or the faith which unites the soul to the righteousness which is life.
　(6) Of the man in whom the process is realized, or the σάρξ as the seat

ii. But Paul does not allow his doctrine to remain simply abstract, at most personalized in Adam and Christ; he boldly works it into what we have called a philosophy of history— *i.e.*, a theory of the laws or forces that have governed the development of man, individual and collective. For these two are incapable of separation; the whole is realized by the individuals composing it; the individuals are what they are through the whole. And here the correlation of the universal or fontal persons and their respective derivative races assumes a new meaning. Each fontal person is an epitome of his race; each race is an expansion of its creative person. And in each case the person and the race exhibit in a similar manner, though on an absolutely different scale, the operation of the laws that first in the region of sense, then in the region of the spirit, regulate the process and the stages of the racial development. Adam is man κατὰ σάρκα, Christ is man κατὰ πνεῦμα; viewed apart, they typify the dualism within the organic unity, the war of the flesh against the spirit, of the spirit against the

of sin, and the πνεῦμα as the seat of righteousness, or the ἄνθρωπος σαρκικός and the ἄνθρωπος πνευματικός : or the ἔξω and the ἔσω ἄνθρωπος.

(7) Of the method by which sin and righteousness are respectively revealed, or the νόμος on the one hand, and the ἐπαγγελία or the εὐαγγέλιον on the other, or Law and Gospel. The law makes the sinner ὑπόδικος τῷ θεῷ; but by the Gospel he attains the δικαιοσύνη διὰ πίστεως, or he is ὁ δίκαιος ἐκ πίστεως.

(8) Of the requirements which these two respectively make, ἔργα and πίστις, or works and faith.

(9) Of the state which they respectively create—δουλεία and ἐλευθερία or υἱοθεσία, or bondage and freedom or sonship.

(10) Of the character and conduct—παρακοή and ὑπακοή, or disobedience and obedience.

(11) Of the societies—κόσμος and ἐκκλησία, or the world and the Church.

(12) Of the ultimate sources or causes of all their respective results— ἁμαρτία on the one hand, and χάρις or simply θεός on the other.

But it would be a mistake to conclude that, because Paul so strongly emphasizes these antitheses, there is no unity in his conception of man and history. There is the strongest possible unity, but it is realized under the conditions of conflict, yet a conflict which leaves God and His grace victorious and supreme.

flesh; taken together, they typify the unity within the dualism, the natural which precedes the spiritual, the spiritual which succeeds, supersedes, and perfects the natural. But as the races interpenetrate, as all, like Christ Himself, must be of the natural before they can be of the spiritual, it follows that in all the race of Adam there is something of Christ, in all the race of Christ something of Adam. We may represent this by saying that Paul conceives the acts and states personalized in Adam and Christ as forces active alike in the race and in all its members. Sin reigns,[1] exercises dominion,[2] has a law which it enforces both within and against the man and in opposition to the law of God.[3] It operates within the race as an un-divine and a contra-divine power, hides God from man, darkens his mind, blinds him to the truth, tempts him to idolatry, so degrades and materializes his religious ideas that he changes "the glory of the incorruptible God into the likeness of corruptible man, and birds, and four-footed beasts, and creeping things."[4] Once God is expelled from man, falsehood and lust and all basest passions take possession of him, and he becomes the slave of the sin whose end and whose wage is death.[5] But the God who made man in Christ, building, as it were, the race after Him and Him into the race, cannot allow this reign of sin to become absolute; and so He acts against it according to a purpose as old as Himself, which His foreknowledge guides and His foreordination fulfils. The realization of this purpose is gradual, and proceeds on a twofold line—the natural or immanent, and the supernatural or transcendent. The immanent is a personal yet universal law within man, which teaches him at once the knowledge of God and his duties to Him. Every man has this knowledge. God so works in nature, and nature so manifests God, that reason can discover through its visible things His invisible, His

[1] Rom v. 21, vi. 12.
[2] Rom. vi. 14.
[3] Rom. vi. 20-23.
[4] Rom. vii. 22-25, viii. 2.
[5] Rom. i. 18-32.

eternal power and divinity.[1] The reason, therefore, is everywhere on the side of God and against sin. But the reason does not stand alone; there is conscience also. In the heart of man the law is written. Men judge themselves and judge their neighbours; these judgments imply a standard of right and a knowledge of duty, a law known to all and binding all. Sin, therefore, holds nowhere undisputed sway; in every conscience there is such a witness of God as leaves the sinner without excuse.[2]

But the immanent could not live without the transcendent, and this is represented by the constant action of God with a view to the realization of His purpose—the coming of the Christ who is necessary to the completion of the race. This cannot be done all at once; man must be prepared for it. The preparation begins with a promise: man is to be saved; God is to save him. The promise is made to a person— Abraham—who believes it, and his faith is counted to him for righteousness.[3] But man is as yet too sensuous and infirm a creature to be saved by so gracious and gentle a thing as the promise. He still sins, and the law is added because of transgressions.[4] This law comes in not to annul the promise, but to help towards its fulfilment, and is therefore occasional, provisional, transitional.[5] It has many functions, some of them most dissimilar and diverse, yet all of them necessary. It is as an institution disciplinary, intended to restrain men from sinning[6]; educational, tutorial—on the one hand it is the "pædagogus" or schoolmaster of sons who are still pupils,[7] and on the other, the "rudiments" by means of which they are educated and drilled[8]; religious, emphasizing the reign of God and the duty of obedience[9]; symbolical, showing what was necessary

---

[1] Rom. i. 19, 20: cf. Acts xiv. 15-17, xvii. 27.
[2] Rom. ii. 15.
[3] Gal. iii. 16; Rom. iv. 9 ff.
[4] Gal. iii. 19.
[5] Rom. vii. 7.
[6] Gal. iii. 23.
[7] Gal. iii. 10.
[8] Gal. iii. 24, iv. 1, 2.
[9] Gal. iv. 3, 4.

to the recovery of man, impossible to him, possible only through God.[1] But in order to the fulfilment of the promise— *i.e.*, the coming of Christ—and to the existence of the law, a people was necessary; and as these were both from God, the result of His free and transcendental action, so the people must also be His creation. He proceeds by the principle of election, selects Abraham, the man who had believed His promise, to be "the father of the faithful," and of his sons Isaac, of his sons Jacob, and of Jacob's sons He constitutes a state, giving to them the institutions which were necessary to maintain their separate being.[2] They are as His adopted sons, and have the visible presence, the covenants, the law, the service of God, and the promises[3]; they are His organ, entrusted with His oracles[4]; and of them, "as concerning the flesh," Christ is to come. But they were not equal to the honour they had to bear; they took themselves and their institutions for ends rather than means, and in the name of the law "crucified the Lord of glory."[5] But by this very act their law and their own being were ended[6]; for a law which could do nothing better with the Holy and Just than crucify Him, was by an act of so transcendent wrong condemned and abolished; and a people who had so failed to fulfil its mission as to make a victim of the Promised Lord, had most surely set themselves against the counsel and purpose of God.[7] So by one and the same act the old local and provisional order which had done its preparatory work was ended, and the new universal and permanent order, whose work was never to end, was instituted.

2. *The later system.*—In the polemical Epistles the antitheses determine the province as well as the terms of the discussion; and while the principles look out into universal history, the argument moves within the lines drawn by

---

[1] Rom. viii. 3, 4; Gal. iii. 21, 22.
[2] Rom. ix. 6-18.
[3] Rom. ix. 4.
[4] Rom. iii. 2.
[5] 1 Cor. ii. 8.
[6] Gal. iii. 13.
[7] Rom. x. 3, 4, xi. 1 ff.

Judaism. In the Christological Epistles these antitheses are transcended; thought is, alike as regards form and matter, universal. Christ occupies not simply an historical, but a cosmical place; He is the idea or principle constitutive and interpretative of the All. In Him, by Him, and unto Him all things are created.[1] He is the vital bond of uncreated and created being; in Him all things are constituted, and in Him all are re-constituted.[2] As the image of the invisible God[3] He stands in a double relation,—one essential, to God, whose image He is; another formal, to man, who sees the image that he may know God. In Him dwells all the fulness of the Godhead bodily,[4] and out of this fulness He communicates alike in creation and redemption.[5] And the cosmos He creates and governs is not limited to the Nature we know; it is as wide as being, comprehends the heavenly and the earthly, the visible and the invisible, all dignities and all dominions.[6] Men are created and are elect in Him,[7] but through Him the highest principalities and powers discover "the manifold wisdom of God."[8] His significance is absolute; what He does on earth and in time, He does for the universe and eternity. His kingdom is God's,[9] and His name is exalted above every name, both in this world and in the world to come.[10]

But these universal acts become the basis and regulative principle of particular relations and acts. The Creator is so bound to His creation that He cannot allow it to be divided from Him by evil, for this would be its ruin. And so at the touch of evil the cosmology becomes a soteriology; for when sin enters the world, the Creator, who is good, has no choice but to become the Saviour. Hence there

---

[1] Col. i. 15, 16.
[2] Col. i. 17; Eph. i. 10.
[3] Col. i. 15.
[4] Col. ii. 9, i. 19.
[5] Eph. i. 23, ii. 19.
[6] Col. i. 16, ii. 11; Eph. iv. 10.
[7] Eph. i. 4.
[8] Eph. iii. 10.
[9] Eph. v. 5.
[10] Eph. i. 21.

emerges, alike as regards evil and redemption, a significant formal difference between the polemical and Christological Epistles. Evil has as great a place as ever; it is a thing of nature, opposed to God, deadly to man.[1] Yet before it becomes immanent in man it has a being outside and above him, exists, as it were, with an organized kingdom and king of its own, whose spirit, the counterfeit of the Spirit of God, works in the sons of disobedience.[2] The old antithesis of Adam and Christ is not denied, but it has disappeared, or been sublimed into a higher—the Son and the prince of the power of the air, the kingdom of light and of darkness.[3] The categories of time and history have thus ceased to be here applicable; sin is no longer an affair of man or earth, but of the universe. The conflict against it is extra-temporal; its field is the whole realm of mental being, the protagonists God and the devil. The soteriology is as the cosmology; the arena and the range of the creative and the redemptive energies are coincident and coextensive; in other words, what had been earlier conceived as a question of God and man is now conceived as a question of God and the universe. We may represent the change by saying that as before all had been historical in form, now all was cosmical; yet all is so conceived as to compel sin to testify to the wonderful continuity of the Divine action. Thus salvation is the Son's work, just as creation had been.[4] This work, while universal in its purpose and results, is local in its scene. The Incarnation appears an event in time, but was the fulfilment of an eternal purpose, and so had been from eternity before the mind of God as an idea, and to Him idea is the same as reality. The event in time was for us, not for Him; and so while outwardly accomplished on earth, it was yet so above time that on account of it and by

---

[1] Col. i. 21; Eph. ii. 1.   [3] Col. i. 13, ii. 15; Eph. iv. 26, vi. 11.
[2] Eph. ii. 2, vi. 12.   [4] Col. i. 20, ii. 14, 15.

it as means Christ subdues all things unto Himself.[1] In the body of His flesh by death, by means of His cross, He reconciles the men who had been alienated from the life of God,[2] makes them new men, created after the image of God, builds them into a new society, becomes the Head of the society He builds, communicates to it His life, rules it by love, fills it with peace, and distinguishes it by the great unities which are the signs of His presence and victory: "One Lord, one faith, one baptism, one God and Father of all, who is above all, and through all, and in all."[3]

§ II.—THE CHRISTOLOGY OF HEBREWS.

A. ITS SPECIFIC CHARACTER.—The Epistle to the Hebrews is in all its formal and in some of its material aspects a complete contrast to the Pauline Epistles. It is not so much an epistle as an elaborate treatise. It has no author's name superscribed, nor any address; nor can either author or destination be from internal evidences clearly discovered. It is signally impersonal, though there are a few faint biographical traits. The author was no original disciple, no ear-witness of the Lord[4]; knew members of the Pauline circle,[5] some Christians of Italy,[6] and was known to the Church he addressed. It is further clear that his Judaism is not Paul's. Paul's was Pharisaic, scholastic, the Judaism of the doctors and the schools, where the law was ceremonial, but not sacerdotal, where it lived and grew by being interpreted, burdened life by a routine and custom which were made more irksome by verbal niceties and more imperious by dialectical rigour; but our author's was hieratic and hierarchic, the Judaism of the priests and the Temple, where the law was sacerdotal,

---

[1] Phil. iii. 21, ii. 9-11 ; Eph. i. 10.
[2] Col. i. 22.
[3] Eph. iv. 5, 6.
[4] Heb. ii. 3.
[5] Heb. xiii. 23.
[6] Heb. xiii. 24.

realized in worship, concerned with the sanctuary, the services, and the sacrifices, not with the reading and exposition of the Word. The one was the Judaism of the scribe and the schoolman, the other of the priest and the Levite, though not as known in Jerusalem. Our author's is not the Temple as the sordid and secular Sadducaic spirit had made it, torn by the factions begotten of a pride all the meaner that it was so aristocratic, but it was an ideal temple, the worship of the people as it lived in the fond imagination of one who construed the Holy City from afar, and more as she lived in fancy than as she was in reality. It is such a colonial yet conservative idealization of the motherland and its religion as we might have expected in an Alexandrian, and Alexandrian is the method the author uses to educe the new from the old and to sublime the old into the new. He is an idealist whose heaven is the home of all transcendental realities, whose earth is full of their symbols; and these are most abundant where earth is most sacred—in the Temple and worship of his people.[1] And so we are here without the sharp antitheses and clear-cut categories of the schoolman Paul, the contradictions of Adam and Christ, law and gospel, works and faith, legal and evangelical righteousness; but have instead the notions of type and antitype, shadow and substance, symbol and reality. The law is not abolished, but fulfilled. The earthly Temple is transfigured into the heavenly; the multitudinous and historical priesthood is translated into the one and eternal Priest; the ever recurring yet never efficacious animal sacrifices cease in the presence of the perfect Sacrifice "offered once for all," and all the sensuous services find their end in those spiritual realities which they foreshadowed and foretold. Hence the law is not Paul's law, nor are its relations to the Gospel his relations; yet the positions are not contradictory or even contrary, but

[1] Heb. viii. 5, ix. 23.

rather supplementary and corrective. Paul's view left the whole sacerdotal side of Judaism untouched and unexplained. It was the view natural to one who had been educated a Pharisee, and had become the Apostle of the Gentiles. But our author's is the view natural to one who conceived the Temple to be the sum and essence of Judaism, and who therefore felt that the new faith must be read through it and in relation to it. Hence he discovers elements in Christianity Paul had missed, those realities which had their correlatives in the sacerdotal system. The view was necessarily more limited than Paul's, for it had so to move within the terms of sacerdotal Judaism that it could not stretch back to Adam or out to the meanest Gentile; but it was quite as elevated as his, more emphasized the perfection and permanence of the Gospel, if it less emphasized its universalism. Hence Hebrews helps us by its very differences from the Pauline Epistles the better to measure the range and value the variety of Apostolic thought, especially in the point most cardinal to us—the theological significance of the person of Christ. Not only is the construction made fuller by this independence of mind and change of standpoint, but its meaning and its philosophy alike become to us the more intelligible. The person is made to guarantee the truth of the religion; it owes all its majesty and all its permanence to its Founder. The men that contemplate apostasy are brought face to face with Him, and made to feel the immense renunciation apostasy would involve.

B. ITS THEOLOGY.—Hebrews, then, presents us with a quite specific interpretation of Christ, what we may term a theology of His person as at once the archetype and the antitype of Levitical Hebraism. As the archetype it and all it involved were latent in Him; as the antitype it and all it signified became patent and were fulfilled in Him.

THEOLOGY OF THE SONSHIP. 323

As the first He had a Divine and transcendental being, as the second He had a human and historical, and these are both made entirely natural by being through the Sonship united, the one with the idea of God, the other with the idea of man. While this is the philosphical basis of the interpretation, its actual is the belief in the historical reality of Christ. What He had said our author knew only by the testimony of man, but this had been authenticated by acts of God.[1] The manhood is strongly emphasized. Jesus was a partaker in our common "flesh and blood,"[2] made like unto His brethren in all things,[3] was tempted as they are,[4] prayed and cried as they do.[5] Although a Son He suffered, learned obedience, attained perfection,[6] tasted death.[7] But in one thing He stood distinguished from man—He was "without sin,"[8] "holy, guileless, pure, apart from sinners."[9] This moral transcendence is the sign of an essential or personal, which is expressed by His distinctive name: "Jesus, the Son of God."[10] This Sonship is no mere figure of speech, but denotes a reality and rank of nature which qualifies for peculiar and pre-eminent functions. By it His place and work in the universe, in humanity, and in the history of Israel are all determined, as well as the permanence and sufficiency of His religion.

i. As Son He has a certain essential relation to the Father, which can best be expressed by metaphors: He is "the effulgence of the glory," "the image," or, as it were, the stamped or engraved counterpart of Him whom we call God.[11] The change of metaphor is not without reason; the first means that the Son is the radiance or distributed light through which the inaccessible "glory" is revealed

[1] Heb. ii. 3, 4.
[2] Heb. ii. 14.
[3] Heb. ii. 17.
[4] Heb. iv. 15, ii. 18.
[5] Heb. v. 7.
[6] Heb. v. 8, 9, ii. 10.
[7] Heb. ii. 9.
[8] Heb. iv. 15.
[9] Heb. vii. 26.
[10] Heb. iv. 14.
[11] Heb. i. 3.

and known, the second that He is a face reflecting a face we cannot see, a visible being upon whom the exact image and superscription of a being invisible is stamped. The first expresses the notion of a relation as inseparable as that between the centre and seat of light and the light diffused from the centre; the second expresses the notion of a dependence as absolute as that of the figure on the stamp, yet of forms as distinct as the stamp and the figure. The metaphors are changed, then, that the ideas of identity and difference may be expressed; and so construed they are bolder and more explicative phrases than any Paul had attempted. They were destined to suggest later many kindred similes, and, based on the similes, speculations without end. But the metaphors do not stand alone; the writer elucidates them by the deductions he draws. The Father commands all His angels to worship the Son[1]; He is addressed as ὁ θεός[2]; He makes time and all it doth inhabit,[3] sustains all things by the word of His power, and is appointed heir of all.[4] In these phrases, as in the metaphors, the ideas of difference and identity struggle into expression; Father and Son are distinguished, yet each is ὁ θεός, without any conscious breach with monotheism on the writer's part, or the anticipation of any consciousness of incongruity on the reader's. And this Son is the Jesus Christ who sums up in Himself the old covenant and institutes the new, makes purification of sins, and is exalted to the right hand of the Majesty in the heavens: ᾧ ἡ δόξα εἰς τοὺς αἰῶνας τῶν αἰώνων· ἀμήν.[5]

ii. The determinative idea of the Epistle is the Sonship; and what it is used to determine is the spiritual preeminence, perfection, and permanence of the New Covenant, in contrast to the sensuousness, insufficiency, and

[1] Heb. i. 6. [2] Heb. i. 2.
[3] Heb. i. 8. [4] Heb. i. 3.
[5] Heb. xiii. 21.

transitoriness of the Old. The whole matter is stated in the opening verse: it is the same God who has spoken to the fathers in the prophets and to us in the Son; but their revelation, as became its form, was fragmentary and partial, while ours, because its form is perfect, has perfect truth. Hence the Son is the pivot on which the argument everywhere turns; and so the opening paragraph states His significance, defining His relation to God and the universe. This relation is explicated in a series of contrasts.

(*a*) The first is between the angels who had given the Old Covenant and the Son who had instituted the New.[1] He was God's Son, had the name, the throne, the sceptre, the eternity, the authority, of God; but they were only creatures, ministers of God's will. But this Being who was supreme over angels used His supremacy in the most godlike way, not simply to rule as a Sovereign, but to succour as a Saviour. The angel remains an angel for ever, created being can only be what it was created to be; but the essence of Sonship is the permanence of the relation even under variability of form. So, as He would succour men, and men could be succoured only by man,[2] Jesus is made a little lower than the angels, and becomes one with those He would save, and in order to be able to save He suffers and tastes death.[3] For it was a thing that became God to qualify the Saviour for saving by suffering, and a thing necessary to man to have a High Priest "without sin," yet sympathetic through endurance of all the trials and temptations common to man.[4] Hence among men, as over the angels, Jesus, because the Son, stood pre-eminent, now Saviour as before Creator and Sovereign.

(β) But this contrast is general, relates to quality and rank of being, and on it as a basis there come several specific contrasts within the sphere of history; and so of

[1] Heb. i. 4-14. [3] Heb. ii. 9, 10.
[2] Heb. ii. 14-17. [4] Heb. ii. 17, 18.

religion, especially Israel's. First, He stands distinguished from Moses as the Son from the servant, as the Builder of the theocratic house from the house which He builds, as the One who designed the whole from him who executes a part.[1] Secondly, as a Priest He stands distinguished from Aaron and his priesthood in many ways[2]; He belongs to a different order—viz., that of Melchisedec, king and priest in one, the direct creation of God, without any of the accidents of time, independent of descent, independent of descendants,[3] alone, sinless, eternal, without any needs in Himself, sufficient always for all the needs and sins of men.[4] Hence He fulfils all priestly ideas and functions, and by abiding a priest for ever supersedes and ends man's perishable priests and changeable priesthoods.[5] But He cannot displace the persons, and leave all they did and represented standing as before. And so, thirdly, the institutions or religions are contrasted, as were their founders and representatives, yet so as to bring out the new in the old, the permanent in the transitory. The whole ancient apparatus of worship is resolved into a symbolism which dies in the presence of the reality. The Son is sacrifice as well as priest, and it has all the qualities of His person, is one as He is one, is spiritual and perfect, eternal and universal as He is, ends all sensuous sacrifices as He ends all historical priesthoods with their proud inanities of succession and descent. Where the priest and sacrifice are, there must the temple be; Jesus has passed into the heavens, and where He is there is the holy of holies, while the outer and lower courts are where men wait, sure that the Mediator lives within.[6] And the men who have this assurance are men of faith,[7] and the mention of faith

---

[1] Heb. iii. 1-6.
[2] Heb. vii. 4-22.
[3] Heb. v. 5, 6, vi. 20, vii. 1-3.
[4] Heb. vii. 24-28.
[5] Heb. viii. 3, ix. 11-14, 25, 26, x. 10-14.
[6] Heb. viii. 1-4, ix. 11, 24, x. 12, 19-22.
[7] Heb. x. 23, 38.

gives the author the opportunity of transcending these contrasts of his, and showing that beneath the outward difference is an inward harmony. Christ did not begin to be with His birth or incarnation; He had ever been; and the evidence of His permanent being is the being of His people. Judaism did not create the religious life within and before it. Its symbols and shadows had not created spirit or given life. Christ had. What had made the saints and martyrs was not the priests and sacrifices of the law, but faith. Hence faith was no new thing; all the heroes and the saints under the Old Covenant had been made heroic and saintly by faith, and not by the sensuous worship. Faith, which has always and everywhere been the principle creative of obedience, is as old as man, and those who have lived by it form a society at once earthly and heavenly, of all ages and all places, which has been united in Christ, those before as those after His coming being made perfect by Him.[1] And so there is constituted under the new covenant a new Israel, within a new city of God, where, without the audible thunder and the visible pomp of the old, Jesus, the Mediator, lives His gracious life and performs His gracious work.[2] And so, as becomes the Son of God, eternal in heaven, universal on earth, Jesus Christ remains "the same yesterday, to-day, and for ever."[3]

The Christology of Hebrews, as of Paul, is thus quite as much a philosophy of history as a theology—*i.e.*, it is a means of so uniting God and man that the two cannot be divorced, of so conceiving our past that it becomes the realm of His activity. The thought is wonderful for its large outlook and organic unity. There are relations within Deity which are the basis of all the relations Deity can ever sustain. Creation is by the Son and for Him. He is by nature Mediator, all the relations of the Creator to the

[1] Heb. xi.   [2] Heb. xii. 18-24.
[3] Heb. xiii. 8.

creature and the creature to the Creator are through Him and because of Him. His Sonship is the condition of man's; in order to its apprehension man was trained by legal and symbolical institutions; in order to its realization the Son had to partake of a manhood that did suffer, but did not sin. And the man who wrote these things was a Jew, and he wrote them for Jews, and the cause of their being written was Jesus of Nazareth, who had only a generation before been despised by the Jews as a man without letters, and crucified by their chiefs and rulers as a blasphemer against Moses and against God. Certainly there are things here that need explanation, if we are to believe in the reasonableness of man.

§ III.—THE MINOR CHRISTOLOGIES.

A. THE JACOBEAN.—In James we have a complete contrast both to Paul and Hebrews. Its most remarkable feature is not—what so offended Luther—the opposition to Pauline doctrine, but the poverty of its Christology and the paucity of its references to the historical Christ. These things are organically connected; it is because the writer has so little sense of the one that he feels no need for the other. It is an invariable rule in the primitive as in the later Church: where the historical sense is least real, the theological construction is most empty. James, indeed, has more the spirit and attitude of the liberal synagogue than of the persuaded Church; and possibly his book is in the canon to show how large and tolerant the early Church was, and all Churches ought to be. His invisible audience is, as it were, the assemblies of mixed minds, interests, classes that were properly neither Church nor synagogue, but had something of both. We are here without the antitheses of Paul or the contrasts of Hebrews; the Gospel is a new law [1]; men are to be doers of the Word, and not

---
[1] James i. 25.

hearers only,[1] justified as Abraham was by works.[2] This law, indeed, is "the law of liberty,"[3] but his liberty is rather a change in the terms of the law than, like Paul's, "freedom from its bondage." The attitude was thoroughly characteristic of James. He was late in recognizing the Lord, though he had lived face to face with Him longer than any other disciple, and he was always more anxious about the retention of the old than the acceptance or comprehension of the new. He is the Apostolical representative of the historical continuity, that in its devotion to form and letter forgets substance and spirit. The position given to him on account of his kinship he neither deserved nor had earned, and it only enabled him to use in government aims and abilities that hardly qualified him for service. His address in the Apostolic Council[4] and his behaviour to Paul[5] are quite in keeping with his Epistle; and we can well understand the feeling of the man who was brave because he understood Christ, to the man who was timid because of his failure to understand.[6] Yet even in James there are the germs of a Christology. He describes himself as the "servant of God and of the Lord Jesus Christ,"[7] a most significant co-ordination. This same Jesus Christ is "the Lord of glory."[8] He is the One in whose name men pray, and who answers prayer.[9] Of Him ὁ κύριος is used in the most absolute sense,[10] and he passes without any feeling of the unfit from using it of Christ to applying it to Deity.[11] Further, He conceives Him as lawgiver and judge,[12] speaking the word of truth, giving and enforcing the perfect law of liberty. The Christology is so rudimentary because of a double defect,—it is not rooted in the historical Person,

---

[1] James i. 22.
[2] James ii. 21.
[3] James ii. 12, i. 25.
[4] Acts xv. 13-21.
[5] Acts xxi. 18-25: cf. Gal. ii. 12.
[6] Gal. ii. 2, 9.
[7] James i. 1.
[8] James ii. 1.
[9] James v. 13, 14.
[10] James v. 7, 8.
[11] James v. 10, 11.
[12] James iv. 12, v. 9.

has no element distinctive of His consciousness save the inwardness of His law as distinguished from the outwardness of the Pharisaic; and it has no knowledge of the Sonship, or any trace of any sense or idea of what it signified and involved. Yet the thought is significant, as showing how much the living consensus had affected even so timid and conservative a mind.

B. THE PETRINE.—In Peter we have a different spirit and atmosphere. There is a strong sense of the reality of Christ's person, of His sinlessness,[1] His sufferings,[2] His meekness yet endurance under trial[3]—qualities that might well be stamped on Peter's mind—of His death and the cross on which He died,[4] of the offence caused by His death,[5] of His resurrection and the effect it had on the faith and hope of His society.[6] But while his Christology has a character of its own, it is in the spontaneous rather than the articulated stage, the product of a man who took what we may term a vernacular view of both the old and the new religion. He feels the continuity of God's people as only one of the people can. He loves to think of the mode of entering into their number as a new birth,[7] of each member as a "living stone," of the society they constitute as a "spiritual house," of the collective being as a "holy priesthood," and their common function to offer up "spiritual sacrifices."[8] He has no philosophy as to the vocation or institutions of Israel; he has only the most vivid intuition, born of personal experience, into the significance of Christ, who by faith and hope creates the people elect of God.[9] The fundamental fact is the Sonship; God is "the Father of our Lord Jesus Christ," and so "abundant in mercy."[10] Though the appearance of Christ is recent, yet,

[1] 1 Peter ii. 22, i. 10.
[2] 1 Peter i., ii. 21, iv. 1.
[3] 1 Peter ii. 23.
[4] 1 Peter ii. 24, iii. 18
[5] 1 Peter ii. 4, 7, 8.
[6] 1 Peter i. 3, 21, iii. 21.
[7] 1 Peter i. 3, 23.
[8] 1 Peter ii. 5.
[9] 1 Peter i. 2, 5, 9, ii. 4, 9.
[10] 1 Peter i. 3.

the reality He signified is ancient. His Spirit was in the prophets, who were in a sense pre-Christian evangelists, testifying beforehand of His sufferings and the glory that was to follow.[1] In harmony with this he conceived those sufferings as in a sense extra-temporal. While endured at a specific moment they had a being in the mind of God, and were, because of His inspiration, preached by the prophets before they happened.[2] Though manifested only in these last times, He was foreknown before the foundation of the world,[3] had ever been within and before the eternal mind, as it were the medium through which it saw and conceived what was to be. This foreknown Lamb who is without blemish and without spot is a sacrifice; He bears our sins in His own body on the tree, and by His stripes we are healed.[4] He is, too, the Christ, the Messiah, whose coming makes the day the prophets had foretold.[5] With Peter, as with Paul, the name has ceased to be official, and become personal, Christ often occurring alone, Jesus never without Christ. He has passed into the heavens, sits at the right hand of God, and has angels and principalities and powers subject unto Him.[6] He is the Shepherd and Bishop of souls,[7] the Judge of the world,[8] our Lord, absolutely, like God.[9] Here, too, citations from the Old Testament which refer to Jehovah are directly applied to Him.[10] Peter is clear that no inferior dignity can be His, though he may be unable to tell or even clearly to see how His high titles affect the old monotheism. One thing he surely knows—Jesus is to Him now both Lord and Christ.[11]

---

[1] 1 Peter i. 10, 11.
[2] 1 Peter i. 12.
[3] 1 Peter i. 20.
[4] 1 Peter i. 18, 19, ii. 24, iii. 18.
[5] 1 Peter ii. 13, cf. i. 25.
[6] 1 Peter i. 11.
[7] 1 Peter iii. 22.
[8] 1 Peter ii. 25.
[9] 1 Peter iv. 5, v. 3.
[10] 1 Peter ii. 3, 4, cf. Psalm xxxiv. 8; 1 Peter iii. 15, cf. Isa. viii. 13.
[11] Doxology, 1 Peter iv. 11 : cf. Acts ii. 36.

C. THE APOCALYPTIC.—The Apocalypse is the most Jewish book in the New Testament, inspired, as it were, by a passion for the people rather than for a school or a system, and its character is stamped into its language imagery, symbolism, associations, and thought. It loves the holy people, the holy land, the holy city, the old tribal divisions, the Temple as the home not of the priesthood, but of the people's God and His worship. This affects the forms under which Jesus is conceived and represented. He is of the tribe of Judah, and, to indicate His Messianic character, its Lion,[1] at once the Root and the Offspring of David,[2] the Anointed of the Lord.[3] As Son of man He more resembles the vision of Daniel than the Jesus of the Gospels, and He is described more in the terms of the altar and the Temple than of history.[4] He appears in priestly garments, and His most loved name is "the Lamb," slain that He might cleanse by His blood.[5] Yet a significant touch is the use of the historical name, Jesus, qualified now and then by Lord.[6] All the more, because of these characteristics, is its doctrine of the Person remarkable. Christ is conceived as the Son of God; God is in a peculiar and indeed exclusive sense His Father.[7] On the throne beside the Father sits the Son, and indeed it is expressly named "the throne of God and of the Lamb."[8] He is the absolute Lord, exalted above all kings.[9] He is the Holy and the True,[10] receives Divine honour and worship; in the doxologies His name and the Father's stand together[11]; the radiance that surrounds Him is that Divine radiance which no mortal can bear.[12] He is omniscient; like God, He searcheth the heart and the

---

[1] Rev. v. 5.
[2] Rev. v. 5, xxii. 16.
[3] Rev. xi. 15, xii. 10.
[4] Rev. i. 13.
[5] Rev. v. 6, 12, xiii. 8. The term ἀρνίον is applied to Christ twenty-nine times.
[6] Rev. i. 9, xii. 17, xiv. 12, xxii. 20, 21.
[7] Rev. i. 6, ii. 18, 27, iii. 5, 21, xiv. 1.
[8] Rev. vii. 17, xxii. 1, 3.
[9] Rev. i. 5, xvii. 14, xix. 16.
[10] Rev. iii. 7, xix. 11.
[11] Rev. i. 5, 6, vii. 10-12.
[12] Rev. i. 17.

reins, rules and judges the heathen, breaking their strength like a potter's vessel.[1] He is eternal, the beginning of the creation of God, the Ancient of Days, to whom belongs the Divine symbols Alpha and Omega, the first and the last, the unbeginning and the unending.[2] These are extraordinary titles and prerogatives to be claimed by one who has all the monotheistic passion of the Jew, for one who has the simple name Jesus, and is still remembered as the Crucified. Nowhere does the author show any consciousness that the Divine attributes and functions in which he has clothed the Christ can in any way injure either the unity or the supremacy of God. His thought, indeed, is expressed, but not articulated; he does not tell us how to relate or reconcile its antinomies, but simply leaves us in awed yet tender adoration before the throne of God and the Lamb.

[1] Rev. ii. 23, 27, xii. 5, xix. 15.
[2] Rev. iii. 14, i. 8, 11, 17, xxii. 8, 13.

CHAPTER II.

THE HISTORICAL BOOKS.

WHILE the books hitherto studied have aimed at the interpretation of the Person, they have simply assumed His history as known. Now we have to deal with those whose special concern is the history. The Gospels are all the work of believers, and are written for believers and in order to belief. On this point they are frankly sincere, and their sincerity has its own worth. Scepticism is not veracity, and of all the mirrors held up to nature it is the least capable of reflecting nature truly. The guide to truth must himself be convinced; honest belief in the person he testifies of does not disqualify a witness. But what concerns us is, not the criticism of the books or their authors, but simply this—first, how do the men who write the history conceive the Person they describe? and, secondly, how do they correlate the two—the Person as they conceive Him and the events which they narrate?

§ I.—THE SYNOPTIC GOSPELS.

A. MARK.—He is our oldest authority. To him Jesus is the Messiah,[1] the beloved Son of God,[2] who cannot in the most solemn moment of His life deny either His office or His Sonship.[3] The Baptist is the prophet who prepares His way,

---

[1] Mark i. 1.   [2] Mark i. 2.   [3] Mark xiv. 61, xv. 2

and tells what His work shall be.[1] The baptism sets Him apart, the temptation fits Him by trial for His work, which He begins by preaching the Gospel, and so instituting the kingdom.[2] His acts, like His speech, express His Messianic dignity and power. He casts out unclean spirits, and they recognize Him.[3] He forgives sins, which confessedly none can do but God only.[4] He claims to be Lord of the Sabbath, and acts according to His claim.[5] The men He called, once they have learned to know Him, confess that He is the Messiah, and He then explains the destiny of suffering and death involved in the office,[6] His speech growing ever more impressive and explicit.[7] The very people come to recognize Him, and He does not refuse their homage.[8] His words are to endure for ever; He is to return to judgment, to reign in glory, to gather His elect from the uttermost parts of the earth and the heaven.[9] He founds the new covenant in His blood, which is shed for many.[10] The Gospel, then, may be limited in its scope, but is clear in its purpose. It is concerned with no more than the life which unfolds the Messiahship, but what it does unfold is the life of the Messiah. Its moral is in the cry of the centurion: "Truly this man was Son of God."[11]

B. MATTHEW.—Here we have no clearer a doctrine of the Messiahship, but we have it more fully unfolded—placed, as it were, in its historical relations. Matthew sees that the Person cannot appear suddenly on the stage, without antecedents in the past, or any prophet but the Baptist, or other sanction than the Baptism. He was woven into the history of Israel, was indeed the very end of Israel's being; and so the inter-relations are indicated, that He through Israel and

[1] Mark i. 2-8.
[2] Mark i. 10-15.
[3] Mark i. 23, 24, 34, iii. 11, v. 7.
[4] Mark ii. 5-12.
[5] Mark ii. 27, 28.
[6] Mark viii. 27-31.
[7] Mark ix. 12, 31, x. 33, 34, 38, 45.
[8] Mark x. 47, 49, 52, xi. 9, 10.
[9] Mark xiii. 26, 27, 31, 35-37.
[10] Mark xiv. 24.
[11] Mark xv. 39.

Israel through Him may alike be justified. This is the reason of the genealogy which is but an expansion of positions we have found in Paul and the Apocalypse: Jesus is of the Jews, the people were elect for Him.[1] His personal name is made to express His function,[2] and the official name is used with a caution unknown to Mark.[3] Incidents at His birth at once fulfil prophecy and indicate office and rank.[4] And this is characteristic; His history as a whole and in its details, alike as regards His action and His suffering, is a fulfilment of Prophecy,[5] while His work fulfils also the Law.[6] This fulfilment dismisses the form that it may realize the Spirit, and gives to the teaching of Jesus in Matthew a peculiar ethical quality—it is spiritual and prophetic, as distinguished, on the one hand, from the rabbinical, and, on the other, from the sacerdotal.[7] And this quality in His teaching gives a distinctive position and authority to His person. Jesus is in Matthew not so much a prophet as a new lawgiver and king, the regal elements in the Messianic idea being those most emphasized.[8] He is the standard of action; deeds done to His are done to Him, and either condemn or acquit the doer.[9] His person is greater than the Temple.[10] He has all power in heaven and on earth, and in His final words the Son is co-ordinated with the Father and the Holy Spirit.[11] This Gospel then

---

[1] Matt. i. 1, 17. [2] Matt. i. 16, xxvii. 17, 22.
[3] Matt. i. 21. [4] Matt. i. 22, 23, ii. 1-6, 14, 15, 17, 18, 23.
[5] Cf. Matt. viii. 17, xii. 17, xiii. 14, 35, xxi. 4, xxvii. 9, 35.
[6] Matt. v. 17, 18. In this passage the idea of "law" has affinities with Paul rather than Hebrews, but "fulfil" with Hebrews rather than Paul—*i.e.*, the law is not Levitical, concerned with the Temple and the priesthood, but ceremonial, the law as read in the synagogue and interpreted in the schools. To "fulfil" is to translate its ceremonial form into ethical terms: cf. vii. 12.
[7] Cf. Matt. v. 21 ff, ix. 13, xii. 7, xv. 11-20.
[8] Matt. xxviii. 20, xvi. 27. Hence the peculiar quality which we find in Matthew's version of the Sermon on the Mount, and the prominence he gives to the later apocalyptic addresses and parables.
[9] Matt. xxv. 34-46. [10] Matt. xii. 6. [11] Matt. xxviii. 16-20.

exhibits Jesus as the end of Israel, the reason and goal of Israel's history, who by educing the new spirit out of the old forms does not destroy but fulfils the Law. But while Matthew brings Jesus through Israel, he does not limit Him to Israel. The Magi are as symbolical of Matthew as the prophets; they mean that Jesus is for Gentile as well as Jew. Men from the East and West shall sit down with Abraham, Isaac, and Jacob in the kingdom of God.[1] The kingdom is to be taken from the Jew and given to the Gentile.[2] The Gospel is to be preached in all the world for a witness to all nations[3]; and the risen Christ commands His disciples to "teach all nations."[4] Certainly this is no mere Gospel for the Hebrews; there is a universalism in it which corresponds to its notion of Jesus. Since He was no accident, but the result of God's action in history, His work must be as wide as God.

C. LUKE.—He places Jesus, not simply, like Matthew, in relation to Hebrew, but to universal history. His genealogy does not stop with Abraham, but mounts to Adam, "which was the son of God."[5] He comes as "a light to enlighten the Gentiles"[6] and to create on earth peace.[7] He bears from the first the official name, is now Christ the Lord[8] and now the Lord's Christ.[9] Yet His Hebrew descent is not forgotten; He is to sit on the throne of His father David, and reign over the house of Jacob for ever.[10] In Him ancient promises and prophecies are fulfilled.[11] Jesus, then, comes through Israel, but for mankind. The rejected of His own people turns to the Gentiles, and finds room for all[12]; but this not because of their act, but because of His own will and

---

[1] Matt. viii. 11.
[2] Matt. xxi. 43.
[3] Matt. xxiv. 14.
[4] Matt. xxviii. 19.
[5] Luke iii. 38.
[6] Luke ii. 32.
[7] Luke ii. 14.
[8] Luke ii. 11.
[9] Luke ii. 26.
[10] Luke i. 32, 33.
[11] Luke i. 54, 55, 68-80.
[12] Luke xiv. 22, xiii. 24-30.

grace.[1] In Luke, more than in any other Gospel, Jesus is severe to privilege and impious pride, but tender and gracious to the sinner. Here we have the parables, peculiar to this Gospel, of the Lost Sheep, the Lost Coin, the Prodigal Son, the Good Samaritan, the Rich Man and Lazarus, the Pharisee and the Publican, and such incidents as the calling of Zacchæus.[2] The parables spring out of the conditions around Him, but they represent His relations to the world. The Publican is justified in the presence of the Pharisee, the Samaritan condemns the priest and the Levite, and human nature, alike in its commonest and noblest instincts, vindicates the ways of grace. Hence, as Matthew exhibits Christ in His authoritative and royal functions, Luke exhibits Him more in His restorative. He is a Saviour, His mission is to the lost; it is because of the very essence of His character and work that He is offensive to the proud Jew and welcome to the Gentile and the sinner. The emphasis on the soteriology only exalts the Christology. The more universal His person becomes the more special grows His work; in the degree that He ceases to be the Jewish Messiah He becomes the Saviour of men.

§ II.—The Fourth Gospel.

As regards the Johannine writings, the distinction of historical and expository books can hardly be carried out. The Gospel and the First Epistle are here taken together, as if they constituted a sort of organic unity.

A. Relations and Characteristics of the Gospel.— In John we seem to enter into quite another order of ideas than we find in the Synoptics, but it is an order that has grown out of theirs. The development is so legitimate that we may term it inevitable. Mark conceives Jesus as

---

[1] Cf. the words that mark the beginning and the end of His ministry, Luke iv. 24-27, xxiv. 47.

[2] Luke xv., x. 30, 37, xvi. 19-31, xviii. 10-14, xix. 1-10.

the Christ, the Son of God, holy, miraculous in His action, extraordinary in His person, designed of God to a special work. On the basis of this notion Matthew exhibited His relation to Israel, Luke His relation to man, John His relation to God. Mark introduced Him as a sort of unannounced miracle, Matthew made law and prophecy prepare for Him, Luke man wait for Him, John God send Him. There is not so much of the supernatural in John as in Mark—indeed, there is less—but there is more of God and His action, though the action is altogether natural to God. The history of Matthew involves as gracious a cause and as universal an end as the soteriology of Luke, but the form is more special, the colouring more local. In order to do justice to the ideal element in the mind of the Evangelists we must live in their world. Their nature was not the narrow and rigid thing defined by modern physical or scientific law; it was a nature that lived in eternity and was alive with God. Our tendency is to confine God within the laws and limitations of nature; theirs was to penetrate and fill nature with the presence and the energies of God. The more intimately they conceived the New Testament as related to the Old, the less could they allow the Person who was the end of the one and the beginning of the other to remain a Jew or be regarded as a common man. The sacred books of Israel began with the narrative of creation—God created the heavens and the earth, formed all creatures, breathed the breath of life into man; and though they became a special history of Israel, it was only that they might the better show how God was the God of all. So the Evangelists, in relating Jesus through history to Israel and through man to creation, became, as it were, bound to go forward another step, and relate Him to God. This is the mere formal logic of their relations, development obeying its own immanent laws. They, being the men they were, could not refuse to look at the person and history of Christ in and through the Eternal, and the attempt so to look at Him is the Gospel of John. We may with all reverence describe it as the history of Jesus read as a chapter in the life of God.

The distinguishing feature, then, of the Fourth Gospel is this: it comes to Jesus and His history through God. But this statement needs to be corrected and qualified by another— viz., the distinguishing feature in the mind of the Evangelist is that he had read God through Jesus before he attempted to read Jesus through God. The book is a history written from a standpoint which its subject Himself had supplied. In the author's conception of God there are two elements —the one proper to him as a Christian, the other proper to him as a Jew. The first, which he owed to Jesus, was the idea of the Son; the second, which he owed to the mind and history of his people, was the idea of the Word. These two elements gave to his conception of God all its actuality; he could not conceive God without them, or them as existing apart from God. Through them God became to him a real, an active—in a word, a living Being; through God they became eternal, the cause and the end of all things. They were formally differentiated, but materially identical, modes by which God ceased to be an abstract simplicity and became a concrete and manifold energy— as it were, a realm where the only conditions that allow the reason and emotion, the intellect and heart, to exist, were essentially existent and everlastingly active: the conditions of personal distinctions and reciprocal activity. He came to these distinctions within the manifoldness of the Infinite in the only way he could come—from without, through the idea of Sonship given in Christ and through the idea of the Word, creative, prophetic, organizing, given in the sacred literature. Each term was a correlative: Word was the explicit and articulated reason which could not be unless there was an implicit and articulative reason; Son was an object reflective of love which could be only as there was a Father or subject of love active and creative. These were necessary to full and absolute or perfect being; and so, if God were such a being, they were necessary to God. Deity, then, in the full and absolute sense, was not Father without Son or Son without Father—for neither could be without the other, and if either was both must be. Nor was He Word without Reason or Reason without Word—for an inarticulated reason were not rational, were rather a mere characterless potentiality, and no realized actual reason. But He was these as so related and so exercised in their relations, so active and counteractive in their modes of being, as to be constitutive of a living whole. And if God has outward relations, they must, from the very nature of the case, be due to the explicit Reason or the Word, and the objectified Love or the Son. Only through these can He be approached from without, and only through these can what is within God become outward, constitute a universe or reach a universe already constituted.

B. CHRISTOLOGY.—Now, through his notions of Word and Son John binds the historical Christ to the eternal God, and through Him to the whole field of His creative and providential action. The Word, as the vehicle and organ of the immanent reason, is the Creator and Revealer; the Son, as the object and medium of love, is the Saviour and Healer. And so in the Prologue to the Gospel the Word creates— "all things were made by Him"; and He illuminates—is "the light of men."[1] But He who can be so denoted must Himself be uncreated—therefore eternal; and so He is described as existing "in the beginning" and with a self-sufficient being, for "in Him was life."[2] The Son is "the Only Begotten," whose home is "the bosom of the Father"[3]; therefore He has love as the medium and atmosphere of His being. But as "God

[1] John i. 3, 4.   [2] John i. 2, 4.   [3] John i. 18.

is love,"[1] the conditions of love must belong to His very essence—*i.e.*, be as eternal as Himself. And so the Son has been "from the beginning"[2]; for the eternal being of the Son and the truth "God is love," are only the concrete and the abstract forms of the same idea. The process or method by which this love is realized for man is the Incarnation. The Word becomes flesh and dwells among us,[3] the Life which was with the Father is manifested unto us,[4] and of course the only possible means of manifesting life is by means of a living Person. The Person who incarnates the eternal love or manifests the eternal life is the historical Christ. He is, as it were, the Word or Son, appearing under the conditions of created existence or time and place, in order to the completion of His work, which, while capable of being formally distinguished into the stages or processes known as creation and salvation, is yet as essentially one as are the persons of the Creator and the Saviour. Christ as the incarnate Word is the light of men, as the incarnate Son is their life. As the first His symbol is the tabernacle, which was for Israel the home of the visible presence; as the second He has the features of the "Only Begotten of the Father," grace and truth.[5] In His double aspect He "declares the Father"[6]—*i.e.*, as one who has been eternally within God He comes to those who are necessarily without, that they may know God as He is known from within, see God as He sees Himself, and so learn to love God with a godlike love.

Now, the history is written as a sort of commentary on the Prologue; and so has a twofold character—it describes a real which represents an ideal world. In it history and thought become a unity without losing their distinction. The forms and categories are those of time; but the ideas, which are their real contents, are those of eternity. And thus the

[1] 1 John iv. 8.
[2] 1 John i. 1
[3] John i. 14.
[4] 1 John i. 2.
[5] John i. 14.
[6] John i. 18.

history is a sort of acted parable, whose principle or idea is stated at the beginning and its moral at the end. The Fourth Gospel is quite frank as to its purpose; it is written in order that men may believe "that Jesus is the Christ, the Son of God."[1] And to the historical Person the author does not shrink from applying the highest predicates he had used of the Word and the Son. Thomas recognizes Him with the cry, "My Lord and my God!"[2] And we are never allowed to forget his meaning or to ignore his purpose. His book is a work of rarest art; it is a history, a drama, an allegory, a more manifold and complex symbolism than the system so lovingly interpreted in Hebrews. And with his fundamental idea it could not but be these all together and all at once. We move as if within the very consciousness of God; we feel His love, His attitude to man, His sacrifice to save him. We see Jesus living under and among all the most terrible and sordid conditions of space and time, yet somehow as if He were a being of eternity. He works miracles, which are, while sensuous events, all symbols of transcendental truths. He lives in a world which is only blind and crafty Judæa, but yet it broadens into a universe where light and darkness, life and death, wage their awful, unceasing battle. The Jews are real persons, priests and rulers of the people, but they are no less embodied ideas, organs of principles; darkness and hate live in them as light and love in Christ. His body is but a mortal thing of flesh and blood; but it becomes a temple which men destroy,[3] but God again more gloriously builds,—a mystic sacramental food that men may eat and live for ever[4]; a victim that cunning priests do to death for their own safety, but God transforms into the life of the world.[5] His words seem to be but occasional, drawn from Him now by a guileless seeker,[6] now by

[1] John xx. 31.
[2] John xx. 28.
[3] John ii. 19.
[4] John vi. 48-51.
[5] John xi. 49-52.
[6] John i. 49-51.

a nightly visitor,[1] now by a solitary woman void of good yet hungry for it,[2] now by accusing Jews, now by curious multitudes, now by trustful yet perplexed disciples; but His audience is not the men who hear—it is mankind; the world listens by looking, for its light has come.[3] His death seems to be the victory of the meanest jealousies and the most conflicting hates,—priests who through love of ruling forget the service of God and men; scribes who in the passion for words and laws lose the sense of right and the love of truth; a people unstable as water, demanding that the idol of one day be crucified the next because He would not be as they were; the judge willing to be unjust where his master was not concerned, or ready to be relentless where he was. But the cross was not like these its makers, nor was the death like these its authors; the cross was the world's altar, and the death the sacrifice offered once for all. We are in a world of realities where yet all is ideal; the history is from its very nature an allegory, for it means that God, in the poor vehicle of a mortal manhood, is accomplishing His most characteristic work, and the men who attempt to pervert or prevent it only the more contribute to its accomplishment. What proceeds in time belongs to eternity; the outward event is the visible symbol of what is innermost in the Divine nature and ultimate in the Divine purpose; and where the prosaic senses perceive but the men of a moment, the constructive imagination reads a parable which reveals to man the secret of God.

In John, then, we have an interpretation of the Person expressed in the terms of the life; and if the Person was as he conceived Him, the history could not be other than its interpretation. The real was not indeed the counterpart of the ideal, but rather its symbolic realization, a thing limited and futile to him who could not see the spirit for the

[1] John iii. 1 ff.   [2] John iv. 7-26.
[3] John viii. 12.

flesh, but a thing of infinite meaning to him who saw the flesh transfigured by the spirit. So construed, we may say that John's is, while the most speculative, also the most personal Christology in the New Testament. It is distinguished from all the others by its personal character; its motive is a transcendent enthusiasm for a person, and we may, in a sense, name it the apotheosis of love. The theology of Paul is a theology of the intellect. He loves persons as ideas. Jesus Christ is indeed to him the supreme historical reality, but he loves as he honours Him κατὰ πνεῦμα, and not κατὰ σάρκα.[1] He glories in the cross, but it is even more the cross of idea and doctrine than of fact and history. Without the fact and history the idea and doctrine could not have been, and would not be; but his immediate consciousness is of the ideal cross, which has interpreted, transfigured, and glorified the real. With it his associations are more those of thought than those of experience and sense. He has seen the cross through the Resurrection; he has not known what it was to watch it ringed with fanatic hate and with no background but death. He lives for Christ; but his Christ is not one whose historical form so dwells in memory and is so beautiful to imagination that he feels the very place of His feet to be glorious, all the more that over it fall the shadows cast by the dismal surrounding night. As with Paul, so with Hebrews. Christ is to him the Archetype, the Antitype, the Son, the High Priest, the symbol of the most exalted idea; but He is not Jesus, handled with the fondness of a love made tender by memory and sweet by hope. In John all is different; his is the theology of the heart; the terms in which it is unfolded are those of the most real, immediate, and reminiscent, yet living love. And so his speculation is all personal : the Person is never lost in the idea, the idea is ever incarnated in the Person. When he speaks in the Epistle, it is as one to whom love is life;

[1] 2 Cor. v. 16.

when he speaks in the Gospel, it is as one for whom the love has lived. For him the ideals of God have been clothed in flesh; and in the process the flesh has not made the ideals gross, but the ideals have made the flesh divine and glorious. And thus the abstract terms, Word, Light, Life, Spirit, are not abstract to him; they have all a mystic personal quality; out of them looks the face of Jesus, and His look is love. And so it was but natural that the history should be to John most real where it was most symbolical. Christ was to him in very truth the Son of God, and God in very truth the Father of Jesus Christ. And he so read the Father he had not seen through the Son he had known, that eternity was but life with the Son made infinite.

§ III.—THE IDEAL PERSON AND THE REAL HISTORY.

But now we come to our second question: How do the Evangelists correlate the Person they so conceive and the history they write? How do they reconcile His ideal with His actual being? Perhaps the truest reply would be, They do not feel that there is anything to reconcile. It was in and through His history that they found the ideal; and as it was most ideal where most real—viz., in the Passion—they were content to speak as witnesses, leaving the task of conciliation to those who felt it to be necessary. But it may help us to understand their mind the better if we attempt to interpret this, as it were, sub-conscious element of their thought. The positions to be correlated are these:—

1. Jesus is to all the Evangelists a supernatural Person. He is so altogether apart from any question as to the specific mode of His coming. The narratives of the Nativity are peculiar to Matthew and Luke. Mark says nothing as to His birth, though he knows Mary as His mother.[1] Nor does John, though he twice alludes to Joseph as His father,[2] and

[1] Mark vi. 3.   [2] John i. 45, vi. 42.

makes His relation to His mother much more filial, and so
more natural, than any of the other Evangelists.[1] He is supernatural simply because of what they have found in Him,
because He is to them the foretold and expected Messiah,
the Son of God and King of Israel. They differ in their discernment and appreciation of what this belief involves, but
not in the fact or matter of the belief. Mark may show us it
in its empirical form, and John in its most speculative and
developed, but John's faith in Jesus as the Messiah is no
stronger or more real than Mark's. And this means that
He is to both a person who transcends the order of nature,
one whose very being is miraculous.

2. As miraculous in person, so He is miraculous in act. In
all the Gospels He heals diseases, casts out devils, feeds the
multitudes, raises the dead, and is raised from the dead.
These acts correspond to His nature as they have conceived it;
the natural action of the miraculous Person is the miracle. In
the degree that He Himself transcends nature, it is but normal
that His acts should do the same. So far forth, then, as the
Person who is a miracle works miracles, the conception may
be said to be coherent; there is at least, as between its two
parts, a certain logical consistency.

3. This supernatural Jesus exhibits in His own person all
the phenomena natural to the normal human being. On
this point the Evangelists are all equally explicit; if there is
any difference, John may be said to be the most explicit of all.
Jesus is born and grows; has senses and sensuous experiences;
has parents who chide Him, because, childlike, He leaves
them and forgets in His own interests their sorrows. He
grows in mind as in body, in wisdom as in knowledge.[2]
He suffers hunger, thirst, weariness. He experiences joy,

[1] John ii. 3-5, xix. 25-27.
[2] It is worthy of notice that the Evangelist who emphasizes this growth
(Luke ii. 40-52,) is also the only one who applies to the historical Jesus
the name proper to the exalted Christ: ὁ κύριος (Luke vii. 13).

pain, anguish, pity, and inner trouble. He weeps. He is tempted, has to struggle under suffering. Mental is attended with bodily pain, death with physical anguish,—the shedding of His blood and the breaking of His heart. These facts are not concealed, nor is there any sense that they need concealment; for there is no feeling that they are in any way inconsistent with the conception of Jesus as the Christ. On the contrary, the writers feel as if these things were in the highest degree consonant with their conception of Him. He is not the less but the more the Messiah that He suffers, not the less but the more a Saviour that He dies. And so they narrate in the simplest way, as if both classes of phenomena were equally in harmony with their subject, the acts in which He transcended nature and the sufferings and fatalities which show Him under it. Yet they were not unconscious of the difficulty, for they themselves had experienced it in the acutest possible form. They had assumed that He would do other than He did; and when He did not as they expected, some doubted, and some even fell away. If with this keen sense of the contradiction between His transcendental person and His actual experiences they yet write as they do, we have here evidence of two things—first, of the simple-minded veracity which is incapable of concealment, and, secondly, that they had reached a point of view where the contradiction had for themselves not only ceased, but become a testimony to His truth and reality. They looked at the matter through the Person they described; they did not look at Him through a nature science has interpreted and defined. To them He was both nature and law, but to us nature tends to become a law to Him. If we can reach their point of view, we may be the better able to construe both their idea and their history.

A. Now, in their view Jesus was at once a single and a universal person; His being could be construed through the nature and from the side of man, or through the nature and from the side of God. But these were so related that what was possible to Him as the second depended on what He was as the first. The Messiah could not be without the man, and the man must be what all men are to be man at all. On no basis but a natural could the supernatural be built. Of course this natural was made of God; it was sinless, as it were the veritable manhood God imagined. But Christ's moral was not so conceived as to involve and assert His physical transcendence, but rather His obligation to remain in our limited and normal human state. This is distinctly the idea conveyed in the important initial incident known to all the Synoptics[1]—the Temptation. We can hardly be wrong in construing this as even more an allegory than an event, and the more real it is made the more allegorical will it become. It stands between the Baptism and the Ministry, which means, He to whom the Messianic consciousness has come must be proved in order that He may be approved. The Baptism denotes the Person, the Temptation tests His capabilities, and it is as the selected and the tested that He begins His ministry.

We can only mean by the reality of the Temptation that Jesus was really tempted. It was not a drama of which He was a spectator, but a tragedy whose stage was His own soul. Each act in it cost struggle, agony, and sweat of spirit, as in every conflict of sense and conscience, reason and will. But it is evident from the terms which describe the event that it had to do not with the weaknesses common to man, but with Himself and His vocation, the work He was called to do, what He must be to do it, and how or under what modes it was to be done. We must read its reason in the place it holds and the forms it assumes. He was no son of the synagogue or the Temple, no pupil of the scribes or novice of the

[1] Matt. iv. 1-11; Luke iv. 1-13; Mark i. 12, 13. The text follows the narrative of Matthew. Cf. my "Studies in the Life of Christ," pp. 80-98; Wendt, "Die Lehre Jesu," vol. ii., pp. 69 ff. (Eng. trans., vol. i., pp. 101 ff.).

priesthood; His way had been His own; He was the supreme example of those men call the self-taught, often because they have no other term by which to denote the taught of God. But there were traditional ideas of the Messiah and His kingdom—ideas that had worked themselves into the spiritual blood and bone of Israel; and He could not be what He was and stand where He did without feeling their presence and their power. When, then, His vocation came in the Baptism, and the mysterious Spirit within Him stood up in face of His predestined mission, He was, as it were, forced into the conflict or pursued by the problems which we call the Temptation:— How are the person and the mission, Jesus and the Christ, related? In what form is the Messiah to appear? Under what conditions must He do His work? What truth is there in the traditional idea? How far can it be used by the transcendental and incorporated with it? It is through questions such as these that the Temptation must be understood: without them, the tempter could have had no part to play; with them, he played his part so well as to make the struggle the tragic reality it was.

So understood, then, the Temptation represents the conflict through which the Saviour passed relative to Himself and His ministry, or concerning His person in relation to His work. From this point of view let us try to read its meaning.

(*a*) The first temptation was the making of stones into bread. He was "an hungred," and was invited to work a miracle in order to satisfy His hunger. To what was He tempted? To the exercise of miraculous powers for personal ends. It implied the being of such powers, the capability of using them for such an end, the occasion for such use in physical hunger, and the justification for their use in saving from the hunger and its possible issue in death. But to have yielded and used the power would have lifted the Person out of the category of humanity, placed Him above rather than under nature, made the kinship and obedience and fatalities of manhood impossible to Him—in a word, as a being of another order and another system, He would have been completely divorced from man. Hence the trial meant, whether He was to be for Himself as a person filling the office and doing the work of Messiah, altogether as a man, under nature with all its limitations and all its disabilities, under law with all its obligations and all its responsibilities. Jesus was victorious because He refused to emancipate Himself from law, or to live otherwise than as under the conditions common to man.

(β) In the second temptation He was invited to cast Himself down from the pinnacle of the Temple. What was its essence? The claim to special conservation and care from God. It signified that the Person had so peculiar relations and was of such peculiar value to God, that He could, because of these, make extraordinary ventures beyond the natural, that He ought to do what He could, and appear before men as the One miraculously guarded of God. The second was thus the exact converse of the first; it tempted to such dependence on God as no common man could know. If this had succeeded, it too would have separated Him from man; and its failure meant, that Jesus, while doing His work, was to claim from God nothing for Himself that should exempt Him from our common human lot and liabilities. There was to be for Him no special intervention, no exclusive providence, nothing that marked Him as the solitary care and single love of Heaven. He was to take His place in the ranks of men, live as they lived, under the same conditions, sons of the one Father, brothers in dependence on God as on nature; and if He did a greater work than any other, He was still to do it not as made of God independent of law, but as like man bound to all obedience.

(γ) The third temptation was, as it were, the other two reduced by a synthesis to a subtler and more attractive form. He was to receive the kingdoms of the world if He would worship the power which was their master—*i.e.*, He was not to take the way of obedience, but of force and self-will. The question was, whether He would emancipate Himself from God and take the matter into His own hands, or leave Himself in God's keeping to do it in God's way. His victory means that His work is one of obedience, that obedience is the method all through, and in order to it all the ends and all the ways must be God's, but all the acts and all the endurance the free choices of man. He who would be Messiah must be perfect man; the manhood broken from below by sin, or from above by the exercise of miraculous powers or the claim of a special Providence for any end of the Person—both of which would only be another form of sin—would be a manhood incapable of the Messianic office or its essential work. The humanity of the Saviour must be absolutely real.

Now, the idea expressed in these real yet allegorical incidents is this: the terms under which Christ lived His life were those of our common non-miraculous humanity. We know no other. To be perfect and whole man must mean that as regards whatever is proper to manhood He is man, and not something else. Hence the emphasis which writers like Paul and the author of Hebrews lay upon His "being found in fashion as a man," so constituted that He was the First-born Brother, made like unto His brethren in all things, except sin. The Synoptics, without formulating the idea, express it in the strongest possible way—they represent Christ as doing His work within the terms and under the conditions of normal manhood. His supernatural powers are for others, not for Himself. He performs no single self-regarding miracle. The priests mocked Him because, while He saved others, He did not save Himself[1]; and we may add, He could not both save Himself and be Himself. What had made Him in so supreme a personal act cease to be man would have deprived the act of its special character. The physical limitations really represent the transcendent obliga-

[1] Matt. xxvii. 42.

HIS HUMANITY NON-MIRACULOUS.

tions imposed by His work upon His will. What only a man could do remained undone unless a man did it; and so the manhood must be real that the sacrifice may be the same. And this principle is far-reaching; upon it depends the reality of the Person and His history. Whatever touches either touches both. If Christ in His historical life be conceived as a conscious God who lives and speaks like a limited man, then the worst of all forms of docetism is affirmed. For it is one that dissolves Him into infinite unreality. If He knows as God while He speaks as man, then His speech is not true to His knowledge, and within Him a bewildering struggle must ever proceed to speak as He seems, and not as He is.[1] If He had such knowledge, how could He remain silent as He faced human ignorance and saw reason wearied with the burden of all its unintelligible mysteries? If men could believe that once there lived upon this earth One who had all the knowledge of God, yet declined to turn any part of it into science for man, would they not feel their faith in His goodness taxed beyond endurance? Is not much of the modern impatience of theology a just Nemesis upon systems that have in this matter wronged Him they professed to interpret? Had the simple method of the Evangelists been followed, these difficulties would have been unknown. Christ's humanity was as regards the actions and ends proper to it as a humanity altogether normal, and so non-miraculous, subject to all the limitations and liabilities of the common lot. To conceive Him alike in relation to nature or to God as other than His brethren, is to misread the lesson of the Temptation, and so the whole meaning of His person and work.

---

[1] Christ recognizes the limitations of His own knowledge (Mark xiii. 32: cf. xiv. 35, 36). He knew, indeed, what was in man (John ii. 25: cf. Matt. ix. 4; Luke v. 22; Matt. xii. 25; Luke xi. 17). But this was the note of the prophet (Luke vii. 39). There were things in man, too, that surprised Him (Mark vi. 6; Matt. viii. 10); so in nature (Mark xi. 13).

B. But the single was also a universal Person, and had as such a mission altogether supernatural because altogether of God. It could be fulfilled only by one whose nature was human, but it could not be humanly fulfilled. He must by means of nature be the fit person, but He could only by means of God do the fit work. His coming was, as it were, built into history, belonged to the design and action of God. For it Providence had ruled, prophecy prepared, elect men lived and died. To it all the earlier ages had moved; out of it all the later ages were to proceed. We must therefore make a distinction: there was a normal manhood, but a supernatural function, and the function was made possible by two things—the quality of the manhood and the quantity of the Divine action. The quality of the manhood we have seen, but the significance of the action is what we have now to see. It could not proceed on the broad field of history, and never touch the special Person—nay, it must have been in relation to Him that it reached its acutest point. We may describe this point in the terms of John, "The Word became flesh"[1]; or in those of Luke, "The holy thing which is to be born shall be called the Son of God"[2]; or in those of theology, "God became incarnate in Christ." But what to the Evangelists did incarnation mean? It meant the coming to be not of a Godhead, but of a manhood. Its specific result was a human, not a Divine, person, whose humanity was all the more real that it was voluntary or spontaneous, all the more natural that God rather than man had to do with its making. To the Evangelists the most miraculous thing in Christ was His determination not to be miraculous, but to live our ordinary life amidst struggles and in the face of temptations that never ceased.[3] One principle ruled throughout: the motives that governed the Divine conduct governed also the human. This principle and these

[1] John i. 14.   [2] Luke i. 35.
[3] Luke iv. 3, xxii. 28.

motives may be described as the law of sacrifice. The Father denied Himself in giving the Son; the Son denied Himself in becoming man and in living as the man He had become. Looking up from below, it was all one infinite *kenosis*; looking down from above, it was all one infinite sacrifice. But kenosis and sacrifice alike meant that, while He assumed the fashion of the man and the form of the servant, both the manhood and the servitude, in order to either having any significance, had to be as real as the Godhead and the sovereignty.

Hence Christ was to the Evangelists at once normal man and supernatural person—the former in all that pertained to His personal existence and relations, the latter in all that concerned His work. The whole region in which this work lived and moved was the natural of God, but the supernatural of man. All that was done was of God and befitted God. He lived, as it were, in visible presence and audible voice upon the earth. The truth Christ revealed was not man's, but God's. The love that abode in Him was Divine. The life in Him was the uncreated yet creative life. And so, when He acted not for Himself, but as the called of God,[1] His acts were naturally supernatural. His work was a unity, miraculous not at one point or in one thing, but in all things and at all points. The miracle was the normal speech of His will; the right to forgive sin had as its correlate the power to heal. His words and person have acted like miracles in history. His miraculous power is illocal and universal. The normal manhood had its home in Judæa and its history written by the Evangelists; but the supernatural Person has no home, lives through all time, acts on and in all mankind.

The miracle, then, does not belong to the region of His personal being, but of His official activity. And here it is essential and integral. Hence we may note three characteristic facts. First, since He is as Founder of the kingdom super-

[1] Heb. v. 10.

natural, all His acts are here of a piece, and all of God. Miracle and speech, preaching and healing, cleansing and curing men, are signs of the kingdom.[1] Apart from it they cannot be; within it they are in place and have a function. They are co-ordinate and correlative, express one energy in Him, aim at one result for man. Secondly, the conditions of physical help are spiritual[2]; what qualifies a man to be forgiven qualifies him for healing; and all physical help is spiritual good. The miracle is a voice, a witness, a preacher warning men to repent[3]; the Word is a miracle, a spirit that quickeneth.[4] Thirdly, what they speak of is God, the Divine, the presence of the creative will, now the re-creative, on earth.[5]

We may say, then, the miraculous Person is the Person in His office, at His work, standing in His peculiar relations to God. Apart from these, living the personal life, He is the normal man; within these He is the Christ of God. It is here, if such an image may be allowed, as in our English commonwealth. There can be no sovereign without the person, but the person is not the sovereign. Office and person are so mutually necessary that neither can be without the other. But the person within the office is not as the person without it. Without it she is but a mortal woman, with all the characteristics of her kind; but within it she becomes the sovereign who can do no wrong, the source of law and justice, filling and, as it were, possessing the high court of Parliament, clothed upon with the authorities and the prerogatives proper to the head of a great state. With Christ we cannot now

---

[1] Matt. xi. 5; Luke iv. 18-21, xiii. 32.
[2] Matt. viii. 10, 13; Mark i. 40, v. 36, vi. 5.
[3] Matt. xi. 21; Luke x. 13; John v. 36, x. 25, 32, 37.
[4] John vi. 63.
[5] John viii. 28, xiv. 10: cf. Luke v. 17, ix. 43, xvii. 15-18; Matt. ix. 8, xv. 31. It is therefore Christ's own doctrine that His miracles witness not to something peculiar in His own humanity, but to the power of God (Mark v. 19, vii. 34; Matt. xii. 28, xiv. 19; Luke xi. 20).

separate office and person, for these are fused into one. But the standpoint of the Evangelists was not ours. We know the accomplished fact, but they saw the process of accomplishment. And the process is reflected in their histories. The vocation to the Messiahship did not come till the Person had been disciplined and qualified. In the period of obscurity and preparation the large prerogatives of the end were not His. It was only when the suffering was past and the right hand of the Father won, that the Son became an object of worship, possessed of all power in heaven and on earth, able to promise His eternal presence to His people.[1]

[1] Matt. xxviii. 9, 17, 18.

CHAPTER III.

THE CHRISTOLOGY OF CHRIST.

BUT how do these varied interpretations of His person stand related to the teachings of Christ Himself? Have they any reason or justification in any words or claims of His? Is He their creator or only their occasion? In other words, how did Jesus conceive Himself?

§ I.—Significance of His Names.

A. THE CHRIST.—Jesus is to Himself from the Baptism onwards the Messiah. He begins His ministry by a confession of faith: in Him prophecy is fulfilled, the Spirit of the Lord is upon Him, and He is anointed to preach the Gospel to the poor.[1] He does the works of the Messiah, and to confess Him is to be blessed.[2] He institutes by His preaching the Messianic kingdom, and He allows Himself to be saluted as the Messianic King.[3] In the presence of the chief priest and in answer to his solemn abjuration He declares Himself the Christ.[4] But in taking the name He changed the idea, and by means of a most significant question He emphasized the change. How do the scribes conceive the Christ?[5] "As David's son," they said; and they meant that to be his son was to be not simply his descendant,

---

[1] Luke iv. 16-21.   [2] Matt. ix. 27; Mark x. 47-49; Luke xviii. 39, 40.
[3] Matt. xi. 1-6.   [4] Mark xiv. 61, 62; cf. Matt. xvi. 16, 20.
[5] Matt. xxii. 41-46; Mark xii. 35-37. Cf. Wendt's "Lehre Jesu," ii. 436 ff. (Eng. trans., ii. 133 ff.).

but altogether like him, a king after his kind in a kingdom such as his. But Jesus asks, " How, then, does David in spirit call Him Lord?" and He means: " My view of the Messiah is exactly the reverse of yours; to you the main thing is the Davidic sonship, to David it was the lordship. The lordship signified a relation to God, which you forget; but the sonship, which you remember, involved a relation to David that may be interesting, but is not vital, and hardly significant."

The change Jesus effected in the Messianic idea was parallel to the change He effected in the theistic, and the two must be taken together before either can be understood. Neither idea could have been without Judaism, but neither the God nor the Messiah of Jesus was of the Jews. The element He introduced was the most distinctive and constitutive in His thought, and may be described as on the one side the paternal, on the other the filial,—these terms being strictly inseparable and correlative, affecting both the Messianic and the theistic idea. As regards the former, it had a twofold form—a Godward and a manward; the Messiah was Son of God and Son of man, and each in such a sense that it involved the other.

B. THE SON OF GOD.—This phrase had in the Old Testament a sort of official sense. It denoted collective Israel, the son because the elect of God.[1] It denoted, too, the Messiah, the theocratic King,[2] who was in a special sense the creation and care of God, but it was an official title rather than a proper name, applied to the King as distinguished from the man. There are traces of this meaning in the Gospels. Satan uses it in the Temptation[3]; so do the evil spirits when they are cast out[4]; so do the disciples in the ship after the

---

[1] Deut. xiv. 1, 2; Exod. iv. 22; Hos. xi. 1; Isa. lxiii. 16; Jer. xxxi. 9, 20; Mal. i. 6.
[2] 2 Sam. vii. 14; Psalm ii. 7, 8.   [4] Matt. viii. 29; Luke viii. 28.
[3] Matt. iv. 3; Luke iv. 3, 9.

calming of the storm.[1] The usage of the centurion, on the other hand, is pagan rather than Jewish.[2] But it is remarkable that in the Synoptics Jesus never uses this title; and His careful avoidance can only be explained by His aversion to its official sense.[3] With Him the personal relation was primary, the official secondary, and He would not use a name which could be understood of an office, but which had to Him no meaning save as applied to a person. To the Jew the Messianic King was the Son of God, but to Jesus the Son of God was the Messianic King.[4] Hence in strong contrast to His avoidance of the official title is His use of the personal name "Father" for God. He spoke of God in the most impressive forms and exclusive sense as His Father. His usage is too distinctive and exceptional to be an accident. Nothing so marked Jesus as His feeling of kinship with men, His brotherhood, His love of standing in their midst while they prayed "Our Father which art in heaven." All the more on this account is His action significant when He detaches Himself from man and distinguishes Himself as in a pre-eminent sense the Son of God. Thus He warns men that only those who "do the will of My Father who is in heaven" shall enter into the kingdom.[5] None but those who confess Him before men are to be confessed before His Father.[6] Only those plants which His Father has planted shall endure.[7] The confession of Peter is due to the inspiration of "My Father."[8] The angels do always behold His Father's face.[9] His Father answers prayer.[10] The saved are the "blessed of My Father."[11] In the awful moments of Gethsemane and the cross it is to

[1] Matt. xiv. 33.
[2] Matt. xxvii. 54; Mark xv. 39.
[3] Cf. His answer to chief priest, and rapid substitution of his own "Son of man" for the priest's "Son of God" (Matt. xxvii. 64; Mark xiv. 62).
[4] Wendt, ii. 436 (Eng. trans., ii. 133).
[5] Matt. vii. 21.
[6] Matt. x. 32, 33.
[7] Matt. xv. 13.
[8] Matt. xvi. 17.
[9] Matt. xviii. 10.
[10] Matt. xviii. 19, 35.
[11] Matt. xxv. 34.

His Father that He cries.[1] But He speaks still more clearly and impressively. The Lord of heaven and earth is His Father; and to Him He claims exclusive and commanding relations. No one knoweth the Son save the Father, or the Father save the Son, and he to whom the Son willeth to reveal Him.[2] Here is mutual knowledge, perfect openness and access of each to the other, but to none besides; and all who know God or get to Him know Him and get to Him through the Son. It is a son's knowledge, and they who receive it become as He was who gave it. These are personal relations, and out of them spring all His official activities and functions. Save as Son He has nothing to teach concerning God; as Son He has such knowledge to communicate as will make all the world restful and blessed. The last wickedness is to reject the Son[3]; the highest beatitude is to know Him as He is known of the Father.

C. THE SON OF MAN.—But now in what seems strict yet complementary antithesis to "the Son of God" stands "the Son of man." It occurs but once in the New Testament on other lips than His own,[4] but so often on His that it may be described as the title of His own peculiar choice.[5] In the Old Testament the usage is varied; it is now generic, and denotes man in distinction from God, as created, mortal, impotent, imperfect[6]; now specific man, as member of a race, with all the qualities of the race he belongs to[7]; now personal, a man with

---

[1] Matt. xxvi. 39, 42, 53; Luke xxii. 42, xxiii. 34, 46.

[2] Matt. xi. 25-27; Luke x. 21, 22.

[3] Mark xii. 1-11. Under the "beloved son" of verse 6 Christ Himself is to be understood. The ascending dignity of the messengers is to be noted.

[4] Stephen, Acts vii. 56. But cf. Rev. i. 13.

[5] In singular contrast to His avoidance of "Son of God" in the Synoptics stands His usage of "the Son of man." It occurs in Matthew thirty times, in Mark fourteen, in Luke twenty-five.

[6] Job xxv. 6; Psalm viii. 4; Num. xxiii. 19.

[7] Psalm cxlvi. 3; Isa. li. 12.

all the attributes of his kind, directly spoken to and made the instrument or mouthpiece of God.[1] But the most significant use is in Daniel.[2] He sees one like a Son of man come in the clouds of heaven to the Ancient of Days, and there is given to him a kingdom which shall not be destroyed. Now, the "Son of man" is here a symbol or type; He stands opposed to the "four great beasts," "diverse one from another," which represented the older empires. They were the symbols of brute force and cruelty, the ferocious strength that prevailed by devouring; but the new kingdom had as its symbol humanity; its strength was reasonable justice and truth. In four respects it was to stand opposed to the brute empires: first, they were the creatures of the earth, but it was of Divine origin, the gift or creation of the Ancient of Days; secondly, they rose out of violence and stood in wrong, but it lived by the human gentleness which best typified Divine grace; thirdly, they had only a local, but it was to have a universal dominion, over "all peoples, and nations, and tongues"; and, finally, they were merely temporal, but it was to continue for ever.

Now, while this phrase, which signified so much as to the Messianic King and kingdom, passed into the apocalyptic literature, it did not penetrate the Christology of the people and the scribes; but Jesus adopted it, enlarged and enriched all its elements.[3] In His hands it became at once a personal and a Messianic title, the one because the other; the term "man" defined at once a source and a character, the term "Son" a relation which expressed at once His nature, function, and work. The text determinative of His usage is the famous question to Peter[4]: "Whom do men say that I, the Son of

---

[1] Ezek. ii. 1-3, 8, *et passim*.
[2] Dan. vii. 13.
[3] The relation to Daniel seems to be indicated in τὸ σημεῖον τοῦ Υἱοῦ τοῦ ἀνθρώπου (Matt. xxiv. 30, 44; Mark xiv. 62, viii. 38).
[4] Matt. xvi. 13. Cf. Mark viii. 27; Luke ix. 18.

man, am?" The place and time and result of the question are all significant. It was asked at Cæsarea Philippi—*i.e.*, in the region, as it were, of the Gentiles, and in a city whose name ominously joined the Roman and the Herodian, and so in a sense in the world and before the face of Rome, the most terrible and enduring of the ancient empires, and just as He had turned His face to Jerusalem and the Passion. The agony and the death were already in His soul, and expressed in His question. The answer given by Peter was the occasion of what may be termed the solemn and formal institution of the kingdom. From that hour it was not only for Him, but for His people and through them.

This name is made to denote at once the loftiest functions and the lowliest state. "The Son of man" has power on earth to forgive sins.[1] He is Lord of the Sabbath.[2] His coming creates the new age which men so desire to see.[3] One day His angels shall attend Him and do His commandments.[4] He will reign and judge, fixing the eternal destinies of men.[5] But this official majesty has its contrast in the personal lowliness; "the Son of man" lives a humble and suffering life. In this connection the title is used as if it were a personal pronoun, yet it never seems so much a name of majesty as when it connotes the abasement of the Person it denotes. He is poorer than the foxes or the birds of the air, having nowhere to lay His head.[6] He is reproached and a cause of reproach.[7] He lives as a man and not as an ascetic, and is judged gluttonous and a winebibber.[8] He suffers many things, is betrayed, rejected by the chief priests, goes to His destiny, which is death.[9] But this humiliation is the way of His majesty; by its means He seeks that

---

[1] Matt. ix. 6; Mark ii. 10; Luke v. 24.
[2] Matt. xii. 8; Mark ii. 28
[3] Matt. x. 23; Luke xvii. 20-22.
[4] Matt. xiii. 41, xxiv. 31.
[5] Matt. xxv. 31 ff.
[6] Matt. viii. 20; Luke ix. 58.
[7] Luke vi. 22.
[8] Matt. xi. 19; Luke vii. 34.
[9] Luke ix. 22, 26; Matt. xvii. 22, xx. 18, xxvi. 2, 45; Mark xiv. 21.

He may save the lost, and gives His life a ransom for many.[1] It is essentially the name of Him who redeems by the sacrifice of Himself.

The title, then, has at once a personal and an official sense (*a*) Construed as personal, it does two things: emphasizes, (1) the stock whence He springs—man, humanity, mankind; the Son of man is no man's son, is as it were the child or offspring of the race. (2) His own solitude and pre-eminence. He has no fellow, stands by Himself, is an individual who is a genus, a person *sui generis*, not *a* son, but "*the* Son of man." Within the lowliness there lies therefore an extraordinary claim; He transcends every individual, and is, as it were, the equivalent of man. He is the epitome of the race at one point, as its common father was its epitome at another. And as such He is its embodied ideal, bears not only a normal humanity, but the alone normal; in Him man is summarized, and what is alien to man has no being in Him. (*β*) Construed in its official sense the title emphasizes, (1) the character and relations of Him who fills the office. As the alone normal man He is sprung from the collective race, and related to it. (2) The nature and scope of the office. He who fills it so holds and represents man as to be able to serve and save, to rule and judge him. And (3) the forms and terms of service under Him. The normal becomes the normative man. The citizens of the Messianic kingdom must be as its Founder: the men He approves are men who act as He did to those who as men are contained in Him.

§ II.—The Names and the Mission.

How are the terms "Son of God" and "Son of man" related? Both denote, as it were, on the inward side a peculiar and exclusive relation—there is this one Son of God and no other, and no other than this one Son of man; and both denote

[1] Mark x. 45; Matt. xx. 28; Luke xix. 10.

on the outward side a relation personal yet universal—the one Son of the one God is the sole medium of the knowledge of Him, but He is a medium for all; and the one Son of collective man is the sole person in whom all men are, and through whom all manhood is. "God" in the one phrase and "man" in the other denote each a unity, though the unity is in the one case personal, in the other organic; and "Son" expresses the mode in which each unity is realized —the one in knowledge, the other in being. To know God through the Son is to know Him as a Father and so to become to Him as a son; and it is in order to this double result that we have the double sonship of the creative Person. One who is Son of God is alone able to embody the ideal of humanity, and only a humanity conscious of Sonship can be ideal. Man as God conceived him was son, and so only through the Son can man become as God conceived him. Hence as Son of God Christ interprets God to man; as Son of man He interprets by a process of realization man to God. The ideal He embodies is to be perpetuated, not destroyed, and those who are formed after Christ become sons of God while sons of men. His kingdom is but the multiplication of Himself, the realization of the double sonship in a common brotherhood.

But in order to understand the relation of the two names and their significance alike for the Person and the mission we must turn to the Fourth Gospel. Here the organic relation of the two sonships becomes clearer than in the Synoptics. The Prologue prepares us for a more impressive and exalted use of the phrase "the Son of God." It is used by the Baptist, Nathanael, Peter, Martha, the Jews, and the Evangelist himself,[1] who adds emphasis to his usage by recurring to the μονογενής of the Prologue.[2] But Jesus also employs it, though only three times—twice in argument with

---
[1] John i. 34, 50, vi. 69, xi. 34, xix. 7, xx. 31.
[2] John iii. 16, 18: cf. i. 14-19.

the Jews,[1] and once to His disciples when He heard of the death of Lazarus.[2] So far as it has a distinct reference in those cases, it is either as an interpretation of the term "My Father," or as associated with the exercise of re-creative power. But much more significant is the use of the term "the Son" in a sense as distinctive and denominative as "the Father." "The Father loveth the Son"; "the Son quickeneth"; "the Son can do nothing of Himself"; "all may honour the Son as they honour the Father"; "the Son has life in Himself"; "the Son shall make you free"; the Father glorifies the Son, the Son the Father.[3] The two are so associated as to be indissoluble; the correlation involves a unity, which yet does not become identity. He is in the Father, the Father in Him; and to see the Son is to see the Father,[4] for they two are one.[5] Their being is so concordant that the Son can do nothing of Himself[6]; and as the Father has worked hitherto, so He works.[7] Out of this relation His mission has come: He is the sent of the Father[8]; His work is the Father's[9]; to believe Him is to believe the Father and to possess eternal life.[10] His appearance in time and all that belongs to it flows from His Divine Sonship, and without it no part of His work could have been done.

But the names are in John in a peculiar sense and degree epexegetical; each helps to define and explain the other. Turning, then, to "the Son of man," we find that it is here, as in the Synoptics, used exclusively by Jesus, and this is only the more emphasized by its occurrence as a quotation from

---

[1] John v. 25, x. 36.
[2] John xi. 4. In ix. 35 the reading is more than doubtful: in iii. 18 the words are manifestly the Evangelist's.
[3] John v. 19, 20, 21, 23, 26, viii. 36, xvii. 1.
[4] John xiv. 9-11.
[5] John x. 30.   [8] John v. 36, 37, vi. 38, 39, 44, 57, viii. 16, 18, etc.
[6] John v. 19.   [9] John iv. 34, ix. 4, xvii. 4.
[7] John v. 17.   [10] John v. 24, xiii. 15, 16, xvii. 3.

Him in a question by the Jews.[1] "The Son of man" is the sign of the open heaven, the body on which the angels of God ascend and descend.[2] He is the only one who has ascended into heaven, because He alone has descended from heaven.[3] He is lifted up that men may believe on Him and live.[4] Authority to judge has been committed unto Him,[5] and to give eternal life.[6] Men must eat His flesh and drink His blood that they may have life.[7] By His passion and death He is glorified.[8] The connotation is here in every case union with man, as in the other name it had been union with God. "The Son of man" is lifted up—the act of man[9]; but "the Son of God" is given or sent—the act of the Father. The former is palpable—to be discerned and assimilated through sense; the latter is spiritual—the mind must believe and conceive Him. The one expresses the temporal form and relation of the Person and His work, but the other expresses His extra-temporal being, with its essential or inherent life. The Son of God brings the life down from heaven, but the Son of man distributes the life and is the way to heaven. The double Sonship thus expresses a double relation—on the Divine side the unity of Father and Son, on the human the incorporated being of the Son and man. The one represents the mode by which God finds access to man, but the other the mode by which man finds access to God. And this access is only the same thing seen from different standpoints; for the Person is one, though the relations are twofold. It is the Divine Sonship that makes sacrifice possible to God, but the human sonship which makes the sacrifice manifest to man. The real sacrifice is the act and experience of God, the surrender of the Father, the submission of the Son; but the evidential process is the Passion and Death, where the Son of

---

[1] John xii. 34.
[2] John i. 51.
[3] John iii. 13, vi. 62.
[4] John iii. 14: cf. viii. 28.
[5] John v. 27.
[6] John vi. 27.
[7] John vi. 53.
[8] John xii. 23, xiii. 31.
[9] John viii. 28.

man dies for the man whose Son He is. By the unity of Father and Son the life of God is communicated; by the unity of man and Son the life of God is distributed. The doctrine of Jesus in John thus completes and explains His doctrine in the Synoptics. It places the Redeemer in essential relation with God, the source of redemption, and with man, its subject. Its cause is sufficient, for it is Divine; its means normal, yet adequate, for they are human. And so through the one Sonship what is inmost in God comes to man, and through the other what is most ideal in man returns to God.

The inference we draw from this analysis and discussion is simple and obvious: the constitutive idea in the consciousness of Jesus was the filial; round it His thought and character, as it were, crystallized. The ideal man was the conscious Son of God, and His function was by the creation of the ideal consciousness to create ideal men. But the correlative of the filial in man is the paternal in God; and so the God of Jesus is the Father of men. His Fatherhood precedes, creates, underlies their sonship. It is the basis of all duty, involving an affinity of nature that makes it possible for men to be perfect as their Father in heaven is perfect.[1] They are to love their enemies, that they may be the sons of their Father, who maketh His sun to shine on the evil and the good.[2] Prayer is the speech of the filial spirit; needs, therefore, to be simple, sincere, the murmur of a love that seeks only the ear of the loved, and fears to be overheard by the profane.[3] So when He speaks to men of God He calls Him "your Father" or "thy Father."[4] They are to pray trustfully, for if even sinful men may be kind fathers, what shall the gracious God be?[5] Worship must be in spirit and in truth, for only so can it be acceptable to the Father.[6] And the characteristic of

[1] Matt. v. 48.
[2] Matt. v. 45.
[3] Matt. vi. 5 ff.
[4] Mark xi. 25; Matt. vi. 1, 4, 6, 18, 32, x. 29, xxiii. 9; Luke xii. 32.
[5] Matt. vii. 11.
[6] John iv. 23.

Fatherhood is, that while it rejoices in the obedient it cannot surrender the bad. The prodigal does not cease to be a son, and the Father hails his penitent return with weeping joy; and the hard, self-righteous brother is rebuked into gentleness, that he may be waked to brotherhood.[1] God's real relation to man is thus in the view of Jesus the paternal, and so man's perfect relation to God is the filial. Sonship is of the essence of humanity as paternity of God, and so He who is by nature Son of God appears as Son of man, that men through Him may attain the filial state and spirit and relation. What this means will be seen later; meanwhile, it is enough to recognize its being.

§ III.—HIS PERSON AND PLACE.

From this analysis of His names we may infer that His whole message to man was but the interpretation of Himself. And this interpretation represents Him as being at once as necessary to man and as sufficient for all His functions as if He were very God. What He held of the Christ in relation to David,[2] He held of Himself relative to the saints, the prophets, priests, and kings of the Old Testament. He transcended them all. He was greater than Jonah, than Solomon,[3] than Abraham.[4] He was greater even than the most sacred institutions—the Temple, the Sabbath, the Law, and the Prophets—which He at once superseded and fulfilled.[5] And He was not only great as regards the past, but necessary as regards the future—the one Being needful for all men everywhere and needful not simply as an official, but as a person. His very being is a condition of man's chief good. It is not only as a teacher of truth, as a preacher of the kingdom, or as a realized ideal of righteousness that He is necessary; the necessity is so personal that it is by His relation to

---

[1] Luke xv. 11 ff. [2] Matt. xii. 41, 42.
[3] Mark xii. 35-37. [4] John viii. 53-56.
[5] Matt. xii. 6, 7; Mark ii. 28; Matt. v. 17, 18, xxi. 34-37.

men and men's to Him that they are to be judged, saved or lost. If men refuse to hear Him or His, it shall be more tolerable in the day of judgment for Sodom and Gomorrha than for them.[1] To receive or reject Him is to receive or reject God.[2] To be ashamed of Him and His words before men is to have no part or lot in the kingdom of God.[3] Men who would share His life must bear His cross, for the sake of Him and His Gospel all must be sacrificed, and then all will be gained.[4] The service must not be outer, ceremonial, vicarious; must be inner, real, personal, or it is worthless.[5] He is the living bond of unity, necessary to fellowship among men and worship of God.[6] If any one dares to try issues with Him he will be not simply broken, but ground to powder[7]; but blessed are they who are not offended in Him.[8] And as the necessary He is the solitary; no one can take His place or do His work; He stands alone. As the Son He only knoweth the Father, and all knowledge is of His giving.[9] No one cometh unto the Father but by Him.[10] And as necessary and unique He is universal—no local or provincial person, but One who invites all, and promises rest to the all He invites.[11] He is sufficient for every human need, and becomes through His death only the more mighty. By being lifted up He is to draw all men unto Himself.[12] Where the office is a necessity, the person is not; where the person is a necessity, the office is but His exercised functions, the creation and consequence of His being. In the first case the person is but a transient incident in the being of a perpetual institution; in the second case the office is but the form or mode in which a

[1] Matt. x. 15.
[2] Mark ix. 37; Matt. x. 40.
[3] Mark viii. 38; Matt. x. 32, 33.
[4] Mark viii. 34, 35, x. 29, xiii. 13; Luke xiv. 27.
[5] Matt. x. 34-39.
[6] Matt. xviii. 19, 20, xxviii. 20.
[7] Luke xx. 18.
[8] Matt. xi. 6.
[9] Matt. xi. 27; Luke x. 22.
[10] John xiv. 6.
[11] Matt. xi. 28.
[12] John xii. 32.

perpetual person works. With Christ the person is primary, the office secondary; from the perpetuity of His person has come the perpetuity of His office. And so all that He is and all that He does must be construed, as it were, in the terms of His personal being; and before the construction can be speculative it must be historical, the historical supplying the speculative with all its architectonic and regulative principles.

But the necessary and sufficient is also an accessible person. If He was needed by all, it was only fit that He should be open to all. And so He appears as One who did not love intermediaries, but desired direct personal intercourse with men. It was easier to reach the Master than to conciliate a disciple. The disciples would have forbidden the mothers to present their children; but by His rebuke of the men and His reception of the children He justified the confidence of the mothers.[1] One of the earliest and most persistent charges against Him was "the friend of publicans and sinners,"[2] "this man receiveth sinners and eateth with them"[3]; and He vindicated His conduct by what may be described as at once His most beautiful and most characteristic parables.[4] He did not refuse the public homage of the woman who was "a sinner,"[5] or the secret visit of the man who was "a ruler of the Jews"[6]; He mingled with the crowd, and it pressed upon Him[7]; He was touched by one within it, and He Himself touched the sick, the palsied, and the blind.[8] He met and was met of men in the synagogue, the Temple, the mart, the street, the highway, the private house. He spoke to them on the mountain, from the ship,

[1] Matt. xix. 13-15; Mark x. 13-16; Luke xviii. 15-17.
[2] Matt. xi. 19; Luke vii. 34.
[3] Matt. ix. 10, 11; Mark ii. 16; Luke v. 32, xv. 2.
[4] Luke xv.   [6] John iii. 1, 2.
[5] Luke vii. 37-39.   [7] Luke vii. 45.
[8] Mark v. 30; Matt. viii. 3, 15, 29; Mark vii. 33, i. 41; Luke v. 13, vii. 14, xxii. 51.

amid the green fields. He did not deny Himself to Pharisee or Sadducee, to scribe or priest. The lost sheep of the house of Israel, the woman of Samaria, the Magdalene of the city, the inquisitive Greek, the authoritative Roman, the messengers of John, the men of Galilee—all had access to Him. He loved to be sought of men. His dignity owed nothing to mystery; indeed, the most mysterious thing about Him is the increase, with increased knowledge, of the feeling of the awful loveliness and sanctity of His person. And so men are conscious of nothing but harmony in a picture which now exhibits Him as "meek and lowly in heart," and now arrays Him in the dread attributes of the judge. What He was then He was ever to be—an eternal presence in the midst of His people,[1] with all His relations personal and all immediate, an unmediated but always mediating mediator.

[1] Matt. xviii. 20, xxviii. 20.

CHAPTER IV.

THE RELATIONS AND THE REASON OF THE CHRISTOLOGIES.

§ I.—COMPARISON OF THE APOSTOLIC CHRISTOLOGIES WITH CHRIST'S.

WE are now in a position to determine how the Apostolic Christologies stand related to Christ's, whether and to what extent His was the source of theirs, theirs the development and explication of His. We may say of all save James, who hardly had a Christology, that they so construed Jesus as the Christ as to evolve not only a new religion out of the old, but also a new philosophy of history, of man, and of God. The constitutive ideas were His, but the constructive endeavour theirs; with Him all is spontaneous, the expression of an intuitive or immediate consciousness; with them all is reflective, the expression of a mediative consciousness, using the methods of a more or less explicit dialectic. The affinities may be presented under four heads: historical, religious, philosophical, theological.

1. *The Historical.*—The Apostles, like Jesus, conceived the Messiah as of the Jews, but not as Jewish. To all His character and office were alike ethical, His method one of self-denial and obedience, and His end to save from sin and reconcile to God. He is the end rather than the product of prior history; does not so much get meaning from it as give meaning to it. He is before Abraham, and so the

patriarch and the promise are made significant by the Son and the fulfilment. The Davidic descent is to Paul, as to Jesus, a mere outward incident; the material thing is His being as the Son of God. In the Apocalypse David is more an effect than a cause; he is for the Messiah rather than the Messiah through him. As of the fathers and kings, so of the people. The Jews are for Christ; Christ is not in order to the being of the Jews. But as Paul conceives it this is a great honour, the very greatest possible, carrying with it their place in the whole order of Providence, their election of God, the fathers, the promises, the giving of the law, the being entrusted with the oracles of God. This was the reason of their pre-eminence; they were that Christ might be. This was the doctrine of Matthew and John as well as of Paul, and all owed it to Jesus. As with the people, so with the modes which connected Him with the institutions and ideals of Israel. The law was in order to Him, and He by fulfilling it made an end of it. And so Paul conceived it as the schoolmaster who instructed and governed till He came; Hebrews represented it as the type or shadow of the good things He was to bring, and the Apocalypse made the institutions it created the symbols of His perfect and enduring reign. Jesus claimed to be the fulfilment of prophecy, and so Peter represented the Spirit of Christ as in the prophets, who all testified of Him, while Paul and Hebrews, the Apocalypse and Matthew, all cited their words as witnesses to the truth. What Jesus terms tradition Paul often terms the law, which lived by being interpreted in the school, and to both its dominion was the tyranny of impotence, which Jesus represented as ended by the lordship of the Son of man, and Paul by His coming and creating in us the Spirit of His own Sonship.

2. *The Religious.*—This concerned His person, in all its redemptive and normative significance. Jesus predicted His sufferings from the scribes, His death at the hands of the

chief priests and rulers; and Paul not only describes the princes of this world as crucifying the Lord of glory, but also connects Christ's death under the law, which is the abstract of chief priest and ruler, with our redemption from its curse. Christ speaks of His religion as a new covenant in His blood; and Hebrews develops His words into the elaborate contrast of the old covenant and the new, translating all the sensuous elements of the old into their spiritual counterparts. Jesus represents His body as a temple, which is to take the place of the one built with hands; and Paul applies the figure now to the Church, which is His body, now to the men, and now to the bodies of the men who are Christ's; while in the Apocalypse the Lamb Himself is the temple, and in Hebrews the High Priest's presence constitutes the heaven where He is the holy of holies. The form of the thought is Apostolic, but its essence is of Christ. He preaches the kingdom and founds a society for the realization of His ideal, and this becomes in all the Apostles the Church. His society is ethical through and through, and so the terms in which they describe and express the society are all ethical: the ancient ceremonialism is the repealed law of Paul; the old sacerdotalism is the transcended priesthood and ritual of Hebrews. At the touch of His hand, the old religion of the letter has passed away; all has become of the Spirit and the truth.

3. *The Philosophical.*—This element appears mainly in the new anthropology, which develops the ideas connected with the name "the Son of man." These ideas may be divided into two classes—those suggested (a) by its connotation, (β) by its absolute sense. He is, as to (a), in harmony with His own usage, conceived by the Apostles as the end of the law, and as the normative person who creates a normal society or kingdom where the law is love. He reigns and judges, dies for our sins, gives His life a ransom for many, creates a righteousness by faith which exceeds the righteousness of the law;

in other words, the outer law is superseded by the inner life He gives. The distinctively evangelical elements in the Apostolical theology are simply expansions of the ideas which Jesus had made to cluster round "the Son of man." And these were justified and explained by the principles educed from (β) the absolute sense. He became the ideal Man, made in all things like unto His brethren, yet as without sin in a world where all had sinned, transcending all that He might help all. As "the Son of man" he became to Paul the last Adam, the second Man, who stood as a parallel and yet as an absolute opposite to the first,— head like him of a race, but a spiritual, not a physical head; creator of righteousness, not of sin; of life, not of death. Paul's whole elaborate anthropology is but the dialectical explication of this name. In its light man was seen to be an organic unity; the history that divided Adam and Christ exhibited his evolution under forces that were now of God and now of the devil; the deliverance that came by the second Man was unmeaning without the ruin that had come by the first. But its significance ranged into the future as well as into the past. The Son of man was the brother of men, the first-born of the new race. They were to be conformed to Him, made in His image; His privileges, honours, standing, were to be theirs. As was the new Man, such was to be the new mankind; His brotherhood meant man's sonship and God's Fatherhood.

4. *The Theological.*—Here the regulative idea was supplied by the supreme or determinative element in his own consciousness—viz., the Sonship. The idea of "the Son of God" penetrated the Apostolic thought, stamped it with its specific character, created its distinctive theology. Fatherhood became essential to God, sonship to man. Jesus Christ is to all the Son of God, and God the Father of our Lord Jesus Christ. The Father is conceived, studied, interpreted, through the Son. The men who entered into His consciousness

looked at God with His eyes, thought of God in His way, learned to speak of God in His terms, and bequeathed to us as their abiding legacy an interpretation of Christ which was an interpretation of God.

§ II.—Conclusory and Transitional.

1. This Christology was the work of Jews, men who had Monotheism as a passion in their blood; and made its appeal to men, many of whom were of the same race and had the same passion. Yet these men join God and the Son of God together, speak of them with equal honour, and do them equal reverence, using of the Son terms as descriptive of Deity as any they ever use of the Father; and neither they nor the men they address feel any shock or any sense of incongruity in such usage. They all think that God has only become worthier of obedience and love.

2. The Person to whom they ascribe a dignity so transcendent, and for whom they claim a reverence so extraordinary, had a quarter of a century before suffered death on the cross at the hands of His own people, who were the elect people of God. This date is taken from those Pauline Epistles which even the most radical rational criticism has regarded as our oldest authentic Christian literature; but this literature is as high in doctrine as any of the later, and has as its author the most characteristic Jew of them all. As there was nothing in the outward state or fortunes of this Jesus to suggest a dignity so pre-eminent and absolutely singular—indeed, everything to suggest the very opposite—the result must have been due to the transcendent qualities of His person, to His consciousness as expressed in speech, in character, and in action.

3. The Apostolical interpretation of Him was absolutely opposed to what may be termed the science and the philosophy of the time. If ever both educated and common sense would have justified not only scepticism but the most frank

and brutal denial, it was in this case. Men might well have resented it as an insult to their belief in God, and to their own reason; nay, to their very sense of decency. The marvel is not that they were so much but so little offended. The reasonable view seemed to be contained in the scandal of the Jews and the sceptical mockery of Celsus. This view was in every respect the direct and flagrant contradiction of the Apostolic. Jesus was in the broadest sense a child of nature, skilled in Egyptian magic, and able to deceive the simple into the belief that He was a god. He had no real sense of the Divine. The simple people He deceived imagined themselves the special care of Heaven, the only marvellous thing being that they were so easily deceived; yet it was not so very marvellous, as they were one and all ignorant and unlearned men. Their apology was His condemnation. If they had not been men of this order, they would never have believed in Jesus; and their belief only helps to make both them and their religion the more ridiculous.

4. But the two views have a right to be tried at the bar of history. The question what Jesus Christ is cannot be settled by an appeal to the New Testament, either to Himself and His Apostles, or to the Jews and Greeks; but history has a contribution to make that may help towards a settlement. His life is written in the Gospels, but His history is written in the life of civilized man. And before we can even approximately know Him, what the New Testament said of Him must be compared with what history has to say. Its verdict may be summed up in some positions that may be described as commonplaces of the philosophy of history.

i. Jesus Christ is in His own order—viz., the order of the founders or creators of religions—the transcendent Person of history; and to be transcendent here is to be transcendent everywhere, for religion is the supreme factor in the organizing and the regulating of our personal and collective life.

ii. He is the real Creator of Monotheism. Before and apart

from Him we have Naturalisms, Polytheisms, Pantheisms, and a Henotheism, which is the term most characteristic of Judaism as it was and is; but it is only through Him and within Christendom that Monotheism has come to be and has been incorporated in a real and realized religion.

iii. He created a religion in its own order as transcendent as His person, and its order is the universal and ethical. The one God has as His correlative and counterpart the one religion, and in its character the religion could not but be as was the God; and as were the God and the religion, so did they design man to be. By making God a new being to man, man was made a new being for the service of God.

iv. Since the religion was universal and ethical, it stood differentiated from all previous religions by being, on the one hand, independent of special polities, able to create the varied and dissimilar polities or organs needed for its ever-changing work; and, on the other hand, capable of living in all places, under all kinds and orders of government, empires, monarchies, or democracies. The only thing it could not tolerate was the government that, either by civil persecution or by the absorption of the religion into a civil institution, denied its right to live.

v. By means of His religion He created a new ideal of life, bound together the service of God and the service of man. By virtue of the ethical qualities of the God He revealed, love of Him became the mainspring of an obedience which evoked universal beneficence. By virtue of the ethical qualities of His own person, love of Himself became love of all mankind; service of Him, service of the race.

vi. It is this religion which constitutes the difference and measures the distance between the ancient and the modern, the Eastern and the Western worlds. The contrast between the ancient and modern, especially in all that concerns the higher religions and humaner moral ideals, is an impressive witness to the personal pre-eminence and grandeur of Christ. The contrast between the Eastern and Western worlds, especially in those forces that work for order and progress, freedom and mobility, ethical achievement and public conscience, is an invincible testimony to the permanence and efficiency of the moral energies which He embodies.

vii. The most remarkable fact in the history of His religion is the continuous and ubiquitous activity of His person. He has been the permanent and efficient factor in its extension and progress. Under all its forms, in all its periods, and through all its divisions, the one principle alike of reality and unity has been and is devotion to Him. He is the Spirit that inhabits all the Churches, the law that rules the conscience and binds into awed and obedient reverence the saintly men who live within all the communions that bear His name.

viii. Love of Him has remained the inspiration and commanding passion of His Church. Other loves have died, or, by being embalmed in literature, have become means of cultivating the imagination; but this love has been, as it were, an immortal spirit, incapable of death, though capable of being incarnated in infinite modes or forms of moral and social being. It is the only thing in the region of moral motive that can be described as an imperishable yet convertible force, whose changes of form never mean decrease of energy or loss of power.

ix. This love is even more remarkable for its ethical quality than for its energy and persistence. It has changed the bad into the good; has even created in wise, commonplace, or even mean and ignoble men emotions so dissimilar as the passion for holiness, the enthusiasm of humanity, the zeal to save, the hatred of oppression, the love of liberty and of truth. It has quickened the imagination of the poet and the painter, of the warrior and the statesman, and may be described as the one love which has been most universal where most consciously personal: the men who have most absolutely loved Christ have been also the men who have most truly loved all men and the whole of man.

x. But its action on the Godward emotions and acts has been no less marvellous. It has made love of God a reality, has caused men to feel that they are capable of loving Him and He capable of being loved. Without the person of Christ the language of adoration, of gratitude, of wonderment, in which the Church has for all the centuries of its existence spoken its love of God, would cease to have any meaning or any reason or any right to be.

xi. And this means that His person has affected the theistic conception which He originally created. It has prevented the Monotheism becoming a mere abstraction, a Pantheism on the one hand, or a Deism on the other. This is the result that could least of all have been foreseen. The action of the Person might have been expected either to hide the μόνος θεός or dissolve Him into a plurality; but it has done the very opposite—made the μόνος absolute and the θεός real.

xii. The life of the religion, then, lies in the person of its Founder; all that it has done for the race is but a form of His action within and through it. He has given actuality to its theistic beliefs, has been the motive, impulse, and law to all its beneficences. The sense or consciousness of His abiding presence constitutes His Church; the emotions He awakens determines all its worship and all its desires. Even where this seems most concealed, it is yet present as the veritable seat and principle of life. The Virgin may seem to hold the first place in what may be called the more vulgar Roman worship; but she does it not as woman, but as mother; she stands there not in her own right, but by virtue of her Son. The opposite fault has been committed in many an evangelical sermon; the Son has been so preached as to hide the Father, or to deny Him by absorbing those ethical qualities which are most distinctively Divine. But here, too, the Son could not be without the Father, or the Father without the Son; both were needed to the being of either; and so the emphasis on one was only a crude way of expressing their unity. The historical fact then remains—the person of Christ has given reality to the life of the Christian religion, and actuality both to its belief in God and to the God it has believed in.

5. We come back, then, to consider the two views as they stand at the bar of history. The world has for now almost nineteen centuries had experience of the two interpretations of Christ—the Ethnico-Judaic and the Apostolical, the natural and the supernatural; and may we not say with this remarkable result—that the supernatural offers a more reasonable philosophy of this experience than the natural? For the attempt to connect Christ with all men and the whole past of man has been more than justified by His continued creative presence in what was then future and is now past, and His easy pre-eminence over the conscience and the conduct of what is still present. What seemed so incredible then appears so credible now that apology has become the duty of disbelief rather than belief; culture is now almost as coy of denial as it was then of faith. Something surely is due to the foresight, or inspiration, or whatever the quality may be called, of these Apostolical men. If they had been guided by probability, they could never have believed as they did; but apologetics can now argue that all the probabilities are on the side of the then improbable. History is a scene of order and progress. Failure may belong to the individual, but development is proper to the whole. Yet if there be ordered movement in history, then the most necessary person of history is the person most necessary to the movement and the order. And as it does not lie open to doubt that this is Jesus Christ, it follows that He is the last person that can be conceived as an accident or a creation of chance. And what is the Apostolical theology but an attempt to explain His place in the providential order of the world, His necessity on the one hand to God, and on the other to man? And have not the very things that made

the attempt seem then absurd become to-day its best vindication? Wisdom has been justified of her children.

6. The theology which embodied the attempts is marked by singular originality. Its way is its own. In order to be it had to effect equal changes in the current and conventional ideas of God and man. Of these ideas there were many types, though only two that could have influenced the New Testament writers—Judaic or Hebrew Deism, and Hellenic Theism and Mythology; but the apostolic theology most significantly differs from both. In its notion of God it is not deistic, like Judaism; does not so divide God and man that the two can be conceived only as opposites, mechanically related—*i.e.*, as forces and not as spirits, with natures too different and opposite to be capable of interpenetrative being. And it is not on the theistic side monistic, like Greek thought, and on the historical mythological, like Greek religion—*i.e.*, it does not, on the one hand, reduce Deity to the substance that remains unchanged amid all the changes of phenomenal existence; nor, on the other, does it by a process either of apotheosis or of generation abolish all distinction between God and man. Apotheosis implied that God and man were so near in status and in dignity that the gods into whose ranks the man was admitted were as little creators and as little by their own might or right immortal as the man; while he by entering their society did not cease to be a creature, nor did he become in any tolerable modern sense Divine. And so descent from the gods did not involve Deity as the Apostolic writers understood it or as we understand. But the remarkable thing in their theology is that by the way it took Monotheism was made absolute; yet the relation of God to man made real, organic, continuous. God was made man's Father, man God's son; and the very notion of their relation involved the affinities of their natures, the distinctness of their personalities, and the community and connection of their lives. And where both were so conceived

it was really a thing most reasonable, consonant, as it were, to the higher and universal or common nature, that God by the method of incarnation should become fully known to man, and man realize His ideal and organic being before God.

7. The theology did not stand alone; it is but one of the many creations which came from the Spirit of Christ. He created the men who made the theology, the society they formed, the ideals they followed, the things they achieved. And their continued being is but the permanent effect witnessing to the permanence of the cause. Through faith in Him faith in God has lived upon the earth; and the sense of His presence has been not only the life of His religion, but of all its manifold beneficences. Certainly this theology cannot be construed as a mere chapter in the history of speculation, for within it live the forces that have made the religion of Christ the religion of civilized man and man it has civilized.

DIVISION II.

CHRIST THE INTERPRETATION OF GOD.

CHAPTER I.

THE GODHEAD.

§ I.—THE DOCTRINE OF THE GODHEAD AND REVELATION.

THE interpretation of God consists of two distinct yet complementary parts—a doctrine of God and of the Godhead. God is deity conceived in relation, over against the universe, its cause or ground, its law and end; but the Godhead is deity conceived according to His own nature, as He is from within and for Himself. God is the Godhead in action within the sphere of the related and the conditioned; the Godhead is God in the region of transcendental existence, yet with His immanent activities so exercised that His absolute being is concrete and complex, as opposed to abstract and simple. God is an object of natural knowledge—*i.e.*, He can be known from His works, or by a process of regressive and analytical thought; but the Godhead is a subject of supernatural revelation—*i.e.*, can be known only as man is in a sense taken into the secrets of the Divine nature. By the light of reason we may know that God is, but what He is we can know only as He Himself speaks. Yet the natural knowledge is incomplete without the supernatural. What reason reaches is an abstraction, or series of co-ordinated qualities, streams whose course is beneficent, tendencies that make for righteousness; but what revelation discloses is the life within—the motives, the emotions, the inner nature of Him who speaks; in a word, it changes our idea of God into knowledge of the Godhead. But this means that man no longer looks at God through the eyes of nature, but rather at nature through the eyes of God—*i.e.*, he thinks of the Divine in the categories of the Divine, or through a consciousness of its creation. And this constitutes the distinction between natural and revealed religion: the former is God read through nature, or interpreted in its terms; the latter is nature read through God, or interpreted in terms of a consciousness pervaded by His word. The characteristic of a theology reasoned out from the principles of a revealed religion may, then, be said to be this—the inner qualities and constitution of the Godhead are made so to penetrate the notion of God that all His outer action is conceived as a transcript of His inner being. The logical consequence of the revealed doctrine of the Godhead is thus a new doctrine of God.[1]

Now, it must be here quite frankly stated that a doctrine of the Godhead as the basis of a doctrine of God, is possible only as a result of revelation and through it. We are not here concerned with a natural theism, but with a theology whose formal source is a revelation. If we refuse to believe that God has so acted and spoken as to reveal Himself, we can have no data for a positive conception of the Godhead, for we deny that we have any means of knowing what He is. But if belief in God be in harmony with reason, the belief in revelation cannot be contrary to it; nay, the real contradiction would be disbelief. Agnosticism assumes a double incom-

[1] Cf. Butler on "the essence of natural religion" and "the essence of revealed," each taken as an "inward principle"—the former consisting "in religious regards to God the Father Almighty," the latter "in religious regards to the Son and to the Holy Ghost" ("Analogy," pt. ii., c. 1). It seems to me the difference is better indicated by the change worked by the notion of the Godhead in the doctrine of God.

petence—the incompetence not only of man to know God, but of God to make Himself known. But the denial of competence is the negation of Deity. For the God who could not speak would not be rational, and the God who would not speak could not be moral ; and so if Deity be at once intelligent and moral, there must be some kind or form of revelation. And this revelation must, from its very idea, be the testimony of God touching Himself, for what is not this does not reveal. Nothing that man can learn of nature by research into nature, nothing that he can discover of truth by the exercise of his own faculties, however late, unless it be supernaturally communicated, in his personal or collective history the discovery may come, belongs properly to the idea of revelation. Were it, as Lessing conceived it,[1] simply education, a means of hastening and directing human development, then, as adding nothing to what man can find within the terms of nature, it could have no right to its name. Then were this its sphere, its action would be mischievous rather than beneficent Whatever shortens the course of human development stunts it. The search for truth is the inspiration of reason ; it is because man knows that he does not know, that he is compelled to seek for knowledge. Necessity is the mother of invention ; without conscious ignorance there would be no motive to discovery and no discipline from it. Revelation, then, can only concern what is so above nature as to be beyond the power of man to discover or of nature to disclose ; in other words, it must relate to God, proceed from Him, and be concerned with Him. But though it be His testimony touching Himself, yet it must enter the consciousness of man through his history and in the forms of his experience. And it is here that Christ takes His place. He is the supreme revelation ; in Him the consciousness of God and man exist in purity and in perfection. To both He is essentially related. By virtue of His transcendental relations He has the con-

[1] *Supra*, p. 194.

sciousness which qualifies Him to deliver the Divine testimony to the Divine; by virtue of His being in history and within the terms of our experience, He has the generic or racial consciousness which enables Him to deliver His message to man. He is, as it were, the immanent intelligence of God become a corporate intelligible to man; and so is like a middle term created by the reason that would be interpreted for the use of the interpretative reason. He so knows God from within, and so represents what He knows to the humanity He came to live within, that for man to interpret Him is to interpret God as He is to Himself—a Godhead while a God. The interpretation of God in the terms of the consciousness of Christ may thus be described as the distinctive and differentiating doctrine of the Christian religion.

§ II.—THE DOCTRINES OF GOD AND THE GODHEAD.

These doctrines, as they exist in Christian theology, have each a very different history and function. The belief in the Godhead is specifically Christian, but the belief in God as specifically Hebrew. The former was created by the attempt to understand the person of Christ, or explain and unfold the contents of His consciousness; but the latter was inherited, a gift which Judaism gave to Christianity.[1] And the processes which elaborated the beliefs into doctrines were as different as their sources. The doctrine which conceives God as Lawgiver and Ruler had as the main or active agent in its formation the Latin Church. But the doctrine which conceives the Godhead as a Trinity, or a threefold distinction of Persons subsisting in a unity of essence, had as the active agent in its formation the Greek Church. Each Church, as we have seen, exercised its formative activity under different conditions, the plastic agency being Roman law and polity in the one case, and Greek philosophy in the other. The result is

[1] *Supra,* pp. 64-66.

two distinct and very different conceptions, which have not only failed to modify or correct each other, but have even retained what we may term the antipathies of their respective creators. It is significant that the Greek Church was determined by its conception of Christ's person to its doctrine of the Godhead, but the Latin Church by its conception of God to the doctrine of His work. This means that in the former case the material factor of the doctrine was native to the religion, but in the latter case it was alien. And as a consequence the two doctrines have remained in a remarkable degree independent and unrelated, in a state of juxtaposition rather than of mutual permeation. The Latin God has been too forensic, the Greek Godhead too metaphysical, to be incorporated in a single homogeneous notion. God, forensically conceived, becomes the Absolute Sovereign whose will is law, whose function is administration and judgment; the Godhead, metaphysically construed, becomes a number of differentiated Persons, whose unity depends upon a community of essence. The more the stress falls on the legal character and relations of God, the less ethical they grow; and the more metaphysical the construction of the Godhead becomes, it is the more reduced to a series of personalized abstractions, whose relations are logical rather than real. Neither was sufficiently determined by the determinative element in the consciousness of Christ. In the Greek theology Father and Son are so used to denote immanent relations in the Godhead, that their significance for man as a whole is, though not lost, yet weakened and impoverished; and in the Latin theology the ideas of Sovereign and Lawgiver are so emphasized that those of Father and son almost disappear. In the former, Paternity is not allowed to penetrate the whole Godhead over against man, or Sonship to penetrate man as a whole over against God; but Fatherhood is so confined to the first Person of the Trinity and Sonship to the second, that God tends to lose the unity and reality of His moral relations to man, and man the unity and reality of his moral being before God. In the latter, God becomes so much a juristic and judicial person, and man so much a civil subject, that the paternal and filial relations are virtually transmuted into political.

As a natural consequence, neither theology did justice to the affinities and relations of God and man. It is dangerous, where the field is so vast and the opinions are so varied, to make broad statements or use too general terms; but we may say that to both theologies, though for different reasons, the Sonship of Christ was so interpreted as to reduce man's from a reality to little more than a figure of speech. He was Son by nature, we sons by adoption. He endowed the humanity He assumed with the filial dignity and rights proper to His Deity; and so constituted a new type and instituted a new and correspondent order of being. As Son by essential Divine nature, He was Only Begotten; as Son in His assumed human nature, He was First Born. His Sonship as the μονογενής or "unigenitus" was incommunicable, but His Sonship as the πρωτότοκος or "primogenitus" was communicable. As the property of His humanity man may participate in it, and become, like Him, a son, but by adoption, not by nature. But this made the Divine Fatherhood and the human sonship alike unreal. He who is no son by nature can never become a son by adoption. Before a child can be the adopted son of any man, he must be the real son of some man; and so if it was only by adoption that God became our Father and we His sons, then we could never in any true sense be His sons nor He in any true sense our Father.[1]

[1] The question touched upon in the text is very fundamental for the interpretation of the Nicene and post-Nicene theology. There are points that may be raised in correction of the above exposition that really support it. Athanasius, for example, strongly affirms the participation of man in the nature of the Word who created him, but he relates man as a creature to God through the Word rather than through the Son. This means that his governing idea is here philosophical rather than religious, that while

And this means that unless Godhead and God be alike interpreted in the terms of Fatherhood, the interpretation will remain inadequate and incomplete.

This, then, defines the order of our discussion. We must first state the doctrine of the Godhead, and then attempt to bring it into relation with the doctrine of God; in other words, through the immanent nature and relations of Deity we must approach Deity in His outward relations and activities.

§ III.—CHRIST AND THE GODHEAD.

The point, then, from which our constructive endeavour must start is this—the determinative element in the consciousness of Christ is the filial. He directly and intuitively knew His own Sonship, and by its means He made known

he has on the one hand come through the New Testament to the immanent relations of the Godhead, he has on the other approached the relation of man to God through the Schools of Alexandria. Hence the Word makes man in His own image (κατὰ τὴν ἑαυτοῦ εἰκόνα ἐποίησεν αὐτούς), and gives to him something of His own power, that he may be able to abide for ever in beatitude ("De Incar. Verbi," c. 3). And the Maker becomes the Redeemer, is made man that men might be made God, (αὐτὸς γὰρ ἐνηνθρώπησεν, ἵνα ἡμεῖς θεοποιηθῶμεν) (*Ibid.*, c. 54). Cf. "Contra Arian.," I. xi. 39, ἀλλὰ Θεὸς ὤν, ὕστερον γέγονεν ἄνθρωπος, ἵνα μᾶλλον ἡμᾶς θεοποιήσῃ. But though he, of course, with every degree of emphasis and insistence identifies Son and Word, he does not with similar lucid emphasis identify man's participation by nature in the Sonship with his participation in the Word. And even this participation is not by nature or real constitution, but by grace and as a *donum superadditum* (πλέον τι χαριζόμενος αὐτοῖς). Hence Athanasius is here doubly defective, for he did not bring his philosophy and his theology into connection and consistency either with each other or with nature. He does indeed say in a vague way that in Him the whole creation is created and adopted, (καὶ ἐν αὐτῷ πᾶσα ἡ κτίσις κτίζεται καὶ υἱοποιεῖται) ("Contra Arian.," III. xxiv. 9); but when he comes to detailed exposition the filial relation becomes a thing not of nature but of adoption, created thus rather than restored. Cf. "Contra Arian.," II. xix. and xxi., §§ 57-61, I. xi. 37; "De Decr.," VII. iii. 9, 10. His notion of the primary and fundamental relations of God to man are, therefore, even with his *donum superadditum* thrown in, more philosophical than religious; he has applied the philosophical idea to Christ rather than made the religious and filial idea which Christ embodied,

God's Fatherhood. The two were correlative and mutually inclusive; the being of the Son involved the Father's, and the Father was in character and quality as was the Son. The regulative element in His mind became the determinative idea in the Apostolic. The New Testament interpretation of Christ is in its ultimate analysis an interpretation of the Father in the terms of the Son.

In the mind of Jesus, Father and Son were conceived as forming a unity over against man. The relation the Father had to Him He had to no other; the relation He had to the

penetrate and transform his notions of God, of man, and of their mutual relations. And this was the common and accepted position of the Greek Fathers. Cf. Greg. Thaum., "Hom.," iv., ἀλλ' οὐκ ἔστι παρὰ σὲ ἄλλος φύσει Υἱὸς Θεοῦ; Cyril. Jer., "Catecheses," vii. 7,—where Christ's Sonship as κατὰ φύσιν is contrasted with man's as κατὰ θέσιν. Epiphanius, "Ancor.," 49, holds that there is no Sonship like Christ's, or that ought to be compared with His; other sonships are κατὰ χάριν, but He is the φυσικῶς υἱός. Joh. Dam., "De Orth. Fid.," iv. 8, Καὶ ἄνθρωπος γέγονε (ὁ Υἱὸς τοῦ Θεοῦ), γεγόναμεν δὲ καὶ ἡμεῖς δι' αὐτοῦ υἱοὶ Θεοῦ, υἱοθετηθέντες διὰ τοῦ βαπτίσματος· αὐτὸς ὁ φύσει Υἱὸς τοῦ Θεοῦ, πρωτότοκος ἐν ἡμῖν τοῖς θέσει καὶ χάριτι υἱοῖς Θεοῦ γενομένοις καὶ ἀδελφοῖς αὐτοῦ χρηματίσασι γέγονεν. We may express the general idea thus: the primary relation, both as natural and supernatural, stood in the Word, the renewed or restored relation was constituted in the Son—*i.e.*, men were creatures by nature, but sons by grace and adoption. In this case the West followed the East, and made Fatherhood and Sonship as immanent to Deity real, but as external adventitious and more or less figurative. The schoolmen introduced a distinction between Fatherhood *personaliter* and *essentialiter*: the immanent relations—*i.e.*, those of Father to Son within the Godhead—were *personaliter*; but the external relations—*i.e.*, those of the whole Godhead to man—were *essentialiter*. This was described as a distinction not "secundum rem, sed tantum secundum modum"—*i.e.*, the Fatherhood and Sonship were in each case alike real, though differing as to mode. In the one case it was a relation of persons within the same essence; in the other a relation of essences, the one being causative, the other created: the whole Trinity was Father of man, man was son of the collective Trinity. And so under these distinctions room for distinct types of sonship could be found. But see Pearson on this "vulgar distinction," ("On the Creed," Art. I.) Of Patristic thought as a whole we may say, then, it tended so to emphasize Paternity within the Godhead as to obscure and lose God's Paternity within the universe.

Father no other person had. They two were so related that each was known only to the other, and could therefore only by and through the other be made known. The unity was so real that to see the Son was to see the Father, to know the Father was to know the Son. Hence, while Jesus conceived Father and Son as distinct from each other, He also conceived them as having a common being and as sustaining common relations to man. In their mutual relations they were distinct, but in their common relations they were a unity; and in what was mutual there was nothing that involved disruption or division in what was common. The relations were not voluntary, but necessary; the distinctions not matters of choice, but of nature or essence. It is true that in order to the being of a Son there must be a Father, but it is no less true that in order to the being of a Father there must be a Son. Fatherhood is no older than Sonship, the one is only as the other is; in other words, if Fatherhood is of the essence of Deity, Sonship must be the same. And to Christ God does not become Father—He is Father just as He is God; and He Himself does not become Son—He is Son, and were He not Son He would not be. And what the Apostolic writers attempt is to express the notion, which they owed to Christ, of a God who is both Father and Son, who is a unity which is the home of distinctions, the distinctions not dissolving the unity nor the unity cancelling the distinctions. They remain as consciously and even sternly monotheistic as the Hebrews, but they are not Hebrew monotheists. They use language that others may feel inconsistent with monotheism, but that they do not, for they have felt their way into an order of ideas which combines and harmonizes elements that would have seemed alien to the older thought; but all these elements make Deity infinitely more rich and gracious and beautiful than any man or any religion had before imagined Him to be.

What the new order of ideas was we may represent somewhat thus:—God is love; but love is social, can as little live in solitude as man can breathe in a vacuum. In order to its being there must be a subject, bestowing love, and an object, rejoicing in the bestowment; without the active forthgoing and the passive reflection and the return it could not be, for absolute and simple loneliness of being would be a state of complete lovelessness. If, then, God is according to His essence love, He must be by nature social; for if He were an infinite simplicity, then emotion, with all its complex relations and manifold interactions, would be to Him unknown. But the same necessities of thought meet us from another side. God is reason; but a reason that has nothing objective is no active intelligence, and has none of the conditions that make intelligence possible. A speechless reason would be one in which rationality were either latent, and so a mere possibility, or impotent, and so a mere passive reflector, if even so much; it could not be an infinitely perfect mind, which cannot be other than infinitely active. But the mind that is this must have all the conditions and causes of activity within itself and by necessity of nature. For if they are outside or external to the nature, then it is not perfect; and if they are not by necessity, then as matters of will they once were not, and before they were Deity would be imperfect, and they might never have been, which leaves the perfection of Deity an accident or chance, and so no reality. And therefore we need to conceive, beside the Logos that ever abides in God, the Logos that ever goes forth from Him. Without the one the other could not be; the being of both is necessary to the being of either. So much ancient philosophy had perceived, but what Christian theology did was to change the abstract process into the terms of a concrete relation. The translation of the idea of an articulative Thought and an articulated Reason into the notion of the Father and the Son, was the transformation of abstract God into concrete Godhead, which is no simplicity, but a unity where love and thought are ever in exercise, and all the graces and beatitudes of social existence are things of the Divine essence, necessary to the nature of God.

Now, this conception was not reached by a dialectical process, nor was it a creation of scientific or elaborative thought; but it was the result of intuition or inspiration, or whatever we may term the process by which the imagination, possessed and transfigured by a commanding personality, becomes spontaneously creative of other and higher things than it had ever dreamed of. It was a conception of remarkable originality, without parallel or analogue in any religion or philosophy; yet it gave to the idea of God an actuality which every religion and every philosophy had felt after without being able to find. These are matters capable of clearest historical proof. Parallels to the Christian Trinity have indeed been sought both by old and recent scholars and theologians in Greek philosophy and mythology and in Hindu religion; but in each case the differences are radical. The Hindu Trimurti only represents the adaptation of a Pantheistic idea to historical conditions. The co-ordination of Brahma, Vishnu, and Siva is recent, and may be described as the result of a religious diplomacy, all the more real that it was unconscious and undesigned, and a metaphysical speculation that acted here just as it had acted everywhere. Each of the deities had a prior and very ancient history. They run back into the Vedic period, and are the survivals of different mythological schools and tendencies. Brahmā (masculine) is the deification of the priestly idea, especially the act and efficacy of prayer; Vishnu is a form of the sun-god, who as Surya or Savitri moved like a beneficent and radiant spirit across the face of the sky; and Siva is the survivor of the ancient storm-gods, who swept from their homes in the Himalayas with destructive force down upon the plains. These do not represent one religion, but distinct religions, or rather many different religions, each with its own customs, festivals, modes and objects of worship, and even geographical distribution. Then the Brahmă (neuter) in whom they are co-ordinated is the universal substance or soul ; of him or it all phenomenal being is a manifestation. He is no conscious reason, no home of ethical relations and distinctions, but only the ultimate essence or basis of all things. Every god and every man and every creature is in him as much as the sacred triad, and in all he appears or becomes incarnate. In other words, the system is a polytheistic and mythological Pantheism. But the Christian idea is the opposite of all this. God is personal, conscious, ethical; the Godhead expresses this personal, conscious, and ethical being as immanent and essential. Man cannot be absorbed into God, or God individualized and distributed in man. The Persons in the Godhead are incapable of absorption into more abstract forms of being; they represent God not as an ever unfolding and enfolding substance, but as a necessary and eternal communion, the home of life and love.

The affinities with Greece seem more natural, and, so far as real, they indicated necessities of thought which the Christian Godhead satisfied. No modern theologian would maintain with Cudworth that the Christian Trinity could be found in Plato [1]; nor would any modern scholar argue with Vossius that the Godhead was represented by certain triads in the Greek and Latin mythologies,[2] or with Creuzer that there was embalmed in the figures and songs of the temples an ancient intuition of a triad or deity which was three-in-one.[3] But the affinities are now sought in speculative tendencies and phrases, especially those of the Hellenistic and Alexandrian philosophies, which show thought feeling after some mode of breaking up, as it were, the solitude of Deity, and saving Him from the impotence which clings to a mere isolated Absolute. These

---

[1] "Intellectual Sys.," vol. ii., pp. 364 ff.
[2] "De Theol. Gentili.," lib. viii., c. 12.
[3] "Symbolik und Mythol.," vol. i., p. 45.

affinities are represented by the *ideas* of Plato, the *logos* of the Stoics and of Philo, and the *æons* of the Gnostics; and they no doubt signify attempts to discover categories under which the Infinite could be conceived as related to the finite, as actual in Himself and as active within it. In this respect they have the greatest possible significance for the need of the Godhead in order to the conception of a really living God. But their meaning is primarily philosophical, while the Christian idea is primarily religious. It is the creation of our supreme religious consciousness, and it satisfies our supreme religious need. The love which the Godhead makes immanent and essential to God, gives God an altogether new meaning and actuality for religion; while thought is not forced to conceive Monotheism as the apotheosis of an almighty will or an impersonal ideal of the pure reason.

§ IV.—THE GODHEAD AS A DOCTRINE.

There is indeed to be no attempt made here at a scholastic or scientific construction of the doctrine. This would not be a difficult thing to do, for it is easy to combine the ancient terms into reasonable formulæ; yet our purpose is not to express in familiar technical language the conclusions of the schools, but to exhibit and to emphasize the source, significance, and bearings of those essential ideas which every doctrine of the Godhead has aimed at expressing, yet has often failed to express.

1. The doctrine of the Godhead is, in origin and essence, an attempt to represent to thought the determinative element in the consciousness of Christ. He is God's Son; and because Son of God, He becomes Son of man. The filial relation to man is the temporal form of the eternal relation to God. This Sonship is so essential to His consciousness that He would not be what He is without it—*i.e.*, He would not be at all.

2. What is true of Him as the ideal Son of man, is true of the humanity He embodies. It, too, is son of God, exists before the mind and heart of God as son, and has so existed ever since it was conceived—*i.e.*, in our time-conditioned speech, from eternity. But this filial relation of the created to God is made possible by Fatherhood and Sonship being eternal in God—*i.e.*, no matters of will, but of nature, facts of His essence, not results or products of choice or volition. It is this idea that comes into being with Christ. Fatherhood is the essence of God, therefore Sonship is the same; and both are realized in the only forms and under the only conditions possible where God is concerned—outside or above the categories of space and time, where all distinctions of here and there, before and after, alike cease.

3. The distinctions these terms denote are immanent and essential. No theory of external modes or manifestational forms and aspects can satisfy the conditions. For what we need is not a variety in our modes and forms of apprehending Deity, but such a conception as realizes Deity—as, if we may so speak, represents Him to the imagination as an organism whose life is love, active and passive, a loving and being loved. The Sabellian notion is as shallow as it is false; it may satisfy the intellect which thinks that the mysteries of the Divine nature are amply explained if stated in terms which can be worked into the processes of formal logic. But the supreme necessity of faith is one with the ultimate necessity of thought—viz., a God who can be related to the universe, one who is not an infinite abstraction or empty simplicity, but who is by nature a living and, as it were, productive and producing Being. To be this He must have immanent and essential modes and forms of activity, and because He has these He may have outer relations created by energies freely exercised.

4. These inner and essential modes or forms are not known to us by nature, but by revelation. Reason may see that

they must be if God is to be a living God, but what they are can be known only if He spontaneously speak or reveal Himself. This He did in Jesus Christ; and what He showed was the Father-Sonship. There may be other infinite modes and forms, but here we know only what has been made known. The terms used are personal, denote personal relations, and these of the tenderest order; but they are relations realized under the forms of the Divine and Infinite, not of the finite. Beside Father and Son one other such personal mode we know—the Holy Spirit. He proceeds from the Father and the Son, is co-ordinated with them, has the same rank and the same essential being; and has the function, so far as the outer relations are concerned, of being the agent through which the Fatherhood is ever presented that the sonship may be realized without as it exists within.

5. As the conception is peculiarly and specifically a conception of revealed religion, it ought, when articulated into a doctrine, to be stated as nearly as possible in the terms and according to the Spirit of the revelation. The Greek terminology was mainly philosophical, and what it did was to translate the conception into a philosophy rather than into a theology. It is well that we distinguish even the most audacious and brilliant translations from the original and the reality. Οὐσία is the abstract now of God, now of the Godhead; but we shall know better what we mean if we keep to the concrete, and speak of Father, Son, and Spirit as one God. He is one, but not as the atom or monad is one, but as the organism. He is a unity; but a unity and a simplicity are opposites—the one is the synonym of indiscrete and undifferentiated being, but the other of being rich, complex, manifold. An infinite simplicity were incapable of movement or relation, but an infinite unity must be the bosom of all distinction and difference. God is a unity, but He is not a simplicity, and so can be more truly described in the terms of ethical and concrete than of metaphysical and abstract

existence. "Person" may be an excellent name for those immanent distinctions we know as Father, Son, and Spirit, who together constitute the unity of God. It does not mean individual, a single, separated being, incapable of further division, and so may well denote those modes or forms of inner being which realize without dissolving the unity. But we are nearer reality if we conceive God in the terms of the Gospels than if we define Him in the categories of the schools.

6. We have now to see how or in what way the notion of the Godhead affects our conception of God and of the world to which He stands related, and whether it is capable of being formulated into the material or determinative principle of a Christian Theology.

CHAPTER II.

THE GODHEAD AND THE DEITY OF NATURAL THEOLOGY.

§ I.—God in Theism and in Theology.

IN order the better to appreciate in what way the notion of the Godhead has affected the conception of God, we must distinguish two conceptions—the speculative or philosophical, and the positive or religious. There is an idea of Deity which is the last deduction or final dream of a speculative Theism, and there is an idea of Deity which is the primary or material principle of constructive theology; and these two ideas are quite as remarkable for their differences as for their affinities. In the one case Deity is a name for a deduction from certain necessities of thought, but in the other case for the ultimate and causal reality of religion. Theism may be satisfied with the rational basis or scientific form of its conception, but it has no means or instrument that can transform it into the soul of a religion. Theology may assume the legitimacy of the rational processes which have given the theistic result, but it cannot accept the result as adequate or sufficient for its purpose; before it can begin to build it must have a richer and completer doctrine of God.

Theism construes Deity from the standpoint of mind and nature—conceives nature as an effect which needs to be explained, God as its cause or sufficient reason, and mind as the organ which brings the two into reasoned relations or the unity of an intelligible notion. It has to determine whether there is any evidence of His existence; how He is to be conceived, whether as substance or reason or will; how He is related to the world, and whether He exercises over and within it a controlling activity at once intelligent and moral. But in these discussions Theism may with equal truth be described as either the last chapter of a philosophy or the first of a theology. Its methods, principles, formulæ, arguments, are all philosophical: the systems it criticizes are the philosophies; the authorities it invokes are philosophers. God is described in the terms of the schools; He is either an " Ens infinitum" or "absolutum" or "unicum," or a "Causa efficiens prima," or an "Intelligens, a quo omnes res naturales ordinantur in finem"; He is either the "Primum et per se agens," or the "Ultimus Finis," the "Actus Purus," the "Una Substantia," or "Das Sein" or "Der Geist," or the "Unknown Reality," or the "Voluntas," by whose energy all things are. As God is in Theism a metaphysical, so nature is a physical abstraction, as it were the system of things reduced to a synthesis which shall more or less co-ordinate and accommodate both the demands of science and the necessities of religion; while being has its qualities denoted by terms like "good" and "evil," which have an ethical connotation, but not always an ethical sense.

But in constructive theology the questions and the categories are altogether different. Thought here starts with the data and the beliefs, the consciousness and the principles, of a religion and the religious society. God is a being whose existence is accepted and assumed; He has been an object of worship before He has become a subject of thought, and so the thinker has not to create Him for experience, but to interpret Him through the experience which He has created. He is not the unity of physical functions and metaphysical attributes, which Theism seeks to discover and at once to personalize and keep impersonal; but He is the concrete spiritual and ethical

Being of religion, who is for the intellect because He has been for the conscience and the heart, who is for thought because He lives in a religion and has come through a revelation. And the world theology has to interpret is as concrete as the God. It is not the abstract nature of Theism, but the world of actual men, with all that lies as history behind and all that lives as passion, sin, belief, hope, and reason within them—men with all their religions and irreligions, states and institutions of good and evil. Theology, in a word, is the science of a living God and of His work in and for a living world.

Now, the supreme difficulty of Theism and Theology is one: How shall we conceive God? And what we seek from the doctrine of the Godhead is help towards the solution of this difficulty. Of all forms of apologetic, what we may term the *tu quoque* is the most vacant and debased. It is a poor defence for revealed religion to say, " Natural religion has difficulties as many and as grave." Two insolubles, a revealed and a natural, ought to make a man less rather than more contented with his faith; and though revelation does not create the belief in God, it ought to supply us with a conception of Him that shall lighten some of the darkness amid which the spirit gropes when it seeks to see God face to face, and to know His world somewhat as it is known to Him. And so we have meanwhile a twofold question: How does the doctrine of the Godhead affect the conception of God, first, in natural, secondly, in revealed theology?

§ II.—THE GODHEAD AND THE CHARACTER OF GOD.

We may describe the change which the notion of the Godhead effects in the conception of God by saying, that it completely ethicizes the conception. The history, whether of religion or philosophy, shows that there is indeed nothing harder to thought than to conceive God as a moral being, though it is relatively easy to conceive Him as the source of all the moralities. He can be the latter as reason or idea or will, but He can be the former only as it belongs to His essence or nature to exist in a state of conditioned and related, or ethical and social activity. God was to Judaism a lawgiver, the source of His people's morals, but He was not in the strict sense moral. His nature was legalized rather than ethicized. The law He instituted was positive, the creation of His will rather than the transcript of His nature. On this will His relations to Israel and Israel's to Him were based ; it was because He so willed that they were His people and He their God. He was indeed conceived to be holy and righteous, just and merciful, but He was these things within the terms of the covenant and according to the measure of His law. It was not felt to involve any contradiction to the idea of Him that He should be the God of the Jews only, though the writer, whose conception most nearly approached the ethical, showed signs of feeling it. It would be much too unqualified to say that He was to the common mind like the Oriental sovereign, who may be the source both of law and morality without being either lawful or moral ; but at least we may say this—that the law was the regulative idea, and the Divine nature and relations were conceived under legal rather than moral categories. So inveterate was this regulative idea that Paul could not quite emancipate himself from it. When he reasons as a Jew with Jews on the question of their vocation, it becomes to him a matter of will, settled by an appeal to the Divine Sovereignty as absolute and ultimate. His argument as to the election of Israel is a complete contrast to his argument in proof of the righteousness by faith. The essence of the one is the conditioned, of the other the unconditioned, action of God. The field of the action may differ; in the one case it may be the history and function of a people, in the other the change and salvation of a person ; but the significant thing is, that though both fields are moral, the point emphasized in the one case is the unmoral power, but in the other the moral and conditioned grace. The truth is, Paul argues not as an Apostle with Christians but as a Jew with Jews when he says, "God is a potter, men are clay; He can as He pleases make one vessel to honour and another to dishonour, and who can resist His will?"[1] But where Deity is ethicized He cannot be spoken of as a potter or man as clay. The use of the figure means that God's power is conceived as physical, but where it is conceived as moral the analogy becomes not only irrelevant but false.

But in Greece the theistic conception, while more abstract and general, was even less ethicized than in Israel; as in the latter it was more political than moral, in the former it was more metaphysical. The difference was one of nature because of source. The Hebrew state was a creation of Deity; the Greek Deity was a creation of mind. To the Jew God was the head of his state and the being he worshipped, but to the Greek the One God was the last deduction of thought and its supreme object. The reason that reached Him defined Him; He was interpreted in its terms, clothed in its attributes, but did not transcend its categories—*i.e.*, He remained abstract, logical, impersonal. The ideas of reason are its ultimate realities; but it is of their essence to be ideas, to refuse to become actual, to defy ethical impersonation. Out of them ethics may be deduced, but they are themselves metaphysical—beget life, induce action, but cannot themselves live and act. So Plato's God may be termed the good, or the beautiful, or the true; but He is personalized when the philosopher becomes a poet only to be depersonalized when the poet relapses into the philosopher. The invariable tendency in metaphysics is to the de-ethicization of a Deity who can be described in terms neuter and abstract rather than personal and moral.

But in contrast to these stands the Apostolic conception.

[1] Rom. ix. 19-24.

God was one to whom Fatherhood and therefore Sonship were immanent. Personal and therefore moral relation was of the very essence of His being. A God who could not be without a Son was a God who could not be without moral qualities in exercise. The relations that belonged to the very constitution by virtue of which He was God, involved moral character, duties, ends. We shall utterly misconceive the Apostolic mind if we reduce the terms Father and Son and Spirit into rigid ontological symbols; the realities they denote are ethical, metaphors of necessity, but metaphors of the kind the imagination uses when it speaks of a world unrealized in the language of the real. Father and Son do not here denote a Paternity and a Sonship that begin to be, for in the region of the eternal all the categories of time cease; but they denote states, relations, that ever were and ever must be in God. In Him the paternal feeling is eternal, and the paternal cannot be without the filial; and for these to be means that He is the infinite home of all the moral emotions with all their correlative activities. God conceived as Godhead is the very manifold of exercised and realized moral being—a manifold that may be reduced by metaphysics, whether Theistic or Pantheistic, Nicene or neo-Platonic, to the barrenness of the wilderness. The main thing is to adhere to the ethical realities: the thing we cannot afford to lose is what was won for us from the consciousness of Christ and its Apostolic interpretation. To hold the eternal Father-Sonship of God is to hold the essential graciousness of His being, and the necessary grace of all His acts.

§ III.—The Godhead as it affects the Notions of Creator and the Creation.

1. The gravest difficulties of Theism are the initial—those concerned with the idea of the Creator rather than of the creation. The empirical evidences of His being would be

invincible were they not confronted and overpowered by the more invincible antinomies of the pure reason. The categories that describe the Deity of pure thought are rather those of being than of relation and action. The difficulties which the criticism of Kant so emphasized, in the attempt to rise from the phenomenal to the transcendental, have their counterpart in the difficulty of descending from the transcendental to the phenomenal. It is harder to connect the Uncreated with the created than to connect the created with the Uncreated—*i.e.*, the logical process which seeks to prove that contingent being must have had an origin and a sufficient reason, is much simpler and more coherent than the process which would prove that the primary being is a personal Cause, who consciously and freely willed to make the world. For the difficulty in the latter case begins with the very premiss; not merely, How shall it be proved? but, How shall it be formulated? The creation either was or was not eternal. If it was, then as it never began to be, it had no cause, has a being independent, necessary—*i.e.*, is but a form of the only Divine that is. If it was not eternal, then why did it begin to be? The Creator made it; but why did He make it? and what was He doing before creation? Either He was idle or He was active. If He was idle, then He could not be a perfect or even a good being: if He was active, then was not this activity creative, and does not this mean that creation was eternal? Then what moved Him to act? If He was a being of absolute simplicity, He could have no motive within; and as there was no creation, no motive could come to Him from without; and even supposing it had come, it could in His absolute simplicity have found nothing to which it could have appealed. And even then, if it had been able to move Him, it would, as finite and shot out of nothing, have represented only the dominion of chance over the creative and causal Will.

It is evident, then, that the difficulty in the dialectical

process that would reason from the First Cause downwards is initial. If this Cause is conceived to be God, how is God to be conceived? If we use abstract or impersonal terms, we may succeed in elaborating a coherent theory. We may state our notion of the Cause in the terms of Spinoza, and translate " Deus " by " Substantia "; or in the terms of Hegel, and, identifying pure Being with pure Thought, resolve creation into a process of dialectical or logical unfolding; or in the terms of Spencer, and make the Ultimate the Unknown which is manifested to us as persistent force. But these are theories of being rather than of creation, conceiving phenomena as modes of the absolute rather than effects of personal will. If we hold that the Creator is conscious and personal Deity, yet demand that He be as simple as a form of abstract and impersonal being, we are at once involved in all the difficulties of a beginning that cannot be conceived without a negation of Divine perfection, and of motives and movements that cannot be represented in thought without a denial of the Divine simplicity. These are the difficulties that have made our Pantheisms, Materialisms, and Agnosticisms seem so reasonable. From the standpoint of an ordered universe nothing seems so inevitable as the inference of a causal and an ordering Mind; but from the infinite Mind as the standpoint or principle of thought, nothing is so full of perplexities and mutually exclusive or destructive contradictions as the dialectical process that would relate the creative action, on the one hand, to the Creator and His past, and, on the other, the creation to the creative Person or Will.

2. But the Godhead with its completely ethicized Deity mitigates the gravest of these initial difficulties of Theism. It does no more than mitigate, for no more is possible; but this mitigation represents an immense gain to thought. What increases the conceivability of the Divine action makes Theism more rationally credible, and so tends to beget and

develop a view as to the order and end of the universe as moral as the Deity from whom and for whom it is.

A. The Godhead compels us to conceive God as conditioned in His very being. It belongs to His essence to exist under and within relations. No abstract of pure thought, no generalization from our sensuous experiences, can denote or describe Him. The more we attempt in obedience to some process of inexorable logic to rarefy our notion of the causal Being, the less are we able to conceive the Being as cause. Abstract terms like "Being," "Substance," "the Unknown," "the Unconditioned," "the Absolute," are the results or residue of mental processes, but represent nothing that can be conceived as a real causality. If we speak of simple homogeneous matter or force, we speak of something we do not know to exist, that we cannot conceive as existing without our own conscious experience, and that no authentic act of the constructive imagination can make into the cause or sufficient reason of a varied and reasonable universe. Out of an abstract of thought we cannot evolve the concrete of experience; for the very terms that define and express our ultimate abstraction take from it the power or faculty of creative movement. But if we take the supreme religious consciousness of man as our interpretative medium and conceive God as the Godhead, then our primary and causal existence ceases to be simple, abstract, dead, and becomes complex, concrete, living. He is never out of relation; it is His nature to be related, and He cannot be without His related states and distinctions. What we call the Persons of the Godhead are activities, emotional, intellectual, ethical, always related and always in exercise. The Absolute is not mere indifference, or substance homogeneous and indiscrete, but infinite differences belong to His nature. Creation was for God not the beginning of action; He was by essence active because a Godhead. He did not change from unconditioned to conditioned being; His being as related is conditioned in all its activities. To conceive God as Godhead therefore is to escape the paralyzing abstractions of metaphysics, transcendental and empirical, pantheistic and agnostic. Our Cause is a concrete of such infinite fulness and variety that we can well conceive Him as the ideal home and efficient energy of the universe.

B. But the relations and activities immanent in the Godhead are less physical than ethical, denoted by terms expressive of the purest emotions and the most creative and dependent relations known to man—Fatherhood and Sonship. These represent love as native to God, and as eternal as God. For Him it never began to be, for this is the meaning of the eternal Sonship. The love of man has a potential before it has an actual being; he has the capability of loving before the reality of love; but the love of God had always an actual, never a potential being, for only so could it be perfect love. In man love is born of the meeting of susceptible subject and attractive object, but in God the absolute love had ever perfect reason and room for active being. Man can never know a father's affection until he be a father, or woman a mother's love unless she be a mother. The capacity may be there, but only the capacity, the aptitude to be, not the actual being. But the Godhead means that as the Fatherhood and Sonship have been eternal, so also has the love. It signifies that God is not the eternal possibility but the eternal actuality of love. Hence creation did not mean for God the beginning of love, or even any increase of it. It might be an increase in the objects, but not in the affection. The Son was to the Father the universe; infinite, He could absorb without exhausting the affection, while the infinite affection could be distributed without being diminished or withdrawn.

C. But this eternal love explains the causal impulse, the beginning of the creation of God. Love may be described as a need that can be satisfied only by giving. What is needed is another, susceptible, receptive, akin; what is given is the best self of the needing, all of himself he has to bestow. Lotze[1] has defined "the good in itself" as enjoyed or realized felicity; what we term "goods" are means, and become good only as transmuted into this; for outside a feeling, willing, and thinking spirit good has no being. But what in its nature is this good, this realized felicity? "It is the living love which wills the happiness of others." And even this is God; He is the supreme good which is realized beatitude, "the living love which wills the happiness" of all being. But if He wills its happiness, the life must also be willed; there must be existence that there may be felicity. And so He wills to create, that the happiness He has willed may be realized. And this precisely is love, seeking another that He may give to the other He seeks all within Himself that is best worth giving. And this love is creation, which is but God's method of obeying His love in order to the realization of the felicity He has willed. And so Rothe argues that love and creation are alike in this—each is a spontaneous and free giving, a communication of God Himself, proceeding out of His beatitude in order to the being of beatitude. Love is no external attribute, needing created relations in order to its exercise, for it was before creation, and creation was through it; and it is no attribute of pure immanence, for though it lives within Deity, and has there the necessary conditions of its life, yet it ever strives from within outwards, struggles, as it were, towards creation. And so Rothe defines love as the transitive element in the immanent being of God, and, consequently, as the bond which binds together His inner and His outer attributes and action. There must be eternal love that creation may be. Creation must be that eternal love may

---

[1] "Mikrokosmus," vol. iii., p. 608.

realize the happiness it willed. "The whole life and activity of God *ad extra* is a loving."[1]

D. This conception may help us to conceive why and how creation was necessary while the Creator was not necessitated. Franz Hoffmann has most truly said: "Nothing has given to Pantheism a greater appearance of reasonableness, and consequently of truth, than the idea that every theistic theory proceeds necessarily upon the supposition of a certain contingency of creation, and that the affirmation, Creation is a free act of God, is identical with the affirmation, It is a contingent or accidental act of God. But whoever attributes contingency to God subjects Him, only in a manner exactly the opposite of the pantheistic, to blind fate."[2] This is true, for chance and fate are more nearly synonyms than contraries. Both terms are expressive of ignorance, inability to explain the cause or reason of the system or some part of the system to which we belong. Chance is fate in things individual, falling out separately, though concurrently; fate is chance in things collective, so falling out together as to seem a system. Both are blind, neither is a reason for the existence or occurrence of anything, only an obscure way of saying that no reason is known or has been found. If, then, we so conceive the Divine will to create that it appears as arbitrary, or has in it any element of accident or chance, we do not find in God the sufficient reason of creation: He is not the supreme or the first and final Cause, but above Him stands some one or some thing which moves His will, makes Him an instrument, is His God.

This is one of the invincible difficulties of natural Theism which we may justly expect revelation to solve, or indicate whether there be any way to a solution. And the solution lies in the love that must will the happiness of others, and in order to their happiness must will their being. Julius Müller, indeed, argued against the position of Rothe,—his man "einer mittel-

---

[1] "Theol. Ethik.," vol. i., pp. 166, 167.
[2] Baader's "Werke," vol. ii., p. 4, footnote by Hoffmann.

alterlich romantischen Phantasie,"—that "if God had need of the world, therefore of a being different from Himself, in order to be what He is according to His essence—viz., love—then this very love were not absolutely perfect."[1] This is true enough, for it is in a sense the premiss of our argument, but it is not here relevant or in place. What is argued is not that God in order to be love must create, but something altogether different— viz., since God is according to His essence love, He could not but be determined to the creative act. There is an absolute difference between physical necessity and moral need; they are not only opposites, but contradictories. Physical necessity is the negation of freedom; moral need is its affirmation. Physical necessity is objective, the compulsion of a power without and above; but moral need is subjective, a spontaneous and rational movement, obedience to the idea or law of one's own nature. The imperiousness of the need, the measure of the constraint, whether it does or does not leave the possibility of opposed tendencies, depends on the nature which gives the law. Where in a subject hate is as possible as love, both nature and love are imperfect; but where the nature is perfect, so will be the love; the subject will have no choice whether he will love or not love—he must love, the very perfection of his nature not allowing him to do otherwise. Yet this necessity, if we may now so call it, is freedom, the act of a Being so perfect that action and essence, thought and will, intelligence and nature, are unities and incapable of difference or division. So through the notion of the Godhead we are able to conceive a Theism which stands opposed, on the one hand, to an unmotived Deism or reign of chance, and, on the other, alike to the abstract necessities of Pantheism and the mechanical necessities of Materialism; and affirms that creation is due to the moral perfection of the Creator, who is so essentially love that He could not but create a world that He might create beatitude.

[1] "Christliche Lehre von der Sünde," vol. ii., pp. 184, 185.

§ IV.—The Godhead and Providence.

1. The difficulties Theism feels when it tries to conceive God as Creator meet it in another form when it attempts to conceive Him as Providence—or as Deity maintaining relations to the world He has made. How are nature and God related? Do they exclude or include each other? Do its energies supersede His action? and are its laws so adequate to the evolution and maintenance of order as to operate without dependence on His will? Then how does nature affect God? Does not the thing made impose limitations on Him who made it? But can a God so limited by His own creation be as much the infinite as when He had all infinity to Himself? As theistic solutions of these problems we have Deism, or God's absolute transcendence, and Pantheism, or His absolute immanence.

Deism conceived God as above and apart from the world. He had so made it that it was a system complete in itself; its perfection was seen in its ability to do its work for an indefinite period independently of Him. The proper analogy of their relations was the watch and its maker. Without the maker the watch or the world could not be; His was the idea of the whole, His the manufacture of the several parts, the calculations, the adjustments, and the first construction. Once finished, His wisdom was seen in the length of time nature could go on without repairs, and if repairs were needed they could be done only by acts of "intervention" or "interference," stopping the whole or some part of the machine in order to readjust the mechanism. This is very broadly but truly stated; it was the common idea of the eighteenth century, carried out by the deist to its logical conclusion—the complete separation or inter-independence of God and the world, modified with the help of a more or less infirm logic by the apologist, so as to allow Deity some part and nterest in the world He had made. But each had at root the same idea: such complete transcendence, that if God acted in the world at all His action was miraculous, and must be described or discussed in terms that implied He was outside the system, and was able to get inside it only by some process of interference or suspension of law.

Pantheism, on the other hand, reversed this process: God was the *causa immanens*, inside nature, not separable from it, the eternal ground or substance whose infinite modes are our phenomena of space and time. Intelligence was the mode of an infinite attribute which was termed thought, and body the mode of an attribute termed extension. Deity must have an infinite multitude of attributes, but these were the only two revealed in experience, and so all we knew. But this theory as completely dissolved God in nature as the other held Him apart from it. He was but the abstract of our concrete experience, the hidden energy conceived not as energy but as being, which effects or suffers the cycle of changes we call the universe. He was not the *natura naturata*, the begotten or produced nature, our phenomenal existence, but *natura naturans*, the begetting or producing nature, whose infinite modes were ever forming and ever dissolving. He alone was; everything else was but appearance, the swiftly formed and dissolved changes of an infinite kaleidoscope.

2. But to the ethicized notion of God these theories are both alike inadequate and alien. The complete transcendence of Deity involves His essential limitation and moral imperfection. To the extent that He makes nature independent of Himself He does two things: (*a*) retracts His energies or circumscribes His essence, renouncing by the one His omnipotence and by the other His ubiquity; and (*β*) He denies Himself all pleasure in His creation and all normal intercourse with His creatures, so surrendering, as it were, the very joy of being a God who has created. The nature, too,

that has no God within it is a mechanical nature; it may have had a cause, but it has no reason, and the conception of its origin is contradicted by the theory as to its course. Then the complete immanence of Deity is the negation of His being. He becomes but another term for nature; is, like nature, without moral character or freedom; can only be, not do; has attributes, but no action; modes, but no life. Deity so construed has ceased to be Divine; He is but an objectified abstraction, a personal name used to denote an impersonal and indeterminable substance. But both Deism and Pantheism err because they are partial; they are right in what they affirm, wrong in what they deny. It is as antitheses that they are false; but by synthesis they may be combined or dissolved into the truth. With Deism we say, God is transcendent; unless He be He is no God. Transcendence means that He was before and is above nature. It neither sets limits to Him nor is He contained within its limits, but as He is before so He is over all. With Pantheism we say, God is immanent; unless He be nature has no Divine life or reason, and He no infinitude of being or excellence. Immanence means that He is everywhere in nature, and nature has no being save in Him. It does not affirm, He is not apart from nature; it only affirms, Nature is not apart from Him. He is through all and in all; in Him all live and move and are. The transcendent God is Creator, the immanent God is Providence; the one is necessary to the being, the other to the well-being of the world. Creation is no greater a miracle than Providence; Providence is no more miraculous than creation.

To such an idea of the relations between God and His universe the implications of the old rationalistic terminology, whether deistic or apologetical, and the positions of Pantheism in its abstract and exclusive forms, are alike abhorrent. Where God is immanent, His action can never be interference; where His presence is conceived as necessary to the very being of nature, "intervention" is the last word that can be used to describe it, for the miracle were then His withdrawal from nature, not His continuance within it. And where God is conceived as transcendent, He can never be dissolved into nature or become synonymous with it. Distinction and difference are of His essence, belong to the ground or constitution of His being as ethical; and if they are immanent in Him, they make Him transcendent as regards nature,—at once related to it and different from it; akin to all its ethical elements, but alien from all its anti-ethical. If we believe in a living God, we surely believe in a God who lives; but God does not live unless He is every moment and in every atom as active and as much present as He was in the very hour and article of creation.

But if God construed through the Godhead becomes, as we may say, the synthesis of transcendence and immanence, it is necessary that we discuss and determine more fully the relations expressed by these terms. In other words, we must bring the ethicized Deity and His creation more explicitly together.

§ V.—THE GODHEAD AND THE EXTERNAL RELATIONS OF GOD.

1. It is evident, then, that our conception of the relation depends upon our conception of the terms related—*i.e.*, as we conceive God, we conceive the universe; and as these are conceived, so also are their relations. The principle through which we interpret the related terms is this:—The creature is a being who corresponds in quality and kind to the causal instinct or creative impulse to which he owes his existence. God does not love because He created, but He created because He loved. It follows, therefore, that creation in its most real and radical sense is the production of a being capable of being loved, and therefore of loving; for these two are strict counterparts; a being incapable of loving is

incapable of being loved—may be an instrument to be used or a thing to be admired, but is no person able to satisfy affection by giving it.

This distinction between person and instrument is fundamental and characteristic. The instrument can have no being apart from the hand that made or uses it; but the person is independent in his very dependence, fulfils the end of his creation by obeying the law given in his being. Without the engineer the engine is a mass of dead material—*i.e.*, is not an engine; through him it came into being, and through him it continues to be, to live, and do its work—so informed by mind as to seem a living thing. Without the artist the work of art could not be, and it lives only as seen and realized by the sympathetic imagination; change, enlarge, or lessen our senses, and it is a work of art no more. But the person is so an end in himself that once he is he has a being apart from his Maker. The disciple does not die with the master who formed him; he becomes independent, a master himself, his excellence as a teacher but expressing his excellence as a learner. The home fulfils its functions only as it makes not instruments that cannot be without the parent, but persons who grow into the conscious manhood which is possessed of the energies and foresight creative of new times and new homes. The instrument is for use, but the person for action and communion; what disqualifies for either or both spoils the personality. The more perfect the instrument grows, the more necessary to it is the delicate hand or the deft finger; but the more perfect the person becomes, the more he is a causal will and a creative reason, able to form as he was formed. Thus it is the very essence of the instrument to have no being apart from the mind that produced or employs it, but it is no less the essence of the person to have being only as he stands before the creative mind distinct and individual, dependently independent.

We may say, then, that to God two worlds exist—one

instrumental and subjective, the other personal and objective. But of these the former is apparent, the latter alone is real. What we call matter or nature has no real being to God; at best, all the reality it has is relative, such as belongs to the means which a mind made and minds can use, but which have no being without mind. The only universe that really exists to a moral Deity is a moral universe. It alone can exercise and satisfy the energies that gave it being, for it alone is capable of the beatitude that can be willed, and the capability of beatitude is one with the capability of loving and being loved. God can love only a being whose happiness He can will, for love is but the passion to create happiness active and exercised, but this means that its object is a moral person, with a reason and a will of his own. The most perfect of all possible machines may awaken admiration in Deity as in man, but for it neither man nor Deity can feel anything that can be defined as love. God watches sparrows and cares for oxen, but His love is for men. In their joys He is able to participate, and they in His; and when this participation is mutual and absolute there is beatitude, God and man alike blessing and blessed.

2. But these distinctions involve a twofold relation of God—one to nature as instrumental and subjective, and one to man as personal and objective. The being of the instrument is in and through the minds that use it. The maker must be before and above the instrument—*i.e.*, the relation to it is one of transcendence; but he must also be in it, his mind or a mind that understands his as regards the use or function of this special thing, must be present and active in order to its being as an instrument—*i.e.*, the relation is one of immanence, So without God above nature it could not have been, and without God within nature it could not be. According to Kant, man makes nature—*i.e.*, without his architectonic reason it could be no cosmos, a system of order, a realm where what appear as individual and disconnected pheno-

mena are reduced to a co-ordinated and intelligible whole.
But if mind is constitutive of the very nature it interprets,
it means that nature is a middle term between minds. What
intelligence finds in it belongs to intelligence as a discovery
rather than as a creation, but what intellects discover intellect had created. Thus the cuneiform characters of Babylonia
and the hieroglyphs of Egypt can say nothing to the animal;
it has no sense to which they can appeal, and they have
no meaning to any sense it has. In a purely animal world
symbols of thought could have no significance, for thought
has no being. But they do exist to reason, and so are
capable of interpretation by it, and it is by virtue of this
capability of interpretation that they are characters or signs.
As they are read, the language they represent is constituted
or restored. But the language could not be reconstituted
by the interpreting mind if it had not been constituted a
language by the mind interpreted. The cries or characters of
the insane are senseless to the sane, and the language of the
reason is unintelligible to the idiot. The condition, then, of
a language being understood is, that it embody understanding. No bilingual or trilingual inscription would enable
reason to recover a tongue that had no thought or reason in
it. Hence the nature whose speech is intelligible to man
speaks of the intelligence of its Maker; its interpretation is
His. And therefore, if mind makes nature, it is because
mind created nature, constituted it a middle term between
two intelligences. But this is only the metaphysical way of
expressing the transcendence and the immanence alike of
God and man, or of saying that nature is an instrument to
man because one of God. Every act of interpretation is an
act of transcendence, for if man did not so rise above as to
co-ordinate and combine or relate what he reads, he could not
read it; but it also involves the fact of a twofold immanence
—thought within the thing interpreted, and the interpreted
thing within the consciousness of the interpreter. Hence we

may say that nature as an instrument or middle term has no being save as constituted by the mutual and correlative indwelling or transcendence and immanence of God and man.

3. But if nature be the middle term, with a being that is only instrumental, persons or spirits represent the beings that are to God real or objective. With them He can sustain relations that exercise all His energies, physical and moral, emotional and intellectual; and what He can do is what He will. They are beings capable of good, capable of 'evil; therefore fit subjects for the hourly care of Him who made them. And this care is but a form of His creative energy. On the most purely metaphysical grounds we may say that it is not within the power even of the Omnipotent to make a being independent of Himself, for that would mean a second Omnipotent, a created infinite. But omnipotence is not the synonym of God conceived as Godhead. The terms in which He is construed are ethical, and the ethical Deity can never live out of relations, or secluded from those who need Him. He will not dissolve the relations through which alone He can work the beatitude He has willed: were He to do so, He would cancel the very end for which He had made the world.

If this be so, then two things follow: (a) the creative will as a will of moral good is eternal, and (β) universal. These terms but express the same idea—the one under the form of time or duration, the other under the form of space or extension. According to the one, the good-will of God never began to be, and it can never cease from being, or be other than it has ever been. According to the other, His moral energies can never be circumscribed in their action, any more than they can cease to act or be changed in their direction or purpose. God's being is timeless, as it is boundless: His ubiquity does not know the distinctions of here and there, propinquity and distance; there is no place to Him who cannot remove Himself from one point to another, or time to Him who knows only eternity. What can be measured by years or centuries has a beginning and will have an end, but where there is neither end nor beginning there can be no measurement. And so to say that God is eternal is to say that for Him the categories of time are not; He is no older to-day than He was on the morn of creation, or than He will be when its even has come. And in the region of space it is as impossible to restrict His energies as to limit His being. He is pure action as well as pure thought. Creation was for Him no moment of exceptional activity within a defined area. Providence is continuous creation. To maintain a world which is more a process of becoming than a completed result, is as much creation as was its aboriginal production. And so we must conceive God to be just as much and as directly concerned in the becoming and being of every man as He was in the becoming and being of the first. In all time and in all place God worketh hitherto.

But the moral counterpart of an essence that knows no time or space is a character that knows no change. Yet ethical is not as metaphysical immutability. As regards His metaphysical being, God is above our categories of sequence and position; as regards His ethical being, He is the home of relation and activity. The immutability of the former is, as it were, quantitative, but of the latter qualitative—*i.e.*, in the one case there never can be less or more, but in the other there never can be different or opposite. In other words, metaphysical immutability relates to being and energies, but ethical to character and end. This distinction involves another: the modes or forms of activity which express metaphysical immutability are uniform or invariable, but those which express ethical are variable or multiform—*i.e.*, the physical attributes and energies of God have to do with invariable quantities and relations, but the ethical have to do with variable persons, with their varying characters and states. In the realm of physical existence God can never seem different from what

He is—the Almighty, All-present, in a word the Infinite—but in the realm of moral He often seems different, though He always is the same. It depends on the state and needs and character of the person what He will seem, but what He is and does depends only on Himself. The older theology expressed the same idea when it said, The chief end of God, as of man, is the glory of God. The idea is right if our conception of the Divine Being is right; but this conception is primary. As we conceive Him, so also must we conceive His actions and ends. If God be as the Godhead, a Being whose very life is love, then the only ends worthy of the infinitely Good are those of infinite goodness. If He acts as becomes Himself rather than as we deserve, then we shall experience a good proportioned to His immeasurable grace, not accommodated to our own measurable merits. Hence Jonathan Edwards argued that the chief end of God could be expressed in a twofold form—either as His own glory or as the good of the creature. These were not two things, but only the same thing seen from different sides. Yet the glory, as the grander, was the higher point of view. For God to act in a manner that became God was surely for the action to be more creative of good than if He simply regarded a universe which could never cease to be finite. Where all the ends are infinite, none of the acts can be mean or limited. The Creator's primary motive governs His permanent action and determines the creation's ultimate end; and all who live in the universe, and the universe in which they live, will be penetrated with as much of good as it is able to bear or they are willing to receive.

The ethicized conception of God, which we owe to the Christian doctrine of the Godhead, has thus resulted in an ethicized conception of the universe, or of being as related to God. It has thus lifted us to a higher position than is possible to a mere philosophical Theism. God is not in theology, as He is in philosophy, conceived under the categories of metaphysical immutability, but under those of ethical ; and these are defined for us by the terms in which the revelation came. It came in the Son, through the Only Begotten who is in the bosom of the Father. And this means that paternal love, filial love, love communicative, and love dependent, receptive, reflective, are of the essence of God— He incapable of being Himself without love, it capable of describing if not defining His very being. And when we attempt to translate these immanent ethical realities and relations into their external counterpart, what can we say but that the conditions of His inner life constitute the laws and motives of His outer ? God cannot be other to His universe than He is to Himself. He did not create to hate, but to love ; creation continues because He loves, not that He may hate. His affection is not a perishable emotion, can be as little lost by sin as gained by service. His love of the created is something He owes to Himself, not something that can be earned by merit or achieved by success. Were the reason of the love in man rather than in God, it would be in ceaseless change, always mixed, never pure ; but God loves for His own sake, not for the creature's. Were He to hate even the devil, He would while the feeling endured have in Him an element alien to the Divine, and so would be less than God. It is granted to no being to compel Deity to lose the splendid happiness of loving even those who disobey and hate Him. But though the good and the evil may be alike loved, yet the love is not in the two cases of the same quality. Quantitatively there is no more of the love of God in heaven than in hell, but qualitatively the loves differ as much as hell and heaven. The love of the good is complacency, but the love of the evil is pity or compassion. Complacency is twice blessed, gives the mutual joy that is beatitude, happy being in a happy world ; but compassion feels double pain—pain for him who needs help, and pain for the evil that causes the help to be needed. Complacency is the double beatitude of God in the universe and of the universe in God. Pity, too, is double ; it is the shadow which evil casts on the Good, and the promise the Good is ever bound to make to Himself—never to surrender to evil those who are held by evil. But this promise carries us beyond natural into the region of positive or constructive Theology.

CHAPTER III.

THE GODHEAD AND THE DEITY OF CONSTRUCTIVE THEOLOGY.

§ I.—The Theistic Conception and Theology.

THIS discussion started from the distinction between God and the Godhead.[1] The Godhead is Deity as He is in and for Himself, the infinite Manifold who is by His very nature, as it were, a society, the home of ethical relations and activities, of spiritual life and love ; but God is Deity as He is to and for the universe, in His outward functions and relations, a unity over against the manifold of finite existence. The distinctions do not break up the unity, for they are immanent ; nor does the unity abolish the distinctions, for God does not cease to be one because His nature is a rich and complex manifold rather than an absolute and abstract simplicity. In other words, God is not a substance or unit or monad incapable of thought or action ; but an infinite Being, with all the conditions of free, personal, ethical, and conscious existence within Himself. The significance of this notion for the questions raised by a speculative or philosophical Theism we have seen ; what we have now to see is its significance for the primary or material conception of a positive or constructive theology.

God is here a quantitative but Godhead a qualitative term. According to the one, He is an indissoluble unity ; according to the other, He is, to use in a new connotation Butler's term,

[1] *Supra*, p. 385.

an indiscerptible community—*i.e.*, He is by His very essence social, possessed of a life which can be common or communal only as there are personal distinctions. But between God and Godhead there must be an absolute and reciprocal *communicatio idiomatum*. God is capable of receiving the whole Godhead, and the Godhead of absorbing all the attributes and exercising all the functions of God By God the Godhead is unified; but the Godhead is, as regards its essential qualities and life, personalized in God for the government of the universe. Without this complete interpenetration of the two ideas our constructive thought would be without its regulative principle.

We may say, then, that as the Godhead is God interpreted in the terms of the Spirit and consciousness of Christ, so the special task of Christian theology is to reinterpret God in the terms of the Godhead. What He *does* depends upon what He *is*—*i.e.*, all His functions and actions relative to the created are only the outward expression of His inner qualities and character. As Hooker has well said, putting into English the fundamental principle of the Reformed theology of his day, "The being of God is a kind of law to His working; for that perfection which God is giveth perfection to that He doth."[1] And the attempt to approach the doctrine of God through the Godhead means simply that what we wish to know is "that perfection which God is," in order that we may the better understand the "law of His working" and the perfection of His works.

What is fundamental, then, is this: the conception of God in positive or constructive theology is not as in natural or speculative; it has been transformed by the action of the supreme and normative religious consciousness. This theology does not start from a philosophical idea, but from a concrete Person and the Deity as known to Him: in other

[1] "Eccles. Pol.," I, i, 2.

words, we come to the Godhead through Christ, and to God through the Godhead; and through the God so reached we interpret our beliefs and organize them into a theology. Hence the explication of this constitutive idea forms at once the foundation and ground-plan of the whole theological system.

But in dogmatic theology there has been, from causes already indicated,[1] a remarkable tendency, if not to keep the doctrines of the Godhead and God apart, yet to leave them in a state of incomplete interpenetration. The Godhead has had greater ecclesiastical than theological or cosmical significance; while in soteriology it has been accepted more as the means or condition of effecting salvation than as the very truth as to God and His relations to man. The idea of God, on the other hand, has been so construed as to determine the nature, necessity, and limits of the salvation which the Persons of the Godhead have been made to effect. When we think of the Godhead we speak of the Father, Son, and Spirit; when we think of God we speak of the Sovereign, Lawgiver, and Judge. And under this distinction of speech there has lived a distinction of ideas. While our notion of the Godhead has been formally Christian, our notion of God has been formally Hebrew, but materially Roman—*i.e.*, the conception of God is Jewish in its origin, but into it has been read, upon it has been impressed, the spirit, the character, and the categories of Roman law and laws Rome has modified or influenced. And this forensic Deity, instead of being permeated and transformed by the ethical qualities of the Godhead, has imposed, as it were, its yoke upon the Divine Persons, forcing them to serve as names or factors in a juridical process. In other words, the Hebræo-Roman God has so prevailed over the Christian Godhead, that instead of the latter expelling the juristic or forensic element from the notion of the former, the Godhead has

[1] *Supra*, pp. 388-91.

tended to become mainly significant as a convenient mode of carrying out a legal process which the legalized notion of God had made necessary. What is needed is to reverse this process, and penetrate our conception of God with the life and qualities of the Godhead.

§ II.—THE JURIDICAL DEITY.

The juridical conception of Deity has two main forms, corresponding to the two main types of theology—the institutional or political, and the dialectic or constructive. These two forms have as their principal representatives Catholicism and Calvinism. The forces that organized the Catholic system elaborated the Catholic conception of God. The law it incorporated He was made to embody; His character and functions were adjusted to the legislative and administrative system which came to be known as the Church. The plastic ideas worked inward, from the circumference to the centre, rather than outwards, from the centre to the circumference. The notions of the old law were read into Deity rather than the notion of Deity articulated into a new law. The penitential discipline of the Church organized the idea that law could be commutative as well as vindicative, that it could be so satisfied by the loss or suffering of the disobedient as to remit the severer and more flagrant penalty; and in the image of the law God was made. The heavenly and the earthly hierarchies corresponded, just as the pseudo-Dionysius had conceived, only the correspondence was not as he conceived it; it was the earthly that gave its form and quality to the heavenly. In other words, the political character and expediencies of the Church were so reflected in its Deity that He was but, as it were, their ideal embodiment; and the more magisterial its spirit and methods became the more of a magistrate He grew. The Papacy is a delegated magistracy, but the delegates have made the visible authority become a law for the Invisible. To the Catholic mind religion is, alike as regards faith and conduct, a matter of positive or instituted law. The Deity is as the system is; the system is one of ceremonial and sacerdotal legalism, and the Deity is a Being who can be satisfied by a sacerdotal act or process for any failure in legality, whether termed disobedience or sin.

The Calvinistic conception of God was reached by a process exactly the reverse of the Catholic—viz., the dialectical or deductive. He was in the ultimate analysis the supreme or sovereign Will; His highest function was the realization of Himself and His ends, and this was possible only as He ordained and created the necessary means. In a deductive system the essential thing is the premiss; if it be false or inadequate, the conclusion can never be right. And a theology which professes to start with the God given in the consciousness of Christ, can never be justified in the attempt to reduce God to the category of will. And the evil in the initial assumption was intensified by the efforts at mitigation being made, as it were, from without—*i.e.*, by setting limits to God rather than by a change in the conception of Him. As to the ultimacy of the will Calvin is explicit: men are admonished "nihil causæ quærere extra voluntatem."[1] Is He not unjust, then, when He elects some and reprobates others? No; for, as Augustine taught, those He elects merit no favour, while those He reprobates deserve punishment; and so He is "ab omni accusatione liberari, similitudine creditoris, cuius potestate est alteri remittere, ab altero exigere."[2] The very use of such a figure ought to have made the falsity of the idea apparent. Calvin holds, indeed, that the Divine will is not, as it were, mere naked omnipotence, for God "sibi ipsi lex est"[3]; but this law is more judicial and retributive than gracious and salutary. And under the influences of controversy it tended more and more to become detached from the Divine nature or

[1] "Inst.," iii. 22, 11.   [2] *Ibid.*, iii. 23, 11.
[3] *Ibid.*, iii. 23, 2.

character and attached to the Divine function or office. In other words, God was interpreted through sovereignty rather than sovereignty through God. The notion of sovereignty was not always one or uniform. The Calvinist held it to be ἀνευθυνία, absolute and irresponsible; but the Arminian held it to be tempered by benevolence: to the one it was a "dominium absolutum,"[1] to the other a dominium "partim dignitati naturæ divinæ, partim conditioni naturali hominis commensuratum."[2] And it was characteristic that men laid down propositions about the Absolute Sovereign they would have hesitated to affirm as to God. They claimed for Him rights such as were then claimed for kings, but were unworthy of Deity, and defined His relations to man and man's to Him in language more agreeable to the politics of despotism than the truth and grace of religion. For the more the emphasis changed from will to law, from personal power to impersonal government, the more could they speak of Him in the language of the current jurisprudence, and hedge Him within its hard and narrow rules. What Deism did in the physical realm forensic theology did in the moral and religious. God was sacrificed to sovereignty, imprisoned within the laws He

[1] Camero, Opera, p. 41. But especially treatise by Amyraut, "De jure Dei in creaturas," in "Dissertationes Theologicæ." It is characteristic that the more moderate school of Calvinism was the most emphatic in its doctrine of sovereignty; they tried to relieve the pressure of their system on the character of God by substituting for Him and His will theories forensic and judicial.

[2] Episcopius, "Instit. Theol.," iv., sec. ii., c. 28. In this chapter Episcopius directly sets limits from the side of equity and nature to the power of God (cf. *supra*, pp. 169-72). He argued, on the one hand, "justitia hæc est voluntatis actionumque divinorum directrix"; and, on the other, that it followed from the natural congruency and connection which man has with God "ut jus ac dominium Dei in hominem non sit infinitum." Cf. Ritschl, "Geschich. Studien zur Christ. Lehre von Gott," "Jahrb. für Deuts. Theol.," vol. xiii., pp. 67-133. Theories of the Divine sovereignty had the strictest relation to current theories as to the forms of government, or the duties and rights of citizens, and the grounds and limits of the regal power. This means that to the forensic theologian, as was the state, such was the universe and the reign of God.

was supposed to have framed, or reduced to the function of their administrator. In the older Calvinism there was a majesty as of the Infinite; in the later there was a hard and pragmatic spirit as of the lawyer and the law court.

§ III.—Whether and in what Sense God is a Sovereign.

In our modern theology much of the old forensic speech and idea still survives; and so it may be as well to examine its basis in the doctrine of the sovereignty. The last serious attempt to state and defend it was made by the late Dr. Candlish. His position consisted of three main parts:—

1. "God's fundamental and primary" relation to man was that of Creator and Governor; "His rule or government must be, in the proper forensic sense, legal and judicial"; "absolute and sovereign"; "of the most thoroughly royal, imperial, autocratic kind." To conceive it as anything else were "an inconsistency, an intolerable anomaly, a suicidal self-contradiction."[1]

2. The only essential Sonship was that of Christ's Deity, but by its union with His Deity His humanity became participant in the filial relation. And so He was the only historical Person who was really and by nature the Son of God.

3. The only other sons of God were the elect in Christ, who became by adoption partakers in the Sonship of the Only Begotten. Beyond these limits there was no Fatherhood, only sovereignty.

The first position is the fundamental; and with it alone are we meanwhile concerned. Let us, then, ask What a "strictly legal and judicial sovereignty," "of the most royal, imperial, and autocratic kind," means, and How far it is predicable of God? These are terms borrowed from our political history and experience, and must by these be interpreted before they

[1] "The Fatherhood of God," pp. 9, 10, 12, 13, 17 (5th ed.).

can be allowed to pass current in theology. Well, then, the
legal sovereign may be either (α) a sovereign made by law, with
all his rights and functions defined, guarded, and maintained
by the law that made him; or (β) a sovereign who makes the
law, with all his rights and authority rooted in power, in the
force which makes the stronger the king of all feebler men.
The sovereigns of the first kind are constitutional, "strictly
legal and judicial"; the sovereigns of the second kind are
despotic, "imperial and autocratic." As we have the one or
other, we have a different ideal of law and justice, of their
relation to the sovereign and of his relation to them, of the
source, limits, and quality of his power, royal and judicial.
The constitutional sovereign is a creation of law, made by
it for its own ends, an instrument of the order it aims at
securing; bound, therefore, by its terms; going beyond them at
his peril; faced ever by the possible penalty of being unmade
by his very maker. This means that the legal sovereign is
the supreme subject, able to commit treason against the impersonal majesty of the creative law, just as the citizen may
commit treason against the personal majesty of the reigning
monarch. But this sovereignty is a creation of highly civilized
times; designed not to abolish but to secure the equality of
all before the law, so much so that he who most seems over it
is most bound to live under it if he would live at all. But the
"imperial or autocratic" sovereign is the creator of law. He
is its only source; it is but his expressed will. He has only to
change his will, and the law is changed. His authority is not
based on law, but law is based on his authority. He is the
ground and condition rather than the instrument of order.

But this "imperial or autocratic" species of sovereignty
may be of two kinds—either acquired or natural. Acquired
power is power gained by some means—conquest or cunning,
force or fraud, which is only a kind of force, viz., the ability
to deceive by seeming to be other than the reality. The
ultimate basis of authority so acquired is superior strength;

28

and though it may be transmitted, it can never lose the character it owes to its source. But while the authority based on force may be used for moral ends, it is not moral authority; while it may be "royal, imperial, autocratic," yet it is not in the strict sense either a moral or religious government. Indeed, the imperial sovereign is simply the *imperator* become the *rex*, the head of the army changed by virtue of the force behind and beneath him into the head of the state. But the natural sovereignty is of a different order ; its representative or type is the parent or the patriarch. The primitive or aboriginal natural sovereign was the primitive father. The first kingdom was the first family, and its natural head was the first king. That was the sort of kinghood that rested on creatorship; but even so it means that fatherhood is the source and basis of sovereignty. The only absolute natural kingship, therefore, is neither legal, a creation of law ; nor imperial, a creation of power, personal or organized ; but paternal, a creation of nature. Unless we deify force, or leave force to create our deities, we must find in the father the ideal of the king absolute by valid or natural right.

So far, then, this analysis has not resulted in the discovery of any " suicidal contradiction " between the ideas of sovereignty and fatherhood ; on the contrary, in the family, which is the unit of society and the germ of the state, the terms become, if not equivalent, yet complementary and coextensive. The absence of either element involves the imperfection of the other, and imperils the common good. The more perfect a father is, the more of a sovereign will he be ; the better he is as a sovereign, the more excellently will he fulfil his functions as a father. The forms and sanctions of his authority will vary, but the less formal it grows the more real it will become. There is nothing so absolute as the paternal reign in its earliest form. The infant is the most helpless creature in nature; depends for food, clothing, tendance, everything essential to its continued being, on other hands than its own ;

and the parent's sovereignty is then a sovereignty of carefulness, a mindfulness which feels every moment that the child can live only in and through those to whom it owes its being. Here the law governs the parent, though the law be love; and in obedience to it the work, as it were, of creating a subject still proceeds, and only as it is well and thoughtfully done can the subject ever be created. But in due course the new mind and will awake, and sovereignty then assumes a new form, becomes legislative and administrative, frames laws which the child must be now persuaded, now compelled, now beguiled to obey. Here the authority is autocratic, yet with an autocracy which is most tender where most imperious. But the child becomes a youth, and the sovereignty again changes its form, becomes flexible in means that it may be inflexible in end, loving the boy too well to tolerate his evil, so watching him that he may by a now regretted severity and a now gracious gentleness be trained and disciplined to good. And when the youth becomes a man, the sovereignty does not cease, though its form is altogether unlike anything that had been before; it may be the fellowship by which the old enrich and ripen the young and the young freshen and enlarge the old; it may be by a name which filial reverence will not sully, or a love and a pride which filial affection will delight to gratify; or it may only be by a memory which, as the years lengthen, grows in beauty and in power. But in whatever form, the sovereignty of a father who has been a father indeed, is of all human authorities the most real and the most enduring.

The two ideas therefore of paternity and sovereignty are not only compatible, they are indissoluble; either can be perfect only in and through the other. The absolute sovereign without the father is a tyrant, a despot, the symbol of the government that can least of all be suffered by free-born men; the father without the sovereign is a weakling, a puppet or thing made rather than a maker, the symbol of the feeble good-nature which is so prolific a source of evil even in the good. Neither function, then, can be well discharged without the other. A sovereignty without fatherhood may create order, but it is the forced order which is only disguised chaos; not the order of concordant and obedient spirits, but of the coerced wills that are most rebellious when they have to appear most submissive. A fatherhood without sovereignty may beget persons, but can never form characters, or build the characters formed into a happy family or a contented and ordered state. The two, Fatherhood and Sovereignty, must then live together, and be incorporated into a living and effective unity, if we are to have a government of ideal perfection, such as becomes God and is suitable to a universe full of the realities and infinite possibilities of good and evil.

§ IV.—The Sovereignty of Law and of God.

There is, then, no absolute antithesis between sovereignty and paternity; the only perfect form in which we can have either is where we have both. The argument which opposes the two proceeds from the basis, not of nature or ideal truth, but of the policies and expediencies and experiments of our perplexed social and civil life. On this ground it is impossible to reach any clear or coherent conception of God's rule over men. For if we describe His sovereignty as, "in the proper forensic sense, legal and judicial," "thoroughly royal, imperial, autocratic," we simply interpret God in the terms of the government under which we live, or whose form we chance to think best. And this, so far from making His action, as the Christian revelation represents it, more intelligible, really makes it quite inconceivable. For sovereignty is a radically different thing when paternal and when legal or imperial; sovereign, subjects, laws, methods and ends of government, are all, as regards quality and kind, unlike and dissimilar.

Thus the purely legal or imperial sovereign so reigns as to strengthen and extend his authority, but the father so rules as to educate and benefit his child, as to order and bless his home. The relations of the sovereign are all legal; persons to him are nothing save subjects of rights or duties, objects to be protected or restrained; law and order are all in all; all his ends are political, his methods judicial, his instruments most perfect where least personal; his justice is never absolute, always relative, tempered by the expediency which can seldom dare to be abstractly just. But the relations of the father are all personal; his ends are to make good persons; his means must be adapted to his ends; and his reign is prosperous only as he constrains towards the affection that compels obedience or wins from evil by the wisdom of a watchful love.

And as the sovereigns differ, so do their laws. The legal authority does not chastise, only punishes; all its sanctions are penalties, and they are enforced, not to reform or restore the criminal, but to compel respect and conformity to law. But the paternal authority does not so much punish as chastise; all its sanctions are chastisements, and their ultimate aim is to correct and reform, so expelling the evil as to make room for the good. This distinction is fundamental and determinative. Punishment and chastisement agree while they differ. They agree in this:—both are exercised on offenders by those who have the authority to command and the right to be obeyed, and the power to execute the judgment which has been passed on disobedience. But they differ here:—punishment regards what may be variously described as the maintenance of order, the public good, the majesty of the law, or the claims of justice; but chastisement seeks the good of the offender, certain that if it secures this all these other things will surely follow. And this distinction involves another:—under a rigorously forensic or legal and judicial system all penalties punish, but do not chastise; they may be vindicative, exhibiting the power or sufficiency of the law against those who break it, or exemplary and deterrent, warning those who would do as the criminal has done of what will be their certain fate: but under a sovereign paternity all penalties chastise, and do not simply punish—*i.e.*, while doing the same things that legal punishments do, they yet aim at doing something more, so affecting and so placing the offender that he shall cease from his offences and become dutiful and obedient. Hence emerges a further and final distinction :—a government which is "in the proper forensic sense, legal and judicial," is punitive, not remedial; its agencies and aims are retributory and penal, not reformatory and restorative: but a paternal sovereignty is in the true sense remedial in its very penalties; its methods and ends are never merely vindicative or retaliatory, but are always corrective, redemptive. Under a purely legal government the salvation of the criminal is impossible, but under a regal fatherhood the thing impossible is the total abandonment of the sinner. If salvation happens under the former, it is by other means than the forensic and the judicial; if loss is irreparable under the latter, the reason is not in the father. And so we may say, in judgment the legal sovereign is just, but the paternal is gracious. The one reigns that he may prevent evil men from injuring the good, but the other reigns that evil may cease by evil men being saved.

This argument has not been directed against the Sovereignty of God, but against the attempt to bring it into the category of legal, judicial, royal, or forensic governments. These terms denote ideas of the most relative and variable order, and their use tends to beget the notion that the universe is a transfigured court or a magnified forum. There is no intention of denying God's absolute Sovereignty; on the contrary, it is here affirmed in the most earnest and emphatic way; but what is maintained is, that it must be interpreted through God, and not through our autocracies and monarchies. It is

God's Sovereignty, and God must be known that the Sovereignty may be understood. What was before affirmed as to theism must now be affirmed as to theology—the Godhead has completely ethicized the conception of God. And this was as great a necessity in the one case as in the other. The Deity of our forensic theologies is legal, but not moral; by their systems of jurisprudence they have made actions which were morally necessary seem legally impossible to Him. Hence He must be emancipated from legalism that He may be restored to moral reality and truth. But this means that His essential qualities are ethical rather than physical, metaphysical or political. These indeed are necessary to Deity as Creator, but as servants to obey, not as masters to command. The moral attributes are, as it were, the God of God, move Him to act and regulate His action. As such they are the seat of the causal impulse, while the physical attributes are but the instruments they impel and guide. The world owes its existence, not to the omnipotence of Deity, though without His omnipotence it could not have been, but to the moral nature that moved and the intellectual that used the omnipotence. And as creation was a moral act all its motives and ends were in God, for only so could they be worthy of Him. These motives and ends were those of the supreme good. God willed being that He might will beatitude. The willing was a sovereign act, but the motives and ends made the act paternal. It was both at once, and was perfect because it was both. In other words, the supreme act of Sovereignty was the realization of Paternity, for these names only denote the obverse and reverse sides of the same thing. In origin they are simultaneous, in being coincident, in range coextensive, in ends identical. The Father is never without the Sovereign, nor the Sovereign without the Father; conflict or inconsistency in their acts is impossible, for they have one will, and what is done by either is performed by both. There could be no Sovereignty without subjects or Fatherhood without sons, and the act that begat the sons created the subjects. But while Sovereignty may be said to begin with creation, the sovereign will does not, nor the nature which guides the will—is its law and determines its end. Hence, we repeat, we must not construe God through our forensic sovereignty, but the sovereignty through God, and God through the filial and normative consciousness of Jesus Christ.

Here, then, we emphasize once more the significance of the Godhead for the conception of God. God is to Jesus essentially the Father, and He is to Himself as essentially the Son. He would not be what He is without the Fatherhood, nor would God be what He is without the Sonship. Were the Sonship subtracted, there would be no Fatherhood; were the Fatherhood denied, there could be no Son. But the unity in which these relations are is a unity of active and social love. This defines what God according to His essence is :—Viewed from within, as Godhead, He is this love in eternal exercise, existing through personal distinctions, yet in community of life, communicative, communicated, reciprocated, in ceaseless flow and ebb, streaming from its source in the eternal subject, retreating from its bourn in the eternal Object, moving in the unbeginning, unending cycle which is the bosom of the Infinite. What He is as Godhead He must remain as God; the energies exercised without only express the life within. The inward and the outward face of Deity, if we may so speak, is one face; and He whose inner life is a community of love must be in His outer action creative of conditions correspondent to those within. Hence He who is by His essence a society will so act as to create an outward society which shall reflect His inner relations. The law of the Divine working is the Divine nature, and as is the nature such must be the work. The internal Sonship is normative of the external; and as Fatherhood is essential to the Godhead, it is natural to God; all the qualities it implies within Deity are expressed and exercised in His activity within the universe. And therefore, while

Jesus speaks of Himself as the Son and of God as the Father, He teaches men also so to speak. The relation of the only begotten Son, who is in the bosom of the Father, is, as it were, the prototype and idea of the many sons who play round the Father's feet. And so we conclude that God cannot be other without than the Godhead is within; the outer action and relations and the inner being and character must be correlative and correspondent.

§ V.—God as Father and as Sovereign.

If, then, we interpret God through the Godhead, the result will be a conception which, instead of dividing and opposing, unites and harmonizes the ideas of Fatherhood and Sovereignty. These terms denote, not so much distinct or contrary functions which Deity may successively or contemporaneously fulfil for opposite purposes and as regards different persons, but rather the attitude and action of a Being who must by nature fulfil both if He is to fulfil either. We may distinguish them as we distinguish love and righteousness, which we may term the paternal and regal attributes of God; but they are as inseparable as these, and form as real a unity. We may say alike of the attributes and the functions,—Were they divorced, both would be destroyed; and were either denied to Deity, He would be undeified. To love is to be righteous; to be unrighteous is to be incapable of love. Love is righteousness as emotion, motive, and end; righteousness is love as action and conduct. Love is perfect being; righteousness is perfect behaviour; and so they may be described as standing to each other as law and obedience. It is of the essence of both to be transitive. Love regards an object whose good it desires; righteousness is the conduct which fulfils the desire of love. Love as it desires another hates the evil that mars his good; righteousness as it serves another judges the evil that defeats the service. Hence love is social, but righteousness judicial; the law the one prescribes the other enforces. And so they must exist together in order to exist at all. Subtract love from righteousness, and it becomes mere rigour, conduct too inflexible to be living, justice too severe to be just. Subtract righteousness from love, and it ceases to be, becomes mere sentiment, an emotion too pitiful to combine truth with grace. Love makes righteousness active and helpful; righteousness makes love beneficent while benevolent.

Each of these qualities is of course capable of analysis into much simpler elements. Love as the causal impulse or need of another determines the nature of the other that is needed; he must be a being whose happiness can be willed, the happiness of a kind which depends on fellowship with his Maker. For the other that love needs, it needs for fellowship; and fellowship is made possible by affinities; it is the communion of natures akin. Without affinities love cannot live. And so for God to love man, man must be akin to God; for man to love God, God must be akin to man. In all love, then, there must be sympathy, which is a sort of mutual or inter-incorporation of being, of the loved in the loving, of the loving in the loved. In sympathy the soul that loves feels as its own every shadow, every emotion, every experience that passes over or through the soul of the loved. It is, as it were, the vicarious principle; where it is there is substitution by the absorption, ideally, of the object into the subject, such an' inter-penetration of two beings that whatever lives in the one or happens to him becomes a matter of real, vivid, personal experience to the other. In a world of happiness it creates double beatitude; in a world of misery it is to the good the double suffering men call sacrifice. Where it lives we have "one passion in twin hearts," which "touch, mingle, and are transfigured"; and the result is

> "One hope within two wills, one will beneath
> Two overshadowing minds, one life, one death,
> One heaven, one hell, one immortality."

But this identifying or inter-incorporating power of love which we term sympathy involves two opposite elements, whose being is conditioned on the state of the object—where that state is good it gives joy, where evil it creates pity. And these two cannot live inactive and self-centred. Joy is an emotion which will not be suppressed, and for it to be expressed is to be creative, the happiness that does not create happiness turning into misery in the breast that feels it. And pity when it sees misery becomes mercy, the passion of helpfulness, the will that has no choice save to end the evil by the creation of more and higher good. And these two in their one and common activity constitute grace, which is the spontaneous yet inexorable impulse of the ever-blessed God to create beatitude. In this sense grace is only the exercised love of God, acting in the forms needed by a real and dependent world as it had acted in a world ideal and Divine.

Love is essentially the attribute of motives and ends, but righteousness of means and agencies. It may be described as in a sense the executive of love; it is, as it were, the will using the fit means to reach and realize the ends of the heart. Love regards persons and their states, but righteousness the methods by which these can be effected for good. So understood it is purposive, selective; wisdom not simply as advisory, but as effective and efficient, applied to the realization of the means that shall best realize the ends. It is thus a rational will, a power which intelligence guides while love rules. But the will that purposes creates; and what it creates corresponds to its motive and end; it is therefore, as creative of good will, the sole efficient will of good. But in doing this it expresses the moral perfection of Him whose will it is, and this perfection is holiness, or the absolute agreement of act and nature, or character and will. But He who exhibits this agreement cannot demand less than He realizes, and this demand is expressed in a twofold form,—what we may call the legislative, embodied in conscience, which shows the law that governs the will of Deity translated into a law for man's; and the administrative, expressed in the order of history, personal and collective. The former is judgment; the latter is justice; and they are related as law enacted and law enforced. Wisdom as selective determines means, goodness their kind, holiness their quality, judgment their form, justice their vindication or enforcement. These are all necessary to the righteousness of the sovereign will. Remove the wisdom, and it would not be the best; remove the goodness, and it would not be the highest; remove the holiness, and it would not be whole or the will of a sound and perfect nature; remove the judgment, and it would not be directive; remove the justice, and it would not be regnant. God as ethical can never abandon sovereignty; to be indifferent to the moral state of His creatures would be to be false to Himself, to His nature, to His love, to all the ends for which He created. To think of God is thus to think of a Being who can never be gentle or indulgent to sin. The judge does not fear crime as the father fears the very taint of vice; the sovereign does not hate the violation of law as the parent hates the very shadow of coming disobedience. Evil is a more terrible thing to the family than to the state; and so the theology which reduces God's government to one "legal and judicial," "in the proper forensic sense," makes far more light of sin than the theology which conceives it through His sovereign Paternity.

§ VI.—Paternity and Sonship.

Our conclusion, then, is this:—the antithesis between the Fatherhood and Sovereignty of God is fictitious, violent, perverse. The Father is the Sovereign; and as the Father is such must the Sovereign be. Hence the primary and determinative conception is the Fatherhood, and so through it the Sovereignty must be read and interpreted. In all His regal acts God is paternal; in all His paternal ways regal; but His is not the figurative paternity of the king, though His is the real kinghood of the Father.

How we are to define the notion of Fatherhood is a point

on which there has been much barren dialectic. Pearson[1] describes the Divine Paternity thus: "The first and most universal notion of it, in a borrowed or metaphorical sense, is founded rather upon creation than procreation"; and then he amplifies and develops it by the notions of "conservation," "redemption," "regeneration," and "adoption." The late Dr. Crawford, in his "Reply" to Dr. Candlish, framed his definition on Pearson thus: "Fatherhood implies the origination by one intelligent person of another intelligent person like in nature to himself, and the continued support, protection, and nourishment of the person thus originated by him to whom he owes his being."[2] To which Dr. Candlish sensibly replied, "Such a universal Fatherhood I do not care to call in question."[3] For all that we have is a figurative and euphonious way of describing creation and Providence. But our discussions have throughout proceeded upon this principle:—Fatherhood cannot here be stated in the terms of physical creation or procreation, which represents an instrumental or a secondary cause, but only in the terms of ethical motive, relation, and end. It is not the physical act as physical that is constitutive of Paternity, but the act as ethically conditioned and determined. Man is God's son, not simply because God's creature and Godlike, but because of the God and the ends of the God whose creature he is. Fatherhood did not come through creation, but rather creation came because of Fatherhood. The essential love out of which creation issued determined the standing of the created before the Creator and the relation of the Creator to the created. Where love is causal, it is paternal; where it creates a fellow with whom it can have fellowship, the relation of the created is filial. Spiritual and personal relations which have their causes and ends in spiritual and personal needs, cannot be stated in the terms of physical creation or political institution,

---

[1] "On the Creed," sub Art. 1.   [2] "The Fatherhood of God," pp. 9-10.
[3] Candlish's "Reply," p. 8.

but only in those of the heart and the life. And the aboriginal relation of man and God is the universal and permanent; within it all later possibilities are contained. It is the emptiest nominalism to speak of the adoption of a man who never was a son, for the term can denote nothing real. The legal fiction has a meaning and a use only where it represents or pretends to represent something in the world of fact; but to speak of the "adoption" of a creature who is in no respect a son, is to use a term which is here without the saving virtue of sense. The Sonship must be real to start with if adoption is ever to be real, and its reality depends on the reality of the Paternity. If the motives and ends of God in the creation of man were paternal, then man's filial relation follows, and it stands, however unworthy a son he may prove himself to be.

Were we, then, to attempt to form a notion of the Paternity, it would be through the Godhead as determining the act of God, the kind of creatures it produces, and the peculiar and special relations in which He and they will stand to each other. Thus:—

i. The end of creation existed before the creative act. The τέλος was before the actual ἀρχή, and creation was but a means for the realization of the end.

ii. The means were in harmony with the end, but the end in harmony with the Creator. God willed as He was. The idea of the election of one from among an infinite multitude of possible worlds, is a philosophical myth; the only possible world was the one realized. The Divine will is not contingent or arbitrary because it is free; the free action is spontaneous, an action into which the whole nature as a whole, as it were, involuntarily and harmoniously blossoms. God might or might not have acted; but if He did act, the way He took was the only way possible to Him.

iii. The nature which determined the end was the unity which we speak of as the Godhead. In it Fatherhood and Sonship were essential and immanent, and so the end may be described as the realization of external relations correspondent to the internal; in other words, the creation of a universe which should be to God as a son, while He was to it as a Father. As within the Godhead so conceived all love was law, so within the universe He created all law was love.

iv. The universe He thus created is personal and spiritual; all its units are capable of loving as of being loved; and where such capability exists we can best express the causal relation by the term Paternity, and the created by Sonship.

v. But these two notions may seem empty and unrelated if they remain mere notions; the definition that comes of actual being can alone make them real. And here emerges the significance of the historical and normative person of Christ, which we may exhibit thus: (a) His is the normal humanity, God's ideal realized. Hence it follows that all the relations man by nature sustains towards God, He perfectly sustained. (β) Of these the most characteristic and fundamental was the filial. Without it His humanity would not have been perfect, and so it is as Son that He learns obedience and attains perfection. (γ) The Sonship that was necessary to Him is common to man. He is a unit who is universal; and what is here true of His nature is true of man's. On His Sonship His brotherhood is based; and through His brotherhood man's, as real and universal, is guaranteed. (δ) The Sonship He realized is the ideal of the race All God was to Him, He was meant to be and wants to be to every man; all He was to God, every man ought to be and may become. The very reason of His being was to exhibit through the ideal relation of man to God the actual relation of God to man. (ϵ) The embodied ideal is the supreme reality. In Christ we see it, not only within the terms of finitude, but under the conditions of suffering which is sorest sacrifice because of the sins and the states of brothers who will not be sons. Yet we see it that we may be redeemed by being made partakers of His Spirit, and so qualified for adoption out of the sonship of nature into the Sonship of grace.

vi. The truth illustrated by the person is enforced by the teaching of Christ. He makes the Fatherhood the basis of all the duties which man owes to God. Supreme love to God is possible only because God is love. On the ground of mere sovereignty or judicial and autocratic authority, the first commandment could never be enjoined. We cannot love simply because we will or wish or are commanded, but only because we are loved. Supreme affection is possible only through the Sovereign Fatherhood. And what is true of this first is true of all our other duties. Worship is to be in spirit and in truth, because it is worship of the Father. Prayer is to be constant and simple and sincere, because it is offered to the Father. We are to give alms in simplicity and without ostentation, because the Father sees in secret. We are to be forgiving, because the Father forgives. Obedience is imitation of God, a being perfect as our Father in heaven is perfect. In a word, duty is but the habit of the filial spirit; and it is possible and incumbent on all men, because all are sons.

DIVISION III.

A.—*GOD AS INTERPRETED BY CHRIST THE DETERMINATIVE PRINCIPLE IN THEOLOGY.*

CHAPTER I.

THE FATHERHOOD AND SIN.

§ I.—The Formal and the Material Principle of Theology.

THE conclusion from the preceding discussion may be stated thus:—the Fatherhood neither limits nor contradicts, but qualifies and determines the Sovereignty; the King must be construed through the Father, the Father cannot be educed from the King. In other words, the theology which starts from the consciousness of Christ finds that the determinative element in His idea of God is the paternal, and in His idea of man the filial. But this conclusion is only the premiss of a constructive or interpretative science, and all the positions evolved in the science are involved in the premiss. In the older systems there was a familiar distinction between the *principium cognoscendi* and the *principium essendi*; in later systems the former appears as the formal principle or source of theology, the latter as the material or real principle or source.[1] The distinction is, as it

[1] Cf. on this distinction, Dorner, "Gesammelte Schriften," Essay ii., pp. 48-152.

were, between the fountain whence we draw the water and the water we draw. Theologies and Churches have differed both as to the nature and the relation of these sources. The formal source has been conceived as the Scriptures and tradition, or the Scriptures and the Church, or as the Church alone, or as the Scriptures alone. The material source, the *articulus primarius*, or *fundamentalis*, has been conceived to be the Church, or justification by faith, or the Incarnation, or the sovereign will of God.[1] And these sources are so related, that while the material determines the theology, the formal determines the material. If a man holds the Church and tradition to be joint sources of knowledge with the Scriptures, he cannot possibly find his material principle in justification by faith or the sovereign will of God; while if he holds the Scriptures to be the sole formal source, he cannot possibly regard the Church or its decrees as the material. Where a man goes for knowledge really determines what its matter will be, though not where its emphasis will fall.

In these discussions it has been everywhere assumed that our formal source is the consciousness of Christ. This is what we must know if we would find our material or constructive principle. In order to it the Scriptures are necessary, but as a medium or channel which conducts to the source, not as the source itself. They testify of Christ, are His witnesses; but it is as witnesses that they are essential, and their value is in proportion to their veracity. And our material is as our formal source. It is the ultimate deliverance of His consciousness. We cannot accept Luther's article of a standing or falling Church as our *principium essendi*. It is Paul's rather than Christ's; it may be true, but it still remains what it was at first—a deduction by a disciple, not a principle enunciated by the Master. Nor can we accept the Incarnation as the material and determinative doctrine. This was made by many Lutheran thinkers deter-

[1] *Supra*, pp. 155, 156.

minative of their position over against the Reformed, as the older article had determined their antithesis to Rome. And the later doctrine, as much more central and characteristic, tended to supersede the earlier. For one thing, it justified their sacramental theory; for another thing, justification could be more easily evolved from it than it from justification; thirdly, it involved a profounder and truer philosophy of the relations of man and God; and, fourthly, allowed stronger emphasis to fall upon the person of Christ, and through it upon His work. From the Lutherans the notion has filtered through various channels into the modern Anglican consciousness, which loves to describe Christianity as "the religion of the Incarnation,"[1] the Church as naturally of a piece with it,[2] and as continuing its work.[3] But whatever the historical place and function of the person of Christ, it is clear that the Incarnation cannot be the material or determinative principle of Christian thought or theology. For it is a derivative, or secondary and determined doctrine, not one primary, independent, determinative. In the consciousness of Christ the Father is at once primary and ultimate, the normative and necessary principle; but the filial feeling is the dependent and normated. All He does is done because of the Father and for Him. The Father sends the Son, works through Him, abides in Him, raises Him up, and glorifies Him. The Father is first and last, the cause and end of the

---

[1] "Lux Mundi," has as its sub-title, "A Series of Studies in the Religion of the Incarnation." Curiously, the Incarnation is the very thing the book does not, in any more than the most nominal sense, either discuss or construe.

[2] Gore, "The Church and the Ministry," p. 64.

[3] Mr. Lock, in "Lux Mundi," p. 367. Cf. a fine passage in Hooker which the idealism of the Reformed Theology has strongly influenced (bk. v., lvi. 7). We are in Christ ideally and eternally according to the Divine foreknowledge; but from our actual adoption into the body of His true Church, we are, "by virtue of this mystical conjunction, of Him and in Him, even as though our very flesh and bones should be made continuate with His."

Son's appearance and achievements. And so the conclusion is inevitable :—if we attempt to construct a theology which shall be faithful to the consciousness of Christ, the Fatherhood must be the determinative principle of our thought. It is the architectonic idea ; out of it the whole system must grow ; with it all elements and deductions must be in harmony : all else is body ; it alone is the informing soul.

§ II.—The Doctrine of Sin.

The correlative ideas which we have to bring into explicit relations and to explicate into the first lines of a Christian theology are those of the Fatherhood of God and the sonship of man. God is by nature Father, and man is by nature son ; and of these two the normal relation is one of communion or fellowship. But the normal is not the actual ; its realization is hindered by sin. "Sin" is a religious term, intelligible only in the realm of religious experience and thought. "Evil" is a philosophical term, and denotes every condition, circumstance, or act that in any manner or degree interferes with complete perfection or happiness of being, whether physical, metaphysical, or moral. "Vice" is an ethical term ; it is moral evil interpreted as an offence against the ideal or law given in the nature of man : it is the blot or stain left by the departure from nature. "Crime" is a legal term, denotes the open or public violation of the law which a society or state has framed for its own preservation and the protection of its members. But sin differs from these in this respect :—they may be in a system which knows no God, but without God there can be no sin. It belongs to its very essence to be, as it were, transcendental and extra-temporal. Evil, as metaphysical, belongs, whether privative or positive, to being and states of being ; vice, as ethical, belongs to actions and characters which ought to be regulated by nature, but are not ; crime, as political and legal, belongs to acts which can be publicly judged and punished ; but sin, as religious, is the evil person and vicious or criminal act viewed *sub specie æternitatis.* Evil may be collective and common; vice is personal and private, crime personal and public; but sin is at once individual and collective, a thing of nature and of will, common to a race, yet peculiar to a person. Evil may be under a system of necessity, vice in a state of nature, crime in a social or political state, but sin only in a system which knows the majesty and the reign of God. It involves, like evil, the notions of suffering and loss; like vice, the notions of disobedience and blame; like crime, the notions of revolt and wrong, culpability and penalty; but it enlarges almost to infinity all these ideas and elements, and combines them into a unity representative of man's personal and collective being under a Divine Sovereignty he has denied or forgotten. Sin has no meaning without God and His purpose concerning man. It signifies that man has missed the end for which he was made; that he is not in character and state, in idea and reality, in act and function, what he was created to be; and that he himself is the cause of this failure. But not to have God as an end is to have self as centre and law; what is from the standpoint of God disobedience, is from the experience and personality of the creature selfishness. Sin is in its positive character the substitution of self for God as the law and end of our being; in its negative character it is transgression or violation of law. We refuse to obey God's will, and instead we obey our own—*i.e.*, we make ourselves into our god, and attempt to force Him and all He has created into servants to our wills, means to our ends. There is therefore, to speak with the older theologians, something infinite in sin. An infinite act by a finite being, even though done against the Infinite, is indeed absurd; but what the phrase means is this:—sin, alike as act and state, belongs to the relations of man to God, and partakes of the immensity of these relations; with them it lies outside time, and involves issues to which, alike as regards intensity and duration, limits cannot possibly be set. God's end for man is a state which, as eternal fellowship with Himself, is an everlasting progression towards the Divine; and the act which, by the substitution of self for God, hinders this, has in it the quality of infinitude. Hence sin stands distinguished from evil, vice, and crime by all their elements appearing in it under the categories of the transcendental and the eternal.

Sin, as thus defined and conceived, is not simply a religious, but a specifically Christian notion; indeed, we may describe it, whether understood as idea or consciousness or both, as an express and peculiar creation of Christianity. No other religion knows it or has its precise equivalent. Hellenism as philosophical knew vice, and as religious knew defilement, which is a ceremonial rather than a moral idea; but its gods had too little ethical majesty, and their rule was too void of ethical character, to allow it to know anything of sin. Judaism knew crime, which was an offence against the God who had instituted the state, and uncleanness, which was an offence against the ritual of the Temple or the traditions of the schools; but there was too little of the spirit and the truth in its Deity to enable it to comprehend the awful idea of sin. Indeed, nothing so marks the Levitical system, as a whole, as its inadequate sense of sin and its consequent defective notion of sacrifice. There are approximations in Old Testament writers to the Christian idea, but only in those who have transcended the standpoint of the priest and the scribe. Brahmanism, again, knows evil, but as metaphysical rather than moral, man's being in a system of illusion, divided by ignorance from his rest in the Brahma who is the only and universal reality. Buddhism, which has of all religions the most overmastering sense of misery, has also the least sense of sin. Existence is to it a calamity, or even a kind of crime; but in the very degree that it makes misery of the essence of existence it gets rid of sin, for it transmutes evil into the victorious or regnant power from which man escapes only by escaping from the region of personal or conscious being. Islam, too, has the idea of political revolt or resistance, punished by such penalties as a political sovereign can inflict; but sin is not the essence of its hell or holiness of its heaven. Indeed, we may say, the more coarsely and cruelly a religion depicts the pains and miseries of the damned, the less does it feel the infinity of the evil within the sin ; once it feels this, it knows that no physical pictures can represent the horror and the darkness of the lost. And so even within Christendom sin is never so little feared as when hell most dominates the imagination ; it needs to be looked at as it affects God to be understood and feared. It is, as it were, the creature attempting to deny to the Creator the beatitude he was created expressly to give. If man misses his mark, so in a sense does God. He may indeed cause even evil to be His minister, but He can do it only by making manifest to the evildoer what the evil he does is. And it is in its nature so malignant that it may for ever divide God from the spirits He created that He might enjoy their society for ever. For the terms of the external must be those of the internal fellowship of God. The eternal beatitude is constituted by the communion of Father and son ; and beatitude can be to the created only as the created is son in communion with the Eternal Father. It is here, therefore, that the significance of our determinative idea becomes apparent. Sin is the reign of unfilial feeling in the heart that was made for filial love, and where this reigns the created sonship can never fulfil its end, or the creative Fatherhood be satisfied with its unrealized ideal.

§ III.—THE PERMISSION AND DIFFUSION OF SIN.

Out of the many questions which sin, as so conceived, raises, there are two which concern our notion of God : (a) Why did He permit sin? and (β) Why did He so constitute and why does He so govern man that sin has not only a personal but a collective or racial and native being?

(a) "Permit" is a term which has both a physical and an ethical sense; in its physical it has here no relevance, in its ethical it has here no right. The term has its physical sense when construed through omnipotence; the Almighty can hinder anything He wills to hinder. He cannot, indeed, do impossibilities; the possible alone is possible of accomplishment even to the Almighty. And one of the impossibilities is, having made man free, to compel him to act as if he were necessitated. To suspend the will when it inclined to sin were to prevent sin by the destruction of freedom. And sin were in that case not prevented; for the will that had meant to do evil were an evil will, and could never be restored to being without being restored to evil. Evil once intended may be vanquished by being allowed; but were it hindered by an act of annihilation, then the victory would rest with the evil which had compelled the Creator to retrace His steps. And, to carry the prevention backward another stage, if the possibility of evil had hindered the creative action of God, then He would have been, as it were, overcome by its very shadow. Into this discussion, then, omnipotence cannot enter. It did not permit sin, nor could it have prevented it save by either refusing to create or by hastening to uncreate the new created; and even then it would have been the moved, not the motive—the minister that obeyed, not the mind that commanded. But if "permit" in its physical sense is irrelevant, in its ethical it has here no place. God did not "permit" sin to be; it is in its essence the transgression of His law, and so His only attitude to it is one of opposition. It *is* because man has contradicted and resisted His will.

But why did He create a being capable of sinning? Only so could He create a being capable of obeying. The ability to do good implies the capability of doing evil; and both are contained in the idea of sonship. To be a son is to be the image of the father, no mere instrument of his will, but a repetition of himself, constituted after him in nature and faculty. The engine can neither obey nor disobey, and the creature who was without this double ability might be a machine, but could be no child. If, then, there was to be a world of created sons, it must be a world which had evil and good, sin and obedience, as possible alternatives; and the possibilities could be determined only in one way—by the action and the experiment of the new natures. Moral perfection may be attained, but cannot be created; God can make a being capable of moral action, but not a being with all the fruits of moral action garnered within him. Innocence is the attribute of the created, but holiness of the obedient. And, if we may so speak, these alternative possibilities constitute the interest of creation for God; because of them it needs Him more, appeals to Him more, calls more of the resources of His nature into exercise. It may well be that God experiences a deeper and a diviner joy in winning the love of a creature that can refuse His love, than in listening to the music of spheres that cannot choose but play. Nor are we to think of creation as completed; it is only in process. God has made man, is still making him; and His dealings with him can begin only after he is. This thing we call sin has come to be in the first act of the drama; we must see the last before we can judge what it means. But even now we can see this—through it attributes of God have become known that could not otherwise have been manifested, and the beatific vision will be all the richer and the more ecstatic that the Father it sees is one who loved too deeply to surrender the lost. In the parable the sins of the sons throw into grander relief the grace of the father, and the memory of their own evil must have touched them with a deeper admiration for his redeeming good. And the reverence of the moral universe will be in proportion to its knowledge of God; and its stability will be in the measure of its reverence and its love. Only through the possibility of sin could God have sons, and it may be that only through the actuality of sin could the sons know God.

(β) But why was the race so constituted that sin when it entered the world became collective or common as well as personal? This question refers to facts which not only theology but science recognises and seeks to explain, especially by the heredity we are all beginning so dimly to understand. Our inheritance from the past is too ancient for memory to measure; and though it has much of good, it has also its proportion of evil. And the pathetic thing is that the heir enters upon his inheritance all unconscious of its being or his own. The home into which he is born, the family in which he is nursed, the school in which he is educated, the society in which he lives, evoke and exercise his latent qualities; and he discovers that nature is older than his person, the action of collective forces prior to the operation of the will. Now, the evil, whether privative or positive, at once in the nature which incorporates our inheritance from the past and in the conditions amid which it is realized, represents what theology has termed original sin, what science knows in part as heredity, and history as the law of continuity. The principle which underlies these three things is one and the same; all attempt to express the idea that law reigns in nature and in man—that the present rises out of the past, that the forces that mould the person are older than the person they mould. But they differ here:—Science and history are empirical and real, see but the operation of laws within the limits of space and under the conditions of time, unconcerned with anything lying beyond sense and the phenomena it knows; but theology, as transcendental and ideal, looks at man through the universal and eternal, measures him in his collective as in his personal being by no less a standard than the mind of God. And from this point of view theology sees things hidden from those who move on a lower plane. Science knows no holy and profane, only a natural and a real;

history knows no eternal and ideal, only a temporal and an actual; and their judgments are expressed in the language of the laws they know. But to theology neither nature nor time is ultimate; on the contrary, it has to judge both in the light of the Divine ideal. And so it finds in nature, as embodied in man, forces that work for evil—in man, as history shows him, tendencies that create crime and wrong; and these are to it agencies or energies that contend against God, sinful and factors of sin. Theology were the blindest of all sciences if it did not see that evil was something more and mightier than the habits and acts of persons, besetting the will even before it was awake with potent beguilements. "Natura corrumpit personam" expresses a fact which science recognizes without condemning the nature, but theology so formulates that the nature may be expressly condemned.

§ IV.—SIN COMMON AND TRANSMITTED.

Now we have here two questions: (1) In what sense is the common or collective evil sin? and (2) By what law is its distribution or transmission or continued operation governed?

(1) As to the first point, we must return to distinctions already found in Paul. While the common sin underlies and precedes all individual transgressions, yet in itself it is not transgression or offence—*i.e.*, it does not involve culpability or guilt. It may even, while it stands alone, entail privation or loss, but not the penalties which follow upon personal blame. It denotes at once a privative and a potential state; as privative it is a state without merit and without demerit—*i.e.*, all the qualities proper to personal action are absent, and so there is nothing upon which final moral judgment can be based; and as potential it is a centre or seat of the energies, all still latent, stored by the past in the new organism, and waiting only the fit conditions to develop into activity. But this means that the nature does not conform to an absolute

standard; it is not ideal or normal, but has slumbering energies that may wake in actual transgressions. The defective compass will not speak truly, the watch that is wrong goes wrong, and so neither can be trusted; and we condemn not merely the single act, but the whole machine. And so God must judge natures as well as acts. The nature where there is no positive good and much potential evil has too little of the Divine in it to be accepted and approved just as it stands. It has so come through the race as to participate in the evil of the race; and this participation has its sign and seal in the sufferings and the tendencies common to us all. But while all men suffer from these defects of nature, yet for them no man is condemned; from them every one needs to be saved; but on their account alone no one will be lost. The infant, whether baptized or unbaptized, will not perish. Christ calls all little children unto Him, and says, "of such is the kingdom of heaven." And the way into His kingdom is not guarded by any sacrament which men may give or withhold. As the sin is common, the way out of it is common too; the God who judges the irresponsible nature sinful will not deal with it as if it were responsible for its sin. He can only be gracious provided He is just; and He who is Father of all will not forget His Fatherhood where it has been least disowned and where recognition is most needed.

(2) But this question can only find its solution through the discussion of the second. The law which governs the distribution and transmission of sin is one with the law which governs the distribution and transmission of righteousness. The law is one, though the operation is twofold. If men be sons of God, then mankind is a family; and where the family is a whole there the sin or the good of one is the evil or the gain of all. This constitution of the race may be represented by two great ideas—its unity and the solidarity of its constituent members. Its unity is at once real and ideal, the latter being expressed or incorporated in the former. The

great Being of Positivism was collective Humanity; but if Humanity be an organic whole, it cannot be a mere series, successive or co-ordinate, of detached phenomena or accidentally aggregated atoms, but must as an organism embody ideas, be as it were a structure built by mind. What Positivism was too unideal to express had been expressed centuries before under varied forms in the New Testament. The one Creator made all men of one blood and for one purpose—to feel after and to find Him; and so they were all His offspring, constituted, alike as regards origin, nature, and end, a unity, which, as it were, incarnated the thought of the constitutive mind. Science has followed with leaden foot and unquiet eye in the track of faith, and through biology and language and history discovered the unities which religion had found through its belief in God. But the more we conceive the race as a unity, the more are we forced to conceive the solidarity of its members—*i.e.*, all lie under the law of mutual and reciprocal responsibility. We may be unconscious of its operation, but it operates none the less. In the home the vice of the father or the virtue of the mother is a common evil or good; in the state the character of the sovereign, the genius of the statesman, the courage of the soldier, the imagination of the man of letters, the honour of the merchant, the energy of the industrious, the indigence of the indolent, the acts of the criminal, affect the common weal. There is no person so mean or so impotent as to be without effect on the whole. In universal history the villain as well as the hero contributes to the final result. And this law of solidarity finds its supreme illustrations in the sphere of religion: here creative personalities exercise their mightiest lordship, and the evil will its most disastrous influence. The names that in theology embody good and evil for the race are Adam and Christ; through the one sin came to be, through the other righteousness. They are because opposites complementary and correlative. If either was to be, both must be.

If Adam and his sin reigned unto death, then it could not but be that Christ and His righteousness would reign unto eternal life. This means that we cannot construe common or collective sin apart or by itself; it must be taken in connection with the common or collective righteousness. Original sin would not in any one of its forms be tolerable, were it regarded either as a complete or an absolute truth. Its unconditional reign over even a single individual, let alone a whole race, would be abhorrent to the justice which expresses Fatherhood. Its exists, therefore, only through its antithesis, and its very being is a symbol that God has not separated Himself from the race, that He feels its dependence and claim upon Him, that even His justice is a mode in which He works within and upon it to prepare it for His mercy. But if these two, the common sin and the common righteousness, only represent the operation of a law due to the filial constitution of the race, then two consequences follow:—First, the unconscious or irresponsible whose only sin is the common sin stand both in Christ and in Adam, and share in the good as well as in the evil. The race was constituted in the Son, stands together in Him, is His; and all its undeveloped personalties are His by right, by His death redeemed, and by His redemption reclaimed. Secondly, the conscious and the responsible determine their own relations to the sin or the righteousness. By transgression the one is developed into personal guilt; by faith the other becomes a personal possession. By the one the man belongs to the race whose head is Adam, by the other to the race whose Head is Christ. The unity of man is seen in the reign of the common law, with its two opposite effects; the principle of solidarity is seen in the action of the persons whose evil and good the law has distributed. But both were, as regards being and operation, made possible by the filial constitution of the race.

§ V.—SIN AND THE REGAL PATERNITY.

But sin, either in its personal or collective form, cannot be discussed or understood alone; and so we must look at it from a higher point of view—viz., God's action relative to it and to man. In the very degree that it affects man it must affect God. But in what sense or manner can it be said to affect Him? Certain things are from the nature of the case obvious at the very outset. Sin cannot change God's character or ends: what He was before it He is after it; what His ends were they are; and though His action may be changed, it can only express unchanged mind and purpose. Sin is in an equal degree an offence against the paternal love and the sovereign will,—against the love, for it defeats all the motives and intentions of the eternal goodness; against the will, for it contradicts all the means and ends of the eternal righteousness. But it can annihilate neither the Fatherhood nor the Sovereignty, for it cannot annul either the character or the acts through which they are; and if these remain, they must be expressed in fit and relevant action. Hence we are now concerned with the conduct or methods of the regal Paternity relative to sin and the sinner.

1. As to the Fatherhood. The God who created out of love cannot cease to love because His creatures have sinned. This love must be as immutable and universal as God[1]; and it may be said to have a twofold object—persons, and their states or characters.

(*a*) Persons as objects of love have an unchangeable worth to God. They cannot cease to be to His consciousness, and while they are they must be loved. Theologies have been written on the principle that the loss of souls is a loss to the souls and not to God; nay, divines have ventured to speak as if by such loss His glory and the beatitude of His universe could in some manner be promoted. He created heaven and earth

---

[1] *Supra,* pp. 421 ff.

by a word; by another word could He uncreate them, and by a third word call into their vacant places new sons of God, able and willing, like the old, to sing for joy on the morning of their birth. But these are only forms under which the ancient notion survives that the Almighty is the equivalent of God. It is not possible to a being who has once loved to lose and to feel as if the loss were not his, or as if it were one that a new person with the old name could easily repair. It belongs to the nature of love to allow no substitution, for it lives by virtue of its inability to surrender what it possesses. Affection may be transferred, but cannot be distributed; love is capable of distribution, but incapable of transference. Into a home a child may come, live awhile, and die; to him another may succeed, bearing the same name, recalling the vanished face; but to the mother the new is not the old, and the heart trembles while it rejoices in the possession of the living, for it remembers the dead. So loss concerns God even more than man; the loss of the lost soul is not all the soul's—it is God's as well; and where He feels loss He can never be satisfied without attempting to regain. The living sorrow is harder to bear than the dead, for death allows time to heal and distance to soften and memory to adorn with the beautiful things it will not forget; but life allows no healing process to go on, and turns the very love of the evil or the shiftless into an open sore of the heart. Yet in one respect there is a happier difference: with death hope, so far as concerns these modes of being, has died; but where life is hope is, and hope lives because love will not let it die. So the love of God as eternal and universal will not surrender its object to sin; to it the effort after recovery is necessary. To accept the loss were to cancel the love. He who created, because a Father, must even in the face of sin, because of His Fatherhood, seek to save the lost.

(β) But love regards characters and states of being as well as persons; and the purer it is as personal, the intenser its jealousy of evil. As a will of good to the person, it can be satisfied with nothing less than his happiness. In his wasted existence it can never rejoice, nor can it consent to regard as normal his evil and miserable state. But all sin is misery, for misery is but the symptom of a being which has failed to fulfil its end. If man was created for God, then to constitute himself God's enemy is to be a sinner, and to be separated from the source of all the good and all the joy of the universe is to be miserable. But if man fails of his end, God will not fail of His purpose. We may, then, conceive sin as presenting to the Divine will alternative courses,—either man must be abandoned to it and in consequence to misery, or made happy in it, or saved from it. It was not possible that God could find a reason in man for the course to be pursued. The motives must be worthy of Himself, and so could be found only within Himself, in His nature which gives the law to His will. If this, then, be our standpoint, it is evident that the misery of those He loves and will not cease to love, cannot but be abhorrent to God; and against its continuance He will contend with all His moral energies. To abandon souls He loved, even though they had abandoned Him, would be to punish man's faithlessness by ceasing to be faithful to Himself. Nor could He make man happy in sin, for here there were a twofold impossibility: first, happiness is not something that can be made—it must be evoked from within, earned that it may be enjoyed; and, secondly, His own happiness is moral, and He can create happiness only by means of a moral perfection akin to His own. What became Him, then, was to save man from sin. He so loved the world that He could do no other than will to save it. He so pitied man that to redeem him He could not spare Himself. To say "God is love" means He must be the Saviour.

2. As to the Sovereignty. The love which is the paternal attribute regards souls and their states; the righteousness which is the regal attribute regards their acts and qualities. In

other words, while the concern of love is happiness, the concern of righteousness is holiness; in the one case the emphasis falls on the sinner, in the other on the sin. Sin, then, wears a somewhat different aspect to these attributes: to love it is an outrage, because an attempt to ruin its objects; to righteousness it is an offence, because it creates disorder, introduces wrong, insult, licence, self-will, turning the act of one into the injury of all. Now, what is the only attitude righteousness can hold to sin? It can never tolerate it or allow that it has any right to any footing in the universe. The mere existence of sin is a wrong which righteousness must resist, and seek to end in the only way it can regard as right or even possible —viz., by expulsion. To expel the evil which Tertullian named the great interloper, must ever remain the aim and the effort of the eternal righteousness, or evil will become a sort of naturalized or legitimated citizen of eternity. But how is it to be expelled? There is the way of annihilation, expulsion of sin by destruction of the sinner. But this were a ruthless remedy, somewhat in the manner of a rude physician, who, in order to stay a disease, killed his patient. And if this were the method of cure, who would be the victor—God or sin? Would not the victory remain with the evil which compelled God to uncreate His own creation? There are no difficulties connected with the origin of evil at all commensurate with those connected with the ending of it in a way so unworthy of the wisdom and foresight and grace of God. The annihilation of the creature either now or at any moment even inconceivably distant, were a confession by the Creator of utter helplessness, an acknowledgment that the universe, or a part of the universe, had so broken down in His hands that He knew no way of mending it but by ending it. Then, if there is any truth in the Fatherhood, would not annihilation be even more a punishment of God than of man? The annihilated creature would indeed be gone for ever—good and evil, shame and misery, penalty and pain, would for him all be ended with his being; but it would not be so with God—out of His memory the name of the man could never perish, and it would be, as it were, the eternal symbol of a soul He had made only to find that with it He could do nothing better than destroy it. If, then, we cannot conceive destruction as the method of the Paternal Sovereign, can we conceive the way of penalty? Penalty, indeed, there must be. Fatherhood is not infinite good-nature, oblivious of faults, indulgent to the wrongdoer, tolerant of wrong. There is something more terrible in the attitude of the father to sin than of the judge to crime, for the judge sees in the crime only an offence against law, but the father feels in the sin the ruin of his son. The judge regards the criminal only as a person against whom the law is to be vindicated, but the father regards the son as a person out of whom sin is to be expelled. Hence comes in the father's case a severity to sin that does not exist in the judge's to crime. And so sin is the last thing the regal Paternity can be indulgent to: to be merciless to it is a necessity; nothing that defiles purity or threatens obedience can be spared. But this very necessity prevents penalty ever becoming merely retributive or retaliatory. God can never be reconciled to the being of sin, or be anything else than its supreme enemy. Were He at any point of space or moment of eternity to say, "Certain sinners must, in order to vindicative and exemplary punishment, remain sinners for ever," then He would, as it were, concede a recognized place and a function to sin. He would accept it as a thing that must be used, since it could not be overcome. But the righteousness can never cease from its conflict against evil till the evil ceases; and if evil never ceases, then the conflict must go on for ever.

But this argument must not be construed to mean that whether men will or will not they must be saved. Compulsory restoration is only another form of annihilation. Freedom is of the essence of man, and he must be freely saved to be saved at all. Were he saved at the expense of his freedom, he would be not so much saved as lost. For the very seat and soul of personality is will; and were the will suspended, especially in the article of its supreme choice, the personality would be destroyed; what resulted would be not a new man, but another man from him who had been before. And the original man could not be recalled into being; for were the old will, suspended that the man might be saved, restored, the old state would be restored with it. Those alone can freely stand who have been freely saved; and without freedom there can be no obedience, without obedience no beatitude. Hence the argument as little involves universal restoration as it allows partial annihilation. What it maintains is an eternal will of good, and, as a consequence, eternal possibilities of salvation. God will never be reluctant, though man may for ever refuse. But to necessitate were as little agreeable to the regal Paternity as to annihilate. The Fatherhood will ever love and ever seek to create happiness; the Sovereignty will ever govern and ever seek to expel sin and create righteousness; but neither will ever forget that the son is a free citizen, and must be freely won to submission and obedience. Sin is not to be vanquished either by the destruction or the compulsory restoration of the sinner, but by his free salvation; and should this fail of accomplishment, yet God will have been so manifested by the attempt at it, that all the universe will feel as if there had come to it a vision of love that made it taste the ecstasy and beatitude of the Divine.

CHAPTER II.

THE FATHERHOOD AND SOTERIOLOGY.

OUR argument, then, has led us to this—that God, by the ethical necessities of His nature, becomes the Saviour. This does not make His action less, but rather more gracious and free. It is altogether spontaneous; for it has all its motives, though not all its ends, within Himself. He may be said to obey the gentle constraint of love and the imperious demand of righteousness; but in this He is only obedient to His own nature. Yet while He saves by inner or moral compulsion, He will not compulsorily save. If man returns to God, it must be freely; the way of necessity were the way of death. But in order to bring man freely back, God must find some way of so entering his consciousness as to overpower and expel sin. For the only thing that can expel sin is possession of God. And this can be no mere subjective process. More than the sane mind is needed to restore the insane to sanity; he must live in a sane world, be an intelligence to it, while it is an intelligible to him, for only as the reason within is reconciled with the order without can existence become reasonable. And so the process of saving means, not only new persons, but a new order, all things within and without made new. We pass, therefore, from the ethical necessities that govern the action of God to the action itself, or the means by which His ends are to be realized.

§ I.—THE INCARNATION.

1. We have learned to think of the surrender of man the sinner as a thing impossible to God, and of his salvation as a thing possible only to God and through Him. But if God is to save man by a process which shall not destroy but restore and perfect his nature, then the process must be one which uses the nature, works upon it and through it; in other words, He must reach man through men, heal persons by persons. Yet He can do this only as the persons are His agents, as He forms, fills, guides them. Their power to heal will depend upon the degree in which they are possessed of Him, for they can communicate only what they are charged with. Now, in this region degrees of difference easily become differences of kind. The men who have had manifest commissions from God to heal man are an innumerable multitude, and they have done it as His servants, by virtue of what they transmitted rather than what they intrinsically were. But Jesus Christ stands here in an order by Himself; though He appeared as man, His action has been such as became the manifested God. His religious supremacy is a matter of personal and historical experience. From Him has come the God we know, and all of God that fills our lives. Were He removed, our personal religion would be altogether different, and our consciousness of God would lose its specific character. His manhood has this peculiar attribute—while it shows Him one with us, it is yet to us the medium through which we feel one with God. All it has effected as to our ideal of man it has accomplished through its action on our idea of God, and our consciousness of relation to Him. And this is no peculiar experience; it is common to centuries and to whole races. He is the regnant Head of the spiritual society which has been the most efficient agent in the healing of man, and from Him all its sense of divinity and all its motives to

beneficence have been derived. We may say, then, if any one has acted as a Deity to the race, He has so acted; and if anything in the life of His society was inevitable, it was that it should conceive and represent Him as the Divine yet human person it knew Him by experience to be.

The Incarnation may be said to be the counterpart in the field of history of the Godhead in the field of thought. Through the Godhead we conceive Deity as so existing and conditioned that the Incarnation is possible; through the Incarnation we conceive an historical Person as so placed that He realizes the affinities of God and man, and so constituted that He brings them into organic relations. God conceived as Godhead is a Being with life in Himself, communicable and ever in process of communication; Christ conceived as the incarnate Son is a Person so possessed of the communicable life of God as to be the inexhaustible medium of its communication to man. In His being as such a medium two things are involved—personal unity (a) with God, and (β) with man. As (a) He is in possession of the life which has to be communicated; as (β) He is a fit and capable organ for its communication. Were He cut off from God, He could be no source of the life; and what life He transmitted as a channel would be, because of His inadequacy, both quantitatively and qualitatively different from the Divine. Were He cut off from man, He would be no normal or natural, and therefore no universal, medium of distribution. The doctrine of the Incarnation is the theory which, by the union or coexistence of the two natures in His Person, explains His sufficiency for His functions as Mediator and Saviour.

This doctrine may be said to consist of four main divisions or questions.

(a) In what sense was the Person who became incarnate God, and in what sense was the incarnate Person man—or the doctrine of the natures?

(β) In what form did the nature which assumed humanity exist prior to the act of assumption, and in what form posterior to it—or the doctrine of the states?

(γ) Did the natures involve the personal unity or the duality of the incarnate Being—or the doctrine of the person?

(δ) How were the natures as they coexisted within the personal unity related—or the doctrine of the *communicatio idiomatum*?

It is impossible to discuss all these questions within our limits; all that is possible is to explain and exhibit the idea of the Incarnation in the light of our determinative principle.

2. It is as well frankly to confess that no doctrine is more beset with difficulties, all of them grave enough to appal and oppress the most audacious thinker. Yet the metaphysician, when he inquires into the genesis and conditions of knowledge, is confronted by difficulties as many and as grave. And we ought not to expect for religious truth an immunity which is granted to no other. In no region of thought or inquiry do we regard intellectual difficulty as a disproof either, objectively, of truth, or, subjectively, of truthfulness; and least of all ought we to do so in the realm of religion. Nay, in proportion as a doctrine affects and is affected by our deeper problems, we ought to feel that it has a greater value for thought, and a more vital interest for faith. Now, the Incarnation has an equal significance for religion and for speculation, though the significance of these two is not equal; and as regards both the modern mind has another attitude than the ancient. In speculation there is now a clearer insight into the affinities of the Divine and human natures, and in religion a truer perception of the relation which the Fatherhood and Sonship within God hold to the being and constitution of man and his world. The affinities of the natures may be said to be the common principle of our higher philosophies. It was implied in Des Cartes'

attempt to educe from the nature and contents of his own mind the evidence for the being of the Infinite; as also in Spinoza's endeavour to resolve the phenomena of space and time, matter and thought, into the modes of a single substance, which was at once a *res extensa* and a *res cogitans*. The same may be said of Malebranche's theory of the vision of all things in God, and Berkeley's doctrine of nature as a visual language, which was spoken by the creative and translated by the created spirit. The relation of Kant's subjective forms and categories to the interpretation of nature, and of his dialectic to the transcendental ideal, implies, in spite of his own negative criticism, the correspondence or reciprocity of the interpretative mind with the interpreted reality. Schelling's Absolute Identity and Hegel's Absolute Idealism meant the same thing[1]; and it has passed into current thought, philosophical and religious, as the doctrine of the Divine immanence. For this doctrine signifies that God does not lose but rather realizes His being by His immanence in nature and man, and man does not cease to be but rather becomes himself through the presence and operation of the immanent God. The natures are not contradictory or mutually exclusive, but their affinity or kinship expresses their reciprocal susceptibility. God is, as it were, the eternal possibility of being incarnated, man the permanent capability of incarnation.

But the meaning of this speculative tendency becomes more apparent when taken in connection with the religious, which has here only expressed the growing consciousness of our determinative idea. Affinity of nature has its highest expression in Fatherhood and Sonship. The Creator is the archetype even more than the architect of the creation; the Godhead is, as it were, the idea and model after which it is built. He who is according to His essence a society, makes a social universe; and as the inner society is constituted by the co-ordinated

[1] *Supra*, pp. 209-233.

being of Father and Son, the outer is made in the image of the inner. The ideal is, as it were, the uncreated; the real is its expression, its reflection or shadow. The ideal is eternal, belongs at once to the essence and the mind of God, where thought and being are one; but the real is temporal, has a history, is a form which expresses the essence out of which it comes. So the originated nature is like the Originating, spirit as He is Spirit, and they stand related according to the eternal ideal, which is yet an eternal real, as son and Father. The affinity of nature and the filial relation are thus but two sides of the same thing. Man as God's kin is of His kind, the differences being of degree rather than of nature. But this affinity and relation are ideal, as conceived and purposed of God—not actual, as manifested in man and realized in history. In fact and through sin God and man are ethical opposites, though in thought and in intention they are related and akin. But the very aim of the Divine action is to overcome the difference, and realize the ideal. Hence we may conclude from the affinity of the natures that incarnation appears a possible thing, while from the need of ending their ethical division it may well become necessary.

For, as we have already argued, the filial is an ethical even more than a physical relation. Sonship can be realized only where Fatherhood is known, and Fatherhood can be known only where it is seen with all its qualities in fullest exercise. The act of physical generation constitutes only a nominal or legal Paternity; duties of another and higher order must be fulfilled if a man is to be a father indeed. Nor is it enough to feed and clothe the child—the State can do that; or to educate him—the school can do that. The child must, as it were, daily live in the father's soul, be warmed by its generous heat, quickened by its larger life, moved and expanded by its wiser love. And if God's Fatherhood is to be a reality to man, he must see it as it is, know it by experience, by handling it and being handled by it. But the only way in which it can thus come to him is in the form of humanity. He must see a real son, whose knowledge of the Father is inner, and not, like his own, outer only. He must learn what the Father is from one who has lived in His bosom. Even in so high a region personal experience may illustrate a truth. One of the things time has made most obvious to me is this:—that of all the human persons that have contributed to the shaping of the character which is as destiny, the mightiest was that of an obscure man who died years before I was born. But his daughter was my mother; and the daughter so loved and revered the father, so remembered his sayings, so understood his mind, so believed the faith that ruled and guided him, that she had no higher thought for her son than to make him such a man as her father had been. And so, invisible as he was, he became the real parent of the spirit and the character of the man who now writes this book. And if God is to become the real Father of man, and man the real son of God, then all the energies and loves and ideals of the unseen Paternity must be incarnated and organized in a visible sonship, that they may become creative of a mankind which shall realize the filial ideal. It is through the one God-man that the many become men of God. The nature that is in all men akin to Deity becomes in Christ a nature in personal union with the Deity, and the *unio personalis*, which is peculiar to Him, is the basis of the *unio mystica*, which is possible to all.

3. To the positive construction of the doctrine we come, then, through the conception of the Godhead; for where its main difficulty lies, there lies also its explanation. We speak of the incarnation of God, but it were more correct to speak of the incarnation of the Word or the Son. Jesus Christ is neither God nor the Godhead incarnate, but He is the incarnate Son of God. The distinction is cardinal; the Father did not become incarnate, nor did the Holy Spirit, and so far forth as they did not we have an incarnation not of the whole Godhead, but only of the Son. And the reasons for

the distinction are fundamental. What was impossible to the Godhead as a whole may well be possible to the Second Person. For the Father could not be identified with man as the Son could. He was the ideal of the actual world; it existed in Him before it was; He was, as dependent and reflexive and receptive, the symbol of the created within the Uncreated; as the Object of eternal love and Subject of eternal thought, He was the basis of objectivity within the Godhead. And so it was but fit that He should manifest His ideal in the forms of actual being, exhibit under the conditions of space and time those relations of the eternal nature which the created natures were intended to realize. But in order to these a supreme renunciation was necessary; He had to stoop from the form of God to the form of a servant. This act is described as a *kenosis*, an emptying of Himself. Now, this is precisely the kind of term we should expect to be used if the Incarnation was a reality. It must have involved surrender, humiliation; there could be no real assumption of the nature, the form, and the status of the created Son, if those of the uncreated were in all their integrity retained. These two things, the surrender and the assumption, are equal and coincident; but it is through the former that the latter must be understood. We may express what it means by saying that the Incarnation, while it was not of the whole Godhead, only of the Son, yet concerned the Godhead as a whole. And this carries with it an important consequence :—Physical attributes are essential to God, but ethical terms and relations to the Godhead. In other words, the external attributes of God are omnipotence, omniscience, omnipresence; but the internal are truth and love. But the external are under the command of the internal; God acts as the Godhead is. The external alone might constitute a Creator, but not a Deity; the internal would make out of a Deity the Creator. Whatever, then, could be surrendered, the ethical attributes and qualities could not; but God may only seem the more Godlike if, in obedience to the ethical, He limit or restrain or veil the physical. We reverence Him the more that we think the annihilation so easy to His omnipotence is made impossible by His love. No such impossibilities would be known to an almighty devil; he would glory in destruction as much as God glories in salvation. We may say, then, that what marks the whole life of Deity is the regulation of His physical by His ethical attributes, or the limitation of God by the Godhead. But this same principle supplies us with a factor for the solution of our problem. The salvation of the sinner was a moral necessity to the Godhead; but no such necessity demanded that each of the Divine Persons should every moment exercise all the physical attributes of God. And this surrender the Son made when He emptied Himself and assumed the form of a servant, and was made in the likeness of man. The determinative Divine qualities were obeyed, and the determined limited; yet it was, as it were, the renunciation of the less in order to the realization of the more Godlike qualities. " The Word became flesh, and dwelt among us"; but we only the more "beheld His glory, glory as of the Only Begotten from the Father, full of grace and truth."[1]

So conceived, then, the Incarnation may be described as the most illustrious example of the supremacy of God's moral over His physical attributes, and of the relation they hold to the healing and the happiness of man. As such it is of all acts the act that most becomes Him, and so the one we can least conceive as accidental. And therefore, though its special form may be affected by the fact of sin, yet it were mere impertinence to imagine that but for the accident of sin, the universe would have been deprived of its most invincible evidence of grace. Luther, in his picturesque way, has said, that Lucifer, while a good angel, saw in the very countenance of God that He had from eternity determined to become a man, to assume in time the nature of men, not of angels; and hence came the

[1] John i. 14.

envy that caused his fall.[1] But those who see the prophecy fulfilled, feel that there is nothing so majestic as the condescension of God. For as Luther has also said, "seine Ehre ist seine Liebe"; and His honour is so His love that the humiliation to which His love constrained most awakens our wonder and our praise. And this exaltation through His moral attributes has not lessened our sense for His physical. These the Incarnation does not, any more than external nature, so limit as to conceal. Between them there is nothing on this point that deserves to be called radical difference. The physical universe circumscribes the ubiquity of God; the divisions of time annul for us His eternity. There is, in truth, no difficulty involved in His union with human nature that is not equally involved in His relation to material nature, which, however vast, is not so near the Infinite as man, and, however old, has not so much of eternity within it as his mind. The relation must indeed assume different forms, because the terms related are different. There can be no personal union with material nature, for it knows no personality; but with human nature, which must be personal to be, the union which does not become personal is not absolutely real. While, then, the Incarnation does no more violence to the physical attributes of God than creation does, it yet so exalts and glorifies His moral qualities and character that in its presence the voices of nature may be said to lose their music or die into silence.

4. The argument, so far as it has proceeded, has been governed by the determinative idea of God as interpreted in Christ. But as to Christ Himself as the incarnate Person little has been said, though much has been implied. The person, to be real, must be a unity, for two wills or minds were two persons. But the natures, if He is to be qualified for His work, must be distinct. Only their integrity must not be developed into antagonism or incompatibility. The union within the

[1] Opera, vii., pp. 1544-1555 (Walch).

Person is not a work of mere omnipotence, but expresses a real affinity, ethically mediated, though personally realized. And the natures in their union condition each other; because of their kinship a real and reciprocal *communicatio idiomatum* is possible. Hence by its union with the Deity the humanity is not superseded or diminished, but rather exercised, realized, and enlarged; and by its union with the humanity the Deity is not discharged or lessened, but rather actualized, personalized, made articulate. For the work designed the manhood was capable of receiving the Godhood, and the Godhood was capable of personal union with the manhood. The perfection of the humanity, while realized in time, expressed what was of eternity,—the perfection of the Godhood, not the physical attributes which belonged to the Creator, but the inner qualities, the hidden loves and energies which were, as we have said, the God of God. And so He was, in a sense, a double incarnation—of manhood and Godhood. In Him humanity was realized before God and revealed to man; in Him God was revealed to man by Godhood being realized before him. The unity of His person symbolized His work as a unity; to participate in His manhood is to become a "partaker of the Divine nature,"[1] "heirs of God, and joint-heirs with Christ."[2]

§ II.—THE ATONEMENT.

But the Incarnation had a function, and so we must ask, *Cur Deus Homo?*

1. Whatever its function might have been in a sinless world, its purpose in ours was to save the soul from personal and the race from collective sin. In attempting to represent how it was made to do this, we must be careful to maintain its true relation to God. If He is the unity of Fatherhood and Sovereignty, law is not something that can be separated from

---

[1] 2 Peter i. 4. [2] Rom. viii. 17.

Him, and conceived as a sort of independent entity, with claims enforced upon the sinner by sanctions and needing to be satisfied by penalties. The idea of law in the New Testament has very little in common with the idea of law in our juridical theologies. The Roman *lex* was not the synonym of the Greek νόμος, especially when used to translate the Hebrew *torah*. Into *lex* whole systems of jurisprudence were packed; it raised the image of the *Cæsar* who was its source, the *judex* who was its interpreter, the *procurator* who was its guardian, the *lictors* with their *fasces*, and all the *apparitores* who waited to be the agents and instruments of justice, when engaged in its noble but often hard and painful work of vindicating authority. But to a Jew who, though he used Greek, thought in Hebrew, νόμος had other and larger associations. It was primarily instruction, a method of discipline through the truth and ordinances given of God, received and revealed by prophets and priests, written in the sacred books, explained, transmitted, and enlarged in the schools, read in the synagogue, observed in the Temple, incorporated in the religion. When a Roman jurist, even though he had become a Christian Father, thought of law, it was as known in the schools where he had studied and in the courts where he had practised; all its associations were judicial, all its processes forensic, all its judgments aimed at the suppression of crime and the satisfaction of justice by penalties. But when a Jewish scholar who had become a Christian Apostle thought of law, it was as the moral and ceremonial, the social and sacerdotal system in which he had been instructed as a religion and as the peculiar revelation granted to his people. There were points indeed where the ideas touched; but these were incidental, while the points where they differed were essential. Hence if a man reads the Pauline νόμος as if it were Roman and magisterial *lex*, he will radically misread it, especially in all that concerns its relation to the death of Christ. " Christ hath redeemed us from the curse of the law "[1]; certainly, but this was the law which the Jew loved, and which was thus for ever abolished, not the universal law of God. He became "a curse for us"; certainly, but under the same law, for by it He was "hanged upon a tree." But the law that thus judged Him condemned itself; by cursing Him it became accursed. His death was not the vindication, but the condemnation of the law. And this is the characteristic attitude of the New Testament writers. The law which Christ at once fulfilled and abolished was not the law of the judge and jurist, but the law of the rabbi and the priest, the law of ceremonial and service, of works and worship, of prophecy and type. The language which describes His relation to it and its to Him cannot be used to describe His relation to the absolute law or righteousness of God. This relation we must interpret through our idea of God, not through our very mixed notions of law and justice.

But this juridical theory gives us a point from which our discussion may start :—The first step in the process of saving from sin is to execute judgment upon it, and so to do it that the judgment, though God's, shall also become, as it were, the sinner's own. There is not room for two absolute wills—one God's, another the man's; one must reign, if action and character, conduct and being, are to coalesce in beatitude. As is the nature, so is the will; the only absolutely good will is the will of the nature absolutely good. Hence the supremacy of God's will is the supremacy of good, the union of a holy Being with a happy state; while the supremacy of man's were but the tumult of an infinite multitude of colliding atoms, each charged with selfish passions and seeking to live by the destruction of its rivals. Salvation, then, can come only by sin being vanquished, by the surrender of the sinner to God, not of God to sin.

This judgment of sin is a necessity. For sin is not a fact which an act of oblivion can annihilate; facts are not capable

[1] Gal. iii. 13.

of annihilation, especially when they are evil deeds that have by recognition and confession been committed to the keeping of two memories and two consciences, one accusing, the other accused. And so forgiveness cannot make a sinner feel or be as if he had never sinned; he cannot so stand in his own eye, or believe that he shall ever so stand in the eye of God. And strangely yet justly enough, it is less easy to forget an unjudged than a judged sin. We are forced ever to remember what we have never confessed or been called to account for. We live in fear lest the slumbering justice we have hitherto eluded should awake and exact tenfold penalties for the silence added to our sin. And this is only one side of the necessity for judgment. That could not be a grave evil which the Author of all good was willing to pass lightly over. What it cost God no pain to forgive, it would cost man no pain to repeat. Hence, if man's relation to sin is to be changed, if the guilty is to be forgiven, it must be on terms that leave him in no doubt as to the nature and desert of his sin. And so if God saves man, it is certain that His method will be so to judge sin as to condemn and overcome it more completely than would have been possible by any judicial process or any system of cumulative penalties.

But in order to understand how this may be we must recall the true nature and end of His judgments : they are not merely retributory or retaliatory, penal or vindictive, in the judicial sense, but they are corrective, reclamatory, disciplinary. While they vindicate authority, they are intended to be not simply deterrent and exemplary, but reformatory and restorative. This affects the function of the Atonement; it works in the universe as the manifest and embodied judgment of God against sin, but of this judgment as chastening and regenerative rather than juridical and penal. It is designed to create in man all the effects of corrective and remedial sufferings, to do the work of restorative and reformatory penalties, only it accomplishes this in a more efficient mode than could the sufferings themselves. It burns into the soul of the sinner the sense of the evil and the shame of sin, forces him to look at it with God's eyes, to judge it with His conscience, to hate it with His hate—in a word, to change his own attitude to it for God's. And when this is the case the sinner is saved, but so saved that his salvation is the supreme victory of righteousness and sovereignty as well as of love and grace. The Atonement may therefore be described as the method by which God has so judged sin in the very home of the sinful as to achieve the salvation of the sinner.

2. In what measure, now, was the Incarnation, with the passion and death it involved, calculated to fulfil this function, or accomplish these ends? We have to remember that it is to us the externalization of what was innermost in God, the secret of the eternal manifested in time. From it, therefore, comes, first, the complete revelation of God. God as He is in Himself and to Himself stood disclosed to man; and man knew what he had forsaken and surrendered for sin. The Creator and Ruler of the universe now lived to faith as the Father, the home of all the most gracious energies and ends. Secondly, His attitude to man was revealed—His love of him, purposes concerning him, His mercy and truth. And as was His attitude to man, such was His attitude to sin. He could not love it, nay, He hated it, and it was, as it were, the sorrow in the heart of His happiness. Theology has no falser idea than that of the impassibility of God. If He is capable of sorrow, He is capable of suffering; and were He without the capacity for either, He would be without any feeling of the evil of sin or the misery of man. The very truth that came by Jesus Christ may be said to be summed up in the passibility of God. But, thirdly, to be passible is to be capable of sacrifice; and in the presence of sin the

capability could not but become the reality. To confine the idea of sacrifice to the Son is to be unjust to His representation of the Father. There is a sense in which the Patripassian theory is right ; the Father did suffer, though it was not as the Son that He suffered, but in modes distinct and different. The being of evil in the universe was to His moral nature an offence and a pain, and through His pity the misery of man became His sorrow. But this sense of man's evil and misery became the impulse to speak and to help ; and what did this mean but the disclosure of His suffering by the surrender of the Son? But this surrender, as it was the act, represented the sacrifice and the passion of the whole Godhead. Here degree and proportion are out of place ; were it not, we might say the Father suffered more in giving than the Son in being given. He who gave to duty had not the reward of Him who rejoiced to do it. Though we speak but in the limited language of our own conditions, yet, may we not ask, must not the act by which the Son emptied Himself have affected and, as it were, impoverished the Godhead ? The two things are coincident and inseparable ; here, pre-eminently, one member could not suffer without all suffering. The humiliation of the Son involved the visible passion and death, but the surrender by the Father involved the sorrow that was the invisible sacrifice.

And this is the Biblical doctrine. "God so loved the world that He gave His only-begotten Son"[1]; "He spared not His own Son, but delivered Him up for us all"[2]; "Herein is love, not that we loved God, but that He loved us, and sent His Son to be the propitiation for our sins."[3] But what do these verses mean, if not that the essence and act of sacrifice was the surrender of the Son by the Father? It was the measure alike of His love to man and the suffering He endured to save. And so we may say, without the Fatherhood there

[1] John iii. 16.   [2] Rom. viii. 32.   [3] 1 John iv. 10.

could be no Atoner and no Atonement; but with the Fatherhood the Atoner and the Atonement could not but be. By their means He, as it were, invited man to come and see sin as He saw it, and judge its evil by beholding through the eternal Son the suffering it cost the eternal Father.

We may, then, construe the sufferings and death of Christ as if they were the sacraments, or symbols and seals, of the invisible passion and sacrifice of the Godhead. That is a message they deliver now and will deliver for ever; but it is not their only message. They are a revelation of sin as well as of God; they show it as nothing else could have done. And revelation is here judgment; for sin to be discovered is to be condemned. In Christ love and righteousness were incarnate: though hated, He always loved; though wronged, He always obeyed. In Him there was nothing akin to evil, or anything that sin could call its own. But this only made two things the more manifest—the hatefulness of sin to the good, and the hate of sin for the good. In the very degree that Christ's soul was pure He was sensitive to the shame of evil; its very shadow was to Him misery; and it is a thing man cannot forget that the Sinless bears as His distinguishing name "the Man of Sorrows." But this purity of His was the very thing sin could not forgive; it saw Him only to feel, "Here is a sacrifice I must offer." And it offered Him, without shame on its own part, but with such feeling and shrinking on His that He prayed, "Father, if it be possible, let this cup pass." But it could not be allowed to pass, for it was necessary to the saving of man that the inmost essence of sin should be revealed. And so, with the sanction and by the act of those who by misrepresenting religion most represented sin, He was sacrificed. The place was the holy city; the time was the morrow of the great feast; the celebrants were the priests headed by their chief; the spectators who approved were the people gathered for the festival. And so they crucified Him, making Him an offering and a sacrifice. In

His soul He carried the sins of men, and for their sins He died.

And from His death two most dissimilar yet related results have followed—a new consciousness of God, and a new consciousness of sin. We have argued that the sense of sin is a creation of Christianity, and we may now add, the creative factor was the death of Christ. But does not this mean that it has achieved the purpose of God, and so expressed His judgment against sin that man is slowly becoming possessed by that judgment, making it his own? Beforehand the means might well have been judged unsuitable to the end; but their suitability is the very thing that the process of time is making most apparent.

3. In the Atonement so construed many principles are implied that cannot be here made explicit. But we note a few.

i. As God is its cause and the Incarnation its organ or medium, it derives from the one all its validity, from the other all its reality and adaptation to its end. What owes its being to God must be well-pleasing to Him; what is done by One who represents both God and man must be relevant to both.

ii. As the work of One so constituted and representative of God and man, it is in nature substitutionary—*i.e.*, so does the work of the penal yet corrective judgments of God as to create the very sense of sin and attitude to it that they aim at. In those who thus feel its action it has accomplished all the ends of the chastisement that at once vindicates His authority and seeks our correction. God has made us to know sin by making Him who knew no sin to be sin for us.[1]

iii. The Atonement has satisfied both the love and the righteousness of God,—His love, by being a way for the recovery and salvation of man; His righteousness, by vanquishing sin within the sinner and vindicating the authority of the eternal Will. By setting forth Christ Jesus as propitiatory, through faith in His blood, God has shown forth His right-

[1] 2 Cor. v. 21.

eousness in the remission of sins, and proved Himself "just, while the justifier of him who is of the faith of Jesus."[1]

iv. The ends of God in the Atonement are those of the regal Paternity—the creation of an obedient and a happy universe. If these ends are represented as the glory of God, it means that the one thing which can glorify a good God is the good of His creatures; if as the salvation of man, it means that the happiness of the universe is the beatitude of the Creator. The Atonement is, therefore, the creation of grace—does not create it.

v. Christ, as the Head, is the basis and symbol of a new mankind, and so of a new order or law for humanity. His obedience, as racial while personal, is the cause of a collective righteousness which cancels for the irresponsible and guiltless the evil of collective sin. But as regards the guilty and responsible, it makes the salvation of no man actual, but of all men possible, dependent on conditions that men must fulfil. The righteousness which is without works is not without faith; and so the possible salvation is realized by him who believeth. Hence, even under it, man remains free, responsible, saved by grace, but through faith.

vi. This Atonement, in the degree that it exhibits God as a Being who does not need to be appeased or moved to mercy, but who suffers unto sacrifice that He may save, must have exalted in the eyes of all created intelligences His character and majesty. And the higher the character of God appears, the greater the happiness of the universe. And so we may say, the work of Christ has modified for the better the state of all created being—nay, even of the lost.

§ III.—THE HOLY SPIRIT.

But God as here conceived is not a being whose spiritual and remedial activities can be limited to a particular time or special appearance; they must be universal and

[1] Rom. iii. 25, 26.

continuous. Occasional action is only a form of inefficiency; permanent energy is needed for effectual work. And in religion God must always remain the efficient cause, initiating all the good man ever receives. Were man here the only active or causal person, he would very soon cease to be religious. If all his prayers were addressed to an impotent abstraction or an impersonal universe which has mechanically evolved a being that can know it, but it can never know, he would soon tire of speaking into a void that could not even echo the voice of his reason. Mind feels oppressed by the infinities of space and time. When we think of the immensity in which we float, the spaces between star and star that fleet fancy grows weary in trying to traverse, or the worlds massed by distance into constellations, we feel with Kant that, like the moral law within, the starry heaven above fills us with admiration and awe. When we think of the eternity behind, which mind cannot measure because thought cannot limit, in whose presence the age of the oldest planet is only as the life of the fretful midge to the course of creation, we feel lost like one who, though he looks before and after, can discover no limit or end on which the eye can rest. But while these Infinities may awe and oppress, they cannot evoke or receive worship, or move man to religion. In it God must speak as well as man, and our appeal to Him is but the echo of His appeal to us. The atom is only a form of the Divine energy, and religion a mode of the Divine presence. God as power is immanent in nature, as spirit is immanent in man; and without the action of His immanence the Incarnation would be but an isolated intervention, marvellous as a detached miracle, but without universal or permanent influence.

Now, what does the Spirit mean to Christ? The Baptist predicted that He should " baptize in the Holy Spirit."[1] At

---
[1] Matt. iii. 11; Luke iii. 16.

the Baptism the Holy Spirit descended upon Him like a dove.[1] Full of the Holy Spirit He returns from the Baptism, and is by the Spirit led into the wilderness to be tempted.[2] In the power of the Spirit He returned into Galilee, and began His work by reading, "The Spirit of the Lord is upon Me."[3] The only consecration He ever had was the anointing of the Holy Spirit.[4] By the Spirit of God He cast out devils, and did His mighty works.[5] He was, then, so possessed of the Spirit that they may be described as co-efficient energies, or co-essential persons; neither could without the other be what He is, or accomplish what He does. For the correlation means a mutual and common necessity; Jesus without the Spirit would not have been the Anointed, the Christ, and without Christ the Spirit would be without His peculiar function and work. Hence comes the extraordinary place the Spirit occupies in the mind both of Jesus and His Apostles. He is the Comforter, the Holy Spirit, who proceedeth from the Father, but is sent by the Son, and bears witness concerning Him.[6] He is the Spirit of Truth who shall come when the Master leaves, teach all things, convict the world in respect of sin and righteousness and judgment, glorify Christ, and abide with His people for ever.[7] This Spirit God gives without measure.[8] Christ, too, breathed on His disciples and said, "Receive ye the Holy Spirit."[9] He promised that they should be baptized in the Holy Spirit; at His coming they were to receive power and they were to speak in His name and as He taught.[10] As with Christ, so with His people or Church; they live, move,

---

[1] Luke iii. 22; Matt. iii. 16.
[2] Luke iv. 1; Matt. iv. 1.
[3] Luke iv. 14, 18.
[4] Acts x. 38.
[5] Matt. xii. 28.
[6] John xv. 26.
[7] John xiv. 16, 17, 26, xvi. 7, 13, 14.
[8] John iii. 34.
[9] John xx. 22.
[10] Acts i. 5, 8; Luke xii. 12. But see on subject of this paragraph the suggestive discussion of Professor Milligan, "The Heavenly Priesthood of our Lord," Lec. iv.

and are through the Holy Spirit, yet the Spirit distilled, as it were, through the Son.

In this sense the teaching of the Master was repeated by the disciples; theirs was the dispensation and ministration of the Spirit, His the Word they preached and the invitation they gave; He sealed and sanctified their converts, and they were baptized and blessed in the name of the Father, the Son, and the Holy Spirit.[1] His work was as great and as necessary, and expressed attributes as divine, as those of the Father and Son—ubiquity, holiness, truth, infinite energy ever exercised and ever resultful. But the Fathers were slow in discovering what the Apostles had so clearly seen. In this point, as in so many others, though perhaps in this point most of all, the gap between the New Testament and the first three centuries of patristic literature is such as no theory of development can bridge. It is true that in acts and formulæ of worship, in doxologies and simple confessions of faith, the Holy Spirit took His place beside the Father and the Son; but touching His person and work confusion reigned till late in the fourth century, and did not by any means even then cease. What became evident was this—salvation, to be real, must be altogether of God, its cause a unity. And so Athanasius argued, that He who sanctifies all must be sanctified by His own nature; Basil, that He who renews could not be inferior to Him who saved; Gregory of Nyssa, that He who revealed the truth must possess the truth He revealed; Gregory of Nazianzus that the attributes ascribed to the Spirit were as divine as those of the Father or the Son. And so the mind ecclesiastical came to formulate its belief in "the Holy Spirit, the Lord and Giver of life, who proceedeth from the Father, and who with the Father and the Son together is worshipped and glorified."[2]

---

[1] 2 Cor. iii. 8, 17; Acts viii. 15, 17, 19, x. 19, 44, xi. 24, xiii. 2, 4, 9; 1 Cor. ii. 4, 5, 10, xii. 3; 2 Cor. vi. 6; Eph. iv. 30; 2 Thess. ii. 13; 1 Peter i. 2; Matt. xxviii. 19; 2 Cor. xiii. 14.   [2] "Nicæno-Const. Symbol."

In salvation, then, there is a threefold Divine causality—the Father who gives, the Son who is given, the Holy Spirit who renews and reveals. And these are so united as to be inseparable in essence and in act. The Father is the fount, the Son the medium, the Spirit the distributor of grace. The Father is known, because He is manifested in the Son; the work of the Son is a sacrifice, because He is delivered of the Father; and the Spirit is now the Spirit of the Son, and now the Spirit of God. It is the unity of the whole that constitutes the efficiency of each, yet the difference is as suggestive as the unity. While the Son enables us to understand the being and action of personality within the Godhead, the Spirit enables us to conceive its being and action without. There is an immanent presence of God in man, but it represents personal agency, not impersonal energy. The God who abides in us is a person who is of the essence of the Godhead, and is ever translating its inner qualities and life into the forms of our dependent yet related being. Our good is His creation; our truth is of His revealing. Our being is void of Divine content, save in so far as we allow Him to fill it. His function is by realizing God in man to keep man open to God and active in His service. He is, as it were, the energy of the Father and Son in the process of continuous incarnation, and He accomplishes it by so revealing truth as to communicate life and determine conduct. But continuous incarnation is progressive filiation; for the Spirit shapes the later sons, singly, after the image of the First-born, collectively, into a unity which is on the Godward side a sonship, on the manward a brotherhood. In other words, what Christ was essentially, that man through the Spirit ethically and ideally becomes; he realizes what we may term the moral essence or heart of the eternal Sonship, and is constituted a member of the family or household of God. And so we may define the work of the Spirit as twofold—concerned both with the generation and the organization of life. In connection with the first, He is the Giver of all truth and the Creator of all life. The field of His operation is co-extensive with man, its forms with his religious, moral, and intellectual activities. All His action is normal, but its degrees and its spheres vary. He inspires and creates revelation; He enlightens and quickens the souls in and for which it lives. In connection with the second, He renews and creates the Church, inhabiting the souls He has renewed and the societies they constitute. The more intensive His action grows, the holier becomes the soul and the purer the Church. Through the men He has renewed and enlightened He reaches man. By ever bearing witness concerning the Son He is ever creating the spirit of sonship.

But the notion of the Spirit's action will become clearer in the discussion of its two great spheres—Revelation and the Church.

CHAPTER III.

REVELATION AND INSPIRATION.

§ I.—RELIGION AND REVELATION.

REVELATION is necessary to the being of religion, and religion is but the symbol of the kindred natures and correlated energies of God and man. It means that each nature seeks the other, is capable of finding it, and is susceptible to its touch. Religion may be described as man's consciousness of supernatural relations, or his belief in the reciprocal activities of his own spirit and the Divine. The activity of the Divine is creative and communicative, of the human is receptive and responsive. The phenomena correspondent to the former are those of revelation; to the latter, those of faith, worship, and obedience. So inseparable are these ideas both in thought and in reality that a religion can as little exist without something representative of revelation as without faith and worship. The great religions have written revelations, but writing is not necessary to the idea. The faith of China is embodied in its classical books, of India in its Vedas, of Buddhism in its Tripitakas, of Persia in the Zend Avesta, of Islam in the Koran. But the Delphic Oracle or the Oak of Dodona was to Greece the voice of its god; the augur interpreted the divine will to Rome; the Book of the Dead revealed it to the Egyptian; the priest and the astrologer to the Babylonian. The veriest savage would neither flatter nor beat his fetish unless he thought it could communicate with him. Without, therefore, the belief in revelation, religion could not exist; indeed, so necessary is the one to the other that even a faith like Positivism, consciously constructed upon the denial of the supernatural, has to make *Le Grand Être* communicate of his wealth to the unit before the unit can either praise or worship. Of every religion, therefore, the idea of revelation is an integral part; the man who does not believe that God can speak to him will not speak to God.

The belief in revelation, then, is not a peculiar creation either of Judaism or of Christianity; it is a necessity common to all religions. And the higher the idea of God they embody, the more necessary does the belief become. For just in proportion as God is conceived to have care for man or the wish to shape his destiny, will He also be conceived as feeling the obligation to speak. And a spoken is sure to become a written word, with an authority high in the very degree that it is believed to be really God's. And to believe in a written is as rational as to believe in a spoken revelation. The two indeed have been represented as opposites. Thus it has been argued: "The word of conscience is the voice of God"; its light is His "revealing and appealing look"[1]; there His speech is imperative, proclaims an absolute law. This law is so "inseparably blended with the Holy Spirit" that conscience becomes at once "the very shrine of worship" and "seat of authority." "Natural religion is that in which man finds God; revealed religion is that in which God finds man."[2] Revelation is, therefore, "immediate, living God with living man; spirit present with spirit; knowing Him, indeed, but rather known of Him." Revealed religion "is there by the gift of God, so close to the soul, so folded in with the very centre of the personal life, that though it ever speaks it cannot be spoken of."[3] It is "an immediate, Divine knowledge," "strictly personal and individual, and must be born anew in every mind."[4] But

[1] Dr. Martineau, "Seat of Authority in Religion," p. 71.
[2] *Ibid.*, p. 302. [3] *Ibid.*, p. 305. [4] *Ibid.*, p. 307.

does this doctrine exclude, as it is meant to do, or does it render superfluous, an historical revelation, with the authority that belongs to it? Is not its logical outcome the very opposite of the one intended? Is it possible to have such an authoritative revelation in conscience without having far more? The theory is based on the notion of the correlated and co-essential activities of God and man. Religion can be as little without the action of God as without the action of man. Where his action is most unqualified and pure, religion will possess in the highest degree the character of revelation. But what God speaks to the man has more than a mere personal or local significance; it has a universal. The man who has most clearly and certainly heard God has done more than hear Him for himself; he has heard Him for the world, and the world ought to be able to hear God in the man. And may not the word which God has spoken to another become a word which God speaks directly to me, yet which I never should have heard but for the older man of finer ear and clearer soul? If, as Dr. Martineau holds, mind can resolve cosmical phenomena into the speech of the causal mind, why may not conscience find men in history who embody the eternal Will? Are there not persons who have acted, and still act, like a personalized conscience for the most cultivated peoples? And is not this one of the clear functions discharged by Jesus Christ? And if it is, what is He but an authority in religion? And if He is, are not also the men who have been most conscious of God and His law? But if He and they are authorities, must not the record of their consciousness have some value, even of an authoritative kind, for the consciences of less inspired men? Again, the lives which have been created by the Divine law, imperatively heard, must be lives of unusual worth, embodying a higher will; and if worked into a literature, that literature must possess the quality, as it were, of the permanent and abiding personalities. Then, do such men or the literature they create come into being by accident? Dr. Martineau holds that "the initiative of all higher good is with God"; but if so, then the holiest persons are those we most owe to His initiative; and the more clearly a person is the result of God's initiative, the more of God does he reveal. In other words, the more evidently a man is an organ of God for the race, the more ought we to conceive him as possessed of the functions and qualities which belong to such an organ.

§ II.—Revelation and Inspiration.

1. If, then, God ever speaks to the conscience of any man, He speaks at the same moment to all men; and His words do not by being written lose their aboriginal quality. It is true they must come to every later as they came to the first conscience, directly from God; but old words, when He speaks, become new, often with a spirit and life proportioned to their age. The idea, then, of a written revelation may be said to be logically involved in the notion of a living God. Speech is natural to spirit; and if God is by nature spirit, it will be to Him a matter of nature to reveal Himself. But if He speaks to man, it will be through men; and those who hear best will be those most possessed of God. This possession is termed "inspiration." God inspires, man reveals: inspiration is the process by which God gives; revelation is the mode or form—word, character, or institution—in which man embodies what he has received. The terms, though not equivalent, are co-extensive, the one denoting the process on its inner side, the other on its outer. According to the quantity of the inspiration will be the quality of the revelation: the fuller or larger the one, the more authoritative will be the other. But if the medium be man, the double process must be conditioned by the laws which govern human development. The message that comes to a man, he must deliver in the language he knows; as he lives at a given moment in a given place, he must so speak as to be

understood. What is unintelligible to the age that receives it will never become intelligible by mere lapse of time. But this involves the converse: the forms necessary to an earlier may in a later age, if made into the permanent substance of the revelation, be a positive hindrance to belief. Thus a scientific history of creation would have been as incomprehensible, because of sheer mental unpreparedness, to a Hebrew recently won from the desert, as the imaginative narrative he could understand would be, if taken as sober or veiled science, to the modern physicist. So, too, the "Ten Words" must have seemed a most exacting and exhaustive moral law to the still unsettled tribes of Israel, though their inadequacy is the thing that most strikes a Christian. Hence if there is to be any written revelation, flexibility must be as much the attribute of its form as permanence of its material truth.

Inspiration, then, is not concerned simply with the production of a record, nor does revelation merely denote the record so produced; but the one represents the Godward, the other the manward side of the creative process in religion. The creation of a sacred literature is not the only or even the primary function of this twofold process, but, in the temporal sense, a secondary. The essential function of inspiration is the formation of the personalities—both the minds for the thought and the thought for the minds—through whom the religion is to be realized; and the essential function of revelation is to embody in historical form—literature, character, worship, institution—what inspiration has created. The one represents the creative impulse, the other its achievement. Hence a written revelation does not simply mean a treasury of ideas, a sort of higher philosophy, or store-house of the best thoughts of the best minds. Were it only this, it would be simply a means of culture, or at most the institutes of religion according to some eclectic method. But it means a history which represents God's action in time with a view to a given result—say, the creation of fitter and happier relations between

Himself and man. This means that the action which produced the revelation only the more proceeds because of its production. Its existence is not a reason why the process of inspiration should cease, but why it should continue. For the better the terms of communion are known, the more intimate ought the communion to be; the more of God there is within the man, the more will the man be possessed of God. In other words, the conditions necessary to the creation of the Word are necessary to its permanent activity, which is only a sort of continuous creation. The inspiration of the men who read is thus as intrinsic and integral an element in the idea of revelation as the inspiration of the men who wrote. Were the Spirit that gave the Word to cease to live or act, the Word would cease to reveal. The essential idea, then, is that in revelation the living God speaks, not simply has spoken, to living man.

2. But so far the discussion has been general, concerned with the ideas and inter-relations of inspiration and revelation; it must now become more special. And here we may note, that the ideas of a universal or natural and a particular or written revelation imply rather than exclude or contradict each other. The universal is not the uniform, nor the particular the exclusive; but the one admits many modes and degrees, the other many qualities and kinds. If God were not naturally related to all men, He could not be specially related to any man; and if He has special relations to one, it means that He has both common and personal relations to all. If all truth is of God, then the truth in any religion or any philosophy is there by His action and express will. But the only efficient form of universal action is particular, and the voice must be personalized in order to be heard. And so the more strictly we conceive God to enter into history, the more natural does the idea of an historical revelation become; for to affect the whole He must speak through persons. The most highly specialized

action will, therefore, be the most universal. And this is what we have in the Christian revelation; it is a record of the redeeming activity of God culminating in the history of the Redeemer. What we term the Scriptures have no meaning and no function unless as so conceived. They may be described as the mode by which God as He is in Christ lives for the faith of the Church and before the mind of the world. They, as it were, so impersonate, immortalize, and universalize the consciousness of Christ, that it can exercise everywhere and always its creative and normative functions. This is a work they can do, and nothing else can. Tradition could not do it, for the longer tradition lives the less veracious it becomes, forgets the more the Original it professes to remember, and paints Him in the colours of other and later times. Nor can any of the bodies men call the Church, for Churches are in their thoughts the creatures of local conditions; all have mixed memories, all have fallible prides and painful prejudices, and all have had seasons of degeneration that would have ended in death had not the Master issued from the Word, where, as in a shrine, He lives in immortal youth. The Church was created by the preaching of the Word; and the Scriptures are but this Word made permanent, that it may be preservative of the Church it created. It died as oral that it might live as written; and if it had not so died, it could not now be alive. And so the Scriptures, as the impersonated consciousness of Christ, made intelligible by the background of Hebrew and the foreground of Apostolic history, remain to-day, as at first, the organ by which He speaks creatively in and to His Church, rebukes its sin, measures its progress, judges its character and achievements. But the Spirit that was necessary to the personal is the same to the impersonated consciousness. The anointing of the Holy Ghost constitutes Jesus in faith, as in history, the Christ. There is still no revelation without inspiration; and unless God be heard in the soul, He will not be found in the Word.

§ III.—THE SCRIPTURES AND CRITICISM.

But we cannot discuss the revelation and ignore the Book which records it, especially as the Book is passing through fires that are here thought to purify and are there believed to consume. It is a Book which has been made to serve many and dissimilar uses in controversy. In the sixteenth century the Catholic theologian argued against the Protestant thus: 'You reject the authority of the Church, but accept the authority of the Scriptures; yet without the Church you would never have had the Scriptures; their creation and preservation, their arrangement and canonization, the separation of the inspired from the apocryphal books—in a word, the whole process which constituted the canonical Scriptures, is the work of the Church; and surely the mind that formed is the most able to interpret.' Hence the Protestant was met with the dilemma: 'If you deny tradition and the Church, how can you prove the canonicity and the authority of the Sacred Books? If you admit tradition to be necessary to the canon, how can you deny its function in theology?' The purpose of the argument was to maintain the dependence of the Scriptures on the Church, in the Catholic sense, and so the necessity of the Church to authority in religion. In the seventeenth century the question assumed in the hands of the Catholic another form, and he argued thus: 'The Bible is not as necessary to the Church as the Church to the Bible; hence those who have the Church are so far independent of the Bible, but those who deny the Church are completely dependent on the Bible. But by a process of criticism it is possible to show its insufficiency as the sole authority and so prove that the Church is necessary and alone adequate to the maintenance of faith. Then, too, for ourselves this argument has many advantages. It is easier to live under a single authority than under co-ordinate authorities, especially when the one that survives is so ambiguous, variable, and, as it were, polyglottic, as to be capable of such diverse disguised personal interpretations as is "the Catholic creed and tradition." And, happily, the very argument that establishes our authority overturns the one poor pillar of vulgar Protestantism.' But the tool soon proved dangerously double-edged. Criticism of the Bible is less possible to a system bound by Catholic tradition than to a system independent of it—for the one thing you cannot do with tradition is to allow the critical faculty to play freely upon it ; and if to the tradition canons and decrees have been added, then the criticism that proves these inaccurate may not touch the Bible, but is fatal to the Church. The thing tradition authenticates must be accepted in the very terms of the authenticator, or tradition will be even more discredited than what it was supposed to verify. Hence the natural course of events brought a double answer to the double contention : the criticism that affected what was accepted on the Church's authority affected still more the authority of the Church, and the inquiry that learned to doubt what tradition had sanctioned grew into doubt of tradition.

On these points the Catholic has almost ceased to trouble the Protestant ; but his attitude has still its representatives, though in men of very different schools. On the one side stands the rationalist, who argues : 'Criticism has disproved the traditional view of the Scriptures; therefore they have ceased to be an authority in religion.' On the other side stands the conservative theologian, who argues: 'The traditional view must be maintained, or the authority will go.' The logic of the situation is in each case the same : 'Grant that certain conclusions which criticism affirms as to the Scriptures, are proved valid, then they cease to be the Word of God, and the only authority which remains to guide our life and determine our beliefs is the voice which speaks in conscience and reason.' The theologian who so argues makes the authority of Scripture in religion depend on questions that, whatever may be said and done, critical scholarship alone can decide, and will decide in its own way, and so decide as to be ultimately believed. And it is precisely the sort of argument that the older Protestant had to meet from the side of the older Catholic, and was able to meet victoriously in the days when his doctrine of the Scriptures had not, from the exigencies of his own internal controversies, hardened into a polemical scholasticism. As now used by the conservative theologian it is an argument of the order that seeks to preserve tradition at the expense of faith ; it is the kind of defence that loses the citadel by concentrating the forces on the weakest and most superfluous outwork. And between the rationalist and the conservative stands the neo-Catholic, who argues thus : 'True, it is becoming more and more difficult to believe in the Bible without believing in the Church. Modern criticism has made an appeal to it in the old Protestant way as the sole and sufficient authority in religion impossible ; but this need not distress us overmuch. We have the Church, and its authority is strengthened and made more necessary by the weakened supremacy of the Bible. Critical results have in them this element of pure gain—they force us to feel the need and the sufficiency of the Catholic creed and tradition.'

What has created the question in its present form is the rise and growth of what is termed the higher criticism as applied to the Sacred Scriptures. What we have, then, is the same major premiss, though with a changed minor, used to justify three different conclusions. The common premiss is: Criticism has affected the authority of the Bible in matters of religion, —*therefore*, says the rationalist, since criticism is true, the authority is at end ; *therefore*, says the conservative, since the authority must be maintained, criticism must be resisted and its decisions rejected ; *therefore*, says the neo-Catholic, since, keeping as regards the Bible an open mind, we must confess the difficulties created by criticism, let us rest in the authority of the Church. Now, what reply would the older Protestantism have made to all three positions, for with all three it was perfectly familiar? It would have begun—for it had Humanism in its blood, and knew too well its obligations to thought and inquiry—with a plea for the use of learning in religion, somewhat thus :—

'This higher criticism is but a name for scientific scholarship scientifically used. Grant such scholarship legitimate, and the legitimacy of its use to all fit subjects must also be granted. Nobody denies, nobody even doubts, the legitimacy of its application to classical or ethnic literature, the necessity or the excellence of the work it has done, or, where the material allowed of it, the accuracy of the results it has achieved. Without it there would hardly be such a thing as sequence or order in the older Hindu literature, or any knowledge touching the authorship or authenticity of certain Platonic dialogues or Aristotelian treatises. To grant that many of its conclusions are arbitrary, provisional, or problematical, is simply to say that it is a human science, created by men, worked by men, yet growing ever more perfect with their mastery of their material. Now, the Scriptures either are or are not fit subjects for scholarship. If they are not, then all sacred scholarship has been and is a mistake, and they are a body of literature possessed of the inglorious distinction of being incapable of being understood. If they are, then the more scientific the scholarship the greater its use in the field of Scripture, and the more it is reverently exercised on a literature that can claim to be the pre-eminent sacred literature of the world, the more will that literature be honoured.

'But if scientific scholarship be legitimate, the higher criticism cannot be forbidden—the two have simply moved *pari passu*. Hebrew language became another thing in the hands of Gesenius from what it had been in those of Parkhurst; the genius of Ewald made it a still more living and mobile and significant thing. The discoveries in Egypt and Mesopotamia have made forgotten empires and lost literatures rise out of their graves to elucidate the contemporary Hebrew history and literature. More intimate knowledge of Oriental man and nature, due to personal acquaintance with them, has qualified scholars the better to read and understand the Semitic mind. A more accurate knowledge of ancient versions, combined with a more scientific archæology and a clearer insight into the intellectual tendencies and religious methods of the old world, especially in their relation to literary activity and compilation, has enabled the student to apply new and more certain canons to all that concerned the formation of books and texts. The growth of skilled interpretation, exercised and illustrated in many fields, has accustomed men to the study of literature and history together, showing how the literature lived through the people and the people were affected by the literature; and so has trained men to read with larger eyes the books and peoples of the past. With so many new elements entering into sacred scholarship, it is impossible that traditional views and traditional canons should remain unaffected. If ever anything was inevitable through the progress of science, it was the birth of the higher criticism; and once it existed it was no less a necessity that it should have a mind and reach conclusions of its own. Where scholarship has the right to enter, it has the right to stay; and it cannot stay in idleness. What it does and decides may be wrong, but the wrong must be proved by other and better scholarship. In other words, once analysis of the objects or material of faith has been allowed, a process has been commenced by reason that only reason can conclude. And this process the higher criticism did not begin, but those who allowed that scholarship had a function in the interpretation of Holy Writ.'

But once the older Protestantism had affirmed that matters of scholarship must be dealt with by scholars and in the methods of the schools, undeterred by alarms on the right hand or the left, it would have proceeded to the more material questions, and addressed itself first to the rationalist within the Catholic thus: 'What you call the Church is not the Church to me, unless a part can be put for the whole, and a part not all of which belongs to the whole. But even granting your notion of the Church, you make a claim for it which cannot be allowed, for it cannot be made good. So far as concerns the Bible the real starting-point of the discussion is not the abstract idea of canonicity, or the process by which the canon was formed, but the concrete and historical Christ, His relation to the Scriptures and theirs to Him. He created the Scriptures as He created the Church; both are forms of His activity, valid as they derive their being from Him, authentic and authoritative only as possessed of Him and authorized by Him. These two, as derivative, can be in harmony with each other only as they are in harmony with Him, and the Scripture whose authority we obey is not the Book the Catholic Church sanctioned, but the Word which Christ spoke and by which He created the Church. Without the Scriptures we could never stand in the presence of the Founder, know His mind, or see how He laid the foundation of the society that was to be. With them the humblest Christian, as much as the stateliest Church, can reach the Presence, and know and believe. The Scriptures, then, have the prior existence, owe everything to the Master, and do everything for the Church. Then, if the Bible is made to depend on the Church, is it not evident that it is the Bible conceived as a book, and not as a revelation? For these two things are most dissimilar, and indeed opposite. The authority that belongs to the Bible belongs to it not as book, but as revelation; what the canonizing process created was not a revelation, but a book. In other words, the process that created the revelation was prior and causal and material, but the process that created the canon later and sequent and formal. The revelation did not come to be because of the canon; the canon came to be because of the revelation.'

§ IV.—The Bible as the Authority in Religion.

Here our first question is, What gives its authority to the Bible? Does this authority belong to the Book as constituted, or to the constituents of the Book? The Bible, on any theory, did not come into being as it is; it came in many parts, through many persons, out of many places and times. Now, what relation has the canonizing or codifying or constitutive process which made it a whole, and the whole we know, to the religious character and authority of the Book as such, or the several books it contains? Had a book, or even a fragment of a book, no religious authority or function till incorporated and superscribed? If this was so, then the canonizing was an authorizing process; it created the inspiration and the authority of what it sanctioned. If this was not so, then how can the tradition which canonized have affected the intrinsic merits or essential character of the book? and how can the criticism which seeks simply to restore the books to their original form either annul or lessen or even discredit their inspiration and authority? Canonization is like codification; the formation of a code implies the existence of the laws. A law does not become authoritative by being codified; it is codified because it is authoritative. So a book does not become inspired by being authenticated, canonized, or even assigned to an author. Hebrews, for example, was long outside the canon: got into a local before it was received into the catholic canon; was denied to Paul, then attributed to Paul, and is all but unanimously denied to him again. But Hebrews was precisely as much inspired, and possessed of exactly as much authority, though it might be an authority much less recognized, before as after its incorporation in the canon, when it was denied as when it was attributed to Paul. It is not to their co-ordination and codification that the books owe their authority, but to their essential character and contents

The tradition or the polemic that obscures these hides the authority; the criticism that makes them most manifest reveals it. To attempt to make a multitude of books, into a single uniform authority, when almost all the books are, from the nature of the case, of different values, is the surest way to discredit even the most authoritative.

But, secondly, if the canonizing process be so inviolable that one cannot touch it or its conclusions without discrediting the Scriptures or reducing the authority of the Word of God, then let us see who were the canonizing agents, and with what functions and powers we must invest them. These agents, and they alone, had power to constitute the Word of God; what existed before their action was a potential, not an actual, revelation; they translated its potentiality into actuality. On this theory, the real organ of God was not the prophet or apostle who spoke and wrote, but the body who indorsed and authorized their writings. And what was this body? One hard to define; indeed, incapable of definition. The Catholic speaks of it as the Church; but history knows that the Church which is called Catholic was only a late factor in the process of canonization. That process has many factors, some much older than the Church. It was pursued for the Old Testament in rabbinical or Talmudical schools, following the traditions now of the Temple, now of the synagogue, now of certain classes and teachers; for the New Testament by Fathers and heretics, councils and custom, local tradition and exegetical schools. If we would secure the inviolable veracity and authority of the result, we are bound in logic to affirm the infallibility not only of the process, but of all its factors. Were they capable of erring, we could have no sufficient guarantee of the inerrancy of the result. But this becomes an affirmation not simply of the infallibility of the Bible, but of all the schools and agencies that created it as a text and as a book; above all, of those most mixed and heterogeneous Jewish bodies whose action antedated and normated the action of the Catholic Church. Apart from the infallibility of the creating bodies, the infallibility of the created results cannot be maintained.

We come back, then, to the position that authority belongs to the Bible, not as a book, but as a revelation; and it is a revelation, not because it has been canonized, but because it contains the history of the Redeemer and our redemption. Critical questions lie beyond the scope of this book; but it is strictly germane to its theological purpose to say :—Criticism has, by bringing the sacred books into relation with sacred history, done something to restore them to their real and living significance. The negative critic may assail the books that he may the better assail the higher and more Divine elements in the history; but the conservative critic who identifies the veracity of a late and formal tradition with the revelation, tends to lose both the inspiration and the history that are in the book. He may turn the record of God's redeeming activity in the world into a body of evidences, or a repository of proof-texts, but only the more will he fail to see how revelation lives in and through and with the people of God. Criticism has, by binding the book and the people together, and then connecting both with the providential order of the world, given us back the idea of the God who lives in history through His people, and a people who live for Him through His Word. The divorce of God and His people, who must be in each other in order to the continued being of revelation by a continuous process of inspiration, has been a calamitous thing for theology and the Church, especially in their relation to the Bible. The Church has lost the sense of its own continuity and unity, and its dependence for both on the continued activity within it of the God who speaks by His Spirit that He may live in the Word.

§ V.—Whether a Constructive Doctrine be Possible.

We are now in a position to define the positive principles necessary to a constructive theory of the Christian revelation.

i. Its theological basis is the regal Paternity. The God who loves man will not cease to speak to him; revelation, in its widest sense, is the process by which He communicates truth in order to the creation of life and the communion of spirit. But the supreme act of revelation was the Incarnation, or the manifestation of the Fatherhood through the sacrifice of the Father and the self-denial or humiliation or *kenosis* of the Son. This act involved the being of the Son under conditions of humanity, but no less the history that should translate His existence under these local and temporal conditions into a universal and permanent being. We know what He is for ever by knowing what He was then, and to know Him is to know God.

ii. In order to the universality and permanence of this revelation a literature is necessary; it can live only as it is written. But the conditions necessary to the Person being a revelation remain needful to the literature. The completion of the record—*i.e.*, the history that redeems—is not the completion or cessation of the revealing action, but rather the condition of its continuance. The written Word is a medium through which the living God and the living soul feel after and find each other; but in order to this the word must be divorced neither from God nor the soul.

iii. Hence the Bible, to be a revelation, must not only be bound through its books to a completed past, but through the Spirit of God to a living present. Revelation is thus as to its accidents a literary question, but as to its essence a spiritual experience; it denotes a living process, not simply a finished product or completed result. The Word of God is a large term; it does not denote a closed book, but a living spirit—not something that is dead, a letter that can be printed in black on white, a book which compositors have set up and binders have bound and educated people can read. It is living; it has no being without the Spirit of God; were that Spirit to be withdrawn, the Scriptures would cease to exist; where they were, a literature would remain, but not the Word of the living God. The continuance of the Spirit, then, is necessary to the being of the Word, and His continuance is the source and secret of its authority. Christ is of all historical forces and factors of faith and obedience infinitely the greatest, yet He lives because the Spirit lives to speak of Him and show Him unto men. Unless, then, the Spirit that gave the Word inspire the spirits that hear and receive it, it can be no inspired Word. Inspiration belongs to it not as the organized or authorized literature which we call the Bible, but by virtue of its being at once the creation of the Spirit and the condition and form of His continued activity. This was what the Reformers meant by the *testimonium Spiritus sancti internum*, and it was this that made them so independent of the polemic of Rome and the criticial denials to which it attempted to drive them.

iv. But the Spirit can continue and the Word can live only provided each has a medium in and through which to work. The medium for each is the Church, the region or society of holy souls, in which holiness is created and propagated. The Church is a large term; it does not denote Churches; polity is not of its essence, saints and souls are. The priest and the presbyter, the bishop and the preacher, are of the accidents of the Churches, not of the essence of the Church; the sainted father or mother, the holy home, the godly man, the living Spirit, are of the essence of the Church, not of the accidents of the Churches. And it is through what is of the essence of the Church that the authority of God is manifested and His truth apprehended. It is holiness that creates holiness, God in the priest or preacher or parent that creates godliness and obedience in the soul.

v. But the Word which thus lives through the Spirit in the Church has as its function to bring the truth of God to man. In order to this it must convince the Reason, which, though once a proud heatheness, has now a redeemed being. The reason in whose name Martineau criticizes revelation, and the conscience in which he seats authority, are not fresh creations; centuries of nurture are in them; much of what he finds there are inherited riches, wealth derived from remembered and forgotten ancestors to whom the Scriptures were a living authority. He may be content with his inheritance, but what his reason and conscience are, they are by virtue of what he has received, not simply by virtue of what he is and has attempted. This means that reason is now so penetrated with Christian elements that a man even in reasoning against historical revelation cannot purge himself from what he owes to it; and it means more—that he has but to be faithful to his reason to be led beyond it to the source of the older formative influences. Certainly, though a man by reason may reject revelation, he can never without reason either know or accept it. And it is to reason that the living truth makes its ceaseless appeal.

Now, all these elements, concordant and concurrent in action, are necessary to the being of a living revelation, and its authority in religion. Without the living and incorporated unity, realized in and through the Holy Spirit, of a satisfied reason, an inspired society, and a living God seeking the living soul, the written revelation will not reveal. And without these there can be no reign of authority in religion, while with these authority cannot but reign. What is needed, therefore, to a true doctrine of revelation is the restoration of the organic union, in the Holy Spirit, of God, the Reason, the Church, and the Scriptures. Without any one of these the very conditions that make it possible are absent. Without God the Church has no Head and no end, the Word no truth and no function, the Reason no goal to reach and no object to revere; without the Church the Word has no medium to live in; without the Word the Church has no truth to live by; without the Reason the Church has no soul to form, and the Word no subject to address; and without the Spirit no one of them has any capability of being either real or religious. If the reason alone be emphasized, we have rationalism; if the Church, as organized and hierarchical, we have Catholicism, Roman or Anglican; if the Word, as written and a record, we have Scholastic Protestantism; but in none of them have we any doctrine of revelation which makes the authority of God in the sphere of religion living and spiritual.

B.—*GOD AS INTERPRETED BY CHRIST THE DETERMINATIVE PRINCIPLE IN THE CHURCH.*

CHAPTER I.

THE DOCTRINE OF THE CHURCH IN THE NEW TESTAMENT.

§ I.—THE CONCEPTIONS OF GOD AND THE CHURCH.

IN the discussion which has just been concluded the term "Church" has been freely used, and even provisionally defined; but it is too essential to the mind and religion of Christ to receive only incidental mention. In its most general sense it may be described as the society He instituted, and constituted out of those who through faith in Him were elect unto the life and fellowship of God. But what this very general idea means can only become evident when we have discussed certain much more specific questions—such as, What were the laws of this society? How was it to be organized, administered, augmented, and maintained?

Now, in order to bring this question into relation with those already discussed, we must determine the relation in which the three great ideas of God, religion, and the Church stand related to each other both in themselves and in the mind of Christ. A religion always is as its God is, and a society is as its God and its religion are. In other words, the qualities of a deity are invariably reflected in the faith and conduct, the polity and worship of his people. Because of this indissoluble relation the terms must be interpreted together—the society through the religion, the religion through God. Taking these, then, as constituting a living unity, we may say, Jesus Christ was the Creator of three things which were yet one—a Monotheism, a religion, and a society, which were all at once ethical and universal. Monotheism, in the strict and proper sense of the term, did not exist before Him. Certain of the prophets of Israel had been Monotheists, but Judaism was not a Monotheism. For a religion that is so bound up with a tribe and its polity as to be incapable of universal realization, does not really know God as absolutely supreme. The limitations of the polity which is His sole organ, and of the single temple which is His exclusive home, are directly imposed upon God. Their particularism contradicts and cancels His universalism. And this was what happened in the Jews' religion. It made, according to one interpretation, the priesthood and the Temple, according to another, Moses and the law, necessary to the very being of the religion. In order to be possessed of God men had to become Jews, for they were the appointed channels of "His covenanted mercies." Hence the only way by which God could become universal was by man being completely Judaized. But while this may be termed Henotheism—which may be most accurately defined in the terms of Paul, "God is the God of the Jews only," *i.e.*, the Deity which is one, is Deity only for the tribe,—yet it is in no proper sense Monotheism—which means that alike in idea and reality God is the God of all men, open and accessible to all. Moreover, the Deity who is reduced to the proportions of the polity which incorporates Him, is a Deity who suffers more in character than in power, for He is conceived as One who (a) is the Head of a tribe, whose enmities, jealousies, pride and even barbarities, His authority is made to sanction, and who (β) has consented to let His covenant and His mercies be translated out of the terms of His own infinitude into those of a tribal finitude.

We may say, then, that, so far as realized religions were concerned, we had before Christ Polytheisms, Pantheisms, Henotheisms, but no Monotheism. By one and the same act He created the conception of one God, one religion, and one society; but the first would have been inefficient and incomplete if it had not been explicated in the second and incorporated in the third. The religion explicated the God, for it was ethical in nature as He was in character; the society incorporated His ideal, for it was universal as God was one, and filial as He was Father. What marks antiquity is the pride of race made invincible by the pride of racial religion; what marks the faith of Christ is that the ideas of God and man are so bound together by the concrete realities of religion and the Church that they all struggle towards the same end, a relation of sonship to God that shall be expressed and realized in the brotherhood of man.

§ II.—CHRIST AND THE IDEA OF THE CHURCH.

Now, our first question is, How did Christ conceive and describe His society? And here we note as most characteristic that His familiar phrase was not "the Church," but "the kingdom of heaven" or "of God," or simply "My kingdom." The mere figures are significant: the term "kingdom" is used in the Gospels to denote His society 112 times, and almost always by Himself; but "Church" only twice. Now, the names are either synonymous or they are not. If they are synonymous, it must be possible to translate the Church into the terms of the kingdom, and the kingdom into the terms of the Church. If they are not, then the kingdom, as Christ's most used, most emphasized, and most descriptive name for His society, must contain His determinative idea—*i.e.*, the Church must be construed through the kingdom, not the kingdom through the Church. If the first position be chosen, then the neo-Catholics who seem almost with one consent to have forgotten the kingdom, have failed to interpret the Church; if the second, then there is behind and beneath the Church another notion, as it were, the aboriginal ideal of the Christian society, to which they have given no adequate recognition, and for which they have found no fit place. In the one case, their idea of the Church is not adequate; in the other, their Church is not the ultimate normal polity or social ideal of Jesus.

The idea of the kingdom, then, is primary. He comes to found or create it. His instrument is preaching or teaching[1]; His message is the gospel of the kingdom.[2] He is the Sower who casts the seed, which is the Word, into the hearts of men.[3] He defines it by various terms; it is "of heaven"[4] in contradistinction to the "kingdoms of the world"—*i.e.*, it has none of the violence, the policies, the evils of the earth; it is "of God"[5] in distinction from "the kingdom of Satan"—*i.e.*, it is the realm of healing, harmony, love, and beneficence. It is a kingdom of the truth[6]—*i.e.*, He is a King by virtue of His very being, and He bears witness to the truth, while His citizens are the men who, being of the truth, hear His voice. It is present[7]; men may enter it,[8] are even within it[9]; the terms of entrance are obedience to the Word,[10] or the child-like spirit.[11] It comes without observation,[12] spreads quietly like leaven,[13] grows like seed.[14] It is ethical in character; to seek it is to seek the righteousness of God,[15] to pray for its coming is to ask

---

[1] Matt. iv. 17, 23.
[2] Matt. ix. 35; Mark i. 14; Luke viii. 1.
[3] Matt. xiii. 3, 19, 23; cf. xxiv. 7, and John xviii. 36.
[4] Matt. v. 19, xviii. 4, xix. 12.
[5] Matt. xii. 28, cf. 26; Luke xi. 20, cf. 17, 18.
[6] John xviii. 37.
[7] Luke xvii. 21; Matt. v. 3, xii. 28; Mark x. 14.
[8] Matt. xxi. 31.
[9] Matt. xi. 11; Luke vii. 28.
[10] Matt. xii. 19, 52.
[11] Matt. xxiii. 3, xix. 14.
[12] Luke xvii. 20.
[13] Matt. xiii. 33.
[14] Matt. xiii. 31, 32.
[15] Matt. vi. 33.

that the will of God may be done on earth as in heaven.[1] The men it honours and rewards are the poor in spirit, the persecuted for righteousness' sake, those who do the will of God, confess Christ before men, cultivate His spirit, live His life of ministry and grace.[2] The signs of the kingdom are all spiritual and ethical, relate to gracious helpfulness and service, never to officers or acts of ceremonial.[3] It is universal, open to all without respect to place or race.[4]

Now, it is remarkable that in the language of Christ as to the kingdom the emphasis falls, not upon the officials, if officials there be, or on Sacramental acts, if such acts there be, but upon the people, upon persons, their personal qualities, conduct, character, their state and living before God, their behaviour and ministry among men. He, indeed, calls disciples and commissions apostles, but He deals with them as men who must be of a given spirit if they would enter the kingdom; their eminence in it depends, not on office, but on spiritual qualities; and their rewards, not on dignities possessed, but on range and kind of service—none being sacerdotal, all spiritual and human.

And this is made more significant by two things—His example and His instructions. He is their type; they are to be as He is and has been—One who heals, helps, saves, a Minister to all the needy.[5] He is a Teacher, a Preacher, whose word has power. He makes no sacerdotal claim, does no sacerdotal act. His ministry is more in Galilee than in Judæa, more in the synagogue and the home than in the Temple; He is the Rabbi, but never to any man, least of all to Himself, is He the Priest.[6] If the ministry is to be received from Him, and He is to remain the ideal which all who enter it ought to seek to realize, then it must be a ministry that neither renders, nor cultivates, nor practises

---

[1] Matt. vi. 10.
[2] Matt. v. 3, 10, vii. 21, xxv. 1, 34.
[3] Matt. xi. 2-12; Luke iv. 18, 19.
[4] Matt. viii. 11
[5] Matt. xviii. 1-4, xxv. 34-40.
[6] *Supra*, p. 49.

sacerdotal sanctities, but is inspired by the enthusiasm for service, by the love of man, by fear of evil, by the passion to heal and to save, by the gentle hand, the generous heart, the gracious presence, the tongue eloquent to persuade the wicked to become the good. And as was His example, such were His instructions.[1] He sent His disciples out to preach, to heal, to live as He lived, to suffer as He suffered, to seek His ends, to surrender, as He surrendered, all to God; to be prophets, as He was a prophet; to represent Him, as He represented God. Yet nowhere is there a phrase or term that so much as hints at any sacerdotal office, or act, or any official accessories. The only text that may seem to touch on peculiar official functions or powers is the saying to Peter: "I will give unto thee the keys of the kingdom of heaven."[2] But the verse must be read in its connection. Peter had made his confession, "Thou art the Christ, the Son of the living God"; on this rock, this truth confessed, His Church was to be built; and the confessor, the man who stood by this truth, preached it, obeyed it, was, as such, to have the keys. It was not an absolute promise to an official, made to a man who holds an office simply because of the office he holds. Nor is it a promise to his successors, for of succession or successors there is no word; but only to a person who has made a confession, because of the confession he has made. And this is made apparent by the next paragraph, where Peter, because he rebukes Jesus for prophesying of His death, receives the rebuke: "Get thee behind me, Satan!"[3] Each saying is appropriate to the moment, neither is absolute, nor significant of a permanent character, or inalienable office, or indefeasible function, but is through and through conditional, and relevant to the context. Peter, so far forth as he would dissuade Christ from His supreme act of sacrifice, is Satan, an enemy and tempter; so far forth as he confesses the highest truth as to Christ, has committed to him by Christ the

[1] Matt. x. 5 ff.   [2] Matt. xvi. 19.   [3] Matt. xvi. 21-23.

"keys of the kingdom." Both must be conditional, or both absolute; but it were hardly reasonable to conceive Peter as through all time filling the incompatible offices of Satan and the Keeper of the keys. And so this instance but emphasizes the truth. Here is a kingdom without any political framework, without any machinery of chartered officials, or spheres of "covenanted mercies," or "recognized channels," or "authorized instruments of grace," but composed of holy men, distinguished by their love and ministry, extended by the preaching of the Word, and the persuasive influence of spiritual character. It represents a unity which no type of polity can create or express, and which varied and even dissimilar polities need not break up nor dissolve. It is visible, yet invisible; all its springs, motives, ends, the souls in which it lives, the God who reigns through the conscience and the conscience in which God reigns, are all unseen; but all its evidences and fruits, the evils it cures, the good it does, the beneficences it works, are seen. Paul defined it through its distinctive elements once for all: "The kingdom of God is not meat and drink, but righteousness and peace and joy in the Holy Ghost."[1] If we seek its nearest analogy, we shall find it in the visible invisible Church of the Reformers; if we seek its deepest contrast, where is this likelier to be found than in the canonized offices of bodies sacerdotal and ecclesiastical?

§ III.—The Apostolic Idea of the Church.

We come now to the more familiar and distinctively Apostolic name for the Society of Christ—the Church. It occurs in the Acts and the Epistles, including the Apocalypse, exactly the same number of times as kingdom in the Gospels, 112; while kingdom appears in only 29 cases. This seems to indicate either a change of idea or a change of term due to a change of soil. But the latter could not happen without the

[1] Rom. xiv. 17.

former also happening in some degree. However, our first concern is with its meaning, which will also help us to see the reason of its later extensive use. In the LXX. ἐκκλησία had translated the Hebrew *Kahal*, the congregation or assembly of the people; in Greek it was the assembly of the enfranchized and qualified citizens met to transact the affairs of the city or state. Into the New Testament usage both Hebrew and Greek elements entered, but, owing to associations and experience, the Greek were much more potent than the Hebrew. It has a double application—a local or particular, and an illocal or universal; but in both cases the emphasis falls on the community—the people—the constituents, as it were, of the society, rather than the constituted agencies. The local use admits of the plural, but the illocal of the singular only[1]; and in our interpretation of the term it will be easiest to proceed from the concrete and definite to the larger and more comprehensive sense.

i. The local ἐκκλησίαι were essentially societies of the enfranchized or saved. Paul addressed his Epistles, so far as they were not directly personal, to the collective body or Church, which is described, now as "all the beloved of God," now as "those sanctified in Christ Jesus," now as "saints," or as "called saints," and again as "the faithful brethren."[2] The ministers are only once specified,[3] and not as intermediaries or a necessity to the being of the Church. The very purpose of his great Epistles is to instruct or persuade free and autonomous societies. Each body is a unit, but its unity is not secured by any office; it is rather because it is a body

[1] The local usage is very instructive. In cities we have the singular, as the Church in Jerusalem, Acts ii. 47, v. 11, viii. 1; Ephesus, Acts xx. 17; Cæsarea, Acts xviii. 22; Corinth, 1 Cor. i. 2, 2 Cor. i. 1: but in districts we have, as a rule, the plural, as the Churches of Syria and Cilicia, Acts xv. 41; of Galatia, 1 Cor. xvi. 1, Gal. i. 2; of Judæa, Gal. i. 22; of Asia, 1 Cor. xvi. 19; of Macedonia, 2 Cor. viii. 1. In Acts ix. 31 we have an exceptional usage, which is the more interesting because of its difference from the Pauline: cf. Gal. i. 22.

[2] Rom. i. 7; 1 Cor. i. 2   2 Cor. i. 1   Eph. i. 1; Col. i. 1.   [3] Phil. i. 1

that it has many members with varied ministries.[1] The lists of these are significant; they represent preaching, teaching, and various beneficences, but nothing sacerdotal, no sanctity peculiar to the office. The argument in First Corinthians is specially striking. God has set in His Church apostles, prophets, teachers, miracles, gifts; but there is something more excellent than these, without which these are but vacant things—the love that never faileth. Each Church was a brotherhood, for all were sons of God,[2] yet each was a legislative and judicial body. The judgment of a majority was efficient to punish,[3] and "a spirit of meekness" was held necessary to true discipline.[4] In an aggravated case Paul seeks to have his judgment executed, not independently of the Church, but through it.[5] Commendatory epistles were given by the Church[6]; charities and gifts were its common act.[7] If the Church had a representative, it was by election, χειροτονηθεὶς ὑπὸ τῶν ἐκκλησιῶν.[8] And in these respects the Church is in Acts as it is in the Pauline Epistles. The election of Matthias to the place of Judas was by the brethren.[9] The seven deacons were chosen by the whole multitude.[10] It was the Church in Jerusalem which sent forth Barnabas as far as Antioch.[11] It was before the same Church collectively (πᾶν τὸ πλῆθος) that Barnabas and Paul declared what God had done through them, and it was "the Apostles and Elders, with the whole Church" (σὺν ὅλῃ τῇ ἐκκλησίᾳ) which selected delegates to bear their message to Antioch.[12] The Church was thus "the multitude of those who believed," or "all who believed," or "the multitude of disciples,"[13] constituting its officers, not constituted by them. Power, authority, was in

---

[1] Rom. xii. 4-8; 1 Cor. xii. 12-28.
[2] Gal. iii. 26-28.
[3] 2 Cor. ii. 6.
[4] Gal. vi. 1.
[5] 1 Cor. v. 3-7.
[6] 2 Cor. iii. 1.
[7] Phil. iv. 15-20; 2 Cor. viii. 1-8, ix. 1, 6-14.
[8] 2 Cor. viii. 19.
[9] Acts i. 15-26.
[10] Acts vi. 5.
[11] Acts xi. 22.
[12] Acts xv. 12, 22.
[13] Acts ii. 44, iv. 32, vi. 2, xix. 18.

the society, not in its ministers. And here we may understand one of the two cases where Jesus speaks of the Church.[1] The address is to the disciples on offences between brethren. First, He says, the sufferer is to reprove the sinner alone; if the sinner will not listen, two witnesses are to be taken; if he still refuses to hear, the Church is to be told; if he refuse to hear the Church, he is to be treated as a "heathen man and a publican." Now, Church is here used in its strict local sense; it is a single society, and authority is said to reside in it, not in any office or officers. And it is of the Church in this sense, not of the Apostles as a special official body, that Christ uses the words: "What things soever ye shall bind on the earth shall be bound in heaven; and what things soever you shall loose on the earth shall be loosed in heaven." And it is to a similar body, the Church he had built on the foundation, "which is Jesus Christ," that Paul said, "Ye are God's temple," "the Spirit of God dwells in you."[2] The most gracious sanctities, the severest authorities, the highest dignities belonged to the Church, not through any official priesthood—for there was none—but through the personal relation to Christ of the men who formed it, and His presence in their midst.

ii. The ideal of the local is realized in the illocal Church, and we must understand it before we can really measure the dream of the newborn faith with the proud creations of the historical religion. Within the New Testament thought is not stationary, and the great example of progressive enrichment is the idea of the Church. In the earlier Pauline Epistles the actual Christians fill the foreground; but the later may be said to live and move and have their being in the Church, ideal and illocal. The development begins with an individual Church, but ends with a universal; thought, conditioned by experience, starts with a unit, but works towards a unity. At first we have what may be termed a mia-ecclesia, but at last a monê-ecclesia, and these are at once sequents and opposites.

---

[1] Matt. xviii. 15-20.   [2] 1 Cor. iii. 16

The Church of Jerusalem is both one and the whole[1]; the Church of the Ephesian and the Colossian Epistles is also one and the whole[2]; but the former is single and individual, while the latter is collective and universal. The one is a unit, which difference may break and dissolve; the other a unity, which variety will only help to realize. If the one had attempted to become the only Church, no Church universal would have been possible; it was through the manifold of experience that the higher unity was gained.

It is by Paul that the notion of the monê-, as distinguished from the mia-ecclesia, is expressed and explicated; it is doubtful if apart from him it have any representative in Apostolic literature.[3] He appears as the very spirit of difference and independence, but he is the Apostle of comprehension and unity. While his controversy with the Judaic party is most intense, his relations to the Jewish Church are most brotherly. He recognizes a distinction of Christians, both as regards race and place,[4] but he recognizes no distinction in brotherhood, and only the more serves where he is the less loved.[5] In experience the κοινωνία was larger than the local ἐκκλησίαι, and harmonized their differences,[6] but in thought the multitude were so combined as to constitute a richer whole. The point where we can best study the relation of the real and ideal, the local and illocal, in the notion of the Church, is where Paul first elaborates the image of the body of Christ.[7] He had first used it of the local Church, as he had before used the images of the tilled field and the Temple[8]; the local was a microcosm, the image and mirror of the universal. The fellowship of the body of Christ suggested the figure of the Church as His body; union in the act of remembrance

[1] Acts v. 11, viii. 1, 3. Cf. Gal. i. 13; 1 Cor. xv. 9.
[2] Eph. i. 22, iii. 10, 21; Col. i. 18, 24.
[3] In Acts the only verse which has it is Pauline, xx. 28. Of course the idea may be found elsewhere, but not under the form of the Church.
[4] 1 Thess. ii. 14; Gal. i. 22; 1 Cor. xvi. 19; Rom. xvi. 4.
[5] 1 Cor. x 32, xvi. 1-4; 2 Cor. ix. 1 ff.
[6] Gal. ii. 9.   [7] 1 Cor. x. 17.   [8] 1 Cor. iii 9.

involved the unity of the united. The unity was, therefore, one of persons; what all received made all who received it one. But did this ideal agree with the reality? In the Corinthian Church there were manifold differences and even divisions; parties were formed, each with a name as a symbol.[1] There had been grave sins, involving serious discipline[2]; disorder had reigned in the assembly, even on the most solemn occasions[3]; violent strife had raged as to the χαρίσματα.[4] The actual condition suggested by contrast the ideal, and he presented the one as a rebuke and warning to the other. He called upon this much-divided society to conceive itself through its ideal. It was a unity, an organism, a body, the body of Christ.[5] Its life was one, but its parts were many; the meanest part was as necessary as the noblest, and so neither could dispense with the other, while the dignity of the whole dignified the least noble member. The essential idea is that Christ is so in all, so needs all, so works through all, that He is the life of the body, and the body the realization of His life. Each is necessary to Him, but He to all. Yet, while Paul explains the unity through Christ, who is the organizing idea, he explains the differences between the members through the action of God. He has set in the Church apostles, prophets, teachers, so bestowing certain χαρίσματα. He has created thus the differences; but why? With a view to the common good, to the creation of things more excellent than themselves—the love that never faileth, the spirit that induces men to live as if the God who is love were incarnate in the men. The next use of the figure is similar.[6] The many are one body in Christ and severally members one of another, and the difference of gifts is traced to God, each being given in order to the efficiency and unity of the whole. The significant things in both cases are these: —As regards offices the two lists are not identical. Apostles

[1] 1 Cor. i. 12, iii. 4.
[2] 1 Cor. v. 1 ff.
[3] 1 Cor. xi. 17 ff.
[4] 1 Cor. xiv. 26.
[5] 1 Cor. xii. 12-xiii. 13.
[6] Rom. xii. 4 ff.

come first in the one list, but do not appear at all in the other; whence it follows that no fixed system of orders was necessary to the body or known to the Church. Further, no member or person appears as possessed of any sacerdotal name or office or function, either with respect to the body or its activities. Again, the discussion introduces passages that in the enthusiasm of humanity surpass all others in the Pauline writings. The Christ that inhabits the body is the Christ of the Beatitudes and the Beneficences of the Gospels. Sacramental grace is not here, nor the orders that are its channels, nor the political organism which defines the sphere of "the covenanted mercies." What we have here is the grace and truth which dwelt in Him become active and efficient in the men who at His call and through love to Him have gathered into societies, that they may the better, as His incarnated and organized Spirit, continue His work among men.

iii. In the later Epistles this idea is expanded into a sublime universalism, which transcends time as much as space. The thought of the Apostle has risen above its old antitheses,[1] and now contemplates all things through the ideal Christ. In Him, through Him, and for Him were all things created; in Him they are so constituted as to be an order, a system.[2] As He made, He redeems; His coming is no accident, or after-thought; but as He ever was with the Father, man has for the Father ever been in Him. It is through this new standpoint, and its vaster and more synthetic outlook, that the notion of the mystical Church first emerges. It is conceived more as an ideal, yet without ceasing to be real, and is personified in an altogether new way. The Church, personal, yet universal, stands over against the personal yet universal Christ; He is the Husband, it is the wife; He is the Head, it is the body; He exercises authority, it lives in subjection and obedience; He loves the Church, gives Himself for it, sanctifies it, exalts it, makes it beautiful, holy, blameless.[3] These

[1] Cf. *supra*, pp. 316-320. [2] Col. i. 16, 17. [3] Eph. v. 23-27.

attributes, the affections exercised and received, the ideal identity and adequacy to each other of the personal Christ and the personalized Church,[1] are new, though it may be only in the sense of being more explicitly developed, elements in the Pauline theology. With the emergence of the new, certain old elements have either retreated into the background or been so qualified as to appear in changed proportions. Christ is not come as the second Adam or new Head of the race, but as the Husband and Head of the Church; He does not die for all, but gives Himself up for the Church, or becomes an offering and a sacrifice to God for us.[2] Less emphasis falls on the mind and acts of man, more on the will and election of God; instead of the justification by faith and the reconciliation with God of the polemical Epistles, we have the creation of a justified and reconciled humanity, a happy, harmonious, and holy society made after the mind of God, constituted by Christ, filled, guided, united by His Spirit. Unless these new elements and points of view be borne in mind, the Church of the later Epistles cannot be construed. It stands as the symbol of the completed work of Christ, of all that God through it had meant to accomplish; by it was unfolded the mystery of His will; in it was manifested, not simply to earth, but to "principalities and powers in heavenly places," His "manifold wisdom."[3] The attributes and achievements of this Church, then, are so vast that no single institution, or any number of institutions, or even the whole field of human history can exhaust its contents, or be the arena of its full unfolding. It represents the summing up, or bringing to a unity in Christ all things in heaven and upon earth[4]; and is presented under a series of images that strive, as it were, to break the bonds of place and sense and reach immensity. But this "Gloriosissima Civitas Dei" struggles towards eternity through time; the men addressed

[1] Eph. v. 28-33.
[2] Eph. v. 2, 25.
[3] Eph. iii. 10.
[4] Eph. i. 10.

are members of it; yet, as if to show how the Apostle was possessed with the universalism and the idealisms of the Church, he never once in Ephesians uses the term in its local or realistic sense. Its members are "the called"—*i.e.*, they are conceived, not in their temporal, but in their eternal relations; and the notes that ought to distinguish them are "lowliness," "meekness," "forbearance," "longsuffering," "love," "unity," "peace"[1]—social virtues all, not sacerdotal or ecclesiastical. In their collective being they ought to be an ideal society, for they are "one body and one spirit," have one hope, "one Lord, one faith, one baptism, one God and Father of all, who is over all and through all, and in all." The unities are all, as it were, universals, as broad as the sovereignty of God, as penetrative as His ubiquity, as all distributed as His immanence. And in this society every member owes his place and his grace to the gift of Christ, who filleth all in all. And with reference to the perfecting of His saints, in order to the edifying of His body, He has created agencies—apostles, prophets, pastors, and teachers; but these are persons, not offices; men created of God, not orders instituted of men. And the edification of the body is a growth in love, so towards Christ that the nearer it comes to Him the more He possesses it. Within this Epistle, then, the Church is so conceived that the notes of what is called Catholicism are all absent; the Church, in the degree that it is mystical, knows no special polity, consents to no institutional forms, is distinguished by no sacrosanct orders, and has no single note that can with any veracity of speech be termed sacerdotal. The Church is constituted by God in Christ, and is composed of "the called," "the saints," the men of love and peace. To it no priest is necessary, or his "instruments of grace"; grace is the direct gift of Christ; what fills the body is His Spirit; what moves, unites, and enlarges it is His love.

[1] Eph. iv. 1 ff.

§ IV.—The Church as the Kingdom and People of God.

If we have rightly construed the Church in its later Pauline or mystical sense, we ought to be able to understand its relation to the kingdom. The kingdom is the Church viewed from above; the Church is the kingdom seen from below. In the kingdom the society is conceived through its creative and informing will; in the Church the will is conceived through the created and informed society. In the kingdom the king is emphasized; in the Church the citizens: in the one case we see man as he ought to be before God—poor in spirit, seeking His righteousness, doing His will, humble, teachable, without conventional goodness, good only in spirit and in truth; in the other case we see man as he ought to be for God in society—possessed of social virtues, exercising all the beneficences and charities that redeem and adorn life as man lives it with man. Hence Jesus preaches the kingdom—*i.e.*, as King declares Himself, proclaims the kingdom constituted by the presence of the King; but the Apostles, by founding Churches, edify the Church, call men to become saints, and to enter into the society of the saved. Hence, too, come the very different images under which the two are presented: the kingdom of heaven is as a sower who goeth forth to sow, or like treasure hid in a field, or like a merchantman seeking goodly pearls, or like a net cast into the sea, or like a seed, or like leaven; but the Church is a house, or a temple, or a body,—*i.e.*, the kingdom represents the idea of a creative will, and man's relation to it as one of search, or its action in man as one of growth; but the Church represents a structure, the association of once unrelated parts, the organization or combination of once dead atoms into a living whole. The coincidence of the two ideas is seen here: the plan after which the Church is built is the will of God, or the ideal of the kingdom, while the means by which the kingdom is realized is the Church and the Churches. But this involves the correlation of the two ideas: the kingdom is the immanent Church, and the Church is the explicated kingdom, and nothing alien to either can be in the other. The kingdom is the Church expressed in the terms and mind and person of its Founder; the Church is the kingdom done into living souls and the society they constitute.

This idea of the Church, as essentially the new humanity, created and penetrated by Christ, as little dependent for its being on specific forms of polity as was the old humanity, might be proved and illustrated from many sides. For example, this notion of the ideal universal Church is distinctively Pauline, and belongs to the very texture of his thought. The old mankind is an organism because of Adam; the new is a body because of Christ. Each is as its Head is: the old is earthly, like the first man; the new is spiritual, like the Second Man,—the one partakes in Adam's sin; the other is possessed of Christ's righteousness. The mind of Adam penetrates his race; the Spirit of Christ dwells in His body. And His Spirit is the son's; the Church is the filial society, man become son of God through the Son of God who became man. And in this sense it continues the Incarnation—*i.e.*, incorporates the ideal Sonship which Christ realized. The Church, as a body, is not material, but spiritual, just as is its Head. The old race was a $\sigma\hat{\omega}\mu a$ $\psi v\chi\iota\kappa \acute{o} v$, but the new race is a $\sigma\hat{\omega}\mu a$ $\pi v\epsilon v\mu a\tau\iota\kappa \acute{o} v$, with all the qualities and characteristics of Him who is by pre-eminence the $\pi v\epsilon\hat{v}\mu a$ $\zeta\omega o\pi o\iota o\hat{v}v$. To have the Spirit of Christ is to be His. "As many as are led by the Spirit of God, they are the sons of God." And "the Spirit itself beareth witness with our spirit, that we are the children of God."[1] And what are these children in their unity but the continued incarnation of sonship? And does not this mean that as the Head of the Church is spiritual, and its indwelling

[1] Rom. viii. 14-16.

power the Spirit, so it is constituted of spirits, and spiritual in all its constituent elements.

But the conclusion which follows from this discussion of the Pauline idea is only defined and illustrated by the usage of the other Apostolic writers. In Hebrews ἐκκλησία is used only as in the LXX.[1]; in Peter not at all; in James and John and the Apocalypse only in its local sense. But in its place Hebrews, Peter, and the Apocalypse have the idea of the people; they conceive the new through the old society; the new is a royal priesthood, a holy nation, God's people with His law written in their hearts, and all the fleshly sacrifices, official priesthoods, and outer ceremonies of the old abolished by being translated into the spiritual realities they typified. The emphasis, again, falls upon the people; they are a whole before God, needing no officials to constitute their unity, or communicate grace by special instruments of the ancient kind. These writers know nothing of the notion that the Church depends for its being on a special polity; to them such a notion would have seemed like an attempt to change the new law into the old. They would have found all the elements essential to it, all the ideas that most distinguish it—its orders, its authorized channels, its covenanted and uncovenanted mercies, its priestly claims, and its ceremonial sanctities—in the law they had escaped from, whose burdens they and their fathers had not been able to bear. And they would have added: the Church is the people of God; wherever they are He is, and the Church through Him in them; and as God's are a free people, He allows them to organize their own polities, the best polities always being those most deeply rooted in love, and so most creative of the spiritual and redeeming graces.

[1] Heb. ii. 12, xii. 23. In the latter case the use is figurative, but clearly based on the Old Testament.

§ V.—The Church and its Organization.

So much has been said as to the New Testament idea of the Church that we can give but little space to the questions, quite distinct yet related, connected with the organization and administration of the Churches. Only two points need be noted—the one concerns the Apostles and the Apostolic Succession, the other the character and function of the ministry as such. The question connected with the first is this: Did the Apostles constitute and consecrate successors with a view to the transmission of Apostolic authority or powers along given lines to given orders, and to these only? The question connected with the second point is this: Is the New Testament ministry a priesthood? As to these all we can do is to state conclusions.

1. There is no doubt that Christ appointed twelve Apostles, that the number twelve bore an ideal significance,[1] and that they had certain specific and defined functions.[2] But that they were to create or did create a special order of successors; that they were empowered to transmit, or did as a matter of fact either profess or endeavour to transmit Apostolical authority,—are positions, to say the least, quite incapable of historical proof; and to be not proven is, in claims of this sort, to be found not true. The Apostles were preachers of the kingdom of heaven, messengers of Christ, witnesses of His resurrection, but ordination is never described either as their special function, or as their peculiar and exclusive practice.[3] The hands laid on Paul were not those of Apostles, but first those of Ananias,[4] a man otherwise absolutely unknown, then those of the prophets and teachers at Antioch;[5] and he throughout strenuously maintained that he was made

---

[1] Matt. xix. 28.   [2] Acts i. 8-22; Matt. xxviii. 19-20; Luke xxiv. 48.

[3] The act and authority in ordination seems to have been rather the Churches' or their delegates' than the Apostles'. Cf. 2 Cor. viii. 19; Acts xiv. 23, xiii. 2, 3, i. 15, 16, 23-26.

[4] Acts ix. 10, 17.   [5] Acts xiii. 1-3.

an Apostle neither from men nor through man.¹ Barnabas was sent forth, not by the Apostles, but by the Church.² But, indeed, what does the term "Apostles" mean? No corporate body, no college of ordaining officers, no exclusive order, but simply certain persons whose special function was the ministry of the Word.³ Hence of the men Jesus appointed, James, Peter, and John are the only three ever named outside the Gospels⁴; and for the history of the Church and its organization only the two latter are of real significance, and even their significance is personal rather than official.⁵ James, the brother of the Lord, appears as an Apostle,⁶ though he was not one of the Twelve. Paul seems to associate with himself in the Apostleship, Apollos,⁷ Timothy, and Silvanus,⁸ and to apply the name to Andronicus and Junia.⁹ The Apostles were therefore no fixed order, and had no special governmental functions—others laid on hands as well as they; they were simply messengers and representatives of Christ. He preached, so did they; by preaching He established His kingdom, and they planted Churches; by the Word they worked their wonders and did their work. But as to any transmission of authority there is no word, nor is there any evidence of the existence of any official body either authorized or able to transmit it.

---

¹ Gal. i. 1.   ² Acts xi. 22.   ³ Acts vi. 2, 4.
⁴ Of course, Acts i. 1-14 is here regarded as a piece of the Gospel history; it is simply the introduction to the Acts of the Apostles, which really begins with the fifteenth verse. But cf. vi. 2.
⁵ It is very significant that it is the personal eminence and influence, not the official authority, of Peter, James, and John that Paul emphasizes in the narrative that describes his intercourse with them (Gal. ii. 6-10). They were alluded to by name, not as Apostles, but as οἱ δοκοῦντες στύλοι εἶναι. Cf. the remarkable way in which he at once distinguishes and co-ordinates himself and the rest of the Apostles and "the brethren of the Lord, and Cephas" (1 Cor. ix. 5). This latitude in the use of the term is inexplicable on any theory of the corporate being and authority of a defined Apostolical body.

⁶ Gal. i. 19.   ⁸ 1 Thess. ii. 6. Cf. i. 1.
⁷ 1 Cor. iv. 6, 9.   ⁹ Rom. xvi. 7.

2. But the other point is more fundamental. It has been already so far discussed [1] that we need only say here, the New Testament ministry is not a priesthood; in no single feature, aspect, or office has it a sacerdotal character. It is a small question what apostle, prophet, teacher, bishop, pastor, presbyter, deacon, mean, or how some perished and others survived, and how in the process of survival they were changed; but it is a profounder question, full of vaster issues, how into those that survived the sacerdotal idea penetrated, and by changing them changed the character of the religion through and through. There is an exact correspondence between the ministerial office and the nature of the religion, or the offices of the Church and its essential character. Sacerdotalism means that an office is conceived to be so sacrosanct, and so necessary to man's worship of God and God's access to man, that without it there can be no perfect worship on the one side, and no adequate or regular communication of life on the other. It means that the priest, as a priest, and not as a person, and his instruments as his, or as used by him, are the only authorized and divinely constituted media through which God reaches man and man God, or through which the recognized and approved intercourse of the creature with the Creator can proceed. Now, in the New Testament no such ideas are associated with the ministry, or with any person appointed to it. No man bears the priest's name, or professes his functions; the studious avoidance of the name by men who were steeped in the associations of sacerdotal worship is most significant; and so is the care with which they translate sacerdotal customs and ideas into their spiritual antitypes. The priesthood ceases to be official by being made universal. The life of the communities is not bound by any priestly rules or observances,[2] but by the new laws of love. The Church and its ministry, therefore, correspond throughout;

---

[1] *Supra*, p. 101. [2] Gal. iv. 9, 10; Col. ii. 16-23.

the ministry is one of persuasion, that seeks to move the will through the conscience, and both through the reason and heart ; that cares in the new and gracious way of brotherhood for the poor, the sick, the ignorant, the suffering, the sinful, and attempts to help, to love, to win by sweet reasonableness ; while the Church is a society which seeks to realize the beautiful ideal of a family of God, or a household of faith, or a brotherhood of man. The rise of the sacerdotal orders marks a long descent from the Apostolic age, but is certainly nothing of Apostolic descent.

CHAPTER II.

THE CHURCH IN THEOLOGY.

§ I.—The Church and its Polity.

FROM the discussion as to the idea of the Church in the New Testament two positive principles may be deduced: (1) As regards material character the Church is the people, the society of the sons of God; and (2) as regards formal character the Church is described in theocratic, ethical, and social terms, but not in sacerdotal or ceremonial. What is meant by the first is that the Church is composed of those who have the Spirit of the Son; without the filial Spirit no man can be within the filial society, but all are within the society who have the Spirit. This is its substance, this is its essence—it is a family constituted by the younger sons of God being conformed to the image of the First-born. What is meant by the second position is that this society is a theocracy, governed directly by its Divine and Invisible Head, with all the relations between its members determined by their relation to Him. The society of the sons of God is a family of brothers, where each loves the Father supremely and his brethren as himself. The material character is expressed by the term ἐκκλησία, and the formal character by the term βασιλεία. The kingdom is composed of free-born or enfranchized men; the Church is ordered and organized by the will and authority of the King whose love founded it, whose spirit fills and guides, whose life quickens and whose law rules all its members. The citizens who constitute the ἐκκλησία compose the βασιλεία, but the laws of the βασιλεία are the only valid and imperative principles constitutive of the ἐκκλησία. So construed God is the conception determinative of the Church both on its material and formal sides. The sons must be as is the Father—holy as He is holy, perfect as He is perfect ; the kingdom must be as the King—righteous as He is righteous, the realm where His will is law, and the law is love.

But the idea of the Church may be further defined and illustrated by being placed in contrast to its antithesis—the idea that is here called by courtesy the Catholic. This idea is political and institutional; but its polity is not the polity of the kingdom, nor are its constituent members the whole society of the sons of God. We need not here carefully define or exhibit in their mutually destructive negations the systems that call themselves catholicisms, but simply select what is common to both—the notion that a given organization or polity is necessary to the very being of the Church. The episcopate is "organically necessary to the structure of the visible body of Christ,"—" necessary not merely to its *bene esse*, but to its *esse*."[1] The society so organized is "the special and covenanted sphere of His (the Spirit's) regular and uniform operations."[2] The Church, used in this strictly political sense and confined to a special body, has a finality which belongs to its very essence, "expressed in the once for all delivered faith, in the fulness of the once for all given grace, in the Visible Society once for all instituted," " and in a once for all empowered and commissioned ministry."[3] By virtue of the first it is the custodian and interpreter of the truth ; by virtue of the second it possesses the Sacraments, which are its instruments for the communication of grace; because of the third the Church is a political unity into which man must be

---

[1] Liddon, "A Father in Christ," p. 13 (2nd ed.).
[2] Mr. Gore, "Lux Mundi," pp. 321, 322.
[3] Mr. Gore, "The Church and the Ministry," pp. 64, 65.

incorporated to be truly and effectually saved ; in the fourth "the instrument of unity" is supplied, "and no man can share her (the Church's) fellowship except in acceptance of the offices of her ministry."[1] Now, of these the last is the greatest and most essential ; though it may be argued that all are alike necessary, and distinction between necessities cannot be drawn ; yet here this distinction exists, the episcopal ministry is the condition through which the other things are ; it is primary, they are secondary and sequent ; without it there can be no unity, no priesthood, no sacramental grace, no authoritative transmission and definition of truth—in a word, no Church ; with it these things cannot but be.

Now, is this a doctrine which even approximately expresses the idea of the New Testament, and especially the mind of Christ as to the Church ? Does it do even the remotest sort of justice either to the filial society on the one hand, or its theocratic form on the other ? Is it a theory of the ministry or of the community ; of the political system or of the people who live under it, and for whose good it exists ; of the forms under which communion is decreed to be possible, or of the saints who hold communion ? The question as to the relation between the various factors constitutive of the State—the sovereign and the citizens, the magistracy and the people, the polity and the community—is as old as the study of politics, and it is as native and as necessary in the ecclesiastical as in the civil sphere. In both there are the same types of political theory, involving questions identical in principle and substance, though somewhat different in form, as to the origin, basis, limits, conditions, and ends of authority. The types may, after Aristotle, be distinguished into three, each capable of existing in two forms, a legitimate and an illegitimate—the monarchical, the aristocratic or oligarchical, and the constitutional or democratic.[2] (i) If monarchical, the monarchy may be either absolute or limited ; if absolute,

[1] "The Church and the Ministry," p. 86.   [2] "Politics," iii. 7.

it will be in the civil sphere an autocracy, but in the ecclesiastical a papacy, while its attribute in the realm of civil law will be supremacy, but in the ecclesiastical, as the realm of opinion, infallibility. If it be a limited monarchy, the limitation must come either from the law, which stands above the king and makes him a responsible ruler, or from a co-ordinate authority which stands over against his and qualifies it. In the ecclesiastical sphere the former is represented by the Gallican theory, the latter by what we may call the Frankish and the older Teutonic theories or customs, which governed the relations between Church and State before the days of Hildebrand and the Hohenstaufen. (ii) If the political type be oligarchical, it becomes in the civil system an aristocracy, in the ecclesiastical either a hierocracy or an episcopacy. Its distinctive note is that it must be self-perpetuating—*i.e.*, the means of continuing and propagating the order must be within the order, and cannot be delegated to any one or anything without. This is secured in the aristocratic and in certain hierocratic systems by a rigid law of hereditary inheritance, but in the episcopal by an equally rigid law of official succession, ordination or consecration of bishops by bishops; in other words, accession to office by act and sanction of those who already hold it. Of course, each of these systems has a theory of origin corresponding to its own peculiar form and needs. In the civil sphere, where the law of hereditary inheritance reigns, the theory is, either supernatural, an ordination of God through His Vicegerent, as with Laud and Filmer; or natural, due to the superior strength or cunning of some ancestor, as with Hobbes; or to the necessities and will either of the State or of certain classes within it, as with Aristotle; or to some imaginary contract, as with Rousseau. But in the ecclesiastical sphere, the theory of origin must always be supernatural; either, where the succession is hereditary, the creation or election by God of some special family or tribe, as with the Jews and the Brahmans; or, where the law of official succession reigns, the institution by the Founder of an order that shall transmit authority and bestow office as in Catholicism and Buddhism. Levi and all his sons were in the loins of Abraham when Melchisedec met him; all the succeeding bishops were in the spirit of Paul when he ordained Timothy and Titus. (iii) If, again, the political type be democratic, it may either be indirect and representative,· where the authority is delegated to certain persons, either of a special order, or simply as citizens of good repute ; or it may be direct and collective, where the enfranchised, or simply the citizens, act together and as a whole. The former has its counterpart in the civil realm, though only in a very partial degree, in ancient Rome ; in a fuller degree in our modern republics ; but in the ecclesiastical it takes shape as presbytery. The latter may be seen, in its civil form, in the ancient Greek cities ; but in its ecclesiastical, in the Independent or Congregational Churches.

But one thing marks all these political types—they are polities, methods and forms of government, of immense significance as such, but as no more. Taken at their very utmost valuation, they represent the framework of the State, but do not describe its essence ; they affect and condition, but do not constitute its life. A Greek city might change from a tyranny to an oligarchy, or to a democracy, but it remained Greek still. Rome did not cease to be when the Republic became the Empire ; France has tried many polities, but still remains France. The State is the people ; the polity is the system under which they are organized, and which may be changed without any change of the people. Salmasius said, "It is absurd to argue that kingdoms were before kings, for it is through kings that kingdoms are ; did no king reign there could be no kingdom." But Milton replied, "Kingdoms, indeed, were not before kings, but peoples were, and it is for and through peoples that both kings and kingdoms exist." And it is in the ecclesiastical as in the civil realm ; it is neither the bishops nor the clergy that constitute the Church, but the Church that constitutes the clergy. The Church was before they were; they are by it, and through it, and for it; they owe their being and succession to it; it does not depend for its unity upon them, but upon its Head and its relation to Him. The people are His; without His people no polity can be. With His people, some polity must be; but of what sort it shall be it is for His people, not for any special order, to determine.

The cardinal vice, then, of this kind of speculation is that it makes the secondary element primary, the primary secondary, and by inverting the relations perverts the force and the functions of both elements. It turns a mere ecclesiastical polity, which is not primitive and is without connection or affinity with Christ's ideal of the kingdom, into a substantive doctrine of the Church. It makes this polity, instead of the people, the constituent factor or authority. It affirms the Apostolic descent of the clergy, but forgets the Apostolic descent of the Church. It argues concerning the ministry as men in the seventeenth century used to argue concerning the king; the Divine rights once claimed for him are still claimed for priests, and proved in similar methods by the help of similar assumptions. And the similarity is not only with Filmer's Divine right of the patriarchal king. The theory represents too deep a tendency in human nature to be without analogies, as every student of comparative religion knows only too well, in wider and more distant fields. But one thing is clear: no theory of either the Church or its polity can be adequate which forgets the collective Christian people, through whom and for whom all polities are. The best polity for a State is the polity that secures the greatest possible good to the whole, doing completest justice alike to the obscurest citizen and the most illustrious; but the polity that shuts outside the Church as immense a body of holy men as are to be found within it, is a polity that does no justice to the ways of God or the actual condition of man. If is to constitute a state by disfranchizing its free-born citizens, and degrading them into serfs or helots. The method may be logical, but it is one of as violent disregard to right and fact as any known to ancient usurper or tyrant. In all questions of this sort there are two points of view: Men may reason downwards from the polity to the people, and say, "The Maker of the world, the Founder of the society, made this polity which we embody and administer, and you cannot be His people unless you live under His polity; on it, and our administration of it, His grace so depends that without us and our instruments it will not be communicated to you." Or men may reason upwards from the people to the polity, and say, "God made the people; His Spirit renewed them and inhabits them. The polity must express and represent the Spirit of God in the people; articulate, organize, and direct their energies. They are first, it is second; proceeds, indeed, from God, but comes through His sons, and only what is their creation has His sanction." Of these two points of view, the former may be termed the high clerical, the latter the high Church. What begins and ends with the ministry may exalt the clergy; what exalts the Church must never lose hold of the people, the saints called and approved of God.

§ II.—The Church Visible and Invisible.

Enough has been said as to the relation between polity and Church, but its theological and historical significance may be illustrated by a phrase which it is the custom of Catholic, especially neo-Catholic, writers elaborately to despise and to misunderstand—"The Invisible Church." The date of its origin is a small matter. New conditions so combine or affect old ideas as to demand new names. If theology used no terms, or allowed no ideas save those found in the Fathers, its life would soon cease, and nowhere sooner than in neo-Catholicism. One thing is certain, the phrase represents elements and ideas the Reformers owed to Augustine. His doctrine of the

Church was confronted with two great difficulties, one real or social, the other ideal or theological. (*a*) The real was the presence within it of the unworthy, the impure, or the hypocritical—men who did not belong to the Society of the Saved, especially as it existed for the mind and by the will of its Founder. Hence he had to distinguish between the ideal and the actual or the real and the counterfeit Church.[1] The Reformers had to face this contradiction in a far more aggravated form, and they said, "Since these impure, hypocritical men, though they are visibly within are really without the Church, let us cease to use false words, and say—Of the Church as God knows it, they are no members. Our actual is not identical with God's ideal; and here the ideal of God is the alone real." But (*β*) the theological difficulty was more serious: Augustine's Church, as sacerdotal, was conditional—by acts and sacraments men could be incorporated into it; but his theology was unconditional—grace was absolute, and men were saved not simply by being within the Church but by the decree or will of God.[2] If the decree is

---

[1] "De Doctr. Christ.," iii. 32: "Non enim revera Domini corpus est, quod cum illo non erit in æternum. Sed dicendum fuit, De Domini corpore vero atque permixto, aut, vero atque simulato, vel quid aliud; quia non solum in æternum, verum etiam nunc hypocritæ non cum illo esse dicendi sunt, quamvis in ejus esse videantur Ecclesia. Unde poterat ista regula et sic appellari, ut diceretur de permixta (instead of *bipartita*) Ecclesia." Cf. "Unit. Eccl.," c. xxv., § 74: "Multi tales sunt in sacramentorum communione cum ecclesia, et tamen jam non sunt in ecclesia." "Cont. Litt. Petil.," ii. 10: "Dico ad semen Abrahæ, quod est in omnibus gentibus, non pertinere, si quid non recte vobis factum est, fortasse a palea dominicæ segetis, quæ nihilominus est in omnibus gentibus." This division was so sharp in Augustine, that he, like the Reformers, was charged with believing in the existence of duas Ecclesias "Brevic. Coll. cum Donat.," iii. 10). The criticism was just as valid in the one case as in the other, and no more! Cf. Seeberg, "Studien zur Geschichte des Begriffes der Kirche," § 7; A. Dorner, "Augustinus," pp. 276-295.

[2] Cf. with above, Augus., "In Joh. Evang.," xlv. 12: "Secundum istam ergo præscientiam Dei et prædestinationem, quam multæ oves foris, quam multi lupi intus; et quam multæ oves intus, et quam multi lupi foris!" So "de Bapt.," V. xxvii. 38: "Namque in illa ineffabili præscientia Dei, multi qui foris videntur, intus sunt, et multi qui intus videntur, foris sunt."

absolute in a man's theology, he cannot consistently allow his ecclesiology to make salvation conditional; yet a conditional salvation is of the very essence of a Church that saves or communicates grace by the sacraments.[1] Hence Augustine might have argued that men were predestinated to baptism, but he could not consistently argue that men through baptism were regenerated. And as in face of the facts he could not maintain, as his one doctrine required, that there were only the elect within the Church and only the reprobate without, and as in obedience to the other, he had not only to admit, but to contend that there were elect as well as reprobates without, and reprobates as well as elect within,—he had to content himself with affirming both positions, leaving them confronting each other as dexterously concealed, yet unreconciled antitheses, or rather as radical contradictions. In the last analysis, indeed, "Numerus certus sanctorum prædestinatus," or the elect, were the real members of the Church; while the non-elect, though in its communion, were but semblances, weeds in the garden of God.

Now, what the Reformed theologians did was simply to develop Augustine's position into logical consistency by conceiving the Church through its ultimate constitutive factor, the will of God. So construed, it became the society of the elect, or company of the predestinated, or, simply, the Church invisible, while the visible was the mixed body who lived in outward profession. But this only showed that the inheritance of Augustine was divided; the Catholics succeeded to his polity, the Reformers to his theology. The anti-Donatist was the Father of the visible Church, but the anti-Pelagian the Father of the invisible.[2]

But this leaves us with the question, What did the Reformers mean by the phrase "Invisible Church"? We can easily see what they did not mean. They did not intend

[1] *Supra*, pp. 116-119. [2] *Supra*, p. 155.

to reduce, but rather to enhance the reality, necessity, and importance of the visible Church,[1] within which the invisible lived and without which it could not be.[2] Nor did they mean to deny the unity and continuity of the Church; but rather to affirm both, though in a form that aimed at being just to all the facts, and the whole truth as to the redeeming activity of God.[3] Nor did they use the phrases, as Bellarmine with the skilful misunderstanding of controversial genius maintained, to denote two Churches, but rather to express two ideas that were related as the body and soul of man.[4] The "Invisible Church" was no "Civitas Platonica," nor was the visible an organized accident, or series of expediences. Each was necessary to the other, and both to the complete expression of so rich and complex an idea as the Church of Christ. In the first place, that could not be an "ecclesia sensibilis," for did not the Creed say, "I *believe* in the Holy

---

[1] Of it John Calvin said: "Verum quia nunc de visibili ecclesia disserere propositum est, discamus vel uno matris elogio quam utilis sit nobis ejus cognitio, imo necessaria; quando non alius est in vitam ingressus nisi nos ipsa concipiat in utero, nisi pariat, nisi nos alat suis uberibus, denique sub custodia et gubernatione sua nos tueatur, donec exuti carne mortali similes erimus angelis" ("Inst. Rel. Christ.," iv. 1, 4. Cf. Catechis. Major, ii. 3, 42).

[2] Melanchthon, "Loci Communes," i., p. 283 (Detzer's ed.) says: "Quotiescunque de ecclesia cogitamus, intueamur cœtum vocatorum, qui est ecclesia visibilis, nec alibi electos ullos esse somniemus, nisi in hoc ipso cœtu visibili; nam neque invocari, neque agnosci Deus aliter vult, quam ut se patefecit; nec alibi se patefecit, nisi in ecclesia visibili, in qua sola sonat vox evangelii, nec aliam fingamus ecclesiam invisibilem et mutam hominum in hac vita tamen viventium." Hence the formula: "Ecclesia invisibilis non extra visibilem est quærenda, sed illa huic est inclusa."

[3] "Apol. Confes. Augus.," art. iv., p. 146.

[4] The terms denoted distinction, but no division; and so Hollazius, p. 1283: "Non asserimus ecclesiam visibilem et invisibilem esse duas ecclesias specie diversas, aut contrarie oppositas; sed unam eandemque ecclesiam diverso respectu dicimus visibilem et invisibilem, visibilem respectu vocatorum, invisibilem respectu renatorum"; and he explains "cœtus invisibilis renatorum sub visibili cœtu vocatorum continetur." Cf. Luther, Werke, xviii., pp. 12-15 (ed. Walch); Gerhard, "Loci," xi. 81, 82; and "Confes. Cath.," p. 207 (ed. 1679).

Catholic Church"? But the things of faith are invisible; God who loves, Christ who saves, the Spirit which renews the soul, are unseen; unseen, too, is the soul they love and save and renew, and unseen the society constituted of God out of this and all the other souls He has saved. In the next place, the body that claims to be the one Holy Catholic Apostolic Church does not possess any one of the attributes it so proudly boasts; it is not one, for it is divided into many sects, and has been the fruitful mother of divisions; it is not holy, for within and over it are many evil men; and to its working evil forces have contributed almost as powerfully as good; it is not Catholic, for it is Roman; nor is it Apostolic, for it has exchanged the ministry of service for the functions of empire. Over against and within this political and juridical body stands the Society of the Saints of God, enjoying a communion, which, though informal or unconscious, is real in proportion as it is rooted in the Divine. Again, the saving of man is an act and work of grace; all its terms are spiritual and free; its very nature would be changed were it bound to institutions of man's making and ordering. Justification by an institution is the very negation of justification by faith; the more it is magnified the more is the sole ability to justify of the spiritual Person who impersonates the saving energies of God limited and lowered; and the more is His claim to achieve through faith the saving change in man qualified and conditioned. Then, as it is persons God saves, it is a people He constitutes; and as He loves them, and they love Him, they must be able to enjoy His fellowship in spite of anything any political society on earth has done or can do. Under this aspect, there is a double idea to express—the idea that all who love God form a society with and before and under the God they love, and the idea that this society, as bound to no terms of man's making, is realized in the realm of the transcendental and eternal. Now, what term can better express this double idea than "Invisible Church"? It lifts us at once into the region where all the realities are transcendental and all are spiritual, where God is all in all to man, and man lives in conscious fellowship with God and loving obedience to Him.

§ III.—The Church of God—Holy, Catholic, and Apostolic.

We have been concerned, not with the truth or falsity of the idea of the invisible Church, simply with the meaning and import of the phrase; but this much may be said: it has more of the historical and Catholic spirit than the phrase in whose interest it has been so loudly despised. It was an attempt to find an idea of the Church as large and deep as the activity of God, yet as varied and free as the spirit of man. It endeavoured to rescue the people of God from bondage to a juridical letter, and restore them to their rightful place in His spiritual order. There was nothing Luther more loved to say and to emphasize than this— Church meant people, saintly, Catholic, Christian, daily being sanctified and made into a holy Christendom. And in so speaking he agreed with the Catholicity of the Early Ages. As Justin counted all truth to be of Christ, as Clement found prophecy in Hellenic philosophy as well as in the Hebrew Law, as Augustine believed that there had been a Christianity before Christ, so Luther held, translating the Patristic abstract into his own brave concrete, that wherever the holy soul is, whether under the Papacy or amid the Turks, there is the Church. And simply because so transcendental and Divine, it must have a phenomenal form. The finite persons who compose it are men; its Founder was an historical Person, and defined the elements necessary to the visible being of His society. These are two, the Word and the Sacraments, or the Gospel by which men are saved, and the symbols which at once express their relation to a common Head and bind them into a common

Brotherhood. Where these are there is a Church; more than these need not be. Forms of polity are matters to be determined by saved people, not by consecrated priests. The people are primary, the polity is secondary, and the polity which best articulates the religion for the people and best organizes the people for the purposes of the religion, is for the time and place the best polity. Particular Churches with their specific polities do not break the unity of the Catholic Church visible, while their faith and love constitute the unity of the invisible. It is only where accidents are made of the essence of the Church that schisms are created, for schism is but an ordinance of man turned into an imperative law of God, and as such forced upon His free people. The phrase "visible and invisible Church" may be open to manifold criticisms, for the idea was large, and human speech is limited, and the ability to read the mind within it more limited still; but surely we may say that in all the elements of sublimity and Catholicity, official Catholicism, especially in its more sectional and schismatic forms, is alongside this belief of "the new sectaries of the sixteenth century" only as "moonlight unto sunlight, and as water unto wine."

We return then, as we close, to our determinative principle: the ideal of the Church and the idea of God must agree. What does not exalt His infinite Majesty and Fatherhood is but colossal individualism, though it may disguise itself as Catholicism. God's grace is too rich to be confined to any one channel, too boundless to be bound to councils or coteries or orders of men, infirm and fallible like all their kind. It were to affirm no paradox, but rather a position capable of the clearest historical proof, were we to maintain that the higher the theory of the Church the meaner the conception of God, or that the growth of high Church doctrine is always coincident with the decay of the highest theistic belief. For an absolute or infallible Church means a limited God, a God whose working men condition, whose mercies they circumscribe, whose grace they regulate and distribute. Their limitations are imposed on Him; His attributes are not transmuted into their energies. They but repeat on a larger scale the sin of Israel,—God belongs to their Church rather than their Church to God; He is accommodated to its claims rather than its claims humbled only to be the more exalted in the presence of His majesty. For the more worthily Churches think of God, the more will they feel the fallibility of all their popes and pastors; the more they are possessed with the faith of His sufficiency, the less will they build on the idea of their own; the more infinitely good and gracious He seems, the less will they be able to claim to be His sole and adequate representatives. The virtue of a Church does not differ from the virtue of a man: all are but earthen vessels, even though they be vessels that bear the treasure of the Lord. The vessel magnified is the treasure depreciated; the more the vehicle boasts its own rare workmanship, the less it glorifies the wealth it was made to bear.

From the strife of the sects we would return into the calm and gracious presence of Him who is at once the Head and the Heart of His Church. He has given us His peace, and it abides with us even amid the collisions and contradictions of men. These are but of time, while He is of eternity. And in His presence we may not meet negation with negation, and affirm of those who say that there is no Church but theirs, that theirs is no Church of Christ; on the contrary, we shall draw no narrower limits than those traced by the hand of the Son of man: "Whosoever shall do the will of My Father which is in heaven, the same is My brother, and sister, and mother."[1]

[1] Matt. xii. 50.

INDEX.

Abelard, on reason and faith, 120 f.
Adam and Christ, the Pauline antithesis, 311 ff., 529; expresses a philosophy of history, 314, 461 f.
Agnosticism in English philosophy, 203 f.; assumes a double incompetence, 387.
Alexandria, influence of its thought in Epistle to Hebrews, 321; tendencies in, 39, 60; the catechetical school of, 75.
Anglican school in theology, the, 9 f., 14, 155, 176 ff.; compared with the Puritan, 181 ff., 188 n.; its doctrine of the Church, 176 ff., 536 ff.; its Arminianism, 183 f.; its patristic tendency, 10, 184; on the Incarnation, 451; in relation to Newman, 27; its revival, 10, 191 f.
Anselm, the scholastic theologian, 118-126; his problems, 119 ff.; of Northern descent, 113. Cf. 210 n.
Anthropology, characteristic of the Latin Church, 70, 74, 108; the Pauline, 310 ff.; in relation to Christ's own doctrine, 376.
Apocalypse, the, its value to-day, 19; its Christology, 302, 332.
Apologists, the, and Christian theology, 66, 82.
Apostolic succession, 531 f., 540.
Aquinas, an Aristotelian Realist, 124; of Northern descent, 113.
Aristotle, his influence in the Middle Ages, 40, 119, 124; his types of political theory applied to the Church, 537 f.
Arius, his theology, 84; declines to use *homoousios*, 88.
Arminianism, a criticism of Calvinism, 169 f., 431; in the Anglican Church, 184.
Athanasius, his theology, 84, 222, 390 n., 490.
Augustine, his anthropology, 109; his dualism, 115 f., 542 f.; his conditionalism in polity, 116, 155, 542; his absolutism in theology, 116 f., 155, 157, 162, 542; his interpretation of Paul, 188; his influence on Scholasticism, 115 ff., and at the Reformation, 146, 153 ff., 541 ff.

Baur, F. C., his relation to Strauss, 259, 264; founder of Tübingen school, 259; history of his mind, 260 ff; the historian of dogma, 263; his Christology, 264 f.; his problem, 265; his antitheses, 267 f., 272; his tendency theory, 270 ff.

550   INDEX.

Biblical exegesis of sixty years ago, 12 f.
„   theology of to-day, 292; in Herder, 200 f.
Bossuet on development, 31 f.
Broad Church, the, compared with the High Church, 176 ff.; its leaders, 178.
Butler, his works, 11; his doctrine of conscience in Newman, 25; on revelation, 386 n.

Calvin, 143-151; his doctrine of God, 145, 164 f., 430; in relation to Augustine, 155, 162; on development, 27.
Calvinism, a doctrine of God, 149, 156, 162 f., 430 f.; its affinity to Pantheism, 164 ff.; its schools, 163, 168, 173: see Reformed.
Candlish on the sovereignty of God, 432 ff., 445.
Catholicism, early, 27, 62, 107 f., 527; its rise explained by Baur, 269, 272; mediæval, 45, 127; later, 27, 149, 155; its conception of God, 429; and of the Church, 155, 536, 547.
Chemnitz on development, 28 n.³.
Christ, use of the name in New Testament, 306, 336, 337, 358 f.; the Christology of, 358-377; the ecclesiology of, 515 ff.; the monotheism of, 378 ff., 514; the filial consciousness of, 48, 360 ff., 390 ff., 440 ff.; histories of, 17 f., 235, 248, 278 ff.; the verdict of history on, 378 ff.; the recovery of the historical, 4, 6, 19 f., 189, 277, 294. See Jesus, Messiah, Son.
Christology of the New Testament, 302-383; of the Ante-Nicene age, 80 ff.; of Augustine, 118; of Lutheranism, 161 f., 186, 257 f.; of Schleiermacher, 228; in Germany subsequent to Strauss, 257; see under the Godhead, 385-400; and under Soteriology, 470-486; and under Incarnation.
Church, the, doctrine of, 513-548; in relation to theology, 153 ff., 450; in relation to the Scriptures, 450, 499 f., 500 ff; development in, 38 ff.
Clement of Alexandria, 67, 75, 103.
Communicatio idiomatum, in Lutheran Christology, 161 f., 186, 257; between God and the Godhead, 427; in the Incarnation, 479.
Creation, doctrine of, its philosophical difficulties, 406; made intelligible through doctrine of Godhead, 410 ff., 413, 417, 421, 446.
Criticism, historical, 191-297; in relation to the authority of the Scriptures, 500 ff.
Cyprian, as an administrator, 77; his sacerdotalism, 104 f., 106 n.

Daillé on development, 28 n.⁴.
Deism, defined, 414, 416, 431; Judaic, 383; English, 204; German, 193, 224; its historical criticism, 192, 239.
Development, the law of, in theology and the Church, 25-190; definition of, 34; history of the doctrine in theology, 27 ff.
Duns Scotus, a Platonic Realist, 124.

Eastern Church, the, its characteristics, 72 f., 185.
"Ecce Homo," 279 f.
English Church, the, and theology, 176 ff. See Anglican, Evangelical, Puritan.
Episcopacy, 102 ff., 536 ff.
Erasmus, and the Renaissance, 131 ff.
Evangelical school, the, 9 f., 14 f., 176; its genesis, 175; contrasted with the Puritan, 179 f.

Fatherhood of God, the, in the consciousness of Christ, 48, 360 ff., 390 ff., 440 ff.; in Paul, 309; in John, 340 f.; in Greek theology, 91, 389; correlative with the Sonship of Christ, 392 ff., 473 ff.; of the essence of God, 398, 410; determinative of sovereignty, 434 ff., 444, 449; in relation to sin, 449-469, 483 ff.; the material principle in theology, 451. See Son and Sonship.
Fathers, the Greek, 74 ff.; on the Holy Spirit, 490; the Antignostic, 82 f., 187; the Latin, 74 ff.
Fichte, 207 ff.

Geneva, its influence at the Reformation, 150 f.
Gnostics, the, the first theologians, 82; their terminology, 86 ff.
God, the doctrine of, compared with that of the Godhead, 385 ff., 401, 426 f.; inherited from Judaism, 64 ff., 388, 428; in Greek theology, 90 ff., 389; in Latin theology, 96 ff., 389, 429; in Calvinism, 145, 149, 156, 163, 430.
God, conception of, in Theism, 401; in Hebraism, 404; in Greek philosophy, 405.
Godhead, the, 385-447; its significance for the doctrine of God, 385, 401, 403, 417, 421 ff., 427, 440; in relation to the Incarnation, 471; in Greek theology, 91, 389, 394; in the Hegelian philosophy, 218 ff.; as revealed in history, 261.
Goethe, 196 ff.; his conception of Christ, 197 f., 295.
Gore, his theory of the Church, 45 n., 536 f.
Gospels, the, criticism of, 19, 230 ff.; by Herder, 202; omitted by Strauss, 235, 266, 271; in the Tübingen school, 258, 266, 270 f.; after the death of Baur, 278; the Christology of, 334 ff.
Greek Philosophy, a factor in development of theology, 59, 62 ff., 70, 81, 89 ff.; in the ancient Eastern Church, 81 ff., 185; its conception of God, 405; affinities with the Christian Trinity, 396.
Greek Theology, 78 ff., 90 ff., 110; the Godhead in, 91, 389, 394; its Christology, 80 ff.

Hebrew religion, a factor in development of theology, 64 f. See Judaism.
Hebrews, Epistle to, its Christology, 302, 320 ff., 345; its ecclesiology, 530. its symbolism, 321, 326 f., 343, 345; in relation to the canon, 506.

Hegel, 213-223; his importance for modern theology, 214, 221 f.; his influence on Strauss, 214, 216, 222 f., 233, 236 f.; and on Baur, 261.
Hegelianism and Christian Dogmatics, 222; and Christology, 258; and criticism, 215, 236 ff.
Hengstenberg criticizes Strauss, 244 f.
Henotheism, descriptive of Judaism, 379, 515.
Herder, 196 ff.
High Church, the, 176 ff. See Anglicanism.
Humanism, at the Renaissance, 128 ff.; its influence on the Reformation, 137 f., 503.

Incarnation, the, as conceived by Paul, 319; by John, 342; by the Evangelists, 354; in the Lutheran Church, 161 f., 257 f., 450 f.; in the Anglican, 184, 451; doctrine of, 470-479; continued in the Church, 529; as held in German philosophy, by Kant, 206; by Fichte, 208; by Schelling, 211 ff.; by Hegel, 220 ff; by Strauss, 238 f., 250; by Baur, 264 f.
Inspiration, the doctrine of, 496 ff.
Invisible Church, the, 541 ff.
Irenaeus, his Biblical theology, 67, 83; in relation to sacerdotalism, 103.

Jacobi, 206 f.
James, Epistle of, its Christology, 302, 328, 373.
Jesus, use of the name in Paul, 306; in Hebrews, 323, 325; in Peter, 331; in Apocalypse, 332; Jesus in John, 344 ff. See Christ.
John, Gospel of, compared with the synoptics, 338 f.; its characteristics, 340, 345; the Christology of, 341 ff., 346 ff., 354; as viewed by Strauss, 248, 253; by Baur, 269, 278; by Ewald, 278.
Judaism, its various forms, 38; in relation to early Christianity, 50 ff.; to Paul, 304, 310, 320, 404; to Hebrews, 320; in the Apocalypse, 332; its conception of God, 377, 379, 393, 404, 428, 514; of the Messiah, 359; and of sin, 454.
Jurieu on development, 30 n. ².
Justin Martyr, his relation to Greek philosophy, 66, 85.

Kant, 205 f.; his influence on Christology, 205, 473; his criticism of Theism, 407.
Keim's life of Jesus, 284 f.
Kenosis, in the Incarnation, 258, 355, 476; in the Godhead, 484.
Kingdom of God, or of Heaven, founded by Christ, 48, 51, 355, 358, 375, 515 ff.; in the synoptics, 335, 337, 356; in relation to the Church, 515 ff., 528 ff.; in the philosophy of Kant, 206; in Hegelian Dogmatics, 222; in modern Biblical theology, 292.

Latin theology, 74 ff., 93 ff., 186.
Law, Roman, in Latin theologians, 71 f., 98 f.; in the doctrine of the Atonement, 123, 480; in Evangelical theology, 175; and in the doctrine of God, 429, 432 ff., 436 ff.

INDEX. 553

Lessing, 192 ff.; his theory of revelation, 194 f., 387.
Lotze, on the supreme good, 411.
Love, essential to God, 410, 424, 440; and righteousness compared, 441 ff.; motive of creation, 410 ff., 417.
Luke, his Christology, 337, 339, 346 ff., 355.
Luther, the Reformer, 137 ff.; compared with Calvin, 143 ff; on the Incarnation, 477 f.; his doctrine of justification, 138, 140, 159, 450; of the Supper, 138, 161; of the Church, 140, 546; of the Scriptures, 161.
Lutheranism, its Church theological, 155, 159 ff., 450 f.; its service to Christology, 161 f., 184, 257 f.; its inconsistencies, 138, 142.

Magdeburg centuriators, the, on development, 28 n.[1].
Maistre, Joseph de, on development, 32.
Marheineke applies Hegelianism to theology, 222, 233.
Mark, his Christology, 334 f., 339, 346 ff., 355.
Martineau on revelation, 494 ff., 511.
Material and formal principle in theology, 449 ff.
Matthew, his Christology, 335 f., 339, 346 ff., 355.
Messiah, or Messianic idea, in the consciousness of Jesus, 358; how affected by the Temptation, 349 ff.; in the Apostolic Christologies, 306, 310, 331, 332, 334 f., 335, 373 f.
Moehler on development, 32, 210 n.[1], 261 n.[1]
Monotheism, of the Jews, 377, 393, 514; really created and preserved by Christ, 378, 381, 514; in relation to the Godhead, 393, 397; in relation to polity and the Church, 514, 547; in the philosophy of Baur, 261.
Mythical Theory, the, previous to Strauss, 241; as held by Strauss, 240, 248, 253, 255, 265; how criticized, 246, 270.

Neander, 233, 246.
Neo-Platonism and Christianity, 39, 76, 109.
Newman, on development, 25, 32 f., 34, 36, 44; his fear of Liberalism, 178; his search for authority, 26; on Protestantism, 42; his theology how affected by English philosophy, 204.
Nicene theology, characterised, 90 ff., 390 n.
Nominalism, 124 ff.

Occam, William of, a Nominalist, 124 f.
Origen, his theology, 83; on sacerdotalism, 104.

Pantheism, in Calvinism, 164 f.; in Strauss, 244; in Hindu religion, 395; defined, 415; its apparent reasonableness, 412.
Papacy, the, 107 f., 112, 127, 130, 429.
Patripassianism, the truth in, 484.
Paul, his Christology, 302-320; his conception of the sovereignty of God, 404; of sin, 459; of the Church, 520 ff., 529 ff.; his influence on the Antignostic Fathers, 187; on Augustine, 187; on the Reformers, 160, 187; the Tübingen criticism on, 266 ff.

Paulinism, according to the Tübingen school, 270, 272, 274.
Penalty, legal and remedial distinguished, 437 f.; and the Fatherhood, 467; and sin, 482; and Atonement, 486.
Petavius on development, 29 f.
Peter, the Christology of his Epistles, 302, 330; as keeper of the keys, 518.
Philo, importance for Christian theology, 65, 68.
Philosophy, in Scholasticism, 112; in England, 203; in Germany, 204 ff., 209 f., 214 ff., 224; and historical criticism, 203; and modern theology, 472 f. See Greek.
Plato, 65 f., 78, 396.
Polity, Roman, a factor in development of theology, 60, 93 f., 110, 187; and the Church, 529 f., 531 ff., 535 ff.
Positivism, 461, 494.
Priesthood, official, unknown in Apostolic Church, 48 f., 533; origin and action within the religion, 101 ff., and under Sacerdotalism.
Protestantism and development, 27; and Humanism, 137, 503; its attitude to Scripture, 158, 500 ff.
Pseudo-Dionysius and Catholicism, 109.
Psychology in the new Tübingen school, 290.
Puritanism in the English Church, 179 ff, 188 n.

Realism, Platonic and Aristotelian, 124 f.
Reformation, the, 137 ff.
Reformed Church, the, theological, 155, 162, 184; its doctrine of God, 163; and of the Church, 146, 541 ff.
Religion, Roman and popular, a factor of change in Christianity, 61; action on ideas of priesthood and worship, 100-106.
Religions, historical, 7; equivalents in them to conception of sin, 454; their revelations, 493; as viewed by Lessing, 194 f.; by Schelling, 211; by Hegel, 217; by Schleiermacher, 225; by Baur, 260 f.
Renaissance, the classical, 4 f., 127 ff.
Renan's "Vie de Jésus," 278 f., 280.
Revelation, the doctrine of, 493-512; necessary to knowledge of the Godhead, 386 ff., 398; in the theology of Lessing, 194 f., 387.
Roman Imperialism in Catholicism, 107 f., 111 f.
„ Law in theology, 71 f., 98 f., 123, 480. See Law.
„ Polity, a factor in Christian development, 60, 93 f., 110, 187.
Romanticism, 4 f., 199 ff.
Rothe on love and creation, 411.

Sabellianism, 222, 398.
Sacerdotalism, absent from Christ's idea of religion, 49, 517 ff., 533 f.; and from primitive Christianity, 101 ff., 521, 525, 527, 533 f.; transcended in the Epistle to Hebrews, 326 f., 375; the growth of in Christianity, 104 ff.
Schelling, 209 ff.; his doctrine of the Absolute, 209 f., 216.
Schenkel's life of Christ, 284.

INDEX.   555

Schiller, 195 f.
Schleiermacher, 223 ff.; his influence on religious thought, 223 f., 260; his criticism of the Gospels, 230 f., 234; his dictum on Christ, 231; his life of Christ, 283 f.
Scholasticism, 111 ff.
Scotus Erigena, 115
Scriptures, the, as the formal source of theology, 450, 512; in relation to the Church, 450, 499, 500, 505 ff.; and to criticism, 500 ff.; the recovery of the, 131 ff.; the Lutheran doctrine on, 161.
Sin, the Pauline idea of, 311 ff.; distinguished from transgression and offence, 312 n.[1]; defined, 452 ff.; as common, 459 ff.; in relation to the Fatherhood, 449-469; and to the Atonement, 479-487.
Socinianism, 169, 172 f.
Son of God, its use by Christ, 359 ff.; and by writers in the New Testament, 307, 323, 334 f., 340; its relation to "Son of Man," 364 ff.
Son of Man, its use by Christ, 361 ff., 364; in the Old Testament, 361 f.; ideas connected with the term, 375 f.
Sonship of Christ, the Divine, in the consciousness of Christ, 48, 360 f., 365 368 f., 376, 390 ff., 397, 440, 447, 451, 471 ff.; in the New Testament, 307, 310, 323 ff., 330, 332, 335 f., 340 ff.; the condition of man's, 328, 390, 447, 529; in relation to the Fatherhood of God, 392 ff., 406, 440, 473 ff.; as defined by Candlish, 432.
Sonship of men, 48, 328, 368 f., 376, 390, 441, 445 ff., 456; in the Nicene and post-Nicene theology, 390 n.[1].; as defined by Candlish, 432.
Soteriology, of Paul, 310 ff.; of Luke, 338; in the East and West, 74; of Luther, 140; doctrine of, 470-492.
Source, material and formal, of theology, 449 ff.
Sovereignty of God, in Judaism, 404; in Greek theology, 81; in Latin theology, 389; in Augustine, 117, 146, 155; in Calvin and Calvinism, 145 f., 149, 155 f., 163 f., 431; in Puritanism, 181 ff.; according to Candlish, 432 ff, 445; as material source of theology, 450; and sin, 465 ff.; analogues in earthly sovereignty, 433 ff., 437 f.; determined by the Paternity, 434 ff., 444.
Spirit, the Holy, 399, 487 ff.
Stoicism, ancient, 60, 71 f., 85 f., 95 f.; in Calvinism, 145 f., 164.
Strauss, 230-253; his "Leben Jesu," 235 ff.; the mythical theory, 240, 255 influenced by Hegel, 214, 216, 222 f., 233, 236 f.; his new "Life of Jesus," 280 ff.; dissolves religion into humanism, 283.
Sub-Apostolic age, the, 53, 55 ff.
Sublapsarian theology, 168.
Subterlapsarian, 173 f.
"Supernatural Religion," 285.
Supralapsarian theology, 163 ff.

Temptation of Christ, the, 349 ff.
Tendency theory, the, 270, 272, 274.

Tertullian, juristic in theology, 39, 67, 76, 83, 93, 95 ff.; his Stoicism, 96; on sin, 466; his sacerdotalism, 97, 104.
Theism, its conception of God, 401; its philosophical difficulties, 406 ff., 412, 414; its relation to theology, 401 ff., 423.
Tholuck criticizes Strauss, 245.
Tradition in the early Church, 54, 57 f.; as defined at Trent, 158; in relation to the Scriptures, 158, 499, 501 f.
Trent, the Council of, 156 ff.
Trimurti, the Hindu, 395.
Trinity, the Christian, 395 ff., 491; in Greek theology, 91; ethnic parallels to, 395 ff.; as held by Hegel, 218; by Baur, 263 f. See Godhead.
Tübingen school, 254-276; later developments of, 289 f. See Baur.

Ullmann criticizes Strauss, 243, 246; on the sinlessness of Jesus, 279.

Western Church, the, characteristics of, 72 f.; its thought and organisation, 107.
Word, the, in the Gospel of John, 340 ff.; or Logos in Greek theology, 82 f., 85; in Tertullian, 97; in the doctrine of the Incarnation, 475.

www.ingramcontent.com/pod-product-compliance
Lightning Source LLC
Chambersburg PA
CBHW031936290426
44108CB00011B/576